D1266041

MEDIA AND THE MAKING OF MODERN GERMANY

Media and the Making of Modern Germany

Mass Communications, Society, and Politics from the Empire to the Third Reich

COREY ROSS

OXFORD

UNIVERSITY PRESS

Great Clarendon Street, Oxford OX2 6DP

Oxford University Press is a department of the University of Oxford.
It furthers the University's objective of excellence in research, scholarship,
and education by publishing worldwide in

Oxford New York

Auckland Cape Town Dar es Salaam Hong Kong Karachi
Kuala Lumpur Madrid Melbourne Mexico City Nairobi
New Delhi Shanghai Taipei Toronto

With offices in

Argentina Austria Brazil Chile Czech Republic France Greece
Guatemala Hungary Italy Japan Poland Portugal Singapore
South Korea Switzerland Thailand Turkey Ukraine Vietnam

Oxford is a registered trade mark of Oxford University Press
in the UK and in certain other countries

Published in the United States
by Oxford University Press Inc., New York

© Corey Ross 2008

The moral rights of the authors have been asserted
Database right Oxford University Press (maker)

First published 2008

All rights reserved. No part of this publication may be reproduced,
stored in a retrieval system, or transmitted, in any form or by any means,
without the prior permission in writing of Oxford University Press,
or as expressly permitted by law, or under terms agreed with the appropriate
reprographics rights organization. Enquiries concerning reproduction
outside the scope of the above should be sent to the Rights Department,
Oxford University Press, at the address above

You must not circulate this book in any other binding or cover
and you must impose the same condition on any acquirer

British Library Cataloguing in Publication Data

Data available

Library of Congress Cataloging-in-Publication Data

Ross, Corey, 1969-
Media and the making of modern Germany : mass communications, society,
and politics from the Empire to the Third Reich / Corey Ross.
p. cm.
Includes bibliographical references and index.
ISBN 978-0-19-927821-3
1. Mass media—Germany—History—19th century. 2. Mass media—
Germany—History 20th century. 3. Germany—History—20th century. I. Title.
P92.G3R67 2008
302.230943—dc22
2008011955

Typeset by Laserwords Private Limited, Chennai, India
Printed in Great Britain
on acid-free paper by
CPI Antony Rowe, Chippenham, Wiltshire

ISBN 978-0-19-927821-3

1 3 5 7 9 10 8 6 4 2

Preface

One of the pleasures of finishing a long-term project such as this is the opportunity to thank those who have helped bring it to fruition. I first started the research for this book during a series of trips funded by the Nuffield Foundation in 2001–2. In 2002–3 I was fortunate to spend a year at the Zentrum für vergleichende Geschichte Europas (now the Berliner Kolleg für vergleichende Geschichte Europas), kindly sponsored by Jürgen Kocka and Arnd Bauerkämper and funded by the Alexander von Humboldt-Stiftung. Since then the project has been further supported by the British Academy, the Hartman Center for Sales, Advertising and Marketing History at Duke University, the Arts and Humanities Research Council, the School of Historical Studies at the University of Birmingham, and once again by the Alexander von Humboldt-Stiftung. I am very grateful to all these institutions for their generous financial support and for providing such an accommodating place to work.

Various parts of the manuscript were critiqued, commented upon, and improved by many friends and colleagues. A special word of thanks goes to Karl Christian Führer for the ongoing conversation I have enjoyed with him over the past several years. He, Liz Harvey, and Pamela Swett have all read parts of the manuscript in some form or another—I only hope I can return all of the favours I owe them. My thanks also go to Matthew Hilton and Jonathan Wiesen for their careful reading of the entire draft and the many helpful suggestions they have made, as well as to Paul Betts and Greg Witkowski for their hospitality in Berlin during the mop-up stages of research, and to Richard Bessel, John Breuilly and Jim Retallack for their advice and encouragement along the way. Some of the arguments were tested at various forums in Oxford, Berlin, Brussels, Paris, London, and Hamilton, and I am grateful for the comments received there.

I would also like to express my thanks to the editors of *Past & Present* for permission to reprint sections of 'Mass Culture and Divided Audiences: Cinema and Social Change in Inter-war Germany', *Past & Present*, 193 (Nov. 2006), 157–95; to the German History Society for permission to reprint sections of 'Mass Politics and the Techniques of Leadership: The Promise and Perils of Propaganda in Weimar Germany', *German History*, 24 (2006), 184–211; and to Palgrave Macmillan publishers for permission to reprint sections of 'Entertainment, Technology and Tradition: The Rise of Recorded Music from the Empire to the Third Reich', in K. C. Führer and C. Ross (eds), *Mass Media, Culture and Society in Twentieth-century Germany* (Houndmills, 2006), 25–43. This material is acknowledged where it appears in the body of the text. Illustrations are reproduced with the permission of the Bildarchiv Preußischer Kulturbesitz, Bundesarchiv-Bildarchiv, Berlin Cosmetics GmbH, Henkel KgaA, and Unilever plc. Every reasonable effort has been made to contact all copyright-holders; any omissions will be rectified in subsequent printings if notice is given to the publishers.

My final thanks go to Deborah, Alex, and Tessa, who have travelled around a fair bit with this project and who, luckily for me, enjoy that kind of thing.

Corey Ross

Birmingham, November 2007

Contents

PART III. MASS CULTURE, DIVIDED AUDIENCES: MEDIA, ENTERTAINMENT, AND SOCIAL CHANGE IN THE WEIMAR REPUBLIC

PART IV. MASS MEDIA AND MASS POLITICS FROM THE EMPIRE TO THE WEIMAR REPUBLIC

PART V. MASS CULTURE IN THE THIRD REICH:
PROPAGANDA, ENTERTAINMENT, AND NATIONAL
MOBILIZATION

List of Illustrations

List of Tables

List of Abbreviations

AfS	*Archiv für Sozialgeschichte*
BAB	Bundesarchiv, Berlin-Lichterfelde
BayHStA	Bayerisches Hauptstaatsarchiv
BBC	British Broadcasting Corporation
BIZ	*Berliner Illustrirte Zeitung*
BLA	*Berliner-Lokal-Anzeiger*
bpk	Bildarchiv Preußischer Kulturbesitz
BT	*Berliner Tageblatt*
CEH	*Central European History*
DAZ	*Deutsche Allgemeine Zeitung*
DDP	Deutsche Demokratische Partei
DNB	Deutsches Nachrichtenbüro
DNVP	Deutschnationale Volkspartei
DR	*Die Reklame*
DVP	Deutsche Volkspartei
FK	*Film-Kurier*
FZ	*Frankfurter Zeitung*
GG	*Geschichte und Gesellschaft*
GH	*German History*
GStA PK	Geheimes Staatsarchiv Preußischer Kulturbesitz
HZ	*Historische Zeitschrift*
IwKGA	*Internationale wissenschaftliche Korrespondenz zur Geschichte der deutschen Arbeiterbewegung*
JCH	*Journal of Contemporary History*
JMH	*Journal of Modern History*
JWT	J. Walter Thompson Company
KdF	Kraft durch Freude
KPD	Kommunistische Partei Deutschlands
LAB	Landesarchiv Berlin
LBB	*Licht-Bild-Bühne*
MkF	*Mitteilungen aus der kulturwissenschaftlichen Forschung*
NRWHStA	Nordrhein-Westfälisches Hauptstaatsarchiv
NSDAP	Nationalsozialistische Deutsche Arbeiterpartei
OKW	Oberkommando der Wehrmacht
PRZ	*Phonographische, Radio und Musikinstrumenten Zeitschrift*
PZ	*Phonographische Zeitschrift*
RDS	Reichsverband des deutschen Sprechmaschinenhandels

RFB	*Reichsfilmblatt*
RfH	Reichszentrale für Heimatdienst
RH	*Radio-Händler*
RKK	Reichskulturkammer
RM	Reichsmark
RMVP	Reichsministerium für Volksaufklärung und Propaganda
RPO	Reichspresseamt
RRG	Reichsrundfunkgesellschaft
RZ	*Radio-Zeitschrift*
SA	Sturmabteilung der NSDAP
SD	Sicherheitsdienst
SOPADE	Sozialdemokratische Partei Deutschlands im Exil
SPD	Sozialdemokratische Partei Deutschlands
SPIO	Spitzenorganisation der Filmwirtschaft
SR	*Seidels Reklame*
SS	Schutzstaffel der NSDAP
StAH	Staatsarchiv Hamburg
UFA	Universum-Film AG
VB	*Völkischer Beobachter*
VE	Volksempfänger
VfV	Volks-Filmverband
VfZ	*Vierteljahrshefte für Zeitgeschichte*
WTB	Wolff'sche Telegraphen-Büro
ZfG	*Zeitschrift für Geschichtswissenschaft*
ZV	*Zeitungs-Verlag*

PART I

INTRODUCTION

Introduction

No one had seen anything quite like it before. Although it is not every day that an international superstar comes to town, when Charlie Chaplin visited Berlin in 1931 his reception was utterly overwhelming.[1] Around 5:00 p.m. on 10 March the Friedrichstraße train station was likened to a 'besieged fortress', 'inundated by thousands of electrified onlookers: the adjacent squares and streets, doorways and steps, every window packed full'. Hundreds of police, some on horseback, had cleared the platforms long before his arrival and tried in vain to keep the crowds away from the station entrance. Despite all of their efforts, the throngs nonetheless surged forward when Chaplin first appeared in the train window: 'everyone running, storming, pushing forward. Thunderous shouts, arms and hats waving wildly', reported the *8-Uhr-Abendblatt*. After struggling to bring Chaplin from the platform, the police had to repel the crowds 'as if they were trying to prevent an assassination' (*Berliner Börsen-Zeitung*). Once they had beaten a path through the bodies and safely deposited him into a car, officers repeatedly had to pull fans from the running-boards. Although traffic was cordoned off along the short route to the Hotel Adlon, it was still impossible upon arrival to get Chaplin out of the car without physically driving back the throng. In the meantime, mounted police forcibly cleared the central promenade of Unter den Linden, where thousands of onlookers had gathered to catch a glimpse of the celebrity.

Events did not stop once Chaplin was inside the hotel. Over the following days crowds waited outside in the early morning to get an autograph, usually to hear that he was still asleep or had slipped out the back. There was wild press speculation about his secret itinerary in the capital, even a special newsreel about his stay. There was also scathing criticism of the police for their excessive use of force, especially on Unter den Linden. Although the commissioner alleged that political radicals had exploited the opportunity to stage illegal rallies, it was generally thought that the security forces had, as the *BZ am Mittag* put it, 'confused the harmless curiosity and effusiveness of the crowd with political demonstrations and other dangerous incidents'. But if the police were overzealous on the day, they were absolutely right to view Chaplin's arrival as a political event.

---

[1] All following quotes from W. Gersch, *Chaplin in Berlin* (Berlin, 1989), 21–32, 39–40, 64, 112, 130–1.

Whereas the Left triumphantly declared him a working-class genius who 'always felt drawn towards working people more than any other segment of society' (*Die Welt am Abend*), conservatives of all stripes found it 'highly inappropriate' that a mere film actor should be celebrated 'as no king before', and that the masses should 'allow themselves to be misused by all of this publicity through stupidity or the lust for sensation' (*Friedenauer Tageblatt, Märkische Volkszeitung*). On the far Right, where Chaplin was already a hate-figure, the entire episode was violently denounced as a Jewish-capitalist conspiracy spearheaded by liberal publishers: 'Because he is a Jew his arrival has naturally been blown up into a sensation by the Berlin street press belonging to the same race' (*Fridericus*, the newspaper of the veterans' organization Stahlhelm). The Nazis, for their part, hurled the usual epithets at this detested foe. According to Goebbels's *Angriff*, the 'disgusting pandemonium' surrounding the foreign 'warmonger' and 'Jewish film clown' Chaplin was nothing less than a national disgrace. The fact that thousands of Germans were 'pathetic and stupid enough to crowd around the car of this Jew like a bunch of hysterical women' was condemned as the 'most monstrous lack of national dignity ever displayed by a people'.

What on earth was going on? One of the most striking aspects of the whole incident is the fact that anyone could possibly care so much about a film star, however famous, in the midst of the massive economic and political turmoil afflicting Germany at the time. Did ordinary Berliners, let alone political commentators, have nothing more important to worry about? Historians have certainly thought they did. The frenzied Chaplin reception was a dramatic expression of the new culture of celebrity between the wars, but in the bigger scheme of things it has gone down as a trivial occurrence. Despite the extraordinary fervour of the thousands of fans, it receives barely a mention in the mainstream historical record, and certainly nothing like the attention paid to the far smaller crowds drawn by the political demagogues of the early 1930s. The simple reason is that, unlike the radical hordes swarming around Hitler, the throngs who came to see Chaplin exerted no obvious impact on subsequent events. With hindsight, their enthusiasm seems little more than a hollow display of adulation whose effect died out as soon as the star moved on to his next engagement. Chaplin was merely an entertainer, and as we all know, an essential trait of entertainment is the freedom from further obligation.

But should the Chaplin commotion really be dismissed so lightly? After all, the political parties were defining themselves in relation to the film star, not the other way around. The crowds he drew were clearly perceived as 'politically' significant, whether as an expression of working-class hopes for a better society, the irrationality of the feminized masses, or the existence of universal values shared by all. The extraordinary vehemence of the rhetoric suggested a fairly direct connection—if not to say competition—between the world of entertainment and politics, and showed how disconcerting many observers found what was happening. So much attention lavished on an actor simply did not make sense, especially since Chaplin himself clearly did not want it. No doubt the local press was partly to blame by devoting so much space to his visit. But were the papers hyping the whole thing up or merely responding to the intensity of popular interest? The widespread surprise at the magnitude of the Chaplin veneration suggested that the crowd itself was driving the sensation more than any journalists or film advertisers. Was it not supposed to work in the other direction? And if not, what did this say about the role of cultural elites, about the current attempts by political parties to mobilize voters, about the supposed malleability of the masses, about the very nature of communication in a complex, media-based public?

Against this backdrop Chaplin's trip to Berlin reveals much more than first meets the eye. In its own way it highlights not only the vital importance of the media to social and cultural life in the early 1930s but also their political impact, the challenge they posed to traditional values, their transcendence of social and national boundaries, and the complex relationship between cultural producers and their audiences. It was a small manifestation of a much larger and more far-reaching set of developments at whose centre lay the unprecedented expansion of new means of communication.

My primary concern in the pages that follow is to investigate these far-reaching developments and some of the connections between them. The overall aim of this book is to reconstruct how the enormous expansion of the mass media since the latter part of the nineteenth century helped to shape social, cultural, and political life in Germany during the turbulent years up to 1945. It makes no claim to provide a definitive version of events, nor is it concerned with surveying the many different theories of communication on offer. It does, however, offer the first systematic look at the rise of the mass media in Germany by weaving together a wide variety of sub-plots, trends, and patterns into a new fabric of interpretation.

Modern Germany was a society that produced an extraordinary flowering of creativity as well as the most gruesome barbarity of the twentieth century, and the media provide a compelling lens through which to view the many tensions and contradictions involved. Given the acute historical fascination with these tumultuous events, some of the basics of the story will no doubt be familiar. Accounts of German cultural life have long emphasized how rapid urbanization, the impact of industrialized warfare, the establishment of democracy, and swift economic and technological modernization interacted to promote both modernism in the arts as well as the development of a new 'mass culture'. The wide distribution of cultural artefacts via new technologies, encouraged by the competitive pressures of an increasingly commercialized entertainment industry, served to undermine the position of educated elites as the principal arbiters and consumers of culture and gradually began to shake the foundations of traditional class hierarchies in Germany. As Chaplin's Berlin visit so vividly illustrates, the increasing internationalization (or 'Americanization') of commercial culture also threw into question many older assumptions about the boundaries of 'national' culture, often eliciting a strong backlash. Although similar developments could be observed across much of the industrialized world, they were arguably of special significance in Germany, especially after the First World War. Since both artistic modernism and mass culture were closely associated with the Republic, cultural debates became extremely polarized and politically destabilizing, eventually playing into the hands of the radical right-wing movements of the time. And as scholars have long emphasized, the Nazis' intense concern with controlling the media was crucial to the regime's ability to realize its aims under a veneer of entertaining 'normality'.

In short, nowhere in Europe was the rise of the mass media and their impact on society more potent or politicized than in Germany. From the heady atmosphere of mobilization in summer 1914 to the blossoming of 'Weimar culture' to the unprecedented propaganda campaigns of the Nazis, the media have featured centrally in some of the most dramatic episodes of the twentieth-century narrative. Yet even so, our understanding of their place in modern German history has long remained fragmentary, strewn across a broad range of academic disciplines and an abundance of highly specialized studies.[2] Although historians have often remarked on the ever-expanding importance of the media, the diffuse nature of their influence (resulting from their very ubiquity) has made it difficult to integrate them into general accounts, which tend to handle them superficially if at all. The classic overviews of cultural life in Imperial and Weimar Germany focus almost exclusively on the elite and avant-garde.[3] In the case of the Third Reich, the overwhelming focus on the political instrumentalization of art, media, and entertainment *qua* propaganda has tended to obscure most other lines of enquiry, and even recent approaches have focused predominately on elite art and culture.[4] Granted, there is certainly no shortage of literature on the aesthetic content of the new media (especially film studies and commercial art), their organizational history, their regulation by the state, and the wider cultural 'discourse' of conservative pessimism and left-wing idealism that surrounded them. But the audiences, the actual people seeing and listening, have generally fallen between these thematic stools, and the wider social and political impact of the media is largely lost in the plethora of tightly focused studies.

---

[2] See K. C. Führer, K. Hickethier, and A. Schildt, 'Öffentlichkeit—Medien—Geschichte', *AfS* 39 (2001), 1–38.

[3] J. Hermand and F. Trommler, *Die Kultur der Weimarer Republik* (Munich, 1978); P. Gay, *Weimar Culture* (London, 1969); W. Laqueur, *Weimar* (London, 1974); W. Mommsen, *Bürgerliche Kultur und künstlerische Avantgarde, 1870–1918* (Berlin, 1994). More well-rounded are M. Jefferies, *Imperial Culture in Germany, 1871–1918* (Basingstoke, 2003); G. Bollenbeck, *Tradition, Avant-Garde, Reaktion* (Frankfurt a. M., 1999).

[4] F. Dröge and M. Müller, *Die Macht der Schönheit* (Hamburg, 1995); H.-D. Schäfer, *Das gespaltene Bewußtsein* (Munich, 1981). More recently: A. E. Steinweis, *Art, Ideology, and Economics in Nazi Germany* (Chapel Hill, NC, 1993); G. Cuomo (ed.), *National Socialist Cultural Policy* (London, 1995); R. Etlin (ed.), *Art, Culture, and Media Under the Third Reich* (Chicago, 2002).

Much of what follows is taken up with these questions. Tackling them would have been incomparably more difficult were it not for the wave of research on the German media over the past few years. It is a sure sign of the times that a prominent social historian, writing in one of Germany's leading history journals, has recently dubbed the period since the 1890s 'the century of the mass media'.[5] Equally tellingly, the yearbook *Archiv für Sozialgeschichte* recently devoted an entire volume to the 'history of mass media and mass communication in Germany', soon to be followed by a stream of edited volumes.[6] Why the sudden upsurge of interest? A number of factors come to mind. At the most basic level, the rise of the Internet and the huge proliferation of commercial broadcasting since the 1980s have made our world even more unimaginable without the media than it already was. Media use has become the dominant leisure activity in modern societies, and the artefacts they disseminate serve as both a reflection and a principal engine of the 'affluent society'. The immense scope of news and entertainment has also transformed nearly every aspect of politics, in many eyes for the worse. And certain aspects of the modern global economy are unthinkable outside of this context as well, from the rise of mega-brands to the problems of piracy. A whole other set of factors has to do with changes within the historical profession itself. Research on the media has, for one thing, undoubtedly profited from the swell of interest in the history of mass consumption and consumer culture. For the German scene in particular, it has also benefited from the methodological shift away from the traditional structural emphasis of social history towards a more culturally oriented focus on values and mentalities.[7] Simply put, any attempt to understand how popular attitudes and orientations changed over time must consider the actual means through which they were articulated and disseminated. And any attempt to do so for the twentieth century can hardly avoid an engagement with the mass media.

Fortunately, this new surge of attention has begun to transcend the conventional focus on media production to consider also the ways in which they were appropriated by the mass of ordinary people who used them. There has long been an interest in 'reception' among literary and cultural scholars in Germany, so it would be unfair to suggest that audiences had previously remained completely out of the picture. Yet few scholars ever bothered to look beyond the reception of canonical works by elite critics, which is hardly surprising given the source problems.[8] It took a long time for the insights of 1970s 'cultural studies' to percolate into German historiography, and only recently have historians begun

---

[5] A. Schildt, 'Das Jahrhundert der Massenmedien', *GG* 27 (2001), 177–206.

[6] For an overview: C. Ross, 'Writing the Media into History', *GH* **.

[7] T. Mergel and T. Welskopp (eds.), *Geschichte zwischen Kultur und Gesellschaft* (Munich, 1997); also T. Mergel, 'Überlegungen zu einer Kulturgeschichte der Politik', *GG* 28 (2002), 574–606.

[8] Generally: M. Charlton and S. Schneider (eds.), *Rezeptionsforschung* (Opladen, 1997); also Etlin, *Art*.

to tackle the questions they raise.[9] In place of the older 'broadcast' models of mass communication, which largely reduced audiences to passive objects in a unidirectional flow of communication, the adoption of a 'uses and gratifications' approach has turned attention towards the ways in which audiences actively select from among the broad array of cultural artefacts on offer, often imbuing them with their own sets of meanings and using them in unforeseen ways.[10] Viewing developments from this angle tends to relativize the power of media moguls and points to the limits of Foucauldian notions of 'social disciplining' that have so strongly moulded recent scholarship on early twentieth-century Germany.[11] It also asks about the complex relationship between consumers and producers of mass entertainments: how producers attempted to 'identify' with readers and listeners, how commercial interests sought to adapt new media technologies to traditional genres in order to engage audiences, how the actual meanings of media artefacts—like all consumer goods—are not intrinsic but rather a product of social and cultural usage. But by and large the interest in these approaches has produced more questions than answers, and given the difficulties involved their influence on empirical research has been rather limited.[12]

It is perhaps foolish to attempt any synthesis of a topic that is so clearly in a state of flux, for some aspects of the story may have turned out different in a few years' time. One might equally claim, however, that it is precisely during such a phase that wider analyses are most useful. This book was written in the hope that the latter will prove to be the case. In any event it does more than merely put together the existing pieces in a new way. For one thing, it contains a large amount of new material on the uptake and social impact of the media that questions the very notion of 'mass culture' as a socially and culturally 'levelling' force. It also offers a detailed discussion of the medium of recorded sound, which has been all but completely ignored in German historiography. The overlapping fields of commercial advertising and political marketing are another under-researched area to which this study contributes. And the opening section provides a different angle on the rise of the commercial media in Germany from what is found in previous overviews.

But what most clearly sets this study apart is its broad focus. In this sense the book is very much a synthetic work. It not only assembles a wide range of material on the social and cultural history of the media but also treats the expansion of the various media together, which is important for addressing their increasing entwinement over time. More importantly, it draws explicit connections between

---

[9] See, generally, *AfS* 39 (2001); also A. Schildt, 'Von der Aufklärung zum Fernsehzeitalter', *AfS* 40 (2000), 487–509; J. Requate, 'Öffentlichkeit und Medien als Gegenstände historischer Analyse', *GG* 25 (1999), 5–32.

[10] For an overview: A. A. Berger (ed.), *Making Sense of Media* (Malden, 2005).

[11] Pioneered above all by Detlev Peukert.

[12] Notable exceptions are B. Currid, *A National Acoustics* (Minneapolis, 2006); F. Bösch, 'Zeitungsberichte im Alltagsgespräch', *Publizistik* 49 (2004), 319–36.

the realms of popular entertainment and political communication, connections that political historians have largely overlooked by ignoring the evolution of the media, and that cultural historians have often downplayed by approaching the media primarily as conveyors of a 'de-politicized' consumer culture.[13] This is certainly not a socio-cultural history of the mass media with the politics left out. Indeed, it underscores how the frequently undervalued 'democratic' impetus of mass culture—the fundamental need to cater to popular interests and consumer choice—could nonetheless serve various political projects.

Of central significance is also the time-span stretching from roughly the 1890s through the Third Reich, for many of the developments it investigates were part of a longer process that transcended the deep political and social caesurae of this period. As I hope will become clear by the end, it is only against the background of long-term patterns that one can adequately understand the importance of these ruptures to the broader history of mass culture in Germany, and vice versa. Likewise, only against a wider backdrop can we appreciate what was specific to Germany, for the story told here was obviously part of an international phenomenon. Since this is not a comparative study, the occasional glance abroad will have to suffice. But the question of specificity and generality, what was and was not unique, is a recurring theme. Although many of the essentials mirrored developments elsewhere, the basic argument here is that the role of the media in social and political life was not predetermined or inherent but depended very much on evolving circumstances.

In short, by locating the expansion of the media and commercial entertainments firmly within their social and political context, the following account seeks to shed light on the relationship between mass media, social change, and political culture during this crucial period in German history. It does this by focusing on a number of themes that lie at the heart of the history of mass communications. The introductory section surveys the rise of the commercial media and their complex interrelationship with existing cultural traditions in Germany. After briefly describing the social and economic foundations around the end of the nineteenth century, it analyses how the commercial press, cinema, and recorded sound intermingled with existing cultural practices and how the threat they posed to traditional authority provoked sharp criticism from various quarters. Part II then investigates the heterogeneous responses of cultural and political elites to the rise of the media and entertainment industries, focusing first on efforts to reassert elite control through a formal framework of regulation before considering the diverse attempts to harness film, radio, the phonograph, and advertising for the purpose of 'educating' and 'uplifting' popular tastes. But as Part III shows, audiences were not the passive recipients that cultural reformers often took them to be. And the modern media, despite their underlying 'democratic' logic, were not the culturally 'standardizing' and socially 'levelling' forces so often conjured by

---

[13] The primary exception is P. Reichel, *Der schöne Schein des Dritten Reiches* (Munich, 1991).

contemporaries and historians alike. In Part IV the focus shifts to the relationship between the media and the changing nature of popular politics. How political elites adapted to the new terrain of mass communications, and how their efforts were related to evolving currents within the realm of commercial advertising, is the central concern here. Finally, Part V investigates how the social role of the media changed in the very different structural environment of the Third Reich. It considers how the Nazi reconfiguration of the media and popular entertainment, in conjunction with acute pressures of commercial concentration and rapid social change, promoted a far-reaching convergence of the media and their audiences in the 1930s and early 1940s, before eventually collapsing in the latter stages of the war.

This is more than enough to be getting on with, so to avoid any disappointments I should state at the outset that there is only limited coverage of the technological innovations or the ins and outs of the major companies—UFA, Ullstein, Hugenberg's empire—that left such an indelible mark on the history of the German media. Some media are also given more attention than others, especially the cinema, print press, and radio, with recorded sound and advertising methods also featuring significantly.[14] The entertainments themselves are not a primary focus, since critical readings of films, radio plays, and the like are readily available elsewhere. Nor is the aim to write a detailed 'media history' in a narrow sense. As mentioned above, there is a strand of research that helpfully charts the organizational, technological, and commercial history of the media but makes less effort to place them within the general societal context or wider historical processes.[15] By contrast, this book treats the rise of the media as an integral part of 'mainstream' history. It is as much about the transformation of popular culture, entertainment, and political propaganda as anything else, with the media providing the thematic thread that holds it all together. A basic premise of the book is that these social, cultural, and political histories are more fruitfully viewed in concert than in isolation, and that we have at least as much to learn by putting together what we know and looking at it in the light of new research as by digging ever-deeper furrows in increasingly specialized fields of interest. Hopefully readers will find some of the connections interesting.

[14] But not television, which made its debut in Germany in 1935 but remained marginal until the 1950s.
[15] e.g. J. Wilke, *Grundzüge der Medien- und Kommunikationsgeschichte* (Cologne, 2000); W. Faulstich, *Mediengeschichte 2* (Konstanz, 2006).

1

The Rise of the Mass Media: Modern Communications and Cultural Traditions in the Late Nineteenth and Early Twentieth Centuries

A NEW CULTURAL CONSTELLATION: PRODUCERS, CONSUMERS, AND THE MARKETPLACE

However frivolous and trivial they may appear, the countless diversions, titillating scandals and gaudy spectacles conjured by the growing commercial culture industry in the late nineteenth and early twentieth centuries reflect some of the most profound historical changes of the modern era. The enormous expansion of new communications technologies and commercial entertainments was not only a direct outgrowth of industrialization and urbanization but was in many respects their primary cultural expression. In Germany as elsewhere, both of these processes accelerated markedly after the middle of the nineteenth century. Among their myriad social effects, one of the most fundamental changes was the gradual emergence of a new market for cultural consumption among the poorer wage-earning classes, centred above all on the swelling industrial cities. Demand was such that by the turn of the century the new media and entertainments that served this market had become nothing less than a constituent part of urban life itself, and indeed began to influence cultural practices far beyond the big cities. In short, the age of 'mass culture' had dawned.[1]

This was, of course, a gradual, patchy, long-term process in which it is difficult to discern any clear turning-points. It was a phenomenon that stretched across much of Europe and North America, and the pace of cultural change varied considerably in different regions, with the heavily industrialized areas of Britain often acting as forerunners. For the German context, however, there are good reasons to regard the economic boom of the 'Gründerzeit' (c.1870–3, followed by a phase of depression) and the economic recovery from the mid-1880s onwards

---

[1] 'Mass culture' is used here in the sense of 'popular commercialized culture', without pejorative connotation.

as something of a watershed. Although the buying and selling of amusements was in itself nothing new, the rapid demographic and technological upheavals of the period after 1870 dramatically changed the environment in which such cultural activities took place. Indeed, the connections between the growth of industrial cities and the rise of a commercialized, media-based culture can hardly be overemphasized. Over the final third of the nineteenth century Germany's burgeoning industrial centres witnessed the emergence of a strikingly new form of 'public', one that was not composed of a network of educated private individuals, but rather a collective public of labouring masses that has commonly been called a 'mass public'. Unlike the older, nature-bound rhythms of village life, the disciplined and clearly demarcated work times of factory production meant that wage-earners possessed regular and significant (though by today's standards austerely modest) periods of time away from their place of work. Such 'unobligated' time gradually increased for many Germans during these decades with the shortening of working hours, though of course other constraints such as commuting and family responsibilities placed additional limits on leisure opportunities.[2] At the same time, the overall rise in real wages also widened the margins of disposable income on which the growing leisure industry fed. Between 1871 and 1913 average real weekly earnings in Germany increased by 35 per cent, and skilled workers in particular found a larger portion of their income left over after purchasing the necessities.[3]

If this increase of 'disposable' time and money formed the very bedrock of modern commercial culture, rising education levels and various trade reforms served as cornerstones. As early as 1830 nearly all Germans had basic reading and writing skills, and by the end of the century illiteracy was all but obliterated in the Reich, tallying a mere 0.05 per cent (compared to 1 per cent in the United Kingdom and 4 per cent in France). In this regard, German press barons and colportage publishers operated on especially fertile terrain. Crucially, however, this insipient mass market for reading material was only formally opened to commercial development in the 1860s through a series of liberal reforms that allowed so-called 'Berufsfremde' (people from outside a particular trade) to establish new businesses. The removal of guild-like restraints was essential to the growth of the entertainment industry in general, and to colportage and newspaper publishing in particular. Together, the rise in real wages and free time, high levels of literacy, the liberalization of trade, and rapid advances in communications marked the outer parameters of a fundamentally new cultural constellation in the latter stages of the nineteenth century.

This process was inevitably characterized by a mixture of continuity and change, and we must take care not to exaggerate the upheaval. After all, vast swathes of central Europe remained all but untouched by these developments.

[2] L. Abrams, *Workers' Culture in Imperial Germany* (London, 1992), 22–7.
[3] G. Bry, *Wages in Germany, 1871–1945* (Princeton, 1960), 71.

Given the strong historiographic stress on Germany's headlong plunge into 'modernity', it is well worth remembering that in 1890 over half of all Germans still lived in small villages (under 2,000 inhabitants) and that around one-third still made their living directly from agriculture. Many of these people were bound by the same basic work rhythms and cultural horizons as their grandparents, and for most of them the new cultural practices emerging in the cities were more or less unknown. At this time only 11 per cent of Germans lived in big urban settlements (of over 100,000 inhabitants) where the new forms of commercial culture were principally based—roughly an average proportion among central and western European countries, and a mere fraction of the urbanization rate in exceptional Britain.[4] Even in the cities, it is all too easy to let the remarkably lively and experimental avant-garde scene colour our views of popular culture in Wilhelmine Germany. In international comparison, Germany was by no means at the cutting edge of popular cultural innovation, and in many respects lagged well behind Britain, the United States, and parts of France. This question of Germany's 'modernity' or backwardness in the realm of the media and entertainments will be a recurring theme throughout the book, and challenges some of the assumptions that have shaped our understanding of early twentieth-century cultural life.

Nevertheless, there was much that was new around the turn of the century. For one thing, the social context was changing rapidly. Urbanization in Germany proceeded at a breathtaking pace once it got going. In 1871 there were only eight cities with over 100,000 inhabitants; by 1910 the number had multiplied to forty-eight.[5] The explosive numerical growth of urban audiences entailed major qualitative changes too, for what was so unprecedented about the emerging cultural constellation was that its production was largely pitched to ordinary folk, not social elites. Despite frequent attempts on the part of entertainers to achieve elite recognition, it was primarily the common people who partook of the pleasures they peddled. Moreover, this cultural production was also specifically tailored for the 'masses' in the sense that it deliberately sought to satisfy their wishes and expectations on their own terms, not as secular or religious authorities wished them to be. The new entertainments were geared first and foremost towards pleasure, not education or spiritual enrichment. In order to entice the average man or woman in the street to part with hard-earned money, they had to be. The underlying prerogative was sales, and in many respects the most novel and essential characteristic of this new cultural constellation was its increasingly commercial orientation. From the late nineteenth century onwards there emerged a vast new market of cultural artefacts sold for profit. Whether these took the shape of popular tabloids, musical recordings, or films, most were produced not as objects of artistic worth but as commodities whose value was measured by sales.

---

[4] J. Quataert, 'Demographic and Social Change', in R. Chickering (ed.), *Imperial Germany* (Westport, Conn., 1996), 106–7.
[5] Ibid. 105.

Ever since the emergence of pulp fiction and popular newspapers, one of the most fundamental issues surrounding the rise of modern entertainments has been the nature of this new commercial market. Who, if anyone, controls it? What is the relationship between the producers and consumers of moving pictures, mass-circulation newspapers, and popular music? To what extent do the usual laws of supply and demand apply? Or does the intangible nature of what is ultimately being sold—excitement, relaxation, distraction—lend the market for commercial entertainments its own unique dynamic? The arguments over these questions are as old as the phenomenon itself. For some observers the easy accessibility of new cultural 'goods' and the fact that they were bought and sold on an open market ultimately gave consumers the final say. As film producers and press barons continually claimed, the key to commercial success lay in 'giving the public what it wants'. Any attempt to preach to audiences, to ignore their wishes, or impose unpopular views was doomed to fail; enterprises that transgressed this law rapidly went to the wall. Yet as other observers have argued, the predominance of private ownership in the entertainment industry and the seemingly ubiquitous dissemination of its output via modern communications technologies gave media magnates unprecedented power to manipulate audiences. Through selective information, tendentious portrayal, and aggressive advertising, proprietors exercised a form of control over the entertainment market that was all the more powerful for its concealment under the veil of consumer sovereignty.

Clearly, neither of these views does justice to the complex relationship between the creators and audiences of commercial culture. The evolution of culture is, after all, one of the most difficult subjects for scholars to analyse. One reason for the difficulty is that solid evidence is often hard to find, in particular for the consumer side of the equation. Which groups read particular newspapers, saw certain films, or listened to specific radio programmes are questions that, before the surveys of the mid-twentieth century, demand a degree of speculation. This shortage of sources on the structure of demand is one of the main reasons why historians have tended to focus on either the producers of commercial culture or its regulation by the state, both of which have left more evidence to posterity. Yet an even more important reason is that the very nature of the question means that no amount of empirical material will in itself supply a conclusive answer. Supply and demand are ultimately difficult to disaggregate. As one observer remarked in 1932, they are 'at least as intertwined in the realm of culture as in economic matters'.[6] How, for example, should we interpret the unmistakeable conservative/national lurch of German film during 1931 and 1932? As a reflection of ascendant right-wing forces within the film industry, or the shifting tastes of an increasingly radicalized and disaffected audience? Similar interpretive problems remain even if we confine our gaze to the supply side. What values, if any, did the new media promote, and was this deliberate? For instance,

---

[6] E. Jolowicz, *Der Rundfunk* (Berlin, 1932), 20.

did the sports craze of the 1920s and its celebration of individual achievement support or undermine the position of social elites, among them the newspaper owners who devoted more and more space to sports coverage? Did the expanding sports pages promote a culture of performance-based individualism or rather suggest the need for a level playing-field beyond the realm of sport as well? Did anyone—whether the readers in search of entertainment or the entrepreneurs in search of profit—particularly care?

As these few examples serve to show, any attempt to investigate the development of commercial culture, which groups drove the process, and whose interests it served requires some degree of conceptual consideration. For better or worse, there is certainly no shortage of concepts on the workings of the modern media. Several decades of sociological and cultural studies research has produced a wide range of different approaches, far too many to discuss in any detail here.[7] Naturally, when taken alone none of these concepts can fully capture the intricacies and contingencies of developments as they unfolded. For the purposes of this study, which focuses not on the media themselves but on how they fitted into their wider social context, their development in Germany will be approached as a complex set of interactions between producers, consumers, and social institutions (state and non-governmental) that together shaped the face of modern mass culture and politics.

Although the relations between these groups differed markedly from one medium to the next and changed significantly over time, it is useful to conceive of them in general terms as a dialogue between consumers and producers in which neither side is wholly dominant and in which their mutual interaction is so fundamental that it ultimately blurs the very distinction between the two.[8] This is not to say that power was distributed equally; in many ways the forces of cultural production occupied a privileged position. Nevertheless, audiences placed real limits on their power by stubbornly registering their own preferences at the box-office. Media entrepreneurs quickly discovered that the key to commercial success lay in anticipating audience wishes and shaping their fare accordingly. In this sense producers indeed 'gave the public what it wanted', or at least tried to. Over time this pressure to appeal to audiences became ever greater in the face of intense competition by rival firms and by the advent of new media. Yet for a variety of reasons this very same competition also encouraged the increasing concentration of media ownership—and the power that accompanied it—into fewer and fewer hands. Large firms like Ullstein publishers, Deutsche Grammophon, or the UFA film syndicate not only enjoyed the advantages of economies of scale, but could also more easily afford the latest and most efficient technologies in an industry characterized by constant and extraordinarily rapid innovation. In addition, by

---

[7] For a recent introduction, see Berger (ed.), *Making*.

[8] M. de Certeau, *The Practice of Everyday Life* (Berkeley, 1984); J. Fiske, *Understanding Popular Culture* (London, 1991).

spreading their risk more widely they were also better placed than their lesser rivals to survive the consequences of the occasional commercial flop, which could quickly prove lethal to small firms with few financial reserves. Over time, this process of concentration meant less competition, which in turn meant less plurality of views. In this sense the increasing concentration of media control from the late nineteenth century onwards undoubtedly brought with it a degree of power to set political agendas, influence tastes, and shape cultural values.

Yet no matter how concentrated patterns of media ownership might become, by its very nature commercial culture always needed to be geared to audience wishes and actively sold to them. Films, records, and newspapers are not basic necessities; one can forgo them without experiencing hunger, thirst, or cold. In most cases, the worst possible consequence of bypassing a newspaper stand is a boring commute home. Not even the most avid fan truly 'needs' to see a film or purchase a recording, and generally will not do so if it is inconvenient or places an unjustifiable strain on one's resources. Of course, the distinction between 'needs' and 'desires' is notoriously fuzzy and subjective, and one should certainly not underestimate the power of modern publicity to conflate the two. Yet it is nonetheless crucial to recognize that not even a media monopoly has a truly 'captive' audience.

The need to appeal to audiences was thus constantly on the minds of Germany's new entertainment entrepreneurs. In search of profitable custom they purveyed a vast range of cultural forms and practices, sometimes opting for iconoclastic 'shock value', sometimes consciously building on older cultural practices, and invariably publicizing their efforts to the best of their ability. As always, the box-office served as the final judgement of success or failure. Unlike the traditional theatre or intellectual press, popularity was measured primarily in terms of sales, not critical acclaim. Audiences only bought what they liked, so observance of the 'bottom line' therefore functioned as an important conduit of audience feedback. In other words, through the selective opening of their wallets, audiences exerted a powerful influence on both the forms and content of commercial culture. Although media magnates were undoubtedly able to influence popular opinions and cultural preferences, they could only do so within the margins of profitability. Producers were no more able to dictate tastes than audiences were wholly impervious to what they were reading, viewing, and hearing. As D. L. LeMahieu has neatly put it for the British context, 'the economic power of press lords, movie moguls, and their counterparts in other areas of commercial culture remained contingent upon the approval of the audience they sought to inform and amuse'.[9]

The key was, of course, to pitch to the so-called average man or woman, to try to identify with one's intended audience. In order to become commercially successful, an editor or director needed to prioritize the consumer's wishes over his or her own and to approach the audience on its own terms. Given the above-average education level and relatively privileged backgrounds of most creators of

---

[9] D. L. LeMahieu, *A Culture for Democracy* (Oxford, 1988), 19.

commercial culture, these interests were frequently quite different from those of the 'ordinary folk' to whom they were trying to sell. In stark contrast to their counterparts in the classical theatre or the elite press, who considered themselves nothing less than guardians of taste and arbiters of enlightenment, commercial culture entrepreneurs quickly recognized that any form of snobbism or cultural arrogance was lethal. Hardboiled producers could privately hold their audiences in outright contempt, but under no circumstances could they afford to let such views cloud their professional judgement.

The concrete forms and techniques they developed to woo audiences were many and varied, and will be discussed in greater detail below. For now it suffices to say that they did not, as a rule, evolve out of any grand scheme or clearly preconceived plan. For the most part they resulted from the gradual accumulation of experience at the box-office, which over time afforded some insight into what formulas or recipes tended to 'work'. Any such knowledge gained by producers came less from their own clairvoyance than from a relatively mundane process of trial and error. For every hit song, 'must-see' movie, and successful tabloid there were several flops. The occasional botched idea was simply part of the entertainment business, even for entrepreneurs who possessed a knack for it. Not even August Scherl, the conservative newspaper tycoon of the Wilhelmine era, could keep his many other business failures from eventually undermining his powerful publishing empire in 1913.

Nonetheless, by the end of the nineteenth century there had emerged a number of basic characteristics that broadly shaped both the form and content of commercial culture. Most fundamental was the need to couch messages in a common idiom. Whether one dealt in colportage novels, popular newspapers, or hit tunes, it obviously made no commercial sense to exclude a large portion of the possible audience simply on the basis of education. Complex syntax and formal speech were not only unfamiliar to most people, they were also impersonal and even intimidating. This was crucial, for it did not take long for producers to recognize that maximizing one's audience was—paradoxically—best achieved through a personalized form of address. As a number of contemporaries observed, it seems that the rationality and anonymity of the modern industrial city generated a widespread desire for a sense of intimacy.[10] 'The first function which a newspaper supplies is that which formerly was performed by the village gossip,' noted the Chicago sociologist Robert Ezra Park. 'The motive, conscious or unconscious, of the press . . . is to reproduce, as far as possible, in the city the conditions of life in the village. In the village everyone knew everyone else. Everyone called everyone by his first name.'[11] Popular literature constantly let readers in on others' secrets, as did the increasingly common personality portraits in popular

[10] R. Sennett, *The Fall of Public Man* (London, 1986), 259–68.
[11] R. Park, 'The City' (1925), and 'The Natural History of the Newspaper' (1925), in R. Park, E. Burgess, and R. McKenzie, *The City* (Chicago, 1967), 39, 84.

magazines. These were an integral part of the new cult of the 'star', which itself grew out of the same desire for intimacy and familiarity. By conveying personal information about an actress or athlete that was wholly irrelevant to his or her professional role, the practitioners of 'stardom' sought to forge a pseudo-intimate link between the celebrity and the individual fan. The human-interest story, which tended to focus on the triumphs and tragedies of private life, likewise spoke directly to the demand for intimacy, and at the same time vastly expanded the definition of what was newsworthy.

Indeed, the whole concept of newsworthiness was revolutionized by the rise of the mass media. One of the chief novelties of the popular press was the wide range of topics it carried. After all, maximizing its readership was the goal, and only by providing variety was it possible to offer something for everyone: the serial-novel buff, the avid gardener, the homemaker, and the sports fan. As educated critics commonly pointed out, such breadth came very much at the expense of depth. But given the limited education and leisure opportunities of most people, who had neither the time nor inclination to inform themselves about the intricacies of political or cultural developments, this was more an asset than a liability. Providing a plethora of quick and varied impressions in easily digestible portions was the best way to awaken and maintain the viewer's interest.

Among the variety of topics on offer, the stories and themes that generated the greatest popular interest came not from the realms of the exotic and wholly implausible but from current affairs and 'real life'—provided they were presented in an exciting way. Sheer make-believe proved far less gripping than what might be called an 'exaggeration of reality'.[12] The primary building-blocks of mass culture were, in other words, not wholly contrived sensations but rather a host of absurdities and overblown superlatives drawn from everyday life: stories and sensations that were anything but 'normal', but ones to which readers or spectators could relate, however indirectly, through their own lived experiences. New technological wonders, amazing physical feats, gruesome murders: reality was, then as now, sometimes stranger than fiction, and whenever this was the case (or could be presented as such) the very fact that it 'really happened' also made it more intriguing. As Vanessa Schwartz has argued for *fin-de-siècle* Paris, the transformation of 'real life' into such 'spectacular realities' was a key element in the making of modern commercial culture. Although most of Germany's cities were decidedly provincial in comparison to Paris, much the same applies to them.[13]

While many of the forms, techniques, and characteristics of commercial culture were self-consciously—even audaciously—new, many also deliberately built on older traditions.[14] Just as the pioneers of commercial culture found it profitable

[12] 'Überhöhung der Wirklichkeit': R. Schenda, *Volk ohne Buch* (Frankfurt a. M., 1970), 484.

[13] V. Schwartz, *Spectacular Realities* (Berkeley, 1998). For Berlin, see P. Fritzsche, *Reading Berlin 1900* (Cambridge, Mass., 1996).

[14] My understanding of these issues owes much to LeMahieu, *Culture*, 56–99.

to mine the seam between reality and fantasy, they also found it prudent to straddle the border between novelty and familiarity. For all the technological and marketing innovations they introduced, the mass media were also powerfully moulded by ingrained traditions and frames of reference that shaped audience expectations. As we will see below, it was not uncommon for popular newspapers to latch on to the trappings of the traditional intellectual press in order to cultivate an air of old-fashioned dignity. Likewise, early film was strongly influenced by the forms of its vaudeville cradle long after it had developed the technology to transcend them. Although the critics of commercial culture often portrayed it as an alien intrusion, a modern-day plague suddenly descended on civilization, it is worth emphasizing that the new media and entertainments developed very much within the broader web of social relations and cultural practices of the time. They were an integral part of the wider historical context in which they emerged.[15] For this reason their impact on society and the ways in which people perceived them depended in no small measure on how they related to existing cultural practices, traditions, and values.

The shifting relationship between technological and cultural change is always a difficult issue.[16] Technological innovations, themselves products of specific social and cultural circumstances, have often had enormous and sometimes unexpected cultural ramifications. In the case of the modern media, their impact has been so far-reaching as to prompt some of the twentieth century's sharpest minds to ponder their implications for the very role of art and culture in the 'age of mechanical reproduction'.[17] That these changes could pose a threat to traditions has been recognized ever since they first became visible to contemporaries. The immense capability of the modern media to reshape or displace existing cultural practices is often highlighted in narratives about societal 'modernization', and as we will see below, there has certainly been no shortage of apocalyptic visions about the death of venerated customs at the hands of mass culture. Yet this is only one side of the story. Risk-averse entertainment entrepreneurs were often keen to build on older, 'safe' traditions, precisely because they continued to shape audience expectations. Even the most novel ideas were often initially dressed in traditional garb, almost as a means of lubricating their insertion into popular consciousness. And quite apart from these marketing considerations, even the most stunning new sensations generally evolved out of hybrid cultural forms. Whether or not such developments undermined or shored up existing cultural traditions is generally a matter of interpretation. In any event, it is important

[15] K. C. Führer and C. Ross, 'Mass Media, Culture and Society in Twentieth-century Germany', in K. C. Führer and C. Ross (eds.), *Mass Media, Culture and Society in Twentieth-century Germany* (Basingstoke, 2006), 1–22.
[16] Brief yet insightful are J. Agar, 'Medium Meets Message', *JCH* 40 (2005), 793–803; P. Burke and A. Briggs, *A Social History of the Media* (Cambridge, 2005), 1–12.
[17] W. Benjamin, 'The Work of Art in the Age of Mechanical Reproduction' (1936), in W. Benjamin, *Illuminations* (London, 1973), 211–44.

to recognize that the rise of the mass media was not merely a story of cultural destruction and displacement, but also of permeation and adaptation.[18]

To sum up, commercial culture was moulded by a variety of complex social and cultural interactions operating simultaneously on several planes: between producers and consumers, between innovation and tradition, between fantasy and reality. These multiple tensions, in conjunction with the perennially underlying profit motive, were what lent commercial culture its immense energy and creativity. They were the driving forces behind its continual growth from the late nineteenth century onwards. As the following sections of this book seek to show, the *effects* of mass communications and commercial culture were every bit as complex as the socio-cultural interactions out of which they evolved, and were similarly marked by countervailing tensions: between emancipation and exploitation, between rejection and affirmation, between social integration and differentiation. But in order to make sense of these consequences, as well as contemporaries' responses to them, it is first necessary to look in more detail at the development of individual communications media over the crucial decades straddling 1900, the era of the so-called 'second industrial revolution'. For in many ways it was during this period that the basic structures of modern mass culture first developed in Germany (as elsewhere), structures that still visibly shape our culture today.

THE COMMERCIAL PRESS

Printed material designed for wide distribution among ordinary folk was certainly not a novelty of the industrial age. Simple flyers and pictorial pamphlets had been around since the invention of the printing press centuries earlier, and played an important role in politics since the Reformation. By the latter half of the eighteenth century inexpensive books and calendars were reaching audiences far beyond the elite reading public. Itinerant *colporteure* made a living from peddling books, magazines and lexica to people who had no access to libraries or bookshops.[19]

Nevertheless, the breakthrough to a truly 'mass' press undoubtedly came during the nineteenth century as a result of two discrete developments: a string of technological innovations and the expansion of literacy. The introduction of the cylinder press in the 1810s, which replaced the twin flat plates used since Gutenberg's time with a roller over a flat type-plate, was followed several decades later by the huge twin-cylinder rotation presses fed by a continuous paper band. Whereas the average press in 1800 was capable of producing 125 four-page

[18] For similar developments in Britain, LeMahieu, *Culture*, 56–9.
[19] R. Schenda, *Die Lesestoffe der kleinen Leute* (Munich, 1976), 28–9; H. J. Galle, *Groschenhefte* (Frankfurt a. M. and Berlin, 1988).

newspapers per hour, the first cylinder press of 1814 could produce almost 1,000 copies. By the mid-1870s new rotation presses could churn out some 24,000 four-sided copies per hour, and the more sophisticated versions of the latter 1890s close to 100,000. This roughly thousandfold increase in printing capacity over the course of the nineteenth century was capped off by the introduction of 'linotype' from around 1890, which made it possible to set up to 10,000 characters per hour, five times the rate of a skilled hand-setter.[20]

This vastly increased supply of reading material is only conceivable within the context of a parallel increase in demand. Whereas the earliest productivity gains after 1800 primarily served a growing bourgeois readership, the dramatic rise in literacy over the nineteenth century amounted to a 'second reader revolution' among lower socio-economic groups. By the turn of the century the masses had become part of the reading public, and moreover had money to spend on reading material. The Reich-wide liberalization of the publishing industry in 1874 meant that a vast new market was waiting to be opened. There were clearly fortunes to be made if a publisher could produce a paper or magazine that the average person wanted to buy. The huge commercial success of a number of US publishers since the 1830s had already proven that it could be done, as did the stunning success of the weekly magazine *Die Gartenlaube*, Germany's leading 'family paper', founded in 1853 and boasting a circulation of around 382,000 by 1875.[21] Tapping this market would require not only the development of new cultural genres attractive to the average reader, but also new commercial approaches designed to keep prices down. It was out of these twin imperatives that the mass commercial press emerged.

The popular newspapers of the 1880s and 1890s differed markedly from their predecessors in terms of form, content, and self-understanding. Throughout the nineteenth century, and indeed well into the twentieth, perceptions of the press and the role of journalism in Germany differed markedly from those in Britain and the United States (and to a lesser extent in France). The emergence of the so-called 'Meinungspresse' (political press) during the Napoleonic Wars shaped German publishing for more than a century. As Joseph Görres, founder of the *Rheinischer Merkur*, remarked in 1814, newspapers should be more than 'just a meagre, inane, and feeble index of events'. In the absence of basic rights and freedoms it was a 'servile (*knechtisch*) principle . . . that they should convey mere facts and refrain from making any judgements'.[22] Over a century later, the editor of a leading liberal newspaper still proclaimed that 'it would be false to assume that the primary purpose of the press is to provide information . . . What the

---

[20] Figures from H. Heenemann, *Die Auflagenhöhen der deutschen Zeitungen*, Diss., Leipzig (1930), 132.

[21] R. Stöber, *Deutsche Pressegeschichte*, 2nd edn. (Konstanz, 2005), 267.

[22] Quoted from K. Dussel, *Deutsche Tagespresse im 19. und 20. Jahrhundert* (Münster, 2004), 25–6.

newspaper wishes to provide is views'.[23] Newspapers were therefore ideally seen 'not merely (as) a source of news information, but also an organ of instruction'.[24] Accordingly, aspiring journalists in Germany were not drilled in an objective and distanced mode of reporting, but were encouraged to print their own opinions. They saw themselves as bearers of culture (*Kulturträger*), even popular educators, not mere reporters. German editors were unambiguously part of the educated elite; in the latter decades of the nineteenth century over three-quarters possessed university degrees, half of them doctorates. 'The German newspaper writer . . . prefers to regard himself as an intellectual (*Gelehrter*),' remarked one journalist who had previously worked in England. 'The dignity and importance of political scholarship are continually conveyed to us with dramatic earnestness, yet we search in vain for a fresh and colourful mode of presentation.'[25] Catering to the interests and educational level of the masses was simply not their calling. Nor, for that matter, was it economically necessary, for the majority of editors actually earned their living from independent wealth or other activities.[26] For most of the nineteenth century the majority of German newspapers pursued cultural and political, not commercial, aims. They were a central institutional pillar of the German 'Bildungsbürgertum', which itself constituted the bulk of their readership.

All of this began to change with the emergence of mass-circulation dailies from the 1870s onwards. They not only challenged the idea that newspaper publishing was different from any other business, but were also explicitly geared towards popular appeal. Although the 1874 Press Law marked an important caesura by liberalizing the publishing business, in many ways the foundations of the commercial press were laid by the advertising reforms of 1850. From that year onwards advertising became increasingly important as a source of income for newspapers. As the proportion of advertising revenue grew, a circular momentum was set in motion. The wider the readership of a periodical, the greater was its advertising value, which thereby allowed it to charge more for its space. In turn, any additional advertising income enabled publishers to expand the readership yet further, either by enhancing the content or lowering the price. Any rise in circulation of course led to a further increase in the paper's advertising value, which set the cycle in motion once again. Whether one viewed this as a vicious or virtuous circle depended very much on one's aims, for the heavy reliance on sales and advertising revenue placed certain constraints on editorial freedom. The editor of a traditional 'Intelligenzblatt', or intellectually oriented paper, was loath to tie his hands by worrying about what the 'man in the street' might think. Newspapers, in this view, were sources of information and opinion,

---

[23] M. Eksteins, *The Limits of Reason* (Oxford, 1975), 73.

[24] G. Bernhard, 'Die Deutsche Presse', in *Der Verlag Ullstein zum Welt-Reklame-Kongress Berlin 1929* (Berlin, 1929), 59.

[25] J. Requate, *Journalismus als Beruf* (Göttingen, 1995), 143, quote 155.   [26] Ibid. 209–12.

and ideally should be free from all forms of censorship *and* self-censorship. If, however, one conceived of a newspaper primarily as a business, such issues were of little concern. What mattered was winning over new readers, and the best means for achieving this was by offering attractive entertainment at the lowest possible price.

The first German publishers to adopt this approach wholeheartedly were Rudolf Mosse and August Scherl. It was no coincidence that Mosse, founder of the *Berliner Tageblatt* in 1871/2, started his career as an advertising man. In the economic boom of the early 1870s his advertising office needed a mass-circulation daily as a vehicle for its expanding list of clients; the '*BT*' was tailor-made for this purpose. Although it eventually became one of the most respected broadsheets in Germany, the *Berliner Tageblatt* started as a commercial venture, not a political one.[27] While this alone made it unlike other papers of the time, what further distinguished it was its aggressive marketing (including thousands of free trial copies) and its modest price of only RM 4.50 per quarter, around half the average newspaper subscription. Here was a recipe that clearly worked. Within half a decade the *Berliner Tageblatt* was already the most widely read paper in Germany, with a circulation of around 50,000.[28]

Characteristically, however, Mosse's lead in the Berlin newspaper market did not go unchallenged for long. In 1883 August Scherl founded the *Berliner-Lokal-Anzeiger* as a direct competitor. Like Mosse, Scherl too was a businessman, not a journalist. Indeed, among all of the big commercial publishers in Imperial Germany, he most clearly epitomized the hard-nosed, profit-oriented approach to the publishing business. First and foremost he was an entertainment entrepreneur, having previously worked as a colportage publisher before opening a gambling establishment, the first roller-skating rink in Cologne, and a vaudeville theatre for his actress wife.[29]

Given this professional background, it is hardly surprising that Scherl found the bulk of German newspapers stodgy and boring. He therefore took to reading British and US dailies for their broader coverage and accessible style. It was while reading these papers at the Cafe Bauer in Berlin that Scherl first met Hugo von Kupffer, a young journalist who had previously worked for the *New York Herald* and shared his views about the dryness of the German press. Eventually the two teamed up to found the *Berliner-Lokal-Anzeiger*, which Kupffer edited for almost forty-five years. The paper was launched with an enormous *gratis* distribution of some 200,000 copies, and was packed with local news and advertisements, the classic formula of the *Generalanzeiger*. It soon appeared daily with a circulation of 150,000 and a subscription price of only RM 3 per quarter, significantly less than the *Berliner Tageblatt*. Although Mosse's new *Berliner Morgen-Zeitung* (founded in 1889) was in many ways a direct response to the challenge,

---

[27] E. Kraus, *Die Familie Mosse* (Munich, 1999), 179–80.
[28] Dussel, *Tagespresse*, 86–7.   [29] H. Erman, *August Scherl* (Berlin, 1954), 35–6.

there were nonetheless noticeable differences between the competing papers. The *Berliner-Lokal-Anzeiger* did not slavishly imitate the *Berliner Tageblatt* or, for that matter, Leopold Ullstein's successful *Berliner Zeitung*. Scherl regarded the former as too serious and the latter as too politically oriented. From the outset Scherl wanted the *Berliner-Lokal-Anzeiger* to be more 'popular'—to carry more entertainment, more human-interest stories, and above all more advertisements.[30] Interestingly, its large editorial board (numbering thirty-four in 1899) was relatively heterogeneous in its social composition: around one-third had not even been to university, and some even had previous criminal convictions unrelated to their journalistic activity.[31] On the eve of the First World War 70 per cent of its revenue was derived from advertisements, only 30 per cent from sales.[32] With this thoroughly commercial formula, the *Berliner-Lokal-Anzeiger* became Germany's most successful mass circulation daily before 1914.

As Scherl's move from Cologne to Berlin indicates, commercial publishers did not merely seek to open up new markets in their own locality, they actively went in search of opportunities. This approach was exemplified by publishers such as Wilhelm Girardet and above all August Huck, the so-called 'Generalanzeiger-King' of Imperial Germany, who owned or possessed a controlling interest in scores of provincial papers by the 1910s.[33] Businessmen rather than journalists (Girardet was trained as a bookbinder and Huck owned a type foundry), they essentially applied Mosse's and Scherl's Berlin formula to other cities in the Reich, at least those in which the old-established local papers had failed to open up a mass readership themselves. Whereas Leipzig, Dresden, and Hamburg presented fertile soil for such a venture, other cities—notably Munich and Cologne, where the long-established *Münchner Neueste Nachrichten* and *Kölnische Zeitung* expanded their markets far beyond their traditional readerships—looked far riskier. The fate of Joseph La Ruelle's short-lived *General-Anzeiger der Stadt Köln* was a lesson in the importance of choosing the right place.[34]

No matter where a particular Generalanzeiger was founded, however, the basic idea was the same: to acquire the largest possible readership and the highest advertising rates at the lowest possible subscription price. But how, more concretely, did they try to appeal to a mass readership? The creation of a new reader–paper relationship was crucial, for another fundamental difference between the Generalanzeiger and the traditional press was that they could not rely on political affinity to forge this link. A truly mass readership could not be established on the basis of shared opinions between editor and readers. One possibility was to offer insurance coverage to subscribers, a ploy first devised in

[30] Erman, *August Scherl*, 55–6, 66–7, 73.   [31] Requate, *Journalismus*, 154.

[32] R. Stöber, 'Der "Berliner Lokal-Anzeiger" und sein Blattmacher Hugo von Kupffer', *Publizistik*, 39 (1994), 314–30; id., *Pressegeschichte*, 258.

[33] See H.-W. Wolter, *Generalanzeiger* (Bochum, 1981).

[34] J. Requate, 'Zwischen Profit und Politik', in D. Ziegler (ed.), *Großbürger und Unternehmer* (Göttingen, 2000), 170–2.

Fig. 1. The face of the 'Generalanzeiger': Mosse's *Berliner Morgen-Zeitung*, 24 February 1891. bpk Berlin.

England in the 1880s before spreading to the continent in the 1890s. By 1911 there were just under 300 'insurance newspapers' in Germany, catering to the full range of political outlooks.[35] But most of the large commercial dailies manufactured their reader–paper bond by anticipating readers' interests and catering to the growing demand for entertainment *without* printing partisan views that could cause political offence.

This required substantial innovation in both form and content. As Rudolf Stöber has put it, the Generalanzeiger was characterized by three essential traits: topicality, universality, and publicity.[36] Their topicality and 'up to date' image were based on the latest printing technologies and an emphasis on 'hot off the press' news. This spirit was epitomized by Ullstein's *BZ am Mittag* (founded 1904), which made speed and late-breaking stories its signature image. Claiming to be the fastest newspaper on earth, it boasted a state-of-the-art distribution system replete with an army of automobiles, the latest and fastest presses, even several airplanes that dropped bundles of copies at reception sites in other cities. Its crowning achievement came—legend has it—in early 1919, when the Republic's new president, Friedrich Ebert, who was due to give a 3 o'clock address to the constitutional assembly in Weimar, was approached shortly beforehand by a paperboy brandishing a copy of the *BZ* flown from Berlin that already contained the full text of the speech he was about to give.[37]

The 'universality' of the Generalanzeiger lay in the broad range of topics they covered, which translated into more items of correspondingly shorter length. As the first issue of Girardet's *General-Anzeiger für Leipzig und Umgebung* (1886) explained: 'In an effort to inform our readers about the most important and interesting events in all aspects of public life, we will constantly report the latest news of the day in concise form. The omission of longer expositions of the material puts us in a position, however, to offer more diversity.'[38] In this way the Generalanzeiger were able to provide 'something for everyone' and to convey basic information without the risks of extended editorial comment and without placing many demands on the reader. The flip-side of creating this common denominator was of course the lack of a distinctive political profile. Since an obvious party-political line placed narrow limits on a newspaper's readership, big commercial dailies made a point of proclaiming their 'unpartisan' status. Although this usually translated into the adoption of a safe nationalist tone, there were also successful Generalanzeiger of unmistakeable left-liberal coloration, such as the *Generalanzeiger für Hamburg-Altona* and the *Berliner Tageblatt*.[39] It was eventually regarded as axiomatic that 'the best premise for the growth of the circulation figures of any newspaper is the absence of all narrow-minded party

---

[35] G. Reuveni, *Reading Germany* (Oxford, 2006), 117–22.
[36] Stöber, *Pressegeschichte*, 259.
[37] G. Kauder, 'Bezett—Bezett am Mittag!', in Verlag Ullstein, *50 Jahre Ullstein, 1877–1927* (Berlin, 1927), 200.
[38] Repr. in Wolter, *Generalanzeiger*, 320.   [39] Ibid. 276–8.

politics'.[40] For the commercial press, the principle of universality meant not only breadth of coverage, but also, to quote again from the *General-Anzeiger für Leipzig*, 'a strictly neutral standpoint wholly independent of the influence of party doctrine'.[41]

By the turn of the century this diversity of news was increasingly supplemented by an emphasis on entertainment. In the major urban centres in particular, expanding leisure time and disposable income generated a huge demand for amusements which commercial publishers sought both to satisfy and further stimulate. The family magazines founded in the 1850s and 1860s, such as *Die Gartenlaube* or *Daheim*, had long made entertainment their *raison d'être*, filling their pages with novellas, poems, popular science articles, and sketches of faraway lands: 'Far from all political wrangling and the clash of opinions, . . . we want to entertain you and inform you in an amusing manner', promised *Die Gartenlaube* in its 1852/3 debut edition.[42] Following their lead, a number of newspaper publishers had already made moves in this direction well before 1900. The *Berliner Tageblatt*, for instance, added a weekly 'home and garden' supplement in the 1880s ('Haus, Hof und Garten'), followed by a new technical magazine ('Technische Rundschau') in the 1890s.[43] At its launch in March 1894 the *Düsseldorfer Neueste Nachrichten* promised to bring 'pleasurable entertainment, instruction, and relaxation to every household each evening through gripping novellas, thrilling stories, sketches and features, public announcements, problem columns, and much more'.[44] Serialized novels (Fortsetzungsromane), already a mainstay of the colportage industry,[45] grew increasingly common as well, and proved an exceptionally effective means of 'binding' readers to a particular newspaper. They were—unsurprisingly, given Scherl's colportage background—a cast-iron component of the *Berliner-Lokal-Anzeiger*, which took the commercial exploitation of reader suspense to new heights by suddenly introducing a new character or plot just before the end of the subscription period in order to hook its readers into renewing.[46] Yet arguably the primary trendsetter for a more entertaining format was Ullstein's *Berliner Morgenpost*, founded in 1898, whose distinctly modern and accessible visual format, along with its sizeable section of picture games and crossword puzzles, clearly struck a chord with Berliners. Within only two years of its launch it reported a daily circulation of around 250,000 copies.[47]

As the success of these examples demonstrates, newspapers and magazines were no longer just a source of information, but were an indispensable companion

---

[40] Bernhard, 'Deutsche Presse', 68.   [41] Wolter, *Generalanzeiger*, 320.

[42] Quoted in Stöber, *Pressegeschichte*, 268.   [43] Kraus, *Mosse*, 183.

[44] Repr. in Wolter, *Generalanzeiger*, 325.

[45] M. Storim, 'Einer, der besser ist, als sein Ruf"', in W. Kaschuba and K. Maase (eds.), *Schund und Schönheit* (Cologne, 2001), 252–82.

[46] Erman, *Scherl*, 110–11.

[47] Figures from A. Bernstein, 'Wie die "Berliner Morgenpost" wurde', in *50 Jahre Ullstein*, 149–50, 186.

for leisure time. The act of reading was, like the new urban pastime of window-shopping, not merely a means to an end but was becoming an end in itself. For many people, the sheer enjoyment of reading was just as important as the acquisition of information. Browsing through local stories, advertisements, and advice columns represented in many ways a new form of virtual *flânerie*, and indeed one in which both men and women of all classes could easily take part.[48]

If this growing demand for entertainment influenced the content of commercial newspapers, it also shaped their form. As a means of enhancing the 'publicity' of their products, commercial publishers not only relied on straightforward language and playful commentary, but also experimented with more eye-catching layouts. As the leading publishers' journal put it some years later, before the Generalanzeiger most papers had 'a very calm appearance. The three columns of text on each page contained no more than absolutely necessary by way of article and section headlines, and there had to be something very unusual going on for a report to appear in bold typeface or spaced out on a page. This was all changed in one stroke with the emergence of the Generalanzeiger.'[49] Although the shift hardly happened overnight, how these papers displayed their content was just as important as the content itself. Whereas the dense columns of print that characterized the political press demanded considerable time and energy to decipher, striking visual headlines or illustrations could convey basic information quickly and easily, without the reader necessarily having to 'read' very much in the traditional sense of the word. As publishers soon recognized, this ability to 'browse' headlines was potentially attractive to the bulk of readers who lacked the time or energy to plough through vast fields of text. The importance of catching the eye through the use of white space, bordering, and different script styles was particularly acute for newspapers geared towards street sales instead of subscriptions. Even more than the average Generalanzeiger, their success depended on their ability to attract sufficient interest to trigger a sale. Although pictorial illustrations were still rare before the First World War, it was nonetheless recognized that appealing to a wider audience required greater accessibility, and that greater accessibility required not only plain language but also new visual prompts.

Nowhere was this more clearly manifested than in the huge expansion of illustrated magazines around 1900. These magazines came in all forms, from clever satire to pioneering photojournalism to cheap titillation and soft porn. At the lower end of the scale, rags such as *Satyr* and *Flirt* specialized mainly in nudity and tales of sex scandal. Sharing the bottom rack were a range of crime-reporter magazines inspired by London-based forerunners: *Reporter, Criminal-Reporter, Neue Detektiv-Zeitung*.[50] Moving up the scale, magazines such as *Simplicissimus*

---

[48] G. Reuveni, 'Lesen und Konsum', *AfS* 41 (2001), 114–15; Kraus, *Mosse*, 283.
[49] 'Das Gesicht der Zeitung', *ZV* 20 (25 July 1919), 1242–3.
[50] H. Gebhardt, 'Halb kriminalistisch, halb erotisch', in Kaschuba and Maase (eds.), *Schund*, 184–217.

Fig. 2. Eye-catching layout: *Illustrirte Zeitung* (Leipzig and Berlin), 7 October 1897. bpk Berlin.

or *Fliegende Blätter* specialized in biting political and social satire. Yet as far as future developments were concerned, the most important illustrated magazines were the range of general-interest periodicals founded in the 1880s and 1890s, weeklies such as the *Münchner Illustrierte Zeitung, Leipziger Illustrierte Zeitung,* Scherl's *Die Woche,* or Ullstein's *Berliner Illustrirte Zeitung.*[51]

By far the most successful of these was the *Berliner Illustrirte Zeitung* (*BIZ*), founded in 1891. Equipped with a specialized staff, image archive, and picture production unit, the *BIZ* was Germany's first truly mass-circulation weekly. As one of the first periodicals to offer subscription-free sales and free delivery, it achieved print-runs of around 1 million copies by 1914.[52] Yet the chief pull of *BIZ* (and of Scherl's *Die Woche,* which perennially occupied second place) was the quality and quantity of its illustrations (though engravings continued to outnumber photographs before the First World War). For many observers it was the illustrated magazines rather than the mass dailies that embodied the spirit of the age. As Kurt Korff (Kurt Karfunkelstein), the long-term editor of *BIZ,* remarked, the magazine's success rested not only on its own merits, but also on the general shift towards a more visual culture: 'In a time in which living life "through the eyes" began to play a more central role, the demand for visual illustration had become so strong that one could hardly avoid using images themselves as conveyors of news. That meant a totally new relationship to the visual image.' Pictures required little or no formal education, and they conveyed a message quickly and convincingly. Perhaps most important, they generated a sense of authenticity and 'reality'. Seeing was believing, and photographs in particular gave a sense of 'direct' experience that the written word could not match: 'Without illustrations the things that happened in the world were reproduced incompletely, and often seemed hard to believe—it was above all the image that conveyed the strongest and most lasting impression.'[53] Pictures thus played a key role in the sensationalizing of 'real life', in the creation of 'spectacular realities'.

Through the use of more illustrations, accessible layout, easily comprehensible language, and entertaining content, the commercial press in Germany both fulfilled and further expanded the popular demand for reading material. From 1862 to 1914 the number of newspapers more than trebled, from around 1,300 to 4,221. Although sales figures are somewhat unreliable (publishers often inflated them to maximize advertising revenue), it is nonetheless clear that circulation, too, grew rapidly over the same period. Whereas the average newspaper circulation in 1885 is estimated at 2,604, by 1906 it had more than doubled and by 1914 nearly quadrupled (see Table 1). Of course, these aggregate

---

[51] See generally H. Knoch, 'Living Pictures', in Führer and Ross (eds.), *Media,* 217–22; C. Zimmermann and M. Schmeling (eds.), *Die Zeitschrift* (Bielefeld, 2006); S. Schlingmann, *'Die Woche'* (Hamburg, 2007).
[52] K. Korff, 'Die "Berliner Illustrierte"', in *50 Jahre Ullstein,* 283.   [53] Ibid. 290.

TABLE 1. *Growth of the press in Germany, 1885–1914*

Year	Number of newspapers	Number of municipalities with newspaper	Newspapers with circulation < 1,000	Newspapers with circulation > 20,000	Average circulation
1885	3,069	1,554	1,044	31	2,604
1906	4,183	2,161	727	127	6,139
1914	4,221	2,321	226	159	8,609

Source: Muser, *Statistische Untersuchung*, 10–15, 58–63.

TABLE 2. *Number of newspaper editions per week, 1885–1914* (% age of titles)

Year	1×	2×	3×	4/5×	6×	> 6×	Other
1885	18.9	27.14	22.91	2.54	22.35	4.2	1.95
1906	14.21	15.03	26.63	3.69	34.87	4.4	—
1914	11.5	11.60	25.80	3.80	42.30	4.5	—

Source: Muser, *Statistische Untersuchung*, 43–7.

statistics mask immense variations between the many dwarf provincial papers and the popular dailies in the big cities. Yet the overall trend is unmistakeable: while only a tiny handful of papers in 1860 printed more than 10,000 copies, by the turn of the century there were twenty-five with print-runs over 35,000, several of them over 100,000. These larger newspapers were, moreover, appearing far more frequently. Whereas most newspapers in the 1880s appeared no more than three times per week, by 1914 42.3 per cent were published every day but Sunday, with a further 4.5 per cent adding a seventh edition. And some appeared far more often than that. By 1897 there were ninety-one papers with over ten editions per week; topping the list was the *Frankfurter Zeitung*, with nineteen weekly editions (three per day Monday to Saturday, plus a Sunday edition).[54]

Again, the bulk of this growth came in the form of entertainment, local news, and advertisements. Whereas in 1800 over three-quarters of newspaper space was devoted to politics, by 1900 the proportion had sunk to just over one-third, with most of the change occurring after 1850.[55] By the 1920s even the chief editor of the staunchly traditional *Vossische Zeitung* made no secret that 'the only way of achieving higher circulation figures is to give the political contents the character of human-interest material and to add supplements which, by

[54] Figures from Muser, *Statistische*, 43–7; R. Stöber, *Die erfolgverführte Nation* (Stuttgart, 1998), 84.
[55] G. Meier, *Zwischen Milieu und Markt* (Paderborn, 1999), 53.

catering to the interests of every class of reader, will attract wide circles of the population'.[56]

It is, therefore, unsurprising that the publishers of old-established papers perceived the commercial press as a huge threat. In 1894 the Association of German Newspaper Publishers (Verein Deutscher Zeitungsverleger) was founded for the express purpose of protecting them from what they dismissively called 'Scherlism'. Their worries were thoroughly understandable, for the threat they faced was twofold: the rise of popular dailies challenged not only the economic viability of their publications, but also, more importantly, the very understanding of journalism that they embodied. In many contemporaries' eyes, the entire matter boiled down to a struggle between 'Gesinnung' and 'Geschäft', convictions and commercialism. Because journalism in Germany was conceived very much as a matter of the former and not the latter, the commercial press was decried for undermining journalistic traditions. Placing profit before principle was, for one thing, a renunciation of their educational mission. Instead of informing and edifying readers, commercial newspapers supposedly catered to their ignorant mindsets and 'base instincts', and in the process granted their views an unwarranted air of legitimacy.[57] While their content represented a 'dumbing down' of intellectual standards, their eye-catching format was also an affront to serious journalism, insofar as it prioritized appearance over substance. At one level such criticisms were an integral part of more widely held reservations about the rise of capitalism itself, reservations common among the educated middle class in Imperial Germany. Yet in the case of the press this scepticism was magnified because of the decidedly intellectual self-understanding of journalism. As Jörg Requate has put it, commercial publishers 'were scolded for doing precisely what other entrepreneurs were celebrated for: namely, opening up new markets through innovation'.[58] For traditionalists, Germany's press landscape was a central battlefield in the wider struggle between culture and commerce.

As understandable as such fears were, they were also significantly overblown. The rise of mass dailies and illustrated magazines may have reconfigured the publishing industry and reinforced the ongoing changes to German reading culture, but they hardly sounded the death-knell for Germany's political press. For one thing, the highly politicized party newspapers also experienced a significant upswing over the same period. The Social Democratic press rebounded with a vengeance after the lapse of the anti-socialist laws in 1890, though it admittedly never nearly kept pace with the party's electoral success. From a total of twenty-three papers in 1876, their number leapt to sixty in 1890, of which nineteen were dailies. Over the same period their combined circulation more than doubled

---

[56] Bernhard, 'Deutsche Presse', 68.
[57] Stereotypical: W. Hammer, *Die Generalanzeiger-Presse kritisch beurteilt als ein Herd der Korruption*, (Leipzig, 1911), 8–11.
[58] Requate, 'Zwischen Profit', 167.

from around 100,000 to 260,000, expanding further to around 400,000 by 1900. Even more successful was the party's satirical magazine *Wahrer Jacob*, whose circulation of 380,000 in 1912 dwarfed all other Social Democratic publications. The Catholic Centre Party press likewise experienced rapid growth, especially after the repressive Kulturkampf of the 1870s. Its overall circulation was in fact significantly higher than that of the SPD, numbering over 600,000 by the 1880s and around 1 million by the turn of the century.[59] Far from succumbing to the 'apoliticism' of the mass dailies, Germany's party-political press was thriving. Insofar as the growth of the press represented a threat to traditional socio-cultural hierarchies, it was arguably these SPD and Centre publications that posed the more direct challenge to the interests of educated elites—at least those of the Protestant majority—rather than the bulk of mass dailies, whose avoidance of political controversy in some ways functioned to conserve the status quo.

Moreover, the bulk of traditional newspapers not directly affiliated with a particular party also thrived into the First World War and beyond. As we will see in more detail below, the distinction drawn between the 'political press' and 'commercial press' was never as clear in practice as in theory. From the very beginning, there was considerable cross-fertilization and overlap. By 1900 some of the traditional papers began adopting certain props from the popular press in order to enhance their appeal, though never too much to tarnish their solemn reputation. At the same time, many mass dailies sought to ennoble their image by deliberately adopting traditional-sounding names, for instance, the *Breslauer Generalanzeiger* rechristening itself the *Breslauer Neueste Nachrichten*, or the *Generalanzeiger für Halle* transforming into the *Hallische Nachrichten*.[60] New publishing innovations could be harnessed to bolster time-honoured conventions, and borrowing from inherited customs could enhance the appeal of new cultural forms.

Most importantly, the exaggerated threat posed by the commercial press rested in large part on a misconception about its readers. The bulk of its growth came not from poaching older subscribers away from their 'serious' papers but rather from seeking out new readers who would never have bothered with the staid publications of the old-established press in the first place. From this point of view, the contemporary jeremiads about the erosion of cultural standards by the commercial press could be turned on their head. For as far as the promotion of reading per se was concerned—a sacred activity among the German Bildungsbürgertum—the many innovations introduced by the mass-circulation papers rendered a greater service than all of the well-meaning workers' libraries and popular-education associations combined.

---

59 Figures from Dussel, *Tagespresse*, 99, 101.
60 Requate, 'Zwischen Profit', 172; see also S. Matysiak, 'Zwischen Traditionsbildung und Traditionsverweigerung', *Jahrbuch für Kommunikationsgeschichte*, 7 (2005), 122–46.

EARLY FILM

'It is no coincidence that the development of the cinema and the development of the *Berliner Illustrirte Zeitung* have run more or less parallel to each other,' noted its editor Kurt Korff in the 1920s. 'To the extent that life became more restless and individuals were less inclined to leaf through a magazine in calm contentment—to this same extent it was necessary to find a sharper and more striking form of visual depiction.'[61] As many of his contemporaries observed, the growing emphasis on layout and illustration reflected not only the expansion of the reading public and the faster pace of urban life, but also the increasingly prominent role of motion pictures. For it was during the same period that the visual spectrum of the press was expanding that the cinema first developed into a new and remarkably successful form of entertainment.

Despite its popular image as a quintessentially modern form of communication, the roots of cinematic technology reached back many decades before its breakthrough in the 1890s. The first experiments with capturing movement in images were already carried out around the middle of the nineteenth century. Around the same time, the development of electrical lighting led to a number of innovations such as the panorama and diorama, in which spectators viewed brightly illuminated images painted on surrounding screens or on the walls of a darkened room. More closely related to subsequent cinematic technologies were the popular slide shows and 'magic lantern' displays, which first projected luminous images on to a blank screen. By the 1880s Étienne-Jules Marey's 'chronophotographic gun' could conserve a series of photographic stills suitable for rapid, 'moving' reproduction, and other optical contraptions, such as Ottomar Anschütz's 'tachyscope', were capable of generating moving pictures by mounting photographs on spinning discs.[62]

Yet cinematic technology made its most rapid strides after the development of celluloid film. In the 1890s, as Thomas Edison was experimenting with his 'kinetoscope' and the Lumière brothers were developing their 'cinématographe', the German photographers Max and Emil Skladanowsky began using a new 'film camera' loaded with Kodak celluloid strips. In 1895 they unveiled their own 'Bioscop' projector, which in November of that year treated Berlin to the world's first public film screening at the Wintergarten theatre.[63]

[61] Korff, 'Berliner Illustrierte', 290.

[62] K. Bartels, 'Proto-kinematographische Effekte der Laterna magica in Literatur und Theater des achtzehnten Jahrhunderts', in H. Segeberg (ed.), *Die Mobilisierung des Sehens* (Munich, 1996), 113–47.

[63] R. Fielding (ed.), *A Technological History of Motion Pictures and Television* (Berkeley, 1967). Anschütz was actually the first to show moving Tachyscope images to a paying audience in spring of 1895, though the first use of film for public entertainment is nonetheless attributed to Skladanowsky: S. Hake, *German National Cinema* (London, 2002), 10.

The new Bioscop act was an immediate hit. Composed of several brief vaudeville-style numbers, it basically provided a short virtual reproduction of the live show that it capped off. What most fascinated the audience was thus not the content of the images so much as their technological novelty and uncanny sense of authenticity. In the words of the *Berliner-Lokal-Anzeiger*: 'What plays itself out before our eyes is the fullness of life, depicted in stunning detail. Every scene is a vivid portrayal of nature, so precise down to the last detail that it appears to us as if we are viewing the real world itself.'[64] After the successful Wintergarten premiere, moving pictures rapidly became a standard part of vaudeville programmes across Germany. By 1900 it was already reported that no big Varieté was without a film act.[65] And over the following years the selection of films and projectors swelled rapidly.

Yet in spite of film's vaudeville roots, the bulk of the early cinema audience was not found in the big cities but rather in the countryside and small towns where most Germans still lived.[66] Before the growth of film rental companies around 1905, cinema operators generally had to buy outright all of the films they showed, and therefore tried to exhibit them as many times as possible until they were literally worn out. In any given locality the Varieté theatres could only show a film for a few weeks at most, thus making it difficult to recoup the costs of purchase. Operators quickly recognized that changing localities on a regular basis was a more profitable means of maintaining audience interest in their films. Cinema was therefore an ideal new attraction for the itinerant entertainers who plied the annual circuit of local fairs and carnivals that punctuated the social calendar in Germany's small towns. For around RM 0.30 locals gained entrance to a tent or other portable structure where they were treated to a variety of short films showing acrobatic stunts, speeding locomotives, and the like, usually by means of a fairly primitive projector. Some of the more enterprising 'Wanderkinos' also sought audiences beyond the temporal confines of the yearly fairs, occasionally hiring auditoriums in hotels and inns.[67] Despite their considerable aesthetic and technological shortcomings, these roving cinema shows formed the foundation of the German film industry for around a decade, and helped to popularize the medium far beyond the urban centres.

Whether screened at the vaudeville theatre or the fairground, the attraction of these films lay in their ability to capture the sense of events whose very essence was movement. Capitalizing on the ability to show viewers things they

[64] *Berliner-Lokal-Anzeiger*, 24 Apr. 1896, quoted from J. Toeplitz, *Geschichte des Films*, vol. 1 (Berlin, 1992), 20.

[65] C. Müller, *Frühe deutsche Kinematographie* (Stuttgart, 1994), 20; id., 'Anfänge der Filmgeschichte', in Segeberg (ed.), *Mobilisierung*, 314–15.

[66] Generally, M. Kullmann *Die Entwicklung des deutschen Lichtspieltheaters*, Diss., Nuremberg (1935), 33–5; G. Stark, 'Cinema, Society, and the State', in G. Stark and B. K. Lackner (eds.), *Essays on Culture and Society in Modern Germany* (College Station, Tex., 1982), 122–3.

[67] See Toeplitz, *Geschichte*, 36–43; Müller, *Frühe*, 11–12; D. H. Warstat, *Frühes Kino der Kleinstadt* (Berlin, 1982), 18, 27–9.

could not see on stage, early filmmakers focused largely on current events and documentaries rather than narrative storytelling. Natural phenomena, in particular those involving movement, were intrinsically suited to the medium. Realistic images of a fire alarm or a steaming locomotive were a sensational novelty for audiences (though despite myths to the contrary, never so much as to cause panic at the sight of a train racing towards the camera).[68] Even well before the development of celluloid film, Étienne-Jules Marey was capturing the movement of birds in flight, and Eadweard Muybridge recorded galloping horses with his 'Zoopraxiscope'.[69] Filmmaking pioneers focused much of their attention on natural phenomena or news events involving movement (like the launching of a ship). 'The cinematic portrayals of natural occurrences, such as waves breaking in the sea, flowing rivers and waterfalls, the thundering arrival of a locomotive or a team of horses cannot be surpassed in terms of clarity by any other means of depiction', remarked an enthusiast in 1911.[70]

As this quote indicates, the subjects covered by early films included everything conceivable, from royal weddings to natural wonders to bullfighting.[71] The key, however, was the screening of 'Aktualitäten', short depictions of current events or issues that tapped viewers' interest in the happenings of the wider world. The activities of the royal family were a regular feature on Germany's cinema screens. Oskar Messter began to make the first newsreels (his famous 'Messter-Woche') in 1897 after successfully filming scenes of the centenary ceremonies of Kaiser Wilhelm I's birth. That same year one of the earliest 'Messter-Woche' films showed the first moving close-up of Wilhelm II in the dockyards of Stettin. Guido Seeber, renowned for his pioneering use of a moving camera, also made films about the Kaiser.[72] Wilhelm was so enchanted by the results that he began to cancel events if the weather was not suitable for filming.[73] Yet even more popular were short films dealing with sensational incidents of the type so beloved by the commercial press. Among the top hits of the 1908–9 season were 'The Berlin Elevated-Railway Catastrophe of 26 September 1908', 'The Earthquake in Messina', 'Zeppelin in Berlin', and 'The Spanish Judicial Murder of Francisco Ferrer'.[74]

In many ways these films made a virtue of necessity. The technical limitations of early cinematography, in particular the length of celluloid rolls and the film capacity of projectors, placed tight constraints on the aesthetic exploitation of

[68] Toeplitz, *Geschichte*, 18–19; Müller, 'Anfänge', 299.

[69] Fielding (ed.), *Technological*, 2–3, 7.

[70] H. Lehmann, *Die Kinematographie*, (Leipzig, 1911), quoted in W. Jacobsen, 'Frühgeschichte des deutschen Films', in W. Jacobsen, A. Kaes, and H. H. Prinzler (eds.), *Geschichte des deutschen Films* (Stuttgart, 1993), 24.

[71] Generally, Jacobsen, 'Frühgeschichte', 16–18; Toeplitz, *Geschichte*, 22–35.

[72] M. Loiperdinger, 'Der frühe Kino der Kaiserzeit', in U. Jung (ed.), *Der deutsche Film* (Trier, 1993), 21–50.

[73] Jefferies, *Imperial*, 226.

[74] Müller, *Frühe*, 109. On the early development of non-narrative films, U. Jung and M. Loiperdinger (eds.), *Geschichte des dokumentarischen Films in Deutschland*, vol. 1 (Stuttgart, 2005).

the medium. The vast bulk of films before 1910 were between 15 and 30 metres long, which corresponded to a playing time of around three to six minutes. Only few films exceeded this length, running to a maximum of around fifteen minutes. Despite the occasional production of short fantasies and humour sketches, it was difficult to develop a plot in this length of time. By contrast, the 'optical reporting' of current events lent itself ideally to the capabilities of the medium.

Yet it was not merely technological limitations that encouraged the pastiche programmes of early cinema. There were good reasons for screening a variety of shorts in rapid succession. Vaudeville theatres had proved the popularity and commercial success of this format, which entertainers and academics alike deemed uniquely suited to the hectic environment of Germany's burgeoning urban centres. As the sociologist Georg Simmel famously argued in 1903, in the big city the 'swift and uninterrupted change of outer and inner stimuli' led to an 'intensification of nervous stimulation'. In his view, the new mode of perception in the modern metropolis was characterized above all by 'the rapid crowding of changing images, the sharp discontinuity in the grasp of a single glance, and the unexpectedness of onrushing impressions'.[75] As the writer Otto Julius Bierbaum had noted two years earlier, these changes inevitably affected people's leisure preferences: 'The contemporary city-dweller has vaudeville nerves; he seldom has the capacity of following great dramatic continuities, of tuning his senses to the same tone for three hours. He desires diversity—Varieté.'[76] So successful were the vaudeville theatres around the turn of the century that it seemed only obvious for cinema operators to copy them. 'One of the main reasons for the popularity of the cinematographic theatre resides in its many-sidedness,' noted the cinema reformer Ernst Schulze. 'The Varietés have already made this their primary principle, because their owners know that people nowadays, namely the city-dwellers exhausted by the monotony and stress of the workday, are very receptive to quick diversions.'[77]

Early film and Varieté were downright made for each other. In many ways vaudeville provided film with an ideal home by drawing in large crowds in search of precisely what early film could offer: a quick series of brief and rapidly changing impressions. Film programmes followed a quintessentially vaudeville rationale, namely to hook the audience with an opening number and keep it in suspense before building up to the main attraction. The standard formula, as described by the cinema journal *Licht-Bild-Bühne*, was as follows: '1. Musical piece. 2. Current affair. 3. Humour. 4. Drama. 5. Comedy.—Interval.—6. Nature film. 7. Comedy. 8. The big attraction. 9. Science/knowledge. 10. Off-colour comedy.'[78] At the same time, film also represented an ideal attraction

[75] G. Simmel, 'Die Großstädte und das Geistesleben' (1903), trans. in K. H. Wolff, *The Sociology of Georg Simmel* (Glencoe, 1950), 410.

[76] Quoted from P. Jelavich, *Berlin Cabaret*, (Cambridge, Mass., 1993), 24.

[77] Quoted from Müller, *Frühe*, 11.   [78] Toeplitz, *Geschichte*, 39.

for Varieté. It not only enriched the programme with images and topics that could not be seen on stage, it also, unlike human performers, did not mind being the final act of the evening, and indeed helped transform the last slot from a kind of exit accompaniment into a real finale.[79]

It was around 1905 that the first permanent cinemas appeared.[80] The buoyant market for films, the vast increase in their supply and—crucially—the establishment of distribution firms allowing owners to change their programme on a regular basis meant that there was big money to be made for operators who settled in a suitable place. It was remarkably easy to open a so-called 'Ladenkino' (shop cinema) during these boom years. Despite the flammability of the celluloid films, there were no safety regulations; all one needed to do was set up a projector and screen in a vacant shop or pub. The result was a veritable explosion of moving-picture houses in German cities. From the end of 1905 to the end of 1907 the number of permanent cinemas in Berlin grew from twenty-one to 132, with continuing (if somewhat slower) growth over the following years.[81] The bulk of these establishments were fairly primitive, and according to one contemporary account were chiefly distinguishable by the 'better or worse quality of their ventilation'.[82] Yet by 1908 the first purpose-built cinemas and luxurious 'cinema palaces' also began to appear. Located in city centres or near traffic hubs, and equipped with lavish decoration, upholstered seats, and musical orchestras, they sought to attract a stratum of customers unlikely to visit the seedy Ladenkinos: 'the difference in terms of furnishings and decor between a small neighbourhood cinema and one in, say, Berlin W(est) is absolutely enormous', noted a contemporary survey.[83] The first cinema chains also emerged in this period, starting in 1906 with Paul Davidson's 'Union-Theater', which rapidly spread from Frankfurt am Main to other cities.

The growth of permanent cinemas was closely related to the emergence of feature-length films. Inspired by trendsetters such as the 1910 Danish film *Weiße Sklavinnen*—at 600 metres (or up to around two hours) by far the longest production to date—filmmakers increasingly experimented with the narrative possibilities of the medium, mainly in the form of social dramas and sensational films about love, adventure, and criminality.[84] There were, apart from the technological improvements that made it possible, two primary reasons for this shift. First of all, many filmmakers sought to legitimate their medium in the eyes of the cultural elite, to lay claim to a respectable artistic status hitherto denied them (on which more below). Although cinemas had for years tried to present themselves as 'cinema-theatre', the inability to make longer narrative films rendered such claims unconvincing. The aim of feature

---

[79] Müller, *Frühe*, 20.
[80] Only a tiny handful came earlier: A. Jason, *Der Film in Ziffern und Zahlen (1895–1925)* (Berlin, 1925), 20–1.
[81] Ibid. 21, 31.   [82] E. Altenloh, *Zur Soziologie des Kino* (Jena, 1914), 51.
[83] Ibid. 19.   [84] Toeplitz, *Geschichte*, 70.

Fig. 3. The early 'Ladenkino': staff at the entrance to the Nord-Kino cinema in Berlin, c.1910. bpk Berlin.

films was to be 'abendfüllend', or to take up the whole evening, which for
the traditional theatre meant around two to three hours. It was hoped that by
adopting this recognized aesthetic form the feature film would 'generate just
as much expectation and premiere-fever, would mobilize precisely the same art
critics as perhaps "Der Rosenkavalier". Then film will become a theatre event,
a literary and artistic work.'[85] Underpinning this bid for elite recognition was,
secondly, the desire to raise profits. Only when films could acquire the status of
'valuable art' could they demand the kind of prices theatre did. In this sense the
narrative 'cinema drama' played the same role for film producers that the cinema
palace played for exhibitors: the point of both was to tap a well-heeled audience.

The success of the 'cinema drama', which by 1914 had become the most
popular film genre, had a profound impact on nearly all aspects of cinema. For
one thing, their length of an hour or more meant that they no longer fitted
into vaudeville programmes, which further boosted the trend towards permanent
cinemas. It also affected the average size of cinemas, for longer films meant
less audience turnover, and lower turnover meant that maximizing audience
size required a larger auditorium.[86] It is no coincidence that the half-decade
before the First World War witnessed the construction of ever-larger cinemas
in Germany's major cities; by 1914 Berlin alone had three theatres with seating
capacities over 1,000. Entertaining audiences for this length of time also required
better plots and scriptwriters. Given that a large proportion of the spectators
were women, many of these early 'cinema dramas'—especially those starring the
Swedish-born actress Asta Nielsen—were deliberately geared towards women's
concerns, often revolving around gender and social relationships and a woman's
struggle for happiness.[87] While the films themselves (and at least some of the
cinemas) came to resemble certain aspects of the traditional theatre, so too did
the audience. The fact that good seats in the finer 'cinema palaces' could cost
around RM 5 (as much as a theatre visit) was taken as 'evidence that the cinema
has long ceased to be exclusively the theatre of the little man'. As a result, even
the mode of reception in these venues became more genteel: 'The visit becomes
an official act that one undertakes exactly as one would a theatre visit. There is
none of the casual coming and going as in the smaller local cinemas.'[88]

As we will see below, it was precisely with the emergence of drama and
'artistic' cinema that the German cultural elite became more interested in film,
in both a positive and negative sense. But in the meantime the attempts by
filmmakers to gain the sympathy of the educated classes by no means severed
all of cinema's vaudeville and fairground roots. Although the bid for artistic

---

[85] *Licht-Bild-Bühne* (*LBB*) (22 Apr. 1911), from C. Müller, 'Variationen des Kinoprogramms',
in C. Müller and H. Segeberg (eds), *Die Modellierung des Kinofilms* (Munich, 1998), 70.

[86] Müller, 'Variationen', 71.

[87] See generally H. Schlüpmann, *Unheimlichkeit des Blicks* (Basel, 1990); also Altenloh, *Soziologie*,
58.

[88] Quotes from Altenloh, *Soziologie*, 19–20.

recognition was celebrated in some quarters, not everyone was happy about it. In fact, the advent of the long film met with considerable scepticism, even within the industry. The problem was not so much that longer films meant fewer showings and potentially less revenue (which was a concern), but rather that they represented a break from the previous variety format that had made the cinema such a success in the first place. In 1913 Kurt Tucholsky remarked that the tried-and-tested formula of rapid and brief impressions 'seems to be the only form in which the cinema can be endured: three minutes, parody, grotesque, superhuman hand movements, a smiling mouth but no spoken word, joy, attempt, hope, happiness, fall, thump, defeat, live with it. Three minutes.'[89] Audiences still craved variety, and programmes with up to ten numbers did not die out overnight. Indeed, some cinemas even sought a competitive advantage by retaining the Varieté format. In 1913 Berlin's plush *Kammerlichtspiele* actually banned the long drama from its programme on the grounds that 'the experience with numerous, lavishly made dramatizations has prompted the *Kammerlichtspiele* to be one of the first movie theatres of the capital *to return to the original aim of the cinema*, which is primarily to satisfy the audience's desire for entertainment, its demand for knowledge and its curiosity'.[90] The forms of early film were not determined solely by the technological capabilities of the medium. The Varieté traditions of pastiche and diversity shaped audience expectations and film production long after the technical barriers to feature-length films were overcome. Mixed cinema programmes including dances, acrobatic numbers, and live sketches carried on well into the 1920s, especially in cities with a vibrant vaudeville scene.[91] Ironically, it was only when film could finally claim to be 'cinema theatre' that it first began deliberately presenting itself as 'cinema-Varieté'.

Film, then, remained very much a popular phenomenon. In spite of the new artistic pretensions, for the most part it continued to function as the 'theatre of the little man', where the public wilfully insisted on seeing what it was used to and regarded aesthetic experiments with scepticism. Action, adventure, and romance were—then as now—the stock-in-trade of the film industry. They were, as the film journal *Licht-Bild-Bühne* put it, 'what modern nerves need, what they avidly crave'.[92] As such, it was almost inevitable that the cinema would attract criticism from an educated elite defined in large part by an appreciation of 'art' and 'culture'. Although recent research has shown that the early cinema

---

[89] P. Panter (K. Tucholsky), 'Moritz und Max', *Die Schaubühne* 9 (27 Nov. 1913), repr. in J. Schweinitz (ed.), *Prolog vor dem Film* (Leipzig, 1992), 390–1.

[90] 'Reform im Kino', *Der Kunstwart* (Nov. 1913), quoted from Müller, *Frühe*, 227, italics in original.

[91] 'Kino-Varietés', *Reichsfilmblatt* (*RFB*) (29 Nov. 1924), 41; also Landesarchiv Berlin (LAB), A Pr. Br. Rep. 030, Tit. 74, Nr. 1357.

[92] 'Die Karriere des Kinematographen', *LBB* (10 Dec. 1910), quoted from A. Kaes (ed.), *Kino-Debatte* (Tübingen, 1978), 7–8.

audience was far less proletarian than many contemporaries assumed,[93] it was nonetheless generally shunned by the German Bildungsbürgertum. The bulk of the audience was drawn from urban labourers and the lower-middle classes, and was also disproportionately young.[94] Once it became a profitable entertainment industry for the masses, film was suddenly perceived as a social and cultural 'problem'. By around 1910 various professional groups such as teachers, clergy, doctors, and writers unleashed a flood of pamphlets and books expressing their concerns about the social and cultural ramifications of the cinema.

In many ways the resulting anti-cinema discourse of the 1910s grafted directly on to the anti-Varieté discourse of the 1890s.[95] In both cases, their mixture of different genres and the compilation of numerous short features was itself an affront to elite cultural sensibilities. Deliberately conceived as entertaining diversion, the standard film programme flagrantly transgressed the categories and structures of traditional art forms. The sense of uniformity and linearity that characterized great musical or theatrical works met its antithesis in the hodgepodge of 'cinema-Varieté'. Worse still, this filmic trampling of aesthetic standards occurred by and large through visual means, thereby sidestepping the authority of the word. This is not to say that early film was wholly devoid of a verbal element: captions conveyed both dialogue and narrative skeleton, and some cinemas employed live announcers (*Erklärer*) until around 1910.[96] But most films nonetheless relied on a new vocabulary of gestures and visual cues—cues to which the culturally initiated were unaccustomed. The sudden cutaways to a wholly different scene or different camera angle were often perceived by the art aficionado as profoundly disruptive. 'I cannot imagine anything more artless and devoid of style than this constant jumping from picture to picture, this completely unjustified change of scale to which the eye is supposed to adjust so quickly,' remarked a Dresden curator in 1913. 'This continual change of perspective, of lighting, of tempo gradually drives the viewer into a condition of nervous agitation.'[97]

If the forms of early cinema did not accord with elite notions of culture, its content was deemed no better. As critics often argued, the very nature of film as a visual medium made it intrinsically sensationalist. Relying so heavily on images and gestures to convey meanings carried an inbuilt tendency towards exaggeration and lurid thrills. Critics feared that this propensity, in combination with film's unique sense of authenticity, would erode viewers' sense of reality. The many 'sensation films' in circulation were therefore a particular target of

[93] See esp. C. Müller, 'Der frühe Film, das frühe Kino und seine Gegner und Befürworter', in Kaschuba and Maase (eds.), *Schund*, 62–91; P. Jelavich, 'Darf ich mich hier amüsieren', in M. Hettling and S.-L. Hoffmann (eds.), *Der bürgerliche Wertehimmel* (Göttingen, 2000), 283–303; K. Maase, 'Massenkunst und Volkserziehung', *AfS* 41 (2001), 39–77.

[94] Altenloh, *Soziologie*, 92.   [95] Jelavich, 'Darf ich', 286–7.

[96] Kullmann, *Entwicklung*, 35.

[97] *Berliner Tageblatt* (16 Mar. 1913), quoted from Jelavich, 'Darf ich', 293.

scorn, especially those dealing with sexual or criminal themes. While erotic titles such as *Sinful Love, Burning Love,* and *Queen of the Night* posed a clear danger to moral values, the often sympathetic portrayals of daring and resourceful criminals threatened to undermine respect for the law.[98] Government officials in Württemberg, for instance, worried that:

when people constantly see scenes of criminality and suicides, acts of viciousness, gross sensuality, and the many other unethical things that recur with sickening regularity in our so-called 'criminal and sexual films', then their sense of what is ethically reprehensible is gradually blunted. This danger exists especially for children and adolescents, whose ethical perceptions are still in the formative stage, and also for adults whose characters are insufficiently developed or whose mental faculties are weak.[99]

Cinema was thus the last place in which such themes should be aired, packed as they were with youth, women, and manual labourers—precisely the groups deemed most susceptible to such moral corruption and most in need of patriarchal guidance. The fact that the masses partook of such damaging fare under cover of darkness, and therefore free from supervision, only heightened suspicions about its detrimental effects.

Early cinema thus challenged traditional bourgeois values on a multitude of levels. As Peter Jelavich has emphasized, the nature of cinema in many ways presented a nightmare scenario in the eyes of cultivated patricians. In dark and crowded rooms, an audience drawn mainly from the lower social strata gawked at frivolous sensation films with subversive sexual or criminal themes, or gave itself over to social dramas featuring independent and strong-willed women, and all of this without the primacy of the word, without a clear plot or message, and—given the highly improvised nature of early film production, in which actors and actresses often exercised as much creative influence as directors—without even unambiguous artistic origins.[100] To make matters worse, film also posed a danger to bourgeois institutions. The ever-growing popularity of the cinema threatened to undermine not just the morally dubious *Tingel-Tangels* (the German equivalent to music halls) and fairgrounds frequented by the urban masses, but also the 'legitimate' theatre. For it was precisely when the cinema tried to re-create itself in the image of the stage that it attracted the ire of the theatre world. Critics also worried whether the cinema might overtake the schoolroom in terms of social influence, and thus undo all the good work of Germany's prized education system.

Yet, as we will see below, the problem was not so much with film per se as with the specific ways in which it was manifested: as a largely unregulated commercial enterprise whose primary social function was 'mere entertainment'. Nearly all contemporary observers—whether supporters or opponents, regular

---

[98] Titles from Stark, 'Cinema', 130; see also J. Goergen, 'Der pikante Film', in T. Elsaesser and M. Wedel (eds.), *Kino der Kaiserzeit*, (Munich, 2002), 45–61.

[99] Quoted from Stark, 'Cinema', 132.   [100] Jelavich, 'Darf ich', 296.

movie-goers or abstainers, progressives or traditionalists—agreed that film was an immensely powerful new form of mass communication. More than newspapers, magazines, or books, film was seen as an ideal vehicle for conveying messages and values to a mass public that often lacked the education or inclination to absorb large amounts of information through reading. It was not only decidedly user-friendly, but its unique ability to show the 'genuine article' lent it a degree of credibility and persuasiveness that—though potentially dangerous if left to the machinations of commercial entrepreneurs—made a more indelible imprint on the thoughts and opinions of an audience than any other medium. It was, in short, regarded as an ideal means of popular education, and the aim was to harness it for this purpose. Whether social reform was the only justification for its existence, whether it was legitimate at all to convey 'mere entertainment', how film should be shaped for more edifying purposes—these were all questions that had to be grappled with.

CONSERVING SOUND: PHONOGRAPH
AND GRAMOPHONE

If the years around 1900 saw a significant shift towards a more visually oriented culture, the concurrent changes in the 'landscape of sound' were hardly less important.[101] Admittedly, the medium of recorded sound was far less widespread than the cinema or press at the turn of the century. But even so, its gradual emergence marked a major milestone in the development of a media-based commercial culture. It is perhaps the relatively slow development of recorded music that explains the lack of attention historians have paid to it. For all the recent interest in mass communications, the history of recorded sound in Germany has remained relatively uncharted territory. For the early years in particular, little has been written about the spread of the phonograph and its relationship to broader patterns of social and cultural change.[102] The following section will offer a brief overview of these issues, focusing first on the growth of the recording industry in Germany before considering the popular reception of recorded sound and its effects on existing cultural traditions.

Like the cinema, phonographic technology underwent a lengthy process of evolution prior to its breakthrough as a popular form of entertainment. When Edison first presented his 'phonograph' to the world in 1877, a mechanical device capable of reproducing sounds conserved on etched metal cylinders, it

---

[101] See L. Tournès, 'The Landscape of Sound in the Nineteenth and Twentieth Centuries', *Contemporary European History*, 13 (2004), 493–504.

[102] See C. Ross, 'Entertainment, Technology and Tradition', in Führer and Ross (eds.), *Media*, 25–43; S. Fetthauer, *Deutsche Grammophon* (Hamburg, 2000); far narrower is R. May, 'Die Schallplatte als "Kult"-mittel', *MkF* 15 (1992), 182–225.

was conceived primarily as a means of business communication. Once it became clear, however, that the business world was uninterested in the contraption, other entrepreneurs began to focus on its potential for popular entertainment. At the same time, a number of engineers experimented with different techniques and materials in an attempt to improve sound fidelity and lower costs. Most notable was the German-American inventor Emil Berliner, whose 'gramophone', unveiled in 1887, introduced the flat shellac discs that eventually came to prevail.

It was around 1900 that the German recording industry made its breakthrough. After Berliner founded his 'Berliner Grammophone Company' in Philadelphia in 1887, he soon established production facilities in Europe, first of all in his hometown Hanover. Other firms soon followed, and over the first decade of the twentieth century the production of records swelled in Germany from around 2.5 million in 1902 to 18 million by 1907. Despite such impressive growth, however, the recording industry proved highly prone to fluctuations in the wider economy. Records production declined precipitously during the First World War, and only rebounded to pre-war levels during the latter half of the 1920s, reaching a peak of some 30 million records in 1929, around half of them for export.[103]

Though an unusually volatile industry in the early twentieth century, recorded sound was becoming big business. In 1907 the German record and gramophone industry already numbered 181 enterprises employing around 4,600 people (not including the various supply firms closely related to the industry). At the industry's inter-war peak around 1930, it was estimated that some 40,000 manual labourers and 7,000 white-collar workers were directly or indirectly employed in the record industry, making it approximately the same size as the shoe industry.[104] Most of the firms were concentrated in Leipzig, Dresden, Hamburg, and above all Berlin, which by the early 1920s was home to no fewer than seventy firms.[105] This geographic concentration was based not only on the cheap labour and large local public afforded by the large cities, but also on the high concentration of actors and singers (again, particularly in Berlin) on whom the recording industry relied.

By the mid-1920s the medium of recorded sound was an integral part of Germany's cultural landscape.[106] During the economic upswing after 1924 it became both more affordable and more widespread, especially among the middle classes. At the same time, it catered to an ever more complex palette of tastes, ranging from popular dance music to the classics. Yet from early on many educated elites regarded it with concern. Although this did not

---

[103] Figures from K. Blaukopf, *Massenmedium Schallplatte* (Wiesbaden, 1977), 26.

[104] W. Leubuscher, 'Normalisierung in der Sprechmaschinenindustrie', *PZ* 31 (15 Mar. 1930), 448. For earlier figures: R. Krebs, *Die phonographische Industrie in Deutschland unter besonderer Berücksichtigung ihres Exports*, Diss., Greifswald (1925), 40; G. Braune, *Der Einfluß von Schallplatte und Rundfunk auf die deutsche Musikinstrumentenindustrie* (Berlin, 1934), 32.

[105] Figures from Krebs, 'Industrie', 32.

[106] The following section is drawn from Ross, 'Entertainment', with the permission of Palgrave Macmillan.

Fig. 4. Young Berlin couple pondering the purchase of a gramophone, late 1920s. bpk
Berlin.

keep the gramophone out of many a bildungbürgerlich household—Thomas
Mann himself was an avid listener—to many it represented at best a dubious
compromise with mechanization and cultural commercialization, and at worst
another threat to genuine *Kultur*. This sense of elite ambivalence was eloquently

expressed by the journalist Paul Schlesinger, who, though clearly delighted with his new gramophone in 1924, nonetheless found it difficult to accept its social and cultural implications: 'A particular conception of what constitutes a respectable way of life lasts for only a limited number of decades—then one has had enough of it and buys a gramophone. One has his convictions, and has championed them for years; then he goes and blissfully does the opposite. None of what one has ever thought or said against the talking machine is retracted. It was a noble and splendid fight, and the defeat was literally a noisy one.'[107] Purchasing a gramophone is portrayed here as a betrayal of one's values, and there is a certain pang of conscience about finally succumbing to the medium of recorded music, which he likens to a 'sweet poison', an addictive drug at once dangerous and irresistible.

As Schlesinger's comments suggest, elite aversion to the gramophone arose on a number of levels. First of all, as a primary reflection of the wider mechanization of music, it was seen to pose a threat to the bourgeois ideal of the cultivated lay musician. The practice of making music at home (*Hausmusik*) was second only to reading in the bourgeois hierarchy of cultural virtues. By eroding the idea that one must play music in order to appreciate it, the gramophone was perceived by many as 'the death of living music, especially music in the home'.[108] At the same time, it was held in either grave suspicion or outright contempt by the bulk of professional musicians, for whom 'the word mechanization currently carries the same horror as the word machine did for many workmen one hundred years ago'.[109] Simply put, the ability to conserve sound over time rendered the act of performance less important. Similar complaints were voiced by the musical-instrument industry, which had long been in decline and tended to blame this on the rise of recorded sound.[110]

But even more alarming to cultural conservatives was the central role of recorded sound in the 'internationalization' of music, and in particular the popularization of American jazz. Enthusiastically embraced by much of the avant-garde and grudgingly accepted by many liberal-minded listeners, jazz was contemptuously rejected by conservatives of all shades, who regarded it as little more than primitive 'negro-music' and therefore quintessentially un-German.[111] The fact that jazz was associated with urban living by both supporters and opponents alike did nothing to reduce its polarizing impact. Whereas supporters celebrated its rhythmic affinity with modern life, for opponents it was one of the more egregious outgrowths of 'asphalt culture'. As if the ability of records to

---

[107] Sling [P. Schlesinger], 'Die Tonkneipe' (Dec. 1924), repr. in Sling, *Die Nase der Sphinx* (Berlin, 1987), 182–3.

[108] Quote from 'Rundfunk, Schallplatte und individuelle Musik', *PZ* 34 (25 Feb. 1933), 87. See also 'Schallplatte und Hausmusik', *PZ* 34 (25 Mar. 1933), 156; G. Reuveni, 'The "Crisis of the Book" and German Society after the First World War', *GH* 20 (2002), 438–61.

[109] F. Warschauer, 'Musik im Rundfunk', *Musikblätter des Anbruch*, 8 (Oct.–Nov. 1926), 374.

[110] *PZ* 30 (15 June 1929), 918; see also G. Braune, *Einfluß*, 111–16.

[111] M. Kater, *Different Drummers* (New York, 1992), esp. 3–28.

transport jazz across the Atlantic were not bad enough, the efforts of German recording companies to stimulate interest in the genre seemed nothing less than an act of treason against the German cultural heritage.

Given the conservative perception of America as a land of soulless commodification, shallowness, and 'massification', the very 'Americanness' of jazz also resonated with another strand of criticism: the commercial nature of the recording industry. Although the threat of commercialization applied to the entire spectrum of popular culture, it was, given the strong sense of national pride in the German musical legacy, of particular concern with regard to recorded sound.[112] Recording firms were naturally more interested in selling music for profit than in shoring up cultural traditions. There was, after all, big money to be made by hits such as *Yes, We Have No Bananas*, which by 1929 had sold 3 million copies. Quite obviously, sales for even the most popular symphonies, like Beethoven's Ninth, paled in comparison. As a result, 'hit' music soon came to dominate the industry by the 1920s, accounting for around 75 per cent of all recordings by 1929.[113]

The problem in the eyes of cultural conservatives was not so much that such hit songs were popular. Even the most hidebound traditionalist agreed that popular 'hits' in some form had been around for centuries. The issue was rather where this popularity originated, and it was the commercial nature of the modern 'hit' that caused offence. For one thing, it trampled the idea that a 'successful' piece of music should possess some degree of enduring cultural value. The goal of achieving timelessness was simply not the aim of hit tunes, which consciously opted for the immediate reward of momentary appeal. During the runaway inflation of the early 1920s the notoriety of such timely hits as *We're Boozing Away Granny's Little House* and *Who Rolled the Cheese to the Station* testified to the commercial success of this approach.[114] Moreover, unlike the folkloric origins of many traditional songs, the 'popularity' of the modern hit was seen primarily as a reflection of its consumption, not production. As the critic Herbert Connor put it, whereas popular songs had previously emerged from 'the people', in the mechanized and commodified twentieth century they had become the 'product of a deliberate calculation'. Their texts and melodies were not derived from oral or musical tradition, but were written by publishers and composers in such a way as to maximize royalties. Thus, despite the common suggestion that modern dance hits somehow compensated for the stress of the modern workplace,[115] it was incorrect to ascribe this 'mass production of aural trash' to the current Zeitgeist since it actually originated from purely commercial

---

[112] Generally, P. Potter, *Most German of the Arts* (New Haven, 1998).

[113] Figures from H. Schröder, *Tanz- und Unterhaltungsmusik in Deutschland 1918–1933* (Bonn, 1990), 317; P. Wicke, *Von Mozart zu Madonna* (Leipzig, 1998), 98.

[114] 'Wir versaufen unsrer Oma ihr klein Häuschen'; 'Wer hat denn den Käse zum Bahnhof gerollt': W. Haas, *Das Jahrhundert der Schallplatte* (Bielefeld, 1977), 138.

[115] e.g. H. Stumme, 'Von der Psychologie des Schlagers', *Die Stimme seines Herrn* (*Die Stimme*), 13 (June 1928), 103–4; J. Damanski, 'Über Unterhaltungsmusik', *Die Stimme*, 13 (Aug. 1928), 143.

considerations: 'It was first in the modern metropolis, which has forfeited all communal ties, that the musical hit, by its very nature a product of the people, has become an object of cheap entertainment.'[116] As the primary vehicle of such 'aural trash', as a central conduit for the 'Americanization' of popular music, as an allegedly remorseless destroyer of live performance, the gramophone was in many eyes guilty by association.

Yet for all the venerated cultural traditions potentially threatened by the rise of recorded sound, its effects were in practice much more ambivalent than such Cassandra-calls suggest. Overall, the relationship between recording technology and cultural traditions in Germany followed a pattern not at all dissimilar from that in Britain, where, as D. L. LeMahieu has shown, recorded sound did not so much destroy musical traditions as reconfigure them, often in unpredictable ways.[117] There were three primary aspects to this, relating to the transcendence of time, the transcendence of space, and the general mechanization of music.

First, there can be little doubt that the ability of recorded sound to transcend time relativized the act of musical performance. Professional musicians and concert-hall regulars were quite right to fear the impact it would have on the long-term viability of individual orchestras, especially in view of the dwindling subsidies available after the First World War. At the same time, it was also understandable that musicologists should feel uneasy about the ability of recording technology to transform music from a social activity into a consumer good that could be deployed by individuals at almost any time. However, in the years before the dominance of studio recordings the vast bulk of records were in fact based on live performances. It was fairly common to purchase recordings of performances that one attended oneself, almost as a memento of the occasion.[118] Even after the large firms established special recording studios, their recording sessions were regularly open—and advertised—to the public.[119] The line between recording and live performance was therefore not so clear as one might assume.

The implications of sound conservation differed quite substantially for individual musical genres. It is telling that sound conservation was by no means regarded by tradition-minded musicologists as singularly negative. As early as 1900 commentators recognized how beneficial it would be if recordings of Beethoven conducted by Hans von Bülow were available, or recordings of *Parsifal* made during Wagner's lifetime.[120] Beyond the classical canon, however, the effects looked somewhat different. As LeMahieu has pointed out, although recording technology in one sense immortalized a popular tune, the ability to replay it as often as one wished actually tended to *shorten* the life-span of a 'hit' by

---

[116] H. Connor, 'Haben Schlager künstlerischen Wert?', *Die Musik*, 24 (July 1932), 750–1.
[117] LeMahieu, *Culture*, 88–98, on which the following paragraphs also draw.
[118] Wicke, *Mozart*, 99.
[119] 'Künstler—Schallplatte—Publikum', *PZ* 36 (Dec. 1935), 512.
[120] 'Die Phonographie im Dienste der Musikpädagogik und Musikwissenschaft', *PZ* 1 (Oct. 1900), 33–5.

diminishing the intervals between hearing it. No longer having to wait very long to hear a beloved melody, the public quickly had enough of it. It appears that this trend accelerated markedly during the 1920s with the rapid expansion of radio and gramophone use. Whereas midday radio programmes in the mid-1920s often featured 'the hits of the season' (including songs from over the past year or two), by the end of 1929 the Berlin broadcaster was playing only 'the newest hits of the month' on its midday programme.[121] Thus the increasingly rapid turnover of hit songs was not just an industry ploy for stimulating demand, but was also rooted in the very usage of recorded sound within the wider cultural context.

Secondly, although the ability of recorded sound to transcend space made the music scene in one sense much more international, it also served to 'nationalize' popular tastes and to reaffirm the boundaries of national culture. This was clearly manifested in August 1914, as recording firms and popular composers quickly made the shift from foreign dance music to 'war production' in order to satisfy the exploding demand for patriotic songs. Among the most popular hits of the era were Walter Kollo's *Immer feste druff!*, Paul Lincke's *Fürs Vaterland*, and Bogumil Zepler's *Das deutsche Schwert*.[122] The 'nationalization' of tastes was also in evidence during the Ruhr crisis of 1923, which witnessed a huge surge in demand (and supply) for Rheinlieder.[123] The Wall Street crash in 1929 likewise triggered a noticeable shift, as German Lieder, military marches, and waltzes increasingly supplanted jazz-inspired 'hits', which themselves became more distinctly German around 1930: titles such as *Das Schützenfest, Alt-Heidelberg*, and *Einmal am Rhein* give a sense of the trend.[124] One should not, however, overemphasize this shift, for despite the polarizing disputes over jazz, it is important to note that waltzes and Volkslieder had always been the popular favourites in Germany in any event, and this in spite of (or rather because of) their complete lack of international appeal.[125] Moreover, much of what counted as 'jazz' in Germany had little to do with the genuine American article. As a German dance journal explained in 1925: 'What is nowadays played as jazz has nothing to do with negro music. It is, in reality, nothing more than syncopated music, and sometimes nothing more than a somewhat rhythmically wilful manner of playing the percussion instruments.'[126]

Thirdly, although recorded sound undoubtedly constituted a quantum leap in the mechanization of music, it also served to boost live performance by stimulating the demand for hit songs and promoting the wider dance craze that

---

[121] L. Stoffels, 'Rundfunk und die Kultur der Gegenwart', in J.-F. Leonhard (ed.), *Programmgeschichte des Hörfunks in der Weimarer Republik*, vol. 2 (Munich, 1997), 988.

[122] See 'Die Geschäftsstöckung', *PZ* 15 (Aug. 1914), 621; F. Ritzel, 'Hätte der Kaiser Jazz getanzt', in S. Schutte (ed.), *Ich will aber gerade vom Leben singen* (Reinbek, 1987), 278.

[123] *PZ* 24 (June 1923), 532.   [124] Ritzel, 'Hätte', 290.

[125] See L. Koch, 'Schallplattenindustrie, Staat und Volksbildung', *Die Musik*, 22 (Apr. 1930), 516; also W. Mühl-Benninghaus, *Das Ringen um den Tonfilm* (Düsseldorf, 1999), 274.

[126] C. Schär, *Der Schlager und seine Tänze im Deutschland der 20er Jahre* (Zurich, 1991), 41, n. 21. See also Kater, *Different*, 3–28.

swept Germany after the First World War.[127] Records could very successfully popularize tunes, but before the advent of electrical recording they were ill-suited to performing them in public due to the inability to achieve the necessary volume levels.[128] Because the phonograph served to heighten demand *without* being able to satisfy it in a public setting, the overall effect was to boost live music. Although these technological obstacles were largely overcome in the second half of the 1920s with the advent of electrical recording and the mains plug-in set (which first introduced electrical amplification as we know it today), the cost-saving potential of these devices could hardly outweigh the appeal of a live band. There was, as the record companies argued, no reason to assume that the gramophone would kill off live music any more than previous mechanical inventions had done, whether the medieval Glockenspiel, the orchestrion, the organ, or the mechanical piano.[129] At the end of the 1920s there were still armies of musicians and singers employed in Germany's dance halls: 21,000 in Berlin, 19,000 in Hamburg, 15,850 in Hanover, 11,000 in Leipzig, and 10,800 in Dresden.[130]

Much the same can be said for the impact of the gramophone on music-making in the home. For all the complaints about its supposed displacement by records, it seems that Hausmusik was becoming more, not less, popular after the First World War.[131] It was widely acknowledged by all but the most irretrievable pessimists that the desire to hear music (whether recorded or otherwise) or to play it oneself were quite different urges.[132] Indeed, records arguably *aided* the revival of Hausmusik after the First World War in the form of special accompaniment ('Spiel mit') recordings of duets and quartets minus one instrument.[133] And apart from the sheer quantity of music played in the home, many music critics also welcomed the qualitative improvements of recorded sound. In 1905 the composer Engelbert Humperdinck expressed the hope that 'mechanized' Hausmusik would supersede the 'vain bungling' prevalent in most households: 'The great painting masterpieces are not there to be copied but to be viewed; could it not be the same with musical works?'[134] As for lay musicians, many found it difficult 'to master an instrument to the point where one's own playing can even remotely fulfil his own musical standards. One is eventually happy that the gramophone

---

[127] Schär, *Schlager*, 43–9; Wicke, *Mozart*, 86–8.

[128] 'Die Sprechmaschine als Tanzmusik', *PZ* 6 (Jan. 1905), 23.

[129] K. Sonnemann, 'Der erste deutsche Schallplattentag', *PZ* 31 (15 Dec. 1930), 1730.

[130] Schär, *Schlager*, 49.   [131] Potter, *Most*, 6, 42–4.

[132] See Braune, *Einfluß*, 111–16.

[133] See esp. 'Neue Abnehmerkreise für Schallplatten', *PZ* 34 (June 1933), 281; also 'Die Schallplatte als Förderin der Hausmusik', *Die Stimme*, 19 (Nov. 1934), 136–7; *PZ* 39 (Jan. 1938), 13; 'Hausmusik und Schallplatte', *Die Stimme*, 20 (Nov. 1935), 117–18. Record retailers were surprised to find that the campaign 'Foster German Hausmusik' boosted rather than hindered record sales in the early 1930s: *PZ* 35 (Jan. 1934), 4; 'Zum Tag der Hausmusik', *PZ* 35 (Nov. 1934), 543–4; 'Die Lehren des Tages der Hausmusik', *PZ* 36 (Dec. 1935), 484–6.

[134] E. Humperdinck, 'Die Zukunft der mechanischen Musik' (repr. from *Kunstwart*), *PZ* 6 (Oct. 1905), 876.

dispenses with the necessity of having to listen to oneself plonking away.'[135] As another critic pointedly remarked: 'the phonograph has rendered greater services to Hausmusik than all of the piano lessons in the world.'[136]

However hyperbolic such assertions may have been, they nonetheless demonstrate an important point. The relationship between the gramophone and musical traditions was—and was perceived by many contemporaries as—not merely one of destruction and displacement, but of recasting and transfiguration, in some respects even rejuvenation.

CULTURAL AUTHORITY AND THE ENTERTAINMENT MARKET

Despite widespread contemporary fears about the effects of the new media, closer inspection shows that their impact on cultural traditions, patterns of social distinction, and popular tastes was rarely straightforward, and depended crucially on the precise nature of their technology, the changing composition of their audiences, their variegated uses, and the wider social and cultural context in which they were embedded—factors which the following chapters will consider in detail.

Yet there can be no doubt that the growth of commercial culture represented a serious threat to certain traditions. Above all, it questioned the social position of the Bildungsbürgertum as the principal arbiters and consumers of culture. At the most fundamental level, commercial entertainments and mass media undermined the authority of cultural elites by making the marketplace their most important measure of success. Cultural value was no longer determined solely by aesthetic standards, but also by sales. By deliberately catering to the tastes of a mass audience, commercial entertainments effectively took the judgement of artistic merit out of the hands of a cultural oligarchy and put it to a popular referendum. At the same time that the marketplace usurped this authority 'from below', the increasingly international scope of commercial culture also challenged it 'from without'. The mounting cross-border traffic of music, films, and the values they embodied threw into question many older assumptions about the boundaries of 'national' culture, and along with them the role of an educated elite as custodians of a distinct national heritage.

Given what was at stake, these developments naturally elicited a strong response. The fundamental challenge they posed to the cultural hegemony of the

---

[135] E. Ackerknecht, *Bildungspflege und Schallplatte* (Stettin, 1930), 2–3; also Jolowicz, *Rundfunk*, 13; E. Hanisch, 'Wie steht der Dorfbewohner zur Musik?', *Musik und Gesellschaft*, 1 (July 1930), 82–3.

[136] H. H. Stuckenschmidt, 'Erziehung durch Sprechapparate', *Musikblätter des Anbruch*, 8 (Oct.–Nov. 1926), 370.

educated elite prompted heated debates among a wide range of different groups. As we will see in the next two chapters, the concrete responses to the challenge of commercial culture varied widely, and were by no means confined to outright rejection and the 'politics of cultural despair'.[137] Yet it is nonetheless fair to say that mass communications and commercial culture were generally viewed with scepticism among the bulk of the Bildungsbürgertum, and were regarded by many as a social and cultural 'problem' that required urgent solutions.

Although similar developments could be observed across much of the industrialized world, these debates were particularly vehement in Germany, for two closely related reasons: the changing self-understanding of the German educated elite, and the unique importance of culture in bourgeois conceptions of German nationhood. The fact that the rise of the new media and commercial culture coincided with a broader sense of crisis among the Bildungsbürgertum strongly coloured perceptions. Over the course of the nineteenth century the German educated elite had grown accustomed to exerting a remarkable degree of cultural and political influence. The traditional process of elite formation among the German bourgeoisie revolved largely around the Humboldtian tradition of humanistic education in Gymnasium and university. At the top of the social hierarchy stood academic occupations such as professors, lawyers, and physicians, whose social prestige derived primarily from their educational qualifications rather than material wealth. During the latter part of the nineteenth century rapid industrialization in Germany gradually undermined their position as a non-economic middle class. The rise of a new industrial and technical elite threatened to displace the values of *Bildung* (education) by the power of *Besitz* (material possessions), and at the same time the expansion of higher education threatened to dilute academic standards.[138]

In response, Germany's non-economic elites tended to defend the status symbol of humanistic education by drawing a clearer distinction between *Bildung* and *Ausbildung*, or education as self-cultivation (and a virtue in itself) as opposed to the acquisition of practical knowledge.[139] In this context an appreciation of art and culture for their own sake represented an ideal weapon for asserting social superiority. This weapon was all the more potent for being able to draw on older Romantic conceptions of art as a kind of window to the divine, the creation of inspired genius that demanded a quasi-religious form of veneration (along with the requisite education) to be fully appreciated. The resulting dichotomization between 'serious' art and that which merely sought to 'entertain' was thus not new to the Wilhelmine era, but it was accentuated by the rapid social changes under way. It was also related to the increasingly strident nationalist claims to

---

[137] F. Stern, *The Politics of Cultural Despair* (Berkeley, 1961). For a corrective focused on mainstream reformers, K. Repp, *Reformers, Critics and the Paths of German Modernity* (Cambridge, Mass., 2000).

[138] F. Ringer, *The Decline of the German Mandarins* (Cambridge, Mass., 1969), 44–6.

[139] See W. H. Bruford, *The German Tradition of Self-Cultivation* (Cambridge, 1975).

German exceptionalism from the 1890s, to the supposed profundity of German *Kultur* over the superficial mannerliness of Western *Zivilisation*. The nationalist jingoism of the Wilhelmine period posited a unique appreciation of culture as a distinguishing characteristic of the national soul.[140] This, too, rested on older ideas about the centrality of culture to the definition of German nationhood. Although the sense of sharing a distinct cultural heritage has of course played a key role in the construction of national identities across the globe, it was particularly acute in Germany, where the idea of a *Kulturnation* was long celebrated as a surrogate to actual political unification prior to 1870, especially among the educated elite. A deep reverence for 'culture' was thus an indispensable badge of both national and social distinction. The intense veneration of art by the Bildungsbürgertum therefore reflected art's role as both 'a medium of national cultural integration and as a confirmation of their own cultural hegemony'.[141] By the turn of the century much of Germany's educated elite had begun to perceive itself more specifically as a *cultural* elite whose duty was quite literally to act as guardians or 'bearers' of German national culture against the alleged soullessness and sterile rationality of modern industrial society.[142]

In many respects the rise of commercial entertainments embodied the most regrettable ills of this society. As mere commodities devoid of intrinsic value, they were a primary symbol of the new technological civilization and its 'cultural decadence'. Although elite criticisms of commercial culture were many and varied, it is useful to conceive of them as the product of four distinct sets of concerns that were closely interrelated in practice: aesthetic, social-pedagogic, medical, and economic.[143]

For the initiated, the vast bulk of cultural artefacts peddled by the mass media were simply worthless. As we have already seen, intellectuals by and large judged popular culture according to the artistic criteria of literature, painting, theatre, and classical music. In these terms, the stuff in the popular press and cinemas could never be educational or uplifting; it was simply rubbish. During the decade or so after 1900 the concept of *Schund*, loosely translatable as 'trash', came to replace the label 'kitsch' as the operative term of derision. Though it may seem trivial, the shift in terminology is in fact quite revealing. Whereas 'kitsch' was used to disparage a work of poor artistic quality, 'trash' implied a more fundamental form of rejection, a denial that the object in question had anything to do with artistic quality at all.[144] Even the thousands of cheap oil paintings on pub walls and the deliberate provocations of the avant-garde were still—however tasteless and whatever traditions they set out to trample—comprehensible within the categories and conceptual vocabulary of conventional aesthetics. The fact that

---

[140] Generally, H. Glaser, *Bildungsbürgertum und Nationalismus* (Munich, 1993).

[141] Bollenbeck, *Tradition*, 165.

[142] See generally G. Bollenbeck, *Bildung und Kultur* (Frankfurt a. M., 1994); K. Vondung (ed.), *Das wilhelminische Bildungsbürgertum* (Göttingen, 1975).

[143] This categorization partly follows Bollenbeck, *Tradition*, 166–71.   [144] Ibid. 161.

the artefacts of commercial culture largely resisted such categorization, or rather were not concerned with it in the first place, caused even greater offence to aesthetic sensibilities. Unlike 'great art'—or, for that matter, attempts that fell well short of it—it did not seek the veneration of the viewer but rather his or her participation. Any claims that it made to cultural value were not based on its intrinsic merits, but on its ability to entertain. The aim of the season's new dance hit was to give pleasure, not to inspire awe. The whole point of popular film was, as the critic Béla Balázs approvingly put it, to 'abolish the distance between the spectators and an art-world closed off unto itself'.[145] In this sense, the aesthetic problem presented by commercial culture went well beyond that of kitsch. It not only met with the disapproval of the distinguished panel of judges, it also ignored their laws and even refused to recognize the legitimacy of their court.

This was all the more galling to an educated elite that saw the spiritual guidance and betterment of 'the people' as its natural calling. As Fritz Ringer pointed out long ago in his study of the German academic elite, the sense of cultural malaise that plagued many *fin-de-siècle* mandarins did not diminish their claims to the moral and spiritual leadership of the nation. Their decidedly patriarchal inclinations, which if anything intensified as they came under threat, meant that they 'were never content to cultivate their own gardens. They thought of themselves as a priestly caste, and they meant to legislate ultimate values to a peasant population.'[146] Although Ringer was referring here specifically to academic luminaries with their own particular gripes about the erosion of spiritual values in a technological age, much the same could be said of the Wilhelmine educated elite more generally, and certainly of their perceptions of commercial culture. The fact that the mass media did little to improve popular aesthetic sensibilities was bad enough. What made them even worse was that they actually threatened to undermine the elite's ability to shape popular tastes. 'Edification' and 'entertainment' were, in this view, a zero-sum equation: every hour of leisure time spent watching sensation films or reading local crime stories was one less hour available for self-improvement. Worse still, their continuous portrayals of sensuality, unbridled passion, crime and violence could hardly contrast more starkly with the values of self-control, moderation and reason that bourgeois social reformers sought to inculcate. In this sense, concerns about the content of commercial culture reflected the vague but very real *fin-de-siècle* fears of an irrational rabble governed not by reason and intellect but by instincts and impulses.

Admittedly, emotions and passions were the stock-in-trade of commercial entertainments. They deliberately appealed to the senses, they promised immediate pleasure, and they frequently titillated audiences with action and eroticism. As critics commonly argued, this was a major factor behind the ever-multiplying

---

[145] B. Balázs, *Der Geist des Films* (Halle, 1930), quoted from Kaes (ed.), *Kino-Debatte*, 34.
[146] Ringer, *Decline*, 268.

signs of spiritual 'brutalization' (*Verrohung*) among the masses. From this socio-medical point of view, the careless unleashing of emotion and fantasy was nothing short of a public health hazard. Too much excitement and nervous stimulation was, so the argument went, detrimental to the physical and psychological well-being of the nation, and that of youth in particular. And the danger this posed to psychological health was not confined to nervous excitement alone: watching or reading too many implausible action adventures or contrived love tales could, it was feared, erode one's very sense of reality. Although concerns about the overexposure of young people to sexually explicit material was a standard element of the decades-old moral crusade against obscene literature,[147] the rise of the cinema added a new sense of urgency to such criticisms. This was not only because of its unprecedented vividness, but also due to the simple fact that it took place in darkened rooms where, as the physician and writer Alfred Döblin put it, 'couples squeeze into corners and are lost in the reverie of each other's obscene fingers'.[148] Even in the relatively 'respectable' cinemas where one was unlikely to encounter such behaviour, the overexertion of the eyes due to the flickering images on the screen was still deemed a significant health hazard.

In many ways this socio-medical line of criticism likened commercial entertainments to a narcotic. They were a temptation that, once sampled, could become addictive. Pathological terms such as 'reading frenzy' (*Lesewut*) and 'cinema addiction' (*Kinosucht*) clearly expressed this analogy. Users, it was feared, could 'succumb' to the alluring pleasures pushed by the commercial media and thereby forfeit their own self-control. In an age marked by an increasingly biological conception of the nation—and a correspondingly Darwinian conception of international relations—this presented a danger not only to individuals but to society as whole, to the very 'strength of the nation' (*Volkskraft*).[149] Obsessive concerns about population growth and the rising interest in eugenics ensured that the expansion of the commercial media would also be judged according to its effects on 'national health'. Needless to say, most such judgements were harsh. Instead of encouraging self-improvement and a sense of civic duty (as the Bildungsroman, for example, deliberately set out to do), the shallow, sensual appeal of commercial entertainments pandered to sloth and self-indulgence. From the utilitarian perspective of racial hygiene, their invitation to unbridled fantasy and hedonistic pleasure was at best useless, and most likely harmful by diverting the nation's creative energies into the fruitless channels of instant gratification. Worse still, if too much erotic stimulation encouraged excessive

[147] See P. Major, 'Trash and Smut', in Führer and Ross (eds.), *Media*, 234–50; G. Wilkending, 'Die Kommerzialisierung der Jugendliteratur und die Jugendschriftenbewegung um 1900', in Kaschuba and Maase (eds.), *Schund*, 218–51; D. S. Linton, *'Who Has the Youth, Has the Future'* (Cambridge, 1991).

[148] A. Döblin, 'Das Theater der kleinen Leute' (1909), in Kaes (ed.), *Kino-Debatte*, 38.

[149] K. Maase, 'Krisenbewußtsein und Reformorientierung', in Kaschuba and Maase (eds.), *Schund*, 308–9.

masturbation or a blasé attitude towards sex, it could even dampen the natural urge to procreate. As Robert Gaupp argued in his 'medical and psychological' study of the cinema, failure to tackle such problems would leave little choice 'but to demand that the state eliminates a poison that undermines the health of our younger generation'.[150]

For many critics, the idea that all of this was driven by the pursuit of profit was the final straw. The imperative of the 'bottom line' was the root cause of the unrepentant indifference shown towards aesthetic standards, social well-being and moral values. Of course, in some respects this criticism was not so wide of the mark, for giving free rein to the market left little room for scruples. Seemingly unencumbered by the constraints of traditional morality, press lords and movie moguls were constantly decried as 'ignominious wheeler-dealers' who 'fill their pockets by appealing to the base instincts of the masses'.[151] At one level this strand of criticism was part and parcel of the conservative anti-capitalism so prevalent among the German Bildungsbürgertum, a set of reservations and prejudices rooted in the prioritization of *Kultur* and *Bildung* over practical knowledge and material wealth. Yet in many ways these criticisms of the mass media were also of special significance, since they had to do with the realm of culture itself. If riches made from speculation were filthy mammon, then profits drawn from the manipulation of the nation's cultural life were the filthiest of all. Fighting such debasement was therefore not just any old battle in the war between culture and commerce. If anything, it was less a struggle *between* culture and commerce than against their increasing *overlap*, and especially against the perceived corruption of the cultural realm by the cynical practices of capitalist profit-seeking.

On this point in particular—though not only on this point—there was little disagreement between conservative anti-capitalists and their socialist counterparts.[152] For all their ideological differences, most political and cultural elites from across the spectrum had few doubts that the new media and commercial entertainments represented a threat to the spiritual health of the 'masses'. How elites attempted to deal with these issues is the subject of the next section.

[150] R. Gaupp, 'Der Kinematograph vom medizinischen und psychologischen Standpunkt', in K. Brunner and R. Gaupp, *Der Kinematograph als Volksunterhaltungsmittel* (Munich, 1912), 12.

[151] K. Brunner, *Der Kinematograph von heute—eine Volksgefahr* (Berlin, 1913), 3.

[152] On the Left's difficulties with popular culture, G. Eley, 'Cultural Socialism, the Public Sphere, and the Mass Form', in D. Barclay and E. Weitz (eds.), *Between Reform and Revolution* (New York, 1998), 315–40.

PART II

TAMING MASS CULTURE: STRATEGIES OF CONTROL AND REFORM

Introduction

As we have just seen, the expansion of commercial culture and the emergence of new communications technologies threatened the position of cultural elites on a number of levels. One of the most visible effects of these developments was a new brand of cultural interventionism among the educated elite, a belief not only in their ability to improve the tastes and cultural practices of the masses, but indeed in their right—even duty—to do so. While the use of censorship as a means of social control was of course nothing new at the time, the unapologetic commercial orientation of popular amusements and their unprecedented dissemination added a new dimension to the problem during the late nineteenth and early twentieth centuries. Following Jörg Schönert and Ute Daniel, it is helpful to conceive of this as part of a wider shift in the relationship between, on the one hand, the dominant discourses surrounding cultural life and, on the other, the actual socio-cultural practices prevalent in society. Whereas the previous century or so had been characterized by a close relationship between the two—that is, elite expectations and standards of judgement strongly shaped how cultural artefacts were perceived and used—after around 1870 these connections were smothered amidst the swelling market for cultural consumption. Although such a generalization unavoidably simplifies matters, it is fair to say that the growth of a popular cultural industry meant that entertainment value partially displaced aesthetic and ethical value: 'the connections between discourses and socio-cultural practices lost their importance whereas the interactions between these practices and "the market" became more intense.'[1]

Faced with this new cultural constellation, anyone determined to assert elite standards of merit against the spread of market forces effectively had two courses of action available to them: either to increase the intensity of the dominant discourse surrounding cultural life (via efforts to 'edify' popular entertainments and 'educate' popular tastes) or to decrease the potency of the market (via state censorship and commercial regulation). There were many different interests and motivations behind such intervention, ranging from a conservative defence of traditional hierarchies to progressive visions of 'democratizing' culture. Broadly

---

[1] J. Schönert, 'Zu den sozio-kulturellen Praktiken im Umgang mit Literatur(en) von 1770 bis 1930', in Kaschuba and Maase (eds.), *Schund*, 286. Although Schönert, drawing on Daniel, refers specifically to literature, the point can be generalized.

speaking, whereas conservatives tended to focus on limiting the spread of mass culture, the more liberal-minded concentrated on improving its content 'from within'. Yet in practice, the boundaries between these initiatives were fluid, and as we will see, the stark differences in motivation did not preclude the possibility of making common cause. The following two chapters will survey these responses to the rise of mass communications in Germany, first investigating efforts to reassert elite authority via new mechanisms of control before considering attempts at reforming mass culture itself.

2

Reasserting Control: The Regulation of Mass Culture

Whatever critics thought of mass culture and what it stood for, no one doubted that it was here to stay. It was, however lamentably, a part of social reality, and needed to be treated as such. The problem was that there was only so much one could do to guard against what many perceived as its corruption of cultural values. 'Refining' the content of commercial culture was, as we will see in the next chapter, a difficult task. Combating its corrosive effects through informal suppression—a clearer demarcation between 'high' and 'low' culture, denigration as 'base instincts'—also had its limits. The need for some kind of formal control was therefore a point of general consensus among cultural reformers. The central difficulty, however, was that the growing popularity of the commercial press, pulp fiction, and the cinema had already made the imposition of far-reaching restrictions both politically and economically impractical. Well before the turn of the century, the most one could realistically achieve through such 'negative' controls was to banish the most egregious excesses, to set at least minimum standards of taste and decency. This, too, would prove to be a challenging task, and those who took it upon themselves could draw scarce comfort from the thought that their endeavour was a never-ending one, that all societies must continually negotiate what is and is not acceptable, and that in this sense the rise of commercial culture was no exception. For what *was* exceptional was the sheer scale of the challenge they faced, the wholly unprecedented circulation of cultural artefacts that needed to be vetted, and proscribed where necessary. The scope of the problem required urgent solutions. This chapter surveys the efforts of individuals, civic organizations, and state agencies to find them.

'SMUT AND TRASH': CENSORSHIP AND YOUTH PROTECTION IN THE EMPIRE

Although censorship is often derided as illiberal, puritanical, and backward-looking, it is in fact something we humans seem unable to live without. Just as the individual's suppression of unacceptable thoughts can help maintain mental stability, the suppression of certain ideas and images at a collective level helps guarantee the smooth functioning of the social order. Not even the most extreme libertarian would want to do away with censorship entirely, especially in cases of libel or child pornography. Deep down we are all, as Peter Jelavich reminds us, in favour of censorship in some form or another.[1] Yet it is nonetheless fair to say that censorship is, as a rule, a repressive and conservative measure. It is usually employed for the purpose of shoring up a set of values or ideas perceived to be under threat, and for this reason it is a particularly attractive course of action for embattled elites during periods of upheaval and instability. As we have now seen at length, the decades around 1900 were just such a period. It is hardly surprising, therefore, that Wilhelmine Germany witnessed a rash of attempts to tighten state control over what people—especially young people—read, saw, and heard. By the end of the nineteenth century 'smut and trash' (*Schmutz und Schund*) had become the rallying-cry of all who sought to curtail the influence of commercial culture.

The German states already had a long tradition of artistic and press censorship; the theatre had long been subjected to pre-censorship, the written word to 'Nachzensur' since 1848. Yet the proliferation of newspapers, magazines, pulp fiction, and film nonetheless presented a whole new set of problems and opportunities.[2] Not only did it increase the amount of material subject to censorship, it also multiplied the number of people affected by it. Whereas the mischievous transgressions of naturalist writers, avant-garde painters, and theatre directors were largely confined to the chattering classes, the commercial entertainments of the late nineteenth century reached an incomparably wider audience of workers, women, and young people. The conviction that these were precisely the groups most in need of social discipline prompted Germany's moral guardians to focus their attention more acutely on the entertainments peddled to the common folk.

Thus the new attempts to regulate commercial culture were aiming at a different target. Whereas the censorship of elite literature and theatre revolved primarily around challenges to religious or political authority, the control of commercial entertainments was chiefly a matter of upholding morality and taste. After all, the publishers of popular dailies or pulp fiction were, unlike the artistic avant-garde, unlikely to cause deliberate offence to political or religious sensibilities. The occasional ill-judged scandal story notwithstanding, regulating their output rarely involved the suppression of blasphemy and *lèse-majesté*, but rather the curtailment of the obscene, the immoral, or merely the vulgar. Controlling commercial culture was thus rarely about preserving the authority of religious or secular institutions, but rather had the more ephemeral aim of

---

[1] P. Jelavich, 'Paradoxes of Censorship in Modern Germany', in M. Micale and R. Dietle (eds.), *Enlightenment, Passion, Modernity* (Stanford, 2000), 266.

[2] On censorship before the 1870s, see K. Koszyk, *Deutsche Presse im 19. Jahrhundert* (Berlin, 1966), 45–65, 120–6; also H. Göpfert (ed.), *'Unmoralisch an sich . . .'* (Wiesbaden, 1988).

maintaining the ability of social and cultural elites to set the standards of taste and decency.

As a result, one of the biggest problems faced by the anti-*Schund* campaign was the difficulty of defining 'smut and trash' for legal purposes. Although Article 184 of the Penal Code allowed local authorities to ban anything that fell under the term 'obscene' (*unzüchtig*), this law was scarcely applicable to the bulk of publications and images deemed merely immoral or tasteless. In an attempt to expand the legal definition of obscenity, representatives from the Catholic Centre Party and other conservatives in the Reichstag tried to pass the so-called *Lex Heinze* bill in 1900, whose wording threatened to suppress not only what most lawmakers regarded as 'trash', but also much of 'serious' modern art. Although supporters of the bill eventually succeeded in banning the sale to minors of anything deemed acutely offensive (but not necessarily 'obscene'), in many ways it proved counter-productive, for the more important outcome was widespread public opposition and a furious debate about the nature and extent of moral censorship that prompted parliament to water down the bill.[3]

Undeterred by this legal setback, Germany's moral crusaders redoubled their efforts after the turn of the century. During the decade after the *Lex Heinze* affair they proved remarkably successful at lobbying local censorship boards to tighten their enforcement of existing anti-obscenity laws, helping to coordinate policing efforts, and, on a general level, keeping the problem of *Schund* on the political agenda. The defence of public morality was an extremely popular cause in Wilhelmine Germany, eagerly taken up by a paternalistic elite keen to improve the spiritual well-being of its social inferiors. Nearly every city had its local association for combating 'smut' and public immorality, and over the years they became increasingly organized. Efforts to coordinate the diverse initiatives across the Reich culminated in 1911 in the Central Agency for the Fight Against Trashy Literature (Zentralstelle zur Bekämpfung der Schundliteratur) based in Berlin. The previous year a Central Agency for the Fight Against Obscene Images and Texts (Zentralstelle zur Bekämpfung unzüchtiger Bilder und Schriften) had also been established, whose remit included not only books and periodicals but also offensive advertising. Well before the First World War, the struggle against 'smut and trash' had grown into a formally institutionalized and state-sponsored effort at cultural intervention.[4]

Before the war campaigners focused above all on popular reading material, especially that designed for young people. Itinerant *colporteure* had for decades hawked their serialized 'backstairs novels' (*Hintertreppenromane*) to adults and young people alike. By the 1870s the production of adventure novels for boys

---

[3] R. Lenman, 'Art, Society and the Law in Wilhelmine Germany', *Oxford German Studies*, 8 (1973), 86–113.

[4] D. Peukert, *Grenzen der Sozialdisziplinierung* (Cologne, 1986), ch. 11.

and so-called *Backfischromane* (young maiden novels) for girls had become a lucrative segment of the expanding book market.[5] Whether in the form of a love story, Wild West adventure, or detective mystery, what most distinguished this genre was its easy affordability and complete lack of literary pretensions. Mass produced by publishing houses such as the Mühlheim-based Bagel-Verlag or the Berlin Weichert-Verlag, they generally came with brightly coloured covers and numerous illustrations, were thirty-two or sixty-four pages in length, and cost anywhere from around 10 to 25 pfennig (though more plush productions were also available). A number of authors, such as Oskar Höcker and Clementine Helm, specialized in the genre, producing dozens of books in which, as one critic put it, 'gruesome, improbable stories of adventure, shipwrecks, negroes, red indians and cannibals are portrayed with consummate skill'.[6] By the end of the century the rise of the so-called *Groschenheft* (consciously modelled, as the name suggests, on the American dime novel) marked a new phase in the evolution of popular literature. Following the adventures of heroes such as Nick Carter, John Drake, or Buffalo Bill, they not only offered a self-contained story with each instalment but were also sold at kiosks and tobacconists alongside the other products of the commercial press.[7] Deliberately priced for working-class youth and no longer reliant on door-to-door sales, dime novels were seen to pose an even greater danger, since they could be easily purchased and read without parental supervision.

Because youth was widely regarded, then as now, as a phase in which one's character is most impressionable, the ethical corruption of young people was a matter of deep concern to social reformers of all stripes. The anti-*Schund* campaign thus comprised a heterogeneous mix of organizations: temperance groups, religious associations, women's commissions, leagues against public vice, even local police forces.[8] Economic interests were hardly absent either, as publishers of 'good' literature (such as Reclam of Leipzig) seized every opportunity to complain about the competition of the colportage publishers.[9] Yet it was teachers who provided the primary driving force. The roots of the campaign against *Schund* can indeed be traced back to the efforts of elementary school teachers (*Volksschullehrer*) in the 1870s and 1880s to influence the reading habits of their pupils by drawing up lists of recommended titles. In 1893 a handful of these local vetting commissions founded the journal *Jugendschriftwarte* as a means of coordinating their activities and disseminating their verdicts on individual publications. The following year they also established the Association of German Vetting Commissions for Youth Publications (Vereinigung deutscher

---

[5] See generally Schenda, *Lesestoffe*; id., *Volk*; Wilkending, 'Kommerzialisierung'; Storim, 'Einer'.

[6] E. Fischer, *Die Großmacht der Jugend- und Volksliteratur* (1877), quoted in Wilkending, 'Kommerzialisierung', 232.

[7] Generally, Galle, *Groschenhefte*; R. Fullerton, 'Toward a Commercial Popular Culture in Germany', *Journal of Social History*, 12 (1979), 489–512.

[8] Generally, Maase, 'Krisenbewußtsein'.   [9] Schenda, *Lesestoffe*, 87–8.

Prüfungsausssschüsse für Jugendschriften), which by 1914 included 135 local groups and exerted a powerful influence on the youth literature market.[10]

It was Heinrich Wolgast, an elementary school teacher and chairman of the Hamburg vetting commission, who in 1896 wrote the first programmatic statement on 'The Wretchedness of our Youth Literature'.[11] In many ways his pleas for the aesthetic education of young people expressed a consensus among the entire cultural reform scene. Wolgast's basic argument was that youth literature must have artistic merit, a view that was based on the broader conviction that the common folk should be educated to take part in the cultural life of the nation. The innumerable adventures and love-stories not only failed to deliver on this demand, but were an exploitative attempt to make money by selling cheap sensations. As a corrective, Wolgast argued for both 'negative' controls over their production (a position shared by critics across the political spectrum) as well as the 'positive' encouragement of a canon-oriented form of literary education (which naturally met with the outspoken approval of 'good' publishers).

Although many of these arguments had a conservative and nationalist ring, the anti-*Schund* campaign also included many social-liberal and decidedly progressive elements, not least Wolgast himself. His unsparing criticism of pulp fiction was accompanied by a similar aversion to literature with a strong patriotic or religious bias.[12] His promotion of canonical literature included not only classics such as Goethe and Schiller, but also decidedly modern authors such as the arch-realist Zola and, more controversially, literary naturalists such as Richard Dehmel.[13] It was well known that many members of his reform-oriented 'Hamburg movement' were sympathetic to Social Democracy. The coexistence of such tendencies alongside more conservative and nationalist currents underlined the limits to the anti-*Schund* consensus. In 1899 the Hamburg Patriotic Society launched a pointed attack against Wolgast's entire concept of literary education, culminating in the accusation that behind the veil of aesthetic interest lay 'a hostile tendency towards religion and Fatherland'. Such criticisms were echoed several years later as a number of teachers' associations distanced themselves from the Hamburg commission for cooperating with organizations deemed to be 'socialist'.[14] For many on the Right, the struggle against depictions of violence in youth literature made a notable exception for novels that glorified war and dying for the Fatherland.[15]

In 1910 Karl Brunner, a gymnasium teacher and leading critic of the 'Hamburg movement', founded the journal *Die Hochwacht* as a counterpart to Wolgast's

---

[10] Maase, 'Krisenbewußtsein', 298–9; Peukert, *Grenzen*, 175–7.
[11] H. Wolgast, *Das Elend unserer Jugendliteratur* (Hamburg, 1896).
[12] Wilkending, 'Kommerzialisierung', 235–7.
[13] Ibid. 244–5. For background, G. Stark, 'The Censorship of Literary Naturalism, 1885–1895', *CEH* 18 (1985), 326–43.
[14] Wilkending, 'Kommerzialisierung', 220–2, 251.
[15] For a detailed discussion, Schenda, *Lesestoffe*, 78–104.

Jugendschriftwarte. As it turned out, Brunner's rise to prominence symbolized not only the increasingly uncompromising tone among conservative-minded youth-protection activists, but also the expansion of anti-*Schund* efforts towards other forms of popular commercial culture. Appointed by the Berlin police as expert literature consultant in 1911, Brunner soon became the most powerful film censor in Germany as well.

It took some time before film came into the sights of the anti-*Schund* campaign. Although the struggle against trashy literature was already in full swing, the cinema made remarkably few enemies during its first decade of existence. Neither its mode of presentation nor its content gave Germany's moral custodians much cause for concern. At this stage its audience was essentially that of the established vaudeville theatres and annual fairs. Moreover, the 'infotainment' format of most films placed them more in the realm of popular education than 'smut and trash'. Early cinema was recognized as a valuable means of learning about the wider world. Yet for a number of reasons this benign perception began to change after the establishment of permanent cinemas from around 1905. The fierce competition unleashed by the cinema boom led not only to an explosion of garish film advertisements, but also to deliberate attempts to lure in young viewers through special shows and discount tickets, thereby attracting the keen attention of anti-*Schund* campaigners. Concerns about targeting young audiences were compounded by the gradual shift in film content towards storytelling, drama, and fantasy. The fact that many of these narrative films revolved around the well-worn pulp-fiction themes of adventure, crime, and romance placed them, unlike their *Aktualitäten* predecessors, firmly in the 'smut and trash' category.[16]

Unsurprisingly, then, the so-called 'cinema reform movement' was essentially composed of the same groups as the campaign against trashy literature: clergy, cultural reformers, leagues against public vice, and teachers. It was also similarly characterized by a variety of perspectives and motivations, not all of them backward-looking and puritanical. Even its organizational forms were broadly similar, centred on local initiatives by teachers and/or school authorities to control what pupils could see on the silver screen. In a number of cities local teachers' associations formed special commissions to view and rate individual films, thus copying the established *modus operandi* for vetting youth literature.[17] These commissions were instrumental in lobbying local authorities to introduce new cinema regulations. Starting in 1906, police forces in most of Germany's major cities began to censor objectionable material or at least place age-limits on audiences.

The censorship of film was on firmer legal ground than the restriction of trashy literature, based as it was on existing laws pertaining to the theatre.

---

[16] See esp. Müller, 'Der frühe Film', 62–4; Maase, 'Massenkunst', 40–4.
[17] Müller, 'Der frühe Film', 67–76.

Yet the specific regulations varied considerably from place to place. Whereas some cities enforced strict pre-censorship of all films shown in public cinemas (Berlin), others required that children be accompanied by an adult (Hamburg, Strasbourg), and still others only allowed children into specially pre-approved programmes (Leipzig, Dresden).[18] The resulting patchwork of regulations gave rise to a number of problems. Not only were many police forces overwhelmed by the need to vet dozens of films each week, but their efforts were often in vain since films banned in one locality were sometimes freely screened in a neighbouring town. It also meant that production companies could submit a film to police scrutiny in towns with relatively lax standards, since films already passed in one locality were more likely to be accepted elsewhere.[19]

By around 1912 most states tried to close these loopholes by centralizing film censorship under a single territorial authority: Munich for Bavaria, Leipzig for Saxony, Stuttgart for Württemberg, Berlin for Prussia. By far the most important was Berlin, whose judgements tended to prevail throughout the Reich. Under the supervision of Karl Brunner, who made no bones about his distaste for the popular cinema, the Berlin censorship office suppressed anything that, in its view, might threaten public order, undermine state and religious institutions, or damage public morality, especially that of young people. As Gary Stark has argued, in practice this affected five different types of material: films that glorified crime or violence; scenes portraying seduction or extra-marital relationships; politically subversive or blasphemous material that could offend segments of the public; scenes of excessive violence, cruelty, or brutality; and anything that might exert a psychologically or pedagogically undesirable influence.[20] Although film producers did their best to avoid the censor's scissors, Brunner's Berlin office nonetheless found plenty to complain about, banning around 2 per cent of films in their entirety and making cuts to around half.[21]

But even so, popular film remained miles from the healthy popular amusement dreamt of by cinema reformers. Indeed, the rise of the film drama after 1910 drew increasingly shrill criticism from anti-*Schund* campaigners, who feared the harmful effects of a 'cinema of illusion' on its hapless viewers. In contrast to many teachers' commissions, which sought not only to suppress trashy films but also to encourage producers to raise their standards, a number of hard-core critics such as Konrad Lange and Hermann Häfker were unwilling to concede any legitimacy at all to the cinema as a means of entertainment. Brunner himself leaned in this direction, regarding the feature film as both 'the antithesis of art' (*Unkunst*) and a 'danger to the nation' (*Volksgefahr*).[22] For these most unsparing critics, the inherently sensational nature of the cinema drama was itself the problem, and deserved to be banned outright in favour of strictly educational fare. But since this would have ruined the film industry and caused a public uproar, reformers

---

[18] Stark, 'Cinema', 135. [19] Ibid. 137–8. [20] Ibid. 141–6.
[21] Maase, 'Massenkunst, 57–8. [22] Generally, Brunner, *Kinematograph*.

had to satisfy themselves with suppressing the worst excesses. Even Brunner said that around one-third of the films passed by his censors were still reprehensible.[23]

This strident current of criticism coincided with the emergence of an increasingly organized theatre lobby that perceived the cinema as a serious menace. The thrust of their complaint was that the cinema not only represented a danger for the legitimate theatre, but its exemption from existing commercial regulations meant that it enjoyed an unfair competitive advantage. In 1913, as the imperial government studied proposals to extend the commercial code, a number of local authorities took matters into their own hands by introducing surcharges on cinema tickets ranging from around 5 to 20 per cent. This new amusement tax (*Lustbarkeitssteuer*) proved a highly popular source of revenue, and soon became a staple feature of municipal finances, despite the protestations of the film industry. The industry suffered a further blow in February 1914 when the Reich government submitted a draft bill that mandated strict licensing for all cinemas. Borrowing directly from the arguments of the theatre lobby and cinema-reform movement, and commanding broad support across the political spectrum, the bill would surely have passed if the tumultuous events of summer 1914 had not intervened.[24]

If film producers and exhibitors were thus spared new legislation in August 1914, their relief was short-lived. For the outbreak of hostilities and the exceptional circumstances it imposed on the home front gave an enormous boost to ongoing efforts to curb commercial culture in Germany. As in all the belligerent countries, German authorities quickly tightened control over all forms of public discourse. On 31 July Wilhelm II proclaimed a legal state of siege that was to last for the next four years. Under this law the commanders of the twenty-six military districts into which the Reich was divided exerted immense influence over all aspects of social and cultural life, including strict control of the press and public amusements. For the duration of the war it was expressly forbidden to publish or perform anything that could divulge valuable information to the enemy, weaken the nation's determination to fight, or undermine public confidence in the military and civilian authorities. Military commanders were also authorized to ban public gatherings and even close down leisure businesses (including cinemas, music halls, and the like), thus exerting far-reaching powers over both the content of public amusements as well as their availability.[25]

Given that most of Germany's military commanders, like its police chiefs, regarded popular entertainments with either scepticism or outright contempt, it was not difficult for anti-*Schund* campaigners to persuade them to use this power. In the immediate aftermath of Germany's declaration of war on 4 August,

[23] Maase, 'Massenkunst', 58.   [24] This paragraph is based on Stark, 'Cinema', 148–54.
[25] See G. Stark, 'All Quiet on the Home Front', in F. Coetzee and M. Shevin-Coetzee (eds.), *Authority, Identity and the Social History of the Great War* (Providence, RI, 1996), 57–80; R. Chickering, *Imperial Germany and the Great War, 1914–1918* (Cambridge, 1998), 48–9, 136–9.

the bulk of public amusements (music halls, cabarets, theatres) were summarily closed. It was widely felt that their frivolous fare was singularly unsuited to the 'gravity of the times'. As Berlin's district chairmen complained to the police on 10 August, 'it is a mockery of these grave times when the upright citizen reads the decrees and appeals on the advertisement pillars through teary eyes while behind him others are playing raucous tunes and telling smutty jokes'.[26] The Berlin police wholeheartedly concurred, decreeing that 'in music halls and cinemas, only performances will be permitted that correspond to the seriousness of the times'.[27]

Such tight restrictions were by no means confined to the capital. All across Germany the extraordinary circumstances of the war fundamentally altered the terrain in favour of the anti-*Schund* struggle. Almost overnight, the sense of moderation that prevailed before the war was suspended until further notice. Previous concerns that stricter regulations would cause an adverse public reaction were blunted by the exigencies of mobilization. If popular amusements were regarded as morally hazardous before the war, they were now suspected of undermining the war effort by wasting the energies of the population and squandering scarce resources. To the enthusiastic applause of 'the best circles of the public',[28] military commanders introduced a raft of new regulations that shortened opening hours, tightened controls on advertising, and, in many areas, mandated strict pre-approval for nearly all public performances. Many in the entertainments business perceived the wave of new regulations—somewhat justifiably—as little more than the settling of old scores by local authorities that had long sought an excuse to undertake such drastic measures.[29] Certainly the swiftness with which the police seized the opportunity suggests that the outbreak of the war was more a pretext than a genuine cause for their actions. Even when amusement enterprises were allowed to reopen over the following months, the situation did not revert to the *status quo ante*. After the initial bans were lifted, a whole array of stricter controls was left in place for the duration of the war.

These sharper restrictions were motivated by a number of interrelated concerns. Throughout the fighting, amusements of any kind were frequently decried as inappropriate, even offensive. In 1916 the Kaiser himself castigated the 'shameless misconduct' of Berlin pleasure-seekers in view of the heroic self-sacrifice of German soldiers.[30] Moreover, as the war dragged on and ever larger numbers of men were called up, the control of public amusements became part of wider fears about the moral dissolution (*Verwahrlosung*) of young people in the absence of parental guidance—all the more so as growing numbers of mothers were

[26] LAB A Pr. Br. Rep. 030, Tit. 74, Nr. Th 1622, fo. 1.

[27] Quote from Stark, 'All Quiet', 62.

[28] LAB A Pr. Br. Rep. 030, Tit. 74, Nr. Th 1622, v. Jagow to v. Kessel, 31 Aug. 1914, fo. 60.

[29] See, e.g. LAB A Pr. Br. Rep. 030, Tit. 74, Nr. Th 1622, fo. 33. A point echoed by Abrams, *Workers' Culture*, 106–7.

[30] Stark, 'All Quiet', 63.

recruited into the work-force, thus leaving many adolescents to their own devices for much of the day. Against this backdrop, the shortening of school hours caused by the chronic shortage of teachers further exacerbated the problem—and this on top of a dramatic wartime increase in truancy. Worse still, the entry of many working-class adolescents into full-time employment meant that they also had more money to spend on amusements, thus prompting compulsory savings plans in many urban centres.[31] The wartime situation therefore intensified the fight against 'smut and trash' in two ways. It not only gave authorities additional powers to curtail its distribution, but also additional reason to fear its adverse effects.

This synergy of means and motive was clearly manifested in the suppression of pulp fiction. Over the winter of 1915–16 military commanders issued a number of decrees against trashy literature and images, which by spring 1916 were coordinated around a list of banned texts compiled by the Prussian Interior Ministry. Initially numbering 135 titles, the list grew to well over 200 by the summer of 1917, when the Supreme Command ordered the few district commanders who had not yet issued bans to do so.[32] By the summer of 1918 the Prussian Interior Ministry (enthusiastically supported by the Association of German Vetting Commissions for Youth Publications) began to draft legislation allowing for the continuation of most wartime controls after the cessation of hostilities—a law that, as we will see shortly, would eventually come to fruition in the Weimar Republic.

In the meantime, the cinema was also subjected to a series of tighter restrictions. By the end of 1914 the military authorities had become sufficiently annoyed with the frivolous potboilers and adventure films to begin banning them. In a drastic step, the Imperial government also halted the import of foreign films in 1915, which had hitherto constituted the bulk of supply in Germany. Deprived of their most profitable sensation films, cinema owners engaged in an increasingly fierce advertising battle, literally plastering their façades with ever-larger and more eye-catching posters, and eventually prompting the authorities to introduce new regulations on film advertisement as well. Military commanders also tried to clamp down on child admissions by mandating special youth matinees and raising the minimum age of entry for certain films. By March 1918 the imperial government even submitted a draft bill to the Reichstag that would codify these ad hoc wartime measures and continue them into peacetime—another law that would be resurrected in the Weimar Republic.[33] Yet, as Karl Brunner himself discovered in 1916, the results of all these efforts were mixed at best. For wartime audiences the cinema not only provided a welcome respite from the drabness of the home front, but was also one of the few pleasures on which to spend one's money amidst the constant shortages of consumer goods. At the same

---

[31] E. Rosenhaft, 'Restoring Moral Order on the Home Front', in Coetzee and Shevin-Coetzee (eds.), *Authority*, 81–109; also Chickering, *Great War*, 120–6.

[32] Peukert, *Grenzen*, 175–6; Stark, 'All Quiet', 65–6.   [33] Stark, 'Cinema', 160.

time, the short supply of coal that left millions of sitting-rooms cold made the warmth of a darkened projection room all the more attractive. As a result, movie theatres in the major cities were frequently overfilled and full of under-age children. They regularly disregarded censorship regulations and continued to screen low-grade adventure and detective films that young people liked. 'One can find here nothing, or almost nothing, of all the official efforts over the years to guard against the endangering of young people through improper cinema performances', Brunner complained.[34] Yet as far as the military authorities were concerned the news was not all bad: the recent decision to harness the cinema's popularity for the war effort (which will be discussed later) seemed far more promising than efforts to throttle it.

Wartime attempts to combat musical 'trash' were similarly futile. This was not for lack of effort on the part of local authorities, most of which suspended the licensing of new music halls and cabarets and brought forward closing times from 11 p.m. to 10 p.m. Yet many music halls and theatres enjoyed remarkably good business during the war—by some accounts better than before.[35] The fact that the music industry as a whole—entertainment halls, recording industry, writers, and producers—popularized a flurry of new jingoistic tunes may well have mitigated the ire of nationalist anti-*Schund* crusaders. Jumping on the patriotic bandwagon was not only fashionable with audiences, it was also a good way to avoid unwanted criticism during these 'grave times'. In any event, there were practical limits to regulating the musical scene. As one contemporary remarked, the authorities could do little to restrict the performance of 'hideous couplet and *Tingeltangel* nonsense' short of taking the unrealistic step of banning all public entertainment music for the duration of the war, 'because they certainly cannot play "Die Wacht am Rhein", "Deutschland, Deutschland über alles" and "Ich hatt' einen Kamaraden" for hours on end, day in and day out'.[36]

For all their failings, however, the string of wartime controls represented a significant advance for the decades-old campaign against 'smut and trash'. Both the will and the means to regulate public amusements were greatly enhanced under the pressures of war. Yet in other ways the period from 1914 to 1918 also marked the beginning of a new era in German elites' engagement with mass culture. Despite all the cultural-pessimistic muttering, the bulk of the pre-war Bildungsbürgertum had possessed a deep-rooted belief in progress and in the ability of society to rectify its shortcomings through the redemptive power of art and culture. Whether their target was dime novels, cinema thrillers, or the bawdy antics of the music-hall stage, most culture-reforming busybodies could feel relatively certain of the correctness and security of their own position. Put differently, they were criticizing from a position of strength. This sense

---

[34] LAB A Pr. Br. Rep. 030, Tit. 74, Nr. Th 1265, report of 17 Jan. 1916, fo. 49.
[35] Stark, 'All Quiet', 63.
[36] P. Marsop, *Öffentliche Unterhaltungsmusik in Deutschland* (Munich, 1915), 1.

of socio-cultural stability—guaranteed by the authoritarian state—helped to generate the relatively 'conciliatory climate' of the imperial era, a sense of calm assurance about the future in spite of the many cultural blemishes of modern society.[37] But this air of optimism, already gradually dissipating before 1914, was largely shattered by the experience of industrialized total war, and what little remained after the fighting was further worn down by the trauma of revolution and inflation.[38] For many middle-class conservatives, the post-war cultural landscape looked as bleak and unpromising as the treeless mire of no-man's land, and the prospect of social chaos at the hands of an increasingly violent and uncontrollable working class gave even forward-looking cultural reformers cause for concern. Amidst unprecedented social upheaval and widespread political radicalization, the government's tighter wartime restrictions lost nothing of their appeal. Having finally upgraded their tools to control mass culture, cultural and political elites were hardly going to relinquish them now.

MORALITY AND CENSORSHIP IN THE REPUBLIC

Amidst the fierce political conflicts of the immediate post-war years, there were two matters on which nearly everyone agreed: first, that Germany was undergoing a process of moral decay; and second, that it was witnessing an unprecedented explosion of pleasure-seeking. Although the two issues were not necessarily connected, they were nonetheless conflated in people's minds. It seemed that four years of industrialized war had not only shattered many moral certainties, but also engendered a widespread desire to live it up again after the end of wartime restrictions. When the prohibition on dance entertainments was officially lifted in Berlin on New Year's Eve 1918, the *Berliner Tageblatt* reported that 'the people hurled themselves upon the long-awaited pleasure like a pack of hungry wolves. Never before has Berlin danced so frequently, so furiously.'[39] The fact that most families had suffered great personal and/or financial loss did nothing to dampen this demand for amusements. On the contrary, it reinforced the sense that one should enjoy life while one can. 'Our German nation—nay, the whole world—has become sick through the war, is sick from the very times', a Bavarian official disapprovingly remarked. 'And, craving like addicts, the masses of people clutch at a narcotic that can blind them at least for a while from their present misery. . . . If a sensible physician does not intervene soon they will wretchedly perish from it.'[40]

---

[37] 'Conciliatory climate' from Bollenbeck, *Tradition*, 189. See also Jefferies, *Imperial Culture*, 221–3; S. L. Marchand and D. F. Lindenfeld (eds.), *Germany at the Fin de Siècle* (Baton Rouge, 2004).

[38] Generally, M. Eksteins, *The Rites of Spring* (Boston, 1989).

[39] *Berliner Tageblatt* (1 Jan. 1919), quoted in Wicke, *Mozart*, 131.

[40] Bayerisches Hauptstaatsarchiv (BayHStA) MK 15274, 'Entwicklungslinie für ein neues Filmunternehmen', undated, 1.

With the shock of defeat and political revolution in autumn 1918, ongoing concerns about the corruption of youth quickly mushroomed into a general moral panic about the deterioration of social norms and traditional authority. During the war itself, the rising tide of food protests and industrial disputes had already indicated the crumbling power of the imperial state that eventually culminated in the mutinies and political upheaval of autumn 1918. Other kinds of authority—of men, of parents and teachers, of employers and churches—had been visibly challenged too, and this further aggravated post-war perceptions of moral decay.[41] Although parties across the political spectrum largely agreed on the symptoms, their diagnoses differed dramatically. Whereas the socialists and left-liberals attributed it to the brutalization of the war and its corrosive effects on the family, conservatives tended to blame the revolution itself.[42] Nonetheless, there was widespread agreement that the country was in need of moral renewal after the war, and that the flourishing amusements industry was a primary cause of Germany's moral decay.

It is worth noting that all the talk of an amusement epidemic and 'pleasure addiction' (*Vergnügungssucht*) was more than just the imaginary ravings of backward-looking moralists. There clearly was a huge increase in demand for amusements of all kinds, a demand that entertainment entrepreneurs were all too eager to satisfy after years of chafing under wartime regulations. As observers have often remarked, the so-called 'film fever' and 'dance craze' of the early 1920s seemed in many ways a reflection of pent-up demand. In many eyes the resuscitation of public amusements represented the symbolic return of a degree of 'normality'—or what passed for it in post-war Germany—after the 'grave times' of national emergency. There was also a strong sense among former soldiers and civilians alike of an inalienable right to amusement that could no longer be denied after their immense sacrifices for the national cause. In the words of a local official near Aachen, 'the extraordinary and utterly rampant pleasure addiction' was nourished not only by the poor economic situation, but also by a 'greatly diminished sense of authority'.[43]

Yet probably the most important reason for the wave of pleasure seeking was people's fundamentally altered relationship to money. Ever-rising inflation meant that money was no longer something to be relied upon. The relentless depletion of the mark meant that saving—preached as a moral and financial virtue in the pre-war era—had lost its rationale. The growing urge to spend what one had was further compounded by the wartime experience of continual shortage, which had conditioned people to buy what they could when they could. In this situation, 'going without' as a means of investing in the future no longer

---

[41] R. Bessel, *Germany After the First World War* (Oxford, 1993), 252.

[42] C. Usborne, *The Politics of the Body in Weimar Germany* (Basingstoke, 1992), 74.

[43] Nordrhein-Westfälisches Hauptstaatsarchiv (NRWHStA), Reg. Aachen 22755, Landrat Schleiden to Reg. Pres. Aachen, 25 Feb. 1920, unpag.

made much sense, for, as Martin Geyer has put it, 'whoever did not consume today would have nothing tomorrow, and what would be available tomorrow was uncertain anyway'.[44] Looking back on the immediate post-war years, Hans Ostwald, the renowned observer of Berlin's nightlife, discerned a close parallel between the declining value of money and changing cultural norms: 'it was a time of great revaluation (*Umwertung*)—in the economic as in the cultural sphere, in material and in spiritual matters.'[45] Inflation encouraged people to spend money in the here and now, and in conjunction with the eight-hour day, the end of military conscription (summer 1919), and an acute housing shortage, it helped generate unprecedented demand for public amusements.[46]

The regulation of commercial entertainment was thus an ongoing concern for Germany's new leaders. Many of the wartime controls were left in place or reintroduced in the course of 1919. Dance halls were the most frequent targets, and in some areas were only allowed to operate two or three days per week.[47] Such tough restrictions were not just the work of the many conservatives and closet monarchists who still packed the Republic's bureaucracy, but also of liberal and socialist officials. It was, for instance, the SPD defence minister Gustav Noske who introduced midnight closing times in November 1919, and the following month it was a SPD-dominated cabinet that authorized a police crackdown on the notorious *Animierkneipen* (hostess bars).[48] Although most bans were lifted or at least eased in the course of 1920, local police continued to wrestle with allegedly indecent performances and breaches of existing regulations. Some cities witnessed a pitched battle between fairground operators and police forces intent on curtailing or closing their establishments altogether.[49] When the German and French governments fell out over the extraction of resources from the Ruhr in late 1922, there was a wave of closures and bans once again justified on account of the 'gravity of the times'.[50] Throughout the 1920s German police forces increasingly coordinated their efforts through the new Central Police Agency for Combating Obscene Pictures, Publications, and Advertisements (Zentralpolizeistelle zur Bekämpfung unzüchtiger Bilder, Schriften und Inserate).

The continuation of such restrictions under the peacetime republican government was based on the fact that they did not legally constitute 'censorship'. Although the National Assembly formally abolished 'censorship' in Article 118 of the Weimar Constitution, this pertained specifically to political intervention in a narrow sense, and did not cover other forms of social control such as

---

[44] M. H. Geyer, *Verkehrte Welt* (Göttingen, 1998), 266.
[45] H. Ostwald, *Sittengeschichte der Inflation* (Berlin, 1931), 7.   [46] Bessel, *Germany*, 250.
[47] See, e. g. BayHStA MWi 736, *passim*; BayHStA MInn 72671; NRWHStA Reg. Düsseldorf 30479; Reg. Aachen 22755; also Schär, *Schlager*, 150–2.
[48] Usborne, *Politics*, 77.
[49] LAB A Pr. Br. Rep. 030, Tit. 74, Nr. Th 1623, 1624; BayHStA MInn 72680, 72678.
[50] Quote from BayHStA MInn 72671, Bekanntmachung über Einschränkung der öffentlichen Lustbarkeiten, 12 Nov. 1922, 1.

licensing, confiscation, and bans, which police forces were still authorized to carry out for the sake of upholding public order and, from 1922, protecting the Republic itself.[51] Moreover, the constitutional provisions on censorship made a number of exemptions. The SPD, liberals, and Centre Party made a difficult compromise on Article 118, which in the end upheld the basic right to freedom of expression without maintaining a complete ban on censorship for particular forms of amusement. In the words of the Article: 'Every German has the right to express his opinion freely through word, writing, print, imagery, or other manner within the boundaries of the general laws. . . . Censorship will not be exercised, but by law exceptional measures can be imposed on film. Legal measures are also permitted for the suppression of trashy and smutty literature as well as for the protection of young people regarding public performances and amusements.'[52] The cause of youth protection and the control of film and pulp fiction remained live issues after the war, and lawmakers' decision to exempt them from the constitutional ban on censorship left the door wide open to further legislation.

The most significant piece of legislation to emerge from this exemption was the 1926 Law for the Protection of Young People from Trashy and Smutty Literature (Gesetz zur Bewahrung der Jugend vor Schund- und Schmutzschriften), the single greatest success of the anti-*Schund* campaign. This law, which grew directly out of tightened wartime controls, triggered the most contentious battle over censorship during the entire Weimar era. Initially proposed in December 1923 and finally passed by the Reichstag three years later, it mandated a fine and/or prison term for anyone selling or giving prohibited publications to persons under the age of 18. The list of banned works, which numbered 143 by 1932 and included such popular series as Nick Carter and Buffalo Bill, was compiled by several vetting bodies (*Prüfstellen*) answerable to the Interior Ministry, each chaired by a senior civil servant and staffed by eight experts from the fields of art, literature, the publishing trade, the teaching profession, and youth organizations.[53] Hailed by its supporters as a bulwark against the rising flood of sleaze, and decried by its critics as a shameful breach of artistic freedom, the law marked an important milestone not so much for the actual control of pulp fiction as for legitimating the idea that popular amusements should be subjected to some form of moral censorship. The 1926 'smut and trash' law was, like the *Lex Heinze* of 1900, a litmus test for how far the state could legitimately intervene in the cultural life and leisure pursuits of its citizens. But unlike the successful opposition against *Lex Heinze*, critics of the 1926 law were clearly in the minority. The 'conciliatory climate' of the pre-war era had turned far cloudier by the 1920s; it was now widely agreed

[51] K. Petersen, *Zensur in der Weimarer Republik* (Stuttgart, 1995), 38–9, 41–2.
[52] Quoted from ibid., 31–2.
[53] M. Stieg, 'The 1926 Law to Protect Youth against Trash and Dirt', *CEH* 23 (1990), 49, 52; Petersen, *Zensur*, 56–67.

that literary sleaze was dangerous enough to justify forcible controls. Typically, however, there was far less agreement on precisely what constituted 'smut and trash' and how it could be restricted without trampling constitutional rights to privacy and freedom of expression. In the end, the enforcement of the law foundered on these very issues.[54] Yet its true importance lay in the fact that it could pass at all. Even if its actual effects failed to meet the expectations of its supporters, it still represented a powerful symbolic victory for the forces of moral protection. Not only did it affirm the pre-eminence of their cultural values over others, it also validated the imposition of these values—at least in principle—on to society at large.

Much the same can be said of the Law for the Protection of Young People Regarding Amusements (Gesetz zum Schutz der Jugend bei Lustbarkeiten), which placed stricter age-limits on a range of entertainments. Planned from the early 1920s, this law was finally passed by the Reichstag in May 1927, only to be dismissed by the upper house (Reichsrat) due to its exorbitant costs and practical infeasibility. But again, the fact that it progressed this far at all is indicative of the changed climate. During the 1920s there were numerous attempts to close down fairgrounds and other public entertainments by banning anyone under 16 or enforcing early closing times.[55]

Yet it was undoubtedly the film industry that attracted the most attention. As we have seen, the growing popularity of cinema before 1914 had already unleashed calls for an organized system of censorship, culminating in a draft bill that was sidelined by the outbreak of hostilities. After the war, film was generally recognized as the most powerful medium of the age and therefore in need of careful supervision. The immediate problem was that in November 1918 all such supervision suddenly collapsed with the abolition of wartime controls. Not since the early 1900s had the industry operated so freely. In the words of a Bavarian official, the 'colossal upswing of the smut film'[56] that resulted from this regulatory hiatus provided incontrovertible proof of the need for tight restrictions. The remarkable speed with which film producers exploited the opportunity confirmed all the negative stereotypes about their moral bankruptcy. Particularly rankling was the wave of titillating 'education films' and 'morality films' (*Aufklärungsfilme* and *Sittenfilme*) that purported to inform the public about the dangers of promiscuity and venereal disease.[57] As the Social Democratic interior minister Wolfgang Heine declared in November 1919, 'the excesses brought about in the realm of cinema by the unscrupulous profit-hunger of a number of filmmakers bent on exploiting the masses' instincts make it advisable to take immediate and energetic measures against any further

54 Stieg, '1926 Law', 53–6.
55 LAB A Pr. Br. Rep. 030, Tit. 74, Nr. Th 1623, *passim*; BayHStA MInn 72680, *passim*.
56 BayHStA MK 15274, 'Entwicklungslinie für ein neues Filmunternehmen', undated, 1.
57 M. Hagener, J. Hans, 'Von Wilhelm zu Weimar', in M. Hagener (ed.), *Geschlecht in Fesseln* (Munich, 2000).

poisoning of people's minds through cinematic trash'.[58] The suppression of the 'smut film' was indeed one of the few issues on which Left and Right could agree in the immediate post-war years. Tellingly, when the licensing of new cinemas was debated in the Munich city hall, the left-wing USPD's motion against any further 'anarchization and spiritual depravity' was supported without alteration by the arch-conservative BVP.[59]

The fact that the Reichstag passed the Reich Film Law (Lichtspielgesetz) less than a year after the constitution came into effect demonstrates the sense of urgency and cross-party agreement on the need to control the popular cinema. Building on pre-war legislation, the Film Law of May 1920 mandated strict pre-censorship for all films shown in the Reich. In contrast to the pre-1919 censorship regime, all decisions were to be made by a central commission, thus taking the matter out of the hands of police. The precise wording of the law gave the censors considerable latitude. Films could be banned in whole or in part if they were considered likely 'to endanger public order or security, to offend religious sensibilities, to exert a brutalizing or morally degrading effect, or to undermine German prestige or German relations with foreign states'. However, in order to ensure compliance with Article 118, it was expressly forbidden to ban a film 'on the basis of a political, social, religious, ethical, or ideological tendency (*Weltanschauungstendenz*)', or indeed 'for reasons that lie outside the content of the film'. For the purposes of youth protection, no film could be shown to minors 'which gives rise to the apprehension that they may exert a harmful influence on the moral, intellectual or physical development of young people or cause an over-stimulation of the imagination'.[60] In addition, the Film Law also sought to influence film content through a new rating system, whereby a special commission (the 'Lampe-commission', chaired by Professor Felix Lampe) could award tax exemptions for films it regarded as educationally or artistically valuable.

This new system of film censorship quickly eradicated the excesses of post-war 'education films', but it inevitably failed to meet the diverse expectations of the various groups that supported it. The need to strike a balance between competing interests meant that the censorship regime often appeared even to supporters as 'more capricious than the most spoilt *prima donna* and more unpredictable than April weather'.[61] Socialists repeatedly complained that the decisions of the rating commission were one-sided and essentially amounted to informal censorship. They also accused the censorship board of double standards when Russian films were censored while countless examples of 'mendacious monarch-kitsch, abominable Old-Heidelberg swindle, wretched Fridericus humbug, and

[58] NRWHStA Reg. Köln 8119, Minister des Innern to Regierungspräsidenten, 22 Nov. 1919, unpag.
[59] Geyer, *Verkehrte*, 75.
[60] Petersen, *Zensur*, 52–3; also P. Jelavich, *Berlin Alexanderplatz* (Berkeley, 2006), 126–55.
[61] C. Moreck, *Sittengeschichte des Kinos* (Dresden, 1926), 40.

military-reactionary newsreel palaver' were passed in their entirety.[62] In the wake of the Nazis' electoral breakthrough in September 1930, systematic right-wing intimidation and heightened concerns about public order gave additional credence to such complaints, most notoriously with the banning of the Hollywood version of Remarque's *All Quiet on the Western Front*. When the film premiered in December 1930 on Berlin's Nollendorfplatz, gangs of Nazi brownshirts, flushed with confidence from their recent successes, launched a series of violent demonstrations that, in conjunction with pressure from the army and Foreign Office, prompted the censorship board to reverse its earlier decision and ban the film after only one week—clearly breaching the legal provision that films should not be prohibited 'for reasons that lie outside the content of the film'. The fact that the government caved in to such thuggery was rightly seen by pro-Republican forces as a serious blow to its authority, and was particularly galling given that the right-wing film *Das Flötenkonzert von Sanssouci*, whose message amounted to a call-to-arms against the treachery of the Versailles Treaty, was cleared for general release only shortly thereafter.[63]

Yet prior to the more restrictive atmosphere of the early 1930s, German censors were arguably the most liberal in Europe, especially in terms of political intervention. Germany was one of the few countries in which Sergei Eisenstein's masterpiece *Battleship Potemkin* was publicly screened, in spite of vociferous conservative protests.[64] The majority of Soviet films, which in many countries were subjected (either in law or in practice) to a blanket ban, were passed by the Berlin censors with a minimum of alteration. By contrast, youth-protection regulations were relatively strict. Whereas the French authorities banned only 5 to 8 per cent of films for youth audiences, in Germany it was around 25 to 30 per cent. These bans were also rigorously enforced; police forces often enlisted local teachers' commissions to ensure that cinemas observed age-limits and advertising requirements. Yet above the age-limit of 18 moral censorship in Germany was comparatively permissive. Of the approximately 3,000 films vetted in 1928, only thirty-seven were banned. Most censorship involved merely cutting particular scenes, though even this was relatively light-handed.[65]

As a result, most conservatives were every bit as disappointed by film censorship as socialists and communists. Throughout the 1920s conservative and religious

---

[62] Quote from 'Politischer Film', *Hamburgischer Correspondent* (21 Mar. 1928); see also K. Kreimeier, *The Ufa-Story* (New York, 1996), 95.

[63] The film was rereleased in summer 1931 to closed audiences only: 'Zum Film-Bürgerkrieg. Müssen wir uns reaktionäre Filme gefallen lassen?', *Vorwärts* (11 Dec. 1930); Bundesarchiv Berlin-Lichterfelde (BAB) R43I/2500, fo. 148; Petersen, *Zensur*, 263–5.

[64] BAB R43I/2498, fo. 260; R43I/2499, Reichswehrminister to Int. Min., 7 Apr. 1927, fo. 17. British authorities were far less permissive: N. Pronay, 'The Political Censorship of Film in Britain Between the Wars', in N. Pronay and D. W. Spring (eds.), *Propaganda, Politics and Film, 1918–45* (Basingstoke, 1982), 98–125.

[65] W. Petzet, *Verbotene Filme* (Frankfurt a. M., 1931), 109; P. Monaco, *Cinema and Society* (New York, 1976), 54; Staatsarchiv Hamburg (StAH) 376–2, Gen IX F 19, fos. 4–8.

organizations constantly railed against the lax moral standards of the Berlin censors and their failure, as one critic put it, to 'protect segments of the populace that have retained a greater degree of moral sensitivity'. As the Catholic Association in the Rhineland town of Viersen complained, 'films that pass censorship as being acceptable by Berlin standards can still be perceived as thoroughly immoral in a place like Viersen'.[66] Such provincial prudery led to frequent calls for tighter standards and the establishment of regional censorship boards, in particular in Bavaria and Württemberg, where older state laws had in fact been stricter than the Reich Film Law. It was, in the words of one South German official, 'an outrageous imposition to allow different states to show a smut film that is perhaps only tolerable among a portion of Berlin modernists'.[67]

But as always, one person's smut is another's entertainment. As Carl Bulcke, the director of the Chief Vetting Agency (Oberprüfstelle), remarked in 1921, the task facing the censorship offices was to strike a balance between these views.[68] Though never easy, this was especially difficult in the highly polarized cultural landscape of Weimar Germany. For many conservatives, what counted as cinematic 'trash' included not only obscene or indecent material, but also films that were aesthetically worthless or morally degrading. Even many liberal politicians tended to conflate these categories in their aversion 'against *Schund*, against kitschiness (*Kitschigkeit*)', as a DDP delegate tellingly put it.[69] The 1920 Film Law may have removed the most offensive films from the silver screen, but within the constitutional framework of the Weimar Republic it did not give censors the power to stem the constant flow of second-rate kitsch through German cinemas.

In the eyes of cinema reformers, the basic problem was that the film industry had quickly learned how to operate within the new censorship regime. Although the boundary between the acceptable and the unacceptable was never perfectly distinct, the low percentage of prohibited films shows that producers soon acquired a feel for it. Indeed, the threat of a ban made it financially imperative to do so, and in this sense the censorship system was highly effective at channelling the industry's self-interest into self-restraint. Yet the same commercial self-interest that prompted filmmakers to play it safe also led them to continue making the sensational adventures and romantic tales that had always pulled in the crowds. Below the threshold of obscenity and indecency, censors were not authorized to legislate taste, and so long as the film industry was allowed to meet popular demand, it could hardly be expected to engage in risky attempts at raising the aesthetic expectations of audiences. 'Giving the public what it wanted' remained the key to commercial survival. And in the eyes of most cultural elites, what

---

[66] Both quotes from BAB R43/I/2499, fos. 63–4.

[67] BAB R43/I/2498, Interior Ministry to Reich Chancellery, 15 Feb. 1924, fo. 135.

[68] See *Deutsche Allgemeine Zeitung* (6 July 1921); also BAB R43I/2498, fos. 54–6.

[69] Gertrud Klausner, 6 Nov. 1925, from A. v. Saldern, 'Massenfreizeitkultur im Visier', *AfS* 33 (1993), 34.

the public wanted remained stubbornly poor. As the SPD newspaper *Vorwärts* despairingly put it: 'If audiences pay to see old-Heidelberg, Rhine and Vienna kitsch, lieutenant schlock and (Queen) Luise balderdash, sweet girl-around-the-corner nonsense and military rubbish, then the film industry produces this tripe without the slightest trace of a cultural conscience. If audiences pay to see something else, then they produce something else. The private capitalist film industry has a right to screen trashy films if valuable films are not desired.'[70] So long as the German cinema was governed by the 'dictatorship of plebeian demands', cinema reformers would be fighting an uphill battle.[71]

STATE AND COMMUNAL OWNERSHIP

This was precisely the logic behind efforts to bring public amusements under state control. Given the anti-capitalist tendencies of many educated elites, the idea of putting a stop to all this by depriving the entertainment industry of the very basis of commercial speculation was a remarkably appealing prospect. Only by abolishing the market mechanism would it be possible to improve the content of mass culture, or so the argument went.

Immediately after the war, it was once again the cinema that generated the most serious discussion about the possibilities of state-owned entertainments. In early 1919 there were various calls to place the film industry under state or municipal control.[72] Amidst the spate of 'education films' that came on the market, such suggestions enjoyed widespread sympathy across the political spectrum.[73] But in the event, dreams of socializing the film industry effectively ended with the suppression of the Soviet government (Räterepublik) in Bavaria in April 1919. It was never seriously considered by the Reichstag, the Economics Ministry, the Nationalization Commission, or even the trade unions, largely because of doubts about its practical feasibility.[74] On balance, the fear that it would produce a bureaucratic nightmare generated more scepticism than enthusiasm, even among many who supported the idea in principle.

Yet if state control over film *production* appeared unworkable, socializing the *exhibition* branch still seemed a plausible prospect. This was not least because there already existed an organization along these lines: the Cinema League of German Cities (Bilderbühnenbund deutscher Städte), whose aim was to raise the quality of films through municipal involvement at the point of exhibition.[75] Support for the scheme was widespread and progressed furthest in

---

70 H. Bauer, 'Statistik der Geschmacksverirrung', *Der Abend, Spätausgabe des 'Vorwärts'* (25 May 1928), 3.

71 P. Medina, 'Die Diktatur des Zuschauerraums', *FK* (21 Nov. 1921), 1.

72 J. Kinter, *Arbeiterbewegung und Film (1895–1933)* (Hamburg, 1985), 187.

73 J. Spiker, *Film und Kapital* (Berlin, 1975), 28–9.

74 Kinter, *Arbeiterbewegung*, 188.   75 Spiker, *Film*, 30–1.

Munich, where communal control over local cinemas was actually passed by the city administrative commission. Yet once again, these ideas foundered on the practicalities. The few concrete attempts at municipal cinema management were not very promising, for as officials quickly discovered, even cinemas free from market competition still had to take audience wishes into account. When, for example, the city council of Frankfurt an der Oder took over the local programme and filled it with educational films, the result was a total box-office meltdown: 'The public felt it had more or less outgrown such schooling and therefore showed little inclination to sit through two hours of cinematic further education lessons after a hard day's work', reported the journal *Licht-Bild-Bühne*.[76] When an attempt was finally made to draw a crowd by screening the French Revolution drama *Madame Dubarry* (1919), the first German blockbuster since the end of the war, it was so successful that the suspicious city councillors viewed the film themselves and prudishly decided to cut the final act—an extremely unpopular move that effectively ended the experiment at municipal control. Yet few local officials were willing to undertake such an experiment in the first place. Beset with the difficulties of demobilization and an acute housing shortage, most were reluctant to bear the additional costs of buying out the cinemas while at the same time suffering a drastic reduction in the amusement tax revenues on which they so heavily relied.[77] Because municipal authorities thus stood to lose out on two counts, in the end most voted down communal control as impractical—even in Munich, where city delegates pointlessly consoled themselves by doubling the amusement tax and thereby unleashing a general cinema strike in the city from September to December 1919.[78]

Nevertheless, the notion that the market mechanism was ultimately to blame for the moral and aesthetic depravity of the mass media did not go away. If nationalization of the film industry proved unworkable, the underlying principle that public ownership presented a remedy against the proliferation of 'smut and trash' was by no means discredited.

So when the German government began to organize the new medium of radio in the early 1920s, the premise that it should operate under close state control was essentially taken for granted. From early on the Reich government claimed its sovereignty in the realm of broadcasting (*Funkhoheit*), which was explicitly designed to set radio on a fundamentally different footing from the free-market economy that prevailed among the other media. Like their counterparts in Britain, the architects of German radio consciously sought to avoid the supposed chaos that had plagued the unregulated explosion of broadcasting in the United States after 1920.[79] As things turned out, this did not exclude the involvement of

---

[76] 'Das städtische Lichtbildtheater', *LBB* (3 Jan. 1920), 10.
[77] Spiker, *Film*, 31–2.   [78] Kinter, *Arbeiterbewegung*, 187–8.
[79] For an international perspective, E. Lersch and H. Schanze (eds.), *Die Idee des Radios* (Konstanz, 2004).

private companies and commercial investors, who were encouraged to sink their money into the venture. But the tight restrictions placed on their activities meant that the main players were the Interior Ministry, which was ultimately responsible for regulating cultural production, and in particular the Postal Ministry, whose energetic young state secretary Hans Bredow became the single most influential figure in the early development of German radio.

After the first regular services were broadcast from Berlin in October 1923, a group of nine regional programme companies were founded over the following year, each offering a medium-wave service within a particular radius. Each programme company effectively had a broadcasting monopoly within its respective region, an arrangement that was designed to avoid the deleterious effects of market competition. The Drahtloser Dienst (Wireless Service), or Dradag, was also founded in 1923 as a central news agency to support the regional companies. Later, in January 1926, the Deutsche Welle began the first long-wave service intended to reach all areas of the Reich. In order to produce and broadcast their programmes, all of these companies required a special operating licence from the Postal Ministry, which required them to hand over a 51 per-cent majority of their shares in order to acquire a permanent operating licence. At the same time, it also stipulated that operators must become part of the Deutsche Reichs-Rundfunk-Gesellschaft mbH (RRG, which formally began activity in January 1926), a holding company that supervised the economic, technical, and organizational affairs of the broadcasters (in which the Postal Ministry also held a controlling interest). In order to keep the radio waves free from partisan influences, political parties, foreigners, and any person or company with a commercial interest in the production of radio receivers were banned from holding shares.[80] Special supervisory commissions (*Überwachungsausschüsse*) were also established to oversee the political content of the programmes. Composed of representatives from the Reich Interior Ministry and Länder governments (which constitutionally exercised *Kulturhoheit*, or sovereignty in the realm of culture), the commissions exerted indirect pre-censorship over all political aspects of the programme. Other segments were to be supervised by Cultural Advisory Boards (*Kulturbeiräte*), though in the event these remained insignificant.[81]

By 1926 German radio was for all intents and purposes a state-run broadcasting system. Jealously guarding its new competences, the German Postal Ministry built, operated, and owned the broadcasting stations, created the legal framework within which they operated, and determined (and disposed of) the fees levied from radio users.[82] All contemporary talk of the 'mixed economic' structure of German radio, implying a hybrid between a private and public enterprise, was

---

[80] Generally, K. C. Führer, *Wirtschaftsgeschichte des Rundfunks in der Weimarer Republik* (Potsdam, 1997); W. Lerg, *Rundfunkpolitik in der Weimarer Republik*, (Munich, 1980); K. Dussel, *Deutsche Rundfunkgeschichte* (Konstanz, 2004), 28–45.

[81] Dussel, *Rundfunkgeschichte*, 37–8.   [82] Lerg, *Rundfunkpolitik*, 267.

fundamentally misleading. In reality this meant no more than that broadcasting companies were organized according to civil law, not public law, and that private persons could own shares in them (though even dividend payments were limited to 10 per cent). As Winfried Lerg has argued, 'it had become a state institution, a part of the Reich administration'.[83] All that kept it from being a 'state radio' in its entirety were the continued involvement of private investors and the indirect nature of government control over its content. It was not long before even these residual non-state elements were abolished. In 1932, under the government of Franz von Papen, the Postal Ministry and Länder governments bought out the private shareholders and acquired sole possession of the broadcasters' assets in an attempt to ensure that their content supported the reactionary cabinet's policies. By the end of 1932 German radio companies thus formally became the public enterprises they had already been in practice since 1926. Thus, when the Nazis came to power in 1933 it required only one further step—the transfer of the Länder shares in the RRG and regional companies to the Reich—for German broadcasting to become a completely centralized state radio system, ultimately the sole preserve of the Reich Propaganda Ministry.[84]

There were a variety of reasons why the Weimar authorities were determined to manage radio as directly as they did. The fledgling republic of the early 1920s was, for one thing, still a precarious entity. The enactment of Laws to Protect the Republic (Republikschutzgesetze) in July 1922, following the high-profile assassinations of Matthias Erzberger and Walther Rathenau, expressed both a fear of its numerous enemies and a resolute willingness to uphold the democratic state against them. As the Interior Ministry wrote to Bredow in July 1923, it was crucial that a medium as powerful as radio should 'not be handed over to some or other private companies whose attitude towards the current Reich government is sceptical and shaky, but rather be used first and foremost for the strengthening of the Reich and its influence'.[85] Alongside this high-minded defence of democracy, there were also purely practical reasons for the Postal Ministry to guard its control over radio: namely, to use it as a source of revenue for offsetting deficits in other areas.[86] Most importantly, however, sheltering radio from the full force of the market was seen as the best means of harnessing it for popular education and cultural improvement. Hans Bredow himself regarded radio as an 'instrument to spread culture' and to maintain Germany's 'intellectual standards'.[87] The architects of Weimar broadcasting—epitomes of the liberally educated Bildungsbürger to a man—instinctively saw the role of the new medium as that of a 'cultural factor', a bearer of knowledge and spiritual

---

[83] Ibid. 270.
[84] Ibid. 438–523; A. Diller, *Rundfunkpolitik im Dritten Reich* (Munich, 1980), 84–9.
[85] Dussel, *Rundfunkgeschichte*, 31.   [86] Führer, *Wirtschaftsgeschichte*, 105–11.
[87] Quotes from K. C. Führer, 'A Medium of Modernity? Broadcasting in Weimar Germany, 1923–1932', *JMH* 69 (1997), 728–9.

refinement. Opening up radio to the laws of supply and demand would inevitably hinder its ability to fulfil this lofty mission.

In this sense, state management of radio, like the laws against 'smut and trash' and the system of film censorship, was very much a part of the wider attempt to reassert elite cultural standards through a formal framework of control over communications. As the following chapter shows, however, elite responses to the challenge of mass culture were by no means limited to merely curtailing it.

3

Attempting Reform: Legitimation, Education, and Uplifting Tastes

For good reason, historians have long emphasized the turbulent currents of anti-modernism and cultural pessimism in their accounts of Wilhelmine and Weimar Germany. Without a doubt, Germany was home to a particularly clamorous strand of cultural criticism and a remarkably broad array of organizations dedicated to the regulation of commercial culture. But as the following pages seek to show, this is only one—albeit important—part of the story. While some set their sights on throttling the growth of the commercial media, others sought to meet the challenge through a strategy of constructive engagement. Even if the imposition of certain restrictions was more or less universally accepted, this hardly exhausted the range of possibilities. For those who wanted not merely to stem but to reverse the perceived tide of sensationalism and superficiality, mass culture would have to be reformed from within.

As part of the broader movement for 'rational recreation', an army of reform-minded organizations and activists attempted to develop wholesome alternatives to mainstream commercial amusements.[1] The overall goal was to create a 'valuable mass culture' that would appeal to popular tastes yet still meet certain standards of aesthetic quality. Instead of borrowing its forms from the familiar repertoire of the music hall or popular fairground, valuable mass culture would draw primarily on the classics, on real or imagined 'folk' traditions, and, to a lesser extent, on the experiments of the avant-garde—all of which would obviously need to be remoulded to suit popular tastes. Ideally, these alternatives would help raise audience expectations so that 'smut and trash' would gradually lose its allure. More realistically, the goal was at least to minimize the negative side-effects of cheap sensationalism and appeals to 'base instincts'.

These pro-active efforts at cultural reform, which stretched across the political spectrum, were essentially composed of two interrelated strands. On the one hand, there were diverse attempts by progressive politicians, critical intellectuals, and cultural conservatives to educate and uplift popular tastes. Ranging from

---

[1] J. Reulecke, ' "Veredelung der Volkserholung" und "edle Geselligkeit" ', in G. Huck (ed.), *Sozialgeschichte der Freizeit*, 2nd edn. (Wuppertal, 1982), 141–60; Abrams, *Workers' Culture*, 139–68.

independent film to pedagogical radio programming, these initiatives were based on either the financial support of enlightened patrons, the founding of cooperative organizations, or state-run structures that circumvented the market mechanism altogether. Closely related to this project were, on the other hand, a variety of efforts among the avant-garde and critical intelligentsia to explore the potential of the new media as a means of artistic expression. Despite the vulgar uses to which they were commonly put, the mass media were treated here as nothing other than particular forms of cultural communication that deserved serious attention. At one level, the aesthetic experiments of writers, actors, and graphic artists were conceived as a means of legitimating the new media in the eyes of their social peers. Yet at the same time they were also part of the wider progressive agenda to synthesize 'high' and 'low' culture. This chapter will survey each of these strands in turn, focusing first on attempts to enlist the mass media for the cause of popular education before briefly discussing the creation of new cultural forms suited to the unique requirements of modern communications.

COMMERCIAL CULTURE AND SOCIAL REFORM

It was only towards the end of the nineteenth century that the rise of commercial culture became a central concern among Germany's social-reform movements.[2] The huge upheavals caused by rapid industrialization meant that groups such as the Central Association for the Welfare of the Labouring Classes (Zentralverein für das Wohl der arbeitenden Klassen) and the Association for Social Policy (Verein für Sozialpolitik) focused their attention on more basic issues such as housing and health facilities. At the risk of sounding unduly precise, in many ways the year 1890 marked a watershed in the perception of commercial culture among the German middle classes. The lapse of the socialist laws in September 1890, which allowed the Social Democratic Party and its affiliated unions to operate in the full light of day, capped off a string of new legal provisions that significantly decreased working hours. As a result, the period after 1890 was characterized by a simultaneous expansion of both the labour movement and the commercial leisure industry. The concurrence of these two developments meant that debates about commercial culture quickly became an integral part of ongoing efforts at social reform. Put differently, the parallel rise of mass culture and social democracy reinforced the tendency to regard both as part of the broader 'social question'.

The first conference on leisure time in Germany, organized in 1892 by the Central Agency for Workers' Welfare Facilities (Berliner Centralstelle für Arbeiterwohlfahrtseinrichtungen) to promote the 'expedient (*zweckmäßig*) use

---

[2] Reulecke, '"Veredelung"'; also J. Reulecke, *Soziale Friede durch Soziale Reform* (Wuppertal, 1983).

of Sundays and leisure time', was expressly convened as a means of 'gaining the upper hand over the dissatisfaction and revolutionary ideas among the working classes'.[3] In many ways the synchronous campaign against 'smut' literature grew out of precisely the same concerns: campaigners focused especially on the spiritual and moral protection of working-class youth who might otherwise turn to social democracy.[4] Paternalistic employers also became more involved in leisure provision around the turn of the century as a means of defusing work-force discontent and raising productivity. Meanwhile, for the increasingly powerful labour movement, the reduction of working hours triggered a similar concern for what workers did with their leisure time. Labour activists were understandably worried that the chief beneficiary of this hard-won victory might be the amusements industry, long regarded as one of the main obstacles to workers' education efforts. For all of these reasons, issues surrounding popular culture and leisure pursuits were inseparable from wider concerns about social reform. Improving mass culture was, as the prominent democrat Theodor Heuss later put it, a form of 'social policy for the spirit' (*Sozialpolitik der Seele*).[5]

Notwithstanding the long-term battle against pulp fiction (a reflection of the peculiar veneration of the written word among the Bildungsbürgertum), it was the huge expansion of film that attracted the most attention. As we have already seen, the growth of the film industry had already given rise to a vociferous cinema reform movement during the decade before the First World War. It is important to recognize, however, that not even the most rancorous complaints by the likes of Konrad Lange and Karl Brunner were directed at the medium of film *per se*. The tenor of debate was characterized less by hysterical denunciations of cultural mechanization than by the more or less universal assumption that film, as a uniquely powerful channel of communication to the masses, represented an ideal means of popular education. The main current of thought among cinema reformers was therefore not a churlish cultural pessimism, but rather a 'paternalistic modernism'.[6]

In some ways it is misleading to speak of pre-war cinema reformers as 'a movement' at all. Not only were their efforts largely uncoordinated, but they encompassed a multiplicity of views. At one extreme stood a handful of enthusiasts who emphasized the pedagogical potential of film. The most energetic and radical proponent was Hermann Lemke, an elementary-school rector in the Brandenburg town of Storkow, who in 1907 founded the journal *Der Kinematograph* to promote the use of film—even entertainment film—for educational purposes.[7] Most cinema reformers were more sceptical, especially regarding the value of narrative films. After 1910 the increasing concerns about

[3] Reulecke, 'Veredelung', 143.   [4] See generally Linton, *Youth*.
[5] Heuss to the Reichstag, 27 Nov. 1926, quoted in v. Saldern, 'Massenfreizeitkultur', 24.
[6] The term from Maase, 'Massenkunst', 42.
[7] On Lemke, see Müller, 'Der frühe Film', 71–6.

feature-length dramas led some to doubt their very right to exist. Yet it was clear to most reformers that blanket bans were wholly untenable, and only a small number of hardliners such as Lange and Hermann Häfker argued that the cinema was only justifiable in an explicitly educational format.[8]

No one doubted the pedagogical value of motion pictures as such. The promotion of *Lehrfilme*—short films about technological, scientific, historical, or geographic subjects—was something on which all cinema reformers could agree. The incipient 'education film movement' in Germany, which first emerged around 1905, took on a whole new dimension with the wartime increase in German production and the establishment of UFA's Culture Film Department in 1919. During the 1920s German educational films experienced something of a heyday. On the production side, German firms had established themselves as global leaders. The major film journals commented regularly on educational films, and the *Kinematographischen Monatshefte* even printed a special Lehrfilm supplement.[9] On the exhibition side, attempts to bring documentary films to a wider audience became more organized. Cinema clubs and trade unions—especially the Free Union Cultural Film Association (Freigewerkschaftliche-Kulturfilm-Gemeinde)—regularly arranged special screenings, and by the end of the 1920s they acquired an international dimension with the International Education Film Chamber in Basel and the new International Institute for Educational Film in Rome.[10]

Both the production and exhibition of educational films thus made significant progress in the 1920s. As a massive recent study has made clear, the documentary format was far more popular than has often been assumed, especially travel films and shorts set in exotic locations.[11] Equally clearly, however, the bulk of movie-goers were primarily interested in other things. During the early 1920s education films were sold almost exclusively to schools, special associations, or clubs, with few takers among commercial cinemas. The lack of state support made them relatively unprofitable, and apart from a handful of popular works such as Arnold Fanck's *Das Wunder des Schneeschuhs* (1920, on Alpine snow-skiing) or Robert Flaherty's *Nanook of the North* (1922, *Nanuk der Eskimo*, about survival in the Arctic environment) and *Moana* (1926, about everyday life in Polynesia), most were all but unknown outside the cinema clubs.[12] The big break for commercial production came in 1926, when an amendment to the Reich Film Law reduced amusement tax levies on educational and cultural films. Thenceforth they became

---

[8] See H. Häfker, *Der Kino und die Gebildeten* (Mönchen-Gladbach, 1915); K. Lange, *Der Kinematograph vom ethischen und ästhetischen Standpunkt* (Munich, 1912); generally, Müller, 'Der frühe Film', 82–4.

[9] *Der Lehrfilm. Beilage der Kinematographischen Monatshefte* (1920–6).

[10] A. Hübl (ed.), *Dritte Internationale Lehrfilm-Konferenz in Wien, 26. bis 31. Mai 1931* (Vienna, 1931), 38–9; *Der Lehrfilm*, 2 (Apr. 1921), 29; also Kinter, *Arbeiterbewegung*, 270.

[11] See generally K. Kreimeier, A. Ehmann, and J. Goergen (eds.), *Geschichte des dokumentarischen Films*, vol. 2 (Stuttgart, 2005).

[12] Toeplitz, *Geschichte*, 415–16.

an increasingly common element of cinema programmes, usually included as one of several shorts screened before the main feature. Documentary producers like Hans Cürlis naturally hailed the change as a major contribution to popular education, 'providing the broad masses of cinema-goers with small but continuous doses of valuable information that would otherwise remain unknown to them'.[13] Cinema owners, though verbally supportive of such educational efforts, had a rather different perspective. Their daily experience with audiences showed that most viewers were quickly bored by anything less than top-notch productions, which themselves could only be screened 'in small doses', more precisely in a ratio of around 1 : 20 to entertainment films. Efforts to replace a larger portion of entertainment films with documentaries were generally deemed a non-starter. As one cinema operator put it, this could only lead 'to the depopulation of the cinema and the complete ruin of the entire film industry'. In the end, the need to keep audiences happy meant that exhibitors were generally uninterested in anything more than 'small films as little accompaniments that don't cause him any pain and that don't bore his audience'.[14]

If efforts to improve cinema standards were to have more than a marginal effect, they obviously could not focus solely on documentary films. This became abundantly clear during the war, as official attempts to boost home-front morale via the cinema were predicated on the popularity of entertainment films. By 1916 at the latest, the 'discovery' of the cinema's propagandistic potential meant that opponents of entertainment films found fewer allies in government. Despite the noble claims of the semi-official film agency Bufa 'to combat kitsch and material of poor quality and thus to elevate and refine cinematography', officials quickly concluded that it was necessary to screen around ninety minutes of light entertainment for every half-hour of documentary material.[15] In November 1917 this official embrace of feature film culminated in the founding of UFA, which was explicitly conceived as a means of producing and distributing patriotic entertainment.

After the war, the main concern of cinema reform was thus to *combine* education and entertainment. In contrast to the conservative focus on censorship, most left-wing activists and critical intellectuals clearly favoured this approach. Ranging from radical democrats to socialists and communists, these reformers were motivated by a desire to improve aesthetic standards and to harness film as a means of political persuasion. Despite the deep political divisions over the Left's response to film, a number of practical schemes were launched after the end of the socialization debate of 1919–20.

One such initiative was the SPD Education Committee's Lichtbildzentrale, conceived as a distribution agency for 'worthwhile' films. Starting with only a

---

[13] H. Cürlis, *Vom Deutschen Lehrfilm* (Berlin, 1928), 11.
[14] R. Ott, *Wie führe ich mein Kino?* (Berlin, 1922), 29–30; 'Lehrfilm und Publikumsgeschmack', *FK* (11 Mar. 1920), 1.
[15] Stark, 'Cinema', 162; quote from Maase, 'Massenkunst', 71.

handful of pictures in the early 1920s, its stock reached nearly 2,300 films in 1929, enough to cause concern among commercial distributors and even an attempted boycott against it.[16] The actual *production* of films was a different matter. Following the demise of Rolf Gärtner's short-lived Soviet Film Company for Proletarian Culture (Sowjetfilmgesellschaft für proletarische Kultur m.b.H.), a number of trade unions founded the People's Picture House (Volksfilmbühne) in 1922 as a means of supporting the creation of 'edifying' films.[17] But due to a lack of financial resources, it never really moved beyond the distribution of existing productions. As cinema reformers quickly recognized, the hurdles to independent film production were prohibitively high. Filmmaking required both a sizeable capital basis and a far-reaching distribution network, since many films were only financially viable if they could be shown over a wide area of the country.

As a result, efforts to raise the quality of film were by and large concentrated on consumer cooperation. By far the most important initiative along these lines was the Volks-Filmverband (VfV), founded in 1928 for the purpose of 'organizing the broad masses of working-class cinemagoers and educating them to a critical understanding of film'. Proceeding from the assumption that film was justifiably the most popular entertainment medium of the day, the founders of the VfV nonetheless maintained that 'amusement need not be identical with trash, and that relaxation need not mean spiritual impoverishment'.[18] According to its president, the novelist Heinrich Mann, art had a duty to educate people even if the loyalties of a commercial industry were primarily to its investors. The aim was therefore to organize a 'bloc' of consumers that wanted an alternative, thus reducing the financial risk involved in making more demanding films. If producers could be assured of screenings to such an organized mass audience, this would remove one of the primary reasons for the aesthetic poverty of popular cinema.[19]

Although the VfV boasted some forty-four branches in Germany by 1930, fourteen of them in Berlin alone, it never came close to achieving the mass impact it sought. The original membership goal of 200,000, the number thought to make the organization commercially significant, proved wholly unrealistic. In the event, the VfV attracted only a few thousand followers, most of them socialist- or communist-party members with a sprinkling of radical intellectuals such as Heinrich Mann himself. One of the main assumptions on which the association was based, namely the idea that there were large numbers of working-class cinema-goers dissatisfied with the selection of 'bourgeois' films on offer, was clearly erroneous. As early as 1929 the association's journal *Volk und Film* already acknowledged that it was little more than a federation of local film clubs,

---

[16] Kinter, *Arbeiterbewegung*, 263.   [17] Ibid. 204.
[18] VfV Foundation Appeal, quoted from W. L. Guttsman, *Workers' Culture in Weimar Germany* (New York, 1990), 267.
[19] H. Mann, 'Der Film' (26 Feb. 1928), repr. in Kaes, *Kino-Debatte*, 170.

'a society of cinema fans which sold cheap tickets for progressive films to its members'.[20] Originally conceived as a vehicle for progressive cinema reform, it never became much more than an association of progressive cinema reformers.

As was so often the case, this well-meaning attempt to improve the standards of mass culture was based on a misunderstanding of popular tastes. But instead of blaming the failure on their own false assumptions, the left-wing reformers in the VfV—not unlike their conservative counterparts—tended to regard the mass of uneducated cinema-goers as the real culprit. As the Volksbühne director Siegfried Nestriepke complained in 1929, 'the masses flock to films that crudely provide ridiculous sensations and strained happy endings through the mutilation of all psychological depiction and logic of plot'.[21] The apparent lack of popular demand for 'edifying' film was, as the SPD daily *Vorwärts* concluded, 'not a blot on the film industry, from which cultural achievements cannot rightly be demanded, but rather on film consumers'.[22] Even the most liberal-minded reformers concluded that a more pro-active approach was required. As one commentator typically put it, 'the cinema public has its wishes and demands that should not be brusquely rejected or ignored. This is not to say, however, that one should always give in completely to the demands of the audience. By going along with the audience, one can gradually divert its tastes and thereby purify and elevate them.'[23] As these remarks clearly illustrate, the conflicting requirements of entertainment and education were still a central concern in the 1920s, even among those who were prepared to concede that the public had a right to amusement.

This very same tension between didacticism and diversion also shaped the development of early radio, though the tight regulation of German broadcasting rendered the interplay between these forces quite different. Weimar cultural reformers held great hopes for the new medium of broadcasting. Unlike the cinema, its state-controlled monopoly position had established what many regarded as ideal conditions for balancing educational pretensions and customer satisfaction. As the psychologist Ernst Jolowicz put it: 'The wishes of listeners and audience tastes must of course be taken into account, even when these tastes do not meet the demands that experts at the pinnacle of their fields are justified to place on them. On the other hand, deliberate pedagogical efforts are undertaken to elevate the cultural wishes of the audience and to facilitate its ability to distinguish between good and bad.'[24]

This was very much how the founders of German radio viewed the matter. As we saw in Chapter 2, Hans Bredow and his associates shared a vision

---

[20] Quote and figures from Guttsman, *Workers' Culture*, 268.

[21] S. Nestriepke, 'Die technischen und kulturellen Möglichkeiten des Films', in *Film und Funk* (Berlin, 1929), 20.

[22] Bauer, 'Statistik', 3.

[23] W. Schmitt, *Das Filmwesen und seine Wechselbeziehungen zur Gesellschaft* (Freudenstadt, 1932), 124.

[24] Jolowicz, *Rundfunk*, 58–9.

of the new medium as a vehicle of knowledge and cultivation, a champion of civility and sobriety that would help generate a sense of commonality in a starkly polarized society. These enthusiastic advocates of the wireless were convinced that it could, if deployed properly, help overcome some of the ills of the modern industrial civilization that had given birth to it. In the eyes of Weimar programmers, broadcasting was intended to keep people at home, aid family togetherness, and above all to spread the fruits of education among the common folk. As Carl Hagemann, director of the Berliner Funk-Stunde (the largest of the regional broadcasters), proclaimed in 1928, the ultimate goal of broadcasting was to 'mould self-contained human beings (*in sich geschlossene Menschen bilden*). . . . Radio should serve the broad mass of the populace as a reliable elementary school (*Volksschule*), informal yet at the same time continually open'.[25] Unlike in the United States, superficial amusements should not roam freely on the airwaves in the land of poets and thinkers. Although radio was undoubtedly conceived as a 'mass medium'—a means of communicating with a socially and geographically diverse public—its architects were determined to keep it from becoming another element of 'mass culture'. This aim of popular education and cultural improvement was, more than anything else, what shaped radio programming in the Weimar era.

Broadcasters pursued these aims in a number of ways. Throughout the 1920s a particular emphasis was placed on classical music and lectures, both of which were lovingly cultivated by the regional stations and occupied a large chunk of the evening programme (the programme will be discussed in more detail in Chapter 5). There were two interrelated reasons for this. Transmitting the treasures of the symphony hall and lecture theatre not only brought *Kultur* to the masses, but also served as a means of acquiring elite approval for the medium. This was by no means a minor consideration during the early years, for there was no shortage of elite concern that radio might range itself alongside other modern evils such as the popular press and cinema. As the conservative publicist Wilhelm Stapel put it, with typical pessimistic flourish, 'the cinema has destroyed the culture of the theatre, and the radio will destroy our concert and lecture culture. The wheels of progress race forward with the speed of an automobile.'[26] In order to allay such fears, broadcasters constantly professed their commitment to the 'higher things', and indeed their actual programming left little doubt where their cultural allegiances lay. Lectures, classical symphonies, and other demanding fair formed the spine of the programme throughout the 1920s, and although their share of airtime gradually decreased in purely quantitative terms, they thoroughly dominated the peak listening hours between eight and ten o'clock in the evening. The centenary commemorations of Beethoven's death were, though perhaps

[25] C. Hagemann, 'Die künstlerisch-kulturelle Zielsetzung des deutschen Rundfunks' (1928), in Hans Bredow (ed.), *Aus meinem Archiv* (Heidelberg, 1950), 228.
[26] C. Lenk, *Die Erscheinung des Rundfunks* (Opladen, 1997), 137–8.

unusually relentless, symptomatic of this highbrow tendency. In March 1927 the Berliner Funk-Stunde broadcast music by Beethoven every single night for a whole week, while the Mitteldeutscher Rundfunk in Leipzig even embellished the composer's repertoire with a series of twelve evening lectures on 'The Age of Beethoven in the Mirror of Culture'.[27] Anyone fearful that radio would destroy traditional concert and lecture culture could hardly have felt less threatened.

Securing elite recognition was of fundamental importance not only for legitimating the new technology, but also for commercial reasons. Educated professionals not only spent significant amounts on cultural goods, they also continued to set the standards for wide segments of the populace. 'One should never forget the influence that these very circles exert on their surroundings', remarked the journal *Radio-Händler*, the mouthpiece for radio retailers. 'The fact that a porter might recently have acquired a radio still constitutes no compelling reason for the well-heeled occupant on the second floor to become a radio listener. However, the probability is obviously much higher the other way around.'[28] Efforts to win over this most discerning group of listeners thus promised a handsome dividend, and the best means of gaining their approval lay in demonstrably catering to their tastes. This explains why, during the infancy of broadcasting, even retailers eager to open up a mass market for radio sets were at pains to emphasize their vision of radio as 'a kind of further education college. . . . Whoever wants a mere talking machine should buy himself a gramophone; a radio apparatus is too valuable to be used for such a lowly purpose.'[29]

By bringing the arts and sciences to a mass audience, Weimar broadcasting was a bulwark against both the plebeian colonization of the public sphere as well as the further dilution of Germany's national and regional heritage. Amidst the growing popularity of jazz and dance music, radio was to embody the very antithesis of the 'Americanizing' film and recording industries. As Bredow himself remarked in October 1924, radio would 'gradually eradicate Negro music and, through the elevation of tastes, both deepen and widen the sense of repulsion against poor foreign music'.[30]

But there were limits to the educational focus of broadcasting, and it was obvious even to the most zealous proponents of 'Bildung' that modern dance music and catchy hits could not be fought solely with the weapons of the symphony and lecture. In their search for surrogate forms of entertainment, Weimar programmers thus increasingly turned to Volk and Heimat traditions as a wholesome substitute for 'Americanized' commercial culture. It was a fitting partnership, for as Adelheid von Saldern has pointed out, radio programmers and

[27] Führer, 'Medium', 747–8.
[28] W. Heymann, 'Und die Intellektuellen . . . ?!', *RH* (27 Aug. 1929), 798.
[29] *RH* (30 Sept. 1924), 103.
[30] Lenk, *Erscheinung*, 186; see also M. Stapper, *Unterhaltungsmusik im Rundfunk der Weimarer Republik* (Tutzing, 2001), 95–6; Stoffels, 'Rundfunk', 961.

advocates of Volk and Heimat culture shared a number of common interests.[31] For one thing, the regional structure of German broadcasting meant that there was an inbuilt interest in promoting regional dialect and culture. In the early 1920s radio executives had deliberately chosen a decentralized system that would reflect the cultural differences between North and South and between Catholic and Protestant regions.[32] During the latter part of the decade the Hamburg-based NORAG in particular tried to develop a distinctive regional profile by devoting a substantial proportion of its airtime to local themes. Its assistant director, Kurt Stapelfeldt, regarded the promotion of Heimat culture as 'one of the most responsible tasks of radio broadcasting', and as a trained philologist he laid special emphasis on the use of Low German in the programme.[33] Another important affinity between programmers and Heimat advocates lay in the hope that such customs might overlay the social divisiveness of proletarian culture. The notion that even the major cities represented a form of Heimat with a distinctive local culture and set of folk traditions was highly appealing to radio executives, who sought to use broadcasting as a 'unifying band' that would overcome class divides. It also resonated with the avowedly 'apolitical' stance of German radio, for the advocates of Volk and Heimat culture similarly sought to transcend party politics by focusing on values and practices that people supposedly held in common. Finally, it even dovetailed with radio executives' efforts to promote radio-listening in rural areas, where it was thought that Volk culture would naturally find a receptive audience.[34]

Unsurprisingly, however, such broadcasts were not to everyone's taste, and many who wholeheartedly supported the educational mission of radio were strongly opposed to the promotion of Volk and Heimat culture, not to mention the 'apolitical' conception of radio that underpinned it. As SPD spokesmen repeatedly argued, such transmissions were wholly irrelevant to the lives of most manual workers. The attempt to subsume the tensions of modern society under a veneer of folksy sentiment was hopelessly romantic. In time, the 'bourgeois' character of German radio that was reflected in such programming led the more militant segments of the Left to reject the Weimar broadcasting system altogether. The Arbeiter-Radio-Bund, which advocated a separate workers' radio network, saw no point in trying to make radio more relevant to a working-class clientele through gradual, piecemeal reform. But in the absence of viable alternatives this was precisely what the majority of socialists and critical intellectuals sought to do. After all, there were broad areas of agreement with the existing system: by

---

[31] A. v. Saldern, '*Volk* and *Heimat* Culture in Radio Broadcasting During the Period of Transition from Weimar to Nazi Germany', *JMH* 76 (2004), 319–20.

[32] Führer, 'Medium', 730.

[33] Generally, H. Halefeldt, 'Ein Sender für acht Länder', *AfS* 41 (2001), 145–70; quote from Saldern, '*Volk*', 324.

[34] D. Münkel, 'Der Rundfunk geht auf die Dörfer', in D. Münkel (ed.), *Der lange Abschied vom Agrarland* (Göttingen, 2000), 177–98.

and large they shared the conviction that radio should chiefly act as a bearer of culture and education, not as a vehicle of unconstructive pleasure-seeking.[35]

Overall, the educational discourse that permeated Weimar radio meant that broadcasting made only minimal concessions to popular tastes. By the middle of the 1920s German radio was already recognized as remarkably didactic and 'heavy' in international comparison. Whereas the BBC was characterized by a mixture of entertainment, music, and current events, the Dutch, French, and Italian services by an emphasis on music, and American radio by a shamelessly 'light tone', German broadcasting was distinguished by a 'pontificating (*dozierend*) tendency'.[36] Complaints about the programme rarely criticized its poor quality, but rather that it was, as one observer put it, 'too high in quality, that is to say, not popular enough'.[37] Developing the radio as an instrument of cultivation resulted in a stodgy and unmistakeably elitist programme.[38] Karl Christian Führer is quite right to characterize the pedagogical impetus of Weimar radio as a form of 'defensive modernization', as one of the many instances in which German elites utilized modern concepts and techniques as a means of shoring up the status quo. In view of the threat posed by commercial culture, it is hardly surprising that the dyed-in-the-wool Bildungsbürger who oversaw German radio regarded the new medium as a means of promoting the cultural values that they themselves venerated, a tool for upholding 'the hegemonic claims of traditional high culture'.[39] In some ways the state-sponsored protection of the airwaves, the supposedly 'ideal conditions' for maintaining a balance between education and popularity, hindered rather than helped the cause of cultural reform. For the limited need to cater to consumer wishes meant that pedagogical programming could quickly go over the top, that the achievement of a genuine compromise could all too easily be sacrificed on the altar of Kultur.

Quite obviously, no media organization operating in a competitive market could afford to do what the radio corporations did. For this reason the development of the recording industry took a very different trajectory. As we saw in Chapter 1, the industry's fortunes swung wildly over the first third of the twentieth century, capped off by ruthless price wars during the depression years as companies frantically chased after dwindling customers. Catering to popular tastes was an absolute necessity for commercial survival, and no amount of derision by cultural conservatives was ever going to halt the continued proliferation of short-lived and aesthetically undemanding hits.

---

[35] F. Merkel, *Rundfunk und Gewerkschaften in der Weimarer Republik und in der frühen Nachkriegszeit* (Potsdam, 1996); also P. Dahl, *Arbeitersender und Volksempfänger* (Frankfurt a. M., 1978), overestimates the movement.

[36] H. Engel, 'Völkerpsychologie und Rundfunk', in R. Lothar and A. Ihring (eds.), *Radio-Almanach 1926* (Berlin, 1926), 53–4.

[37] (P.) Lertes, 'Rundfunk aufs Land!', in R. Lothar and A. Ihring (eds.), *Radio-Almanach 1927* (Berlin, 1927), 70.

[38] K. C. Führer, 'Auf dem Weg zur "Massenkultur"?', *HZ* 262 (1996), 777.   [39] Ibid. 777.

Yet the new technology of sound conservation nonetheless had its advocates within the educated elite. Among left-leaning musicologists there was a keen interest in expanding its use beyond the conservation of formulaic tunes. The aim of such efforts was, as with the popular cinema, to enhance the artistic potential of the medium and to demonstrate that, in the words of one reformer, 'records also have an *educational* mission'.[40] The benefits they could bring to musical tuition were a regular topic of discussion in the music press in the 1920s and early 1930s. Far from lowering musical standards, records were promoted as 'an unforgettable form of illustrative material for training the ear about the texture of different instruments, about musical lines . . . and about musical standards themselves'.[41] Their usefulness was, moreover, by no means limited to schools and amateurs, but could even be employed at the highest level by conserving virtuoso performances from which professionals themselves could learn.[42] In order to realize this potential, music-pedagogical efforts required both better organization and more generous support from the state, whose only action by 1930 was to establish a small 'records advice bureau' within the Central Institute for Education and Teaching (Zentralinstitut für Erziehung und Unterricht).[43] Such official recognition would, it was thought, also enhance the 'image' of recorded sound. And for those purists who still harboured doubts about the compatibility of art and mechanical reproduction, the pedagogical potential of the medium was by no means confined to music education. Further applications ranged all the way from foreign-language tuition to readings for the visually impaired to physical-fitness regimes not at all unlike modern-day aerobics.[44]

The reformist promotion of the gramophone dovetailed with the interests of recording companies in two interrelated ways. Not only did it help gain elite recognition, it also supported companies' efforts to penetrate this most demanding segment of the market. It is therefore unsurprising that the campaign to promote recorded sound for musical education found its most generous patrons in the very companies that were criticized for producing and marketing 'musical trash' in the first place. Nowhere was this more clearly manifested than at the German Record Convention in 1930, co-organized by the cultural department of the firm Carl Lindström, the Mannheim Committee for Folk

---

[40] The following four paragraphs are drawn from C. Ross, 'Entertainment', with the permission of Palgrave Macmillan. Quote from L. Koch, 'Schallplattenindustrie, Staat und Volksbildung', *Die Musik*, 22 (1930), 518, emphasis in the original.

[41] E. Ackerknecht, *Bildungspflege und Schallplatte* (Stettin, 1930), 2; also 'Musik im eigenen Heim', *Die Stimme*, 13 (1928), 163.

[42] Stuckenschmidt, 'Erziehung', 370.

[43] Koch, 'Schallplattenindustrie', 518, italics in original; see also H. Pasche, 'Die Schallplatte als Unterrichtsmittel', *PZ* 31 (1 May 1930), 652–4.

[44] 'Sprachunterricht durchs Grammophon', *PZ* 25 (1 Nov. 1924), 898. By 1924 there were already at least two aerobics-style products on the market, replete with fold-out illustrations of the movements: *PZ* 25 (15 Aug. 1924), 708.

Music, and the Mannheim Adult Education Centre. This was the first public event in Germany to focus explicitly on the 'problem of the record as a cultural and educational factor'.[45] Discussions about the wider potential of recorded sound also regularly featured in Deutsche Grammophon's house periodical *Die Stimme seines Herrn*, and from 1929 to 1931 Lindström's cultural department, under its energetic director Ludwig Koch, even produced a special journal entitled *Kultur und Schallplatte*. By the latter 1920s most of the large firms had 'cultural' or 'educational' departments that organized special concerts and events specifically designed to woo the Bildungsbürgertum. While Electrola and Deutsche Grammophon invited audiences into their studios to listen to orchestral recordings taking place, Telefunken and Lindström staged live matinee concerts featuring various artists on their labels.[46]

Such publicity exercises were, however, no substitute for concrete action. The goal of gaining elite recognition ultimately required an expansion of the companies' classical repertoires. The problem was that this cost money. The inclusion of many 'highbrow' recordings could thus only be justified as either a long-term sales strategy or, more plausibly, as a public-relations exercise in itself. As the *Phonographische Zeitschrift* remarked in 1930, many classical recordings functioned as loss leaders: 'Every record company has in its catalogue recordings that never cover their own costs and that are included only in order to ensure that the company is not perceived as a gang of un-artistic and uncultured philistines.' For the recording firms, elite patronage and profit were not always easily reconcilable. By and large, such recordings were 'produced only grudgingly and in limited numbers'.[47]

Yet they were not without success on the public-relations front. One of the keys to elite acceptance was to achieve coverage in the 'respectable' press. The recording industry had by and large failed to do this before the First World War, the sole exception being the *Neue Wiener Tageblatt*, which began publishing a weekly gramophone supplement in 1914. It was first in the early 1920s that German newspapers began to cover musical recordings, most notably the *Deutsche Allgemeine Zeitung* and *BZ am Mittag*, whose Sunday editorial sections included headings for 'phono-art' and 'music and dance'.[48] By the closing years of the decade the situation had changed dramatically. As the Reich Association for the Phonographic Trade (Reichsverband des deutschen Sprechmaschinenhandels) gleefully noted in 1928, 'whereas the German newspapers merely used to carp and crack jokes about the screech-music of the talking machine, nowadays the press engages with serious critiques of new recordings just as fulsomely as it does

[45] Sonnemann, 'Schallplattentag', 1730–1.
[46] 'Sprechmaschinen-Konzerte', *PZ* 6 (4 Oct. 1905), 873; *PZ* 24 (1 June 1923), 524; 'Künstler–Schallplatte–Publikum', *PZ* 36 (1935), 512.
[47] *PZ* 31 (1930), 160.
[48] M. Eisler, 'Spaziergänge eines Grammophonisten', *PZ* 24: 9 (1 May 1923), 450; *PZ* 24: 10 (15 May 1923), 488.

for concerts and theatre'.[49] Though records still featured less prominently than radio or film, they had finally become *pressefähig* (worthy of coverage).[50] Indeed, their coverage was not just confined to the mainstream dailies, but also included leading music journals such as *Die Musik*, which by the 1930s ran special sections on both 'radio' and 'mechanical music'. The medium of recorded sound had, like the cinema and the radio, become an integral part of Germany's cultural landscape in the inter-war years. Although it functioned primarily as a purveyor of popular songs and dance music, it was also gradually finding a place in the realm of elite culture.

NEW MEDIA AND NEW GENRES

As the case of the gramophone makes especially clear, the related tasks of raising popular tastes, refining public entertainments, and promoting the cultural benefits of new communication technologies were, though notionally distinguishable, all but inseparable in practice. Whether in the realm of sight or sound, the attempt to create alternatives to commercial culture depended not only on the support of political or economic elites to shield them from the financial pressures of the commercial market, but also on the involvement of the educated middle classes as a core constituency of consumers. In order to elicit such patronage, reformers needed first of all to overcome the sense of ambivalence felt towards the new media and the material they conveyed. Their association with plebeian audiences was—though somewhat erroneous—well established by the turn of the century, and proved remarkably persistent over the following decades. The goal of reforming 'mass culture' thus required the development of new forms that could both uplift popular tastes and convince an art-worshipping elite of the expressive potential of the new media. It was, in other words, not only a social project but an aesthetic one as well.

The challenges this presented were immense, and the stakes could hardly have been higher. Superseding the ingrained cultural hierarchies in German society represented nothing less than the 'democratization of culture' itself, the Holy Grail for progressive intellectuals and artists. The ultimate goal was to overcome the chasm between 'E-Kunst' (elite art) and 'U-Kunst' (*Unterhaltung*, or entertainment) through the creation of a so-called 'A-Kunst' (*Allgemein-Kunst* or universal art) available and accessible to all. The aim of achieving universal appeal meant that such efforts were primarily focused on the new media of communication rather than the older and more exclusive theatre or concert hall. By forging new art forms specifically suited to their technological attributes,

[49] H. Wünsch, 'Die Lage der deutschen phonographischen Industrie', in RDS, *Jahrbuch für den deutschen Sprechmaschinenhandel* (Berlin, 1928), 11.

[50] D. Bassermann, 'Schallplatte und Musik-Kritik', in RDS, *Jahrbuch*, 33.

reformist artists sought to give ordinary people a greater share of the aesthetic pleasure that was previously confined to the higher strata of society. In this sense, enhancing the aesthetic content of the media closely paralleled the efforts of associations such as the Werkbund and Dürer-Bund to enhance the design quality of mass-produced goods after the turn of the century. Both projects were geared towards uplifting popular tastes and flattening cultural hierarchies, and both directly contributed to the modern project of beautifying everyday life.

From the very beginning there was a direct relationship between these two strands of early twentieth-century reform. Around the turn of the century the growing interest among industrialists in the problems of aesthetic representation meant that many of the earliest initiatives for a 'universal art' came in the realm of commercial advertising. Its unique combination of artistic and commercial potential made it especially appealing as a means of elevating popular tastes, all the more so given the transformation of advertising during the economic boom of the Wilhelmine era. Throughout most of the nineteenth century the bulk of advertisements were carried in newspapers rather than posters or billboards. Most were based solely or predominantly on text, with a conservative layout that exerted little visual effect. The improvement of printing techniques made pictorial images increasingly common from the 1870s onwards, but they were largely limited to company logos or insignia intended to embellish the textual message, which remained the primary communicative factor.[51]

All of this began to change around the mid-1890s, in large part through the adoption of the so-called *Kunstplakat*, or art poster, a genre pioneered in France in the 1880s by painters such as Henri de Toulouse-Lautrec and Jules Chéret. Characterized by the sharp juxtaposition of large, simple fields of colour, the art poster aggressively sought the attention of onlookers. It found its first and most vociferous champions among the small groups of bohemian artists (especially those associated with the journals *Simplicissimus* and *Jugend*), who saw in this mode of depiction an ideal means of liberating art from the confines of the museum and bringing it to the masses. Deliberately attention-grabbing, the Kunstplakat was ideally suited to the visual landscape of the modern city and was soon recognized by commercial artists for its obvious advertising potential. First taken up by figures such as Ernst Growald (Berlin) and Thomas Theodor Heine (Munich), it promised to give artists a competitive edge in the increasingly lucrative advertising market—especially in the form of the so-called *Sachplakat* ('object poster') first popularized by Lucian Bernhard in Berlin.[52]

In the meantime, the sheer growth of advertising made it an ideal vehicle for bringing such aesthetic innovations to the masses. For once, the supposedly antagonistic realms of art and commerce appeared to work in synergy. Although

[51] D. Reinhardt, *Von der Reklame zum Marketing* (Berlin, 1993), 49; C. Lamberty, *Reklame in Deutschland 1890–1914* (Berlin, 2000), 166.

[52] Reinhardt, *Reklame*, 52–8; Lamberty, *Reklame*, 185.

Fig. 5. Typical *Sachplakat*: advertisement for Manoli cigarettes, by Lucian Bernhard, 1914. bpk Berlin.

only a handful of companies were initially willing to pay extra for ads with artistic pretensions—above all for new brand-name products such as Odol mouthwash, Continental tyres, Bahlsen biscuits, and Pelikan ink—their number grew rapidly after 1905. Whereas the vast majority of Kunstplakate commissions had previously been for exhibitions, theatre productions, and other events within the art scene itself, henceforth the bulk of patronage emanated from private businesses.[53]

This unusual convergence between art and commerce was very much a mutual endeavour, simultaneously pursued from both sides. Artists and designers, for their part, went out of their way to cultivate closer relations with firms that invested in advertising. The basic thrust of the Jugendstil movement—namely to re-enliven the aesthetic quality of craft trades—meant that its many adherents were predisposed to this type of cooperation in any event. As soon as one jettisoned his disdain for mixing art and commerce, there was no compelling

[53] Reinhardt, *Reklame*, 58–60.

reason not to make a good living from it. Indeed, since many commercial artists—including even leading lights such as Lucian Bernhard and Ludwig Hohlwein—were autodidacts with little or no connection to intellectual circles (and often snobbishly unaccepted within them), they had little to lose by way of 'genuine' artistic reputation in doing so. The Poster-Lovers Association (Verein der Plakatfreunde), founded in 1905 with the explicit aim of 'promoting the artistic poster among the public and business world', provided a crucial organizational home for these efforts; its journal, *Das Plakat*, appearing from 1910, likewise furnished an important forum for information and exchange.[54]

Business leaders, for their part, were eager to promote these artistic initiatives for their own purposes. Without a doubt, the founding of the Werkbund in 1907 represented a milestone in the confluence of art and industry. Motivated by a desire to uphold German national culture against the threat posed by industrialization, the Werkbund rejected the anti-modernist pessimism so common among conservative intellectual circles, seeking instead the harmonization of art and industry through new forms of cooperation. Bringing together liberal politicians such as Theodor Heuss and Friedrich Naumann, progressive industrialists like Robert Bosch, and noted architects and artists such as Hermann Muthesius and Henry van de Velde, the Werkbund represented a curious amalgam of progressive cultural aims and distinctly nationalist economic interests. At base, its aim was to strengthen the German economy and boost exports through improving the design quality of German goods. This would, in turn, lead to a more highly skilled work-force, higher wages for workers, and thus higher standards of cultural taste and material prosperity. To some extent this can be seen as a quasi-Fordist project of achieving social harmony through a virtuous circle of high incomes and high levels of consumption—the main difference being an emphasis on consumer quality rather than quantity. Forging a new community of interest between industry and labour was a central feature of this vision.[55]

Advertising was an important factor in the equation, for the sought-after community of interests was not confined to employer–employee relations but also implied a closer link between producers and consumers. Harmonizing social and economic relations would clearly require the integration of consumer wishes into the national economy, and the best means of achieving this was seen to lie in effective, artistically inspired advertising. Raising the aesthetic standards of mass society required improvements in retailing no less than in manufacturing. The activities of the German Museum for Art in Commerce and Trade (Deutsches Museum für Kunst in Handel und Gewerbe), founded in 1909 with the close involvement of the Werkbund, clearly expressed the

---

[54] Ibid. 61; on graphic artists generally, Lamberty, *Reklame*, 273–87.
[55] J. Campbell, *The German Werkbund* (Princeton, 1978); F. Schwartz, *The Werkbund* (New Haven, 1996).

importance attached to tasteful advertising. During the half-decade before the war the museum organized numerous travelling exhibits and regularly lent out its collections to trade associations, business schools, and art colleges, including the new College of Decorative Arts (Höhere Fachschule für Dekorationskunst) that the Werkbund helped to establish in Berlin. At the same time, these organizations also sponsored improvements in product display, including a series of shop-window competitions held in various German cities.[56]

Admittedly, such efforts were centred on large manufacturing firms and up-scale department stores. The vast majority of small, semi-artisanal manufacturers and corner retail shops were barely aware of them. For the most part, the enamel signs gracing their store entries and the chaotic jumble of posters plastered on advertising columns hardly enhanced the aesthetic standards of the visual environment, as opponents of advertising long complained.[57] Yet the cooperation between commercial artists and progressive business leaders nonetheless had a significant and lasting effect on commercial advertising, an effect that could be felt long after its pre-war pinnacle.

The situation changed dramatically after 1914. During the war itself advertising budgets plummeted due to rationing, and once the fighting was over the no-nonsense rationalization rhetoric of the post-war world left industry far less interested in artistic self-representation than before. But despite all of the changes, advertising was still perceived as an ideal means to 'bring the two poles together, to give a spiritual dimension to the mechanical-economic realm, and to promote art, knowledge, and the pursuit of the common good through the power of material property'.[58] Throughout the 1920s German advertising associations continually sought to enhance the image of the profession through the prestige of artistic recognition. It was quite a coup when advertising posters and sketches were first displayed at Berlin's Grand Art Exhibition in 1922, which had previously excluded all forms of applied art.[59] The extent to which advertisers continued to eye contemporary artistic movements was clearly evident at the 'Art and Advertising' exhibition held in Essen in 1931, a celebration of modernist impulses and their assimilation in commercial art.[60] True, the gradual trend towards a more 'advertising-technical' as opposed to 'artistic' orientation in mainstream publicity was unmistakeable. The semantically revealing displacement of the Poster-Lovers Association by the League of German Applied Artists (Bund deutscher Gebrauchsgraphiker) clearly indicated the changes under way.[61] Yet throughout the 1920s German advertisers still tended to judge their work

[56] Lamberty, *Reklame*, 328–77; Reinhardt, *Reklame*, 69–76.

[57] K. Repp, 'Marketing, Modernity and the "German People's Soul"', in P. Swett, J. Wiesen, and J. Zatlin (eds.), *Selling Modernity* (Durham, NC, 2007), 27–51.

[58] E. Freyer, 'Nach dem Weltkriege', *DR* 11 (Mar. 1918), 40.   [59] *SR* 7 (June 1922), 69.

[60] *DR* 24 (June 1931), 402–6; *SR* 15 (July 1931), 308.

[61] Reinhardt, *Reklame*, 77–8. Equally revealing was the displacement of the journal *Das Plakat* by *Gebrauchsgrafik*.

according to artistic rather than purely marketing criteria. As Hanns Kropff, one of the leading exponents of a utilitarian approach, complained in 1924: 'They seldom concern themselves over whether their work is good from an advertising standpoint. They draw or paint a design and then fill the precious space with it. And the odd thing is that the commissioning firm accepts and publicizes the design simply because the artist says it is good and because it was made by *him*. Advertising is produced not for the person paying for it, but rather for the reputation of the artist.'[62] The hard-nosed American advertisers who began setting up branch offices in Germany in the latter 1920s were also struck by the importance still attached to artistic criteria: 'merely to fill the space is apparently enough, provided the advertising is striking in appearance.'[63]

If advertisers still conceived of their work in artistic terms, many artists—at least among the avant-garde—were growing more and more interested in the expressive potential of advertising. To some extent this was the product of sheer necessity, as runaway inflation meant that big business was one of the only reliable sources of patronage left. Yet on an intellectual level it also reflected the social and aesthetic programmes of various art-isms of the Weimar era, all of which, despite their many differences, rejected elitist conceptions of art and the values that underpinned them. In practice this meant either ignoring 'art' altogether or turning one's attention to the masses, or both.[64] Many avant-garde artists saw in advertising a useful social language and an effective means of reaching a mass public. In the words of Georg Friedrich Hartlaub, the art historian who coined the term 'New Sobriety' (*Neue Sachlichkeit*), 'advertising art (*Werbekunst*) is a social, collective and genuinely mass art form: the only one that still exists today. It shapes the optical customs and habits of the nameless collective of the public.'[65]

As such, advertising was embraced by groups as far apart as Expressionists and Functionalists. During the immediate post-war years there was a spate of Expressionist advertisements that attracted unusual attention—though their insistence on visual effect over actual marketing considerations (in many cases it was difficult to work out what was being advertised) consigned them to a short-lived niche existence.[66] Various rebels working within other artistic movements likewise dabbled in advertising: the Constructivist El Lissitzky, whose ads for the Pelikan ink firm acquired considerable notoriety; the Dadaist painter Kurt Schwitters, who founded his own ad agency in Hanover in 1927; or the

[62] H. Kropff, 'Götterdämmerung der deutschen Reklamekunst', *DR* 17 (Oct. 1924), 674–5, emphasis in the original.

[63] J. Walter Thompson Company Archives: Rare Book, Manuscript, and Special Collections Library, Duke University (hereafter JWT): JWT Research Reports, Microfilm Collection 16 mm, reel 232, A. E. Hobbs, 'Advertising in Germany' (Jan. 1928), 1.

[64] See Hermand, Trommler, *Kultur*, 353–5.   [65] Ibid. 405.

[66] R. Hösel, 'Expressionistische Reklameentwürfe', *SR* 6 (Feb. 1921), 37–40; also Reinhardt, *Reklame*, 78–9.

photo-montage pioneers Jan Tschichold and Max Burchartz, the latter of whom also ran an advertising studio.[67] But not even the involvement of big names like Lissitzky could hide the fact that such initiatives were marginal. The post-war utilitarian impulse had largely sapped the appeal of aesthetic experimentation. By 1931 even Ernst Growald, one of the earliest champions of the Kunstplakat, thought that the poster was only justifiable if it was 'not only artistically, but also technically' effective, and that such an outcome required 'an experienced advertising professional to collaborate with an artist'.[68] In some respects the situation had reverted back to 1900, in that the bulk of consciously 'artistic' advertisements were once again commissioned from the art scene itself, whether for exhibitions, theatre productions, or the film industry.[69]

This was not, however, a case of history repeating itself. The fact that the film industry had emerged as a key advertising patron in the 1920s also reflected how much had changed since the turn of the century. The reliance of the venerated Kunstplakat on cinema commissions poignantly symbolized the intervening shifts in the realm of visual culture. Given the unrivalled popularity of motion pictures in the 1920s, many artists now turned their attention to the cinema as the most promising workshop for the creation of a universal art.

It had taken nearly two decades for film to be recognized as an 'art' form at all, let alone one capable of spanning the cultural divides in German society. As we saw in Chapter 1, the emergence of the feature-length drama first attracted the keen attention of artists and intellectuals. The transition from variety formats to narrative film after 1910 made cinema a matter of intense critical scrutiny, not only among social reformers but also artists, writers, and academics, who saw this as an attack on literary culture itself. Despite its increasing affinities with the traditional theatre, most pre-war observers regarded film as a technology, not an art form. The absence of the spoken word precluded the possibility of any genuine depth of feeling or meaning. Moreover, its reliance on visual representation favoured shallow sensationalism, and its commercial character only underscored its materialistic artlessness.[70] As such, the cinema was doomed to remain nothing more than the 'theatre of the little man', a temple to mediocrity and philistinism.

Yet already before the war there were other voices—admittedly a minority—that promoted a more positive engagement with the medium. By and large they were found among the artistic avant-garde, though not everyone in that milieu was a supporter of the cinema.[71] The raw vitality and expressive power

[67] J. Willett, *The New Sobriety, 1917–1933* (London, 1978), 137; Hermand, Trommler, *Kultur*, 399.

[68] E. Growald, 'Das Künstlerplakat seit 1896', *SR* 15 (Feb. 1931), 83.

[69] Reinhardt, *Reklame*, 83.

[70] See generally Schweinitz (ed.), *Prolog*, 6–7; Müller, *Frühe*, 200–9.

[71] H. Heller, *Literarische Intelligenz und Film* (Tübingen, 1985); H. Segeberg, 'Literarische Kinoästhetik', in Müller and Segeberg (eds.), *Modellierung*, 193–219.

of the moving picture made it an object of considerable fascination among a generation of intellectuals and artists steeped in Nietzschean ideas about the regenerative power of intense experience. The sheer 'visual pleasure' (*Schaulust*) of the cinema proved irresistible to many Expressionist rebels, exasperated as they were with staleness, elite isolation, and encrusted constraints of bourgeois formality. On a more practical level, film was also becoming big business before 1914, and began to engage recognized authors who were lured as much by the lucrative contracts as the artistic challenge.

The years 1913–14 are often viewed as a turning-point, for they not only saw the first serious investigations of an autonomous 'film aesthetic' (most notably Kurt Pinthus's *Kinobuch*), but also the first feature-length adaptations of famous writers.[72] These so-called *Autorenfilme* were deliberately conceived to cleanse the cinema of its plebeian odour and disarm its many educated critics. The first such film, Paul Lindau's *Der Andere*, featured the renowned actor Albert Bassermann as a Jekyll-and-Hyde lawyer by day and criminal by night—an ideal scenario for exploiting Bassermann's expressive versatility on film. Paul Wegener's *Der Student von Prag*, a classic Doppelgänger tale in which the student protagonist sells his reflection to the devil, presented cameraman Guido Seeber with an ideal opportunity to display his pioneering techniques of lighting and filming doubles. Over the following years a string of other Autorenfilme were produced, including Nobel-prize winner Gerhart Hauptmann's *Atlantis*, Hugo von Hofmannsthal's *Das fremde Mädchen*, and Arthur Schnitzler's *Liebelei*.[73]

For obvious reasons, these films occupy a prominent place in the annals of cinema history, representing a milestone in the recognition of cinematic art. At the time, however, they were not particularly successful either with the critics or at the box office. Such acknowledgement as they acquired was largely bought at the price of popular indifference—apart from a few exceptions such as *Der Andere* and *Atlantis*. While they may have helped mitigate elite scepticism, they also attracted withering criticism as a cynical and money-grabbing act of treason against genuine art. As the theatre critic Alfred Kerr mockingly wrote: 'Not just sorry minor scribblers! | Gerhart Hauptmann; Arthur Schnitzler, | All reluctance dissipated— | For they're well remunerated!'[74] In March 1912 the Association of Script Writers (Bühnenschriftstellerverband) resolved that members should lend no support of any kind to the film industry. By borrowing from highbrow literature and theatre, Autorenfilme directly challenged such quarantine efforts. Paradoxically, it was the very attempt to gain elite recognition that elicited such scorn. Traditionalists were understandably concerned about a cinematic

---

[72] K. Pinthus, *Das Kinobuch. Kinodramen* (Leipzig, 1914).

[73] On *Autorenfilme*, C. Müller, 'Das "andere" im Kino?', in Müller and Segeberg (eds.), *Modellierung*, 153–92.

[74] 'Nicht nur winzig schofle Kritzler! | Gerhart Hauptmann; Arthur Schnitzler, | Widerstreben eingestellt— | Denn die Sache trägt a Geld!': Alfred Kerr, 'Sieg des Lichtspiels': Bollenbeck, *Tradition*, 174, my translation.

trivialization of the classics. Unlike the 'cinema-Varieté', Autorenfilme were perceived as an act of trespass on to their home territory, a 'shameful debasement of dramatic art, a barbaric flirtation with mob instincts'.[75]

With the outbreak of the war, the frenetic debate about cinematic art—which had produced literally thousands of texts between 1911 and 1914—disappeared as quickly as it had emerged.[76] By the time these questions resurfaced in the post-war world, film had become a taken-for-granted feature of the cultural landscape. If anything, the shoe was now on the other foot, as film began to exert an unmistakeable influence on inter-war literature and theatre. As a result, filmmakers in the 1920s were no longer so interested in genuflection to traditional art forms, but instead sought to find cinematic forms that would make full use of its technological attributes. As the scriptwriter Carl Hauptmann summed it up in 1919, 'as a mere copy of the theatre, film is led into a cul-de-sac from the very outset, even if this is based on the most successful dramas'.[77]

The overall outcome of these endeavours was without doubt one of the most creative and innovative episodes in film history. 'Weimar cinema' rightly counts as an early high-point of motion-picture art, a springtime of new techniques, perspectives, and individual talents whose likeness has rarely been seen since. Of course, German cinema in the 1920s produced a great amount of dross as well, but this does not detract from the many remarkable films that were immediately recognized—and still are—as milestones of cinematic art. Whether in the gritty social criticism of G. W. Pabst's *Die freudlose Gasse*, Bruno Rahn's *Dirnentragödie*, or Piel Jutzi's *Mutter Krausens Fahrt ins Glück*; the eerie Expressionist worlds of Robert Wiene's *Das Kabinett des Dr Caligari* or F. W. Murnau's *Nosferatu*; the budget-exploding futuristic vision of Fritz Lang's *Metropolis*, the pioneering 'subjective' camerawork of Murnau's *Der letzte Mann*, or the intriguing documentary portrayal of everyday life in Walther Ruttmann's *Berlin—Sinfonie einer Grossstadt* and *Menschen am Sonntag*; Weimar cinema influenced a whole generation of filmmakers, including many in Hollywood, whose executives quickly recognized the challenge and eventually succeeded in poaching much of the best talent for themselves.

All due accolades aside, however, it is important for our purposes to recognize that most of what counts as 'classic' Weimar cinema was not all that appealing to mainstream audiences. It has certainly generated far more interest among film historians than it did among contemporary cinema-goers, few of whom would have seen these films unless, as Walter Laqueur has put it, 'they strayed by accident into a West End cinema of the few big cities'.[78] In many respects classic

[75] E. Oesterheld, 'Wie die deutschen Dramatiker Barbaren wurden', *Die Aktion* (26 Feb. 1913), 261–5, repr. in Schweinitz (ed.), *Prolog*, 263.

[76] Müller, 'Der frühe Film', 86.

[77] C. Hauptmann, 'Film und Theater', *Die neue Schaubühne* (June 1919), 165–72, repr. in Kaes (ed.), *Kino-Debatte*, 124–5.

[78] Laqueur, *Weimar*, 232–3.

Weimar film represented an attempt by the increasingly ambitious film industry to gain artistic recognition, tap well-heeled markets, and colonize new cultural space. As the left-wing art critic Adolf Behne noted, 'the fact that there is no shortage of tendencies to cultivate the "exclusive film" in Germany, in the land in which the book or the possession of the book is an attribute of belonging to a particular class, more or less goes without saying'.[79] Unsurprisingly, such aesthetic experimentation went down better among the cultural establishment than at the box office. As the cinema reformers in the Volks-Filmverband also discovered, the demand for such alternative fare was limited. Given the availability of hundreds of films per year, even the most avid fan could see only a fraction, and if given the choice between the skewed nightmare world of *Caligari* or a detective thriller starring the beloved Harry Piel, most people preferred the latter. It is telling that *Caligari* itself, universally regarded as an artistic highlight of 1920s film, ran in only 101 theatres in Germany. Similarly, Murnau's 1926 film adaptation of *Faust*, starring Emil Jannings, covered only 75 per cent of its production costs, with most of the revenue coming from abroad. An even bigger box-office flop was the 1926 production *Geheimnisse einer Seele*, an ambitious psychoanalytical film starring Werner Krauss, which recovered only 15 per cent of its production costs. All but one of the celebrated Erich Pommer productions of the 1920s had to make up for domestic losses with income on the world market, including all of Murnau's films (the sole exception was Ludwig Berger's 1925 *Walzertraum*).[80] By and large, films that scored highly at the box office and with intellectual critics remained rare in the 1920s: notable exceptions were *Walzertraum*, Lang's *Dr. Mabuse*, and E. A. Dupont's *Variété*.[81] In the eyes of cinema reformers, the key was to bridge this divide.

But how could one achieve the fusion of art and commercial success? This was the fundamental question facing German filmmakers in the 1920s. Of course, this issue was by no means unique to film, but it was in the cinema that it was most dramatically played out. The film press constantly criticized the dualistic thinking that pitted aesthetic quality firmly against profitability. As the director Richard Oswald pragmatically argued in 1922, a film was a success if people went to see it, regardless of what the critics might say. Artistic 'successes' could spell financial ruin, and attempts to uplift or even gauge public tastes were fraught with peril.[82] For Béla Balázs, too, the very essence of film lay in its ability to collapse the distance between producer and consumer: 'The perspective of film is the close-up view of the participant.'[83] Ferdinand Bausback, the general director of UFA in the mid-1920s, stated the issue thus: 'What the problem boils down to is taking the taste of the masses into account without slavishly following it, if

---

[79] A. Behne, 'Die Stellung des Publikums zur modernen deutschen Literatur', *Die Weltbühne*, 22 (1926), 774–7, repr. in Kaes (ed.), *Kino-Debatte*, 163.
[80] Figures from K. Klär, *Film zwischen Wunsch und Wirklichkeit* (Wiesbaden, 1957), 108.
[81] Ibid. 110.   [82] R. Oswald, 'Film-Erfolg und Film-Geschäft', *FK* (9 Dec. 1922), 1.
[83] B. Balázs, *Der Geist des Films* (Halle, 1930), 215, repr. in Kaes (ed.), *Kino-Debatte*, 34.

possible decontaminating it and raising it to a higher level. But latching on to popular tastes as they currently are remains under all circumstances an absolute necessity for the economically responsible film producer.'[84]

Not everyone who wanted to overcome the perceived bifurcation between art and popularity subscribed to this view. For critics on the far Left, the key to bridging the divide lay not in tinkering with audience tastes but rather abolishing capitalist production altogether. Communist Party doctrine held that the capitalist foundations of the film industry precluded any usefulness for the working class. Not only did the pressure to make a profit inevitably produce mounds of trash, but the films themselves were bound to reflect the conservative world-view of the people making them. Although many non-communist critics were also critical of the commercial nature of the film industry, such an uncompromising assessment was rare among the bulk of left-leaning artists and critical intellectuals, many of whom took an avid interest in the subversive and liberating potential of certain popular genres, especially slapstick.[85] Unlike the communists, most reformists thought that individual films should ultimately be judged on their aesthetic merits rather than their mode of production, and that the cinema could in principle serve the interests of the working masses. This split was mirrored in the contrasting views of left-wing intellectuals. Whereas Max Horkheimer and Theodor Adorno emphasized the industrial character of the cinema and thus gravitated towards the communist view, Bertolt Brecht and Walter Benjamin saw in the cinema an escape from the veneration of art and the socially exclusive cult of the classics. For the latter, the impact of film was not confined to the political messages it could convey, but lay predominantly in the collective nature of production and consumption which eroded the very foundations of the individualistic work of art and, along with it, the 'bourgeois' separation of art and life, beauty and utility. The utopian hope arising from this diagnosis was for a new mass culture based on the working class, a more democratic and truly enlightening means of collective communication.

Whether emanating from intellectual critics or filmmakers themselves, all of these views were—whether they acknowledged it or not—strongly influenced by the challenge posed by Hollywood.[86] After the currency stabilization in 1924 American films made rapid inroads now that the industry was no longer shielded from international competition by high inflation. This unleashed a frantic debate about a German 'film crisis' and the competitive strategies that should be adopted. By the middle of the 1920s Hollywood was viewed as the cutting edge of a much broader process of Americanization, a spearhead of cultural imperialism that had to be resisted in the interests of national cultural sovereignty. As the renowned

---

[84] 'Dr. Bausback über Filmproduktion', *FK* (6 May 1926), 1.
[85] T. Saunders, *Hollywood in Berlin* (Berkeley, 1994), 194.
[86] Generally, Saunders, *Hollywood*; also V. de Grazia, *Irresistible Empire* (Cambridge, Mass. 2005), 284–313; id., 'Mass Culture and Sovereignty', *JMH* 61 (1989), 53–87.

theatre critic Herbert Ihering put it, 'the number of people who watch films and do not read books runs into the millions. They are all becoming subjugated to American tastes, becoming uniformly standardized.'[87] How, German producers constantly complained, could they possibly compete with an industry that could amortize the costs of even the most lavishly made motion pictures on its well-to-do domestic market, thus allowing it to underbid any competitors abroad? The imposition of import quotas in early 1925 clearly reflected the sense of anxiety over the long-term survival of the German film industry (by the 1920s the largest in Europe) in the face of the Hollywood onslaught.

Yet this fear of American domination was also accompanied by an unmistakeable mixture of envy and admiration, not just for Hollywood's filmic techniques and prosperous home market, but also, more importantly, for the wider American cultural context in which artistic and commercial success were not viewed as mutually exclusive. For influential film critics such as Hans Pander, Roland Schacht, Kurt Pinthus, and Béla Balázs, none of whom advocated a Hollywood hegemony, the supposed malaise of German film resulted not merely from economic factors and legal constraints, and certainly not from a lack of talent, but rather from ingrained assumptions about the relationship between 'art' and 'popularity'.[88] As Schacht argued in 1926: 'The German who makes art is unconcerned about whether the company financing him is thereby economically ruined. The American says to himself: how can it be art and what use is it if no one wants it, if people don't even voluntarily want to lay out the price of admission to see it?'[89] Only by overcoming the distinction between 'art' and 'entertainment' would it be possible for German filmmakers to meet the challenge of Hollywood. Ultimately, this meant that the oft-cited dilemma between commercial and artistic success was a chimera. As the journal *Film-Kurier* put it: 'Whoever still draws a distinction between audience tastes and the higher advancement of film—nowadays, after he has seen Chaplin, Buster Keaton, Lilian Gish, Emil Jannings, Douglas Fairbanks—is quite simply committing a crime against film.'[90]

But as Schacht's comments clearly indicate, such a revolution in artistic sensibilities could hardly be brought about by filmmakers alone. Many critics regarded the 'glass wall' between artists and audience as a 'tragic fate of German culture'.[91] Unlike his German counterpart, the American director did not consciously aim at public tastes and thus feel pangs of conscience about betraying his own ideals, because he was supposedly rooted in popular tastes himself. To quote once again from Adolf Behne, 'the important thing is that, from its

[87] H. Ihering, 'UFA und Buster Keaton' (1926), repr. in Kaes (ed.), *Kino-Debatte*, 15.
[88] Saunders, *Hollywood*, 161–70.
[89] R. Schacht, 'Deutsche und amerikanische Filme', *Der Kunstwart*, 39 (1926), 267–9, quoted from Saunders, *Hollywood*, 163.
[90] 'Publikum und Kritik sind einig!', *FK* (9 June 1926), 1.
[91] H. Michaelis, 'Die gläserne Wand', *FK* (11 Mar. 1924), 1.

very inception, film is democratic. . . . Film began as art for the masses . . . and film production against the masses is always out of the question.'[92] Ironically, for many of these advocates of the 'film for all', what began as a means of resisting Hollywood domination in many ways implied an argument for cultural Americanization on a more general level. After all, apart from the rarely recommended Soviet example there were no other obvious models for 'democratizing' culture. Even more ironically, the seemingly progressive goal of forging a German 'national cinema' that would cater to popular tastes yet satisfy the cultural establishment became a cornerstone of National Socialist film policy after 1933 (to which we will return later). But in the meantime, it was increasingly clear that the so-called 'film crisis' of the 1920s, rooted in the perceived tension between art and popularity, was a reflection of deep-rooted orientations among Germany's cultural elites.

This was the very same reason why the medium of broadcasting, despite its non-commercial foundations, also exhibited symptoms of the wider aesthetic problem during the 1920s. By the middle of the decade the celebrated trend towards sober functionality had shifted the creative focus more and more towards the social and political environment, and farther than ever from the ideal of pure art. Whether in the form of the reportage novel or the tubular steel chair, a vast new swathe of cultural production was pointing the way towards a truly 'public' art. In many eyes the radio was ideally suited to this project. But German broadcasting companies were barely cottoning on to the trends. Quite the opposite: their obsession with gaining credibility among traditional cultural elites tended to stifle their interest in the development of new aesthetic forms. The overarching definition of radio as a medium of Bildung and Kultur prompted broadcasters to favour the classics and the didactic lecture in their programming schedules: 'performances that appeal to the intellect', as one commentator put it.[93]

It was by and large writers who pressed for a new radio style that would both promote the medium and satisfy a mass audience of listeners. With few exceptions—most notably Fritz Walther Bischoff[94]—broadcasters were hardly involved in this during the 1920s. 'Radio art is already emerging away from the radio!' remarked the writer Arno Schirokauer in 1929.[95] The problem was not that broadcasters shunned the literary elite. In their continual search for cultural acknowledgement they actually paid handsome sums to big names such as Alfred Kerr, Walter Mehring, Bernhard von Brentano, Thomas Mann, and Arnold

---

[92] A. Behne, 'Stellung', from Kaes (ed.), *Kino-Debatte*, 163.

[93] Graf v. Arco, 'Der deutsche Rundfunk', *RH* (20 Jan. 1925), 22–4.

[94] Bischoff was director of the Schlesische Funkstunde, whose pioneering 'Hörspielsymphonie', *Hallo! Hier Welle Erdball!*, was broadcast from Breslau in February 1928: partially repr. in I. Schneider (ed.), *Radio-Kultur in der Weimarer Republik* (Tübingen, 1984), 124.

[95] A. Schirokauer, 'Kunst-Politik im Rundfunk', *Die literarische Welt* (1929), quoted in Schneider (ed.), *Radio-Kultur*, 18.

Zweig to read from their works—though of course reading into a microphone hardly represented much of an artistic innovation. Nor did broadcasters avoid all literary experimentation. Over the course of the 1920s the so-called *Sendespiel*, a radio adaptation of existing theatrical and literary works, became an increasingly common feature on the regional programmes. The best of these, such as Arnold Bronner's 100-minute rendition of Schiller's *Wallenstein* trilogy or Bertolt Brecht's radio version of *Macbeth* (both broadcast by the Berliner Funkstunde in 1927) could even make a plausible claim to artistic novelty.[96] Both represented Herculean efforts of adaptation, and from here it was a relatively small step to the creation of works specially designed for broadcasting.

The earliest forays into such 'radio art' revolved around making listeners 'earwitnesses' of major events or experimenting with the idea of 'acoustic film'.[97] The most important new genre, however, was the radio drama or *Hörspiel*, regarded as the true 'radio form . . . the goal of the multifaceted artistic work in the studio'.[98] Radio dramas in fact found a small niche in programmes from early on, though far smaller than the volume of Hörspiel manuscripts submitted to the radio stations might have allowed. A competition organized by the RRG in 1927 resulted in nearly 1,200 submissions, though none were awarded any prizes due to the jury's inability to reach a verdict. As this lack of consensus suggests, part of the problem was disagreement over what 'radio art' should look (or rather sound) like, with opinions divided between an emphasis on acoustic phenomena and a preference for the spoken word. The quality of many Hörspiel submissions also left much to be desired; for every bright new experiment there were dozens of duds.[99] Yet the crux of the problem was financial: throughout the 1920s the legal ambiguity surrounding royalty fees was the chief hindrance to closer cooperation between writers and broadcasters.[100]

The search for solutions culminated in 1929 in a star-studded conference held in Kassel on the problem of 'literature and radio'.[101] Co-organized by the RRG and the Prussian Academy of Arts, it was effectively a meeting of Germany's cultural 'officialdom'. Featuring luminaries such as Arnold Zweig, Alfred Döblin, and Herbert Ihering, the conference covered everything from epics to dramas to lyric poetry. Whatever their various political leanings, all of the writers and executives at the convention shared a common desire to harness broadcasting as a means of disseminating art to a mass audience. Staid readings by authors and demanding Sendespiele were, though aesthetically admirable and perhaps

---

[96] See generally T. Wittenbrink, 'Rundfunk und literarische Tradition', in Leonhard (ed.), *Programmgeschichte*, 996–1097.

[97] Schneider (ed.), *Radio-Kultur*, 146–7.

[98] Quote from H. Bodenstedt, 'Spiel im Studio' (1929), repr. in Bredow (ed.), *Archiv*, 146.

[99] Generally, C. Hörburger, *Das Hörspiel der Weimarer Republik* (Stuttgart, 1975); on the RRG competition T. Wittenbrink, 'Zeitgenössische Schriftsteller im Rundfunk', in Leonhard (ed.), *Programmgeschichte*, 1163–7.

[100] Generally, Wittenbrink, 'Zeitgenössische', 1098–1195.

[101] See the reprinted convention contributions in Bredow (ed.), *Archiv*, 311–66.

enjoyed by a certain stratum of listeners, less than ideally suited to this end. As Döblin put it rather pointedly, 'there is a huge cleft between an unadulterated and already over-artistic literature and the great mass of the people. . . . Once again radio steps before us and challenges us to forsake printed type and to abandon our small cultivated clique.'[102]

Given the plethora of different interests and viewpoints, the Kassel conference could hardly yield a consensus on what shape 'radio art' should take. Nevertheless, it signalled a more intensive experimentation with new forms and helped clear a path for closer cooperation between writers and broadcasters. The years 1929–30 indeed marked something of a breakthrough for 'radio art' in general, and for the Hörspiel in particular. Works by Arno Schirokauer, Hermann Kasack, and Alfred Döblin, whose literary output owed so much to the forms of the new media, lent the Hörspiel a new air of prestige.[103] The format of the *bunter Abend*, or variety entertainment show, also began to crystallize around this time. Although even its proponents found little merit in such programmes to date, the variety show nonetheless promised to amalgamate the genuinely popular and the culturally uplifting. As Stuttgart's broadcasting director Alfred Bofinger put it: 'What is entertaining can self-evidently contain artistic qualities, just as what is artistic can include elements of entertainment.'[104] The new genre of radio reportage, directly borrowed from current literary trends, also came into its own around the end of the 1920s (though it never acquired the same prominence as in the print press). From its beginnings in the coverage of sport and other public events (for example, the Rhineland *Karneval*), by 1930 high-quality radio reportage—in which the representation itself became as important as the event being represented—had grown into something of an art form as well, 'contemporary theatre in the best sense of the word'.[105]

Crucially, the peculiar economic structure of German broadcasting meant that 'radio art' could develop at a safe distance from the pressures of the commercial market. Yet the underlying challenge was essentially the same as in the realms of film, advertising, and recording. Creating a genuinely 'universal art' between the poles of elitism and entertainment not only required new aesthetic forms. It also called for new standards of judgement and, more generally, a new structure of cultural sensibility, including among many of its own proponents.

This brief survey of efforts to create a 'valuable mass culture' has sought to convey a sense of the wide-ranging nature of cultural reform in early twentieth-century Germany. The goal of developing alternatives to commercial culture spanned the entire political spectrum, and the attempt to create a universal art was pursued

---

[102] A. Döblin, 'Literatur und Rundfunk', repr. in ibid. 314.

[103] Wittenbrink, 'Zeitgenössische', 1106–89; see also Jelavich, *Alexanderplatz*, 62–92.

[104] A. Bofinger, 'Bunte Abende' (1929), repr. in Bredow (ed.), *Archiv*, 310.

[105] H. Bodenstedt, 'Reportage' (1930), repr. in ibid. 164; see also F. W. Odendahl, 'Die ersten Schritte des Rundfunks als aktueller Berichterstatter' (1928), in ibid. 160–4.

in a variety of different ways within all artistic genres and communications media. In at least some cases it achieved impressive results. The creativity and innovation displayed by graphic artists, radio dramatists, and film directors gave a new, more vernacular dimension to the remarkable cultural fermentation among Germany's avant-garde. In the process, they undoubtedly brought new aesthetic perspectives and sensibilities to a far wider audience than the museum or theatre could ever reach. The determination shown by German politicians, union activists, intellectuals, and artists to transcend social barriers through cultural reform—and the novel artefacts that resulted from their labours—have decisively contributed to the posthumous fascination with 'Weimar Culture'.

Yet in spite of all this, it is difficult to escape the conclusion that such efforts ultimately failed to offer viable alternatives to commercial entertainments, let alone to sculpt a 'universal art' blending popular appeal and aesthetic merit. This is perhaps due in part to the utopian nature of the aims themselves. After all, avant-garde artists are not generally known for the practicality of their ideas, and the febrile intellectual atmosphere of the 1910s and 1920s hardly discouraged such fanciful thinking. Indeed, the notion that art and aesthetic experience could help (re)create a sense of spiritual and social wholeness for a nation racked by the strains of modernization was a mainstay of elite cultural discourse during this period. It was not just an article of faith for Wagnerian romantics like Hitler or for conservatives eager to shore up what remained of their cultural authority. As the *Film-Kurier* sarcastically suggested in 1922, reformers often seemed to inhabit a never-never land of unrealistic expectations:

Just think how the world would look if people in the cinema only wanted to *learn* something. If the average Herr Meyer suddenly decided to buy a lexicon of the same name. If the gentlemen in *Zum blauen Affen* [a successful 1921 collection of criminal stories by Walter Serner] politely exchanged business cards instead of stabbing one another. If a tram conductor happened upon the idea of politely offering an arm to an old lady or gentleman to help them in![106]

To some extent it was the very failure to transcend this mode of thinking, the failure to question their own faith in the edifying power of art and education, that hamstringed such efforts from the outset. But more importantly, most of the alternative products offered by reformers simply did not appeal to popular audiences. Many of the initiatives revolved as much around impressing educated critics as actually entertaining the masses. It is highly unlikely, for instance, that the makers of Expressionist films really expected their productions to be box-office hits, just as radio authors were surely aware that two-hour adaptations of classical theatre were not everyone's idea of amusement.

To be fair, these proponents of a 'middlebrow' culture were in many ways caught between two worlds. Seeking to impress a sceptical cultivated elite while

---

[106] 'Wer Augen hat, zu sehen,—der sieht doch nicht', *FK* (4 Apr. 1922), 2, emphasis in the original. W. Serner, *Zum blauen Affen* (Hanover, 1921).

catering to popular tastes meant that they were usually doomed to please neither in the end.[107] In the eyes of their more tradition-minded peers, the desire to appeal to the masses and the programme of 'democratizing' culture was at best naive, probably subversive, and at worst a blasphemy against all that was spiritually sacred. Meanwhile, for the bulk of manual labourers, secretaries, clerks, and housewives in search of entertainment, such fare was often too abstract, demanding, or simply boring to separate them from hard-earned cash. The social divides that reformers sought to bridge were, it seems, still too wide to be overcome during the 1910s and 1920s.

In practice, if not always in theory, most of these efforts to edify mass culture amounted to an embourgeoisement of popular tastes. The didactic and moralizing impulses that underpinned them were a central feature of cultural reform throughout the Wilhelmine and Weimar eras, stretching from a conservative defence against plebeian tastes to a progressive-socialist determination to bring the 'finer things' to subaltern social groups.[108] Against the background of ongoing censorship, and amidst the shrill pessimism emanating from some quarters, the attempt to engage positively with mass culture and elevate it from within was a relatively progressive alternative. Yet in essence these initiatives were still based on a fundamentally patriarchal and authoritarian view of the 'masses', whose tastes and expectations needed a close guiding hand.

What audiences actually wanted to see or hear was rarely asked by any of these reformers, regardless of their political inclination. The point was to give them what they needed, whether the stabilizing certainties of conventional morality, the intellectual cultivation of the individual, or the collective spirit of revolutionary fervour. The fact that even reformers adopted such a patriarchal posture demonstrates the profound inability of most German elites at the time to conceive of audiences in other than authoritarian terms. Even more importantly, it also reflects an almost universal perception of media consumers as fundamentally passive and undifferentiated. Throughout the 1910s and 1920s audiences were widely treated as a monolith, a faceless collective of undiscerning spectators defined by a desire for aesthetically mediocre entertainment—and all too frequently in a wilfully mythical incarnation as the 'Volk'. From this point of view, it is little surprise that reform efforts made such a meagre impact on mainstream commercial culture. For as we will see in the next section, had reformers ever bothered to enquire into mass cultural audiences and their wishes, they would have found much more variety, much less passivity, and infinitely more social complexity than the omnipresent cliché of the 'masses' allowed them to imagine.

---

[107] See also v. Saldern, 'Massenfreizeitkultur', 44; LeMahieu, *Culture*, 178.
[108] Generally, v. Saldern, 'Massenfreizeitkultur'.

PART III

MASS CULTURE, DIVIDED AUDIENCES: MEDIA, ENTERTAINMENT, AND SOCIAL CHANGE IN THE WEIMAR REPUBLIC

Introduction

That the cultural history of the Weimar Republic has been primarily associated with the avant-garde is easily understandable. Germany (and in particular Berlin) was a centre of cultural experimentation before 1933, a crucible of new ideas and movements. Though somewhat less illustrious, the expansion of the mass media and the continued growth of commercial amusements in the 1920s has also attracted attention as part of the overall contemporary debate about Germany's plunge into 'modernity'. As the previous two chapters have shown, the expansion of mass culture was an object of intense interest among contemporary critics and cultural commentators, whose insights, pontifications, and frequent diatribes offer a fascinating reflection of the seismic cultural shifts under way. Over the past two decades or so considerable effort has gone into refining our understanding of the discourse about mass culture and the positions adopted by participants in the contemporary debates on cultural issues. But most of this cultural-historical work has remained on the level of discourses about the new media and mass entertainments, without examining assumptions about their social impact, distribution, transmission, and reception. By approaching the expansion of the media solely or predominately from the perspective of elite discourse, one runs the risk of allowing the polarized contemporary debate to distort our perceptions of cultural life in the inter-war years.[1]

The remarkable vehemence of contemporary debates is perhaps the reason why social-historical approaches to the new media have been slow to develop. The fascination with the 'new' and the 'sensational' in inter-war discourse has strongly influenced cultural-historical research on the mass media and commercial entertainments, often to the detriment of the rather unsensational everyday uses of film, radio, and the popular press.[2] The social availability of the media and their influence on the life-styles and cultural horizons of the 'masses' they were

[1] A point emphasized by E. Harvey, 'Culture and Society in Weimar Germany', in M. Fulbrook (ed.), *Twentieth-Century Germany* (London, 2001), 58–76. Useful inroads into this vast literature: N. Krenzlin (ed.), *Zwischen Angstmetapher und Terminus* (Berlin, 1992); v. Saldern, 'Massen-freizeitkultur'; A. Kaes, M. Jay, and E. Dimendberg (eds.), *The Weimar Republic Sourcebook* (Berkeley, 1994); most recently G. Merlio and G. Raulet (eds.), *Linke und rechte Kulturkritik* (Frankfurt a. M., 2005).

[2] See Schildt, 'Jahrhundert', 196; also K. Maase, *Grenzenloses Vergnügen* (Franfurt a. M., 1997), 115–17.

intended to reach are barely, if ever, touched on in the standard cultural histories of the period. Insofar as the social impact of mass culture has featured at all in the historiography of the inter-war years, it has generally been regarded as a powerful modernizing force that eroded regional and class-based patterns of leisure and helped to establish a more international, 'class-transcendent', and 'socially standardizing' culture shared by all.[3]

Broadly speaking, the literature on mass culture in early twentieth-century Germany has tended to fall into two general categories. On the one hand, there are numerous studies tracing the 'artistic' or aesthetic development of the new media, especially film. On the other, there is a sizeable literature on the organizational history of the media, the changing technical and economic framework that shaped them, and the state policies that regulated their structure and content. But the audiences, the actual people seeing and listening, have by and large fallen between these two stools. For inter-war Germany, as elsewhere, audiences have largely remained 'the missing link, the forgotten element in cultural history'.[4]

The following three chapters attempt to shed some light on this missing link. Their focus is not the discourse surrounding the new media, but rather the patterns of media availability and uptake, their potential to exert any socially unifying effect, and the wider social and economic context in which they were embedded. Together, they demonstrate that audiences were certainly not the passive and amorphous entity many contemporary reformers had in mind when they devised their schemes to uplift popular tastes. They also show that the growth of commercial culture, despite its underlying democratic logic, was not the straightforward 'levelling' or 'homogenizing' force it is often taken to be. 'Mass culture' in the Weimar Republic was mediated through older social structures and cultural frameworks, and as a result was much more variegated and contingent than is often assumed. The rise of the mass media did not necessarily signal an inexorable trend towards a more universal mass culture that bulldozed class boundaries and flattened cultural distinctions in German society. Rather, these processes had a wide range of possible social implications, including the potential to unite or to divide audiences, to weaken or reproduce existing social distinctions, and, of course, to create new ones.

---

[3] Quotes from K. Wernecke, 'Kinobesuch als Freizeitvergnügen', *MkF* 15 (1992), 92–100; D. Peukert, 'Das Mädchen mit dem "wahrlich metaphysikfreien Bubikopf"', in P. Alter (ed.), *Im Banne der Metropolen* (Göttingen, 1993), 167.

[4] L. Levine, 'The Folklore of Industrial Society', *American Historical Review*, 97 (1992), 1379.

4

Technology and Purchasing Power: Media Availability and Audiences

One of the primary characteristics of the mass media is their expansionist character, their tendency to seek out new groups of spectators, readers, or listeners. Although this is partially a function of straightforward profit-seeking, it is also due to the fact that mechanical art, whether commercial or otherwise, is inherently extensive rather than intensive. Lacking the specific aura of the 'real thing'—the sense of exclusivity and originality surrounding the museum piece or live performance—it compensates for this limitation by reaching so many people. Although this might on the one hand be regarded as a loss of artistic authenticity at the level of the individual user, who has to satisfy him- or herself with a mechanically rendered reproduction, on the other hand it represents a huge gain at the collective level in terms of the sheer availability of cultural artefacts.

Without exception, the primary application of the new communication technologies of the early twentieth century was to bring art and entertainment to consumers, to make events and occurrences that were previously fixed in a particular time and place available to geographically and temporally dispersed audiences. While the radio brought the wider world into one's home, the cinema literally set out in search of its audiences by setting up in residential neighbourhoods and city centres. The new media were, especially in highly competitive sectors such as film, strongly sales oriented. Whatever affinities they had or sought to cultivate with traditional art forms were always bound to remain superficial because their success rested on precisely what distinguished them from the representative functions and social conventions of the traditional cultural event. The key to growth was a decidedly 'modern' emphasis on user-friendliness and accessibility, which in practice meant designing entertainment for people whose everyday schedules were structured by the discipline of the industrial workday and its division between labour and leisure time.

For all their expansionist tendencies, however, the actual ability of the media to tap new social constituencies and colonize new cultural space was constrained by a range of factors. Over the first part of the twentieth century the print press was the only form of communication that managed to achieve anything close to a universal reach or market saturation in Germany, with overall circulation roughly corresponding to one newspaper per household.[1] By contrast, the availability of all the other media was powerfully moulded by technological limitations, commercial considerations, ingrained cultural attitudes, and household leisure budgets.

CINEMA DISTRIBUTION AND HOUSEHOLD BUDGETS

Until recently these constraints have rarely attracted the attention they deserve, not even in the case of film, the flagship mass medium of the period.[2] For many years accounts of film simply cited the ever-rising numbers of cinemas and admissions as proof of the rapid growth of film in the early twentieth century. Without a doubt, the figures are impressive. In 1910, around five years after the first permanent cinemas were established, there were already 1,000 cinemas in Germany, with a total of 200,000 seats; by 1919 capacity had multiplied to 2,836 cinemas with 980,000 seats. Much of the growth came during the austerity of the war years, first because film offered some distraction from the worries and increasingly bleak conditions on the home front, and secondly because the shortages of consumer goods encouraged spending on entertainment. During the 1920s the cinema continued to grow by leaps and bounds: by 1928 the number of movie theatres had jumped to 5,267, with a total of 1,876,600 seats, or about thirty seats per thousand inhabitants. By the end of the 1920s it was estimated that Germans went to the cinema around 6 million times per week and 320 million times per year, which corresponded to seven admissions per adult.[3] In the meantime, a wave of newer, larger, and more lavish 'film palaces' were built, many with seating capacities of over 1,000 and all boasting grandiose architecture to match any theatre.[4] The first large cinema chains also emerged at this time, most notably UFA (the largest chain in Europe) and Emelka.[5] Little wonder that film is perceived as the quintessential 'mass' medium of the 1920s.

As impressive as such statistics are, however, film was by no means a universal phenomenon in this period. At the most basic level, the highly uneven regional distribution of cinema capacity meant that audiences did not represent a cross-section of society. Obvious though it seems, it is worth emphasizing that film was an overwhelmingly urban phenomenon. Whereas most municipalities over

[1] See K. C. Führer, 'Die Tageszeitung als wichtigstes Massenmedium der nationalsozialistischen Gesellschaft', *ZfG* 55 (2007), 411–34; Stöber, *Pressegeschichte*, 161.
[2] The following section is drawn in large part from C. Ross, 'Mass Culture and Divided Audiences', *Past & Present*, 193 (Nov. 2006), 157–95.
[3] A. Jason, *Handbuch der Filmwirtschaft, Jahrgang 1930* (Berlin, 1930), 61, 69; Warstat, *Frühes Kino*, 71–2.
[4] See S. Hänsel, *Kinoarchitektur in Berlin 1895–1995* (Berlin, 1995); P. Boeger, *Architektur der Lichtspieltheater in Berlin* (Berlin, 1993); B. Schneider, *100 Jahre Koblenzer Filmtheater* (Koblenz, 1995).
[5] Monaco, *Cinema*, 30. By the end of the 1920s UFA ran seventy-four cinemas and Emelka fifty.

TABLE 3. *Cinema availability in Germany, 1910–1935*

Year	Number of cinemas	Number of seats × 1,000	Average capacity	Seats per 1,000 inhabitants
1910	*c*.1,000	200	200	4
1913	2,371			
1914	2,446			
1917	3,130			
1918	2,491			
1919	2,836	980	345	17
1920	3,422			
1921	3,792			
1922	3,647			
1923	4,017			
1925	3,734	1,319	352	21
1928	5,267	1,877	356	30
1931	5,071	1,899	373	35
1935	4,782	1,808	378	37

Source: Jason (ed.), *Handbuch 1935/36*, 134, 136.

10,000 inhabitants had at least one cinema in 1925, only 1,462 of the 63,057 towns with populations under 10,000 (in which over half of all Germans lived) had any cinema at all. Some rural areas, especially in eastern Germany, were still regarded as 'cinema deserts' (*Kinowüste*) in the mid-1920s (under one cinema per 1,000 square kilometres).[6] Though it is impossible to know how many rural residents travelled to the nearest town to go to the movies, contemporary efforts by rural welfare associations to bring 'the cinema to every village' suggest that this was rare. The widespread cash poverty in the countryside, the inconvenience of travel, and the long working hours meant that film played very little role in everyday rural leisure activities.[7]

The situation was, of course, dramatically different in the larger cities, especially Berlin. In the mid-1920s the capital was home to roughly 10 per cent of all cinemas in Germany (396 cinemas, with a total of 189,692 seats in 1929), and boasted approximately eighteen annual admissions per capita.[8] On the most basic level of seating capacity the accessibility of cinema in the cities was utterly incomparable to that in the provinces. Moreover, this huge difference was further accentuated by the fact that most cinemas in smaller towns (and over half of cinemas altogether) were not open every day, but rather played only on certain nights of the week, usually Friday to Sunday. And even when they were open, these 'non-daily' cinemas generally offered only one or perhaps two showings

[6] Jason, *Der Film*, 25–56, 74.
[7] F. Lembke, *Jedem Dorf sein Kino!* (Berlin, 1930); see also Münkel, 'Der Rundfunk', 179–80.
[8] Jason, *Der Film*, 65, 36; *Statistisches Jahrbuch der Stadt Berlin 1932* (Berlin, 1932), 156.

per evening. This stood in stark contrast to the numerous showings in the larger urban cinemas, which as a rule operated at least six days a week, many opening in the early afternoon and running until around 11 p.m.[9] Although there are no solid figures on itinerant cinemas or occasional film events organized in village pubs during the 1920s, it seems clear that such shows did not significantly diminish the immense disparity between urban and provincial Germany. Despite early hopes that film would help bridge the gap between city and countryside, it rather appears that the overwhelming concentration of cinemas in the larger towns actually *widened* this cultural cleft during the 1920s.[10]

This does not mean, however, that Germany's cities presented a uniform cinema landscape. Quite the contrary: in a number of ways they showed some rather puzzling differences. The density of available seats varied greatly even among cities with over 100,000 inhabitants, whereby the industrial centres of the Ruhr and Rhineland fared particularly poorly. Whereas Leipzig and Hanover topped the list in 1925 with one seat for every thirty-one inhabitants, the ratio in Barmen was 1:92, in Gelsenkirchen only 1:116, and in Mönchen-Gladbach only 1:152. Though it is tempting to attribute this 'cinema poverty' to the predominately industrial or working-class character of these cities, this explanation seems doubtful given the very different picture in other Ruhr industrial centres with a roughly average seat-per-inhabitant ratio. Urban cinema landscapes differed significantly in other ways as well. Whereas some were dominated by a small number of mid-sized and large venues, others were characterized by a plethora of small neighbourhood establishments. For example, while Königsberg, Breslau, and Lübeck had no cinema over 1,000 seats in the mid-1920s, Münster already boasted two such 'cinema palaces'. And whereas Altona and Braunschweig had none with fewer than 300 seats, over three-quarters of all cinemas in Munich still fell under this category.[11] There were also marked differences in the number of cinema visits per capita, which corresponded only loosely, if at all, with the density of seats. Statistics from the early 1930s showed the most film-friendly cities to be Berlin, Düsseldorf, and Hamburg, with between 12.4 and 10.4 annual visits per capita. At the other end of the scale, annual cinema attendance in Stuttgart, Bochum, Nürnberg, and Würzburg averaged only 6.1 to 6.5.[12] There are no obvious explanations for these differences, which do not neatly correspond to social, economic, or confessional patterns.

Within individual cities too, cinema attendance was influenced by a range of social, economic, and cultural factors that completely escape the aggregate statistics. The problem is that contemporary source material is far too thin to allow a detailed reconstruction of cinema audiences. This dearth of contemporary

---

[9] A. Jason (ed.), *Handbuch des Films 1935/36* (Berlin, 1935), 141.
[10] On the town—countryside cleft generally, see Maase, *Grenzenloses*, 16–17.
[11] Figures from Jason, *Der Film*, 61, 65.   [12] Jason (ed.), *Handbuch 1935/36*, 158.

sources was not due to a lack of interest: as we have seen, bourgeois reform groups were acutely concerned about the popular effects of film. Journalists and cultural critics also occasionally discussed the film-viewing public, most notably Siegfried Kracauer, whose penetrating and oft-cited descriptions of the 'cult of distraction' and the 'little shop girls going to the cinema' have profoundly shaped our views of Weimar cinema.[13] Yet such observations about the social structure of cinema audiences are not only exceedingly rare, but also highly impressionistic, at times transparently prejudiced, and often contradictory. Apart from occasional discussions in the film press, on which the following discussion will draw heavily, there is little evidence against which to test them. Outside the United States there was limited empirical research on free-time activities in the inter-war period, and certainly nothing like the market-analyses conducted after 1945.

The closest thing to a sociological survey of film audiences is the classic study by Emilie Altenloh carried out in 1912 in the city of Mannheim. Based on over 2,000 questionnaires answered mainly by 14–18-year-olds in elementary (Volksschule) or vocational school, it could hardly claim to be demographically representative. The study also visibly suffers from the common educated-middle-class prejudice against film as a working-class amusement.[14] But for what it is worth, the picture painted by this study is of a predominately young, male, and working-class audience. Among working-class youths, 32 per cent went to the cinema every week and 29 per cent at least once a month, with the unskilled going most often. There was also a gender divide, with girls going less than boys, in spite of similar levels of interest: whereas only 21 per cent of boys questioned had never been to the cinema, this was still the case among 67 per cent of girls, no doubt because of the higher degree of parental supervision to which they were subjected. Among older age groups (which showed less interest in film on the whole), women seemed to be more fascinated by the cinema than men despite the fact that audiences were predominately male.[15] This was arguably due to both the stigma attached to unaccompanied women in public as well as the fact that women had fewer leisure opportunities than men. Yet apparently 'women of the higher strata' went to the pictures frequently, not least in order to keep up with the latest fashions. The educated middle classes were also clearly represented in cinema audiences, though Altenloh suggests that this was often accompanied by 'a feeling of shame and embarrassment with oneself'.[16] Few people went because of the quality of the films on offer: boredom, courtship, relaxation, and having nothing better to do seemed the predominant motivations. Recent research on film in Imperial Germany has both reinforced and significantly enhanced this picture by showing that audiences were less proletarian and more bourgeois than

[13] S. Kracauer, 'Kult der Zerstreuung' (orig. 1926); 'Die kleinen Ladenmädchen gehen ins Kino' (orig. 1927), in *Das Ornament der Masse* (Frankfurt a. M., 1977), 279–94, 311–17.
[14] See the surgical critique by Müller, *Frühe*, 748–9.
[15] Altenloh, *Soziologie*, 59, 64, 79.   [16] Ibid. 91–6.

previously thought.[17] Overall, there can be little doubt that cinema's frequent association with the lower orders was more a reflection of bourgeois fears and snobbery than of real consumption patterns.

But even so, elite aversion towards film was particularly strong among the Bildungsbürgertum. 'Most people declare film to be the antithesis of art (*Unkunst*),' remarked the renowned linguist Victor Klemperer, 'and when they find that they do like it, they dare not admit it.'[18] As the journal *Film-Kurier* cheekily put it, 'the film aversion among educated and respectable circles is based on the indigenous dogma that tedium (*Langeweile*) is a necessary attribute of art . . . Because film strives above all for entertainment (*Kurzweiligkeit*), the German Bildungsbürger does not include it among artistic matters.'[19] Despite such cultural barriers, the inroads into the bourgeoisie over the 1910s and 1920s were readily apparent in the construction of plush new film venues, the artistic experimentation of 'classic' Weimar cinema, and above all the wide range of ticket prices. A visit to the palatial city-centre venues cost up to ten times more than going to the neighbourhood cinema. After currency stabilization in the mid-1920s, tickets in Berlin cost anywhere from RM 0.50 in the local fleapit to RM 6 for a box seat in the West End.[20] Though the price-span was not so wide in all cities, there was a significant range everywhere. Most tickets cost between around RM 0.60 and RM 1.50, which made the cinema considerably cheaper than a visit to the theatre or opera, especially once cloakroom and travel costs were factored in.[21] In principle, then, the cinema was affordable for all social groups, especially during the early 1920s when owners were slow to raise their prices in line with inflation for fear of scaring off customers.[22]

How often one could afford the cinema, and whether one had the time and inclination to do so in the first place, were other matters entirely. Although there is little statistical data on which to rely, a detailed survey of household budgets from the latter 1920s leaves little doubt that any 'cinema mania' (*Kinowut*) as was perceived by contemporary critics disproportionately infected those with higher disposable incomes. Monthly entertainment budgets for low-income households were on average only around 1 mark for the entire family. Among middle-earning working-class households this sum increased to only around RM 2.50, though high-earning workers' households might have as much as RM 6 per month to spend on amusements. On average, white-collar households spent around 50 per cent more on the cinema than working-class households; civil servants, despite their higher average income, spent only marginally more, generally preferring the

[17] See esp. Müller, *Frühe*, 194–201; also id., 'Der frühe Film'; Peter Jelavich, '"Darf ich"'; K. Maase, 'Massenkunst'; H. Schlüpmann, *Unheimlichkeit*.

[18] V. Klemperer, *Leben sammeln, nicht fragen wozu und warum* (Berlin, 1996), 767.

[19] F. Schulz, 'Definitionen zum Film: Das Publikum', *FK* (27 Apr. 1923), 2.

[20] Jason, *Der Film*, 79.   [21] G. Paschke, *Der deutsche Tonfilmmarkt* (Berlin, 1935), 145.

[22] 'Erhöhung der Kinoeintrittspreisen', *FK* (23 Aug. 1922), 1; also *FK* (9 Dec. 1922), 1.

theatre to the cinema.[23] In the countryside entertainment budgets were lower still, and among rural labouring households they were all but non-existent.[24] Time was also a crucial constraint. Among female textile workers, for example, over 80 per cent of those who spent money on commercial amusements were under 26 and a further 15 per cent under 31; most of those over 30 were too busy with work and household duties to go to such amusements even if they had the money for them.[25] Not that young, single women could afford to go often: a study on female white-collar workers in the latter 1920s found that roughly half could not go to the theatre or cinema at all, and most others only infrequently.[26] Although invitations from young men presumably compensated for this (how much is impossible to know), the average RM 2.69 per month left over for entertainment among male white-collar workers kept any cinema attendance within 'extremely modest limits'.[27] Against this background, contemporary reports in the film press that the 'regular crowd' (*Stammpublikum*) at many cinemas was composed 'mostly of older people who go to the pictures once or twice a week'[28] make sense: not only did disposable income tend to increase with age, but the time-constraints of parenting also diminished with older children. Indeed, despite the lamentations of social workers, teachers, and churchmen about a supposed 'cinema addiction' (*Kinosucht*) among young people, a survey from the early 1930s still found that only 16.6 per cent of young people in Berlin went regularly to the cinema (weekly), 48.9 per cent occasionally (monthly), and 34.5 per cent not at all.[29]

Going to the cinema could not, therefore, be such a proletarian or youthful phenomenon. Older people, skilled workers, and the middle classes were well represented.[30] Yet, as in most areas of social life, the inflation of the early 1920s appears to have reshuffled the hierarchies of cinema audiences, at least during the hyperinflation of 1922–3. As the traditional theatre became increasingly unaffordable for those segments of the middle class worst affected, it seems that the cinema siphoned off at least some of this audience, albeit far less than most theatre advocates feared at the time.[31] For the self-confessed film addict

---

[23] Statistisches Reichsamt, *Die Lebenshaltung von 2000 Arbeiter-, Angestellten- und Beamtenhaushaltungen* (Berlin, 1932), 57. This survey is problematic insofar as it included households with a below-average interest in amusements. For a more detailed discussion, see Führer, 'Auf dem Weg', 751–2.

[24] M. Hofer (ed.), *Die Lebenshaltung des Landarbeiters* (Berlin, 1930), 91.

[25] L. Lueb, *Die Freizeit der Textilarbeiterinnen*, Diss., Münster (1929), 36.

[26] S. Suhr, *Die weiblichen Angestellten* (Berlin, 1930), 45.

[27] O. Suhr, *Die Lebenshaltung der Angestellten* (Berlin, 1928), 22–3.

[28] 'Wenn man vor dem Kino steht', *FK* (10 Feb. 1926), 1.

[29] A. Funk, *Film und Jugend* (Munich, 1934), 48.

[30] See L. Eger, *Kinoreform und Gemeinden* (Dresden, 1920), 9; also K. Dussel and M. Frese, *Freizeit in Weinheim* (Weinheim, 1989), 147.

[31] See K. C. Führer, 'German Cultural Life and the Crisis of National Identity During the Depression, 1929–1933', *German Studies Review*, 24 (Oct. 2001), 461–86; J. Blochert, 'Gibt es einen internationalen Durchschnittsgeschmack?', *FK* (25 Apr. 1922), 3.

Victor Klemperer, cinema represented in 1922 'both diversion and stimulation, it is a substitute for theatre, opera, concert, and travel'.[32] Moreover, the 'great disorder'[33] of 1922–3 was manifested inside the cinemas in a kind of world upside-down. One article from 1923 playfully recounts how a middle-class woman spotted her cleaning lady occupying one of the expensive box seats that usually stayed empty at the time: 'I've never had a central box seat before. But now I only take third class—the better sort seem to sit there.'[34] Many financially strapped cinema-goers resorted to the controversial and rather unappealing practice of eating sandwiches during the show, an obvious indignity for middle-class patrons but one that was defended as a necessary evil.[35] In view of such sentiments, it is hardly surprising that filmmakers tended to avoid the topic of middle-class proletarization over the following years.[36]

The fact that social factors such as class, age, and income so strongly shaped attendance patterns casts considerable doubt on the notion that the cinema, the primary manifestation of 'mass culture' at the time, functioned as a homogenizing force in the Weimar Republic. Although the cinema audience drew on all social strata, patterns of uptake and availability varied greatly between different groups and arguably reproduced social and regional differences as much as undermined them. True, the cinema was frequented by a wider range of social groups than the traditional theatre, opera, or *Tingel-Tangel*, with their more strictly class-bound clienteles. Yet the complex constraints of time, money, and availability still visibly shaped the social outlines of the cinema audience. For this reason alone—though not only for this reason—film could hardly function as the universally 'democratizing' or 'massifying' force so frequently conjured by contemporary enthusiasts and opponents alike.

NEW TECHNOLOGIES AND NEW LISTENERS: GRAMOPHONE AND RADIO AUDIENCES

The various obstacles posed by cost and availability were even more pronounced in the realm of sound. At the end of the 1920s neither the gramophone nor the radio could truly be regarded as taken-for-granted features of everyday life. Although recorded sound, by far the older of the two technologies, was already beginning to alter patterns of leisure before the First World War, for the most part its pre-war expansion remained confined to the well-off. Even in the 1920s the gramophone was still far from being a common household appliance.

---

[32] Klemperer, *Leben*, 626–7, diary entry 22 Oct. 1922.
[33] G. Feldman, *The Great Disorder* (Oxford, 1993).
[34] C. Seibert, 'Mittel-Loge', *FK* (7 Feb. 1923), 3.
[35] 'Die Theaterstulle', *FK* (15 Dec. 1922), 2.
[36] W. Lyon, 'Mittelstandsnot und Spielfilm', *RFB* (13 Nov. 1926), 35.

In its early years gramophone use was in fact not centred on the household at all. Initially it was popularized as a fairground attraction, and found many of its first buyers among the army of publicans and innkeepers keen to entertain their clientele. By 1910 it was already reported that 'one can hardly find an inn without a talking machine or some other mechanical music contraption for entertaining the guests'.[37] Energetic salesmen were busily bringing them 'into the smallest and most far-flung villages'.[38] Yet the key to long-term growth was undoubtedly the expansion of home use. Not only did private owners constitute a far larger market than publicans, but the very nature of the technology lent itself most readily to a private mode of reception. Before the advent of electrical amplification in the latter 1920s, low volume capabilities made recorded music less suitable for noisy entertainment venues than for quiet sitting-rooms. Moreover, unlike books or newspapers, which could be taken nearly anywhere, gramophones were cumbersome objects before the introduction of easily portable models in the 1920s. Although this 'home-centredness' placed certain constraints on the growth of the recording industry, in some ways it also helped generate sympathy among Germany's cultural and political elite. Morality and temperance groups enthusiastically welcomed the gramophone—as they subsequently would the introduction of the radio—as a wholesome alternative to the pub or fairground: 'It is capable of generating great enjoyment, and indeed in the place where it is least likely to exert any damaging side effects: namely, in one's own home.'[39]

Throughout the early twentieth century the expansion of gramophone use faced two main hurdles, cost and quality. Advertised prices for home-use sets in 1900 ranged from around RM 15 to 50 (during the following years prices ranged from around RM 12 to 125), with cylinders and discs costing anywhere from RM 0.75 to over RM 3. For the average industrial worker earning just under RM 25 per week (the vast bulk of which was spent on vital necessities) this was hardly a trifling outlay.[40] Although gramophones became less expensive in real terms in the 1920s, they still represented a major leisure investment for most households. In 1929 the simplest tabletop model still cost at least RM 50, and a reasonably sturdy model considerably more. Meanwhile, fancier cabinet models might cost anywhere up to RM 500, while the new combination radio-record apparatuses went for RM 800 or more.[41]

Nor were the records themselves inexpensive, though prices varied depending on one's tastes and expectations. During the latter 1920s high-quality recordings of popular tunes and dance music cost around RM 3.50 for 25 cm discs, and RM 5

---

[37] 'Die drohende Lustbarkeitssteuer in Berlin', *PZ* 11 (29 Sept. 1910), 885; 'Der Sprechautomat', *PZ* 11 (20 Oct. 1910), 937.

[38] 'Der Sprechautomat', *PZ* 11 (20 Oct. 1910), 937.

[39] 'Ein Phonograph in jedem Haus', *PZ* 2 (22 May 1901), 124.

[40] Prices from *PZ* 1 (19 Dec. 1900), 78; *PZ* 2 (14 Aug. 1901), 210. Wage figure from Bry, *Wages*, 58, 71.

[41] *PZ* 31 (1. Jan. 1930), 40, 42; *Die Stimme* 13 (Dec. 1928), 244–5.

for 30 cm. Recordings involving large orchestras cost slightly more, and some classical symphony recordings could cost as much as RM 7.50. Admittedly, the early 1930s saw a marked decrease in prices as orchestral records went for as little as RM 2.80 and simple dance tunes for RM 1.50.[42] But despite the depression-era drop, records still represented a significant expense for most Germans. As we have already seen, monthly entertainment budgets for working-class households in the latter 1920s rarely exceeded RM 2.50.[43] How much was spent specifically on records and gramophones cannot be accurately reconstructed, but subtracting the amounts spent on cinema and radio from the overall leisure budget left little if anything over. This remained the case well into the latter 1930s. Among 350 working-class households surveyed in 1937, only eleven (3 per cent) spent anything at all on records or musical instruments of any kind.[44] If one compares record and gramophone prices with that of the average cinema ticket—around RM 0.75—it is easy to understand why.[45]

Even more problematic than affordability were the shortcomings of fidelity. In the early years sound quality was so poor as to make recordings suitable for little more than showman attractions or small pubs, where, as one observer put it, 'more often than not the "concert" was such that musical people quickly decided to vacate the locale'.[46] Over the years engineers experimented with a variety of solutions, including heavier pick-ups, higher rotation speeds, and needles made from different materials. But before the advent of electrical recording the advantages of such innovations were almost invariably cancelled out by their disadvantages. Heavier pick-ups achieved higher volumes but caused greater wear to records and needles. Faster rotation speeds increased sound fidelity, but at the cost of a corresponding decrease in playing time. As a result, many would-be owners continued to view the gramophone as both inconvenient and unsatisfying: inconvenient in that it was necessary to change records and needles frequently, and unsatisfying in that sound fidelity was greatly diminished by the stubborn problem of surface noise.

To the discerning ears of the concert hall *Abonnent*, the gramophone therefore remained little more than a contemptible *Krächzapparat* ('croaking machine'). Despite the fact that classical music dominated early recording repertoires (in 1907 63 per cent were of opera, chamber music, and symphonies),[47] this was insufficient to redeem the gramophone's image as a folly for the tasteless. A single experience of a 'cheap pub-machine with a miserable pick-up and worn-out

---

[42] Prices from advertisements in *Die Stimme*, 13 (1928), *passim*; 17 (Jan. 1932), 1–4, 105–8; 18 (Nov. 1933), 145.

[43] Statistisches Reichsamt, *Lebenshaltung*, 57.

[44] Arbeitswissenschaftliches Institut der Deutschen Arbeitsfront, 'Erhebung von Wirtschaftsrechnungen für das Jahr 1937', in id., *Jahrbuch 1938*, vol. 2, (Berlin, 1938), repr. by M. Hepp and K. H. Roth (eds.), *Sozialstrategien der Deutschen Arbeitsfront*, vol. 3.2 (Munich, 1986), 347.

[45] Jason (ed.), *Handbuch 1935/36*, 146.

[46] M. Randewig, 'Radio, Wirt und Gäste', *Deutsche Hotel-Nachrichten*, 33 (Sept. 1929), unpag.

[47] Wicke, *Mozart*, 98.

records' could make an enemy for life. Many of the pre-war culture journals seemed to regard the gramophone 'as the most diabolical torture instrument of the twentieth century'.[48] Such elite derision was reinforced by the fact that classical music was particularly ill-suited to early recording technology, whose narrow band-width drastically flattened the range of tone that characterizes symphony performance. Even more importantly, the short playing time (around three-and-a-half to four minutes per side) of the standard 78 r.p.m. discs was equally unsuitable for classical works. The fact that even single symphonic movements had to be accommodated on several discs not only made them expensive, but also marred their presentation by constant interruptions. The launch of the long-play record (14 minutes per side) in 1931 did little to solve this problem in the medium term, as the players for such records remained unaffordable to all but the wealthy.[49]

By contrast, the bulk of popular entertainment music was ideally suited to early recording technologies. Not only were most popular tunes short, they were also dominated by vocals or forms of instrumentation that were well suited to early recording technology. In comparison to a classical symphony recording, songs drawn from the variety theatre or operetta sounded much closer to the original, and generally had less subtlety and complexity to lose in the first place. Dance music also lent itself particularly well to recording: 'the modern dance rhythms—with their tonally bizarre instrumentation, the texture of the saxophone, and the recitative of the refrain—resound from the trumpet without distortion or adulteration.'[50] Recording firms were quick to capitalize on the swelling demand for new dance tunes after the turn of the century. During the 1900s African-American music (especially cakewalk and ragtime) and popular tunes from the English music hall became a standard component of music publishers' repertoires. The Deutsche Grammophon company already devoted an entire category to the cakewalk in its 1905 catalogue, and by 1910 the tango was also making the rounds. But before becoming a 'mass' phenomenon in the 1920s, pre-war interest in foreign dance tunes was largely confined to the 'smart set', the up-market vaudeville crowd that could afford a gramophone in the first place.[51]

The fact that most gramophone owners belonged to the middle classes did little to alter their plebeian associations among the Bildungsbürgertum, where 'the talking machine was downright scorned as "tenement music" (*Hinterhaus-Musik*)'.[52] If anything, its growing popularity among the middle and upper

---

[48] Quotes from M. Chop, 'Das Grosse im Lichte zeitgenössischer Kritik', *PZ* 11 (22 Sept. 1910), 867–70.

[49] C. Riess, *Knaurs Weltgeschichte der Schallplatte* (Zurich, 1966), 243.

[50] Jolowicz, *Rundfunk*, 14.

[51] See F. Ritzel, 'Synkopen-Tänze', in Kaschuba and Maase (eds.), *Schund*, 164–7, 172–3; Ritzel, 'Hätte', 268–9.

[52] Wünsch, 'Die Lage', 11.

classes probably heightened the sense of alarm among traditionalists, who feared that it might serve to hollow out German musical culture from its very social core. As the music critic Karl Storck bitterly complained in 1911, it was not the uncultivated labouring 'masses' who were primarily responsible for this decline of standards, but rather the well-off leisure classes who should have known better: 'Listen sometime to the music that is played evening after evening in the "better" restaurants. Consider the stock of gramophone records in the bourgeois pubs that lures the money from the pockets of those philistines who are otherwise so unapproachable for art donations. Or do you think it is "workers" who make the hundred thousand copies of the "hit of the season" possible?'[53] As Storck's tirade suggests, the gramophone was, despite its fairground associations, almost exclusively a bourgeois luxury before the war. Even in the 1920s, the sheer costs meant that the middle classes still accounted for most of the market.

In terms of its availability and social distribution, recorded music was therefore not the 'mass medium' that contemporary enthusiasts and historical accounts have sometimes taken it to be. The desire of left-wing intellectuals to 'democratize' music and make it accessible to the Volk led many to an over-optimistic view of the medium as classless and egalitarian, enabling all to participate. But as Jost Hermand and Frank Trommler remarked long ago: 'The fact that this "Volk" possessed neither the same education nor the same financial basis as the bourgeoisie was usually overlooked.'[54]

If these issues were generally overlooked by intellectuals, they were very much on the minds of gramophone and recording companies keen to open up new markets. These companies in fact helped to pioneer a number of new turn-of-the-century marketing techniques such as the introductory model and payment by instalment. As early as 1900 many were deliberately selling cheap models near cost in order to hook consumers and hopefully sell them a more expensive model later on. As the *Phonographische Zeitschrift* remarked, the best way to expand the market was to sell inexpensive models, 'even if they are primitive and do not remain flawless for long. After the initial cheap model there usually follows a second more expensive one, which never would have been purchased without having had the first one.'[55] Manufacturers estimated that a mere 20 per-cent decrease in the price of equipment would lead to a 200 per-cent increase in sales.[56] Since price sensitivity was the main problem, the perceived solution lay in a mixture of special offers and repayment schemes. By the 1920s these new marketing techniques had become too much of a good thing, causing serious cash-flow problems for manufacturers and retailers.[57] It was partly thanks to

---

[53] K. Storck, 'Volkslied und Gassenlied' (1911), quoted from S. Giesbrecht-Schutte, 'Zum Stand der Unterhaltungsmusik um 1900', in Kaschuba and Maase (eds.), *Schund*, 136.

[54] Hermand, Trommler, *Kultur*, 323.   [55] 'Billige Phonographen', *PZ* 1 (Sept. 1900), 25.

[56] 'Phonographische Leihbibliotheken', *PZ* 2 (31 July 1901), 182; also 'Billige Platten', *PZ* 6 (Mar. 1905), 283.

[57] See e.g. *PZ* 30 (1 Aug. 1929), 1124.

such innovative salesmanship that the gramophone could penetrate new social strata and widen its appeal in the latter 1920s. After finally recovering to pre-war levels by 1924, annual record sales reached an interim peak of 30 million in 1929, a figure that would not be surpassed for nearly three decades (and which plummeted during the depression years, reaching a low of only 5 million in 1935). Sales of gramophones also experienced enormous growth during the latter half of the 1920s, rising from 196,000 in 1925 to 427,400 in 1929.[58]

This rapid expansion after the mid-1920s was based not only on new sales techniques and the general economic upswing, but also on a series of technological improvements. In particular, the introduction of electrical recording from 1926 onward signalled a huge breakthrough in both sound quality and compatibility with the new medium of radio. By the close of the 1920s mass production of the 'combination' gramophone/radio set using a common electrical input and common loudspeaker made both media more accessible and convenient to use than before. The changing design of these new sets, which increasingly hid their technical innards behind a conventional wooden façade, was a clear expression of how both media were becoming a more established part of everyday life. From this point on, the fate of recorded sound and broadcasting became closely linked. After years of industry trepidation that the radio might displace the gramophone, by the early 1930s their relationship was increasingly perceived as one of complementarity rather than competition.[59] In the midst of the acute sales crisis after 1929, latching on to the ever-growing medium of radio was a practical survival strategy. By the 1930s this marriage of audio media was further manifested in the broadcasting of 'record concerts', in common radio/recording exhibitions, and even in the rechristening of the Reichsverband der Deutschen Sprechmaschinen- und Schallplatten-Handels to the Reichsverband des Deutschen Phono- und Radio-Handels in 1932.[60]

Ever since the advent of broadcasting there were certain connections between radio and recording. The first broadcasting corporation in Germany, the Berliner Funkstunde, was located in the 'Voxhaus', the premises of the leading German recording firm on Potsdamer Straße 4. It was here that the first German radio broadcast took place on 29 October 1923, consisting of a live transmission followed by the 'Deutschland-Lied' recorded on a Vox record.[61] The overlapping skills required to work in the two industries also led to a certain exchange of personnel; soon after its launch, the Berliner Funkstunde managed to poach some of Vox's employees.[62] Yet before the introduction of electrical recording and the mains receiver the two technologies remained largely distinct from each other. Radio was entering new technological terrain, and for all the recording

---

[58] Figures from Blaukopf, *Massenmedium*, 16, 26.

[59] *PZ* 31 (1 Jan. 1930), 23–4; (15 May 1930), 730–2; (1 June 1930), 786–8; (1 July 1930), 893–4.

[60] P. Wiggers, 'Der RDS: seine Bedeutung und seine Aufgaben', in RDS, *Jahrbuch*, 10.

[61] Haas, *Jahrhundert*, 138.   [62] Lenk, *Erscheinung*, 89.

TABLE 4. *Registered wireless sets in the German Reich,*
1924–1933 (Postal Ministry figures)

Year	Registered sets × 1,000	Sets per 1,000 inhabitants
1924	10	0.2
1925	780	12.0
1926	1,205	19.0
1927	1,636	25.0
1928	2,235	35.0
1929	2,838	44.0
1930	3,238	50.0
1931	3,732	58.0
1932	4,168	64.0
1933	4,533	70.0

Source: Koch, *Wunschkonzert*, 53–4.

industry's problems with sound fidelity, the technological obstacles confronting the spread of radio totally dwarfed those of the gramophone.

During the early years of broadcasting these obstacles constituted the single most important factor shaping radio audiences. Admittedly, the growth of this audience was both rapid and remarkably consistent, rising by an average of around 500,000 per year and defiantly bucking the depression-era trend of contraction affecting all the other media.[63] Yet in order to understand the contours of this growth it is important to recognize that early radios were totally unlike modern sets, and that the experience of listening was also very different. The ability to receive and transform radio waves into audible sound generated a profound sense of awe in the 1920s. Constantly referred to as a technical 'miracle', the early wireless had crowds queuing in department stores and tourist offices just to have a brief moment at the headphones. As a consummate item of conspicuous consumption, a radio set could confer on its proud owner a considerable degree of neighbourhood celebrity, especially if he magnanimously allowed his neighbours to have a turn listening to it.[64] Popular fascination with this technical marvel is understandable given its intriguing and somewhat frightening appearance, an assemblage of glass valves, wires, and batteries quite unlike anything most people had ever seen.

These contraptions were also exceedingly awkward compared to their modern descendants. Listening required one's undivided attention. Early radios demanded continuous adjustment to hold a frequency, and the operator also had to take care not to overheat the valves. The batteries that supplied the power were far more temperamental than the simple wire plug-in that came later, and the use of headphones rather than a loudspeaker (which

---

[63] Führer, 'Medium', 731.   [64] See Lenk, *Erscheinung*, 74–6, 79.

Fig. 6. The 'miracle' of the wireless: listening via headphones to an early crystal wireless set in the garden, 1925. bpk Berlin.

only became standard in the later 1920s) was also constraining. Worse still, they were very fragile: the expensive valves were easily damaged by excessive heat or slight bumps. As a reward for all the effort involved, reception was often marred by static and interference. As the retailing journal *Radio-Händler* remarked in autumn 1924, the expansion of the wireless was seriously hindered by such inconveniences: 'People wanted a simple apparatus that would work by, say, plugging into the electrical network, but instead they were confronted with a complicated piece of equipment that required considerable effort and patience to get something from. . . . What people wanted from the radio was a musical instrument, an improved gramophone.'[65] This was a fitting analogy, for many gramophone enthusiasts were put off by their initial experiences with the wireless. 'A number of my friends are happy owners of a radio set and constantly go

---

[65] 'Welches waren die Ursachen für die Schwierigkeiten auf dem Radio-Markt?', *RH* (30 Sept. 1924), 103.

into raptures over the pleasure that it gives them,' remarked one such sceptic. 'But strangely, as often as I visit them, the thing does not seem to work "just now". Bad weather, electrical interference, a nearby radio owner—there is always something to blame for the disrupted broadcast and the pleasure is always a rather dubious one . . . That's why I'm sticking with my gramophone!'[66] Overall, early radio listening was not everyone's idea of a 'leisure' activity. In many respects it was a more of a technical undertaking, a hobby that required considerable patience and dedication. For this reason it appealed above all to the male enthusiast, a specimen more akin to the ham radio operator than the distracted pleasure-seeker, who might spend hours indulging in the novel (but curiously familiar-sounding in the Internet age) pastimes of 'station hunting' (*Senderjagd*) and 'frequency strolling' (*Wellenbummel*).[67]

For most people, radios were also prohibitively expensive. Around the mid-1920s prices for a standard three-valve set capable of receiving distant transmissions hovered around RM 300, dropping only slightly over the following years. As indicated earlier, this was roughly equivalent to the entire monthly income of a white-collar clerk or a skilled worker, which put such sets well beyond the reach of most German households.[68] There was a far cheaper alternative in the so-called *Detektor* or crystal set, which in 1925 could be had for only RM 15 to 40 and did not even require a power source. But buyers of *Detektoren* got what they paid for. Unlike the valve sets, which could receive airwaves that travelled some distance from broadcasters, detectors were capable of receiving only the relatively strong ground waves that emanated a mere 5 to 10 kilometres from the transmitters.[69] As such, they were only an option for listeners in the immediate vicinity of a broadcasting station, though even here reception was often poor. Matters improved somewhat in 1926 with the introduction of the *Röhrenortsempfänger*, which was equipped with a new kind of valve and available for as little as RM 40. Although this quickly became the most common type of radio set after 1926, it too was only able to receive ground waves and was therefore of no use beyond a short radius around the transmitters. In 1931 over half of all registered sets were still either *Detektoren* or *Röhrenortsempfänger*.[70]

These closely interrelated problems of cost and technical availability meant that radio audiences in Weimar Germany were overwhelmingly concentrated in urban centres—that is, in areas close enough to transmitters for the less expensive sets to be used. Before the construction of more powerful transmitting stations in the 1930s, the area in which ground waves could be received was very small, amounting in 1927 to only 1.4 per cent of the territory of the Reich.[71] For the

---

[66] *Die Stimme* 13 (Jan. 1928), 12.   [67] Lenk, *Erscheinung*, 232–3.
[68] See Dussel, *Rundfunkgeschichte*, 41; Führer, 'Medium', 735.
[69] *RH* (30 Sept. 1924), 106.
[70] Figures based on a Postal Ministry survey, reprinted in *RH* (7 Apr. 1931), 316; see also K. Steiner, *Ortsempfänger, Volksfernseher und Optaphon* (Essen, 2005).
[71] Führer, 'Medium', 736.

approximately 70 per cent of Germans who did not live in these densely populated areas, a costly set—usually with at least three valves—was necessary for passable reception, though few households could afford one. Against this backdrop it is scarcely surprising that rural listeners remained few and far between. Surveys conducted in 1927 found that of the 1.7 million registered sets, 1.4 million were located within the twenty-one cities where a transmitter was situated. Assuming that each of these radios was used by an average of four people, it was estimated that there were around 5.6 million listeners within these twenty-one cities, which amounted to around 40 per cent of their population. The remaining 300,000 registered sets were dispersed among the 50 million Germans living elsewhere in the Reich. Even if one reckoned that each of these radios had an average of five listeners due to the larger family sizes outside the major cities, this still amounted to only 1.5 million listeners, or 3 per cent of the population living there. In sum, over the first four years of broadcasting slightly under one-tenth of the population belonged to the radio audience: around two-fifths of those in the largest cities and less than one-thirtieth elsewhere. In spite of all the hype about the rapid expansion of the wireless in Germany, sober radio officials had no illusions that 'this view, if applied to Germany as a whole, is thoroughly mistaken'.[72]

This was not for lack of effort to popularize the radio in the countryside. Agricultural organizations were quick to recognize its usefulness for farmers, and successfully lobbied regional broadcasters to carry regular weather and price reports. In the Hamburg region, the North German Broadcasting Company (NORAG) even introduced a special 'Farmers' Hour' in 1924. The various farming journals frequently carried articles on the radio, and from 1924 onwards the German Agricultural Society (Deutsche Landwirtschaftsgesellschaft) also included a special feature on 'radio and agriculture' in its travelling exhibitions.[73] In 1927 the RRG itself began to focus its attention on the countryside, dispatching a fleet of 'radio buses' into the hinterlands to offer small-town and rural residents a taste of the new medium. By May 1929 radio buses had managed to visit every broadcasting district except for Leipzig and Munich, and by 1930 the fleet was being expanded.[74] Unfortunately, what they offered was often 'so deplorable, so flawed in every regard' that it actually 'strengthened the aversion against the radio among everyone who did not yet own an apparatus'.[75]

The potential of such advertising efforts was in all events severely limited by the high costs of radio listening in the countryside, the dearth of free time among farming households, and the lack of electrification in rural areas. In 1930 only half of Germany's households had electricity. This meant that the vast majority

---

[72] Lertes, 'Rundfunk', 69.   [73] See Münkel, 'Der Rundfunk', 184–5.
[74] H. Schlee, 'Rundfunkwerbung durch Werbewagen', 8 (25 June 1930), 539–40.
[75] 'Wie die Reichs-Rundfunk-Gesellschaft wirbt', *RZ* 7 (25 Mar. 1929), 309–11; also A. Hach, 'Rundfunkwerbung auf dem Lande', *RZ* 7 (10 May 1929), 485–8.

of would-be listeners in the countryside needed batteries, which added another RM 2 per month to operating costs.[76] Thus it was not the alleged backwardness of rural folk (commonly suggested by urban contemporaries) or a mistrust of unfamiliar gadgets that explains the low participation rates, but rather the stark economic and technical barriers. Radio thus tended to be least widespread in the sparsely populated eastern areas, where rural incomes were lower and signals weaker. Whereas listening rates in Cologne's broadcasting district had reached 19 per cent in 1929, around Königsberg the figure was only 3.2 per cent.[77] On a national level, only 7.9 per cent of rural households owned a radio set in 1932, compared to 46 per cent in the large cities.[78]

Yet within the cities too, radio was unevenly spread. The costs alone meant that the Weimar radio audience had a distinctly bourgeois profile. In 1930 around two-thirds of all registered subscribers were categorized as entrepreneurs, civil servants, and white-collar employees, with blue-collar workers accounting for only one-quarter of registered sets, far below their proportion of the general populace. Put differently, around one-half of all civil-servant and white-collar households were equipped with a radio at the end of the 1920s compared to only one in seven working-class households.[79] In a big conurbation like Berlin, these stark class discrepancies could be mapped more or less neatly on to the social geography of the city. The fact that 40 per cent of Berlin residents owned a radio in 1933 masked huge differences between the various municipal districts. In the lead was leafy Dahlem, where 82.8 per cent of households had a radio, closely followed by fashionable Charlottenburg, Pankow, Grunewald, Siemenstadt, Berlin W9 (the area around Potsdamer Platz), and Lichterfelde—all relatively upmarket areas. As the survey emphasized, 'the other Berlin districts follow after a more or less wide gap, whereby the listener density tends to decrease . . . the further east one goes'—that is, entering predominately working-class districts such as Wedding, Kreuzberg, Friedrichshain, and Neukölln. Apart from solidly middle-class Pankow north-east of the centre, the only other 'islands' of significant radio density in eastern Berlin were found in Johannistal, Karlshorst, Niederschöneweide, and Treptow—again, all relatively desirable suburban areas. Although these differences can partly be ascribed to industrial interference and the antenna limitations imposed by the large rental blocks characterizing the most densely populated areas, it was clear to all that the main reason was income difference.[80]

In spite of retailers' efforts to woo working-class households, most seem to have been put off by the sheer costs. True, a *Detektor* or *Röhrenortsempfänger* set was relatively cheap, and moreover could be purchased on instalment; in 1930–1

---

[76] Dussel, *Rundfunkgeschichte*, 72–3.
[77] 'Landbevölkerung und Funkhandel', *RZ* 7 (10 Feb. 1929), 118.
[78] Figure from *Rundfunk und Landwirt* (Berlin, 1932), 1.   [79] Führer, 'Medium', 738.
[80] 'Berlins Hörerdichte', *Phonographische und Radio Zeitschrift* (continuation of *PZ* from Oct. 1933, hereafter *PRZ*), 34 (1 Oct. 1933), 523–4.

around 80 per cent of all radios were sold on repayment schemes.[81] But there was always the RM 2 monthly licence fee to pay, regardless of how much one actually listened. One possibility was of course to ignore the fee by cancelling the original subscription and tuning in on the sly. Such 'Schwarzhören' seems to have been fairly common, though hardly epidemic.[82] The far more common response was simply to forgo the radio altogether. Although RM 2 per month for a radio licence seems a paltry sum to save, we must recall that this alone would have almost completely exhausted the average RM 2.50 at the disposal of a middle-earning working-class household.[83]

In practical terms, this meant that radio did not represent an additional source of amusement for most people, but could only be a replacement for something else. Whereas the radio could offer unique economies of scale for large families by bringing daily entertainment to an entire household for only RM 2 a month, for others the equivalent of three or four cinema tickets often seemed a more attractive alternative. But even for families with sufficient disposable income, lack of time often dampened interest in the radio. A 1934 survey of listeners in and around Berlin found that children were the single most significant factor. Childless households showed by far the highest rate of ownership at 89.4 per cent, followed by families with older children (around 60 per cent). By contrast, families with small children were by far the least likely to own a radio; in households with more than one small child it dropped as low as 6.5 per cent. As one young father put it: 'I already have two little "loudspeakers" at home, and that's enough for me.'[84]

By the early 1930s the decidedly urban and middle-class constituency of early radio gradually began to broaden out, thanks to a series of technical improvements. An important breakthrough came in 1930 when the Postal Ministry began unveiling a new generation of more powerful transmitters (*Großsender*). Whereas the average broadcasting strength in 1926 was only 0.85 kW (reaching 2.79 kW in 1929), by 1930 it leapt to 8.21 kW and by 1933 to 21.89 kW. When the last of these transmitters was completed in early 1934, around 70 per cent of the German population was capable of receiving ground waves with an inexpensive set.[85] In 1931 the Deutsche Welle, Germany's only 'national' radio service broadcasting on long wave, also got a new transmitter that enabled it for the first time to reach the entire Reich, thus giving audiences a choice of at least two stations.[86] In the meantime, radio sets themselves were becoming both cheaper and easier to use. By 1928–9 the mains

---

[81] Führer, *Wirtschaftsgeschichte*, 58; Dussel, *Rundfunkgeschichte*, 72.
[82] See *RH* 1 (2 Sept. 1924), 75–6; *RH* 2 (7 July 1925), 268; (23 June 1925), 246; (1 Sept. 1925), 351; (10 Nov. 1925), 474. The number of monthly fines reported in the mid-1920s numbered in the hundreds, not thousands.
[83] Statistisches Reichsamt, *Lebenshaltung*, 57.
[84] W. Hensel and E. Keßler, *1000 Hörer antworten* (Berlin, 1935), 47–8.
[85] Lerg, *Rundfunkpolitik*, 357, 370–1.   [86] Ibid. 305–10.

plug-in had become the industry standard, and most new sets were equipped with a built-in loudspeaker that liberated listeners from headphone cables.[87] Reception and volume were also improving rapidly. In 1924 RM 300 bought a set with 1 : 30 frequency selectivity and 1000× sound amplification. In 1929 the same amount bought 1 : 50 selectivity and 50,000× amplification, and in 1933 it cost only RM 220 for a set with 1 : 100 selectivity and 1,000,000× amplification.[88] Meanwhile, these vast technical improvements were increasingly hidden behind wooden housings and fabric covers that transformed the once formidable contraption into a domesticated piece of furniture. 'In general one can say that the radio marvel has gradually entered the consciousness of the masses,' remarked one commentator in early 1933. 'One already sees it with normal eyes, or rather with "normal ears". And this familiarity has established itself where one previously saw something supernatural, colossal.'[89]

Yet this did not change the fact that German radio audiences remained both socially and geographically skewed on the eve of the Nazi takeover. A radio still was not a 'must' in the early 1930s, especially in the summer months when people spent more time outside. The continual growth figures tend to hide the fact that every year hundreds of thousands of listeners cancelled their subscriptions due to financial difficulties, poor reception, or simply lack of interest.[90] For the majority of German households in the Weimar period a wireless set was quite simply an extravagance, especially in view of the many other free-time activities available.

And these alternatives were not, of course, limited to the other media of communication, but also included sporting associations, hobby clubs, choirs, and the corner pub. In the 1920s such non-media leisure activities still accounted for the bulk of free-time budgets in Germany. Among young people sport remained the single most popular leisure occupation, involving at least two-thirds and, according to some estimates, well over three-quarters of boys and girls.[91] For male manual workers and female white-collar employees alike, sport and hobby clubs were far more affordable and took up far more of their time than listening to the radio or going to the cinema.[92] Although the 1920s undoubtedly witnessed a significant expansion of media-based entertainments, it was only later that the bulk of the German populace became a regular part of the media audience.

---

[87] See the contemporary overview, 'Zur Entwicklung des Rundfunks in Deutschland', *RH* 6 (2 Jan. 1929), 30.

[88] 'Radio im Jahre 1933', *RH* 11 (10 Jan. 1934), 20.

[89] 'Rundfunk, Schallplatte und individuelle Musik', *PZ* 34 (25 Feb. 1933), 87.

[90] Führer, 'Medium', 739–40; 'Achtung, das Programm—Hörer melden ab!', *RZ* 10 (15 Oct. 1932), 599; Justus Horn, 'Der Funkhandel und die Radioflucht', *RZ* 10 (10 Dec. 1932), 703.

[91] See R. Dinse, *Das Freizeitleben der Großstadtjugend* (Eberswalde, 1932), 85–111; G. Krolzig, *Der Jugendliche in der Großstadtfamilie* (Berlin, 1930), 139 f.

[92] Dussel and Frese, *Freizeit*, 132; Suhr, *Angestellten*, 46.

5

Meeting Demand: Consumer Preference and Social Difference

Audiences for the new media in the 1910s and 1920s were not the indistinct 'mass' collectives of consumers they have sometimes been taken to be, but were crucially shaped by technological, economic, and social factors. Yet as we will now see, the ways in which the wider social context influenced the distribution and usage of the media went much further than their sheer availability. Determining the social composition of media audiences—their class, generational, and geographic makeup—addresses only part of the question. For even among the regular media audiences (that is, those who commonly used a particular medium at all), patterns of uptake and differences in supply visibly reflected the many social distinctions in Weimar society. What films one saw, what paper one read, what parts of the radio programme one tuned into—all of these choices were profoundly shaped by class, age, gender, and milieu.

Nor were the media themselves all of a piece. Depending on the nature of their technology and the framework of regulation, they could offer a different degree of variety and could therefore exert quite diverse social effects. As a rule, the more competitive and commercialized the medium was, the more it sought to meet consumer preferences. And the more it tried to meet consumer preferences, the more it tended to reflect differences in audience tastes. In order to meet—let alone enlarge—popular demand, it was necessary to offer differentiated fare. For this very reason, any lack of sensitivity towards consumer tastes effectively hindered audience growth. In other words, the expansion of a medium of communication tended to entail greater heterogeneity in its content and uses, which increasingly tended to reflect and/or reproduce social differences of taste and expectation. By the same token, the more uniform and standardized the content of a medium remained, the less it was able to expand, thereby limiting its audience to certain groups. Either way, the important point to recognize is that one cannot assume that the rise of the mass media per se necessarily denoted the arrival of a more homogeneous and socially levelled 'mass culture'. The growth of mass communications in the Weimar era had a wide range of possible implications, and there was nothing simple or predictable about their social and cultural impact.

BETWEEN POPULAR APPEAL AND PARTICULARISM:
THE PRINT MEDIA

As we saw in Chapter 1, commercial publishers' aim of opening new reading markets gave rise to a string of innovations around the turn of the century. In terms of form, the new mass dailies were couched in a common idiom accessible to those with only limited education, and were presented through a more eye-catching layout than the dense columns of text that characterized the traditional broadsheets. Through the use of white space, headlines, and subtitles they allowed readers to browse their contents quickly and easily, and to grasp the gist of a story without ploughing through fields of print. This was crucial, since different readers might search out very different sections of their coverage, which included not only politics and cultural events, but also sports, human-interest stories, word puzzles, local news, recipes, gardening tips, and, of course, advertisements. The goal was to offer something for everyone while giving no one cause for offence. From the outset, this encouraged a 'non-political' tendency among the mass-circulation press. As the right-wing media magnate Alfred Hugenberg remarked in 1927, 'over the long term there will be no great German periodical that acts as a representative for such a [party political] group or organization—for the simple reason that the readers would abandon it'.[1] In short, the point was to find a broad common denominator as a means of achieving universal appeal.

By the start of the 1920s the German commercial press had already been pursuing this strategy for several decades, and would continue to do so for the foreseeable future. Yet amidst this basic, underlying continuity there were also a number of important changes under way. During the Weimar years the overall trend towards providing more entertainment and achieving greater visual impact became both more widespread and more pronounced.

The First World War undoubtedly accelerated these changes. It was widely agreed among newspapermen that the German press was, on balance, more 'sensational' after the war than before, with more headlines and images, different typography, and a more urgent tone. There were a number of explanations for this. First, many thought that the experience of the war destroyed or at least weakened many of the earlier barriers against such 'sensationalism'. The outbreak of fighting swiftly ended the discussion about the so-called 'Americanization' of the press, as the huge demand for up-to-date war reports boosted the use of street sales and more attention-grabbing headlines. At the same time, the 'hurrah-patriotism' that inundated much of the German press also encouraged a more sensational and emotional style of reporting. A second explanation was that the

---

[1] Quoted from J. Requate, 'Medienmacht und Politik', *AfS* 41 (2001), 93.

more sensational style of the 1920s resulted from the nervous exhaustion of the war, the over-stimulation caused by years of constant battle reports and the worry they occasioned. A third reason was the heightened competition in the publishing trade after the war, brought on by a combination of lower purchasing power, plummeting advertising revenues, and higher paper prices.[2]

But whatever the reasons for this sensationalizing trend (and it seems that all of these factors contributed to it), its most conspicuous manifestation was the proliferation of tabloids during the post-war years. With their yelling headlines and numerous illustrations, this brash new genre was deliberately geared for the hyper-competitive market of big-city street sales. Lacking a regular subscription base, the only way to sell boulevard papers was by catching the attention of passers-by. Most appeared around noon or in time for the evening rush hour, and were specially designed for rapid browsing during lunch-breaks or while commuting home. As a result, they sought to convey their news quickly and in easily digestible form through the use of rubrics and the visual categorization of contents—or as one contemporary put it, 'more via structure and layout than via commentary'.[3] They also put a strong emphasis on entertainment, scandalizing their readers with hair-raising crime stories, dissecting recent sporting events, and indulging in the latest gossip. By the second half of the 1920s there emerged a standard tabloid formula of around ten to sixteen pages in total, two devoted to politics, three on local news, three or four on culture and entertainment, not more than three on sport, around two on business, and any further space filled with advertisements.[4] The aim was to appeal to as broad an audience as possible, 'from Gustav Stresemann to the taxi-driver', as the *Berliner Nachtausgabe* slogan went.[5]

Although the first boulevard paper in Germany, Ullstein's *BZ am Mittag*, had been around since 1904, it was only after the First World War that tabloids began to take off more generally. As early as January 1919 the *BZ am Mittag* was confronted by a new challenger, the *12-Uhr-Blatt*, which on its debut actually outdid the self-styled 'fastest newspaper on earth' by being the first to report the murders of communist leaders Kare Liebknecht and Rosa Luxemburg.[6] In 1922 came the left-wing *Welt am Abend* and the conservative *Berliner Nachtausgabe*, and by the end of the decade Berlin readers could also choose from Goebbels's *Angriff* and Ullstein's ultra-modern *Tempo*. In the meantime, tabloids were also launched in a number of other cities: the *8-Uhr-Blatt* in Nuremberg in 1918, *Der Mittag* in Düsseldorf in 1920, and the *Hamburger 8-Uhr-Abendblatt* in 1921. But it was undoubtedly in Berlin where tabloids flourished most. Their formula of eye-catching layout, numerous illustrations, sensationalist headlines,

---

[2] See M. Mende, *Sensationalismus als Produktgestaltungsmittel* (Cologne, 1996), 51, 77. Stöber, *Pressegeschichte*, 181.

[3] Kauder, 'Bezett', 194.

[4] B. Fulda, 'Press and Politics in Berlin, 1924–1939', DPhil. thesis, Cambridge (2003), 50.

[5] Meier, *Zwischen*, 74.

[6] B. Fulda, 'Industries of Sensationalism', in Führer and Ross (eds.), *Media*, 183.

and entertaining content was clearly working, and stood in stark contrast to the stagnating circulation figures of the old-established papers in the Reich capital. From 1925 to 1930 Berlin's tabloids nearly tripled their readership, rising from around 350,000 to just under 1 million. This almost equalled the *combined* sales figures of the mass commercial dailies, which stabilized in the 1920s at just over the 1 million mark. Over the same period the city's political broadsheets saw their combined circulation drop from just over 600,000 to under half-a-million, only to fall even more precipitously during the early 1930s.[7]

Gradually, the success of the tabloids and the after-effects of the war prompted the political dailies to adopt some of their competitors' techniques. Among the first to make this move were the Social Democrats, though the process was—as among all segments of the political press—marked by tension between a sense of political mission and the need for popular appeal. 'It is self-evident that our party press must remain first and foremost a political weapon and a means of political education', declared the SPD press commission in 1919. Yet in order to enhance its influence on the masses, it was necessary to borrow a leaf from the big bourgeois dailies. 'Much of their success and circulation is due to the very clever selection and application of their so-called headlines, and we must take the good where we find it. A skilful layout is by no means necessarily an encouragement of the desire for sensation.'[8]

The SPD had long recognized that the circulation of its papers lagged far behind the party's electoral support. Taken together, the SPD press had seen its Reich-wide circulation plummet from a pre-war high of around 1.8 million to merely 1.1 million in 1925, or about the same as the sales of the big commercial dailies in Berlin alone. It was clear that the 'non-political' Generalanzeiger papers were widely preferred to the socialist press, not least in working-class neighbourhoods. Why this was the case, and how one could remedy it, was no great mystery. As Wilhelm Sollmann, the chief editor of the *Rheinische Zeitung*, put it in 1926, 'the vast majority of people are more excited by local events and issues than by high politics'. It was imperative that socialist newspapers devote less space to politics and more to light entertainment. This was especially important for appealing to female readers, who tended to make the subscription decisions in most households. Only by printing more human-interest stories, women's supplements, serialized novels, and sports coverage would the party press maintain its influence against the encroachment of the commercial dailies, whose formula clearly suited workers' tastes. As things currently stood, 'we argue and rant too much, and we chat far too little'.[9]

Although concrete evidence of reader expectations is scarce, the notion that traditional political papers needed to modernize was emphatically confirmed by a 1924 Communist Party enquiry into why so few workers were buying the *Rote*

---

[7] Figures from Fulda, 'Press', 34.   [8] Quoted from Meier, *Zwischen*, 55.
[9] W. Sollmann, *Wir und die Leserwelt* (Berlin, 1926), 7–12, quoted from Fulda, 'Press', 41–2.

Fahne, the official organ of the KPD. To the acute discomfort of the paper's editors, the survey responses were utterly damning of the communist press, from its rabble-rousing tone to its obvious tendency to distort the facts. Although a number of these shortcomings were peculiar to communist publications, the most common complaint was applicable to the political press as a whole: namely, that they failed to deliver entertainment. Even many loyal party members found the communist papers tediously one-sided: 'I want to hear something about natural science, about politics, literature, criminology; in short, I want to feel something of the pulse of life, not always just politics, politics, politics.' Most of the women surveyed were even less complimentary, and a significant number of men responded that they did not subscribe to the *Rote Fahne* because their wives would object. It was not unusual for quarrels to break out over the issue, with wives cancelling the subscription in favour of a more entertaining paper such as the *Berliner Morgenpost*.[10] As the ex-communist Theodor Richter remarked in his 1932 exposé of the KPD, 'man cannot live from this communist reading material alone, and even the most loyal communist, the most zealous class-warrior has substituted his party organ with a bourgeois newspaper simply in order to recuperate from the phrases of his party paper. Not to mention the women!'[11]

As this survey suggests, the political focus of the party press not only thwarted any possibility of expansion but was failing to satisfy the expectations of its current readers. In order to retain market share they needed to become more consumer-oriented, which essentially meant broadening their thematic scope and introducing a more eye-catching format. By the mid-1920s the pressure to make such concessions had prompted many a 'serious' metropolitan newspaper to add 'a few rich dashes of colour': sports coverage, women's sections, local news, cinema, radio, and travel.[12] As we saw in Chapter 1, even editors of traditional political broadsheets readily conceded that the only realistic mear of increasing circulation was to spice up the political section with personalized portraits and current events, and to expand a newspaper's subject matter through additional sections and special supplements. Effective layout and page design were also becoming recognized as a 'necessity of the new era', and became a hot topic in the German publishing world by the middle of the 1920s. 'Clear script arranged in an easily legible manner, set apart in a modern style and standing in white space' was the key for attractive headlines and advertisements alike.[13] At the same time, the use of visual images also expanded. Despite concerns that this

---

[10] Quotes and survey material taken from Fulda, 'Press', 39–40.

[11] T. Richter, *Hinter roten Kulissen* (Berlin, 1932), 56.

[12] Quotes from H. Walter, 'Die Zeitung als Persönlichkeit', *ZV* 27 (20 Aug. 1926), 1799–802; see also M. Meyen, *Leipzigs bürgerliche Presse in der Weimarer Republik* (Leipzig, 1996), 136–8, 280–3.

[13] A. Franke, 'Das Gesicht der Zeitung', *ZV* 27 (29 Oct. 1926), 2327–30; 'Wie wirkt und wirbt die Zeitung durch ihre äußere Form', *ZV* 27 (31 Dec. 1926), 2797–802; R. Gonter, 'Das Gesicht der Zeitung', *DR* 20 (Mar. 1927), 159.

represented a 'dumbing down' of journalistic standards, by the end of the decade one-fifth of German newspapers regularly used photographic illustrations.[14] Similar debates surrounded the use of more informal language in the 1920s, which was another means to enhance the popular appeal of newspapers.[15] In sum, the so-called 'Gesinnungspresse' was becoming more and more like the once-maligned 'Geschäftspresse'. Insofar as this distinction was ever very clear, the highly competitive newspaper market of the Weimar Republic blurred it further.

To what extent did this gradual standardization of form and content render a more universal, consumer-oriented, and socially inclusive readership? As scholars have rightly pointed out, the expansion of print advertising and the habit of 'browsing' through headlines and rubrics were undoubtedly hallmarks of an emerging consumer culture, and tended to appeal to interests and identities that cut across class, confession, or political affiliation.[16] But one should not exaggerate the changes under way. For one thing, they were largely centred on the major metropolitan newspapers, with much of the provincial press lagging far behind. And even in the Reich capital there were limits to how far the 'respectable' mass dailies were prepared to go. Mosse's *Berliner Tageblatt*, which frequently printed multi-column headlines during the war, actually reverted to a more traditional layout after 1918 for fear of jeopardizing its reputation with too many 'Americanisms'. Although long and conspicuous headlines grew more common throughout the 1920s, there was no radical switch to thematic rubrics printed on the title-page, let alone to different sizes and types of headlines. Nor was the number of photos very spectacular, rising on average from only one in every third paper in 1923 to about one per paper in 1928.[17] Admittedly, the unabashed sensationalism of tabloid newspapers pointed in quite a different direction from the reticence of papers like the *BT*. But in most cities tabloids failed to establish themselves, and even where they did take root they did not always achieve a mass circulation. Düsseldorf's *Mittag*, based in the middle of Germany's most densely populated conurbation, reached a circulation of only 50,000 throughout the entire Rhineland. Similarly, Nürnberg's *8-Uhr-Blatt* never achieved even half the sales of the old-established *Nürnberger Zeitung*, the leading subscription-based broadsheet in Franconia. In terms of its tabloid market Berlin was wholly exceptional, accounting for over half of the entire tabloid circulation in Germany in the early 1930s.[18]

---

[14] The illustrated magazines still remained the primary carriers of photographs: Knoch, 'Living', 222–4. On the contemporary controversy: 'Zeitungsbebilderung', *ZV* 30 (22 June 1929), 1277–8.

[15] A. Esbach, 'Die Sprache der Zeitung', *ZV* 27 (18 June 1926), 1439–42.

[16] G. Reuveni, 'Reading, Advertising and Consumer Culture in the Weimar Period', in Führer and Ross (eds.), *Media*, 204–16; id., 'Lesen', esp. 114–15; id., *Reading*.

[17] Mende, *Sensationalismus*, 79–83.

[18] Fulda, 'Industries', 188; see also P. de Mendelssohn, *Zeitungsstadt Berlin* (Berlin, 1959), 268–9.

The move towards entertainment and general consumer appeal was only one of many factors that shaped publishers' calculations in Weimar Germany. Local interests moulded reader expectations just as much as entertainment. This was even the case in the large cities, most of which boasted a plethora of small local papers alongside the big dailies. After the communal reform of 1920, Greater Berlin was home to around thirty district papers each serving a particular area of the capital. In many ways these neighbourhood periodicals were analogous to small-town papers, with their emphasis on local announcements and advertisements.[19] Germany's press landscape as a whole was remarkably fragmented. As the editor Georg Bernhard explained to foreign advertisers in 1929, 'the German still retains to a very great extent his "small-town patriotism." Thus it happens that almost every German town has a newspaper. If the size of its own and the surrounding rural population offers a good market, it has at least two.'[20] Hence the vast majority of papers were small and without much potential to grow. In 1928 Ullstein counted 3,356 daily newspapers in Germany, 114 in Berlin alone. In 1932 the Institute for Newspaper Studies counted no fewer than 4,703, a figure that included non-dailies.[21] As American advertising agencies complained in the later 1920s, Germany did not have any national newspapers that offered adequate Reich-wide coverage for marketing purposes. The average circulation in Germany was only 50 per cent that of England, and the vast bulk of newspapers served a distinctly local readership, including even the large Berlin dailies, which were rarely read outside of the capital. As for the 4,500 magazines counted in 1929, the *BIZ* was the only publication remotely approaching the circulation figures of the big American weeklies such as the *Saturday Evening Post* and *Ladies Home Journal*.[22] Compared to other highly developed countries, Germany was a land of distinctly local readers.

The barriers of social and confessional milieu also remained a crucial factor shaping readerships in the Weimar Republic, especially in the provinces where Generalanzeiger, illustrated magazines, and tabloids were not common. Recent studies have shown that the SPD and communist press were firmly anchored in the working classes and centred primarily on their party memberships. In 1932 62 per cent of SPD press readers were categorized as industrial workers, and a further 21.3 per cent as white-collar workers or civil servants; the figures for the communist press were 69.6 and 14.1 per cent, respectively. By contrast, papers with a conservative-nationalist bias found around one-third of their readers among the lower middle class, one-quarter among white-collar workers and civil servants, and just under a fifth among farmers, with less than 15 per cent among industrial workers. Liberal and 'bourgeois' dailies exhibited a

[19] Fulda, 'Press', 17–18.   [20] Bernhard, 'Deutsche Presse', 68–9.
[21] *Handbuch der deutschen Tagespresse*, 4th edn. (Berlin, 1932), 27*; Bernhard, 'Deutsche Presse', 69.
[22] JWT Research Reports, Microfilm Collection 16 mm, reel 224, 'The German Press' (1929), 4, 15.

similar social profile to the conservative press, with a slightly higher readership among industrial workers and a far lower one among farmers.[23] Generally speaking, the conservative end of the spectrum appealed to industrial and agricultural interests, the more liberal papers to civil servants, professionals, and businesspeople. Although this 'intra-bourgeois' segmentation was more fluid than that characterizing the relatively ghettoized socialist and Catholic press, in some cities it was remarkably stark, for example in Munich, where the centrist, DVP-supporting *Münchner Neuesten Nachrichten* was read by over 90 per cent of professionals, civil servants, white-collar workers, and trades people, compared to the predominance of Hugenberg's right-wing, DNVP-affiliated *München-Augsburger Abendzeitung* among academic elites and the upper echelons of industry and commerce.[24] The only segment of the political press with clear cross-class appeal was that of the Centre Party, though it remained almost completely limited to Catholic readers: 81 per cent of its newspapers appeared in overwhelmingly Catholic areas.[25] For many publishers, especially those within the socialist and Catholic milieus, meeting demand involved not only more sports coverage and serialized novels, but also following a certain political line. In this sense, the attempts to make the political press more attractive through concessions to entertainment did not encourage an erosion of milieu boundaries, but rather reinforced them.

Even most of the mass-circulation dailies had recognizable and more or less distinctive social profiles. Although German editors had always possessed a sense of their core readerships, it was not until the later 1920s that the first surveys were carried out, initially by the American advertising agency J. Walter Thompson (JWT). Among Munich newspapers, for instance, JWT researchers made a clear distinction between the readership of the *Münchner Neueste Nachrichten*, with its 'good middle class', 'businessmen', and 'first importance for cars', and the *Münchner Zeitung*, which was more popular among 'small trades people, lower middle class, some workers'. Hamburg's big newspapers were similarly distinctive. Whereas the *Hamburger Fremdenblatt* boasted 'good class readers' and was a 'leading paper for all products', the *Hamburger Anzeiger* was read by 'workers and middle classes . . . many housewives', and the *Hamburger Echo* mainly among the working class. In Cologne the 'best and richest class' read the *Kölnische Zeitung*, which was especially 'good for high priced cars'. More middle-of-the-road was the *Stadt-Anzeiger*, followed by the 'socialist' and 'low class' *Rheinische Zeitung*. Unsurprisingly, it was the Berlin press that exhibited the greatest diversity. Whereas the *Berliner Morgenpost* was primarily anchored among 'democratic readers with small incomes: labourers, lower middle class,

[23] Meier, *Zwischen*, 347–8.
[24] P. Hoser, *Die politischen, wirtschaftlichen und sozialen Hintergründe der Münchener Tagespresse zwischen 1914 und 1934*, vol. 2 (Frankfurt, 1990), 990–4.
[25] Meier, *Zwischen*, 348.

etc.', the *Berliner Tageblatt* was more prevalent among merchants, Jews, and wealthy readers, while the moderate-nationalist *Berliner Lokal-Anzeiger* was deemed to have a 'better class [reader] than the *Morgenpost*', including many former officials and military officers. Significantly, the *BZ am Mittag* was the only Berlin paper deemed to be 'popular [among] all classes', in stark contrast to the socialist *Vorwärts*, whose overwhelmingly working-class readership made it 'not good as [an] advertising medium'.[26]

A similar degree of variegation could be found among the many magazines and illustrated weeklies flooding the German market. According to JWT researchers, there was a very clear social hierarchy among the leading women's magazines. Using the standard pyramidal income scale of A to D, the readership of *Die Dame* was far and away the most exclusive with a mark of A, compared to C+ for *Fürs Haus* and *Hausfrau* and C for *Deutsche Frau*. The core readership of the satirical magazines and illustrated weeklies all hovered around the B range, with the *Münchner Illustrierte Presse* slightly more upmarket than, say, *Hackebeils Illustrierte* or the incomparably more popular *BIZ*. There was somewhat more variegation among the general-interest magazines, ranging from the A-class readerships of *Querschnitt* and *Westermanns Monatshefte* to the more middlebrow *Uhu* and *Gartenlaube* to the C-rated *Allgemeiner Wegweiser* published by the Scherl-Verlag.[27] Among the cultural periodicals such income differentials were of course far less important than their political slant. On the left were the highly acclaimed *Weltbühne* and *Tage-Buch*, whose perspective on events could hardly be more different from the cluster of conservative periodicals such as *Die Tat, Kunstwart, Preussische Jahrbücher*, and *Süddeutsche Monatshefte*, not to mention Catholic journals such as *Hochland* and *Historisch-politische Blätter*.[28]

It was not only the famous general-interest magazines such as *BIZ* and *Die Woche* that flourished during the Weimar years. There was also a proliferation of target periodicals that catered to a whole range of different political groupings and cultural interests, from women's journals and sport to popular science and art. Even within these topical categories there was often a visible hierarchy or division of labour between the individual magazines. In this respect they were similar to the differentiated market for daily newspapers, whose readerships remained somewhat distinct in spite of the basic trend towards entertainment versus narrow political affiliation. Such renowned mass-circulation titles as the *BZ am Mittag, Berliner Morgenpost*, or the *BIZ*, with their large and relatively diverse readerships, were very much the exceptions that proved the rule. In Weimar Germany the market for printed matter was shaped as much by structures of class, confession, and local milieu as by a universal desire for entertainment.

[26] JWT Research Reports, 'The German Press', 29, 33, 35, 40, 56.
[27] Ibid. 22–5; for general background, W. Marckwardt, *Die Illustrierten der Weimarer Zeit* (Munich, 1982).
[28] See H.-C. Kraus (ed.), *Konservative Zeitschriften zwischen Kaiserreich und Diktatur* (Berlin, 2003).

Fig. 7. Catering to every imaginable taste: newspaper kiosk in Berlin's Kaiserallee, 1932. bpk Berlin. Photo: Friedrich Seidenstücker.

EDIFICATION AND AMUSEMENT: RADIO PROGRAMMING AND ITS CRITICS

While editors were busily competing for market share in the 1920s, radio executives also sought to broaden their audience and stimulate demand for the wireless. But unlike their counterparts in the publishing industry, who operated in a highly competitive market, broadcasting directors could reach out to the audience more on their own terms.

Throughout the 1920s broadcasters tried to find ways of widening the appeal of radio without compromising its 'educational mission'. As we have already seen, one means of achieving this was by publicizing the wireless in rural areas. A somewhat more successful effort was aimed at women, more specifically at housewives, through a whole range of programmes specially designed to fit with the average domestic routine of shopping, cooking, and cleaning.[29] By the end of the 1920s such 'target group' broadcasts—which also included programmes for children, parents, churchgoers, even teachers—accounted for around 8 to 10 per cent of most stations' airtime.[30] But appealing to minority audiences through group-specific programmes was only tinkering at the margins, since the vast bulk of listeners tuned in at the same time, namely in the evening. Hence, any serious effort to broaden the appeal of radio inevitably had to confront the issue of popular tastes, above all the expansion of light entertainment. But what precisely constituted suitable 'entertainment' for a mass radio audience, how much airtime should be devoted to it, and which time-slots were most appropriate—these were all issues that had to be tackled.

In view of the thousands of hours of programming broadcast by nine separate stations, each relying for the most part on its own productions, any generalizations about Weimar radio programmes are bound to oversimplify matters. Nevertheless, a number of basic patterns seem clear enough. For one thing, broadcast times changed markedly over the 1920s. Starting from only a few hours a day at first, daily programming reached around ten hours by the latter 1920s, usually beginning around four in the afternoon and terminating around midnight with an additional one or two hours at midday. By the early 1930s the typical broadcast day began at six or seven in the morning, with a break lasting from around eight until ten or eleven o'clock. After the midday resumption the programme generally continued until around midnight.[31] Although there was some variation between summer and winter programmes, it was only on Sundays that the broadcast day looked significantly different, offering up to eighteen hours of service interrupted only during the main churchgoing times of nine to eleven o'clock.

As for content, the proportion of different types of programming varied little between the individual broadcasters. More or less typical for 1929 was the programme in Munich, around half of which was taken up with music, 10 per cent by lectures, 15 per cent by news and reports, and a further 10 percent by 'target group' broadcasts, with advertising and service announcements accounting for most of the rest. Within the broader category of 'music', 30 to 35 per cent was classified as 'light entertainment', around 10 per cent 'musical education', and just over 10 per cent as 'demanding entertainment' (the latter two categories were hard to distinguish). The fact that 'literary education' accounted for just over 4 per cent of airtime—that is, almost half of the total time taken up by lectures—demonstrates the special attention devoted to the humanities by Weimar programmers.[32] This overall pattern proved fairly constant over the

---

[29] Generally, K. Lacey, *Feminine Frequencies* (Ann Arbor, Mich., 1996).
[30] R. Schumacher, 'Programmstruktur und Tagesablauf der Hörer', in Leonhard (ed.), *Programmgeschichte*, i. 383.
[31] Ibid. 360–1.   [32] Ibid. 383; also Führer, 'Medium', 751.

course of the 1920s, apart from the continual reduction in lectures, which initially took up as much as a quarter of broadcast time.

At first sight, the provision of twice as much 'light entertainment' as 'demanding' material would seem to contradict the vaunted educational mission of Weimar radio. However, one glance at the broadcast times for these different categories confirms that the goal of cultural enrichment remained at the heart of the programme. A survey from 1931 showed three peak listening times: the earliest between 7 and 8 o'clock in the morning, a second between noon and 1 o'clock in the afternoon, and by far the most valuable broadcast time falling between 8 and 10 o'clock in the evening. As a general rule, 'light entertainment' and news were broadcast in the morning or at midday, when most people were at work. The bulk of dance music and contemporary hits occupied little more than a niche in the late evening slot, often only after midnight. By contrast, the evening prime time between around 6:30 and 10:00 p.m. was jealously reserved for the 'higher things'. The segment before 8:00 usually featured lectures, sometimes accompanied by a bit of music or target group programmes. The key hours from 8:00 to 10:00 p.m., when most people were at home and finished with dinner and chores, were thoroughly dominated by 'demanding music', 'literary education', and 'musical education'. Only after this main attraction (as the programmers saw it) did the focus shift once more to news and less demanding music. Detailed sample surveys show little change in this basic recipe over the course of the 1920s and early 1930s, with only a slight shift towards light entertainment during popular listening times. The only obvious exception was Saturday evening, which tended to be geared for general entertainment.[33] In sum, 'light' fare clearly outweighed 'demanding' programming in terms of overall airtime, but classical music, lectures, and literary features still constituted the core of the programme. As Edmund Nick, the musical director in Breslau, put it in 1929, 'it is primarily the evening hours between 8:00 and 10:00 p.m. that determine the artistic physiognomy of the radio, and entertainment music is mostly broadcast before or after this time'.[34]

The extent to which this programming formula matched listener expectations is difficult to ascertain, given the scarcity of sources. Yet the evidence we have suggests that listener satisfaction was low after the honeymoon period in the early 1920s. The first listener survey, conducted in July 1924, actually found that demanding music rated high on the audience wish list. In first place was operetta with 83.3 per cent, followed by current events with 72.6 per cent, time announcements with 71.3 per cent, and, surprisingly, chamber music in fourth place with 63.8 per cent. Dance music and opera followed some distance behind, with 48.7 and 48.2 per cent, while both sport and political news lay just below 40 per cent. This early listener preference for 'culture' over 'entertainment' broadly

---

[33] Schumacher, 'Programmstruktur', 344–51, 364–6, 412–13.
[34] E. Nick, 'Unterhaltungsmusik' (1929), in Bredow (ed.), *Archiv*, 305.

corresponded to programming priorities, though it seems likely that the survey results, based on only 8,000 responses (or 8 per cent of listeners), reflected the predominately educated middle-class audience at the time.[35]

As the audience grew, so too did demands for more light entertainment. It was, according to the *Radio-Zeitschrift*, perfectly obvious what most people wanted to hear: 'Above all, light entertainment music!! But also dance music, marches, variety shows and the occasional operetta and comedy. And of course the transmission of events of general interest.' It was also obvious why: the average working person simply wanted to relax in the evening, and the last thing they wanted to hear was 'heavy chamber music or great operatic works or boring lectures that barely interest 3 per cent of the listeners'.[36] These impressionistic findings were largely confirmed by the first detailed listener survey in 1934. Among the 1,000 people questioned, by far the most popular segment of the programme was light entertainment and dance music. Preferences for 'demanding' versus 'light' music were strikingly class-related. Whereas classical concerts were listened to by 80.4 per cent of professionals and higher civil servants, this was true of only 7.9 per cent of unskilled workers and 10.5 per cent of skilled workers. By contrast, dance music was tuned into by 41.4 per cent of skilled workers and only 13.7 per cent of professionals and higher civil servants. Whereas one of the professional respondents liked to 'dress up in the evening to listen to radio concerts or operas and drink a little wine to create a festive atmosphere', one manual worker colourfully remarked that 'I like to listen to entertainment music, dance music and good hits, just no boring music in shit-minor and allegro!'[37]

Overall, listener preferences and habits were extremely varied. This reflected not only educational levels but also the specific role of the radio within the wider palette of leisure activities available to different social groups. The results from the 1934 survey suggest that different classes tended to have a somewhat different relationship to the wireless. For working-class listeners in particular, it helped transcend the educational and leisure constraints imposed by lower incomes. As one young working-class woman remarked, 'I think I'd die if I didn't have the radio anymore'.[38] Whereas 57.1 per cent of unskilled workers and 44.2 per cent of skilled workers viewed the radio as a substitute for the cinema, theatre, or live music, this was true of only 24.6 per cent of white-collar workers and mid-level civil servants. Among the highly educated (higher civil servants, professionals, commercial elites), the fact that radio was merely an 'enjoyable supplement to other means of education, stimulation, and entertainment' meant that their

---

[35] Lenk, *Erscheinung*, 181; see also K. Dussel, 'Deutsches Radio, deutsche Kultur', *AfS* 41 (2001), 122.

[36] E. Rellseg, 'Zur Programmefrage!', *RZ* 8 (10 July 1930), 582–4.

[37] 'Shit-minor' (*Schis-Moll*) is a wordplay on *Cis-Moll*, or C-sharp minor: Hensel, Keßler, *1000 Hörer*, 53–4.

[38] G. Thann, 'Von der sozialen Bedeutung des Rundfunks', *Soziale Praxis*, 44 (28 Mar. 1935), 379.

relationship to it was 'generally much cooler, much less emotional than that of the other social groups'.[39]

This huge diversity of listener expectations confronted radio executives with a difficult dilemma. As the Munich programme director Kurt von Boeckmann concluded in 1929, 'the more we focus on the cultural side of our task, the more we alienate ourselves from the majority of listeners, and the more we cater to the wishes and instincts of the great majority, the less we will be able to fulfil our role as bearers of culture (*Kulturträger*)'.[40] There was no clear consensus on which strategy to adopt. While everyone recognized that the economic basis of broadcasting was ultimately to entertain listeners, there was little agreement on what it should look like. By the later 1920s a handful of broadcasting directors openly supported a 'lighter' and more 'modern' programme, among them Hans Flesch in Berlin and Alfred Bofinger in Stuttgart. 'What should the radio bring?', Flesch asked in 1930. 'Good programming—that is a simple answer that says nothing and behind which, shrouded in grey tedium, lurk the dangerous popular education phrases of days gone by.'[41] Bofinger, too, was concerned not to drift too far from popular tastes, and grew increasingly impatient with the incessant discussion about the 'balance' between art and entertainment: 'In my view, the radio does not need to decide whether to create "artistic" entertainment or none at all, but rather must determine whether it wants to create "entertaining" entertainment or none at all.'[42]

But as was typical for Weimar broadcasting, a wholesale capitulation to popular tastes was never at issue. It was, as we saw in Chapter 3, more a matter of trying to break down the polarities between 'serious art' and 'entertainment', of maintaining a pious hope in the ability of radio 'to help bridge the divide between artistic music and popular tastes'.[43] Although programmers gradually made more room for light fare from 1928 onwards, this did not imply any fundamental change to the pedagogical character of Weimar radio. As the Berlin artistic director Carl Hagemann declared in no uncertain terms, the prime-time slots were to remain sacred: 'The constantly repeated demand to broadcast light entertainment music in the afternoon (ideally from 4:30 to 7:00) for the women and children at home, and to offer a varied, popular and undemanding programme for the entire family from 8:00 p.m. onwards naturally cannot be fulfilled.'[44]

---

[39] G. Thann, 'Von der sozialen Bedeutung des Rundfunks', *Soziale Praxis*, 44 (28 Mar. 1935), 381.

[40] K. v. Boeckmann, 'Grundlegende Fragen der allgemeinen Programmgestaltung' (Jan. 1929), quoted from K. Dussel, and E. Lersch (eds.), *Quellen zur Programmgeschichte des deutschen Hörfunks und Fernsehens* (Göttingen, 1999), 40.

[41] 'Der Berliner Rundfunk-Intendant sprach' (1930), quoted from L. Stoffels, 'Kulturfaktor und Unterhaltungsrundfunk', in Leonhard (ed.), *Programmgeschichte*, i. 628.

[42] A. Bofinger, 'Bunte Abende', in Bredow (ed.), *Archiv*, 310.

[43] Nick, 'Unterhaltungsmusik', 308.

[44] C. Hagemann, 'Die künstlerisch-kulturelle Zielsetzung des deutschen Rundfunks' (1928), in Bredow (ed.), *Archiv*, 235.

Naturally. But even if this demand were nominally met, it is by no means certain that programmers and audiences had the same understanding of 'light entertainment'. 'What counts as entertainment music is difficult to formulate', noted Max Butting, a composer and member of the Berliner Funkstunde cultural advisory council (*Kulturbeirat*). 'For each different stratum of the populace there is entertainment music.'[45] The fact that in May 1931 the Berliner Funkstunde gave the label 'entertainment music' to an eighty-five-minute potpourri of waltzes, operetta tunes and—bizarrely—excerpts from Wagner's *Tristan und Isolde*, clearly demonstrates that programmers' ideas of 'entertainment' were not necessarily shared by everyone.[46] So, too, does the fact that the modern dance hits so popular among working-class survey respondents were kept at arm's length.[47] Insofar as such music made it at all on to Weimar radio, it was largely thanks to recording firms, not broadcasting companies. Throughout the 1920s it was common for recording firms to hire broadcast time as a means of publicity. Their 'record concerts' were very helpful for keeping broadcasters' production costs down, but they too were confined to the margins.[48]

Given the obvious failure—or refusal—of programmers to cater to popular tastes, there was remarkably little criticism from listeners, most of whom expressed any dissatisfaction they felt by cancelling their subscription or, more frequently, simply switching off broadcasts they found boring. By far the most vocal critics were radio retailers, who had a direct interest in the expansion of the audience. A 'horrifyingly large' number of potential customers remained uninterested, they claimed, quite apart from the armies of radio owners who 'leave it unused to gather dust in the corner'.[49] As the retailers' associations repeatedly argued, the basic premise of Weimar radio was flawed. Surely, the goal should not be to educate a small minority, but rather to win over as many listeners as possible.[50] During the years of acute depression they grew increasingly exasperated by the paternalistic stance of the broadcasting corporations. Reporting on the second annual radio music conference in 1931, *Radio-Händler* gave open vent to these frustrations: 'It obviously makes no sense to indulge in sophistic hair-splitting about how things should be. Rather, one must proceed from the facts as they currently exist, that is, what the public wants from the radio in exchange for the money it pays. The directors of the broadcasting corporations must be "servants of the community of

---

[45] Quoted from Stapper, *Unterhaltungsmusik*, 67.   [46] Führer, 'Medium', 744.
[47] Generally, Stoffels, 'Rundfunk', 948–95.   [48] Dussel, *Rundfunkgeschichte*, 56.
[49] E. Schlesinger, 'Allgemeine Rundfunkkritik', *RH* 7 (22 Apr. 1930), 387–90; see also *RH* 9 (5 Apr. 1932), 304–5; 'Achtung, das Programm—Hörer melden ab!', *RZ* 10 (15 Oct. 1932), 599; J. Horn, 'Der Funkhandel und die Radioflucht', *RZ* 10 (10 Dec. 1932), 703.
[50] A. Hach, 'Schlußwort zum Thema "Händler und Programmgestaltung"', *RZ* 9 (27 June 1931), 461–3; 'Marktanalyse und Absatzforschung', *RZ* 7 (25 Oct. 1929), 1129; Schlesinger, 'Allgemeine'.

listeners", not its dictators who high-handedly use the radio as an educational whip.'[51]

But programmers shrugged off such criticisms, and Weimar radio continued to reflect the interests and values of its educated bourgeois producers. By placing 'serious art' and the classics above light entertainment, they prioritized the interests of the privileged few above the wishes of the vast majority. Measured against the broad diversity of listener expectations, prime-time programming was remarkably monochrome. It is therefore little wonder that the radio audience remained disproportionately middle class well into the 1930s. The social profile of the radio public was, it seems, shaped not only by the constraints of cost and technological limitations, but also by the programme itself.[52]

But despite all of the educational effort invested in it, contemporary surveys leave little doubt that Weimar radio failed to cultivate a shared appreciation for the 'higher things'. The common assumption that 'the great mass . . . is in essence thoroughly compliant' completely overlooked the fact that consumers were also active agents in the equation.[53] Most listeners were simply not interested in hearing a further-education course after a hard day's work, and stubbornly insisted on light music and entertainment. For those working in the commercially oriented recording industry this was self-evident. As the *Phonographische Zeitschrift* remarked in 1930, 'if the broadcasters were suddenly to succumb to a popular education attack and transmit nothing but works by Palestrina or Sebastian Bach for two solid weeks, this would hardly affect the overall tastes of the listening public'.[54] But among radio programmers, improving the taste of the audience by 'gradually but deliberately exposing it to higher and greater things' was precisely the goal.[55] This unswerving pedagogical orientation means that German radio in the 1920s and early 1930s can hardly be viewed as part of a new, universal 'mass culture'. Quite the opposite. As Karl Christian Führer has argued, Weimar radio 'can justly be regarded as a determined attempt to *prevent* the development of such a commercialized and standardized culture in Germany'.[56]

CINEMA PROGRAMMES AND FILM PREFERENCES

Film was an altogether different matter.[57] Both producers and exhibitors were in a fundamentally different situation from the state-sponsored shelter enjoyed by radio executives. Operating in a highly competitive market, they ignored popular tastes at their peril. The underlying commercial imperative of the film industry

---

[51] C. Borchardt, 'Tagung für Rundfunkmusik', *RH* 8 (11 Aug. 1931), 610.
[52] Führer, 'Medium', 751–2.   [53] Hagemann, 'Zielsetzung', 235.
[54] *PZ* 31 (1 Feb. 1930), 160.   [55] Hagemann, 'Zielsetzung', 235.
[56] Führer, 'Medium', 753, my emphasis.
[57] This section is drawn in large part from Ross, 'Mass Culture and Divided Audiences'.

offered little scope for arrogant audience tutelage. Rather, the entire incentive structure was geared towards meeting popular demand, whatever and wherever it was. As a result, inter-war cinema exhibited an extraordinary variety of different genres and modes of presentation, whose sole aim was to give audiences what they wanted. The range of options available to German movie-goers in the 1920s was of a wholly different magnitude from that open to radio listeners. This breadth of consumer choice meant that film audiences were especially active audiences, whose preferences were duly registered at the box-office. It also meant that film, unlike radio, offered a relatively sensitive reflection of popular demand, and hence of the social complexities of audience preferences. Precisely because of its uniquely broad appeal, the cinema landscape in Weimar Germany plainly reflected existing social distinctions. Where one went to the pictures, what films were shown there, and how they were presented were powerfully moulded by older structures of class and milieu.

Despite all the conservative jeremiads about cultural 'massification' (*Vermassung*), perceptive contemporaries were well aware of such differences. According to a 1928 study on Cologne and Danzig, there were three quite distinct film markets: the renowned premiere cinemas, the 'cinemas of the middle class, officials, and pensioners', and the 'workers' theatres'.[58] In the premiere cinemas (average ticket price: RM 1.65) the biggest hits tended to be either American blockbusters or big-budget German films, with German 'mediocre films' (*Mittelfilme*) making up the rest. By contrast, in the 'cinemas of the middle class' (average ticket RM 1.50) US films were relatively unpopular (with the exception of slapstick) in comparison to German standard films, particularly the many military films that glorified the 'Prussian virtues' and were execrated by left-of-centre critics. Among the 'workers' theatres' (average ticket RM 0.53) it was clear that American standard fare, especially westerns, was far more popular here than elsewhere (as were the handful of Soviet films that passed the censors), and regularly accompanied the German comedies and other medium-budget films that comprised the bulk of this market. The fact that military films performed ambivalently here and that Soviet films were rarely, if ever, shown in the 'cinemas of the middle class' is perhaps the clearest—though by no means only—indication that these audiences often saw films promoting very different values.[59]

This picture of a deeply segregated cinema audience is by and large confirmed by the contemporary film press. After venturing into a working-class cinema near Berlin's Humboldthain, a reporter for the *Berliner Tageblatt* remarked in summer 1928 that 'there are occasionally films here that one does not even see at all in the West'.[60] Earlier that same year the journal *Film und Volk* put it in even starker

---

[58] I. Guttmann, *Über die Nachfrage auf dem Filmmarkt in Deutschland* (Berlin, 1928), 13.

[59] Ibid. 18, 25, 32–6.

[60] H. Horkheimer, 'Badstraße 58', *Berliner Tageblatt* (1 July 1928), quoted from Mühl-Benninghaus, *Ringen*, 59; see also 'Badstraße 58', *RFB* (7 July 1928), 12.

terms: 'For the ordinary folk *A Day of Roses in August* and syrupy Courths-Mahler schmooze [*sic*], for the bourgeoisie films with literary ambitions . . . The world of the [working-class] Wedding cinema and the [upmarket] Kurfürstendamm film palace have nothing to do with each other.'[61] Cinema owners were keenly aware of such differences and planned their programmes accordingly. For example, the owner of the 'United Northern Pictures' in proletarian Wedding showed only what he called 'tomfoolery, but good for a laugh!'; all attempts at showing dramas, especially the costume dramas beloved in many a 'middle-class' cinema, proved disastrous.[62] Whereas the bulk of working-class cinemas showed 'adventure films, sensational films, and gripping, flashy kitsch analogous to a penny dreadful', the educated middle classes in particular preferred the 'high-society film' and 'adaptations of famous novels'.[63] Even in cinemas showing a wide mix of different film genres, the audiences changed according to what was on offer. Whereas the 'fashionable film subjects' tended to draw in the 'Kurfürstendamm *trotteur* and the Tauentzien girl', comedies and artistic dramas were frequented more by 'solid middle-class regulars'.[64] Political films also had a divisive effect, though this was largely limited to contentious *causes célèbres* such as *Battleship Potemkin*, *Fridericus Rex*, and *All Quiet on the Western Front*. As one might expect, whereas Soviet films were especially popular among communists and left-wing socialists, there was a clear preference for military and 'Prussian' films among bourgeois party supporters and National Socialists.[65] Yet it was also clear that many well-organized, class-conscious workers loved the so-called 'Fridericus' and 'old Heidelberg' films, the former glorifying Prussian militarism and the latter revolving around life in the right-wing student fraternities. As one cinema owner in Berlin's Danziger Straße remarked, whereas political films were mostly box-office flops, military films were highly popular in spite of the pronounced left-wing political orientation of the neighbourhood.[66]

   In addition to class barriers, regional differences also segregated cinema audiences in Weimar Germany. The nature of cinema programmes varied considerably from city to city, with some composed solely of films and others mixing films with live sketches and revues. Whereas local police generally allowed mixed programmes in Berlin, Cologne, and Düsseldorf, they were rare

   [61] L. Korpus, 'Kinoentwicklung', *Film und Volk*, 1 (Mar. 1928), 31, quoted from Mühl-Benninghaus, *Ringen*, 59–60. Hedwig Courths-Mahler was Germany's most famous pulp-romance writer, Wedding a pronounced working-class area in northern Berlin, the Kurfürstendamm the leading shopping mile in Berlin's West End.
   [62] 'Wie man's macht', *RFB* (10 Mar. 1928), 10–11.
   [63] J. Blochert, 'Gibt es einen internationalen Durchschnittsgeschmack?', *FK* (25 Apr. 1922), 3.
   [64] W. Lydor, 'Unser Publikum wünscht', *RFB* (28 Aug. 1926), 17–18. The Tauentzienstraße is a less exclusive extension of the Kurfürstendamm, commonly associated at the time with the young flapper.
   [65] E. Fromm, *Arbeiter und Angestellte am Vorabend des Dritten Reiches*, ed. W. Bonß (Stuttgart, 1980), 161.
   [66] 'Wie man's macht', 10–11; also ' "Klassenbewußte" Kinobesucher', *FK* (12 Dec. 1925), suppl. 2.

in Hamburg and non-existent in Frankfurt and Munich.[67] As for the films themselves, the taste discrepancy between audiences in Berlin and elsewhere was a constant theme in the film press. In the Rhineland film-goers were reportedly less impressed by sensationalist advertising than in the capital, and were positively put off by 'references to huge successes in Berlin.'[68] Cinema owners in Munich found time and again that 'films which cause a sensation in Berlin can flop in Munich, and vice-versa'.[69] This was due not least to the *berlinerisch* captions of many German films, which were not only unpopular among Bavarian viewers, but sometimes downright incomprehensible.[70] With the introduction of the sound film from 1929 onwards, foreign talkies fared much better in Berlin than elsewhere. Provincial audiences were 'far more film-nationalistic'[71] when it came to hearing their own language in the cinema. As one commentator in Düsseldorf sarcastically put it, the fad-driven Berliner 'becomes as undemanding as an Australian aborigine when a foreigner tells him something about progress. In Berlin one could show Chinese talkies—indeed, with the right presentation they would probably even be "big business".'[72]

As such comments clearly demonstrate, film was not a straightforward purveyor of a thoroughly standardized international or even national 'mass culture' in the Weimar Republic.[73] Surveys on box-office successes continually showed that German films were preferred to foreign ones. Although there were some big foreign hits that were popular in all areas and among all social groups, these were the exception rather than the rule. Significantly, the most successful US feature films tended to be set in Europe or the ancient world (*Ben Hur, Noah's Ark*), frequently featured European stars like Greta Garbo or Emil Jannings, and sometimes were even given tragic conclusions in place of the 'happy endings' of the original US versions (as with *Anna Karenina* and Chaplin's *Gold Rush*).[74] In addition, the strong, liberated women and 'ghastly love scenes'[75] of many Hollywood films could cause painful offence to small-town audiences, especially in Catholic areas where cinema owners were understandably hesitant to screen anything that might attract accusations of moral turpitude. Such provincial

---

[67] LAB A Pr. Br. Rep. 030, Tit. 74, Nr. 1357; 'Kino-Varietes', *RFB* (29 Nov. 1924), 41; StA Hamburg, Gen IX F 17, Hamburg Polizeibehörde to Stuttgart Polizeipräsidium, 2 Aug. 1930, unpag.; Lydor, 'Unser Publikum wünscht', 17–18.

[68] W. v. Köln, 'Das rheinländische Publikum', *FK* (11 June 1924), 1.

[69] W. Jerven, 'Die Stimme Münchens: Schafft Filme statt Kinos!', *FK* (22 Sept. 1926), 1; also 'Die Provinz und der Berliner Filmgeschmack', *FK* (12 Nov. 1926), 1.

[70] W. Jerven, 'In Münchener Kinos erlauscht', *FK* (27 Dec. 1928), 3.

[71] E. Rehse, 'Amerika in der "Provinz"', *FK* 269 (14 Nov. 1925), 4.

[72] 'Das Reich will keine Fremdsprache treffen', *FK* (2 Aug. 1930), 2.

[73] Also the overall argument of Führer, 'Auf dem Weg'.

[74] See J. Garnacz, 'Hollywood in Germany', in Jung (ed.), *Der deutsche Film*, 167–97; Saunders, *Hollywood*, 150–8; B. P. Schulberg, 'Amerikanischer Tonfilm und europäische Filmstars', *RFB* (26 Oct. 1929), 8; 'Kinomüdigkeit?', *FK* (18 May 1926), 1; 'Amerika, hörst Du die Pfiffe?', *FK* (10 Sept. 1926), 1; H. Correll, 'Tonfilm und Internationalität', *FK* (1 June 1929), suppl. 5.

[75] Rehse, 'Amerika', 4.

prudery was also a problem for German filmmakers, many of them urbane Berliners hardly aware that there were, as one producer put it, 'whole areas in which the powder puff and lipstick are stigmatized as tools of the devil'.[76] As we have already seen, conservatives and church organizations frequently demanded a decentralized censorship system more attuned to the traditional social values that pertained in many areas.

Yet despite such complaints about 'Americanization' and 'Berlinization', the annual production of several hundred films in Germany meant that cinema owners did not have to screen anything that might be regarded as 'smut', and indeed could show films that appealed to regional and local interests. Although Germany was home to the largest film company in Europe, UFA, the vast majority of production companies remained small. At the end of the First World War there were 131 production firms in Germany; by the end of the 1920s there were 424. On average, around one-quarter of all films were made by small firms producing only one film per year, around half by firms annually producing two-to-five films, and the rest by the big names such as UFA, Emelka, National, and Phoebus.[77] Before the advent of sound, the relatively modest production costs meant that films geared for regional audiences could still be profitable. In the mid-1920s the market was awash with 'mediocre films' that cost only around RM 40,000 to 60,000 to make, some of them never intended for nation-wide distribution.[78] Berlin cinemas regularly screened dramas and comedies set in the archetypal *Mietskasernen* milieu (literally 'rental barracks'), that were, because of widespread anti-Berlin sentiments, rarely shown elsewhere. Documentaries parading the charms of individual towns or landscapes were also common components of the cinema programme, and frequently played on regional stereotypes and local allegiances.[79] The fact that such locally oriented films generally flopped at the national level[80] only highlights how the supply of films was not as uniform or culturally standardizing as is sometimes assumed. The decline of such films with the higher production costs of sound pictures was actually perceived as a significant loss after 1929. In 1932 UFA even considered equipping its cinema directors with small cameras for making local films about 'topical matters of special interest to his audience'. Alongside the glamour of the wider world, it was thought that 'the presentation of a small film showing locally familiar events and perhaps even capturing the visitor or his friends and acquaintances on camera certainly exerts a powerful attraction for the public to visit the cinema'.[81]

The ultimate aim of Weimar film producers was, as always, to find the lowest common denominator that would appeal to the widest possible range of

---

[76] 'Großstadt und Provinz', *FK* (22 June 1927), 3.   [77] Figures from Monaco, *Cinema*, 29.
[78] 'Die wahre Krise. Das Fiasko des "Mittelfilms"', *FK* (22 Oct. 1926) 1; R. Ott, 'Das schwarze Jahr', *FK* (1 Jan. 1926), 2.
[79] Führer, 'Auf dem Weg', 758–60.
[80] L. Abrams, 'From Control to Commercialization', *GH* 8 (1990), 288.
[81] BAB R/109I/5370, Ufa-Palast Erfurt to Theaterverwaltung Berlin, 22 Feb. 1932, unpag.

viewers. Yet as a rule they had to approach audiences as they were, pitching their production to part of the film market and hoping for the best. Predicting which films would be hits was hardly possible, 'for the audience is so unpredictable that even most experts fool themselves when it comes to judging the precise strengths of a film in advance'.[82] Deliberate attempts to influence demand through advertising and the promotion of 'stars' were also viewed with scepticism by cinema owners well versed in the day-to-day problems of filling their theatres. As one operator in Berlin remarked, 'simply put, our audience has its own tastes and will not change its mind through any amount of advertising'.[83] Apart from Charlie Chaplin and Greta Garbo, stars appeared to have little or no effect on the popularity of a given film: 'German film suffers from an immeasurable overestimation of its stars.'[84] While it was sometimes possible to lure in the occasional passer-by with a clever poster or slogan, in general such efforts were in vain: 'you can advertise until the fences drip with blood-red paint, make the streets impassable with walking poster-men, send donkeys and apes on to the streets, deafen the whole neighbourhood and put up neon lights until the entire square on which your cinema is located basks in the glow of a volcanic eruption—if the average pedestrian has something else in mind he will not be taken in by your advertising.'[85]

Weimar cinema audiences were, then, 'active' audiences that selected from the broad array of films on offer and thereby (re)produced patterns of social distinction. Indeed, this diversity of audience expectations even went beyond the question of film selection per se. The very act of going to the cinema reflected a range of different motivations. At the most basic level, contemporary observers clearly distinguished between 'cinema audiences' and 'film audiences', the former consisting of people more interested in the cinema itself than in what was playing (the inter-war equivalent of the modern 'couch-potato') and the latter seeking out a particular film based on hearsay or newspaper critiques.[86] Generational differences were also apparent. For many young people the cinema created a unique sense of independence from adult authority amid the anonymity of a darkened projection room, quite apart from the romantic opportunities it afforded them.[87] As always, class was also a crucial factor. According to some observers, many working-class movie-goers went not least in order to escape their intolerably crowded housing conditions.[88] In the winter months, and especially

---

[82] Ott, *Wie führe*, 29.   [83] 'Wie man's macht', 11; also Ott, *Wie führe*, 31–60.

[84] H. Wins, 'Der überschätzte Filmstar', *FK* (1 Oct. 1927), suppl. 3; also H. Marschall, 'Rund um das Tageskino', *RFB* (28 Feb. 1931), suppl. 3; C. Frigo, 'Der Zugkraft der Stars', *RFB* (9 July 1927), 8–9.

[85] G. C. Wallis, 'Die Psychologie des Theaterpublikums', *FK* (7 Aug. 1922), 6.

[86] Erbus, 'Das Kino des guten Films', *RFB* (4 Oct. 1924), 18–20; Paschke, *Tonfilmmarkt*, 52.

[87] 'Die jungen Mädchen und das dunkle Kino!', *FK* (20 June 1925), 5; Funk, *Film*, 54; Moreck, *Sittengeschichte*, 209–15; Altenloh, *Soziologie*, 74; H. Nickol, *Kino und Jugendpflege* (Langensalza, 1919), 10.

[88] F. Henseleit, 'Das notwendige Uebel. Zum Thema Zweischlagersystem', *RFB* (19 Nov. 1927), 14.

during the coal shortages of the immediate post-war years, the prospect of spending two hours in a well-heated room was reason enough to buy a cinema ticket.[89] There is also plenty of evidence that the cinema represented different things to metropolitan versus provincial audiences. While it was little more than an entertaining distraction for many urbanites, for residents of small towns it often represented one of the few opportunities to 'satisfy one's urge for knowledge and keep oneself up to date about political and cultural developments.'[90]

Overall, the preferences and motivations of cinema audiences in 1920s Germany were as diverse as the different social groups from which they were drawn. It was, as some critics pointed out, useless to talk about the 'average' cinema-goer:

This strange creature unites within itself the attitudes and interests of a big-city dweller, a resident of a small town and a village, and indeed in the North of Germany as in the South; it is a pious adherent to both the Catholic and Protestant faiths and at the same time espouses a humanist point of view; it blushes whenever a respectable lady would blush, yet can appreciate certain crudities as a *Stammtisch*-regular. No one has spotted it as yet, but the members of the censorship board know with certainty that in spite of its astounding complexity it is lamentably stupid and completely misunderstands everything that they themselves naturally comprehend and correctly assess.[91]

Fortunately for movie fans, the unceasing efforts of filmmakers to meet these diverse expectations produced a huge and highly differentiated supply of films. Yet, contrary to conventional wisdom, the end-result was not an increasingly homogenized film audience consuming a standardized cultural product, but rather a deeply segregated market that was still visibly divided along the lines of region, milieu, and class. Despite the uniquely broad appeal of the cinema, the structure of film demand in the 1920s clearly reflected the fragmented character of Weimar society.

---

[89] 'Vor neuen Überraschungen?', *LBB* (3 Jan. 1920), 9.   [90] Eger, *Kinoreform*, 9.
[91] Petzet, *Verbotene*, 43.

6

Media Publics Between Fragmentation
and Integration

By collapsing space and transcending time, the modern media of radio, film, recording, and the popular press brought common information and shared experiences to a larger and more diverse audience than ever before. Thanks to these new technologies, cultural artefacts in the early twentieth century could reach geographically dispersed audiences that had previously been separated by the insurmountable obstacle of physical distance. In some respects this was nothing new. The broadening of a reading 'public' had been taking place since the seventeenth century at the latest, and the swift rise in literacy rates during the nineteenth century also meant that it was gradually deepening to include the lower social orders. In Habermas's classic formulation, the idealized liberal 'public sphere' of the eighteenth century consisted of an assemblage of different media and forums for rational debate that was, at least in principle, open to everyone.[1] During the nineteenth century the continual representation of news and events through the press cultivated a new sense of national belonging or 'imagined community' that gradually helped bind together various local cultures and allegiances.[2] The emergence of a national and international public sphere over the past few centuries was thus always a matter of forging stronger links between local or regional networks of communication. Yet what was new about the early part of the twentieth century was both the vast acceleration of this process and the further tapping of the human senses by the new visual and aural media. In conjunction with the growth of the popular press, the technologies of radio, recorded sound, and cinema promised to build broader and more densely integrated networks of communication than ever before—in short, the creation of a 'mass' public sphere.

But just as Habermas's critics have faulted him for downplaying the exclusion of ordinary men and women from the public discourse of the eighteenth century, we can still readily observe mechanisms of segregation well into the twentieth. Of course, the expansion of communications and the widening of a public sphere

[1] J. Habermas, *The Structural Transformation of the Public Sphere* (Cambridge, Mass., 1989).
[2] B. Anderson, *Imagined Communities* (London, 1983); E. Gellner, *Nations and Nationalism* (Cornell, 1983).

are integrally related; the former functions as the infrastructure of the latter, and the latter as a crucial stimulant to the former. Yet, as we have already seen, the mere existence of the mass media does not necessarily create a more uniform mass culture, but can also reinforce social and cultural distinctions. This is precisely why some scholars have criticized the notion of 'the public sphere' itself, emphasizing instead the existence of various 'semi-publics' (*Teilöffentlichkeiten*) based on factors such as class, gender, or religion.[3]

In Wilhelmine and Weimar Germany networks of social and cultural communication were complex and multi-layered. And for this reason, it is useful to conceive of them as an 'ensemble' of different media that together structured the public sphere—not a single or universal forum of exchange, nor a series of discrete 'semi-publics', but rather a mixture of different layers of communication.[4] In practice, this meant that any expansion of the media denoted not only a process of coalescence and standardization but also an element of differentiation. Over time, these ongoing tensions between social integration and cultural fragmentation, the contradictions between shared experience and private pleasure, became ever more pronounced as the media came to play an increasingly prominent role in everyday life. And once again, the different media, because of their unique technological capabilities, specific modes of usage, and particular frameworks of regulation, could exert quite diverse effects within the rapidly changing public sphere.

SOCIAL SEGREGATION AND THE CINEMA

As the flagship 'mass medium' of the inter-war period, film clearly embodied this tension. During the 1920s the universality of its appeal was more than matched by the bewildering diversity of its offerings. Although the printed word reached a far larger number of people, and indeed on a more regular basis, no single publication boasted as wide an audience as a cinema blockbuster. Box-office hits like *Ben Hur* and *Gold Rush* were seen by millions around the world, and the genre of slapstick even managed to transcend popular and elite tastes. These films were novel cultural artefacts, unrivalled in their ability to traverse social and cultural boundaries. But once again, such mega-hits were very much the exception, and were no more representative of the popular cinema than the *BIZ* was of the multitude of German magazines. As Chapter 5 has shown, film as a 'national' or even 'international' phenomenon was still mediated through structures of class, location, and neighbourhood.

---

[3] For an overview, C. Calhoun (ed.), *Habermas and the Public Sphere* (Cambridge, 1992); on 'semi-publics', N. Fraser, 'Rethinking the Public Sphere', *Social Text*, 25/6 (1990), 56–80.

[4] Schildt, 'Jahrhundert'; also Requate, 'Öffentlichkeit'.

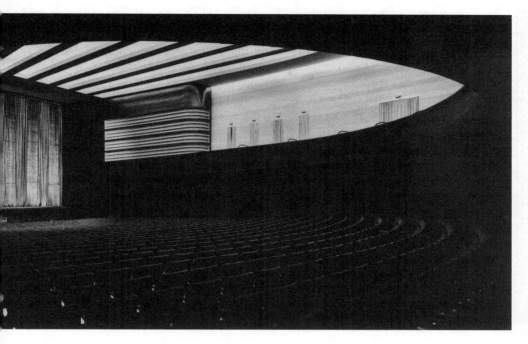

Fig. 8. Cathedrals of cinematic refinement: palatial modern interior of the Universum-Kino on Berlin's Lehninerplatz, by Erich Mendelsohn, 1928. bpk Berlin.

These structures influenced not only what audiences saw, but also how and where they saw it.[5] The large and imposing 'cinema palaces' located at major traffic junctions represented only a small minority of theatres in the 1920s. The vast bulk of cinemas were located outside the city centres and catered to a specific 'regular crowd', whose continual custom was generally regarded as the key to commercial success.[6] According to the cinema operators' journal *Reichsfilmblatt*, most cinemagoers had 'their so-called regular cinema (*Stammkino*), which is usually not far from their flat and which . . . they regularly visit on certain days of the week'.[7] And these 'Stammkinos' were extremely diverse. The deliberate adoption of props and customs from the traditional theatre by cinemas catering to the middle classes (the technically superfluous screen curtain, pauses between 'acts', cloakroom attendants, and opulent décor) stood in stark contrast to the poorly ventilated and often dangerously overcrowded 'Kintopps' of working-class

---

[5] The following discussion is based on C. Ross, 'Mass Culture and Divided Audiences'.

[6] Ott, *Wie führe*, 61–2; 'Halte dein Publikum', *FK* (20 July 1926), 2; A. K. v. Hübbenet, 'Neuzeitliche Kinowerbung', *RFB* (19 Apr. 1930), suppl.

[7] Erbus, 'Das Kino', 18–20; also 'Ein Jahr Kinopolitik', *LBB* (1 Jan. 1927), 22–4.

neighbourhoods, where audiences came and went as they pleased, ate, smoked, and drank as if they were at home, and commonly sat in the aisles if there were no available seats or no room on the bare wooden benches.[8] Unlike the quiet film-palace audiences reminiscent of the bourgeois theatre, the mode of reception in such Kintopps was far more participatory than it is today, as for example in a small Dresden cinema where 'the audience was really into it heart and soul! . . . The whole scene was characterized by laughter that repeated itself frequently, without inhibition, loudly and clearly, and accompanied by more or less pointless remarks.'[9]

Quite apart from their obvious differences with the plush cinema palaces, there was a remarkably wide range of small neighbourhood theatres, as a series of journalistic forays into Berlin's 'Unknown Cinemas' in 1926 vividly illustrates. At one end of the spectrum was a small theatre in the Schlüterstraße in Berlin's West End, a 'clean, quiet, and friendly establishment' with a polite ticket collector, 'excellent' picture projection, and an audience 'with such exemplary conduct. Here one still finds a sense of reverence towards film.' At the other end was a small cinema in a working-class district near Alexanderplatz, where 'the air is so thick you could cut it with a knife; it contains an indefinable jumble of scents in which the smell of fresh laundry is the least recognizable'. Unlike the subdued middle-class patrons in the West End, the audience here was incomparably more boisterous:

The atmosphere in this theatre is as cheerful as can be. It is in no way impaired by the more than modest, dim projection. Absolute delight is aroused by a scene in which Harry [Harry Piel, a popular German actor in the 1920s] kicks a gang of hoodlums one by one in the stomach, twirls them around in the air, and throws them out of the window into the water. The orchestra accompanies the scene with a potpourri from Mozart's *Don Giovanni*, and the audience encourages Harry with shouts like 'look at that!', 'harder' or 'give it to him'.[10] There is a constant to-ing and fro-ing. Whoever feels he has seen enough dons his hat and goes out.[11]

While bourgeois enthusiasts were busy debating such matters of etiquette as whether clapping was appropriate in the cinema,[12] audiences in thousands of local Kintopps were still wholly untamed.

Even when such small neighbourhood cinemas showed the same hits that had first been released months earlier in the premiere theatres, it is highly questionable whether these different screenings can actually be considered the same film. Apart

---

    [8] On overfilling: StA Hamburg Gen IX F19a, *passim*; LAB A Pr. Br. Rep. 030, Tit. 74, Nr. 1384, *passim*.
    [9] 'Ein Besuch im Kleinkino', *FK* (26 May 1928), suppl.; similar is E. Grau, 'Berliner Kinos', (14 Mar. 1923), 2.
    [10] The Berlin dialect of the original is untranslatable: ' "Kiek mal!", "Feste" oder "Jieb ihm Saures".'
    [11] 'Das unbekannte Kino', *FK* (30 Oct. 1926), suppl.
    [12] M. Lyon, 'Claque im Kino?', *FK* (17 May 1924), 2.

from the divergent physical surroundings, the so-called '2-hit system' prevalent in most Kintopps, whereby owners crammed two feature films into a single two-hour showing (usually with a newsreel and several shorts), meant that films were often projected at ridiculous speeds that made actors' movements unnatural and captions all but illegible. Quantity prevailed over quality in many cinemas, whose regular crowd insisted on seeing 'as many acts and kilometres of film as possible in a short amount of time'. Woe betide the operator who refused to cater to such demands: 'many owners know that they cannot under any circumstances shorten the show—for instance by dropping the pauses—by even ten minutes; the audience controls it all with a watch and insists on sitting out its full time.'[13] And this tendency did not stop with 2-hit programmes; in the latter 1920s there were reports of 3- and even 4-hit shows.[14] In cinemas of this ilk, if a film were not already ruined by such projection speeds, the musical accompaniment by a 'discount orchestra' or an amateur duo of violin and old piano often killed off whatever artistic merits remained.[15] By contrast, musical accompaniment in large city-centre cinemas could be of very high standard indeed, led by an experienced conductor and performed by a professional orchestra of up to thirty musicians.[16]

The mistakenly named 'silent' films of the 1920s were not just 'shown' in cinemas: the final product, as it were, was decisively shaped by its visual and acoustic presentation *en locale*.[17] Although historians have tended to forget this, contemporary critics were well aware of it. Some purists actually suggested that the acid test of a 'big film' came not amid the palatial surroundings of a premiere theatre but rather in the Spartan local cinema where, 'in the unadorned presentation of a badly worn-out copy and with the musical accompaniment of an old, out of tune piano—here the big film either survives its ordeal by fire or it does not'.[18] As Kaspar Maase has fittingly put it: 'The film palace, which adopted all of the rituals of the theatre, was not the well-behaved brother of the small working-class neighbourhood cinema, but rather its antithesis.'[19] And such cinematic differences were by no means confined to Berlin. In Cologne too, the 'haze and fumes', the 'perspiration and dubious fragrances', the 'uninhibited remarks of the spectators' were wholly absent 'in the few first-class, refined cinemas'.[20] Even a mid-sized city such as Augsburg boasted a highly diverse cinema landscape, ranging from the central Emelka-Theater with 900 seats and

---

[13] Quotes from H. Bingel, 'Der Vorführer an das Publikum', *FK* (30 Oct. 1926), suppl.; F. Henseleit, 'Das notwendige Uebel', *RFB* (19 Nov. 1927), 14.

[14] 'Unerfreuliches aus der Provinz', *RFB* (24 Sept. 1927), 20.

[15] Horkheimer, 'Badstraße 58'; see also 'Das Tageskino', *FK* (30 Oct. 1926), suppl.

[16] Or even 110 musicians in Berlin's Ufa–Palast am Zoo: *RFB* (28 June 1930), 3. Generally, Ott, *Wie führe*, 64–7; U. Rügner, *Filmmusik in Deutschland zwischen 1924 und 1934* (Hildesheim, 1988).

[17] See also Führer, 'Auf dem Weg', 765.

[18] S. Fingal, 'Großfilm im Kleinkino', *FK* (10 Mar. 1925), 2.

[19] Maase, 'Massenkunst', 47.

[20] BAB R43/I/2497, 'Bericht über das Ergebnis der Kinobesuche in Cöln durch Beauftragte von der Volksgemeinschaft zur Wahrung von Anstand und guter Sitte', 27 Feb. 1920, fo. 260.

a twelve-piece orchestra to the modest 255-seat Metropol-Lichtspiele on the outskirts of town, all the way to the Hofbräu-Lichtspiele, which, as the name suggested, was located in a pub.[21]

Instead of positing Weimar cinema as a vehicle of a new standardizing 'mass culture', it is more useful to view it as a constituent part of a local 'Quartiersöffentlichkeit', or 'neighbourhood public', which itself helped structure the various social and cultural milieus that have attracted so much scholarly attention for the Weimar period.[22] The small cinemas with their 'regular crowd' were in this sense an integral part of the neighbourhoods in which they were located. Especially in working-class districts, where film often functioned as 'relaxation, amusement, "education", and summer holiday', the screening of a hit film was the talk of the neighbourhood.[23] In contrast to respondents from middle-class areas, most residents of proletarian districts could immediately and correctly answer what film was currently playing in which cinema. This sense of neighbourhood belonging was acutely sensed by bourgeois cinema reformers during their expeditions into working-class neighbourhoods. When, for instance, the 'Society for the Maintenance of Decency and Morality' in Cologne visited a range of neighbourhood cinemas in 1919–20 they were 'gazed at with annoyance, viewed as not belonging there, and often loudly criticized'.[24] Although the feverish construction of new city-centre amusements during the 1920s can be interpreted as a geographical centralization of leisure and entertainment, much of the evidence suggests that they did not cause a dramatic migration away from neighbourhood venues.[25] Not only did their pomp and formality erect a threshold of social inhibition, but the more expensive tickets and additional travel costs also made such ventures rare. Operators found that people were generally prepared to travel only for exceptional films, and for the most part waited until films came to their regular cinema.[26] As one commentator put it in 1930, among the 'muddled and divided cinema audiences' in Berlin, 'every cinema-quarter actually has its own individual character and success or failure turns out differently in each case'.[27] Clearly, any talk of a 'homogenous metropolitan audience' is well off the mark.[28]

---

[21] F. Schülein, 'Augsburger Kinostreife', *RFB* (2 Mar. 1929), 12–13.

[22] See A. v. Saldern, *Häuserleben* (Bonn, 1995), 16; also Fritzsche, *Reading*, 249. The mass media are hardly mentioned in the many studies on social and political milieus in the Weimar Republic: S. Weichlein, *Sozialmilieus und politische Kultur in der Weimarer Republik* (Göttingen, 1996); N. Back, *'Zeitgemäßer Fortschritt'* (Frankfurt a. M., 1998); M. Kittel, *Provinz zwischen Reich und Republik* (Munich, 2000); T. Adam, *Arbeitermilieu und Arbeiterbewegung in Leipzig 1871–1933* (Cologne, 1999).

[23] Quote and following point from Guttmann, *Nachfrage*, 32.

[24] BAB R43/I/2497, 'Bericht über das Ergebnis der Kinobesuche in Cöln', fo. 260.

[25] Cf. Abrams, *Workers' Culture*, 178.

[26] 'Wie man's macht', *RFB* (10 Mar. 1928), 10–11; also Erbus, 'Das Kino'; Paschke, *Tonfilmmarkt*, 145.

[27] 'Der Kinobesuch an den "4 Sonntagen"', *FK* (27 Dec. 1930), 1.

[28] So the misleading formulation of Kracauer, 'Kult der Zerstreuung', 313.

Against this background, the widespread notion that the consumption of film by diverse social groups necessarily contributed to the gradual dissolution of milieu boundaries in the 1920s is not very convincing. Indeed, it is doubtful not only on the basis of what was happening in the cinemas, but also how these milieus are conceived.[29] Such views are based, at least implicitly, on a typological conceptualization of a 'social milieu' as a more or less discrete social space that, while perhaps useful as an analytical tool, obscures the fact that milieu boundaries are in practice highly permeable, overlap in numerous, cross-cutting ways, and are therefore characterized by a mixture of openness and exclusion. As a rule, social identities are not 'closed' and monolithic but are rather a kaleidoscope of 'partial' identities that shift in accordance with different social situations. From this perspective, the supposed ability of the mass media to erode milieu boundaries and act as a socially homogenizing force appears even more questionable. For even when such permeable social membranes were crossed—say, in the case of the *grande dame* seeing the same film in the same cinema as her cleaning lady—this is not necessarily tantamount to a blurring of social boundaries.

How such 'situative' identities worked in the context of Weimar cinema can be illustrated by a 1925 interview with a young housemaid working in an exclusive neighbourhood in western Berlin. Although she usually went to her regular cinema, where the owner knew her by name and where she felt very much at home, 'she also greatly enjoys going to a big cinema, though at the most on a Sunday after she has dressed herself up. And someone has to go with her, preferably her boyfriend. That way the 50 marks [her monthly wage] stay untouched, and it looks better too.' These occasional outings to a 'big' cinema were more of an event than a visit to her regular cinema, and required adopting a totally different demeanour:

Admittedly, she does not feel as comfortable among all of these distinguished people as in her small cinema . . . All of the women look like madame and all of them have haughty expressions. No one knows anyone else and no one says to her at the door 'Good-bye, did you enjoy the show, Miss Anna?' Here you cannot even properly laugh. You don't dare let out a loud noise because no one else does either. And if one slips out you feel embarrassed about it afterwards. One can occasionally act refined on a Sunday, but all of the time—for heaven's sake, that's too strenuous.[30]

Although even the young housemaid could occasionally revel in the glamour of the cinema palace, she understandably felt out of place among 'all of these distinguished people' and was, more importantly, quite aware that it was no more than wearing a different public face.

The intention here is not to exaggerate the social segregation of Weimar cinema audiences or to downplay the important shift that the expansion of film

---

[29] A point emphasized by Führer, Hickethier, and Schildt, 'Öffentlichkeit', 31.
[30] 'Kinobesucher: Das Dienstmädchen sagt. . .', *FK* (10 Oct. 1925), 9.

and other mass media implied. However differentiated the new 'mass cultural' audiences may have been, their very creation and existence was, as some scholars have emphasized,[31] itself significant insofar as they constituted new collectivities that differed at least to some extent from those associated with traditional and more rigidly class-bound leisure pursuits. Yet as Pierre Bourdieu pointed out long ago, even in the context of a widely shared set of cultural goods, social distinction is still produced through their variegated appropriation by different groups.[32] It is thus significant for our purposes here that people tended to view films in their neighbourhoods, and moreover consumed them not just as anonymous individuals within a 'mass' audience but rather as members of a social group that existed outside the cinema as well. In this sense, the rather predictable finding that the overwhelming majority of youth visits to the cinema in the early 1930s were undertaken in groups (usually with friends, occasionally with family members) is by no means trivial: such collective attendance not only affected the reception of a film in an immediate sense (cinema owners regularly complained about the disruption caused by rowdy groups of young people), but also influenced how cultural meanings were ascribed to a film through discussion about it afterwards.[33]

The point, then, is that film in 1920s Germany did not exert a straightforward or easily predictable effect, but was rather mediated through older structures of class, neighbourhood, and milieu, which profoundly affected its social impact and how it was experienced.[34] This becomes even clearer if we consider the far-reaching changes that occurred during the early 1930s, as both social structures in general and the film industry in particular came under immense strain with the onset of the Depression and the technological changes of sound conversion.

The advent of the sound film, which first came to Germany in 1929, was nothing short of revolutionary for the film industry. It signalled a fundamental restructuring not only of production and projection techniques, but also of the web of financial relations that sustained this high-risk business.[35] There can, moreover, be little doubt that the sound film brought about a certain 'levelling of cinemas among one another' and made the experience of film more uniform.[36] The conversion to sound over the course of the early 1930s signalled the death-knell for the '2-hit system' by making it impossible to vary projection speeds and by making a double-feature unprofitable given the much higher rental fees. Higher production costs also meant that many small producers'

---

[31] LeMahieu, *Culture*, 17–26; generally, Schwartz, *Spectacular*; Fritzsche, *Reading*.

[32] P. Bourdieu, *Distinction* (London, 1984); id., 'Structures, Habitus, Practices', in *The Logic of Practice* (Cambridge, 1990), 52–65.

[33] Funk, *Film*, 60. Only 17% of boys and 6% of girls reported going to the cinema alone.

[34] The same was true in the USA and Britain: L. Cohen, *Making a New Deal* (Cambridge, 1990), 99–158; R. McKibbin, *Classes and Cultures* (Oxford, 1998), 419–56.

[35] Generally, Mühl-Benninghaus, *Ringen*; also P. Bächlin, *Der Film als Ware* (Frankfurt a. M., 1975); Spiker, *Film*.

[36] Paschke, *Tonfilmmarkt*, 132–3.

days were numbered, and approximately halved the number of films on the market within a year or so.[37] Quite obviously, the live musical accompaniment that varied so dramatically was also brought to an end, which meant not only greater uniformity between cinematic presentations but also unemployment for thousands of cinema musicians.[38]

Yet arguably the key difference brought about by sound film was a dramatic reduction in audience participation. Once films began to speak, spectators fell silent. There were no more captions allowing viewers to follow a plot amidst noisy surroundings, and as a result the very nature of film reception became more passive, individualized, and disciplined. As one commentator lamented in 1931, whereas 'with silent films people could cough as much as there were colds in the room, the sound film has now done away with this final liberty'.[39] Just as the rowdy theatre crowds of the eighteenth century were transformed into the silent and reverent audiences of the mid- and late nineteenth century, the sound film largely killed off the spontaneity of the Kintopp, and within a short period of time brought about a remarkable convergence in the mode of reception across the social spectrum.[40]

Due to the fundamental changes this implied for film consumption, it is, however, easy to overdramatize the shift. The change was, for one thing, not immediate, and so long as the smaller cinemas could not afford to convert to sound (which generally took one to three years) it actually accentuated divisions. Small establishments still needed to offer an attractive programme in order to compete with the sound cinemas, and since the fees for silent films were dropping anyway, the short-term effect was actually an expansion of the 'multi-hit' programme.[41] Even among the cinemas that quickly converted to sound there remained significant differences, and not only in terms of furnishings and ticket price. Because the smaller cinemas generally received second-rate copies for projection, both visual and acoustic quality were significantly reduced. Indeed, the abysmal sound in many cinemas was widely bemoaned in the early years, and represented a decisive step backwards in the eyes of silent-film enthusiasts.[42]

In addition, the sound film had very different effects at the national and international levels. Although it meant greater uniformity of supply and reception within Germany, it simultaneously brought about a 'de-internationalization'

---

[37] Jason (ed.), *Handbuch 1935/36*, 105; on rental fees: Paschke, *Tonfilmmarkt*, 127; on the '2-hit system': 'Eine Abstimmung gegen zwei Schlager', *FK* (7 Sept. 1931), 1.

[38] W. Winnig, 'Kinomusik-Tonfilm', *RFB* (28 June 1930), 3; also Mühl-Benninghaus, *Ringen*, 52–3.

[39] 'Die Revolte des Publikums', *FK* (30 Jan. 1931), 1.

[40] On earlier theatre audiences: R. Dreßler, *Von der Schaubühne zur Sittenschule* (Berlin, 1993); Sennett, *Fall*. For similar developments in the USA: D. Crafton, *The Talkies* (Berkeley, 1997).

[41] 'Die katastrophale Lage der Kleinkinos', *RFB* (15 Feb. 1930), 1; '2-Schlagersystem wieder in Blüte', *FK* (16 Oct. 1931), 1; 'Kinos nördlich vom Alexanderplatz', *FK* (6 Sept. 1930), suppl.

[42] V. Klemperer, *Leben*, ii. 2, 701–2 (4 Apr. 1931); 'Schlechter Ton führt zu Sturmszenen', *FK* (6 July 1931), 1; F. Staar, 'Tonfilmgeschäft und Publikum', *RFB* (7 June 1930), suppl.

of film. German talkies or German-language versions of foreign films (which Hollywood already stopped making in 1931 because of the high costs) were by far the most successful. Synchronized films performed poorly at the box-office, and original versions in foreign languages, even with subtitles, were almost completely rejected. The proportion of foreign films thus dropped dramatically after 1929, and US-firm labels on film advertisements actually proved counterproductive among the bulk of cinema-goers who wanted to hear their own language. The suggestion that the introduction of the sound film strengthened Hollywood's lead in Germany is simply incorrect.[43]

The fact that the advent of the sound film coincided with acute economic depression inevitably affected its introduction and social impact. In terms of film content, it is worth noting that the tide of political disaffection was clearly reflected in German film production of the early 1930s. Both contemporaries and historians have discerned a pronounced conservative-nationalist shift from 1931 onwards, two years *before* the impact of Nazi censorship.[44] At a more fundamental level, falling wages and rising unemployment caused a sharp drop in cinema attendance during the early 1930s, as the zenith of 353 million admissions in 1928 shrank to only 239 million in 1932.[45] Ticket prices fell as well, though this varied dramatically in different regions and among different kinds of cinema.[46] Whereas the large cinema palaces with their limited competition and relatively well-off patrons felt comparatively little pressure to lower prices, most smaller cinemas faced intense competition and tended to serve groups more adversely affected by the crisis. These pressures triggered off price wars in some hard-hit areas, where tickets could go as low as RM 0.30 or even RM 0.20 before some form of price regulation was agreed.[47] Yet despite these unprecedented commercial pressures, the overall effect on the introduction of the talkie was ambiguous. While it made the costly transition to sound more difficult, the higher profits among sound cinemas—one of the few branches of the economy that was actually growing in 1930—simultaneously increased the pressure to convert. And while attendance dropped overall, rising unemployment actually improved business for some small 'silent' cinemas by making their inexpensive

[43] Cf. Peukert, *The Weimar Republic* (London, 1991), 171. On the decline of foreign films: Jason (ed.), *Handbuch 1935/36*, 106–11; 'Mitteldeutschland lehnt den Tonfilm ab', *RFB* (14 Dec. 1929), 18; C. Riechmann, 'Tonfilm und Kinogeschäft', *RFB* (7 June 1930), 2; 'Münchner Tonfilmdebatte: Publikum verlangt Dialogfilme, lehnt aber Synchronisierung ab', *FK* (12 Mar. 1930), suppl.; H. Simon, 'Tonfilmenttäuschungen—Warum?', *FK* (10 May 1930), suppl.; 'Das Reich will keine Fremdsprache treffen', *FK* (2 Aug. 1930), 2.

[44] H. Korte, *Der Spielfilm und das Ende der Weimarer Republik* (Göttingen, 1998), 121, 423–6; Jelavich, *Alexanderplatz*, 156–90.

[45] Jason (ed.), *Handbuch 1935/36*, 28.

[46] BAB R/109I/5370, 'Vorlage zu einem Vortrag über die Eintrittspreispolitik der Ufa', 7 Dec. 1931, 2.

[47] 'Mannheimer Eintrittspreise', *FK* (25 Apr. 1931), suppl.; 'Die Eintrittspreise', *FK* (30 Apr. 1931), 1; 'Köln regelt Eintrittspreise. Vorbildliche Geschlossenheit', *FK* (5 June 1931), 1; Mühl-Benninghaus, *Ringen*, 197.

TABLE 5. *Cinema admissions in Germany, 1925–1935* (in millions)

1925/6	1926/7	1927/8	1928/9	1929/30	1930/1	1931/2	1932/3	1933/4	1934/5
271.5	332.4	337.4	352.5	328.3	290.4	273.1	238.4	247.0	287.9

Source: Jason (ed.), *Handbuch 1935/36*, 161.

showings more attractive to impecunious customers and by enabling them to fill seats from as early as 10 a.m.[48]

As was also the case during the economic crisis of 1922–3, there was increasing talk of an audience shift after 1929. While many previous cinema-goers were frequenting cheaper cinemas and/or attending less often, it was often remarked that 'the sound film has brought in new customers who showed no interest in silent films'.[49] Talkies possessed a novelty value of their own, especially in the case of vaunted hits like *Das Flötenkonzert von Sanssouci*, the first sound film for over half of those who saw it in the Rhineland, among them many who had never been to the cinema at all.[50] It generally appears that the middle-classes became more prominent in the cinemas as the working classes were harder hit by the crisis. It also seems clear that the audience shift intensified the existing crisis of the traditional theatre. Whereas earlier fears that the cinema would kill off the theatre had proven unfounded, based as they were on the erroneous assumption that their audiences significantly overlapped, both the heightened aesthetic appeal of the sound film and its modest price worked very much in favour of it siphoning off theatre visitors under the pecuniary pressures of the economic crisis.[51]

Along with this overall audience shift, mass unemployment also contributed to a new segmentation of cinema audiences *within* hard-hit areas. Although many of the jobless apparently continued to visit the cinema,[52] they tended to go to inexpensive matinees that became increasingly common as unemployment spread. The price differences between matinees and evening programmes grew starker than ever before, as did the new audience divisions this caused. Since the unemployed had plenty of time and little money, it made sense to fill up the early matinees by slashing prices and to leave evening prices much higher for those with money but no free time in the afternoons.[53] The heavily frequented

[48] C. Riechmann, 'Tonfilm und Kinogeschäft', *RFB* (7 June 1930), 2; F. S., 'Im Tageskino', *RFB* (11 Apr. 1931), suppl.

[49] Riechmann, 'Tonfilm', 2.   [50] 'Das Kino sieht neue Besucher', *FK* (12 Jan. 1931), 1.

[51] On the theatre crisis, Führer, 'German Cultural'; 'Theater-Intendanten nehmen Stellung zum Tonfilm', *FK* (25 Oct. 1930), suppl. On cinema audiences, Paschke, *Tonfilmmarkt*, 40–1; Mühl-Benninghaus, *Ringen*, 199.

[52] This impression is conveyed by the film press and also suggested by earlier findings that expenditure on 'amusements and other social occasions' (under which cinema was categorized) dropped less than overall expenditure among the unemployed: Statistisches Reichsamt, *Lebenshaltung*, 79.

[53] BAB R/109I/5370, 'Vorlage zu einem Vortrag über die Eintrittspreispolitik der Ufa', 7 Dec. 1931, 4, 7.

gratis morning shows organized by local trade unions further contributed to the division of cinema audiences along the lines of those with or without work. Admittedly, the widespread introduction of unemployment discounts for evening shows limited this segmentation. But jobless visitors were often treated as second-class customers by suspicious proprietors well aware of how common it was to loan out the identity card entitling one to a reduction.[54]

Taken together, all of these changes during the early 1930s reflected the erosion of the older structures that had shaped the social role of the cinema over the preceding decades. The high costs of making sound films and the concurrent decline in cinema-going meant that the number of films produced and distributed in Germany (as elsewhere) decreased dramatically, which in turn reduced the differences between individual cinemas' programmes. At the same time, the rise of the sound film and the displacement of live music meant that the actual presentation of films also became more uniform. Amidst all of these changes there were, of course, many underlying continuities that should not be lost from view. Patterns of cinema-going still reflected—and themselves helped to produce—social distinctions in German society. The cinema landscape in Germany remained highly variegated, with the plush 'cinema palaces' still functioning as paragons of cinematic edification amidst the thousands of cramped and seedy neighbourhood cinemas. Yet overall, the shifts of the early 1930s in the number of available films, the nature of audience uptake, and the character of cinematic presentation made the act of film-viewing more uniform than it had previously been. Although contemporary critics and subsequent historians have often dated the breakthrough of a new, socially levelling 'mass culture' in the 1920s, it was the changes of the early 1930s that marked the more significant watershed in the social history of the German cinema.

THE FRACTURED PRESS

Throughout the Weimar period the print press was also characterized by a fundamental tension between the processes of standardization and fragmentation. Despite the immense diversity of the German press, the years after the First World War were marked by an acceleration of news centralization and commercial concentration that tempered this variation.

At the basic level of newspaper circulation, the period after 1914 witnessed a clear trend towards fewer, larger periodicals. As a rule the wartime increase in circulation (of around 15–20 per cent) tended to benefit large newspapers rather than small ones, many of which stagnated or went out of business. At the

---

[54] 'In München: Kino der Arbeitslosen', *FK* (17 Jan. 1931), 1; 'Ermäßigungen für Erwerbslose. Ein stark umstrittenes Thema', *FK* (27 Dec. 1930), suppl.; H. Herzfeld, 'Kinobesuch und Erwerbslosigkeit', *RFB* (1 Aug. 1931), suppl.

same time, the more nationalistic newspapers benefited more than the politically moderate. Whereas the *Vossische Zeitung*, which adopted a more nationalist tone during the war, saw its circulation nearly double, the centrist-liberal *BT* grew by less than 10 per cent and the socialist *Vorwärts* actually shrank from 154,000 to 100,000 (though this was partially due to a party schism). In terms of average newspaper size, wartime growth was in fact little more than an acceleration of ongoing trends. Whereas only 10 per cent of newspapers printed over 5,000 copies in 1885, by 1914 it was 35 per cent.[55] As for the number of different titles, however, the war clearly marked a new period of contraction. Of the roughly 4,200 papers in circulation in 1914, around 500 to 700 were discontinued by the end of the war, and by 1927 the total number lay just over 3,200. This figure then remained more or less stable until 1933, when the new press controls imposed by the Nazi regime reduced the number of newspapers once again. In the meantime, German magazines experienced a similar fate. After decades of immense growth, the 6,421 titles circulating in 1914 were roughly halved over the following decade of war and inflation. Although magazine figures had bounced back by 1929 (7,303 titles), they too tailed off once again during the depression and the Nazi takeover.[56] This process of commercial concentration would surely have gone further had the wartime Supreme Command not arranged for the semi-official news agencies to give small newspapers as much information as possible. A similar arrangement continued after the war as well, as the new government effectively subsidized small newspapers as distribution outlets for its news agencies.[57]

But if the central news agencies helped to keep many provincial papers afloat, their growth still amounted to a concentration of information sources. By the 1920s the semi-official Wolff'sche Telegraphen-Büro and Hugenberg's Telegraphen-Union supplied the lion's share of news to Germany's small and mid-sized papers, often in the form of special matrices that did not require any typesetting.[58] This represented a considerable savings for small papers, many of which wrote their own material only for the local pages and relied completely on the matrix services for their political sections. But it came at a considerable price. For one thing, it accelerated the disappearance of regional dialect in German newspapers, which by the 1920s was largely confined to a few South German papers.[59] Moreover, as Georg Bernhard complained, 'a respectable part of these matrix concerns is in the hands of certain nationalistic circles', which meant that much of the apparent diversity of small newspapers 'exists only officially'.[60] The simultaneous trend towards syndicated columns and the

---

[55] Stöber, *Die erfolgverführte*, 81; id., *Pressegeschichte*, 161.
[56] Meier, *Zwischen*, 155; Stöber, *Pressegeschichte*, 159, 164.
[57] Bernhard, 'Die Deutsche Presse', 70–1.
[58] On the WTB, D. Basse, *Wolff's Telegraphisches Bureau 1849 bis 1933* (Munich, 1991).
[59] A. Franke, 'Die Mundarten in der Presse', *ZV* 27 (17 Sept. 1926), 1999–2000.
[60] Bernhard, 'Die Deutsche Presse', 73. The awkward English translation is in the original.

existence of so-called *Kopfblätter* (local newspapers published as sub-editions of a larger paper, merely with a different title and local section) ran in much the same direction.

The growing influence of these 'nationalist circles' in many ways symbolized the process of commercial concentration during and after the war. The roots of these developments reached back to around 1900, as the large urban markets became saturated and publishers began to shift their tactics towards buying shares in pre-existing papers or purchasing them outright. Independent newspapers were thus tapping outside financial support well before 1914. But it was the structural crisis brought on by the war, in particular the high price of paper and the collapse of advertising revenue, that forced many newspapers—in spite of rising circulation—to seek new financial partners in order to stay in business. By the end of the war the publishing branch as a whole was in financial difficulties. This meant that struggling papers were less likely to be bought up by publishing firms, which had their own problems and usually lacked sufficient capital for such purchases, but rather had to be bailed out by companies from outside the newspaper industry—usually in heavy industry.[61]

This was where Alfred Hugenberg and industrialists such as Hugo Stinnes stepped in. Their motive in buying up stricken newspapers was not primarily to make money but to gain political influence. In this regard they differed completely from the hard-nosed business approach of August Scherl, whose media concern, including the *Berliner Lokal-Anzeiger*, became one of the first parts of Hugenberg's press empire in 1916.[62] By this time Hugenberg had already founded the advertising bureau Auslands GmbH with financial help from various Ruhr magnates. In 1917 it was recast into the ALA, or Allgemeine Anzeigen GmbH, as a direct competitor to Rudolf Mosse's advertising bureau and a means of influencing the press via the placement of ads. In the same year he also founded the VERA Verlagsanstalt GmbH as a consultancy for small papers. One of its principle services was to secure a constant supply of ads and news, naturally via ALA and the Telegraphen-Union, the latter of which also came under Hugenberg's control in 1916. After the war the buying spree continued. In 1922 Hugenberg set up the Altertum Kredit-AG and Mutuum Darlehens-AG as a means of buying shares in newspapers, as well as the Wipro (Wirtschaftsstelle der Provinzpresse), a matrix service that provided literally all one needed for the entire political section of a provincial paper. In 1925 Wipro was joined by the newly acquired Deutsche Reichs-Korrespondenz, an established news agency whose previously liberal-democratic orientation was gradually shifted to the right.[63] By the middle of the 1920s the Telegraphen-Union had become the

---

[61] On the post-war publishing crisis, Hoser, *Die politischen*, ii. 795–856.

[62] Requate, 'Zwischen', 174–6.

[63] H. Holzbach, *Das 'System Hugenberg'* (Stuttgart, 1981), 259–85; D. Guratzsch, *Macht durch Organisation* (Düsseldorf, 1974).

second largest news agency behind the WTB, and supplied material to around half of all newspapers in Germany.

Hugenberg's empire therefore symbolized not only the concentration of the German press but also its increasing penetration by business interests keen to enhance their political clout. The fact that commercial companies were exerting more and more control over newspapers was yet another blow against the traditional distinction between the 'Geschäftspresse' and 'Gesinnungspresse'. As Jörg Requate has suggested, in many ways it turned this distinction on its head, for it was ironically the archetypal 'commercial' publishers Ullstein, Mosse, and Huck—not the traditional 'conviction press'—that most successfully resisted the influence of heavy industry and retained the greatest degree of editorial independence.[64]

This was quite simply because the popular, non-party newspapers were the most commercially successful segment of the press. As we have seen, the big commercial dailies were far ahead of their rivals in keeping up with broader cultural trends—namely, the prioritization of pleasurable 'browsing' over the mere acquisition of information. But this growing consumerist orientation among readers raised a fundamental question: could the press really exert as much political influence as many people thought? Was the attempt by Hugenberg and other industrialists to buy political influence via the press a poor investment?

Measuring the influence of a medium on its users is notoriously difficult. But for what it is worth, there are some indications that newspaper reading had less and less to do with political orientation during the Weimar period. One need only compare the very different fates of particular papers and the parties with which they were implicitly or explicitly affiliated. Contrary to conventional wisdom, paper sales were a thoroughly unreliable guide to political leanings.[65] Indeed, during the Weimar years there was a stark *incongruence* between market share and electoral results. At the national level, the circulation of SPD- and KPD-affiliated papers always lagged far behind their electoral success, as did the miniscule circulation of the Nazi press. By contrast, the circulation of left-liberal newspapers far exceeded the number of votes cast for the centrist parties, and remained buoyant even when electoral support for the DDP/Staatspartei and DVP collapsed in the early 1930s. Much the same can be said of the nationalist-conservative press, whose circulation declined only modestly compared to the plummeting electoral support for the DNVP from 1924 to 1932. This incongruence was most visible in the capital, where the liberal Jewish publishing houses of Ullstein and Mosse held over 50 per cent of the Berlin market, or 1.3 million readers, while fewer than 10 per cent of Berliners voted for the DDP, the party to which these publishers were closest. By contrast, the meteoric rise of support for the NSDAP in the early 1930s made only a faint impression on overall circulation figures. The Berlin edition of

---

[64] Requate, 'Zwischen', 182–3.   [65] Cf. Mende, *Sensationalismus*, 48.

the *Völkischer Beobachter* actually had to be temporarily discontinued in March 1931, seven months after the Nazis' big breakthrough in the September 1930 Reichstag elections.[66] In Munich too there was little correlation between voting patterns and newspaper reading. Although the *Völkischer Beobachter* was more successful here than in Berlin, the two dominant local newspapers, the *Münchner Neueste Nachrichten* and Huck's *Münchner Zeitung*, still accounted for around half of the entire local market, despite the fact that the parties they backed, the DVP and DDP/Staatspartei, performed miserably at the ballot-box after 1928, sinking below 3 per cent of the vote by 1932.[67] Calculated in terms of subscriptions per voter, the fortunes of newspapers and their affiliated parties differed wildly between the competing political camps. This was especially evident in the Reichstag elections of 1932, when the 'liberal-bourgeois' press tallied 8.2 subscribers for every comparable vote, national-conservative papers 1.4, Centre Party papers 0.3, SPD papers 0.2, KPD papers 0.1, and National Socialist papers only 0.04 subscriptions for every vote cast for the Nazis.[68]

How can one explain this conspicuous variance? As some contemporaries recognized, one reason was that roving voters kept buying a particular paper out of habit. Subscribers did not necessarily agree with the political views of their daily paper, and would sometimes supplement it with something closer to their own opinions, nonetheless continuing with their old standby for its familiar layout and content.[69] But the broader explanation is that, as we have seen, political papers were becoming increasingly unsaleable to a more consumer-oriented public. By the 1920s the act of newspaper reading was about far more than informing one's political views, and this gradual shift in reading habits meant that newspapers became increasingly detached from voting behaviour, at least in terms of party affiliation.[70] By forging a reader–paper bond through entertainment rather than argument, newspapers were appealing to consumer values and expectations that transcended many of the social and political barriers dividing German society.

The combination of an increasingly consumerist orientation with the ongoing process of commercial concentration undoubtedly encouraged a degree of 'standardization' within the German press of the 1920s. More papers shared the same wire reports and catered to the same general interests than was the case during previous decades. Yet it is important to keep the changes in perspective, for many factors in the 1920s pulled in precisely the opposite direction. Despite all of the empire-building and buy-outs, the sheer span of the daily press in Weimar Germany was still enormous. In the early 1930s one-third of all

---

[66] See Fulda, 'Press', 35–7.

[67] Hoser, *Die politischen*, ii. 981–6; Requate, 'Zwischen', 183–4. On electoral results: J. Falter, *Hitlers Wähler* (Munich, 1991); R. Hamilton, *Who Voted for Hitler?* (Princeton, 1982); T. Childers, *The Nazi Voter* (Chapel Hill, NC, 1983).

[68] Figures from M. Bestler, 'Das Absinken der parteipolitischen Führungstätigkeit der deutschen Tageszeitungen', Diss., Berlin (1941), 109.

[69] Bernhard, 'Die Deutsche Presse', 63.   [70] Fulda, 'Press', 37.

newspapers still had a circulation under 2,000, and another third between 2,000 and 5,000. Only 1 per cent, or around forty papers, exceeded 100,000 copies.[71] Of course, the large newspapers accounted for a disproportionate share of total circulation. Yet the survival of so many small newspapers nonetheless highlights their continued importance within their local areas. Moreover, the broad array of sectarian papers and the milieus in which they were anchored represented distinctive networks of communication in a starkly polarized society. This was, as noted earlier, most observable among the socialist, communist, and Catholic press, though it was by no means confined to them. True, there were areas of overlap between such networks: for instance, the many communist workers who turned to Ullstein's *Berliner Morgenpost* for a little light amusement. But it is telling that the same workers were far less likely to buy a Hugenberg paper like *Tag*, let alone a conservative broadsheet like the *Deutsche Zeitung*, whose readers operated within a totally different universe.[72] Moreover, these diverse networks became increasingly antagonistic in the political hothouse of the latter 1920s and early 1930s. As the communications scholar Emil Dovifat remarked in 1930, the deep fragmentation of the press meant that there were many different 'publics' in Germany: ' "Public opinion" is dead. I mean the concept, not its content.'[73]

From this point of view, the centralization of news services, the concentration of ownership, and the subtle convergence of styles and formats did not so much *overcome* the fragmentation of the German newspaper market as *overlay* it. A single newspaper, whether a big metropolitan daily or a small provincial sub-edition, could simultaneously operate at a number of different levels. Put differently, it could include multiple layers of 'public sphere' within its pages: on one level, local news or a particular editorial slant catering to a certain geographical or political group, and on another, the provision of entertainment and human-interest stories that exerted a more universal appeal. In this sense, the levelling tendencies of the Weimar press were still mediated through the structures of locality and milieu. As was also the case with film, most consumers experienced the 'mass press' in a manner that was tailored for them.

Moreover, the fact that reader expectations went well beyond the purpose of informing political views did not entail a total depoliticization of paper content. Although the aim of maximizing newspaper sales had long relied on a 'non-partisan' stance, there were always pressures pulling in the opposite direction. For example, when Ullstein launched the *Berliner Morgenpost* in 1898 it sought to pre-empt any accusations of political fence-sitting by advertising itself as 'partisan, not party follower' (*Parteinehmer—nicht Parteigänger*).[74] After the upheavals of 1918–19 there was strong pressure to take a stance on current

---

[71] *Handbuch der deutschen Tagespresse*, 25*.   [72] Fulda, 'Press', 22–4, 38–40, 57.
[73] E. Dovifat, 'Die öffentliche Meinung' (1930), repr. in B. Sösemann (ed.), *Emil Dovifat* (Berlin, 1998), 493.
[74] A. Bernstein, 'Berliner Morgenpost', 147–90.

political issues, which meant that the boundary between the 'Gesinnungspresse' and 'Geschäftspresse' was rapidly eroding from *both* directions—that is, the commercial press was also becoming more political, not just the other way around. In the politically charged atmosphere of Weimar Germany, publishers increasingly needed to print clear political views—not necessarily consistent or following a single party line—in order to sell well. Once again, profit and politics were not exclusive alternatives.[75] Of course, the so-called 'non-political' papers had always adopted a certain political tone, for the most part a populist, Fatherland-oriented conservatism. In the Weimar years the label 'non-partisan' (*parteilos*), which was bestowed on around half of all titles, included many papers openly hostile towards the Republic.[76] By this time the supposedly 'non-political' press seems to have *heightened* the politicization of its readers through its more sensational tone. Tabloids in particular found that politics could be made very entertaining indeed.[77] As the journalist Gerhard Schultze-Pfaelzer remarked in 1928: 'The sensational papers in particular have entered the fray of opinions with remarkable effect. Even if they often hide their true faces behind a veil of gossip, in certain decisive cases they nonetheless come to the fore all the more crassly with their propaganda.'[78]

Indeed, if one considers the market for tabloids it is possible to discern a far closer correlation between voting patterns and newspaper sales than a narrow focus on the party press would suggest. As Bernhard Fulda has recently argued, the most successful Berlin tabloids were clearly those that espoused 'anti-system' politics, whether from the Left or Right. Interestingly, their growth ran parallel to the combined electoral fortunes of the anti-democratic KPD, NSDAP, and DNVP.[79] Whereas the strong showing of the KPD in Berlin contrasted with the stagnation of *Rote Fahne*, it was closely paralleled by the growth of the communist-oriented tabloid *Welt am Abend*, published by the Münzenberg concern. At the same time, the lack of a socialist-oriented tabloid in the capital (the boulevard-style *Abend* never really came off) may help explain why the SPD's electoral performance in Berlin was below Reich average. On the Right, the success of Hugenberg's *Nachtausgabe* seems to have cushioned the DNVP's fall in the 1930 elections in Berlin, which was not as precipitate as in most of Germany. And in the meantime, the shift to 'fundamental opposition' by the *Nachtausgabe* (as the rest of the Hugenberg press) after the DNVP's departure from government in 1928 seems to have benefited the Nazis, whose tabloid *Angriff* was in many ways made redundant by the larger *Nachtausgabe* that

---

[75] See esp. Requate, 'Zwischen', 182–5.

[76] R. Stöber, 'Emil Dovifat in der Weimarer Republik', in Sösemann (ed.), *Emil Dovifat*, 69–92; also Meier, *Zwischen*, 48; Eksteins, *Limits*, 312.

[77] Fulda, 'Industries'.

[78] G. Schultze-Pfaelzer, 'Neue Formen des Meinungskampfes in der aktualisierten Zeitung', *Deutsche Presse*, 23 (1928), special edn., 277.

[79] This paragraph is based on Fulda, 'Press', 54–9.

occupied a similar position on the political spectrum. As for the dwindling middle ground, there was admittedly little correlation between the continued success of the Ullstein and Mosse papers and the electoral collapse of the parties they backed. But it is worth noting that they too occasionally exploited the marketability of anti-politics, for example in the sensationalist coverage of the 1929 Sklarek scandal by Ullstein's tabloid *Tempo*, whose circulation leapt as it became one of the most zealous critics of corruption in the SPD-led Berlin municipal government.[80]

Although similar electoral patterns could be observed in areas where tabloids were unknown, these findings nonetheless suggest a correlation between the increasingly shrill political coverage of the popular press and the growing radicalization of the electorate. If the circulation of traditional political broadsheets showed little direct relation to a party's electoral results, this reflected the fact that 'politics' in the latter stages of the Weimar Republic was spilling out everywhere, manifesting itself in places—the streets, the pub, the silver screen—well beyond the forum of representative party politics.[81] Entertainment, sensationalism, and political radicalization blended into a potent elixir during the crisis of the early 1930s. On balance, it seems that the impact of the popular press during these years was, unlike the cinema, more divisive than unifying. Despite the broadening of reader expectations and the intense pressures of commercial concentration, the shrill tones of sensationalized politics helped to polarize German readers as never before.

LISTENING IN PUBLIC AND PRIVATE

Nowhere was the tension between the opposing forces of integration and fragmentation more readily observable than in the realm of the aural media. While the radio generated intense excitement as a potentially 'universal' medium of communication, the gramophone was also becoming an integral component of the media ensemble. Yet the very nature of their reception and usage differed profoundly from the cinema and press. By and large the radio and gramophone were used not in public spaces but in the private sphere, where they were thought to promote a 'domestication' of leisure. The private nature of their reception thus gave them an ambiguous status: the wider 'listening public' they promised to create was largely located in domestic space. These were, in other words, collective yet solitary media. In this sense the technological marvels of modern sound also had the potential to unite and to divide audiences.

---

[80] Ibid. 191–4. On the declining manifestation of Ullstein's liberal traditions: Eksteins, *Limits*, esp. 114.

[81] Generally, P. Swett, *Neighbors and Enemies* (Cambridge, 2004); P. Fritzsche, 'Did Weimar Fail?', *JMH* 68 (1996), 629–56.

Ever since the inception of radio, contemporaries recognized its dual potential to promote public discourse as well as a retreat into the private sphere. During the early years of broadcasting—as notions such as 'public radio' and a 'radio public' were still vague and uncertain—these issues attracted intense interest.[82] In these formative years the future seemed open, and there was a sense that important precedents were being set, perhaps unwittingly. The question of how radio was, or should be, used by listeners had significant implications for its broader social and cultural impact.

From the very beginning, the unique ability of the wireless to bring the wider world into one's home was regarded as a major step in the history of communication. Of course, newspapers and magazines had long performed this function as well, but the sense of 'real time' gave broadcasting a whole new dimension. For some contemporaries this domesticity was welcomed as a means of keeping people at home and away from the pubs. This was not just wishful thinking, for many listeners actually reported that the radio encouraged a 'renewal of family life'.[83] Yet, for other observers the radio's colonization of hearth and home represented a dangerous problem. Not only did broadcasting threaten to undermine sociable music-making (for example, amateur musical clubs), it was also seen to erode personal liberties and privacy. 'What does the radio mean in the context of the domestic sphere?' asked the cultural philosopher Viktor Engelhardt in 1924. 'Nothing other than that the public realm has penetrated our homes. . . . For the individual, the only means of defence is total resistance: switching off, removing the headphones, nothing else.'[84] The supposed powerlessness of the atomized radio audience was a point of continued criticism in the 1920s, and clearly resonated with Bertolt Brecht's condemnation of the unidirectional nature of broadcasting that precluded genuine communication (as opposed to mere 'distribution') between sender and receiver.[85]

Yet, despite its predominant use within domestic space, radio listening was never an exclusively solitary activity, since friends and family would often listen together. Nor was it a solely private experience, especially early on as the radio was still partly geared for public consumption. While upmarket department stores set up radio-listening displays and chic cafés made headphones available to customers, special listening cabins were erected in exhibition parks such as Munich's Theresienhöhe or Berlin's Lunapark.[86] On the evening

---

[82] K. Lacey, 'The Invention of a Listening Public', in Führer and Ross (eds.), *Media*, 61–79.

[83] Hensel and Keßler, *1000 Hörer*, 46; Thann, 'Bedeutung', 379.

[84] V. Engelhardt, 'Die kulturelle Bedeutung des Rundfunks' (1924), repr. in Bredow (ed.), *Archiv*, 88–93.

[85] B. Brecht, 'Radiotheorie 1927–1932', in id., *Gesammelte Werke*, 20 vols., vol. 18 (Frankfurt a. M., 1971), 129. Similar: L. v. Wiese, 'Die Auswirkung des Rundfunks auf die soziologische Struktur unserer Zeit' (1930), repr. in Bredow (ed.), *Archiv*, 98–111.

[86] Lenk, *Erscheinung*, 74–6.

of the Reichstag elections on 4 May 1924 a number of Berlin publishing houses and cafés set up loudspeakers so that passers-by could hear the latest results; crowds apparently grew so large that the police had to disperse the throngs.[87] Among the earliest plans for German radio was the development of 'Saalfunk', whereby loudspeakers were installed in community halls and auditoriums where audiences would pay an admission fee to hear music or lectures transmitted from a nearby broadcaster.[88] Although these ideas foundered on technological and commercial difficulties, collective listening outside of the home was common in the latter 1920s, including special school services as well as various programmes tailor-made for collective listening. In June 1932 the *Hamburger Echo* counted at least 749 'Hörgemeinden' (listening communities) throughout Germany.[89]

In terms of its wider social impact, however, collective radio-listening tended, like the press, to reinforce rather than undermine political and ideological divides. This was precisely the aim in many instances, most notably the various workers' radio clubs (the largest movement of this kind) organized by socialist and communist unions and committed to breaking the 'bourgeois' monopoly over the airwaves. By the early 1930s their events drew crowds of several hundred, prompting the journal *Arbeiter-Radio-Bund* to publish special guidelines for collective-listening programmes.[90] The radical Right also began to organize listening communities in response to the 'Marxist' radio clubs, above all through the nationalist Reichsverband Deutscher Rundfunkhörer.[91] By and large, collective radio-listening in Weimar Germany tended to take place within, not across, established political boundaries.

But for most contemporaries the radio was an instrument of unity rather than division. More than any other medium of the age, it had the potential to embrace everyone regardless of class, locality, or education. As Hans Bredow declared in 1924, the radio could 'bring together the different classes of the people, separated by political and religious differences, and forge them into a spiritually united listening community'. On the international level too, broadcasting would ideally function as a 'worldwide auditorium' that could encourage the important task of international reconciliation.[92] If the gramophone already enabled people to hear the same sounds at different times in different places, the radio took this a step further by allowing a physically dispersed audience to listen simultaneously, thus generating a novel sense of 'being there'. It was, as one contemporary put it, 'this feeling of direct experience (*Miterleben*)—the bridging of space and

---

[87] H. Wulff, 'Radio im Wahlkampf', *RZ* 2 (10 May 1924), 706–8.
[88] C. Lenk, 'Medium der Privatheit?', in I. Marßolek and A. v. Saldern (eds.), *Radiozeiten* (Potsdam, 1999), 206–17.
[89] Merkel, *Rundfunk*, 239.
[90] Ibid., 238–40; Dahl, *Arbeitersender*, 39–83.   [91] Lacey, 'Invention', 72–4.
[92] Quotes from Dussel, *Rundfunkgeschichte*, 52; Lacey, 'Invention', 65.

time—that makes us shudder at the significance and colossal power of this miracle of sound-carrying waves'.[93]

Measured against such superlatives the gramophone never generated quite the same level of excitement, largely because it possessed far less potential to unify audiences. Compared to the simultaneity of radio-listening, gramophone users were independent of each other. Of course, the fact that they were not beholden to a programme was also the great advantage of the gramophone. As the *Phonographische Zeitschrift* argued, radio was less of a threat than many recording executives feared: 'imagine a small group of people at home who want to dance a waltz. Someone switches the [radio] speaker on and hears "Ave Maria". A second attempt with another station finds "useful tips for the housewife", infant care, a violin solo, and similar things.'[94] The commercial orientation of the recording industry also meant that it catered to a wide range of musical tastes. This element of consumer choice, in conjunction with the ability to listen to what one wanted *when* one wanted, differed profoundly from the 'monologic' tendencies of radio.

Yet it would be too simplistic to contrast the collective impulses of radio with the individualized character of recorded sound. The gramophone's independence from a centralized programme also made it a useful prop for sociable events, from dinner parties to impromptu dancing. 'When the weather is nice and the evenings are longer, we pull out our gramophone and dance to the latest hits,' remarked a teenage seamstress in 1930. 'Our building has a big courtyard where we can romp to our heart's content.'[95] The expansion of gramophone use was also an important catalyst of the 'dance craze' after the First World War. As we saw in Chapter 1, records were instrumental in popularizing tunes *without* undermining public venues or live music. Certainly, the wave of new openings during the second half of the 1920s suggests that the gramophone was more an ally than an enemy. By 1930 Berlin authorities counted no fewer than 899 dance locales in the capital, which together accounted for around half of the city's amusement-tax revenues.[96]

It is worth noting that the 'dance craze' of the 1920s furnishes yet another example of the tensions between audience integration and fragmentation. Dancing was undoubtedly a 'mass' phenomenon in the latter 1920s; between 1924 and 1929 around 7 million Germans enrolled in dance courses. The bulk of large city-centre locales were also built during these years, including such renowned establishments as the Café Schottenhaml (later renamed Moka Efti), the Delphi, and most famous of all, Haus Vaterland, the epitome of mass pleasure-seeking in Weimar Berlin.[97] Yet the extent to which the classes actually mixed in such

---

[93] F. W. Odendahl, 'Die ersten Schritte des Rundfunks als aktueller Berichterstatter' (1928), repr. in Bredow (ed.), *Archiv*, 164.
[94] 'Unnütze Angst vor dem Radio', *PZ* 30 (1 Mar. 1929), 440.
[95] Dinse, *Freizeitleben*, 32.
[96] K. Wolffram, *Tanzdielen und Vergnügungspaläste* (Berlin, 1992), 20; Schär, *Schlager*, 49.
[97] Wolffram, *Tanzdielen*, 22; Schär, *Schlager*, 147.

venues was limited. Even among the big locales there were huge differences between, say, the elegance of the 'Femina' in Berlin's West End and the uninhibited carnival atmosphere of the 'Resi' in Friedrichshain.[98] Although visitors to these different locales could often see the same steps and hear the same tunes, *where* one went dancing nonetheless tended to fall along class lines. Only around one-third of Berlin's dance establishments were located in the central amusement areas of Mitte and the West End. The vast majority were small, neighbourhood venues serving a local clientele. Moreover, these neighbourhood venues became increasingly dominant as the Depression crisis hit the central establishments hardest. From 1930 to 1931, as around half of the dance venues located in Mitte went out of business, the number of locales actually rose in working-class districts such as Friedrichshain and Lichtenberg, as well as in the petty-bourgeois areas of Steglitz and Zehlendorf.[99] As Christian Schär has concluded, 'apart from a few exceptions . . . the middle and lower classes, just as the cosmopolitan set, danced among themselves'.[100]

As Part III has now demonstrated at length, 'mass culture' during the Weimar era was still closely tied to class, region, and milieu. The mass media and commercial entertainments, despite their inherent expansionism and universalist logic, were not the culturally 'standardizing' and socially 'levelling' forces so often conjured by contemporaries and historians alike. Undoubtedly, the press, cinema, radio, and recording had become an integral part of German society by the 1920s, and if anything their importance continued to grow. But the very fact that they formed such an elemental part of public life and everyday leisure meant that they were affected as much by the social and cultural context as the other way around. That this was even the case with film and radio, the most 'modern' cultural forms of the age, shows how limited the cultural 'modernity' of the Weimar era actually was. It also shows how crucial it is to approach the media and their audiences firmly within their historical contexts.

Any evaluation of the social role of the media in inter-war Germany must therefore abandon assumptions of a standardized cultural product consumed by an increasingly uniform audience. Although their rapid expansion during this period is often cited as prima facie evidence for their supposedly standardizing or 'massifying' impact, Karl Christian Führer is certainly correct to argue that 'the existence of modern media of mass usage alone by no means denotes a universal mass culture'.[101] The distinctions may well have become more subtle, but this does not mean that they were any less important. Indeed, as recent research on the contemporary relationship between media and social change has

---

[98] C. Moreck, *Führer durch das 'lasterhafte' Berlin* (Leipzig, 1931), 116–30, 186–210. For contemporary literary portrayals: D. Smail, *White-collar Workers, Mass Culture and Neue Sachlichkeit in Weimar Berlin* (Bern, 1999), 121–8, 165–80.

[99] Wolffram, *Tanzdielen*, 20.   [100] Schär, *Schlager*, 237.

[101] Führer, 'Auf dem Weg', 781.

emphasized, the more developed and ubiquitous a medium becomes, the more users it acquires; and the more users it acquires, the more differentiated they and the possible uses of the medium become. From this point of view, the expansion of a particular medium does not necessarily lead to greater cultural uniformity, but also to more variegation.[102]

The argument here is not that the mass media had no socially or culturally standardizing effects, since their very expansion implied an overlaying or even displacement of more traditional, hierarchical leisure pursuits.[103] The point is rather that they could act as both an integrative *and* disaggregating force—or, to use Victoria de Grazia's terms, they could exert both 'Fordist' and 'post-Fordist' effects: integrative and 'Fordist' in that they promoted a standard set of cultural artefacts that transcended societal divisions, and disaggregating or 'post-Fordist' insofar as they could segment audiences (or at least reproduce their divisions) by engendering different frameworks of perception through their very diffusion among a wide range of social groups.[104]

It is also important to recognize that the social impact of different media varied significantly according to their degree of regulation, their level of development, and their relationship to certain cultural traditions. Film, as we have seen, operated in an exceedingly competitive market and was acutely sensitive to audience preferences. Although this helped to generate immense popular appeal, the wide palette of films that were produced, where they were shown, and how they were consumed tended to reflect and reproduce social differences more than undermine them. By contrast, Weimar radio, under strict state regulation and protected by a monopolization of supply, could afford to be stodgy and highbrow, and was in practice shaped by the interests of a relatively narrow segment of the population. In both cases, the topography of their audiences reflected social differences: in the cinema through the huge variety of its programme, and in broadcasting through the skewed social makeup of its audience. There is no neat formula for evaluating the social impact of different communications technologies in any given time or place.

Put differently, the frequently assumed potential of the media to exert any socially 'levelling' or 'homogenizing' influence lay not in their widespread usage per se, but rather in the precise nature of their production and consumption, which could change significantly over time. Whether media programmes were produced regionally or solely for a national audience, and how they were mediated to actual audiences, greatly influenced their social effects. Target radio programmes, regionally oriented films, or the dominance of local newspapers in

---

102 S. Kombüchen, *Von der Erlebnisgesellschaft zur Mediengesellschaft* (Münster, 1999).

103 The otherwise superb study by Führer, 'Auf dem Weg', arguably underplays these changes.

104 V. de Grazia, 'Introduction: Changing Consumption Regimes', in V. de Grazia and E. Furlough (eds.), *The Sex of Things* (Berkeley, 1996), 11–24; id., 'Changing Consumption Regimes in Europe, 1930–1970: Comparative Perspectives on the Distribution Problem', in S. Strasser, C. McGovern, and M. Judt (eds.), *Getting and Spending* (Cambridge, 1998), 59–83.

Germany were not just reflections of an increasingly standardized 'mass media public', but could also bolster local allegiances and social differences. Such mass cultural artefacts were long mediated through older social structures, which profoundly affected their cultural meaning and how they were experienced.

The implication of this argument is that a shift in the structures of production and consumption would have a significant effect on the social role of the media. We have already encountered this in the case of the cinema, which underwent profound change during the early 1930s with the conversion to sound. Given that such shifts are most readily visible over longer stretches of time, we must return to this question for the 1930s and 1940s. As we will see in Part V, the combined effects of technological innovation, commercial pressures, and the fundamentally altered political environment under the Nazi regime tended to promote the 'integrative' over the 'disaggregating' qualities of the media, and thereby reduce the salience of class and milieu structures as mediators of mass culture. In the meantime, Part IV will shift the focus to the central role of the modern media in the volatile political culture of early twentieth-century Germany.

PART IV

MASS MEDIA AND MASS POLITICS FROM THE EMPIRE TO THE WEIMAR REPUBLIC

Introduction

The explosion of modern communications not only reconfigured German cultural life, it also had enormous political consequences. By the dawn of the twentieth century the effects could be seen nearly everywhere: in processes of political mobilization, in electioneering techniques, in the changing nature of political leadership, and in the very perception of the political realm. Over the past couple of decades scholars have rightly emphasized how people's political orientations and behaviour are moulded as much by past experiences, social conventions, and cultural practices as by 'social reality' and material interest.[1] The political relevance of the new media therefore involves more than the supposed 'effect' of media messages on audiences or the implications of specific structures of ownership and control (though these structures undoubtedly influenced content). Equally important to consider are the consequences for the character of political communication itself, in both a quantitative and qualitative sense.

In quantitative terms, the sheer scale of potential influence over public opinion was unprecedented. Never before did political elites dispose of such effective instruments for disseminating and popularizing their ideas. But at the same time, never before did public opinion matter so much. In the era of 'total war', civilian morale became a key component of warfare, and after the war its importance rose further with the introduction of universal suffrage and a new democratic constitution. The expansion of the media thus carried contradictory implications: while they promoted a more democratic political culture by opening access to matters of public interest, they also provided new and more powerful tools for the manipulation or 'management' of public opinion.

Even more important than the magnitude of modern communications were the qualitative changes they entailed. As Walter Benjamin famously observed in the 1930s, the vast expansion of cultural distribution had transformed the nature of its appropriation: 'quantity has been transmuted into quality. The greatly increased mass of participants has produced a change in the mode of participation.'[2] Whereas the newspapers of earlier eras essentially functioned as a means of transporting information across long distances, the pervasiveness of

---

[1] For trenchant analyses: Fritzsche, 'Did Weimar Fail?'; Swett, *Neighbors*; M. L. Anderson, *Practicing Democracy* (Princeton, 2000).
[2] Benjamin, 'Work of Art', 232.

the media in the twentieth century was seen to represent or even create 'public opinion' itself. In addition, the huge complexity of the modern world meant that they could only transmit a highly condensed version of events that scarcely enabled users to make well-informed judgements. Although the media had always conveyed a compressed version of 'reality', the great surfeit of information in the twentieth century meant that news was exceedingly selective. 'One might think that the events of the world take place and then glide automatically into the newspapers; from actuality to the press, from reality into reproduction,' noted Kurt Tucholsky in 1921. 'That is not the case. Because the reproduction of reality is incomparably more important than the event itself, reality has long been busy presenting itself to the press as it would like to be seen.'[3] This problem of tailoring information 'flows' was a central theme of Walter Lippmann's famous 1922 book *Public Opinion*, which argued that the unavoidable process of selection made it easier for political elites to 'set the agenda' and greatly encouraged the use of simplifying stereotypes.[4] Lippmann was clearly on to something, for scholars have often noted the growth of political metaphors and symbols during this period as part of a broader trend towards a more visual popular culture. At the same time, there was a powerful new sense of verisimilitude attached to photographs, moving pictures, recorded sound, or live radio broadcasts. All of these modern wonders seemed (or purported) to convey the 'real thing'. The political importance of the new media therefore lay not only in their ability to reach a larger audience, but also in their deployment of a new language of imagery and supposedly 'direct' experience.[5]

This had profound implications for the nature of modern politics. Following the 'Frankfurt School' tradition of cultural criticism, scholarly discussion of the relationship between mass culture and mass politics in Germany long viewed the rise of fascism as confirmation of the anti-democratic and depoliticizing character of the 'culture industry'. More recently, however, historians have emphasized the multifarious impact of the new media, more in line with Walter Benjamin's nuanced observations about their simultaneously emancipatory and anti-democratic potential. The power of images and the technical reproduction of 'reality' had the potential to enhance or displace rational political discourse, which helps explain the widespread contemporary ambivalence surrounding them. As Peter Fritzsche has argued, 'politics' in inter-war Germany was 'as much the product of desire and imagination as of function and interest'. Although it is difficult to document and impossible to quantify, it seems that the encouragement of new desires and patterns of perception (via new media and forms of cultural consumption) helped to root political mobilization in

    [3] I. Wrobel (K. Tucholsky), 'Presse und Realität' (1921), quoted from Stöber, *Die erfolgverführte*, 13.
    [4] W. Lippmann, *Public Opinion* (New York, 1922).
    [5] This follows E. Rosenhaft, 'Lesewut, Kinosucht, Radiotismus', in A. Lüdtke, I. Marßolek, and A. v. Saldern (eds.), *Amerikanisierung* (Stuttgart, 1996), 119–43.

the imagination and expand the 'emotional register of politics' during the early decades of the twentieth century.[6] These changes were, in other words, part of a far-reaching transformation in cultural expectations and practices. Although the rise of 'politainment' is often dated to the television age, the shifting symbols and vocabulary of political articulation in the early twentieth century were integrally related to the sensual appeal of mass communications and commercial entertainments. The key—for political campaigners, entertainers, and advertisers alike—was to tailor one's message accordingly. How political elites sought to adapt to this new cultural terrain, and how their efforts were related to current thinking about communicating with mass publics, is the focus of this section.

[6] Quotes from Fritzsche, 'Did Weimar Fail?', 632, 645.

7

Propaganda and the Modern Public

Gaining popular sympathy has always been a key element in the art of government. But over the later decades of the nineteenth century a series of interrelated changes made 'public opinion' a matter of supreme political importance in the industrialized world, including the autocratic German Empire. The immense growth of the media was but one of the factors behind this. Equally important were an increasingly literate electorate and a more urbanized industrial work-force, both of which were integrally related to the surge of political mobilization following the lapse of anti-socialist legislation in 1890. Along with the explosion of the popular press and the growing popularity of the cinema, this bundle of interwoven developments signalled a fundamental change to the framework of political life. By the opening of the twentieth century not even a dyed-in-the-wool autocrat could afford to ignore public opinion completely, and by the 1920s any lingering misgivings had been obliterated by the war and subsequent political upheavals. If modern politics had become a battle for hearts and minds, it was natural that politicians and governments would try to improve their media relations and avail themselves of modern techniques of persuasion. The advent of mass politics thus spawned an acute fascination with 'propaganda' that spanned the fields of politics, journalism, psychology, and commercial advertising. This chapter will briefly survey the evolution of these ideas in Wilhelmine and Weimar Germany, focusing on the relationship between the media, perceptions of public opinion, and the changing understanding of political leadership.

FROM PRESS POLICY TO 'PATRIOTIC EDUCATION': STATE PROPAGANDA IN IMPERIAL GERMANY

Although the German Empire may have been founded on 'blood and iron', the print media could claim at least a small portion of the credit. In early 1870, when the French government objected to the prospect of a Hohenzollern king on the Spanish throne, the political constellation in some ways resembled that of the previous crisis of Spanish succession over a century-and-a-half earlier. One of the key differences in 1870, however, was the incomparably greater political role of the press. Unlike the earlier crisis, the dynastic problem of 1870 was itself quickly resolved when the Hohenzollern candidate (from the Catholic

Sigmaringen line of the family) withdrew at the behest of the Prussian king. But Bismarck had other ideas, and continued to stir the issue as a means of engineering a confrontation with France. When the French ambassador appealed to the Prussian king to furnish a guarantee against a Hohenzollern candidature, Wilhelm declined the demand in ameliorative terms calculated to defuse the conflict. Currently on holiday in Bad Ems, he then sent a message about the meeting to Bismarck—the famous Ems Telegram—suggesting that his response be circulated in the press as a means of dampening the dispute. But Bismarck dramatically condensed the dispatch to make it appear as if Wilhelm had been insulted and had sent the French ambassador packing. When the story hit the papers it caused a scandal, precisely as Bismarck intended, and triggered a chain of events that culminated in the French declaration of war and, in 1871, the foundation of the German Empire.[1]

Of course, the press can hardly be regarded as a primary cause of the Franco-Prussian War. There were a host of reasons why both Bismarck and the French were happy to escalate the matter into a confrontation. But the incident nonetheless highlights the expanding role of the press in political life, for it was above all the *publication* of Wilhelm's alleged humiliation that turned it into a diplomatic crisis.

Bismarck clearly had an appreciation for the new tools of mass communication. As the Ems Telegram episode shows, he did not confine his attention to old-style censorship but also pro-actively fed the press. In the 1870s and 1880s the main vehicles for this were the political weekly *Provincial-Correspondenz* (replaced by the *Neueste Mitteilungen* following a reorganization in 1882), the small Press Department of the Imperial Foreign Ministry, and the semi-official Wolff'sche Telegraphen-Büro.[2] But compared to other countries, Germany not only lacked a well-coordinated system of press relations, it also spent relatively little on it. During the 1880s government press activities swallowed anywhere from around RM 600,000 to RM 1 million—about the same as in Britain but considerably less than the press budgets in Russia and Austria and far less than France's RM 2.1 million. At no point was Bismarck's government at the cutting edge of press relations.[3]

Once again, the year 1890 marked something of a watershed in government propaganda efforts. For one thing, after Bismarck's dismissal there was a concerted—though unsuccessful—attempt to centralize press relations in the Foreign Ministry's Press Department, directed from 1894 by the well-connected

[1] L. Gall, *Bismarck* vol. 1 (London, 1986), 356–9; K. Koszyk, *Deutsche Presse im 19. Jahrhundert* (Berlin, 1966), 239–41.

[2] R. Stöber, 'Die "Provinzial-Correspondenz" 1863–1884', *Publizistik*, 44, (1999), 165–84; id., 'Bismarcks geheime Presseorganisation von 1882', *HZ* 262 (1996), 423–51; also Koszyk, *Deutsche Presse im 19. Jahrhundert*, 232–5

[3] B. Sösemann, 'Publizistik in staatlicher Regie', in J. Kunisch (ed.), *Bismarck und seine Zeit* (Berlin, 1992), 302, 305.

journalist Otto Hammann. The efforts of Wilhelm II to stamp his personal authority on government policy—which, for constitutional reasons, proceeded largely in the form of public announcements—also added a new dynamic, though the scandals surrounding members of his political entourage and the almost comical unfolding of the 1908 *Daily Telegraph* affair did more harm than good.[4] Most important, however, was the lapse of the anti-socialist laws. Although the circulation of the SPD press paled in comparison to the party's electoral success, it nonetheless grew into a powerful organ of opposition, printing scathing editorials, embarrassing scandals, and leaking confidential material that damaged government credibility. After 1908 a new party press bureau syndicated such material in order to distribute it more widely, further augmenting its journalistic efforts through the production of leaflets, calendars, and other printed material.[5]

It was largely in response to the growing socialist 'threat' that the Imperial government redoubled its efforts to win over public opinion. While some segments of the Wilhelmine elite clung to their authoritarian habits, others emphasized the need to cultivate popular support for the government's position. The growth of the mass press itself exerted a certain 'democratizing' effect on the forms of political communication in the Imperial era.[6] As Interior Minister von der Recke remarked in 1898: 'No government can make do without effective representation of its views and interests in the press for any length of time, without doing damage to its position and prestige.'[7]

Any such efforts faced a number of problems. Not only would blatant intervention be more likely to serve the SPD than the government, but the machinery of official press relations remained meagre by international standards. Even Hammann's press agency in the Foreign Ministry consisted of only himself and three assistants.[8] Furthermore, the established practice of feeding articles to the elite press was never going to reach many of the 'healthy' segments of the population that might, if neglected, succumb to the 'forces of subversion'. For this task the government depended on a network of independent or semi-official organizations that shared an interest in countering the effects of socialist propaganda. The non-socialist parties, though obvious candidates for this role, were of little use. Both the National Liberal and Conservative parties were essentially associations of notables, with neither the inclination nor capacity to engage in sustained populist agitation.[9] The Centre Party likewise focused on its core clientele.

---

[4] M. Kohlrausch, *Der Monarch im Skandal* (Berlin, 2005), 186–263. The affairs revolved around a number of ill-judged and mysteriously unedited comments made by Wilhelm II in an interview that was published in the *Daily Telegraph*. In one fell swoop, he not only alienated British, French, Russian, and Japanese opinion, but also severely damaged his own prestige within Germany.

[5] Generally, A. Hall, *Scandal, Sensation and Social Democracy* (Cambridge, 1977); id., 'The War of Words', *JCH* 11 (1976), 11–42.

[6] F. Bösch, 'Katalysator der Demokratisierung?', in F. Bösch and N. Frei (eds.), *Medialisierung und Demokratie im 20. Jahrhundert* (Göttingen, 2006), 25–47.

[7] Quoted from A. Hall, 'War', 19.   [8] Dussel, *Tagespresse*, 111.

[9] See J. Retallack, *The German Right, 1860–1920* (Toronto, 2006), 225–72.

The bulk of publicity work thus fell to the handful of nationalist associations that supplied and distributed government-friendly material in the wider public domain: the veterans' organizations, the Young Germany Union, and the Fatherland League. By far the most important of these was the Christian Periodical League (Christlicher Zeitschriftenverein), founded in 1880 for the distribution of patriotic Christian literature. Despite its formal independence, it essentially functioned as a branch of the Prussian administration. By the turn of the century the Christian Periodical League involved some 12,000 local agents distributing over 230 separate publications with a combined circulation of around 700,000.[10]

The activities of these organizations, though useful for the government, never strayed very far from traditional modes of political communication. More innovative in their approach were the handful of 'radical nationalist' groups such as the Navy League, the Pan-Germans, and the Colonial Society, which harboured few misgivings about dirtying their hands with direct popular agitation.[11] Without a doubt, the Navy League proved most adept at it, combining a conventional focus on printed matter with an emphasis on visual appeal. By far the greatest novelty was the Navy League's deployment of film, which began in 1901 and was steadily built up over the following years, peaking in 1905 with 1,599 screenings in 572 towns reaching an audience of over 870,000. In this sphere the Navy League was well ahead of the other nationalist organizations, and even began to spice up its cinema programmes with short films on subjects with little or no relation to the navy. There can be little doubt about the popularity of the film shows: local cinema operators frequently complained about the competition they posed.[12]

Yet the employment of such modern, visually oriented agitation techniques posed certain risks, for it meant fighting the SPD on its own terrain. This was a daunting prospect given the Social Democrats' undeniable successes since 1890. Before 1907 the SPD had managed to increase its share of the vote in every election it was allowed to contest. Its strong showing in 1903, which increased its share of Reichstag seats from 56 to 81, prompted a group of German Conservatives, Free Conservatives, and right-wing National Liberals to establish the Imperial League Against Social Democracy (Reichsverband gegen die Sozialdemokratie) as a means of directly challenging the SPD on the working-class doorstep. Financed by heavy industry, the League quickly set about distributing pamphlets and calendars and supporting like-minded newspapers, eventually founding its own news agency.[13] For a while it seemed as if these efforts were paying off. In the

[10] Hall, 'War', 23–5; G. Eley, *Reshaping, the German Right* (orig. 1980) (Ann Arbor, Mich., 1991) 214–15, 217 f.

[11] Generally, Eley, *Reshaping*; R. Chickering, *We Men Who Feel Most German* (London, 1984).

[12] M. Loiperdinger, 'The Beginnings of German Film Propaganda', *Historical Journal of Film, Radio and Television*, 22 (2002), 305–13. On Navy League propaganda, W. Deist, *Flottenpolitik und Flottenpropaganda* (Stuttgart, 1976).

[13] Hall, 'War', 30–2.

1907 elections the SPD lost seats for the first time, dropping from 81 to 43, and it seems reasonable to attribute at least part of the electoral success of the 'Bülow Bloc' to its publicist activities.[14] But this electoral success was as ephemeral as the Bloc itself. In 1912 the SPD rebounded with a vengeance, becoming for the first time the single largest party in the Reichstag.

This result was a shock to the entire Wilhelmine establishment. It not only accelerated the tactical realignment of the Right into a closer political cartel, it also encouraged a broader rethinking of government publicity policies to counter the red menace.[15] As Chancellor Bethmann-Hollweg admonished his ministers in summer 1912: 'The political parties and economic interest groups are making more and more use of the press as a means of pursuing their goals. At the same time, the competition for sensation between the newspapers has also continually grown. If government leaders do not follow this trend it will become increasingly difficult for them to achieve the necessary public support for the preparation and execution of their policies.'[16] Although his attempt to set up a central news office foundered on ministerial turf wars, the government nonetheless acted swiftly when it perceived a threat to its press interests. When the Scherl concern slid into financial difficulties in 1913, ministers blocked the sale of the *Berliner-Lokal-Anzeiger* to the liberal Mosse publishing house on the express grounds that the *BLA* was 'the only *big* paper on which we can still exert a certain influence'.[17] And what they meant by a 'big paper' was precisely something like Mosse's *Berliner Tageblatt*, whose annual turnover of around RM 8 million totally dwarfed the RM 300,000 of the semi-official *Norddeutsche Allgemeine Zeitung*.[18]

German political elites were thus already becoming more interested in press relations and propaganda on the eve of the war. Yet the crucial turning-point undoubtedly came in 1914. For it was during the First World War—the first war in which not only armies but whole societies were mobilized for the production of violence—that the deliberate shaping of public opinion was first perceived as an indispensable weapon of modern statecraft. More than all previous wars, this conflict was to be won or lost not only on the battlefield, but also on the home front, in the factories and villages. Thus the objective of sustaining one's own morale and undermining that of the enemy was no longer confined to the troops but extended to the entire population. As war henceforth encompassed both the military and civilian spheres, controlling information and influencing public opinion became part and parcel of modern armed conflict.[19]

[14] G. Stöber, *Pressepolitik als Notwendigkeit* (Stuttgart, 2000), 132–42.
[15] Eley, *Reshaping*, 331–4.   [16] Stöber, *Pressepolitik*, 250–1.
[17] Quoted from ibid. 262, emphasis in the original.   [18] Bösch, 'Katalysator', 33.
[19] For a fuller discussion, J. Verhey, 'Some Lessons of the War', in B. Hüppauf (ed.), *War, Violence and the Modern Condition* (Berlin, 1997), 101–3.

Throughout the war, the virtues of national unity and a readiness to sacrifice were officially enshrined in the 'spirit of 1914', the centrepiece of German domestic propaganda. When the Kaiser told the crowds on 1 August that 'when it comes to war all parties cease and we are all brothers', his primary aim was to persuade the SPD's parliamentary delegates to vote for war appropriations in the Reichstag. But this speech—along with his remarks on 4 August that 'I no longer recognize any parties, but only Germans'—soon became the cornerstone of a powerful and long-lived myth of a German nation unified around the Kaiser, whose call to arms was greeted with a wave of enthusiasm that allegedly subsumed the deep social divisions of the past.[20]

If the remarkable popular resonance of Wilhelm's speech came perhaps more by accident than design, there was certainly nothing haphazard about the government's efforts to present the war as a popular call to arms. The German military had long been aware that public opinion would be an important element in any future conflict. Over the course of the July Crisis the government did nothing to discourage the growing impression among journalists that war was the only alternative. Nor did it take exception to the increasingly crude anti-Slavic stereotypes in the papers, soon to be joined by 'perfidious Albion' and the French 'Erbfeind'.[21] Even before the state of siege was proclaimed on 31 July, the police did what they could to hinder the anti-war demonstrations organized by the SPD. Although significant segments of the press were outspokenly critical of the Austrian ultimatum and remained opposed to war during the last week of July, the imposition of strict censorship after 31 July brought a swift end to such dissent. Thenceforth the job of the military censors was to maintain the so-called *Burgfrieden* (internal truce), to protect it against even 'the smallest attempts to upset the unity of the German people and its press'.[22]

From the very beginning, the chief of the General Staff, Helmuth von Moltke, regarded a close alliance with the press as 'an indispensable means of waging war'.[23] Given the immense public thirst for news that sent circulation figures soaring, this required not only censorship of certain information but also the provision of appropriate material. Towards this end the General Staff set up press briefings as early as 3 August, and one week later established a new press service (Nachrichtenabteilung) under Section IIIb of the Supreme Command, run by Major (later Lieutenant-Colonel) Walter Nicolai. At the same time, the WTB also served as an official source of war reports. In February 1915 a Central Censorship Office (Oberzensurstelle) was established to standardize practices across the twenty-six different military districts of the Reich, though it was not until 1917 that information policies were effectively coordinated through

---

[20] See generally J. Verhey, *The Spirit of 1914* (Cambridge, 2000).
[21] B. Rosenberger, *Zeitungen als Kriegstreiber?* (Cologne, 1998).
[22] Quote from Verhey, *Spirit*, 143, on the anti-war demonstrations, 52–7; see also Stark, 'All Quiet'.
[23] Quote from D. Welch, *Germany, Propaganda and Total War, 1914–1918* (London, 2000), 31.

the War Press Office (Kriegspresseamt), directly controlled by the Supreme Command.[24]

While the maintenance of domestic morale was under the control of the army, the parallel attempt to win public sympathy in neutral countries remained a matter for the Foreign Ministry. The cornerstone of its campaign was the Central Office for Foreign Affairs (Zentralstelle für Auslandsdienst), set up in October 1914 with the help of Matthias Erzberger, who was made responsible for foreign propaganda at the outbreak of the war. Staffed by journalists and diplomats with extensive overseas experience (most notably Baron Alfons von Mumm and the journalists/academics Ernst Jäckh and Paul Rohrbach), it monitored the world press, printed millions of leaflets, founded numerous publications for distribution in neutral countries, and provided a constant supply of pro-German material for foreign papers, especially in the United States and neutral Europe.[25]

The Central Office for Foreign Affairs faced a difficult task from the outset. For one thing, Germany's few undersea telegraph cables were immediately cut by the Allies at the outbreak of the war (a predicted move that had already encouraged the development of wireless communication in Germany). More importantly, German violation of Belgian sovereignty, an integral part of the Schlieffen Plan, meant that the German government needed to justify its actions in a way that its enemies did not. Much of the Central Office's material was therefore geared towards explaining the causes of the war from the German point of view, and thus to excuse this clear breach of international law. To make matters worse, from February 1917 onwards it also faced the daunting task of justifying the new policy of unlimited submarine warfare. Overall, the fact that German propaganda had been immediately thrown on to the defensive in summer 1914 meant that it was often reactive in character. The Central Office was certainly kept busy refuting British and French atrocity propaganda, especially that involving the massacres of Belgian civilians and the infamous execution of the nurse Edith Cavell.[26] To be sure, German propaganda often repaid this in kind, portraying England as a 'nation of pirates' and 'vampire of the continent'.[27] But even the seemingly pro-active attempt to parade Germany's cultural and educational achievements can be seen as a response—as in Louis Oppenheim's famous 1916 poster *Wir Barbaren?*[28]—to Allied agitation against the marauding 'Hun'.

Generally speaking, the Central Office was unable to sway neutral opinion, which remained largely anti-German from start to finish. Although the lack of

---

[24] M. Creutz, *Die Pressepolitik der kaiserlichen Regierung während des Ersten Weltkriegs* (Frankfurt a. M., 1996); K. Koszyk, *Deutsche Pressepolitik im Ersten Weltkrieg* (Düsseldorf, 1968).

[25] J. Wilke, 'Deutsche Auslandspropaganda im Ersten Weltkrieg', in J. Wilke (ed.), *Pressepolitik und Propaganda* (Cologne, 1997), 79–125.

[26] Generally, J. Horne and A. Kramer, *German Atrocities, 1914* (New Haven, 2001).

[27] S. Kestler, *Die deutsche Auslandsaufklärung und das Bild der Ententemächte im Spiegel zeitgenössischer Propagandaveröffentlichungen während des Ersten Weltkrieges* (Frankfurt a. M., 1994).

[28] Available at *http://www.dhm.de/lemo/objekte/pict/pl002758/index.html*.

cooperation from the military authorities did not help matters, it is doubtful that the Central Office's propaganda was good enough to succeed in any event.[29] According to Count Bernstorff, Germany's wartime ambassador to the United States, one of the main reasons why Germany never shook off its image as the aggressor was because its propagandists proved unable to couch their message in a more dramatic idiom, failing to capitalize on opportunities such as the French bombing of a Corpus Christi procession in Karlsruhe which killed or injured several dozen civilians, or the increasingly dire effects of the Allied blockade on women and children.[30] Moreover, the central themes of what they did transmit overseas were ill chosen. Whereas British propagandists skilfully propagated the message of 'humanitarian war aims', grounding their appeals in the defence of universal values to which all could relate, German talk of a national mission to spread Kultur came across as arrogant and apologetic, not least in the United States.[31] Despite post-war assertions to the contrary, the shortcomings of German overseas propaganda resulted not from a lack of interest or effort, but rather from a commandeering tone and an ill-conceived message.[32]

Much the same can be said of its domestic propaganda. Although the 'spirit of 1914' helped to mobilize opinion at the beginning of the war, the mantra of national unity alone was hardly enough to sustain morale over the following years. By 1916 at the latest there were clear signs of war-weariness. As the food situation continually deteriorated, strikes and riots became more common and more politicized, especially after the May Day demonstrations of 1916 and the arrest of Karl Liebknecht. This was also the year of the Somme and Verdun, whose terrible toll in casualties for what essentially ended in stalemate quickly turned them into symbols of the futility of the conflict. And what was the message of the government to the long-suffering civilian population, increasingly hungry and constantly concerned about loved ones at the front? By and large it was a mixture of pleas to sustain the 'spirit of 1914' and to 'hold out' against those who were responsible for the food shortages. 'Hold out for what?', many Germans were beginning to ask. Such propaganda utterly failed to address the growing perception that the war was meaningless. By 1916 an increasing number of Germans wanted to know why the war was being fought, and above all what it would take to end it.

In summer 1916 Ludendorff responded by lifting the ban on the discussion of war aims, thereby unleashing a fierce controversy that continued to the end of the war. This issue was inextricably linked to the wider question of political reforms,

---

[29] See the complaints in M. Erzberger, *Erlebnisse im Weltkrieg* (Stuttgart, 1920), 7, 12.

[30] H. Lasswell, *Propaganda Technique in World War 1* (Cambridge, Mass., 1971), 34–5, originally published as *Propaganda Technique in the World War* (London, 1927).

[31] On the mobilization of 'culture', J. Ungern-Sternberg v. Pürkel and W. v. Ungern-Sternberg, *Der Aufruf an die Kulturwelt* (Stuttgart, 1996); H. Lasswell, *Propaganda*, 196–8.

[32] For a contemporary account: A. Pfander, 'Nationale Propaganda', *DR* (Nov.–Dec. 1918), 185–6; generally, Wilke, 'Auslandspropaganda', 123–5.

insofar as a 'victorious peace' involving vast territorial annexations would be seen to validate Germany's authoritarian system and offset the lack of reforms with material gains. By contrast, supporters of a compromise peace argued that the privations of the war should be compensated by democratization and social reform. As they correctly pointed out, visions of conquest sat uneasily with the notion of fighting a 'defensive war', and were moreover broadly unpopular as they only promised to prolong the conflict. The ensuing political fallout came to a head in July 1917, when Hindenburg and Ludendorff threatened to resign unless Chancellor Bethmann-Hollweg was dismissed.

This was a fateful move with a wide range of consequences. What is interesting for our purposes here is that it rested in large part on an assumption about the nature of domestic morale: namely, that its continual deterioration (especially during the so-called 'turnip winter' of 1916–17) resulted less from the war per se than from weak leadership at home, that is, the chancellor and his conciliatory dreams of a 'new orientation' in German politics. In Ludendorff's view, the unthinking masses were there to be led; all that was needed was strong guidance. It was therefore no coincidence that July 1917 also saw the launch of a new 'patriotic education' campaign that sought to steel the nation's nerves. Characteristically, however, this redoubling of propaganda efforts essentially amounted to more of the same—though with the Kaiser, his reputation now much diminished, replaced by the figure of Hindenburg. On the home front, special 'enlightenment divisions' produced yet more pamphlets and posters and organized yet more dry and sparsely attended lecture meetings. For the troops in the field, newly appointed 'propaganda directors' organized mandatory lectures, whose banal content and unimaginative presentation were pedantically prescribed down to the last detail.[33] Soldiers' newspapers were also enlisted for the 'patriotic education' campaign. Having already lost their initial independence with the establishment of the Field Press Office (Feldpressestelle) in 1916, most trench papers now functioned as the official voice of the General Staff, constantly churning out the message of 'holding one's nerve' and replacing the humane images of the soldier with the iconic cliché of the jut-jawed, front-line warrior.[34]

Unsurprisingly, such propaganda did little to improve civilian morale, and was utterly ridiculed by soldiers at the front.[35] Yet the 'patriotic education' campaign nonetheless brought about a number of noteworthy changes. First, press relations were increasingly centralized into the hands of Erhard Deutelmoser, appointed press chief in the Chancellor's Office in September 1917, and subsequently given responsibility for the Foreign Ministry Press Office in

---

[33] Welch, *Germany*, 207–9; also Verhey, *Spirit*, 189–92.
[34] A. Lipp, *Meinungslenkung im Krieg* (Göttingen, 2003); A. Schmidt, *Belehrung—Propaganda—Vertrauensarbeit* (Essen, 2006).
[35] K. Schneider, 'Lehren aus der Frontreklame', *DR* (Apr. 1918), 63–4; generally, Welch, *Germany*, 219–20.

February 1918. Deutelmoser was, secondly, instrumental in setting up the Zentrale für Heimatdienst in early 1918 as a domestic counterpart to the Zentralstelle für Auslandsdienst.[36] Most important, however, was a greater concern with the use of the popular cinema. In 1916 the War Ministry had already commissioned the private firm Deutsche Bioscope to produce entertainment films in support of the German war effort. Soon thereafter it also supported the production of pro-German documentaries and features by the firm Deutsche Lichtbild Gesellschaft (Deulig), which Hugenberg specially founded for this purpose in November 1916.[37] By the beginning of 1917 film was regarded as too important to be left to the private sector. In January the Bild- und Filmamt (Bufa) was set up to coordinate the production and distribution of all visual materials related to the war effort—though the military's secret classification of original front footage meant that many of the films were transparently staged.[38] Somewhat more effective were the 900 or so field cinemas that provided the troops with a mixture of propagandistic documentaries and feature films—a programme that the government tried to force on cinemas back home through threats of closure or the withholding of coal.[39] Yet the biggest step of all was the secret founding of UFA in November 1917 as a means of organizing the production and distribution of pro-German features and documentary films. Although UFA came too late to play a major role in the 'patriotic education' campaign, its start-up capital of around 25 million marks quickly enabled it to buy out a number of smaller firms, thus laying the foundations for the huge film enterprise that emerged after the war.[40]

Amidst all of these changes, the most remarkable feature of German wartime propaganda was not so much its organizational form or its specific content, but the extraordinary degree of faith placed in it by the country's military leaders, especially Ludendorff. Building on the mythical 'spirit of 1914', the emphasis on conviction and belief in victory grew especially acute towards the end of war, as it became clear that Germany could not win by military means alone. Despite its mendacious denials, the Supreme Command, like the civilian government, regarded the military situation as hopeless after the stalled spring offensives of 1918. In this situation, propaganda and the faith that it could supposedly summon represented the last remaining 'weapon' at their disposal. Throughout the closing months of the war Germans were constantly warned against the dangers of subversive propaganda. Civilians and soldiers alike were continually enjoined to reject all signs of defeatism as the work of enemy agents. 'Never before have German newspapers of all political stripes written so much about publicity and propaganda as in the last few months', remarked the advertising

---

[36] K. Wippermann, *Politische Propaganda und staatsbürgerliche Bildung* (Bonn, 1976), 28–9.
[37] S. Kahn, 'Der Film als Propagandamittel' *DR* (July–Aug. 1917), 101–4.
[38] H. Barkhausen, *Filmpropaganda für Deutschland im Ersten und Zweiten Weltkrieg* (Hildesheim, 1982); U. Oppelt, *Film und Propaganda im Ersten Weltkrieg* (Stuttgart, 2002).
[39] Barkhausen, *Filmpropaganda*, 75, 127.   [40] Kreimeier, *Ufa Story*, 38–47.

journal *Die Reklame* in September 1918.[41] 'Belief is victory' was the fundamental message during the closing stages of the war. With sufficient will-power the German people would be able to 'hold out' and break the nerve of the enemy first. Of course, such fanciful appeals to faith could hardly tip the military balance in late 1918, just as they were incapable of restoring the crumbling authority of the Wilhelmine system. But as we will now see, this highly irrational discourse of 'will' and 'spirit' had a number of important consequences, for it powerfully shaped perceptions of leadership, public opinion, and political communication for many years after the war.[42]

PROPAGANDA, THE MODERN PUBLIC, AND THE EXPERIENCE OF TOTAL WAR

'It is no longer possible to fuse the waywardness of individuals in the furnace of the war dance,' noted the American political scientist Harold Lasswell in the mid-1920s. 'A new and subtler instrument must weld thousands and even millions of human beings into one amalgamated mass of hate and will and hope. . . . The name of this new hammer and anvil of social solidarity is propaganda.'[43] Though somewhat melodramatic, Lasswell's assessment of the relationship between modern war and the modern public was nonetheless indicative of a major shift under way. Once and for all, the Great War showed that public opinion was a matter of vital importance. Among liberals and democrats, it furnished hard evidence of the need for meaningful popular input into the running of the state, proof that a genuine 'internal truce' could only come by integrating the masses into the state. Among conservatives, the dependence of the war effort on the sacrifices of the common folk swept away the last vestiges of a semi-aristocratic understanding of political leadership, whereby the state served as a bulwark against the irrationality of unenlightened opinion. Together, the intense intermingling of the military and civilian spheres and the huge mobilization efforts of 'total war' fundamentally remoulded contemporary understandings of the modern public.

On the most basic level, the unprecedented propaganda campaigns of all the belligerent states marked a significant step away from nineteenth-century panoptical and disciplinary forms of governance towards new mechanisms of persuasion and seduction.[44] In place of the conservative governing practice of 'policing', which sought to preserve order within a particular administrative territory, governments became engaged in a more pro-active form of 'surveillance',

---

[41] H. Schmidt, 'Nationale Propaganda', *DR* (Sept. 1918), 129.
[42] See Verhey, *Spirit*, 202–27.   [43] Lasswell, *Propaganda*, 221.
[44] The following discussion is based in part on C. Ross, 'Mass Politics and the Techniques of Leadership', *GH* 24 (2006), 184–211.

which sought instead to transform or 'manage' society, including values and forms of behaviour.[45] In the process, the understanding of political leadership itself changed as the ability to sustain a popular following, not merely to govern in the interests of the state, became the hallmark of modern political power. If the war greatly accelerated these long-term trends, the social and political transformations immediately afterwards further reinforced them through the introduction of a new democratic constitution and the doubling of the electorate with women's suffrage, all of which constituted a fundamental structural transformation of the public sphere. The convergence of these interrelated developments—democratic suffrage, a new appreciation of public opinion in the era of 'total war', the further growth of the mass media—meant that the end of the First World War saw, in Germany as in much of Europe, the advent of a new political form: the modern media democracy.

As a result, the problems of communicating with mass publics became a major political concern in the inter-war period. As the media-studies pioneer Emil Dovifat remarked, this was 'a time in which, unlike any other, "public opinion" is continually cited, referred to, invoked, and mobilized for the purpose of promotion or rejection, protest or support'.[46] The post-war fascination with political communication was by no means confined to Germany. Among her erstwhile enemies too, the scandalous revelations of wartime propaganda had clearly demonstrated that the manipulation of public opinion, and therefore the partial usurping of popular sovereignty itself, was a real danger.[47] Yet, for a number of reasons, these debates took on peculiar coloration in Germany. Unlike in the Allied countries, where the discussion revolved around the perceived moral failures of governments that had knowingly misled the public, in Germany it tended to focus instead on the supposed *lack* of effective propaganda. Whereas the Allied wartime information agencies were quickly closed down in the midst of public criticism, in Germany the idea that propaganda played a crucial role in the country's defeat actually led to a more *open* engagement with it among government and academic circles. Moreover, the fact that this defeat came as a shock to most Germans not only testified to how misled the modern public could be, but also unleashed a fierce controversy about the nature of the defeat itself and the lessons to be learned.[48]

Scarcely was Germany defeated when the myth of a 'stab in the back' had emerged as a means of shifting the blame from conservative and military elites

---

[45] P. Holquist, ' "Information is the Alpha and Omega of Our Work" ', *JMH* 69 (Sept. 1997), 420–1.

[46] Dovifat, 'Die öffentliche Meinung', 493.

[47] On the USA, J. M. Sproule, *Propaganda and Democracy* (Cambridge, 1997); on Britain, M. Grant, *Propaganda and the Role of the State in Interwar Britain* (Oxford, 1994); on France, F. d'Almeida, *La Manipulation* (Paris, 2005).

[48] The scale of the debate is reflected in the vast literature: see F. Scherke and U. Gräfin Vitzthum, *Bibliographie der geistigen Kriegsführung* (Berlin, 1938).

onto the civilian government.[49] According to this legend, the unconquered German military had fallen victim to a collapse on the home front under the influence of enemy propaganda. As Erich Ludendorff contended in his post-war memoirs, the vast material superiority of the enemy had long been compensated for by Germany's greater 'Siegeswillen' ('will to victory'), which was itself the result of strong, resolute leadership: 'We have fought the world, and we could fight the world with a good conscience so long as our *moral* was high.' In this view, the weakness of civilian authority in the closing months of the war created a power vacuum that exposed the German masses to the power of enemy propaganda, which hypnotized them 'as a rabbit is by a snake'.[50] It was this decisive loss of 'nerve', not the ever-growing material superiority of the enemy, that had demoralized the troops and prompted the 'November criminals' (Social Democrats, Liberals, Centre Party) to stab the army in the back. The moral of the story was that propaganda could manipulate the masses at will, and that it needed to be studied carefully to guard the Fatherland against its future enemies, both at home and abroad.

Diametrically opposed to this fanciful view was the idea that propaganda was not the culprit, that morale among the troops had collapsed because of the ever-growing realization of enemy material superiority.[51] Whatever war-weariness emerged on the German home front was less the product of enemy propaganda or socialist agitation than of the relentless deterioration of material conditions and the apparent unwillingness of the Right to countenance anything less than a 'victorious peace'. Over time, the leadership's incessant rallying-calls grew hollow; it was simply impossible to mobilize the masses for ever-greater sacrifices merely through appeals to serving the Fatherland. Ludendorff's self-serving insistence on the power of propaganda was either a cynical calculation or outright delusion. From this point of view, the lessons of the war were quite different. Not only was propaganda of limited usefulness, but such manipulative and deceitful argumentation as was perpetrated during the war had no place in a democratic public realm ideally characterized by certain rules of decent rhetoric. Moreover, the authoritarian conceptualization of public opinion that underlay such propaganda—the understanding of the masses as essentially pliable and in need of a leader—was wholly incompatible with the values of democratic sovereignty.[52]

Hovering between these two poles was the notion that propaganda was indeed a crucial factor in Germany's defeat, but that the military government was itself to blame and that troop morale was affected no less than the home front. This

---

[49] B. Barth, *Dolchstoßlegenden und politische Desintegration* (Düsseldorf, 2003); U. Heinemann, *Die verdrängte Niederlage* (Göttingen, 1983).

[50] E. Ludendorff, *My War Memories, 1914–1918*, vol. 1 (London, 1919), 361, 368.

[51] A. Köster, *Fort mit der Dolchstoßlegende!* (Berlin, 1922); G. Gothein, *Warum verloren wir den Krieg?* (Stuttgart, 1919).

[52] See generally Verhey, 'Lessons', 110 f.

meant there was no 'stab in the back'; it is therefore incorrect to associate all propaganda-centred explanations of Germany's defeat with the militarist Right. The refusal to accept Germany's military defeat and the corresponding insistence on non-military explanations was common among liberal politicians and journalists, reaching even into the SPD. In the words of Edgar Stern-Rubarth, a leading journalist with Ullstein and author of a seminal 1921 treatise on 'propaganda as a political instrument': 'only an insufficient understanding of the ultimate causes of this victory could unleash the fierce controversy over whether the front was "stabbed from behind" or collapsed of itself. For in reality we were defeated by enemy propaganda, by the struggle of words and thoughts.'[53]

Whoever was to blame, the idea that 'the peace of Versailles was ultimately less the penalty for our military defeat than the consequence of our completely defeated publicity policies (*Politik der öffentlichen Werbung*)'[54] was something that most Germans desperately wanted to believe. In a certain sense, the irrational wartime appeals to the nation's 'will' and 'fighting spirit' had their greatest impact *after* Germany's defeat. As Jeffrey Verhey has shown, the notion that German morale was the key to her success was remarkably widespread.[55] When wartime press chief Erhard Deutelmoser admitted in 1919 that 'German public opinion was led in the wrong direction, with grave consequences', he also added that 'it takes two for someone to go down the wrong path: one who points in the false direction, and one who allows himself to be guided'.[56]

Thus, after the war the assumption that the propaganda battle was the decisive one formed a basic precept of the extensive discourse on propaganda in Weimar Germany, not only among the 'scientific' works in the field, but also in journalistic treatises and in the popular press.[57] This had a number of significant political consequences. For one thing, it encouraged a vast overestimation of the power of propaganda; even publicity experts spoke of a 'propaganda psychosis' after the war.[58] Second, by assuming that the masses were seducible and needed to be led, it implicitly rested on an authoritarian understanding of public opinion. Finally, this condescending view of the masses suggested that the perceived morality of propaganda lay more in the cause it served than in the techniques of argumentation as such. If upholding order or consolidating democracy required elites to manipulate public opinion, it made no sense 'to regard agitation per se as something reprehensible'.[59]

---

[53] E. Stern-Rubarth, *Die Propaganda als politisches Instrument* (Berlin, 1921), 3.
[54] G. Schultze-Pfaelzer, *Propaganda, Agitation, Reklame* (Berlin, 1923), 35.
[55] Verhey, *Spirit*, 192 f.
[56] E. Deutelmoser, 'Die amtliche Einwirkung auf die deutsche Öffentlichkeit im Kriege' (1919), quoted from Verhey, *Spirit*, 204.
[57] Generally, T. Bussemer, *Propaganda. Konzepte und Theorien* (Wiesbaden, 2005), 100–51.
[58] A. Zinn (director of the Hamburg State Press Office), 'Kriegspropaganda des Auslandes', 10: StA Hamburg, 135–1, Staatliche Pressestelle, I–IV, 7973.
[59] Schultze-Pfaelzer, *Propaganda*, 63.

On the contrary, it made propaganda a subject worth studying in detail. One of the most visible effects of the post-war propaganda fascination was to stimulate the fledgling academic field of media studies—or 'newspaper science' (*Zeitungswissenschaft*) as it was usually called at the time—which had emerged as an offshoot of sociology after the turn of the century. In the aftermath of the war, its previous focus on the history and economics of the publishing business shifted increasingly towards the study of propaganda, which offered both a broad audience and readily available funding. During the early 1920s a series of new research institutes was founded at various universities, soon followed by the journal *Zeitungswissenschaft* and the appearance of the first standard works on the subject, which effectively established 'newspaper science' as an academic discipline.[60] These research institutes were part of a much larger network of official and semi-official organizations involved in the study of propaganda and press relations, including government agencies such as the Central Office for the Study of the War Guilt Issue (Zentralstelle zur Erforschung der Kriegsschuldfrage) and the Foreign Ministry's War Guilt Section (Kriegsschuldreferat), as well as various research facilities such as the Central Archive for Politics and Economics in Munich and the Stuttgart World War Library (Weltkriegsbücherei).[61]

Yet it was in the established areas of political and social science that the most influential theories of propaganda were developed. After the war propaganda was increasingly regarded not merely as a form of self-interested representation, but as a means of managing the centrifugal forces of modern society. In the view of sociologist Johann Plenge, author of an influential 1922 book on 'German propaganda', propaganda was a vital lubricant for the dissemination of social ideas and the smooth functioning of social organizations. 'The study of propaganda as practical social theory' constituted a core part of the curriculum of the Staatswissenschaftliches Institut which he founded in Münster in 1920.[62] Plenge's views closely paralleled those of Harold Lasswell, widely regarded as the founder of the academic study of propaganda, who drew explicitly on work carried out in Germany, including that of Plenge and Stern-Rubarth.[63] According to Lasswell, the rise of propaganda was a threefold reflection of modernity: first, that the modern world is too vast to forge social cohesion around a tribal fire; second, that it is an educated world that reads news and argument; and third, that in democratic societies individual desires take precedence over bonds of loyalty. In other words, 'propaganda is a reflex to the immensity, the rationality and wilfulness of the modern world. It is the new dynamic of society, for

---

[60] The first standard works were O. Groth, *Die Zeitung*, 4 vols. (Mannheim, 1928–30); E. Dovifat, *Zeitungswissenschaft*, 2 vols. (Berlin, 1931). Generally, J. Heuser, *Zeitungswissenschaft als Standespolitik* (Münster, 1994); L. Hachmeister, *Theoretische Publizistik* (Berlin, 1987).

[61] H. Herwig, 'Clio Deceived', in K. Wilson (ed.), *Forging the Collective Memory* (Providence, RI, 1996), 87–127.

[62] J. Plenge, *Deutsche Propaganda* (Bremen, 1922).   [63] Lasswell, *Propaganda*, 1.

power is subdivided and diffused, and more can be won by illusion than by coercion.'[64]

Different aspects of this argument were indirectly reinforced by a number of German mandarins, most notably Carl Schmitt, who explicitly argued that parliamentary democracy was incapable of forging unity and stability in the era of mass democracy.[65] Schmitt's rejection of liberal parliamentarism was based on the idea that politics was about struggle; what mattered was making decisions that guaranteed the preservation of the state, not generating a lowest common denominator through endless discussion and debate. Moreover, the compromises hammered out by parliaments were by no means a clear reflection of the popular will, subject as they were to the cynical manoeuvring of party machines. In certain circumstances, therefore, a minority government might actually be the most 'democratic' alternative—not least when democrats find themselves in the minority (a real concern in the Weimar Republic): 'Then the familiar programme of "people's education" unfolds. The people can be brought to recognize and express their own will correctly through the right education. This means nothing else but that the educator identifies his will at least provisionally with that of the people . . . Theoretically, this does not destroy democracy, but it is important to pay attention to it because it shows that dictatorship is not antithetical to democracy.'[66] Though Schmitt's arguments were addressing quite different issues from those of Lasswell or Plenge, they nonetheless shared an important implication: propaganda was not of itself immoral or anti-democratic, but rather morally and politically neutral. Indeed, it was on balance desirable, for by enabling leadership in the era of mass politics it presented a pro-active alternative to the 'politics of cultural despair' and the pessimistic diagnoses of an irrational mass public triumphing over educated opinion.[67]

From this point of view, propaganda was nothing less than a modern necessity, in politics as in commerce. It was widely agreed that the huge expansion of commercial markets and the political public required new forms of communication to replace the personal bonds of smaller traditional communities. Just as commercial 'propaganda' enabled producers to communicate with a mass, anonymous market of consumers, so did political 'propaganda' become indispensable with the emergence of a mass electorate. This perception of propaganda as a means of managing the complexities of modern society was, then, nourished by more than just the experience of the war. It was widely thought, for instance, that with the extension of the franchise to women,

[64] Ibid. 222.

[65] C. Schmitt, *The Crisis of Parliamentary Democracy* (Cambridge, Mass., 1985); generally, H. Berking, *Masse und Geist* (Berlin, 1984).

[66] Schmitt, *Crisis*, 28.

[67] Stern, *Politics*; for overviews, B. Beßlich, *Wege in den 'Kulturkrieg'* (Darmstadt, 2000); R. v. Bruch, *Wissenschaft, Politik und öffentliche Meinung* (Husum, 1980); Ringer, *Decline*; also Verhey, 'Lessons', 104–5.

additional guidance was required for this politically inexperienced segment of the electorate.[68] The reacquisition of foreign markets lost during the war likewise pointed to the need for enhanced propaganda efforts abroad, in this case a close intertwining of commercial and state activities. The trauma of revolution and bourgeois fears of an increasingly organized working class also played a role. During the political upheavals of the immediate post-war period, it appeared that only the workers' parties had learned the value of effective propaganda. Hitler himself drew much of his early propaganda inspiration from the mobilization efforts of the SPD before and after the war. In contrast to the 'vividness' of the leftist poster campaign, 'the efforts of the bourgeois parties were dragged down by the lead weight of old-fashioned, hollow ideas from the realm of higher education and suffered from officialese (*Papierdeutsch*)'.[69]

In order to overcome such ballast, it was necessary for political elites to jettison their outdated disdain for publicity and advertising. In spite of the experience of the war, advertising was still widely associated with 'market criers' (*Marktschreierei*) and swindle; as the flip-side of the same coin, political propaganda connoted rabble-rousing, deceit, and playing to the gallery.[70] Most mainstream politicians clung to the view that advertising did not ideally belong in the realm of politics. This was not just a reflection of autocratic hangovers among the bourgeois parties; the bulk of the SPD, precisely because of its Enlightenment roots, held the firm view that politics should be about substance, not appearance. In their efforts to dispel such sentiments, 'newspaper scientists' and sociologists were backed by the advertising industry itself. The need to 'advertise for advertising' and to overcome the scepticism among political and economic elites was a constant theme of advertising exhibitions throughout the 1920s, and was one of the primary motives for staging the 1929 World Advertising Congress in Berlin.[71] At the same time, the Association of German Advertisers (Verband Deutscher Reklamefachleute, renamed Deutscher Reklame-Verband in 1929) undertook extensive efforts at occupational education and self-regulation—consciously following the American industry's 'Truth in Advertising' campaign—in order to improve its image.[72] Building on early ventures in Cologne, from 1920 onwards a series of new advertising institutes and lecture courses controlled entry into the field and weeded out those who gave

---

[68] 'Die Frau und die Tageszeitung', *ZV* 22 (11 Mar. 1921), 293–5.

[69] 'Von der Werbearbeit der politischen Parteien', *DR* (Apr. 1919), 59; also D. Lehnert, 'Propaganda des Bürgerkriegs?', in D. Lehnert and K. Megerle (eds.), *Politische Teilkulturen zwischen Integration und Polarisierung* (Opladen, 1990), 61–101.

[70] See *DR* 24 (Feb. 1931), 129–30; H. Kropff, 'Zur deutschen Reklame', *DR* 24 (May 1931), 281–5; Plenge, *Propaganda*, 69–71.

[71] *DR* 22 (Mar. 1929), 160; A. Stamper, 'Die wachsende Wertung der Reklame', *SR* 6 (1921), 1–2; A. Knapp, 'Wege und Ziele der Organisation des Werbewesens', in A. Knapp (ed.), *Reklame, Propaganda, Werbung* (Berlin, 1929), 11–16.

[72] M. Pauly, 'Truth in Advertising', *DR* 16 (Apr. 1921), 135–7; G. Sherayko, 'The Science of Selling', unpublished paper, Nov. 2003.

it a bad name.[73] These training courses formed part of a wider 'scientification' of advertising which itself was geared towards elevating its status to a genuine 'profession'. The consummate 'professional' advertiser of the inter-war years was thus idealized as a combination of artist and technician, the epitome of the 'modern man' and 'new woman'—an image not at all unlike the professional self-understanding of journalists at the time.[74]

As such self-appointed 'experts' constantly argued, modern and effective propaganda was best left to the professionals. Here too, the experience of the war was cited as evidence. Among the countless post-war ruminations on the superiority of Allied propaganda, all laid special emphasis on its supposedly professional and even scientific character. As advertising organizations continually argued during the 1920s, their success was a direct result of expert involvement. According to Friedrich Schönemann, one of Plenge's assistants at the Staatswissenschaftliches Institut in Münster, the alleged potency of British and American war propaganda was due to its 'ice-cold deliberation' unencumbered by unscientific moral scruples: 'Its creators completely switched off their own feelings and were concerned solely with exerting the desired effect.'[75] This purely instrumental approach was epitomized in German eyes by the British press baron Lord Northcliffe (Alfred Harmsworth) and his 'Enemy Propaganda Department' at Crewe House, whose anti-German leaflets, sketches, and independence proclamations were widely (though mistakenly)[76] credited with the collapse of Austrian troop morale in 1918.[77] Whereas the British in particular had appointed newspapermen like Northcliffe and Lord Beaverbrook (Max Aitken, Minister of Information) to oversee their propaganda campaigns, and thus 'treated the general and the reporter as equally important factors in the war', the German military authorities stood accused of 'initially wanting to pursue the war by themselves. By the time they recognized their mistake, it was too late.'[78]

Although blaming propaganda for Germany's defeat was a comforting thought after the fact, it should be noted that such criticism was voiced well before the end of hostilities. It is simply incorrect to suggest that the notion of Allied propaganda superiority was invented by Ludendorff after the war.[79] This superiority was obvious to many foreign observers; indeed, Lasswell himself concluded that 'what not to do has been nowhere better illustrated than in Germany'.[80] There were numerous calls from 1915 onwards for the establishment of a central

[73] G. Wagner, 'Ziele', in W. Dolge (ed.), *VDR—Handbuch der Reklame 1924* (Berlin, 1924), 26.
[74] W. Schickling, 'Der Verkäufer als Künstler', *DR* 22 (Jan. 1929), 10.
[75] StA Hamburg, 135–1, Staatliche Pressestelle, I–IV, 7973, 8; generally, F. Schönemann, *Die Kunst der Massenbeeinflussung in den Vereinigten Staaten von Amerika* (Stuttgart, 1924).
[76] M. Cornwall, *The Undermining of Austria-Hungary* (Basingstoke, 2000).
[77] A view reinforced by the German translation of S. Campbell, *Secrets of Crewe House* (London, 1920): *Geheimnisse aus Crewe House* (Leipzig, 1922); see also anon., *Northcliffe. Die Geschichte des englischen Propagandafeldzuges* (Berlin, 1921).
[78] Schultze-Pfaelzer, *Propaganda*, 34.   [79] Cf. G. Paul, *Aufstand der Bilder* (Bonn, 1990), 27.
[80] Lasswell, *Propaganda*, 32.

propaganda office staffed with advertising professionals in order to overcome what one advertising journal called the 'complete anarchy' of the German propaganda effort.[81] Although the official propaganda agencies employed a handful of advertisers, it seemed to most observers 'as if the decisions on publicity matters were taken by civilian or military officials with no previous experience in the field of publicity'.[82] Thus, despite all the effort and resources poured into propaganda, the actual product—apart from the striking posters for war bonds and donations to the wounded, mostly created by professional advertisers[83]—was generally regarded within advertising circles as poor. German propaganda needed to involve professionals; it was a grave mistake 'to leave it to those who viewed matters on the world-political stage from their narrow "Prussian-official-military horizon"'. Simply put, German propaganda was 'treated in many ways as a kind of war game (*Kriegssport*), but not as serious publicity science (*Werbewissenschaft*)'.[84] By contrast, the key to the Allies' success allegedly lay in breaking down the very distinction between 'commercial' and 'political' propaganda.

This implied that the shortcomings of German wartime propaganda, and by extension the defeat itself, were ultimately due to the failure of Germany's leaders to adapt to the changing terrain of mass communications. Their conservative instincts and authoritarian tendencies blinded them to the crucial importance of publicity in the modern world. To their acute frustration, propaganda 'experts' still found evidence of this anachronism among political leaders in the continued reverence for policy substance over form. According to Ernst Jäckh, former oriental expert at the Central Office for Foreign Affairs and founding director of the Deutsche Hochschule für Politik, politics (conceived as a mixture of persuasion and responsibility) and advertising (understood as nothing more than the art of conveying a message as effectively as possible) were not only compatible, but 'indeed they need each other and yield . . . a fruitful companionship'.[85] Moreover, the new political constellation of the post-war world fused them together as never before. The military limitations imposed by the Versailles Treaty meant that overseas propaganda represented one of the few 'weapons' that Germany wielded in the international arena: 'The weapon that defeated us—the weapon that remains for us—the weapon that will secure us recovery', as Johann Plenge put it.[86] On the domestic level too, Germany's democratic constitution created an unavoidable synergy between politics and publicity. Both the introduction of universal suffrage and the liberalization of

[81] E. Grube, 'Reklame und Staat', *DR* (July–Aug. 1918), 117. See also F. Soennecken, *Vorschläge für die Errichtung eines Reichswerbeamtes* (Bonn, 1915); W. Bauer, *Der Krieg und die öffentliche Meinung* (Tübingen, 1915); L. Roselius, *Briefe* (Bremen, 1919).

[82] S. B. Banner, 'Die Reklame in der Uebergangswirtschaft', *DR* (Sept. 1917), 121–2.

[83] 'Deutschlands größtes Werbewerk', *DR* (Nov. 1916), 166; A. Walter, '9 Milliarden Kriegsanleihe und—die Reklame', *DR* (Apr. 1915), 107–8.

[84] H. Schmidt, 'Nationale Propaganda', *DR* (Sept. 1918), 132, 134.

[85] E. Jäckh, 'Politik und Reklame', *DR* 24 (Feb. 1931), 113.   [86] Plenge, *Propaganda*, 12.

markets gave individuals new powers of discretion that favoured persuasion over prescription. Advertising—whether for goods or ideas—was thus posited as an expression of freedom of choice, which itself resulted from open competition.

From this vantage-point, propaganda and advertising were not the manipulative tools of hucksters and wartime censors, but rather quite the opposite, primary expressions of democratization. It was not regarded as hyperbole to assert, as the leading advertising journal *Die Reklame* put it in 1929, that 'advertising is the single truly democratic manifestation of public life today'.[87] Although the underlying premise of this wider discourse was difficult to square with notions of democratic sovereignty, the inter-war prophets of publicity were by no means confined to the political Right, but included old-fashioned liberals and committed democrats who regarded propaganda and advertising as natural elements of an open, pluralistic order. While political leadership was of course about substance, in the era of mass politics it simply could not make do without effective presentation. And as far as presentation was concerned, 'it is for the publicity expert of no consequence whatsoever for what kind of merchandise he makes propaganda. . . . It would therefore seem, indeed the conclusion is inescapable, that the generally recognized rules of publicity are also valid for political propaganda.'[88]

ADVERTISING, MASS PSYCHOLOGY, AND THE POWER OF SYMBOLS

What were these generally recognized rules, and how did they apply to the political realm? More than anything else, it was the basic concepts of 'mass psychology' that bound together this disparate body of knowledge on advertising, propaganda, and the modern public.

'Mass psychology' was a curious amalgam of social and intellectual currents in the latter part of the nineteenth century: bourgeois fears of the lower orders, a positivist faith in scientific enquiry, and a growing sociological interest in the impact of industrialization and urbanization. Popularized above all by Gustav Le Bon's *Psychologie des foules* (first published in 1895, translated into English in 1896 and German in 1908), which became one of most widely read 'scientific' works of the era, it was above all an attack on the long-cherished Enlightenment belief in the universal ability of mankind to make rational decisions. In the work of Le Bon and other turn-of-the-century crowd psychologists, the 'mass' constituted a fundamentally different subject from the individuals that composed it. The animalistic drives that governed crowd behaviour overpowered all independent

[87] H. W. Brose, 'Die Königin unter den Werbeträgern', *DR* 22 (Dec. 1929), 908; also Frhr. v. Freytagh-Loringhoven, 'Werbung und Politik', *DR* 25 (Mar. 1932), 192–3.
[88] E. Kwilecki, 'Die Propaganda für die Präsidentenwahl', *DR* 25 (May 1932), 268.

thought. The 'tyranny of the majority' threatened not only to crush the sanctity of the individual, but also to replace enlightened leadership with the rule of mediocrity. In the place of rationality and progress, the modern 'mass'—like the 'mob' of earlier eras—represented dangerous atavistic forces, the antithesis of everything the liberal bourgeoisie stood for. Driven by emotions and primeval urges that were impervious to logical argument, the masses were utterly incapable of governing themselves, and indeed appeared to desire nothing more than being told what to do.

The new 'science' of mass psychology was thus a central element of the broader cultural pessimism that gripped the European bourgeoisie towards the end of the nineteenth century. To some extent it was a reaction to the threat posed by an increasingly organized and self-conscious working class, in particular its demands for political participation. By denying the masses any rationality or capability of self-governance, it amounted to a defence of 'spiritual aristocracy' and the right of an educated elite to run society. As such, it resonated with contemporary thinking across a number of academic disciplines, especially philosophy and the social sciences. From Ferdinand Tönnies to Werner Sombart, sociologists generally agreed on the irrationality of the modern public, even if they rejected other elements of Le Bon's arguments. Mass psychology thus fell on extremely fertile soil in Wilhelmine Germany, where a sense of despair at the erosion of cultural values was *de rigueur* among the educated elite.[89]

Gradually, these gloomy assessments of the 'mass soul' evolved into a more technocratic and pro-active approach. Gabriel Tarde's 1901 book *L'Opinion et la foule* was, in comparison to Le Bon, far more sanguine about the possibilities of steering mass opinion via the press, which he viewed as the modern equivalent of the interpersonal relationships that governed village life. A decade-and-a-half later, Wilfred Trotter's *Instincts of the Herd* (1916) reflected the growing influence of behaviourist theories on social psychology, which approached the actions of the masses—and by implication the responses of media users—as the product of biological urges.[90] Although these later treatises tended on one level to reinforce Le Bon's conclusions about the incapacity of the masses for critical thought, on another they marked a new departure by drawing a clear connection between the irrational public and its assumed manipulability through the channels of the mass media.[91]

After the turn of the century this proliferation of psychological theories began to seep into the commercial realm as well. The new fields of applied psychology and industrial psychology were brought to Germany in the 1910s primarily through the work of Hugo Münsterberg, a German psychologist

[89] See n. 67.
[90] G. Tarde, *L'Opinion et la foule* (Paris, 1901); W. Trotter, *Instincts of the Herd in Peace and War* (London, 1916).
[91] Bussemer, *Propaganda. Konzepte*, 66–72.

who had spent much of his career at Harvard. His influential 1912 book *Psychologie und Wirtschaftsleben*, resolutely behaviourist in approach, dealt not only with psychological testing and performance enhancement but also with the creation of effective advertising. Building on earlier laboratory experiments on memory, repetition, shape recognition, and page placement, his findings offered advertisers a variety of practical techniques to maximize their effectiveness. It was, for instance, Münsterberg who discovered that the upper right-hand corner of a newspaper page possessed twice the advertising value of the lower left corner, thus causing a rapid revision of newspaper fees.[92]

Although it took some years for mainstream advertisers to abandon aesthetics for science, by the 1920s the sub-field 'advertising psychology' (*Werbepsychologie*) began to exert a major impact on commercial advertising. Various journals and research institutes were founded shortly after the war, most notably the Institut für Wirtschaftspsychologie at the Berliner Handelshochschule, whose first director, Walter Moede, edited the journals *Praktische Psychologie* and *Industrielle Psychotechnik*, which regularly published articles on advertising. 'Advertising psychology' was given a further boost with the rise of more utilitarian marketing approaches in the wake of the industrial rationalization campaign. Throughout the 1920s a wave of experiments was conducted on the size, shape, scripts, lighting, placement, and colour combinations of advertisements, as well as the human capacity to absorb information presented in different formats.[93] In order to maximize the test sample, researchers even organized prize competitions to determine the most effective newspaper ads—which, interestingly enough, found immense differences between northern and southern Germany.[94] At the same time, advertising psychology also became part of the curriculum at the new training institutes in Germany, most notably the University of Cologne and the Handelshochschulen in Berlin, Mannheim, and Leipzig. The early 1920s also saw the appearance of the first synthetic works on advertising psychology, most importantly Theodor König's 1922 dissertation *Die Psychologie der Reklame*, which systematically pulled together the latest psychological research, and Christoph von Hartungen's more conventional *Psychologie der Reklame*, a discursive summary of familiar 'mass psychology' and behaviourist theories applied to commercial advertising.[95] While König pointed to the future, von Hartungen better captured the contemporary conception of advertising as a form of 'suggestion' or even 'hypnosis', a decidedly monologic and manipulative

[92] H. Münsterberg, *Psychologie und Wirtschaftsleben* (Leipzig, 1912); this finding was later qualified by experiments in the 1920s:. Reinhardt, *Reklame*, 90, 94.

[93] Reinhardt, *Reklame*, 91–5.

[94] H. Piorkowski, 'Der Anzeigen-Wettbewerb der Dresdner Neuesten Nachrichten', *Industrielle Psychotechnik*, 2 (Nov. 1925), 320–38; F. Giese, 'Die Wertung des Zeitungsinserats beim Provinzpublikum', ibid. 338–48.

[95] T. König, 'Die Psychologie der Reklame', Ph.D thesis, Würzburg (1922); C. v. Hartungen, *Psychologie der Reklame* (Stuttgart, 1921).

means of influencing human actions.[96] The underlying principle was that, as von Hartungen characteristically put it, 'exerting an effect on the psyche of an individual within the mass is most successful when it appeals to the most primordial instincts and desires'.[97]

What therefore distinguished the 'advertising psychology' of the 1920s from *fin-de-siècle* crowd theories was not only its grounding in scientific experiment but also its emphasis on devising techniques for steering consumer behaviour. In order to translate this into practice, however, it was necessary to enhance professional training and organization. As noted above, the advertising industry undertook considerable efforts at education and occupational qualification in the 1920s. Like its organizational counterparts in the United States, Britain, and France, the Association of German Advertisers sought to regulate entry into the field and to ensure wide familiarity with the basics of 'advertising science'.

If the theoretical basis of 'advertising science' lay in the principles of psychology, its chief methodology was found in the new techniques of market research emanating from the United States, where leading firms such as J. Walter Thompson, Ayer & Son, Erwin, Wasey & Co., and McCann had long used market surveys for the products they sold (indeed, the first detailed market analyses in Germany were conducted by J. Walter Thompson).[98] By the second half of the 1920s market research was deemed an integral component of Germany's rationalization efforts, at least in principle. By determining which social groups were most likely to purchase a product, and targeting publicity accordingly, it promised to increase sales at lower costs.[99] In 1928 the Association of German Advertisers sent a study group to the United States to learn about it at first hand, and at around the same time the first German-language works on market analysis were published.[100]

The expansion of market analysis was closely related to the introduction of new advertising techniques that had been developed in the United States around the turn of the century. In contrast to the aesthetically oriented poster-style advertisement, generally characterized by an attention-grabbing visual image and devoid of explanatory text, American advertisers increasingly relied on a new editorializing style that blended textual argumentation with pictorial illustration.[101] Often described as 'salesmanship in print', this new advertising genre was deliberately designed to open up new markets of 'ordinary', thrifty consumers to whom, it was believed, a product's image was less important

---

[96] See also V. Mataja, *Die Reklame*, 4th edn. (Munich, 1926), 26–8; H. Stückel, 'Suggestion in der Reklame', *DR* (Feb. 1922), 62.
[97] v. Hartungen, *Psychologie*, 5.
[98] Generally, JWT Research Reports, Microfilm Collection 16 mm, reel 224.
[99] F. Grüger, 'Grundfragen der Marktanalyse', *DR* (Oct. 1928), special edn., 742–5.
[100] H. Kropff and B. Randolph, *Marktanalyse* (Munich, 1928); A. Kiehl, *System der Markt-Analyse* (Lübeck, 1929); 'Amerika', *DR* 21 (Sept. 1928), 620–4.
[101] V. de Grazia, 'The Arts of Purchase', in B. Kruger and P. Mariani (eds.), *Remaking History* (Seattle, 1989), 230–1; generally, de Grazia, *Irresistible*, 226–83.

than its usefulness. In place of slogans, the new 'reason why' approach sought to persuade consumers to purchase a product by describing its benefits, often enlisting celebrity testimonials or scientific data to back up their claims.[102] Instead of simply grabbing attention, they sought instead to generate need, often by appealing to the desire for beauty, status, and social acceptance. Moreover, these editorializing ads—originally pioneered in US weeklies like the *Saturday Evening Post* and *Ladies Home Journal*—were specifically designed for the print media, which allowed a far more accurate targeting of certain readerships than could ever be achieved by a poster on the street. For their proponents, the adoption of such techniques relegated artistic creativity to secondary status; what counted was not so much aesthetic quality as psychological efficacy.

Armed with both a scientific theory and method, German advertisers, like their counterparts elsewhere, increasingly regarded themselves as modern technocrats, expert sculptors of popular values, expectations, and new lifestyles. The aim of modern advertising was not merely to publicize the name of a firm or product, but rather, as the marketing pioneer (and Erwin, Wasey & Co. employee) Hanns W. Brose put it, to 'win over new segments of society, to penetrate regions which have yet to see the light as to how important proper bodily hygiene, hair care, dental and skin care are for the well-being, self-improvement, and personal performance of the individual'.[103] By carefully managing the decisions of the 'controllable customer', advertising represented a form of social engineering via mass communication.

Such ideas closely resonated with contemporary theories of political propaganda. Undoubtedly the most famous exponent of the so-called 'engineering of consent' was the American publicity guru Edward Bernays, a nephew of Sigmund Freud who is widely regarded as the 'father of spin'.[104] With clients ranging from the US War Department to Ivory soap (whose buoyancy gave Bernays the idea for Ivory's famous soap-boat carving competitions), he straddled the realms of political image-making and commercial marketing like no other. In his books *Crystallizing Public Opinion* (1923) and *Propaganda* (1928), Bernays argued that the expert shaping of public opinion, based on the insights of mass psychology, was necessary for maintaining the coordination and stability of modern economic and political systems.[105] In democratic states, harnessing modern communications for the purpose of propaganda was both inevitable and benign since it enabled political elites, whose expertise and privileged access to information enabled them to make rational decisions, to guide the views of the un- or at best semi-informed majority.

---

[102] R. Marchand, *Advertising the American Dream* (Berkeley, 1985), 10; T. J. Jackson Lears, *Fables of Abundance* (New York, 1994).

[103] Brose, 'Königin', 908.

[104] L. Tye, *The Father of Spin* (New York, 1998); E. Bernays (ed.), *The Engineering of Consent* (Norman, Okla., 1955); S. Ewen, *PR!* (New York, 1996);

[105] E. Bernays, *Crystallizing Public Opinion* (New York, 1923); id., *Propaganda* (New York, 1928).

Fig. 9. Conspicuously 'American-Style' editorializing advertisement for Elida soap, by Hanns Kropff, from *Die Woche*, vol. 28 (1926). By permission of Unilever plc.

Bernays's arguments found a number of parallels in the work of Johann Plenge, whose marriage of psychological approaches with organizational techniques made him the single most influential propaganda theorist in 1920s Germany. Like Bernays, Plenge saw the key to understanding human nature in the insights of mass psychology. Accordingly, he laid particular emphasis on the communicative power of visual symbols ('the sign infused with meaning') which, like the stereotypes simultaneously described by Walter Lippmann, were capable of conveying complex messages in concentrated form and 'enabling the entire meaning to emerge within the inner experience of the observer'.[106] At the same time, Plenge's overarching interest in industrial corporatism meant that he devoted considerable attention to the practicalities of propaganda delivery, much as an advertising director sought to maximize the publicity impact of a limited marketing budget. He likened the practice of propaganda to sowing seed: random dispersal was sufficient to propagate life, but the best results were achieved if the seeds were sown 'in furrows in which they can grow . . . in the correct amount, not too little and not too much. For seeds cost money. The dissemination of propaganda costs a lot of money.'[107] In this respect Plenge was actually ahead of most commercial advertisers in Germany, the bulk of whom began to recognize the benefits of market research only later in the decade.[108]

The most influential propaganda theories of the 1920s thus displayed little of the cultural pessimism of their pre-war predecessors. Plenge, Bernays, and Stern-Rubarth all regarded the creation of 'mass society' not as a threat but as an opportunity to enhance social cohesion and streamline the exercise of power. Nevertheless, their understanding of how to shape public opinion remained firmly rooted in the categories and vocabulary of mass psychology. Though it is impossible to trace the various influences on individual authors, all of the seminal works of the inter-war propaganda discourse—including *Mein Kampf*—reflected the fundamental precepts of Le Bon's *Psychologie des foules*: the conceptualization of the masses as erratic and gullible, their controllability via psychological 'suggestion', the appellant power of emotion over reason and form over content, the attraction of action and violence, and above all the desire of the masses to invest loyalty in others. In contrast to the manly independence of the rational-minded individual, the modern crowd had always been associated with the 'feminine' traits of sentimentality and hysteria. Over time, these gender connotations were further reinforced by the increasing visibility of women among media publics—especially in the cinema—and by the extension of women's suffrage after the war. By the time Hitler wrote *Mein Kampf*, his assertion that 'the people in their overwhelming majority are so feminine by nature and attitude that sober reasoning determines their thoughts and actions far less than emotion

---

[106] Plenge, *Propaganda*, 29.   [107] Ibid. 22.

[108] T. Bussemer, *Propaganda. Konzepte*, 105–24; generally, A. Schildt, 'Ein konservativer Prophet moderner nationaler Integration', *VfZ* 35 (1987), 523–70.

and feeling' was, like most of his supposedly original insights on propaganda, no more than a characteristically brazen way of putting a widely held view.[109] In short, the purpose of political propaganda was to enable leadership in the era of mass politics, and the tools for achieving this lay in the principles and 'laws' of mass psychology.[110]

Modern propaganda, like the bulk of commercial entertainments on offer, was thus concerned primarily with the manipulation of emotions.[111] Its most powerful tools were thus seen to lie not in verbal appeals, which were associated with the intellect, but rather in the same kinds of visual allegories and symbols that drove much of the entertainment trade. This had long been conventional wisdom among advertisers. The need to capture the viewer's attention and make a swift imprint on his or her memory was a maxim of the trade well before the first psychological experiments sought to quantify it. Indeed, subsequent survey research confirmed time and again that images attracted attention more effectively than text, and that the most pleasing advertisements were usually the most visually striking or conspicuous.[112] Whether one welcomed or detested the supposed eclipse of the written word, by the 1920s the triumph of the visual image had become accepted wisdom among the educated elite. 'A picture says *more* than 1,000 words,' remarked Kurt Tucholsky in 1926. 'What 100,000 words are incapable of saying can be conveyed by the visual image, which directly takes hold of the emotions and bypasses mediation by the brain as almost irrelevant.'[113] The proof could be seen everywhere, from the cinema to the display window to the illustrated press, all of which catered to the seemingly insatiable demand for visual pleasure. As the *BIZ* put it in 1921: 'What interests the masses of people are matters of sensory perception. The formation of their opinions proceeds from the visual appearance of life and its occurrences, not through intellectual consideration and speculation.'[114] The ever-rising popularity of the cinema was also attributed to the primordial power of imagery, 'the genuine mother tongue of humankind', in the words of Béla Balázs.[115]

The clearest exposition of this view was the 1932 essay on the *Propagandamittel der Staatsidee* (propaganda for the concept of the state) by the esoteric marketing consultant Hans Domizlaff, by far the most influential propaganda theorist within Germany's commercial advertising circles. As the designer of Reemtsma's highly successful cigarette brands (*Ernte 23, R6, Gelbe Sorte*), Domizlaff was one of inter-war Germany's foremost 'brand technicians'. He has also gone down

[109] A. Hitler, *Mein Kampf*, trans. R. Manheim, (London, 1969), 167.

[110] See also Verhey, 'Lessons', 107.

[111] On media and emotions, F. Bösch and M. Borutta (eds.), *Die Massen bewegen* (Frankfurt a. M., 2006).

[112] Piorkowski, 'Anzeigen-Wettbewerb', 325, 336.

[113] P. Panther (K. Tucholsky), 'Ein Bild sagt mehr als 1000 Worte' (1926), quoted from Paul, *Aufstand*, 290.

[114] Quoted from Schmitt, *Filmwesen*, 113.

[115] B. Balázs, *Der sichtbare Mensch*, 2nd edn. (Halle, 1926), 27.

in marketing history as the inventor of the 'brand personality' and a pioneer of what is nowadays called corporate image (after 1933 he was responsible for the entire corporate design of Siemens).[116] Rooted in what was, even for the time, an uncommonly anti-humanist rendition of Le Bon's theories, Domizlaff's conception of the modern public was as a 'mass brain' characterized by a capacity for reason woefully inferior to that of the individual psyche. Incapable of rational consideration, the 'mass brain' desperately craved the simplification of abstract ideas via symbols and stereotypes perceptible to 'the primitive sensory organs'. This did not, however, mean that the crowd's powers of perception as such were inferior. On the contrary, the flip-side of its irrationality was a remarkably acute appreciation of aesthetic and stylistic qualities.[117] The job of the propagandist was to recognize these qualities, to determine how they were manifested in the particular product or client at issue, and to develop them into a 'brand personality' whose entire aura generated a sense of trust and well-being.[118] For Domizlaff, appealing to the mass brain was a matter of aesthetics as much as science, and as he had previously argued in an advertising treatise published in 1929, the 'typical mistakes' committed by advertisers often derived from a failure to recognize this.[119]

Propagandamittel der Staatsidee was essentially an application of Domizlaff's brand philosophy to the realm of politics. His basic argument was that 'a people can never maintain long-term enthusiasm about an abstract idea such as the state commonwealth if the idea is not objectified by symbols perceptible to the senses'. Rational political appeals were pointless, since 'the great mass of the people has absolutely no idea about the business of governing'. Rather, 'very simple ideas—that by no means need to be sensible, but which match the psyche of the masses in such a way as to arouse psychoses—will always render the most clever and honest government declarations ineffective'.[120] The efficacy of symbolic communication was predicated on what he called a 'uniformity of style' (*Stileinheit*), which generated a sense of commonality and what the state represented. Domizlaff offered a number of concrete (and remarkably 'modern') suggestions for achieving the desired effect, from the bestowal of state honours, to stylistic consistency in communication between the state and its citizens (forms, letterhead, coins, deeds), to an emphasis on user-friendliness and service-orientation on the part of civil servants.[121] Yet the single most important symbol was a state's flag. Domizlaff regarded the 'flag dispute' of the Weimar

---

[116] D. Schindelbeck, 'Stilgedanken zur Macht—"Lerne wirken ohne zu handeln"', in R. Gries, V. Ilgen, and D. Schindelbeck, *'Ins Gehirn der Masse kriechen!'* (Darmstadt, 1995), 45–73; H. Friebe, 'Branding Germany', in Swett, Wiesen, and Zatlin (eds.), *Selling*, 78–101.

[117] H. Domizlaff, *Propagandamittel der Staatsidee* (Hamburg, 1932), 20–1.

[118] Further elaborated in H. Domizlaff, *Die Gewinnung des öffentlichen Vertrauens* (Hamburg, 1939).

[119] H. Domizlaff, *Typische Denkfehler der Reklamekritik* (Leipzig, 1929).

[120] Domizlaff, *Propagandamittel*, 35, 87, 89.   [121] Ibid., 60–4.

Republic—with republicans adopting the *Paulskirche* colours black-red-gold and conservatives holding on to the Imperial black-white-red—as little short of a national catastrophe. In his view, neither flag was appropriate. While black-white-red stood as an emblem of suppression for liberal and regional interests, the republican flag lacked a symbolic focus. Instead, he proposed the traditional black and red Imperial eagle on a gold background (a compromise of colours and symbol), with the shield covering the eagle's breast incorporating the different colours of the federal states. Only through the creation of such commonly shared symbolic fetishes would it be possible, according to Domizlaff, to overcome the 'disastrous spiritual disunity of the German people'.[122]

In today's parlance, this was nothing short of an attempt to 're-brand' Germany, to give it a corporate identity as a focal point for social and political life. What distinguished Domizlaff's ideas from other propaganda theories was not only his focus on aesthetics but also his combination of an elitist conception of politics with a curiously 'modern' attention to personality and image. Yet in the wider context of inter-war propaganda debates his arguments, though novel, ultimately reinforced a point of general consensus: namely, the crucial role of stereotypes, metaphors, and symbols in modern politics. As the seminal propaganda theories of the 1920s and early 1930s clearly demonstrate, Walter Benjamin's oft-cited notion of the 'introduction of aesthetics into political life' was by no means confined to the fascist organization of the masses.[123] The deliberate recourse to political symbols, imagery, and allegory was a fundamental characteristic of the age of the mass media, especially after the experience of the First World War. It expressed a new vocabulary of political communication that corresponded to the shifting modes of cultural perception in a highly medialized public sphere. For many contemporaries, the immense potential—for good or ill—of modern communications and propaganda techniques made it imperative to harness them for the cause of stability and social integration. As the 'experts' constantly warned, it was a missed opportunity, even a danger, to ignore them. How, more concretely, German political elites sought to tap their potential is the subject of the next chapter.

---

[122] Domizlaff, *Propagandamittel*, 45. On the flag dispute, W. Ribbe, 'Flaggenstreit und Heiliger Hain', in D. Kurze (ed.), *Aus Theorie und Praxis der Geschichtswissenschaft* (Berlin, 1972), 175–88.
[123] Benjamin, 'Work of Art', 234.

8

Republicans, Radicals, and the Battle of Images

The propaganda theories of the early twentieth century were, generally speaking, conceived as a means of integrating the masses into a commonly shared network of political communication. Whether in the corporatist *Staatspropaganda* of Plenge or the 'uniformity of style' advocated by Domizlaff, the overarching aim was to promote social stability by harmonizing public opinion with the prevailing political and economic system. At base, modern propaganda techniques sought to enable elites to exercise rational leadership without openly breaching the principles of democratic sovereignty. This was, as we have seen, very much a matter of shaping public opinion to the needs of political elites, not the other way around. It was a deliberate attempt at social engineering via the scientific management of political communication.

But the dissemination of political propaganda via the mass media was no less fraught with ambiguities, contradictions, and unpredictability than the commercial entertainments that existed alongside it. Between the intentions of producers, the interests of audiences, and the concrete context in which it appeared, political propaganda too could exert both integrative and disintegrative effects. The proliferation of symbols, stereotypes, and imagery that accompanied the shift to 'mass politics' had multiple uses: on the one hand to build support, and on the other to distinguish a particular group from its opponents. Moreover, the notion that political elites could use the media as a means of social and political integration seemed conspicuously inappropriate in early twentieth-century Germany, a society whose elites were themselves bitterly divided over what the public needed to be told. In the Weimar era in particular, there was little consensus even on the basic constitution of the state. Judging from the post-war press, by the summer of 1919 the prospects for even a minimal parliamentary consensus already appeared slim.[1] The new forms of entertainment that expanded throughout the 1920s may well have traversed political boundaries, but in many ways the media public was more fragmented than ever along political lines, shocked by the experience of left-wing uprisings and right-wing putsch attempts, and continually inflamed by the violence of conflicting political militias. If

---

[1] B. Asmuss, *Republik ohne Chance?* (Berlin, 1994), 553, 573.

modern propaganda represented a political 'weapon', it was deployed here in a Balkanized war zone.

This chapter investigates how political elites sought to deploy the media and new propaganda techniques during the Weimar years. It first considers the attempts of republicans to devise a more democratic form of publicity distinct from the negative connotations of 'propaganda'. It then analyses the challenge posed by the aggressive and in many ways cutting-edge image campaigns of the radical anti-republican movements, especially the National Socialists, and how both the deepening crisis of the early 1930s and the 'lessons' of the wider discourse on propaganda eventually led many democrats themselves to doubt the possibility of winning public support by democratic means alone.

PUBLICITY FOR THE REPUBLIC: FROM PROPAGANDA TO INSTRUCTION

Although the post-war faith in the benevolence of propaganda was by no means universally shared, most republican politicians agreed on the need for some form of popular political guidance after the upheavals of 1918–19. The SPD, for its part, had long relied on a combination of propaganda and political education as central pillars of its strategy. After the war the bulk of liberals, now deprived of their electoral privileges and somewhat suspicious of public opinion, also began to view propaganda as a matter of priority. In the words of Theodor Wolff, editor of the liberal *Berliner Tageblatt*, 'a people like the Germans, whose political maturity had remained undeveloped under its previous subordination, must be educated above all for its new tasks, its new state form, and its new responsibilities'.[2] The question was, of course, where to draw the line between appropriate 'education' and inappropriate 'manipulation' of public opinion. There were no easy answers, for as Edward Bernays pointedly put it in *Crystallizing Public Opinion* (1923): 'The advocacy of what we believe in is education. The advocacy of what we don't believe in is propaganda.'[3]

During the Weimar years this was not just a matter of abstract debate but of concrete policy. At the most basic level, it was clear to everyone that the collapse of the autocratic regime had produced a fundamentally new situation. As Bavarian press officials remarked in 1919: 'Public opinion is a factor of political life that a government must bear in mind and utilize to a far greater degree than has hitherto been the case.'[4] From the perspective of the new civilian government,

---

[2] T. Wolff, 'Der 1. August 1914', *Berliner Tageblatt* (1 Aug. 1919), from B. Sösemann (ed.), *Theodor Wolff*, (Düsseldorf, 1993), 144–5.

[3] Quoted from Sproule, *Propaganda*, 57.

[4] BayHStA, MJu 17439, 'Die Pressezentrale des Volksstaates Bayern', 13 May 1919.

the war of words by no means ceased with the end of armed hostilities. The task of generating public sympathy and casting doubt on the motives of Germany's erstwhile enemies formed a cornerstone of German diplomatic efforts during the negotiations over the post-war international order. After the armistice the ongoing propaganda struggle took on a new domestic dimension as the fledgling republic was repeatedly threatened over the following months by internal political turmoil. In the circumstances, the question was less whether the government should influence public opinion than how best to do it.

Thus, despite the abolition of censorship in November 1918, the new civilian government retained rather than dismantled the administrative framework inherited from the Kaiserreich. General propaganda activities remained the remit of the Zentrale für Heimatdienst, now rechristened the Reichszentrale für Heimatdienst (hereafter RfH), directed from its inception by Richard Strahl, a former personal consultant to Deutelmoser in the Foreign Ministry news office. Amidst far-reaching discussions about establishing a central agency for 'popular education' (Reichsaufklärungsamt or Reichszentrale für Volksaufklärung), the RfH offered a ready-made tool for propagating the government's policies.[5] In the field of press relations the provisional government actually accelerated the process of centralization that had begun during the war, fusing the press bureaus of the Chancellery and Foreign Ministry into the Reich Press Office (Reichspresseamt, hereafter RPO) in autumn 1919.[6] Henceforth the bulk of press relations were directed by a new Reich press chief, whose job was to represent the whole spectrum of government policy to both the domestic and international press. The importance attached to the RPO was clearly expressed in its size: it employed no fewer than 416 staff in 1919, a wholly different magnitude from the small outfits before 1914.

During the initial months after the war, both the RfH and the government press offices faced two primary tasks: to ward off the spectre of revolution at home and to win as many international friends as possible for the conclusion of a peace treaty. On the domestic front the left-wing press, revelling in its liberation from censorship, was seen as a major culprit for the tide of working-class radicalism that erupted in the Spartacist uprising of January 1919 and the Bavarian soviet republic in April. The main difficulty lay in the limited influence of the coalition parties on the German press, or more precisely the limited influence among working-class readers of the newspapers over which they wielded some control.[7] On an international level, the main focus of attention was the question of German responsibility for the war and liability for reparations

---

[5] BAB R43/I/2490, fos. 23–6; BayHStA, MJu 17435, 'Entwurf einer Organisation für Volksbildung, Aufklärung und Beratung'.
[6] K. Tiemann, 'Reichspressedienst', *ZV* 22 (27 May 1921), 660.
[7] GStA PK, Rep. 90, Nr. 2415, Interior Ministry memorandum, 4 Apr. 1919, fo. 222.

payments. Throughout early 1919 there was considerable disagreement over what approach should be taken: whether to release as many documents as possible, thus demonstrating a clean break with the previous regime in the hope of achieving a more lenient settlement; or to withhold incriminating material and insist on older justifications of a preventive war. In the event, both strategies were pursued. While the socialist Karl Kautsky was commissioned to edit the relevant Foreign Ministry documents for publication, the Foreign Ministry itself established a special War Guilt Section (Kriegsschuldreferat) to supply the press with tendentious material that placed German pre-war policies in a favourable light. During the summer treaty debates it was the latter tactic that prevailed, and by the time the full documentation was made available at the end of the year both the hated Versailles Treaty and the sense of injustice over German 'war guilt' had become branded on public consciousness. Over the following years a variety of nationalist and semi-official organizations—mostly financed by the Foreign Ministry—proved highly successful at keeping the issue alive and generating a wide consensus within Germany about the 'war-guilt lie'.[8]

In the meantime, the propaganda focus of the early 1920s shifted to the series of nationality disputes in Germany's border regions, above all the Saar and Rhineland. The occupied areas along the Franco-Belgian border were home to a host of nationalist organizations that sought to counter the indigenous separatist movement and the French policy of 'pénétration pacifique'.[9] The Rheinische Volkspflege organization, specially set up in 1919–20 by the RfH, became the central coordinating agency for propaganda activities against the French occupation. Masked as a private organization, it was well connected with the local nationalist groups from which it recruited young right-wing idealists such as Werner Best, who would later become a leading figure in the Third Reich.[10] The moment of truth came with the Ruhr dispute of 1923, as the German agencies launched a far-reaching propaganda campaign in support of the government's passive-resistance policy. Although censorship by the occupation authorities made this difficult within the Ruhr itself, the attempt to gain sympathy abroad was important in any event.[11] For this task the government was assisted by a vast range of semi-official propaganda organizations, most notably the Wirtschaftspolitische Gesellschaft, which fed articles to the international press and financed trips to Germany by prominent foreigners. Financed largely by Rhineland industry, it was closely connected to government agencies through its managing secretary Alfred von Wrochem, a former director of Rheinische Volkspflege (and later, in the mid-1930s, head of the foreign press section of the

[8] See Ross, 'Mass Politics', 195–6; also, generally, Herwig, 'Clio Deceived'.
[9] BAB R43/I/2491, French Nachrichtendienst, fos. 3–17; BayHStA, MK 41171; generally, F. Wein, *Deutschlands Strom—Frankreichs Grenze* (Essen, 1992).
[10] U. Herbert, *Best* (Bonn, 1996).
[11] C. Fischer, *The Ruhr Crisis, 1923–1924* (Oxford, 2003), 37.

RMVP).[12] The national chauvinism peddled by the more militant organizations often degenerated into overt racism: the image of the predatory Afro-French soldiers and the 'Rhineland bastards' they fathered was first coined at this time. The Foreign Ministry and Prussian authorities were somewhat more diplomatic, focusing on the distribution of statistics and literature designed to counter foreign claims that Germany had not paid any real reparations and to highlight the shocking rise in mortality rates, food prices, and illness in the Ruhr. This was a promising publicity theme, for it was not difficult to gain coverage and sympathy abroad in view of the near famine-like conditions and resulting evacuation of children during the height of the conflict.[13]

Yet despite such isolated successes and the growing diplomatic isolation of France, the German propaganda campaign as a whole was decried as a failure. The general conclusion was that the government had signally failed to learn the propaganda lessons of the war. Many of the activities of Rheinische Volkspflege were little short of disastrous: it not only alienated local authorities by presumptuously telling them how to deal with the French Ruhr army, it also put off many ordinary people by conveying the distinct—and not wholly inaccurate—impression that officials in Berlin harboured doubts about the patriotism of their Rhineland compatriots.[14] At the same time, the government's international press campaign was also roundly castigated for its half-heartedness and amateurism. As the *Vossische Zeitung* put it, 'Germany is doing far too little in this regard, and whoever does not recognize this is short-sighted and naive'.[15] Instead of letting professionals do the job, 'one satisfies oneself with the appointment of a few recommended journalists into the machinery of government, where they are quickly submerged under the interplay of surreptitious forces and become worn down by office work'.[16] As a result, the government was letting a golden opportunity slip through its fingers, as even foreign journalists remarked: 'If you were doing to the French what they are doing to you—the world would be foaming with rage at you.'[17] Although the French authorities painted a very different picture of a sprawling and well-oiled German propaganda machine,[18] the impression east of the Rhine was of a comprehensive propaganda defeat. And once again, much of the problem was blamed on the complacent conservatism of senior officials such as Chancellery secretary Werner

---

[12] BAB R43/I/2491, 'Vertraulich: Entstehung, Aufgaben und Ziele der Wirtschaftspolitischen Gesellschaft E. V.', fos. 231–5; BAB R43/I/2491, fos. 225–6; BAB R43/I/2509, fos. 27 f; see also A. v. Wrochem, *Die Kolonisation der Rheinlande durch Frankreich* (Berlin, 1922).
[13] BAB R43/I/2491 fos. 159 f; Fischer, *Ruhr*, 37, 108–10.
[14] Wein, *Deutschlands Strom*, 166.
[15] 'Die Kunst der Propaganda', *Vossische Zeitung*, 11 Mar. 1923.
[16] 'Die Zeitung als Waffe', *Hamburgischer Correspondent*, 10 Mar. 1923.
[17] Remarks of an English journalist to a *Deutsche Allgemeine Zeitung* correspondent: 'Propaganda', *DAZ* 29 (Mar. 1923).
[18] BAB R43/I/2491, fos. 3–17.

Freiherr von Rheinbaben, who, when pressed on the issue, reportedly remarked: 'for heaven's sake, no propaganda!'[19]

With the end of passive resistance in the Ruhr, government propaganda efforts abruptly shifted from confrontation towards garnering support for rapprochement with France.[20] This entailed a change of focus back onto the domestic front, where Gustav Stresemann and his government repeatedly sought to enhance their influence on the print media. In 1925 he appointed none other than Edgar Stern-Rubarth as chief editor of the WTB, which by this time was for all intents and purposes a government mouthpiece.[21] Stresemann also supported the purchase of the *Deutsche Allgemeine Zeitung* (the successor to the semi-official *Norddeutsche Allgemeine Zeitung*, temporarily owned by the industrialist Hugo Stinnes) in 1925 as a more direct vehicle of pro-government views. Such pro-active endeavours, especially when measured against those of his predecessors, have led some to regard Stresemann as 'by far the best PR-chief of this republic'.[22]

Yet in many ways the most noteworthy aspect of Stresemann's media-political efforts was the rapid resale of the *Deutsche Allgemeine Zeitung* in 1927, for it symbolized the increasing difficulty that governments faced on the new terrain of press relations. For one thing, it took little time for the secret acquisition of the paper to get out, and once the purchase was revealed it was difficult for the republican government to justify publicly. At a more basic level, it was hardly possible during the Weimar era for a government to exert direct control over a particular newspaper for the simple reason that governments and their policies underwent frequent and far-reaching changes. As the *Frankfurter Zeitung* pointed out in 1926, the times when a new government meant a slightly different shade of conservatism were long gone. No newspaper could shift its editorial position in line with the procession of different governments and still hope to maintain its loyal readership. In contrast to the Imperial era, direct state ownership or financial support of a newspaper no longer made much sense: 'in a parliamentary state, semi-official newspapers are an absurdity.'[23] This situation played very much into the hands of the nationalist Right, insofar as the end of subsidies for the provincial press, on which many small papers relied for survival, allowed cash-rich industrial interests to leap into the breach. The effects were compounded by the fact that Hugenberg's Telegraphen-Union news agency had meanwhile dislodged the WTB from its quasi-monopoly position within

[19] From 'Zeitspiegel', *Hamburgischer Correspondent*, 8 Jan. 1924; on propaganda in the Ruhr crisis generally, K. Baschwitz, *Der Massenwahn, seine Wirkung und seine Beherrschung* (Munich, 1923).
[20] See H. J. Müller, *Auswärtige Pressepolitik und Propaganda zwischen Ruhrkampf und Locarno (1923–1925)* (Frankfurt a. M., 1991).
[21] Basse, *Wolff's*, 217–21.
[22] Rudolf Morsey quoted from Müller, *Auswärtige*, 275; see also Koszyk, *Deutsche Presse 1914–1945*, 143–5.
[23] *FZ* (24 Nov. 1926), quoted from Koszyk, *Deutsche Presse 1914–1945*, 147.

Germany.[24] True, the 1922 Laws for the Protection of the Republic banned the publication of material intended to foment hostility against the Republic, and the Reich president also possessed constitutional powers to limit press freedoms in the interests of upholding public order. But these provisions were only applicable in extreme cases, and moreover were enforced far more leniently in some federal states than in others.

If the swelling influence of Hugenberg's empire were not challenging enough, the visible shortcomings of the government's own press relations only made matters worse. Ministers and journalists regularly complained about the uncoordinated and unnecessarily bureaucratic practices of the RPO, especially during the first half of the 1920s as the position of Reich press chief changed hands with nearly every government prior to Walter Zechlin's lengthy tenure from 1926 to 1932. Yet even under Zechlin the RPO never fully centralized press relations. Several ministries maintained their own outfits, most notably defence and economics, and the federal states too handled press relations independent of Reich authorities. In spite of employing 'an army of officials', as the journal *Zeitungs-Verlag* complained, 'the management of the Reich Press Office is deplorable (*jämmerlich*). Only in the most exceptional cases does it succeed in conveying to the German press a clear and uniform position on matters of foreign and domestic policy.'[25] In addition, over the early years of the Republic this 'army' was systematically reduced from 416 staff in 1919 to 168 in 1922—a figure that included secretaries, drivers, even cleaners.[26]

If the government's dealings with the press were problematic, its engagement with other media was all but non-existent. This was manifestly the case with radio, for two primary reasons. First, the largely 'formal' or procedural understanding of democracy in the Weimar Republic led the architects of German radio to believe that any political broadcasts by one group would have to entail equal broadcast time for others, even anti-republicans, on the basis of 'parity of access'. The principle of 'non-political' airwaves was thus intended to avoid the colossal problems this would cause. This did not, it should be noted, apply in the same way to broadcasts aimed outside Germany's borders; successive governments sponsored frequent pro-German broadcasts in ethnically mixed border regions detached from the Reich after the war.[27] But for domestic listeners, explicitly political programming was to have no place in a broadcasting service whose mission was to serve as a unifying 'cultural factor'. This integrationist understanding of radio was the second reason why the government made so little use of it. In the words of Hermann Schubotz, director of the Deutsche Welle, broadcasting should 'mitigate, not intensify, the internal struggles from which

---

[24] See Chap. 6.
[25] Tiemann, 'Reichspressedienst', 660; see also GStA PK, Rep. 90, Nr. 2415, fo. 240.
[26] BayHStA, MJu 17439, 'Die Presseabteilung der Reichsregierung', 11 Jan. 1922, 2–3.
[27] v. Saldern, '*Volk* and *Heimat*', 335–6.

our nation suffers'.[28] In the volatile political atmosphere of the 1920s, many thought the best way to achieve this was to avoid politics altogether.

Typically, however, Schubotz's 'non-political' vision of radio showed no recognition that this was itself a political position, as critics from across the spectrum continually argued. While right-wing groups from the Stahlhelm to the Nazis whined about the 'Marxist' radio programme, it was the Left that complained loudest, for the 'non-partisan' radio policy largely served—as intended—to keep left-wing views off the airwaves. As the ever-quotable Kurt Tucholsky argued, instead of creating an 'everyday democracy' in which competing views could be heard, the executives retreated into an allegedly non-political 'patriotic radio' programme that effaced genuine differences 'as if one says that we allow the use of new cars but only if driven by generals and nationalistic students'. Ultimately, the problem lay in the unwillingness of elites to cede authority to popular views: 'first we need to have a radio law, regulations for enforcing the law, judicial and literary consultation and twenty-four investigations into the "psychology of radio" before it gets spoken around in Germany that radio has to be neutral. Which it isn't.'[29] But despite such criticisms, and despite the unavoidable inclusion of some 'political' content, on the whole this stance was strictly adhered to throughout the 1920s.[30]

In many ways the cinema seemed a better prospect for government influence given the increasing state involvement in film production during the war. But here too, efforts to use it for republican publicity were paltry. Although Bufa was immediately dismantled at the end of the war, UFA was left entirely intact. To his credit, President Ebert was quick to divulge the secret involvement of the previous government, openly declaring that the Reich still held one-third of UFA shares. But after this frank admission, no moves were made to divest the shares until the journal *Film-Kurier* exposed the failure to list them in a register of government investments in 1921. There could hardly have been any sinister intentions behind this, for during the period 1918–21 the government did nothing to influence production. It not only left UFA's entire board of directors intact, but astonishingly abstained from exercising its own rights to vote. Only four films were produced under government contract in these years: one on tuberculosis, one on artificial limbs, a short on the effects of the Allied blockade, and an anti-Bolshevik film entitled *Der schwarze Gott*. The latter was the only genuinely 'political' film of the four, and even then the government got cold feet and almost banned it before its (very muted) release.[31]

After the sale of the UFA shares there was even less scope for using the cinema for republican propaganda. What is more, the opportunities that still

[28] H. Schubotz, 'Politik und Rundfunk' (1930), in Bredow (ed.), *Archiv*, 170.
[29] K. Tucholsky, 'Der politische Rundfunk' (1926), repr. in Schneider (ed.), *Radio-Kultur*, 207–8.
[30] See generally Lerg, *Rundfunkpolitik*.   [31] Monaco, *Cinema*, 27, 30, 38.

existed were left unexploited. The single most significant move was the Müller cabinet's 1928 bail-out of Germany's second largest film company, Emelka, to prevent its purchase by Alfred Hugenberg, who had taken over UFA the year before. This intervention occurred against a background of increasingly partisan UFA newsreels during the latter 1920s, so-called 'black-white-red newsreels' deliberately geared towards discrediting the republic.[32] Blocking the sale was thus easy to justify on both legal and political grounds, and the liberal press responded without much comment.[33] Yet when Carl Severing, the interior minister who had arranged the purchase, was savagely attacked in the right-wing press, the government did little to counter the scandal-mongering. Even worse, after paying the price of such hysteria it made little use of its leverage over Emelka in terms of either its production or programme in the fifty or so cinemas the company operated in the latter 1920s. The general view within government circles was that the cinema should remain 'neutral', and that government must lead by example. In the words of Carl Severing: 'films that positively promote the republican idea will increasingly be produced by the film industry itself out of its own interest in meeting the demands of the audience. . . . I consider it not only superfluous, but wrong to create such films artificially.'[34] While such reticence was in one sense a laudable expression of republican ideals, in the context of increasing right-wing influence within the film industry it was a luxury that the Republic could scarcely afford.

The bulk of government communications therefore remained centred on the press and the RfH. While the RPO retained a narrowly journalistic focus, the RfH was conceived as a tool for general 'political education' in favour of the Republic—indeed, it was the direct ancestor of the West German Bundeszentrale für Heimatdienst (founded in 1952), which in 1963 acquired its present name Bundeszentrale für politische Bildung. Immediately after the war it supported the new government in a variety of ways: working with the Council of People's Deputies, distributing information on the issue of nationalization, fighting against various strike movements, and later on, agitating against the Kapp Putsch.[35] The first serious problems arose during the Reichstag elections of June 1920, for during the course of the campaign the RfH exposed itself to accusations of making propaganda for the Weimar coalition parties (SPD, Centre, and DDP). This was dangerous territory, for it raised the thorny question of how appropriate such 'state propaganda' was within a democracy and how—indeed whether—it could remain above party politics given that a significant segment of opinion rejected the constitution itself.

---

[32] 'Schwarz-weiß-rote Wochenschauen', *LBB* 21 (16 Aug. 1928), 1–2.

[33] 'Kino und Republik', *BT*, 7 Nov. 1928; 'Filmpolitik des Reiches', *BT*, 14 Nov. 1928; 'Die Reichsbeteiligung bei der Emelka', *Vossische Zeitung*, 15 Nov. 1928: press clippings in StAH, 135–1, Staatliche Pressestelle, I–IV, 5025.

[34] *FK* 11, Sondernummer (1 June 1929), suppl.

[35] Wippermann, *Politische Propaganda*, 70.

As with the radio, the notion that the most 'democratic' course of action was to grant equal representation to all political views put the RfH in a difficult position. If the abstract goal was 'political education', the actual content was open for debate. But despite calls for its dissolution by the extreme Left, the mainstream parties, understandably jittery after the putsch attempt in March 1920 and the recent clashes with the 'Red Ruhr Army', were reluctant to forfeit the republic's main instrument of political education. The RfH was eventually salvaged by a Reichstag decision in July 1921, albeit henceforth under close multi-party control and with a narrower remit: 'The Reichszentrale für Heimatdienst serves the aim of factual instruction (*sachliche Aufklärung*) on issues of foreign and economic policy as well as social and cultural issues, not in the spirit of individual parties, but from the perspective of the state as a whole.'[36]

The key term was 'factual instruction', for it was intended to denote something wholly different from 'propaganda'. As the RfH's official organ explained: 'In contrast to propaganda, instruction is rooted in logic and is based on solid facts, from which each individual can and should draw his or her own conclusions. This instruction does not seek to impose a ready-made opinion as in the case of propaganda, but rather seeks to stimulate one's own judgement and reflection through providing sound and conclusive documentation.' The key distinction was whether it furnished open-ended information for rational deliberation (which was considered 'democratic'), or closed opinions via 'market-crying and the loud ballyhoo of propaganda'[37] (which was not). This principle was soon reflected in the day-to-day activities of the RfH, which deliberately avoided 'extensive methods of mass propaganda' (assemblies, posters, flyers, and so on) in favour of concentrating on 'the "sub-leaders" (*Unterführer*) in the political and economic life of the nation'.[38] In the parlance of communication theory, the RfH consciously opted for a 'two-step' flow of communication via opinion-leaders rather than relying on the 'magic bullet' of direct appeals to the masses. For this task it relied on around 30,000 honorary staff, most of them professionals and/or functionaries of local party associations who distributed pamphlets and helped organize public lectures. To reach them it published its own journal, *Der Heimatdienst*, with some 11,000 subscriptions and a circulation of around 40,000. Yet the main activity of the RfH was its civic education courses, specifically geared for social 'multipliers' such as teachers, administrators, organization-chairpersons, and other professionals. Over the budget year 1928/9 it organized fifty-five such courses involving around 75,000 participants.[39]

[36] Wippermann, *Politische Propaganda*, 169.

[37] O. Schöny, 'Propaganda oder Aufklärung?', *Der Heimatdienst* (Oct. 1921), cited from Wippermann, *Politische Propaganda*, 236–8.

[38] BAB R43/I/2508, 'Die gegenwärtige staatsbürgerliche und wirtschaftliche Aufklärungsarbeit der Reichszentrale für Heimatdienst', Nov. 1922, fo. 55.

[39] Ibid.; also BAB R43/I/2511, 'Tätigkeitsbericht der Reichszentrale für Heimatdienst für das Etatjahr 1928/29', 19 June 1929, fos. 353–63.

The point to recognize here is that this low-key form of targeted 'political education', as opposed to more emotive and visible 'mass propaganda', not only defined the work of the RfH but was symptomatic of republican publicity as a whole. Such efforts were deemed both more democratic and more effective in the long run.[40] The problem was that the long-term prospects of German democracy were less than certain, and in the short term the overwhelming emphasis on rational appeals aimed at opinion-leaders rather than on generating a sense of attachment to the new political system among the population at large contributed decisively to the Republic's oft-cited 'sensory deficit' (*Sinnlichkeitsdefizit*),[41] or lack of rituals and symbols objectifying and supporting the new political order.

Historians were by no means the first to perceive this poverty of symbolic self-representation; it was already obvious to contemporaries, including many republicans, during the flag disputes of the early 1920s.[42] In May 1924 Anton Erkelenz, the DDP's leading publicist, flatly told his party colleagues that 'there must be an active struggle for the Republic and democracy, and it must conform to the new forms of propaganda'. Like other critics proposing a more emotive style, he argued that the 'Republic has been too sober and has had too little to offer the senses; this has to change.'[43] The development of republican symbols and rituals was one of the chief responsibilities of Edwin Redslob in his capacity as 'Reichskunstwart' (Reich art intendant), a position created after the war as a formal link between the artistic community and the national government. Under Redslob's supervision, the Reich staged elaborate republican ceremonies for remembering the war and for 'Constitution Day', 11 August. The tenth anniversary celebrations of the constitution in August 1929 were, at a cost of over RM 100,000, a conscious attempt to showcase the Republic and to counteract the increasingly prominent spectacles of the radical movements.[44]

But despite all the expenditure and careful planning, these attempts at republican political theatre lacked energy and conviction. They lacked energy insofar as they were too cerebral for most spectators. As the *Deutsche Allgemeine Zeitung* put it: 'Always the people will be ready to celebrate with its whole heart . . . when it is given supporting symbols . . . But our celebrations are much too rational. Nobody can identify with them.'[45] And they lacked conviction

---

[40] e.g. Stern-Rubarth, *Propaganda*, 21 ff.   [41] This term from Paul, *Aufstand*, 117.

[42] B. Sösemann, *Das Ende der Weimarer Republik in der Kritik demokratischer Publizisten* (Berlin, 1976), 149; Sling (P. Schlesinger), 'Das Volk ohne Fahne' (June 1922), in Sling, *Nase der Sphinx*, 141–3; Ribbe, 'Flaggenstreit', 175–88.

[43] Quoted from F. Möller, 'Die sich selbst bewußte Massenbeeinflussung', in G. Diesener and R. Gries (eds.), *Propaganda in Deutschland* (Darmstadt, 1996), 14.

[44] Generally, P. Swett, 'Celebrating the Republic without Republicans', in K. Friedrich (ed.), *Festive Culture in Germany and Europe from the Sixteenth to the Twentieth Century* (Lampeter, 2000), 281–302; A. Heffen, *Der Reichskunstwart* (Essen, 1986); E. Redslob, *Von Weimar nach Europa* (Berlin, 1972).

[45] *DAZ*, 28 Nov. 1930, quoted from S. Behrenbeck, 'The Nation Honours the Dead', in K. Friedrich (ed.), *Festive Culture*, 312.

because the endless political compromises that were required between the various parties diluted their symbolism to a pallid common denominator. Even the choice of a national holiday was hotly disputed. Whereas much of the Left favoured 9 November (the proclamation of the Republic) or the traditional May Day, others preferred the 'national' focus of 18 January, celebrating the formal unification of Germany in 1871. The compromise of 11 August, the day the Weimar constitution was enacted, in many ways commemorated a bureaucratic decision. Unlike the emotive power of Bastille Day or October Revolution Day, it was hardly an anniversary capable of firing the imagination.[46] As the *Kieler Zeitung* remarked during the preparations for the tenth-anniversary celebrations, trying too hard to turn this into a national holiday was counter-productive: 'one pushes a large segment of the populace . . . into ever greater opposition to the idea of a celebration for the Weimar constitution.'[47] Much the same could be said for popularizing the Republic as a whole, which many Germans likewise viewed as a 'rotten compromise'.

Of course, no amount of political showmanship could overcome the deep social and political fissures that plagued Weimar democracy. It is easy to understand why the weaknesses of republican self-representation were not a central focus of attention during the 1920s. Given the background of political assassinations and the continual shenanigans of radical paramilitary groups, they hardly seemed to number among the most serious threats to the political system. Yet, as we will see below, perceptions shifted noticeably with the onset of acute economic and political crisis. Only weeks after the 1929 Constitution Day celebrations, the Republic's 'sensory deficit' was increasingly seen as a dangerous vacuum of political communication.

THE RADICAL ONSLAUGHT

The publicity strategies of the radical movements could hardly have been more different from the republican focus on 'factual instruction' and 'political education'. If Weimar democrats conceived of the political realm ideally as a form of rational discourse bounded by certain rules of propriety and evidence, the radical parties on both Left and Right viewed it as an all-out battle, a no-holds-barred war for loyalty, votes, and physical presence on the streets.[48] Throughout this struggle they unequivocally focused on hearts over minds. Unlike their democratic opponents, the radicals had no qualms about manipulating emotions

---

[46] Swett, 'Celebrating', 282, 295; generally, F. Schellack, *Nationalfeiertage in Deutschland von 1871–1945* (Frankfurt a. M., 1990).

[47] 'Wenn Ihr's nicht fühlt, Ihr werdet's nie erjagen', *Kieler Zeitung*, 4 July 1929.

[48] See Swett, *Neighbors*; E. Rosenhaft, *Beating the Fascists?* (Cambridge, 1983); R. Bessel, *Political Violence and the Rise of Nazism* (New Haven, 1984).

and generating a visceral sense of belonging. In many respects their propaganda aims amounted to a mobilization of the very senses that the Republic had largely neglected. In place of the dry, rational language of function and interest, they introduced a new vocabulary of iconography and rituals designed to enthral their supporters, mock their enemies, and generally attract attention. Through the deliberate use of reductive stereotypes and visual metaphors, they represented the political equivalent of a sensationalist tabloid. This was, in short, political propaganda designed for a mass public that had become accustomed to the attention-grabbing techniques of modern media spectacle.

Ironically, it was the SPD, a central pillar of the Republic, that had pioneered such techniques before the war. Its marches, streaming banners, and dramatic iconography had formed a central part of the pre-war socialist movement and proved highly effective at mobilizing members and publicizing the values of the party among the working classes. They provided much of the inspiration for Hitler's own views on propaganda, and were of course the direct forerunners of communist self-representation in the 1920s. But after the war the moderate majority of the labour movement abandoned its previous emphasis on emotive symbolism and rhetoric. While it has been suggested that concurrent aesthetic trends (namely the advent of the 'new sobriety' in the 1920s) may have played a role here, for the most part it was the product of coming into power. The subversive undertones of the SPD's pre-war propaganda techniques ill befitted a governing party.[49] Dealing with the constant stream of political dilemmas and everyday administrative decisions entailed a loss of utopia, a 'secularization of socialism', as Karl Dietrich Bracher has called it.[50] This metamorphosis from a pillar of opposition into a bastion of the new political establishment drained much of the emotion from the SPD's self-understanding and, as a result, its self-representation too.

The Communist Party saw itself as the true inheritor of the revolutionary workers' tradition. Its propaganda and public image thus showed a number of continuities with the pre-war SPD, from its songs (such as the *Internationale*) to its use of the red flag, the labour movement's principal symbol of hope and sacrifice since 1848. The Communist attempt to 'take ownership' of the red flag during the 1920s—manifested in the title of the party's official newspaper, *Rote Fahne*—in many ways summarized the awkward position of the SPD after 1918, caught between loyalty to its own history and to the republican colours of black-red-gold.[51] Yet the KPD also introduced a number of innovations into its iconography in order to demarcate itself from the supposed socialist 'traitors'. The Soviet hammer and sickle was a specifically communist symbol, as were the

---

[49] G. Korff, 'Rote Fahnen und geballte Faust', in D. Petzina (ed.), *Fahnen, Fäuste, Körper* (Essen, 1986), 32.
[50] K. D. Bracher, *Zeit der Ideologien* (Stuttgart, 1982), 114.
[51] Korff, 'Rote Fahnen', 44–54.

five-pointed star and the party greeting of 'Rot Front' with raised fist. And many
of the KPD's symbols represented an amalgam of old and new. The increasingly
prominent symbol of the fist—rising larger-than-life above the factory smoke
or delivering a smashing blow to the fat-cats and militarists—was a militant
variation of the older solidaristic symbol of entwined hands.[52] The hyper-
masculine, muscle-bound proletarian giant similarly recalled the imagery of the
pre-war workers' movement, only now with a far more aggressive demeanour,
punching out the capitalist enemy or heroically slaying the 'dragon' of the
bourgeois press.[53] If the SPD followed the stylistic conventions of 'new sobriety',
the Communists opted for Expressionist provocation.

Fittingly, the KPD was weakest on the cerebral terrain of the written word.
Although circulation figures for the communist press grew significantly throughout the Weimar era, we have already seen in Chapter 5 that its propaganda value
was rather limited, even among party loyalists. By contrast, the pro-communist
papers of Willi Münzenberg, a KPD member of parliament and personal friend of
Lenin, were genuinely popular. This was largely due to the fact that his Kosmos-
Verlag, like the dozens of other Soviet-backed front organizations he set up over
the years through the International Workers' Aid Organisation (Internationale
Arbeiterhilfe, IAH), was not subject to the dogmatic control of party institutions.
A rare breed of committed communist and con man, Münzenberg built the
Arbeiter-Illustrierte-Zeitung (1925) into one of the most innovative and popular
periodicals of the Weimar era. With a circulation peaking at around 300,000, the
AIZ was the Republic's leading left-wing journal, reaching many non-communist
intellectuals whom the party leadership mistrusted and who, for their part, tended
to look down their cultivated noses at the rough-and-ready working-class activists
whose cause they supported. The *AIZ* was no one-off piece of good fortune: a
year after founding it Münzenberg purchased the failing Berlin tabloid *Die Welt
am Abend* and almost immediately turned it into the most popular left-wing
paper in Berlin. Employing the usual techniques of yellow journalism, its surging
circulation of over 100,000 quickly overtook that of the *Rote Fahne*.[54]

Münzenberg is commonly remembered as the maverick mastermind of communist propaganda in inter-war Germany, a pragmatic, commercially savvy
publicist who, unlike his dogmatic counterparts in the party bureaucracy, was
willing to recruit talented non-communists and make concessions to popular
tastes in order to reach beyond the narrow party milieu. As a recent biography
makes clear, however, this is a highly flattering picture. From the very beginning
Münzenberg's media empire rested on unceasing financial bail-outs by Moscow
and utterly unscrupulous business practices that—quite apart from making him

---

[52] Korff, 'Rote Fahnen', 34–44.
[53] K.-M. Mallmann, *Kommunisten in der Weimarer Republik* (Darmstadt, 1996), 235–6.
[54] *Rote Fahne* circulation, claimed to be 100,000, was in reality barely over 20,000: Führer,
'Tageszeitung', 414; Stöber, *Pressegeschichte*, 248, 270. See also S. McMeekin, *The Red Millionaire*
(New Haven, 2003), 211–14, 219–20.

a personal fortune—won him as many enemies as admirers within the communist movement. The common portrayal of Münzenberg as the 'Red Hugenberg' is thus only partially appropriate. While he undoubtedly shared Hugenberg's boundless ambitions and self-promotional instincts, he completely lacked the commercial shrewdness of his right-wing nemesis. The 'red' label could refer to Münzenberg's account books as much as his politics.[55]

Though certainly no business genius, Münzenberg was nonetheless a skilful wheeler-dealer whose propaganda efforts were evidently deemed good value for money. By the latter 1920s his activities expanded from publishing to the cinema, where the constant flow of cheap thrillers and romances in working-class cinemas had long infuriated the radical Left. According to Communist Party doctrine, the capitalist foundations of the film industry meant that it inevitably produced 'trash' and that even the few films of exceptional quality would inevitably echo the conservative values of those who produced them. The only solution was to fight the capitalists on the same terrain by making one's own films. The problem, as we saw in Chapter 3, was that this cost money. The party's efforts were thus initially confined to distributing Soviet-made films via the IAH and Prometheus film company, which Münzenberg set up in 1926. Eventually the IAH began to produce short documentary and propaganda films, most of them directed by Phil Jutzi, who went on to be one of the most prolific documentary directors under the Nazis. Among the most well known were the 1928/9 documentary *Um's tägliche Brot*, a hard-edged reportage about the plight of miners in the Silesian Waldenburg region, and *Blutmai 1929*, a documentary charting the violent May Day clashes in Berlin which Jutzi assembled from eyewitness clips shot with hidden cameras. But the IAH's productions made huge losses, so much so that in 1928 the company Weltfilm was specially founded to soak up the debts. Like Münzenberg's Kosmos-Verlag, the Prometheus and Weltfilm companies were first and foremost communist front organizations, subsidiaries of IAH supported by the Kremlin, and only secondarily commercial concerns.[56]

Thus, the fact that their films lost a lot of money posed no hindrance to further cinematic ventures. In 1928/9 Prometheus finally made the leap to feature-film production with *Der lebende Leichnam*, a co-production with the Moscow-based Meshrabpom. Over the following years it produced a handful of other features, including two classics of Weimar political cinema. The first, *Mutter Krausens Fahrt ins Glück* (Phil Jutzi, 1929), is an overtly pro-communist film about a poverty-stricken widow who commits suicide as her son is arrested for a petty robbery and her daughter considers prostitution. Between the three proletarian fates of death, jail, or joining the communist cause, only the daughter finds the latter outcome. The 1932 film *Kuhle Wampe oder Wem gehört die Welt?*, directed by Slatan Dudow and co-written by Bertolt Brecht, was even more

---

[55] McMeekin, *Red Millionaire*, 204–21.
[56] Ibid. 187–92, 207–12; on the films, see Kaes, 'Film in der Weimarer Republik', 77–83.

overtly didactic. Its political message left little to the imagination, explicitly juxtaposing the misery of working-class life in a depression-era tent colony with the disciplined physical beauty of the workers' sport movement—that is, both the problem *and* the solution. On the train home from the sport festival the protagonists enter an argument with a group of middle-class co-passengers, one of whom smugly asks 'Who will change the world?': 'Those who don't like it', answers the young heroine Anni, with a steely glare.[57]

Although such films were landmarks in the development of left-wing cinema, in practical terms they were little more than drops in the ocean. They made little impact on the entertainment diet of the working masses, who continued to flock to the capitalist-made dream-worlds churned out by UFA and MGM. Yet the KPD used a host of other means to make its mark on the visual environment, from postering and graffiti to the sheer physical occupation of public space. The countless marches and demonstrations were a central concern of the communist movement. They not only gave the rank and file something to do, but also expressed the party's self-understanding as the avant-garde of the revolution, a role which implied a right to put its stamp on any and all manifestations of proletarian life, including a sense of territorial occupation.[58] Marches and assemblies were thus a ritual for both marking territory and demonstrating a visible threat to bourgeois society.[59] Nowhere was the communist assault on the senses more intense than at election time, as agitation troops swarmed the streets in a pitched battle for visual supremacy against their right-wing enemies, plastering every available surface with posters and insignia.[60]

The resulting clash of uniforms, iconography, flags, and banners was the central battleground in the 'war of symbols' that shaped Weimar political culture, especially during the crisis years after 1929.[61] The profound disorientation, anxiety, and polarization of the depression era left little room for rational political communication. The irreconcilable differences between the opposing political camps, nourished by mutually exclusive visions for society, furnished the perfect conditions for deploying the simplifications, stereotypes, and emotional metaphors long prized by the radical parties.[62]

In this respect, the KPD differed little from the National Socialists. Many of the symbols in the opposing political arsenals were strikingly similar, as was the dynamic, naturalistic style in which they were conveyed.[63] Thus, the muscle-bound proletarian giant, to take one example, was by no means the sole property

[57] Toeplitz, *Geschichte*, 440–4.
[58] Mallmann, *Kommunisten*, 238; Rosenhaft, *Beating*, 144–6.
[59] Korff, 'Rote Fahnen', 51–2.
[60] L. Linsmayer, *Politische Kultur im Saargebiet 1920–1932* (St Ingbert, 1992), 192, 231; G. Paul, 'Krieg der Symbole', in D. Kerbs and H. Stahr (eds.), *Berlin 1932* (Berlin, 1992), 27–55.
[61] Paul, 'Krieg'; R. Albrecht, 'Symbolkampf in Deutschland 1932', *IwKGA* 22 (1986), 498–533.
[62] Mallmann, *Kommunisten*, 238.
[63] R. Schoch (ed.), *Politische Plakate der Weimarer Republik 1918–1933* (Darmstadt, 1980); H. Rademacher (ed.), *Plakatkunst im Klassenkampf* (Leipzig, 1974).

of the KPD. As a favoured image of the Nazi artist Mjölnir (Hans Schweitzer), he appears in National Socialist election posters as well, more pumped up and menacing than ever. The anonymous fist also appeared in Nazi imagery, for example in a 1928 election poster *Break the Dawes Chains*, or in a later image of a Nazi fist choking a snake labelled 'Marxism' and 'High Finance' under the caption 'Death to Lies'.[64] As these examples suggest, the portrayal of the parties' enemies also exhibited clear parallels. The podgy, monocled, cigar-smoking capitalist was the physical antithesis of the spartan, athletic proletarian giant. If the Nazis were perhaps more explicit in making this archetypal parasite into a Jew, he looks little different in communist imagery.[65] Even the colours and sense of movement were broadly similar. The red swashes on the Nazis' posters and the red background of its flag carried the same insurrectionary connotations as the red of the communists. These were all images of anti-establishment subversion, of fundamental opposition to the Weimar system, and by the closing stages of the republican era the National Socialists and communists were engaged in a fierce struggle over their ownership.

Although the streets and hoardings were the principal battleground in this struggle, it also reverberated in the press. Like the communists, who founded their central party organ a month before establishing the party itself, the Nazis too were keen to expand their journalistic influence. Despite Hitler's preference for the spoken over the written word, a national newspaper was deemed a priority from the very beginning. In 1921 the *Völkischer Beobachter* (*VB*) was purchased along with its publisher, the Franz Eher Verlag, which was thenceforth chaired by Hitler and directed by Max Amann, a wartime companion of Hitler. The *VB* started out very much like the Nazi Party itself: small, marginal, and centred largely on Munich. Under the editorship of Alfred Rosenberg, it appeared twice weekly before going daily in early 1923, after which its circulation rapidly expanded to around 25,000–30,000 before being closed down after the November 1923 putsch attempt. By the time the ban was lifted in spring 1925, the *VB* had sunk back to a mere 5,000 subscribers. It only regained its 1923 highpoint at the end of the 1920s, by which time the *VB* was only one of many National Socialist publications.[66] The *Illustrierter Beobachter* had started in 1926 as a weekly illustrated newspaper, and the Nazi regional press also gradually expanded to around sixty newspapers by early 1930 (though most remained weeklies and many were short-lived). The big breakthrough came with the party's electoral success in September 1930 and the launch of a Berlin edition of the *VB*. By the middle of 1931 the *VB*'s circulation had swelled to over 100,000 and the number of party periodicals had nearly doubled, most prominent among them *Der Stürmer*, the rabidly anti-Semitic rag

---

[64] See the images in the German Propaganda Archive: *http://www.calvin.edu/academic/cas/gpa/posters1.htm*.

[65] Mallmann, *Kommunisten*, 237.

[66] D. Mühlberger, *Hitler's Voice*, vol. 1 (Bern, 2004), 17–24.

Fig. 10. Propaganda parallels: the Nazi and KPD giants both promise to pulverize their enemies, 1932. bpk Berlin.

edited by the Franconian Gauleiter Julius Streicher, and *Der Angriff*, Goebbels's weekly Berlin tabloid that effectively supplanted the *Berliner Arbeiter-Zeitung* published by his party rival Gregor Strasser.[67]

What was the role of the Nazi press in the party's electoral success? Though it is impossible to gauge precisely, a number of indicators suggest that its impact was slight. The surging circulation figures after 1930 were undoubtedly more a consequence than a cause of the Nazis' electoral breakthrough. Prior to the September 1930 elections total circulation continued to hover under 30,000, the majority for the *VB*—hardly an indication that the party was about to gain over 18 per cent of the vote. Even after this watershed, the combined circulation of the Nazi press was still dwarfed by the large bourgeois dailies. Granted, the most spectacular phase of expansion was still to come: by the end of 1932 total circulation was perhaps as high as 750,000—1 million if one includes weeklies and papers distributed without charge. But these are maximum estimates, and even if accurate they still show that the National Socialist press represented only 5 to 7 per cent of total circulation at a time when the party was achieving one-third of the vote.[68]

---

[67] P. Stein, *Die NS-Gaupresse, 1925–1933* (Munich, 1987); R. Lemmons, *Goebbels and Der Angriff* (Lexington, 1994).

[68] Dussel, *Tagespresse*, 158.

It thus seems that the party press per se—which, it should be noted, encompassed a disparate assemblage of views before the final triumph of the Hitler line in 1933—was largely confined to the hard-core membership. This is hardly surprising, given that most pre-1933 Nazi periodicals were hardly 'newspapers' in the traditional sense of the word—that is, publications conveying information of general interest. They rather functioned as in-house newsletters (not unlike company bulletins) that by and large transmitted political slogans and information of interest only to faithful party followers.[69] This was why, even as circulation rapidly swelled in autumn 1932, Goebbels still regarded the party press as the movement's 'problem child'.[70]

Yet what we might consider the 'national socialist' (as opposed to National Socialist) press was by no means confined to the output of the Eher Verlag. As with the communists, it seems that the party benefited most from papers sympathetic but not directly affiliated with it, in this case the army of conservative-nationalist papers that straddled the increasingly murky boundary between the DNVP and NSDAP. Many of these relied on material from Hugenberg's press agencies, which adopted an increasingly anti-republican stance after the DNVP departed from government in 1928. The same was true of several large right-wing dailies such as the *Rheinisch-Westfälische Zeitung* and *Tag*, which subtly associated the SA street-fighters of the early 1930s with the figure of the front-line soldier, thus harnessing the myth of the unconquered warrior directly to the cause of overcoming the 'November criminals' who stabbed them in the back.[71] As we saw in Chapter 6, Hugenberg's highly successful tabloid *Berliner Nachtausgabe* was at least as helpful to the Nazis as Goebbels's *Der Angriff*, both of which savagely attacked the Republic and the SPD-led governments in Berlin and Prussia.

But if the impact of the party press was negligible before 1933, its cinematic efforts paled into insignificance. This was certainly not for lack of interest: the Nazi predilection for emotive images generated a profound fascination with the cinema. In principle, the party's propagandists viewed film as an ideal means of influencing the masses. Although party propagandists shared the common right-wing hatred of foreign influence and the poisonous 'excesses' of the film industry, on balance the Nazis viewed cinema more as an opportunity than a threat.[72] According to the party's propaganda department, the 'good, German film' represented a primary weapon in the fight against 'cultural Bolshevism', and party members were enjoined to 'place this most modern means of publicity in the service of our movement'.[73] After all, the Bolshevik enemy furnished

---

[69] Mühlberger, *Hitler's Voice*, 22.
[70] Diary entry of 12 Nov. 1932, from R. G. Reuth (ed.), *Joseph Goebbels Tagebücher*, vol. 2 (Munich, 1992), 718.
[71] M. Rass, 'Arbeit, Helden, Straßenkämpfe', in W. Bialas and B. Stenzel (eds.), *Die Weimarer Republik zwischen Metropole und Provinz* (Cologne, 1996), 111–29.
[72] T. Hanna-Daoud, *Die NSDAP und der Film bis zur Machtergreifung* (Cologne, 1996), 9–16.
[73] G. Stark, *Moderne politische Propaganda* (Munich, 1930), 17, 22–3.

some of the most compelling evidence of its potential. Soviet films—especially those of Eisenstein—were held up as models for Nazi cinematic art. After seeing *Battleship Potemkin* in 1928, Goebbels noted that 'this film is wonderfully made. . . . The forceful slogans so skilfully formulated that one cannot raise any objections. That's the actual danger with this film. I wish we had one like it.' The 1929 film *Kampf um die Erde* (1930, English title *Old and New/The General Line*) similarly impressed him as 'dangerous, and we should learn from it. If we only had money. I'd write a n.s. film that would really make a splash.'[74]

As always, money was the perennial problem. Party finances were never sufficient to cover more than small productions, and it was difficult to attract outside backers given the risks posed by the threat of police bans (and thus total loss of revenue). This was especially the case in Prussia, where in March 1931 the Interior Ministry in fact forbade the screening of marching SA columns in the Nazi film *Kampf um Berlin* two years after the censors had passed it.[75] Lack of money was compounded by a scarcity of cinematic know-how. The small handful of films from the 1920s—Hitler's trial in 1924, the party conference in 1926—were amateurish in every sense, and even the eighty-minute documentary of the 1929 party conference was derided by Goebbels as 'awfully poor, Munich kitsch'.[76] Subsequent attempts to organize production bore little fruit, hampered as they were by the endemic intra-party rivalries between regional bosses, Goebbels's Reich Film Agency and Gregor Strasser's Reich Organizational Directorate.

As with the press, however, the Nazi movement probably benefited more from non-party films than it ever could have expected from its own productions. There was, as noted earlier, a clear nationalist trend in film production by the early 1930s including a string of transparently anti-French historical dramas that railed against the injustice of the Napoleonic 'peace' and glorified German 'Wehrwillen'. The parallels with the Versailles settlement were blindingly obvious, and the message closely echoed the increasingly antagonistic foreign-policy rhetoric of the entire nationalist Right. Moreover, the Nazis could hardly have wished for a better cinematic portrayal of their political vision than UFA's sound-film hit *Das Flötenkonzert von Sanssouci* (released in December 1930, only two weeks after *All Quiet on the Western Front* had been banned), starring Otto Gebühr as Frederick the Great, a benevolent and charismatic strong-man who leads his struggling people to victory after being forced by devious enemies to fight against his will.

Although the NSDAP lacked the means to harness film, its use of other visual media was nonetheless remarkably up-to-date. The Nazi penchant to let actions and images do the talking mirrored current thinking in the advertising trade about psychological 'suggestion' and the need to appeal to the senses. Party

---

[74] Reuth (ed.), *Tagebücher*, i. 304 (30 June 1928); ii. 459–60 (16 Feb. 1930).
[75] Hanna-Daoud, *NSDAP*, 226–31.   [76] Ibid., 43–6, 54–61, quote 67.

propagandists made little attempt to hide the influence of commercial advertising on their techniques, from the use of lighting to poster design to the development of concise symbols. As a 1930 handbook from the Reich Propaganda Directorate explicitly recognized, 'the face of the big city as a centre of both production and consumption is shaped by advertising. . . . Everywhere advertising columns, newspapers, billboards, etc. constantly hammer on the victim until at a given time, under the influence of the impressions he has absorbed, he gives in to the will of the advertising firm by making a purchase.' In the struggle for votes and supporters, it was only sensible to tap this body of knowledge: 'the work of the propaganda department consists of studying advertising methods and utilizing them for ourselves.'[77]

One of the main lessons of modern advertising was that nothing should be left to chance. Just as the American ad agencies prioritized the scientific market survey over the 'clever idea', so too did the Nazi leadership emphasize planning and deliberation over spontaneous strokes of genius. A hallmark of rationalized publicity was the 'targeting' of specific groups on their own terms. If, for instance, the most effective flyers and pamphlets in working-class quarters conveyed their message 'in a coarsely forthright fashion', in middle-class areas it was better to proceed 'in a drop-by-drop, camouflaged manner'. Experience showed that paying attention to reading habits was also important: 'the *systematic distribution* of advertising material *in residential buildings* . . . should only take place *very early on Sundays*, so that the compatriot can form his opinion in peace and quiet over his morning coffee.'[78] And above all else, repetition was crucial. As Hitler noted in *Mein Kampf*, 'only after the simplest ideas are repeated thousands of times will the masses finally remember them'.[79] The same messages were thus reiterated via as many media as possible, including slogans, speeches, and above all the pictorial poster, which was specially prized in big cities for its ability to convey a message quickly to passers-by.[80]

Of course, the translation of modern advertising techniques into political propaganda was not the sole preserve of the Nazis. As we will see below, they were gradually influencing perceptions across the entire political spectrum. This was clearest at the opposite extreme, for it was communist propaganda that most closely paralleled 'bourgeois' publicity, in spite of their theoretical contempt for it. During the 1928 elections in the Ruhr, for instance, the local KPD leadership openly recommended that its agitation imitate commercial cigarette ads: 'Bourgeois advertisements of each brand of cigarettes demonstrate the theoretical principle: one catchphrase as brief as possible, one clear illustration or dramatic, pictorially pointed scene.'[81] Yet it was undoubtedly the

---

[77] Stark, *Moderne*, 3, 4.   [78] Ibid. 4, 9, 11, emphasis in the original.
[79] Hitler, *Mein Kampf*, 169.   [80] Stark, *Moderne*, 14.
[81] E. Weitz, 'Communism and the Public Spheres of Weimar Germany', in Barclay and Weitz (eds.), *Between*, 285.

National Socialists who made the most of it. Even the communist showman Münzenberg could not help but be impressed by the Nazis' 'political advertising', in particular the way that it 'unscrupulously uses every available trick, employing all of the refined methods of large-scale advertising in the twentieth century'.[82] Even more telling was the fact that commercial advertisers were more or less united in their praise of Nazi propaganda efforts.[83] Indeed, the inspiration worked in both directions, for some of Goebbels's publicity stunts were occasionally copied by commercial firms. Ullstein's launch of the tabloid *Tempo* in 1928 was a blatant imitation of the advertising campaign for *Der Angriff* a year earlier, which featured a curiosity-piquing series of posters spaced out over a two-week period: first '*Der Angriff*' (in German: 'the attack'), followed by 'When will *Der Angriff* take place?', and finally '*Der Angriff*, the German Monday Newspaper'. The only new feature of Ullstein's campaign was to add a fourth poster: 'You're lacking *Tempo*!', 'You'll soon have *Tempo*!', 'Tomorrow you'll have *Tempo*', '*Tempo*, the up-to-the-minute evening paper'.[84]

Such instances of undeniable advertising flair help to explain the almost legendary status of National Socialist propaganda in popular memory. But conventional views about its seductive genius have always been exaggerated, partly because many contemporary assessments were penned by publicists with an inflated view of their own importance, but also because of the exculpatory implication that the Nazis tricked the German electorate as a slick salesman dupes an unwitting customer. Recent research has shown that Nazi propaganda before 1933 was neither as systematic nor as effective as is often assumed, and that the party's message of national rejuvenation, social reform and strong-man leadership was popular enough in depression-era Germany to 'sell itself' without much political sorcery.[85] This was even recognized by Nazi officials at the time, some of whom disagreed with the prevailing emphasis on suggestive and emotional appeal. Gregor Strasser, for one, laid more emphasis on solid political instruction than agitation, and his brother Otto openly criticized Goebbels's campaigning methods as an 'Americanization of thinking'.[86]

Yet the necessary corrections to the image of Nazi propaganda wizardry do not change the fact that they were well ahead of their rivals in adapting their message to the new sensual landscape of popular culture. They not only plundered the latest ideas on repetition and imagery but were also well versed in brand

---

[82] W. Münzenberg, *Propaganda als Waffe* (Paris, 1937), 12–13.

[83] See, e.g. E. Kwilecki, 'Die Propaganda für die Präsidentenwahl' *DR* 25 (May 1932), 269; I. G. Faber, 'Nationalsozialistische Werbung', *SR* 16 (Aug. 1932), 299; E. Growald, 'Reklame-Fetische an die Front!', *SR* 16 (Sept. 1932), 319.

[84] Stark, *Moderne*, 14–15.

[85] Paul, *Aufstand*, 15 f.; R. Bytwerk, 'Die nationalsozialistische Versammlungspraxis', in Diesener and Gries (eds.), *Propaganda*, 35–50.

[86] Ibid., 51–2.

technique.[87] The Nazis took great care in designing and protecting the symbols of the movement, many of which were sketched by Hitler himself and treated as brands from the outset. Then as now, one of the keys to effective branding lay in consistency and uniformity, for only by propagating the same symbol for a long period of time is it possible to achieve a high degree of recognizability. As Hitler himself wrote: 'All advertising, whether in the field of business or politics, achieves success through the continuity and sustained uniformity of its application.'[88] Another key to branding is exclusivity, for only by confining the use of a symbol or slogan to its 'owner' can it retain the desired associative power. From this point of view, the unauthorized use of party symbols was tantamount to a copyright infringement. Thus, when in 1931 the Leipzig-based recording firm Electrocord, which carried a wide selection of National Socialist songs in its repertoire, produced an advertising leaflet featuring the party slogan 'Deutschland erwache!' (Germany awaken!), Goebbels immediately prohibited both the playing and advertising of its records at all official party events. As the *Phonographische Zeitschrift* remarked, 'if any business is to be conducted under the motto "Germany awaken", then it is apparently to be reserved solely for the party and its own organizations'.[89] Most precious of all the Nazi symbols was the swastika, the movement's corporate brand. In the words of Ernst Growald, it had not only 'proven its effectiveness in the sphere of political advertising', but was 'propagated better than any factory or firm symbol ever was'.[90]

This was praise indeed, especially coming from one of Germany's most renowned advertisers. It reflected the general consensus within the trade that the Nazis were easily the best political propagandists in Germany. But as Growald also noted, their superiority owed as much to the promotional pallor of the competition as to their own merits: 'Hitler's success rests in large part on excellent advertising, which is especially effective since his opponents cannot mount anything nearly as powerful against it.'[91] This criticism brings us back to the apparent inability of the Republic and its chief supporters to communicate a positive and appealing image of the system for which they stood. Although the Republic's 'sensory deficit' was by no means a new idea in the early 1930s, it was certainly brought into sharper relief in the context of the Depression and the radical parties' creeping occupation of the public sphere. By autumn 1930 at the latest there was a growing sense that the shortcomings of republican self-representation were at least partly to blame for the Nazis' electoral successes. There were, of course, more mundane reasons—the swelling economic crisis—that no amount of public relations would solve. But for many onlookers the Republic's publicity deficiencies were allowing the radical movements to punch above their

---

[87] See G. Voigt, 'Goebbels als Markentechniker', in W. Haug (ed.), *Warenästhetik* (Frankfurt a. M., 1977), 231–60; S. Behrenbeck, ' "Der Führer" ', in Diesener and Gries (eds), *Propaganda*, 51–78.
[88] Hitler, *Mein Kampf*, 169.   [89] *PZ* 32 (15 May 1931), 580.
[90] Growald, 'Reklame-Fetische', 319.   [91] Ibid.

weight. Given the constraints under which the Nazis and communists were operating—the chronic shortage of party funds and the constant threat of political censorship—there is doubtless an element of truth to this criticism. But regardless of the reasons, it was up to the republican forces to close the publicity gap.

MAINSTREAM IN CRISIS: THE PROMISE AND PERILS OF PROPAGANDA[92]

In October 1929, the month of the Wall Street crash, the Prussian interior minister Albert Grzesinski wrote a remarkable letter to his Reich counterpart Carl Severing:

Our young republic cannot confine itself merely to the negative task of defending itself against subversive elements, but rather must seek above all to educate the people in democratic thought and action in order to bring about a gradual improvement of the atmosphere that would hinder the emergence of such subversive elements in the first place. This is not a task that can be solved by the schools alone, but rather will require deliberate and long-term influence on public opinion.

The need for more pro-active republican publicity was, he continued, a matter of widespread agreement within his department, and Grzesinski knew that Severing shared his concerns. The efforts of the RfH were by no means sufficient for this task. Rather, it was 'absolutely essential from the outset not to renounce the use of the cinema, radio, press, and theatre for the purpose of positive propaganda in the sense of civic education'.[93]

Of special importance was the cinema, where Grzesinski—like Goebbels—singled out Russian and Italian filmmakers as models to emulate. A first step in this direction might be the deliberate use of the Emelka newsreels, which were screened in 1,200 German cinemas and were now owned by the Reich. There had recently been some success with the newsreels covering Stresemann's funeral, and there was no reason why Emelka could not make an easily understandable comparison of the Dawes and Young Plans. The ultimate goal, however, was 'the production of special feature-length films that should be designed to promote the new state'. Grzesinski also recommended greater government use of radio. Here too, there were recent successes on which to build, above all Severing's address against the Young Plan referendum. As for the newspapers, the traditional practice of feeding information to the press should be complemented by pro-government placards of the type that its enemies were using to such effect. Finally, Grzesinski suggested making special grants available for republican festivities. Given that

---

[92] The following discussion is drawn largely from Ross, 'Mass Politics'.
[93] GStA PK, Rep. 90, Nr. 2415, Grzesinski to Reich Interior Ministry, 21 Oct. 1929, fos. 481–2.

most local authorities and small-town newspapers were not in a position to engage in political education, it would be helpful to give municipalities 'at least a modest little sum for decorations, etc.'. Figuring around RM 50,000 for the cinema, RM 25,000 for press activities and placards, and RM 25,000 for the small grants, the costs of such a scheme amounted to only around RM 100,000 per year. Although resources were admittedly tight, not investing in this area was false economy: 'If we do not embark along this path, we must fear that such an omission will powerfully avenge itself in the long run and in particular might lead to a far greater financial burden for defending against criminal endeavours than the suggestions elaborated here.'[94]

This letter is interesting in a number of respects, quite apart from its unusually forceful advocacy of a pro-republican media campaign. First and foremost is its timing, for it was actually written on 21 October, three days *before* Wall Street's 'Black Thursday'. Grzesinski's suggestions were not a knee-jerk response to the financial panic, but came against the background of an already slumping German economy, radical gains in recent regional elections, and the right-wing anti-Young Plan campaign. Sadly, any such hopes for an amelioration of the political climate were cruelly short-lived, and stood no chance of fulfilment as the reverberations of the American collapse quickly threw the German economy into freefall. Within weeks it was clear that the government's political and financial situation was rapidly deteriorating. If resources for publicity were tight before the Wall Street crash, they soon disappeared completely as revenues dwindled and international credit evaporated.

The second noteworthy characteristic of the letter is its author and recipient. Grzesinski and Severing were two of the most prominent SPD figures of the Weimar era, and were certainly no 'Vernunftrepublikaner' (republicans of convenience). Quite the contrary, they were deeply committed democrats who had spent years protecting the Republic from its enemies. Between 1920 and 1932 they effectively shared the key job of Prussian interior minister, Grzesinski temporarily taking over from Severing (during his appointment as Reich interior minister) before returning to his post as chief of the Berlin police. Like most senior Social Democrats, they firmly believed in the party's tradition of political education and had little patience for shallow political 'advertising'.[95] The fact that two political figures of this ilk were pondering how to redouble the government's publicity efforts well before the depths of the ensuing economic crisis gives some indication of how such issues might be approached as the political situation worsened.

And worsen it did. With the collapse of the last democratically elected government in March 1930, the question for most contemporaries was less how the democratic system in Germany could survive than what would take its

[94] Ibid., fos. 481–2, 484–5.
[95] T. Alexander, *Carl Severing*, vol. 2 (Frankfurt a. M., 1996), 992; A. Grzesinki, *Im Kampf um die deutsche Republik* (Munich, 2001).

place. As the crisis deepened, the 'totalitarian temptation' loomed ever larger; various ideas about leadership cults and mass movements that had previously been only toyed with by the mainstream parties took on a new significance. And as the democratic parties saw little alternative but to tolerate or even support the authoritarian Brüning cabinet as a means of rescuing the Republic from complete collapse, it is hardly surprising that their misgivings about the morality of manipulating public opinion would also gradually be eroded.

But the implications of the shift towards authoritarian government after spring 1930 were by no means clear-cut as far as the perceived role of state self-representation, or 'Staatspropaganda', was concerned. Fundamentally, this shift could imply either a decrease in the importance of publicity efforts corresponding to the diminished input of public opinion (a reversion to a conservative 'policing' regime), or an increase in their importance as a means of shaping public opinion in lieu of following it (a more deliberately transformative 'surveillance' regime).[96] If one were to take the latter alternative of enhancing publicity efforts (which most did), this raised the further question of how best to carry it out: to augment existing efforts at political education or to resort to the kind of agitation techniques culled from commercial advertising and entertainments that the radical political movements, above all the National Socialists, were employing to such effect? In practice, then, there were three alternatives: first, to remain aloof from publicity battles; second, to counter the emotionalized propaganda of the radicals by educating the public about the complexity of the political issues at stake; and third, to imitate the radicals' agitprop techniques in order to fight fire with fire.

The first alternative was in many ways embodied by Chancellor Brüning himself. Unlike his Social Democratic predecessor Müller, who had reversed a decision to cut the RfH budget for fear of creating a domestic propaganda vacuum that could be filled by the Nazis, Brüning radically cut the RfH's budget and had to be dissuaded from closing it down altogether.[97] Given the unpopular nature of his austerity measures, Brüning maintained remarkably little contact with the press. Even the *BT* editor Theodor Wolff, who had far better access to the chancellor than most journalists, spoke of Brüning's 'hermit-like isolation' and encouraged him to make more effort to sell himself and his policies to the public.[98] Brüning's own ministers likewise counselled him to do more. As labour minister Stegerwald wrote to him in December 1931, the government's press policies had to be 'fundamentally reformed' in order to combat the demagogues: 'For I consider it impermissible in a period in which parliament's influence is almost completely eliminated to exclude the press to such a great extent as well.'[99] Although Brüning was eventually persuaded to hold a number of

---

[96] Borrowing again from Holquist, 'Information', 420–1.
[97] Wippermann, *Politische Propaganda*, 344.   [98] Quoted from Sösemann, *Das Ende*, 148.
[99] BAB R43/I/2492, Stegerwald to Brüning, 4 Dec. 1931, fos. 214–15; also Groener to Brüning, 28 Nov. 1931, fos. 212–13.

radio addresses, his instincts always remained those of the autocrat who deemed deliberate publicity efforts to be beneath the dignity of his office, even in the face of vicious attacks by his enemies. This attitude was typified in his response to a suggestion to use free advertising space for publicizing government policies: 'How could you expect me to make propaganda for myself?'[100]

By contrast, the majority of senior officials and government-supporting politicians were soon convinced that enhancing publicity efforts for the government and the state itself was an absolute necessity. But again, views differed on the best means. Many favoured the second alternative: using reasoned explanation as a means of drying up the pool of popular discontent in which the anti-republican parties swam. The most famous example was Theodor Heuss's 1932 book *Hitlers Weg*, a sweeping exposition of National Socialism that by the end of the year had already gone through eight editions and been translated into several languages.[101] It was a devastating critique, dissecting the many contradictions in the party programme and lambasting its racism and anti-democratic spirit. Heuss argued that the strength of the National Socialist movement was primarily rooted in the person of Hitler and the party's skilful propaganda, to which even he was prepared to pay grudging tribute. Without dismissing the threat posed by the Nazis, the thrust of the book was to ridicule them as a lot of hot air. Through systematic and logical exposition of the party's own literature, *Hitlers Weg* portrayed the Nazis as hollow image-artists lacking the substance for actual government.

Yet book-length treatises were hardly an ideal means of reaching the broad mass of voters. For this purpose the third tactic of copying the radicals' own techniques seemed far more promising. During the run-up to the September 1930 Reichstag elections, there were repeated suggestions that the government deploy similar emotive-visual propaganda. The aim, in the words of Adolf Kempkes, a DVP member of the Reichstag electoral scrutiny committee, was 'to create a counter-effect through mass postering as a means of at least partially balancing out the damaging and disastrous effect of the other posters on public opinion'.[102] The problem was that such a campaign was expensive, untested, and, for many mainstream politicians, un-statesmanlike. Despite warnings against 'false economizing', the idea never got off the ground. For one thing, it was estimated that saturation coverage for merely one good placard would require around RM 80,000, far more than the funds at the government's disposal. More importantly, there was a deep sense of scepticism that, as Chancellery secretary Hermann Pünder explained, 'such an officially sponsored election poster, even if very skilfully and professionally executed, would most likely seem rather boring and have little rousing effect among the masses in comparison to a National Socialist or Communist poster, whose arguments and depictions are of course

---

[100] Sösemann, *Das Ende*, 202.   [101] T. Heuss, *Hitlers Weg* (Stuttgart, 1932).
[102] BAB R43/I/2468, Kempkes to Pünder, 29 Aug. 1930, fo. 94.

completely without restraint'.[103] In other words, it was doubtful that the dry prose of rational governance could compete with the emotive poetry of the radical political movements on their own terrain—that is, if translated into dramatic imagery.

In many eyes the radio appeared far more promising than a poster campaign, not least in terms of value for money. From early 1931 the RPO and RfH tried to arrange regular wireless reports about current affairs featuring ministers or other suitable personalities.[104] But such plans faced a number of obstacles, first of all the 'non-political' understanding of German radio. There were few precedents to offer as justification, apart from several ministerial addresses concerning the Young Plan referendum and Stresemann's 1925 broadcast in support of the Locarno Treaty. And if broadcasters were averse to transmitting 'politics' beforehand, by this time they were also anxious to avoid any provocation of the increasingly vociferous minority on the far Right.[105] The best one could realistically achieve was the occasional address by the chancellor, who, as we have seen, was anything but a political showman. Almost in spite of himself, Brüning's radio addresses on 23 June 1931 (dealing with President Hoover's reparations proposals) and 8 December 1931 (in which he explained the fourth emergency decree and directly attacked the National Socialists) were not without impact.[106] But these were very much the exception, and as Hans Flesch of the Berliner Funk-Stunde warned officials, political speeches could easily become counterproductive: 'In place of the scheduled entertainment that the mass of people was looking forward to, there came a lecture that was of course perceived as boring by the listener expecting a little relaxation. The annoyance over the missing entertainment was converted into political disaffection on the part of the disappointed listener; this achieved the opposite of what was intended.'[107]

In comparison to radio, government recourse to the cinema presented a different mixture of opportunities and drawbacks. In the plus column it possessed an audience and a degree of popular appeal that no other medium could match. A further benefit lay in the relatively direct government influence over film censorship, which indeed kept certain films off the screen. But as far as actual production was concerned, the possibilities were severely limited by the crippling costs. From late 1929 onwards there were repeated calls for making Soviet-inspired dramas geared to boost support for the Weimar state.[108] By the time the Reich authorities began making serious plans in early 1932, the financial

    103 BAB R43/I/2468, Pünder to Kempkes, 3 Sept. 1930, fos. 95–7.
    104 BAB R43/I/2001, Niederschrift über die Besprechung in der Presseabteilung am 24. Februar 1931, fo. 45; BAB R43/I/2492, RfH to Pünder, 4 Nov. 1931, fos. 183–8.
    105 Jelavich, *Alexanderplatz*, 114–25.
    106 BAB R43/I/2492, fo. 228: press clipping, *BT*, 9 Dec. 1931.
    107 BAB R43/I/2001, Flesch to Scholz, 9 Mar. 1931, fos. 49–50; also *RH* 9 (5 Apr. 1932), 304–5.
    108 GStA PK, Rep. 90, Nr. 2415, fo. 482; BAB R1501/125683, Weichberger to Interior Ministry, 2 Nov. 1929, fos. 81–5.

situation rendered this utterly impossible. The RM 8,000 initially available at the beginning of 1932 could not even begin to cover the estimated RM 250,000 that a feature film would cost. Shorts and newsreels were thus the only option, and even then current funds only sufficed for five ten-minute films.[109]

This combination of scarce resources, lack of experience, and an entrenched state publicity apparatus meant that the government's self-promotional efforts largely continued in the established vein of rational 'instruction' and argumentation. To be sure, the turmoil of the early 1930s focused unprecedented attention on the problems of public relations. In August 1930, in the heat of the Reichstag election campaign, ministers unanimously agreed to beef up the RPO with a number of experienced journalists.[110] Fritz Klein, chief editor of the *DAZ*, was brought in to help coordinate the government propaganda machinery, which currently supplied articles to 75 per cent of German newspapers.[111] In 1931 the government also became the majority shareholder in WTB, which made it even easier to place pro-government articles in the press.[112] But since the focus remained on journalistic activities, this essentially amounted to more of the same. Furthermore, the intended beneficiary was often the parties supporting Brüning's minority government rather than the state form itself—a tactic that prompted Reich press chief Walter Zechlin, a member of the SPD, to take an extended holiday during the crescendo of the 1930 election campaign.[113] The RfH, for its part, also concentrated on making a 'strong appeal to reason' as an antidote to the political crisis.[114] Despite having its budget cut by well over half, it continued to organize lectures and exhibitions in support of the state. The problem was that, as even sympathetic observers had to admit, 'the material of the RfH is . . . too demanding for the great mass of people', and the 'public propaganda effect is often quite unsatisfactory'.[115] In the meantime its intellectual approach was mirrored within the democratic parties, whose own propaganda efforts likewise continued to emphasize rational persuasion over emotional propaganda.[116] The prevailing goal within the SPD was, as Severing wrote in the *Sozialistische Monatshefte*, 'to shift politics away from the activities of the vocal chords towards the functions of the head'.[117] Insofar as the strategy was to ridicule Nazi propaganda through reasoned argument, the republican parties and the government not only ignored the maxims of the concurrent propaganda discourse but indeed conceived their publicity efforts as an antidote to them.

---

[109] BAB R43/I/2492, fos. 304–5; BAB R43/I/2492, fos. 264, 273, 274–8, 283.
[110] BAB R43/I/2468, Reichskanzlei to Reichsminister, 19 Aug. 1930, fos. 87–8.
[111] Ibid., Pünder to Kempkes, 3 Sept. 1930, fos. 95–7.
[112] Basse, *Wolff's*, 238–47.   [113] 'Der Propagandachef', *FZ*, 31 July 1930.
[114] Quote from BAB R43/I/2492, RfH to Pünder, 19 Mar. 1931, fo. 164.
[115] Quotes from Wippermann, *Politische Propaganda*, 387. In 1930 the RfH budget was slashed from RM 500,000 to RM 200,000, falling to RM 180,000 in 1931 and RM 153,000 in 1932: BAB R43/I/2515, fo. 171.
[116] See D. Harsch, *German Social Democracy and the Rise of Nazism* (Chapel Hill, NC, 1993), 179.
[117] Alexander, *Severing*, ii. 992.

Just as in the immediate post-war years, such efforts were deemed woefully inadequate by professional advertisers and journalists, who increasingly warned against disregarding the insights of modern publicity, above all the need for systematic organization, a wide palette of media, and appealing to emotions and desires. In the mass-political marketplace of ideas the forces of moderation were, so the argument ran, being completely out-advertised by the radical competition. Apart from the handful of welcome radio addresses, the propaganda opportunities of the non-print media were still virtually ignored. 'Has the government never heard of the sound newsreel?' asked the journal *Film-Kurier* in July 1931. 'From [the boxer Max] Schmeling's return to a tour of a naval cruiser, from a Miami swimming party to the Cavalry Day in Dresden, nearly every significant or insignificant occurrence of the last eight days is covered. But on the very thing that most directly affects people, namely the economic situation, there is not a single metre of film in any of the newsreels.'[118] In view of the increasingly partisan UFA newsreels and the spate of militarist features hitting the cinemas, it was an 'unforgivable failure of the Reich government' to leave the field to the far Right out of some misplaced sense of fair play: 'the neutrals are wrong.'[119] The problem, critics suggested, was not merely a lack of money but also a lack of expertise. As one advertiser complained to the Reich Chancellery, in a letter redolent of the 'lessons of the war', 'the government has almost no weapons in the political arena. Propaganda *experts* are not consulted.'[120] This basic argument of the 'experts', repeated time and again in advertising journals, the press and various petitions to the government was, though transparently self-serving, remarkably consistent since the end of the war. *Staatspropaganda* was a modern necessity, and effective *Staatspropaganda* required advertising professionals: 'The requisite specialists, tried-and-tested and practically experienced, are available. They merely need to be deployed.'[121]

From late 1931 onwards the Reich authorities were inundated by such unsolicited advice, much of it castigating the government for having 'no publicity plan, no scientifically trained and *practically* experienced publicity advisors'.[122] A number of advertisers, including the executive committee of Germany's leading advertising organization, the Deutscher Reklame-Verband, offered their services to the government on an honorary or paid basis.[123] The wide range of recommendations essentially boiled down to two points: first, that state publicity efforts needed better organization; and second, that they had to make more use of emotion and suggestion. There were, as during the war, numerous calls

---

[118] 'Kennt die Regierung die Tonwochenschau nicht?', *FK* 13 (17 July 1931), 2.
[119] Quotes from ibid.; E. J., 'Unverfilmtes Deutschland', *FK* 13 (8 Aug. 1931), suppl. 3.
[120] BAB R43/I/2493, Greve to Chancellery, 9 May 1932, fo. 8. Emphasis in the original.
[121] Ibid.   [122] Ibid., emphasis in the original.
[123] BAB R43/I/2492, Deutscher Reklame-Verband to Pünder, 28 Nov. 1931, fos. 243–4; Roebel to Chancellery, 4 Feb. 1932, fos. 324–32; BAB R43/I/2493, Greve to Chancellery, 9 May 1932, fos. 7–11; Krohne to Pünder, 20 May 1932, fos. 20 ff.

for appointing an experienced advertiser to the position of propaganda minister or 'Reichswerbewart' (a counterpart to the Reichskunstwart, Edwin Redslob), answerable to the cabinet and responsible for coordinating the publicity of all the ministries.[124] The idea was to organize state publicity along the lines of a modern commercial advertising campaign, characterized by a single guiding concept and a clear, systematic strategy for disseminating its messages via multiple media outlets.[125] Unlike the RfH focus on opinion-leaders (teachers, professionals, notables), such state publicity *'represents a direct appeal to the mass of the people.* The technical medium of the press office is the newspaper, that of *Staatspropaganda* is the ad text, the slogan, the visual image, film, radio, the poster, flyer, exhibition model; in short: its technical medium is the broad *field of publicity.'*[126] These messages, in turn, had to be grounded in the precepts of 'mass psychology' if they were to have the desired effect. In this view, political education and factual information may be suitable for the RfH, but its efforts touched only elites and were largely preaching to the converted. Since the masses were widely assumed to be clueless about government, rational arguments were out of place. The key was to play on the masses' psychological fears and desires. Failure to do so meant that 'millions meet their Couéist needs for positive thinking, buoyancy, and zest through Hitler'.[127]

Although such *Staatspropaganda* was clearly conceived as a long-term venture, what this advice amounted to in the short term was the imitation of National Socialist propaganda techniques.[128] If the state were to withstand the onslaught, it was seen as imperative to employ the same tools of modern professional advertising: 'systematic and professionally guided state propaganda is a precept of state morality, of wisdom and of thrift.'[129]

In view of the continued growth of the Nazi movement, such sentiments were also on the ascent within the republican political parties. The DDP, as part of its metamorphosis into the Staatspartei, placed great hopes on a more aggressive propaganda style that would 'appeal to the passions of the electors'.[130] By the middle of 1931 leading members such as Gertrud Bäumer and Marie-Elisabeth Lüders were pleading directly with the chancellor for a more dynamic publicity campaign. As Lüders lamented in May 1931, the economic crisis and the massive erosion of support for the Republic meant that 'our methods of political attack and defence are no longer appropriate. The people possess neither

---

[124] BAB R43/I/2493, Greve to Chancellery, 9 May 1932, fo. 9.
[125] Esp. BAB R43/I/2493, Krohne to Pünder, 20 May 1932, fos. 27–8; BAB R43/I/2492, Roebel to Chancellery, 4 Feb. 1932, fos. 324–32.
[126] BAB R43/I/2493, Krohne to Pünder, 20 May 1932, fo. 32.
[127] A reference to French psychologist Emile Coué, prophet of auto-suggestion, who coined the [in]famous phrase 'Day by day, in every way, I am getting better and better': BAB R43/I/2493, Greve to Chancellery, 9 May 1932, fo. 9.
[128] Faber, 'Nationalsozialistische Werbung'; Growald, 'Reklame-Fetische'.
[129] BAB R43/I/2493, Krohne to Pünder, 20 May 1932, fo. 43.
[130] Möller, 'Die sich selbst', 17.

the inner calm nor the energy for rational examination, objective consideration, and independent decision. They do not want to examine, search, and find, but rather want to receive ready-made "solutions", and indeed ones that match their own state of mind, which so far as possible both begins and ends with their own personal fate.' As a result, it was necessary to fight the demagogues with their own weapons: 'We have enough enemies, among them some very clever people. We must be a match for them.'[131]

Within the SPD too, there was a growing realization that, in the words of the Belgian socialist Henrik de Man, 'national fascism appeals to the basic political impulses to which socialism has paid far too little attention over the preceding decades'.[132] Influenced strongly by de Man, the 'Young Right' advocates of a more militant and charismatic political style, such as Carlo Mierendorff, Julius Leber, and Theo Haubach, were gradually gaining ground within the party, thanks in part to the new journal they launched in 1930, *Neue Blätter für den Sozialismus*.[133] The creation of a sharply critical cartoon film entitled *Ins dritte Reich* (1930), a direct riposte to the Nazis' *Kampf um Berlin*, represented a clear attempt to modernize the SPD's propaganda techniques—though, typically, the anxious censorship authorities only allowed the film to be played at closed SPD gatherings for fear of public disturbances.[134] The announcement of the 'Iron Front' in December 1931 (an alliance of SPD, Reichsbanner, the free trade unions and workers' sporting league) was also a direct answer to the right-wing 'Harzburger Front' and the tightening grip of the SA and Red Front Fighters' League over public space. The motorized agitation columns of the Iron Front played a central role in the hundreds of local 'Hindenburg committees' in which the moderate parties joined forces for the presidential elections of April 1932. The propaganda of these committees was remarkably up-to-date, involving ad-vehicles, sandwich-men (carrying over-the-shoulder placards front and back), and even airplane banners. The huge posters and billboards depicting the aging war hero were cleverly designed to awaken a sense of trust and, by association, scepticism about his opponents.[135] More importantly, the eventual adoption of Sergei Chakotin's 'three arrows' motif for the July 1932 elections marked an unambiguous shift towards 'psycho-technical' electioneering tactics. Chakotin, a former assistant to the psychologist Ivan Pavlov and a revolutionary propagandist in the early Soviet Union, had long championed a more scientific approach to party propaganda. Up through early 1932 his suggestions found a mixed response among the SPD leadership, one of the chief criticisms being their similarity to the Nazi gimmickry that the SPD had been ridiculing for years. But Mierendorff wholeheartedly supported

[131] Quotes from Wippermann, *Politische Propaganda*, 388, 390.
[132] H. de Man, *Sozialismus und Nationalfascismus* (Potsdam, 1931), 48.
[133] Generally, S. Vogt, *Nationaler Sozialismus und Soziale Demokratie* (Bonn, 2006).
[134] BAB R1501/125683, fos. 233 ff.   [135] Paul, 'Krieg', 31.

him—indeed, the two co-authored a pamphlet on the 'foundations and forms of political propaganda'—and after Chakotin's appointment as chief propagandist of the Reichsbanner his ideas became increasingly influential as a means of lending symbolic expression to the defence of democracy.[136] Following indications that the use of the 'three arrows' had aided SPD campaign efforts in April 1932, party headquarters finally adopted it as the official symbol for the Iron Front in June 1932, along with the unofficial 'freedom salute' of raised fist with shout of 'freedom'.

In the meantime there were similar discussions within the government about the need to redouble the state publicity effort. While Brüning himself continued to make rather hesitant and infrequent use of the radio, officials within the Reich Chancellery arranged a number of meetings with advertisers to discuss their ideas, though the lack of funds precluded further action.[137] In this regard, the replacement of Brüning's government by von Papen and his arch-conservative cabinet in June 1932 marked an unmistakeable turning-point, for it was first under von Papen that the government as such made a more systematic attempt to gain the popular support it so sorely lacked. The most important changes under von Papen occurred in the area of radio, which was thoroughly reformed and brought under firm state control over the latter half of 1932 (see Chapter 9). As part of this restructuring, interior minister von Gayl ordered a daily 'Government Hour' for all radio broadcasters during which ministers could hold supposedly 'unpolitical' speeches in support of government policies. The perverse result was that, over the six-and-a-half months of his chancellorship, von Papen spoke on the radio eighteen times and went to the Reichstag only once. The contrast with Brüning's aloofness could hardly be starker. This direct political harnessing of radio was very much a part of the wider attempt to fill the power vacuum that the presidential cabinets had themselves created by bypassing parliament. But the attempt by the von Papen government—as well as the Schleicher government that succeeded it in December—to mobilize popular anti-republican sentiment for its own purposes stood virtually no chance of success in 1932, given the huge lead of the Nazis in precisely this area.

In sum, the eventual shift towards more emotionalized publicity was too little too late. It was too little in a number of respects. A large-scale agitation campaign of the kind recommended by advertisers was hindered by both a lack of funds as well as continued reservations about the deployment of 'suggestive' propaganda. This was true not only of the Staatspartei and Centre Party (the latter of which

---

[136] S. Tschachotin and C. Mierendorff, *Grundlagen und Formen politischer Propaganda* (Magdeburg, 1932). See D. Harsch, 'The Iron Front', in Barclay and Weitz (eds.), *Between*, 261–8; also Harsch, *German Social Democracy*, 177–89; R. Albrecht, *Der militante Sozialdemokrat* (Bonn, 1987), 143; id., 'Symbolkampf'.

[137] BAB R43/I/2492, Pünder to Strahl, 24 Dec. 1931, fos. 245–6; Vermerk, 17 Feb. 1932, fo. 334; BAB R43/I/2493, Vermerk, 21 May 1932, fo. 12; Pünder to Greve, 2 June 1932, fo. 58.

did almost nothing to update its publicity), but also of the SPD. To quote once again from Carl Severing, even in the no-holds-barred campaign atmosphere of July 1932 it was best 'not to appeal to the passions of the voters but rather to their intellect. We are well aware how much easier it is to intoxicate hungry and anxious people with the cheap elixir of hollow phrases and empty promises. We condemn this approach.'[138] The new symbols and 'psychotechnical' propaganda devised by Chakotin thus carried little conviction, as many Social Democrats still preferred to temper political debate rather than inflame it. And even among their advocates, a lack of experience in mounting such publicity also posed a hindrance. The 'freedom salute' was widely ridiculed as an obvious imitation of the Nazi and KPD salutes, and the three-arrows motif was decried in the professional advertising press as an amateurish stopgap measure: 'This "symbol", which was probably thrown together at the last minute by some minor artist, triggers off such a chain of unconsciously negative thoughts that it is absolutely incomprehensible how a large party with undoubtedly adequate resources could create such a rallying symbol without prior psychoanalytical examination', noted *Seidels Reklame* shortly after the July elections. Its gravest shortcoming, apart from the ability of the Nazis to disfigure it on posters, was that the arrows pointed downwards, conjuring up the feeling that 'things are going downhill'.[139]

As for the revised publicity strategy being too late, closing the gap between the 'sensory deficit' of the Republic and the forceful visual occupation of the public sphere by the Nazis was not a matter of months, but years. The same applied to the vague visions of a 'new state' harboured by von Papen and his associates. Ernst Growald drew a clear distinction between the long-term cultivation of National Socialist symbols and the feeble symbolic gestures of the moderates: 'Every party that wants to be taken seriously should create a symbolic fetish and start propagating it immediately. There is no point waiting until the elections. If the propaganda is supposed to have an effect at the elections it must already be known and recognized as the party symbol so that it can then emerge as prominently as possible at the right moment.'[140] Political brands, like commercial ones, do not develop overnight.

Perhaps most importantly, any shift to suggestive propaganda was a two-edged sword, for it ultimately meant fighting the Nazis on their own terrain. Their strident, fundamental opposition was, despite its attractiveness to an increasingly hostile electorate, simply not an option for the moderate parties or, for that matter, the gentlemen's-club governments of von Papen and Schleicher. It is telling that the Hindenburg propaganda in April 1932 remained chiefly 'integrative', with little sense of the provocation or tribal demarcation that characterized Nazi and KPD publicity. The Hindenburg committees continued

---

[138] Quoted from Paul, 'Krieg', 29.
[139] H. Bachmann, 'Psychologische Fundamentalfehler', *SR* 16 (Aug. 1932), 304.
[140] Growald, 'Reklame-Fetische'.

to put their faith in rational political argument and the sheer prestige of the incumbent rather than bold new visions of society or impassioned political pleas.[141] As professional observers commented shortly afterwards in *Die Reklame*, the point of election propaganda was not just to mobilize the faithful and sow doubt among one's opponents, but also to 'hammer and funnel' its message into the millions of undecided. Given that the non-incumbents had no record in the job and that voters were not in a position to test the veracity of their claims until well after the election, rational appeals were not recommendable. 'Everything depends on getting as large a number of voters to cast their one-off ballot for a certain candidate. Since it is . . . hardly possible to achieve this via factual arguments alone, one must turn to the realm of feelings.' The result was a political bout that increasingly played to the Nazis' communicative strengths: 'As the National Socialists, who have achieved much by way of propaganda, began with their tried and tested suggestive propaganda, the opponents also moved more and more towards this type of publicity.'[142] It was difficult to see how a party or government claiming to represent the rational interests of the state—whether on a parliamentary or conservative authoritarian basis—could effectively fight an avowedly anti-rationalist party by appealing to emotion over rationality.

This was, however, precisely what the 'experts' had long been prescribing, and as the crisis deepened their ideas seemed increasingly plausible. In this sense the propaganda discourse that underlay these prescriptions helped undermine Weimar democracy not only by nourishing right-wing myths of a 'stab in the back' and anti-democratic notions of a Führer and Volksgemeinschaft,[143] but also by hollowing out democratic conceptions of the modern public from the very centre. The rising tide of posters, slogans, flags, and insignia reflected an understanding of the voter more akin to the 'controllable customer' than the rational citizen. The crisis-ridden experience of parliamentarism and the swelling support for the radical parties had turned even many staunch republicans into what Harold Lasswell called 'despondent democrats', democrats whose trust in the good sense of 'the people' had been disappointed: 'Let us, therefore, reason together, brethren, he sighs, and find the good, and when we have found it, let us find out how to make up the public mind to accept it. Inform, cajole, bamboozle and seduce in the name of the public good. Preserve the majority convention, but dictate to the majority!'[144]

This certainly is not to suggest that the Weimar Republic collapsed primarily because of its public-relations shortcomings. Nor is it to say that refraining from such 'bamboozling and seduction' would have been more effective in the early 1930s. The point is rather that there was no workable solution in the

---

[141] Paul, 'Krieg', 31, 37–8.
[142] Quotes from Kwilecki, 'Präsidentenwahl'; O. Olsen, 'Agitprop!', *DR* 25 (May 1932), 273–4.
[143] As argued by Verhey, 'Lessons'.   [144] Lasswell, *Propaganda*, 5.

circumstances. The Weimar democrats failed to find an adequate answer to the problem of republican self-representation not because they were unwilling, but rather unable to. Unlike their radical opponents, who had no qualms about playing on emotional needs during a period of profound disorientation, Weimar democrats found it unpalatable to argue for a rational form of politics on such a 'suggestive' basis. They also found it difficult to agree amongst themselves on the precise nature of the Republic's self-representation, with anniversaries and symbols derived from the socialist, radical, and national-liberal traditions all vying for prominence.[145] In this sense, the Republic's publicity shortcomings should be regarded more as symptoms than causes of its underlying weakness.[146]

It was therefore not so much a lack of will as a lack of unity that explains why, in spite of the vast post-war propaganda discourse and the significant influence it had on the views of mainstream democrats, the republican forces in Weimar Germany neglected the encouragement of a popular emotional attachment to the new political order and only fully recognized this under the impact of the Nazis' advertising-inspired mobilization efforts. Yet in the circumstances—which involved the supporters of the Republic arduously finding a lowest common denominator—the dismissal of such manipulative propaganda as incompatible with the (ideally) rational discourse of democracy seemed the only consensually 'democratic' course of action.

It was thus no coincidence that the radical anti-democratic movements, with their very different notions about the relationship between political elites and public opinion, found it far easier to mobilize the new cultural vocabulary of images, stereotypes, and metaphors at their disposal. Their utter lack of democratic inhibitions placed no constraints on the deployment of manipulative propaganda, and the quasi-religious self-understanding of their political movements ideally lent itself to the use of ritual and symbolism. The fact that the Nazis in particular followed the same visual, sensual logic that so strongly characterized the realm of commercial entertainments meant that their propaganda was more closely in tune with the wider cultural shift to a highly medialized public sphere than that of their opponents. This is certainly *not* to say that the Nazis were able to 'smuggle' particular messages into people's heads via clever propaganda. This old seduction thesis is not only an egregious form of apologia but also posits an untenably simplistic chain of causality between media message and audience response. Rather, it is useful to conceive of the relationship as a matter of parallels instead of chains, whereby political appeals are in some ways analogous to the logic of mass media and commercial entertainments. In the fierce political battles of the early 1930s, the Nazis not only benefited from

---

[145] Swett, *Neighbors*, chap. 3; id., 'Celebrating'; generally, R. Gerwarth, 'The Past in Weimar History', *Contemporary European History*, 15 (2006), 1–22.
[146] This follows Behrenbeck, 'The Nation', 303–4, 319–20.

the fact that their pleas to emotion and faith were particularly attractive in a time of great uncertainty,[147] but also from the relatively successful adaptation of their message to the new communicative terrain. In other words, the Nazis appealed to people's desires and expectations not only in terms of what they said, but also by how they said it. The forms of the Nazi movement spoke volumes about its content. Or, following Marshall McLuhan, the medium was the message.

The cruel irony is that the lingering doubts about the long-term effectiveness of emotionalized propaganda among democratic sceptics were just proving to be well founded when the Nazis were brought into government. After the November 1932 elections it was clear to Nazi officials and grass-roots activists alike that their propaganda had largely exhausted its possibilities. Goebbels himself despaired at the thought of another election campaign: 'God grant that we do not have to carry it out.'[148] The innumerable posters, slogans, and marches had proven highly effective at whipping up a frenzy of resentment. But as the Strasser wing of the party had previously warned (and republican opponents had always hoped), the overuse of such methods would, as with any stimulant, eventually lead to numbness. Solid, long-term support needed to rest on more than emotion.[149] By the beginning of 1933 moderates were discerning a renewed sense of sobriety that led some to conclude that the worst was behind them. According to the New Year's edition of the *Frankfurter Zeitung*, the demystification of the Nazi Party and the painful lessons of the preceding year had demonstrated once and for all that 'there can be no dictating against public opinion in Germany. The realities of life have forced us to return to that which many were so light-heartedly prepared to throw overboard: to reason.'[150] But tragically, over the following weeks the realization that government could no longer dictate against public opinion eventually prompted the small coterie of conservatives around Hindenburg to throw in their lot with the Nazis. By the end of the month the 'cheap elixir of hollow phrases and empty promises' that helped make National Socialism the most powerful political force in Germany finally achieved its interim goal of a Hitler-led government. The Nazi spectacle had only just begun.

---

[147] Verhey, 'Lessons', 116–8.
[148] Reuth (ed.), *Tagebücher*, ii. 719 (12 Nov. 1932).   [149] Paul, *Aufstand*, 106–8.
[150] Quoted from N. Frei, J. Schmitz, *Journalismus im Dritten Reich*, 3rd edn. (Munich, 1999), 9.

PART V

MASS CULTURE IN THE THIRD REICH: PROPAGANDA, ENTERTAINMENT, AND NATIONAL MOBILIZATION

Introduction

After emerging victorious from the propaganda battles of the early 1930s, the Nazi movement still had its work cut out. The incessant electioneering, disastrous economic slump, and increasingly bitter tone of political intercourse had polarized the country more than ever before. The Nazis were, of course, a primary culprit behind the exacerbation of tensions. Once in power, party propagandists thus faced a very different set of challenges than during the 'period of struggle'. If the immediate task after January 1933 was to consolidate their new position, the long-term aim was to harness the media for the purpose of social and political stabilization, to utilize the means of communication to bridge the divides of German society, much as the propaganda 'experts' had long been counselling. After all, one of the professed goals of National Socialism was to construct a more integrated 'Volksgemeinschaft' that would overcome the deep social and political rifts running through the nation. The aim was quite literally to forge an ethnically based sense of the communal bonds that had become attenuated by the individualizing pressures of modern industrial society. An important part of this was to foster a commonly shared set of cultural values, artefacts, and practices that would transcend social and geographic divides and give expression to the 'healthy' instincts of the national spirit that their movement claimed to represent.

This raises two fundamental questions: how did the Nazis pursue this far-reaching cultural project; and what was the overall effect? As for the first question, the sizeable literature on the Nazi 'coordination' of the press, film, radio, and music offers a detailed reconstruction of the regime's attempt to convey to German audiences an image of itself and the wider world that broadly supported its goals. Although careful research has shown that the orchestration of the mass media was often less organized and direct than is sometimes assumed, it is nonetheless clear that the regime invested an immense amount of time and resources in setting the parameters of mass communication from early on.[1] As for the second question, gauging the actual consequences of Nazi media policies is a more complex matter. At one level the question can be posed in terms of the impact on popular opinion, for which there are a number of

---

[1] For inroads, see D. Welch, *The Third Reich*, 2nd edn. (London, 2002); Etlin (ed.), *Art*.

excellent studies.[2] It has also been addressed as part of the wider debate about the 'modernizing' credentials of the Third Reich, which touches on the extent to which traditional regional and class-based patterns of leisure were displaced by a more universal mass culture.[3] Fascinating though these questions are, they hardly exhaust the topic. The following chapters thus take a somewhat different approach. They do not seek to measure the modernizing (or otherwise) consequences of Nazi communication strategies, nor do they remotely claim to offer a comprehensive overview of mass culture in the Third Reich. They rather seek to investigate, in a more open-ended fashion, how the media fitted into broader patterns of social and cultural change during this fateful period stretching from the traumas of the Depression to the massive upheavals of the Second World War.

In many ways this section grafts directly onto the themes considered in Part III, which showed how the social impact of mass culture was decisively shaped by the broader political and economic context in which it was produced and consumed. The logical extension of this argument is that any substantial shift in this context would have a significant effect on the social role of mass communications. Given the Nazis' avowed aim of utilizing the media for the purpose of national integration, it is tempting to assume that any socially or culturally homogenizing tendencies would be significantly enhanced in the new 'totalizing' political and institutional environment of the Third Reich. Yet, for all the studies on propaganda and the media under the Nazis, the question of how the social meaning of mass culture changed under the combined pressures of *Gleichschaltung* (political 'coordination'), commercial concentration, and technological convergence has not been seriously investigated. Insofar as this issue features at all in the vast literature on the Third Reich, it is generally noted that mass culture under the Nazis did not—apart from the nature and degree of censorship—diverge radically from previous trends or from international developments, and that its chief role was to lull the general public with seemingly 'normal' entertainment while transmitting a modicum of ideology via this otherwise rather unremarkable entertainment industry.[4] While I have few qualms with these arguments, they barely scratch the surface of the wider social impact of the mass media in the Third Reich, from distribution and patterns of usage to their shifting role within German popular culture. This concluding section will thus examine, against the background of longer-term trends, how

---

[2] I. Kershaw, *Popular Opinion and Political Dissent in the Third Reich* (Oxford, 1983); D. Peukert, *Inside Nazi Germany* (London, 1987); R. Gellately, *Backing Hitler* (Oxford, 2001).

[3] Generally, I. Kershaw, *The Nazi Dictatorship*, 4th edn. (London, 2000), chap. 7; R. Bavaj, *Die Ambivalenz der Moderne im Nationalsozialismus* (Munich, 2003).

[4] Maase, *Grenzenloses*, 233; R. Grunberger, *A Social History of the Third Reich* (Harmondsworth, 1974), 475; generally, Reichel, *Der schöne Schein*; Dröge, Müller, *Macht*.

far the reconfiguration of the media and popular entertainment under the Nazis helped to unite, divide, mobilize, and distract German audiences living in what has been dubbed, colourfully if somewhat exaggeratedly, 'the modern era's first full-blown media culture'.[5]

---

[5] E. Rentschler, *The Ministry of Illusion* (Cambridge, Mass., 1996), 21.

9

Political Control and Commercial Concentration Under the Nazis

The Nazi attempt to 'coordinate' every aspect of life in Germany constitutes a central element in any account of the regime. The speed with which existing institutions were 'brought into line' with the vision of the National Socialist movement testifies to both the totalitarian ambitions of its leaders and to the curious mixture of enthusiasm, opportunism, and intimidation that helped translate this vision into reality. No sooner were the Nazis in government than they launched a ruthless campaign to smash the power of their opponents and to establish their supremacy over political, social, and cultural life. As countless studies have shown, this so-called 'national revolution' hardly involved an insurrectionary takeover of government, let alone the overthrow of the existing social order. The need to secure the goodwill of administrative, economic, and cultural elites placed powerful limits on the government's room for manoeuvre. It is indeed questionable how far the 'national revolution' was ever about social and economic change in the first place. As recent research has emphasized, the domestic aims of the Nazi leadership were largely focused on what they viewed as the inseparable challenges of racial and cultural renewal. Accordingly, it was in the realm of cultural life that the most radical transformation was attempted. The overarching aim was nothing less than to recast the values and character of the German nation.[1]

If the goal of cultural renewal presented fewer obstacles than 'hard' social or economic reforms, it was nonetheless constrained by a range of different factors, especially in the sphere of mass communication. True, when we look at the development of leisure and entertainments under the Nazis it is in many ways their interventionist zeal that is most conspicuous. Not even the previous wartime governments attempted such a dramatic transformation of the legal framework and institutions that presided over mass communications. But by the 1930s the media represented a technologically sophisticated and (at least potentially) highly profitable segment of the national economy, that moreover bestowed a certain degree of cultural prestige on the country whose productions could prevail on

[1] For all their differences, R. J. Evans, *The Coming of the Third Reich* (London, 2003) and M. Burleigh, *The Third Reich* (London, 2000) both emphasize the project of cultural renewal.

the domestic and international market. For both political and economic reasons, it was thus something that the government could not afford to turn over to party hacks or suffocate within an ideological straitjacket. What was required was a pragmatic approach—all the more so given the immense commercial pressures and rapid technological innovations during the 1930s, none of which were wholly specific to Germany.

For all these reasons it is helpful to approach the development of mass culture under the Nazis as an interaction between global trends—commercial necessities, technical developments, and the broader economic recovery—and the specific political restructuring of cultural life within Germany. Indeed, it is best not to separate these factors too neatly, for they tended to overlap and reinforce one another. The crucial backdrop to all of these changes was the rise in disposable income—however meagre it remained—after 1932.[2] While the growth in production and employment meant that German households had more money to spend on entertainment, the prioritization of rearmament over living standards meant that leisure would have to soak up much of the excess purchasing power. Expanding media-use as a form of cultural rather than material consumption was thus highly desirable for both political and economic reasons. The catch was that it inevitably required concessions to popular tastes. How these interrelated factors shaped the media under the Nazis is the subject of this chapter.

NATIONAL SOCIALIST RESTRUCTURING OF MEDIA AND LEISURE

Gaining control over the means of communication numbered among the Nazis' first priorities after entering government. It took less than a week for the cabinet to impose drastic limitations on freedom of assembly and expression. On 4 February 1933 the emergency decree 'for the protection of the German people' allowed the police to ban any publication whose content was deemed to threaten public order or insult leading political figures. Along with the SA harassment of opposing editors, this was a highly advantageous campaign tool in the run-up to the Reichstag elections in early March. Three weeks later, on 28 February, the playing-field was skewed even further with the 'Reichstag Fire Decree', which furnished the legal basis for a wave of arrests and an effective ban on KPD and SPD publications one week before polling day (5 March). Thereafter, Goebbels noted, the Nazi election campaign could practically 'run itself'.[3]

But the attempt to use the media for the wider consolidation of Nazi power would require far more than banning orders. Plans to set up a special ministry for

---

[2] On living standards, A. Tooze, *The Wages of Destruction* (London, 2006), 135–65.
[3] Reuth (ed.), *Tagebücher*, ii. 770 (28 Feb. 1933).

propaganda were already under discussion in the early part of 1933.[4] On 6 March, the day after the Nazis failed to achieve an overall majority in the Reichstag elections, Hitler and Goebbels met to hammer out the details. When their plans were presented to cabinet, the only objection came from Hugenberg, now economics minister, who discerned a potential threat to his own media interests. Despite his misgivings, the ministry was formally established on 13 March for the official purpose of disseminating 'enlightenment and propaganda within the population concerning the policy of the Reich government and the national reconstruction of the German Fatherland'.[5] What was meant by this distinction between enlightenment and propaganda was spelled out by Goebbels in a speech to journalists on 15 March: 'Popular enlightenment is essentially something passive; propaganda, on the other hand, is something active. We cannot, therefore, be satisfied with just telling the people what we want and enlightening them as to how we are doing it. We must, rather, replace this enlightenment with an active government propaganda, a propaganda that aims at winning people over.'[6] The point was, in other words, not just to massage public opinion, but to convert the government's erstwhile opponents and unify the nation behind its leadership.

It took only a few weeks before the Propaganda Ministry (RMVP) was up and running. Staffed for the most part by young Nazi activists, and therefore free of the entrenched conservative bureaucrats who dominated most other ministries, it was initially divided into seven departments: a general administrative office, a coordinating department, and five special divisions for broadcasting, press, film, the theatre, and music/fine arts. From the very beginning, the RMVP embodied the far-reaching amalgamation of party and state that would later affect other ministries. Many of its 350 staff held similar responsibilities within the NSDAP propaganda executive: Goebbels himself retained his position as director of party propaganda, a dual role that gave him a distinct advantage over rivals such as Reich press chief Otto Dietrich, the director of the party press Max Amann, Prussian minister president Hermann Göring, and of course Alfred Rosenberg as leader of the 'Combat League for German Culture' (renamed NS-Kulturgemeinde in 1934).[7] So intense were these turf wars that it took the personal intervention of Hitler in June 1933 to clarify the RMVP's competences, after which it quickly became the primary decision-making body for cultural policy in Third Reich.

To facilitate its supervision over general matters of content, the day-to-day tasks of economic and organizational coordination were soon transferred to subordinate agencies. By far the most important was the Reich Chamber of Culture (RKK), founded in September 1933 with Goebbels once again at the

---

    4 Reuth (ed.), *Tagebücher*, ii. 766 (18 Feb. 1933).
    5 Quoted from J. Noakes and G. Pridham (eds.), *Nazism 1919–1945*, vol. 2 (Exeter, 1984), 380.
    6 Repr. in Welch, *Third Reich*, 174.
    7 On these rivalries, see A. A. Kallis, *Nazi Propaganda and the Second World War* (Basingstoke, 2005), 40–62.

helm. The RKK was divided into seven sub-sections for literature, film, theatre, radio, music, press, and fine arts, each directed by a president who was, in turn, personally appointed by Goebbels. These subordinate chambers effectively functioned as professional corporations: they regulated working conditions, remuneration, and entry into the field. The key lever was membership, for the Reich Chambers could exclude any 'undesirables' on racial, political, or artistic grounds. Since only RKK members were allowed to work in a given field, exclusion effectively meant the end of one's career. One of the results was that thousands of artists, writers, and musicians fled Germany after 1933, much to the benefit of the countries willing to accept them.[8] For the majority who were not excluded the RKK brought tangible benefits, above all job security. This helps explain why so many intellectuals and artists were willing to comply with National Socialist measures. While some were genuinely enthusiastic about the regime's aims, in most cases it represented little more than a practical career move.

The great advantage of this regulatory scheme was that it replaced the micro-managerial headaches of censorship with a far more efficient system of self-censorship exercised directly at the point of production, that is, by people fearful of losing their livelihoods. By and large the system worked, though Goebbels eventually found it necessary to issue a blanket ban on art criticism to ensure that officially approved works no longer received negative reviews. After November 1936 only specially licensed 'critics' were allowed to pass judgements, and even these were confined to mere descriptions of content.[9] The dreary result was an even further flattening of creative expression in a country that had boasted the most vibrant art scene in the entire world only half-a-decade earlier. We will look in more detail at the content of the mass media in the next chapter. For the time being it suffices to note that the 'split consciousness' (Schäfer) of the Third Reich—the uneasy coexistence of a repressive, backwards-looking *völkisch* ideology with an enjoyable, 'modern', consumer-oriented lifestyle—was nowhere more apparent than in the sphere of leisure and entertainment. While irreverent cabarets, American-style jazz, and racy depictions of sex and criminality were officially suppressed, the regime actively set about filling the void it had thereby created. The cultivation of sober classics and folksy peasant customs could hardly take up the slack: throughout the 1930s jazz tunes continued to reverberate in the dance locales, and officially sponsored theatre events were just as likely to feature a popular variety format as a classical repertoire. Much the same pattern could be observed across the entire range of leisure provision. The regime quickly created surrogates for the thousands of voluntary associations (*Vereine*) it had banned, most notably 'Strength through Joy' (KdF), the Hitler Youth,

---

[8] H. A. Strauss, 'The Movement of People in a Time of Crisis', in J. C. Jackman and C. M. Borden (eds.), *The Muses Flee Hitler* (Washington, DC, 1983), 45–59.
[9] Though there were ways to subvert this: 'Wenn ein Film nun ganz mißfällt?', *ZV* 39 (3 Dec. 1938), 749.

and the League of German Girls. In the realm of leisure, Nazi 'coordination' was less about transforming the actual content than reorganizing how it was delivered.

This restructuring process did not follow a clear, linear plan, nor was it the product of a single, coherent cultural policy. As in nearly every sphere of the National Socialist bureaucracy, the coordination of the media often proceeded in a haphazard and improvised manner, riddled with conflicting interests and propelled more by the personal ambition of rival administrators than by a consistent set of objectives. It is equally questionable how far one can speak of a Nazi cultural 'policy' at all with regard to popular entertainments. The general set of principles and prejudices that shaped the National Socialist vision could be, and was, translated into practice in many different ways, from a dogged defence of the classics to an unconcealed indulgence of light entertainment. And quite apart from the incessant political infighting and ideological disputes, the commercial necessities and technological advances that transformed communications in the 1930s required a degree of flexibility in any case.

As we will see shortly, the process of political coordination thus differed significantly from one medium to another. Yet we can still discern a number of common features. Nazi control over the mass media was generally pursued through a mixture of intimidation and enticement, whereby the latter was often just as important as the former. By and large, the regime purported to offer—and in some respects did offer—a workable solution to at least some of the ongoing problems in the communications branch in the early 1930s. At the heart of these solutions was a new, corporatist occupational and commercial structure that promised greater protection and financial prospects for all who were prepared to accept the loss of autonomy this entailed. In many instances the Nazis were preaching to the converted. For some would-be reformers the new political and administrative context after spring 1933 presented a long-awaited opportunity to implement the corporatist schemes they had failed to introduce under the Republic. Of course, the fact that they were now carried out under Nazi auspices meant a massive purge of 'Jewish' and 'Marxist' elements. But if the purges were primarily a means of eliminating political opposition, they also tackled a long-standing problem in the media industry: namely, the chronic surplus of journalists, musicians, actors, and producers continually scrambling for work. In short, the Nazis offered a solution to the overcrowding, excessive competition, and insecurity that had long plagued the industry in exchange for tighter regulation and the dismissal of a minority that aroused little sympathy and that had long incurred the wrath of the nationalist Right.[10] Given the intensification of these problems during the Depression, the Nazi restructuring of the media represented in many eyes as much a path out of structural crisis as a new corset of political control.

---

[10] A. E. Steinweis, 'Cultural Eugenics', in Cuomo (ed.), *Cultural Policy*, 23–37.

COMMERCIAL CONCENTRATION, EXPANSION, AND THE TALKING FILM

No medium suffered more from the effects of the Depression than film, and none therefore offered easier justification for Nazi intervention. As we saw in Chapter 6, cinema attendance had fallen dramatically over the early 1930s, dropping from a high of 353 million admissions in 1928 to only 239 million in 1932.[11] The overall result was a huge decline in revenue for the entire film industry, from large-scale producers to small, independent cinema operators. As more and more Germans lost their jobs or saw their wages reduced, expenditure on non-essentials bore the brunt of belt-tightening. Yet the loss of revenue hit the film industry especially hard because it coincided with the costly conversion to sound. For cinema owners who had just invested in new projection and sound equipment, half-filled auditoriums could not have come at a worse time. And for film producers, dwindling box-office returns contrasted cruelly with rising production costs for talking films. The term 'crisis', though perhaps over-used for the early 1930s, seems a thoroughly appropriate description of the German film industry at the time.

In 1932, as the industry was awash in a wave of bankruptcies, the body representing the interests of the big film producers (SPIO: Spitzenorganisation der Deutschen Filmindustrie) published a set of proposals that amounted to a centralization of the entire German film industry. Pushed forward by UFA general director Ludwig Klitzsch, who doubled as SPIO's chairman, the plan revolved around two main points: privileged investment in large producers capable of delivering quality films with a chance of making money abroad, and restricting the domestic sale of such films to distributors and exhibitors who abided by new guidelines on programme format, pricing, and seating. By reducing competition within the branch, this was essentially a recipe for recovery at the expense of smaller firms. The main obstacle was the cinema owners' association (Reichsverband deutscher Lichtspieltheaterbesitzer), which rejected the plan on the grounds that it would ruin many independent theatres. Indeed, this was precisely the aim, for filmmakers had long demanded a radical reduction of seating capacity.[12] While producers complained that exhibitors depressed profits by flooding the market with too many seats and cheap tickets, exhibitors accused producers of overcharging for poor films that lacked box-office appeal.

The fact that this dispute was still simmering in early 1933 made the film industry ripe for state intervention. Yet what kind of intervention was initially unclear, for the squabbles in the industry were mirrored within the party.

---

[11] Jason (ed.), *Handbuch 1935/36*, 28.
[12] On the SPIO-plan, see Spiker, *Film*, 71–5; Kreimeier, *Ufa Story*, 193–5.

While the NSDAP propaganda executive advocated a conciliatory line to avoid spooking the big production companies, other voices (including Rosenberg's) called for a radical overhaul. Drawing on a crude mixture of anti-capitalism and anti-Semitism, a group of Nazi theatre operators led by Adolf Engl and Oswald Johnsen launched a bitter attack against the 'monopolization' of film production by UFA, which, though directed by non-Jewish conservatives, was pilloried as *verjudet* ('Jewified') due to its ties with high finance and its importing of foreign films. To a large degree these efforts were directed against what was perceived—somewhat justifiably—as an attempt by SPIO to centralize the industry under Hugenberg's Economics Ministry, thus keeping it out of Nazi hands. It was therefore ironic that by the time Engl took control of the cinema owners' association on 18 March, the newly appointed Nazi propaganda minister had already made up his mind in favour of a slightly modified SPIO-plan.[13]

The government's approach to the film industry became abundantly clear with the establishment of the Reich Film Chamber in July 1933, the first such chamber of its kind. For all intents and purposes it functioned as a Nazi-controlled SPIO. The appointment of the lawyer Fritz Scheuermann (who was closely involved with the implementation of the SPIO proposals) as its first president gave a clear indication of which way the wind was blowing. So, too, did the disbanding of the film union Dacho in May 1933, which removed the chief institutional hindrance to the reorganization. By the time the Reich Film Chamber was subsumed into the RKK in September 1933 it was already the government's chief lever for influencing the industry. Ultimately under the control of the propaganda minister, it gave Goebbels legal power over the employment of everyone in the movie business, from filmmakers and actors to cameramen and set designers. Not that he needed to exercise this power very often: UFA was already quietly dismissing its Jewish employees in spring 1933, without provoking much protest from their 'Aryan' colleagues. And of course many actors and directors with objectionable racial or political backgrounds leapt before being pushed, recognizing that their prospects under the new regime were bleak. It is frequently pointed out that this haemorrhage of talent was an enormous windfall for the studios in Hollywood (where up to around 500 German-speaking exiles were based) and, to a lesser extent, Paris, London, and pre-annexation Vienna.[14] It is less often noted that the vast bulk of cinematic know-how remained. Although the Nazi takeover deprived the German film industry of some of its brightest stars (Fritz Lang, Billy Wilder, G. W. Pabst), the overwhelming majority continued to work within the new system, including many successful actors, (Emil Jannings, Lil Dagover, Otto Gebühr, Willy Fritsch, Hans Albers), directors (Paul Wegener, Carl Froehlich),

---

[13] Spiker, *Film*, 80–1; Kreimeier, *Ufa Story*, 222.
[14] J. C. Horak, 'Exilfilm, 1933–1945', in Jacobsen, Kaes, and Prinzler (eds.), *Geschichte*, 108.

and scriptwriters (Thea von Harbou, soon to be ex-wife of Lang, who had long gravitated towards the political Right and finally joined the NSDAP in 1933).

Yet officials in the Propaganda Ministry were acutely sensitive to the misgivings such moves could generate. On 28 March 1933 Goebbels tried to assuage industry fears by presenting himself to an assembly of film functionaries 'as someone who has never lost contact with film in Germany: in fact, I am a passionate devotee of the cinematographic art'. The last thing on his mind was to put the future of film production in jeopardy. With the Nazis in charge, 'the film industry has every reason to feel secure'. The films that he singled out for praise included not only the Germanic mythology of Lang's monumental *Die Nibelungen* and the nationalistic vigilance of *Der Rebell*, but also Greta Garbo's artful rendition of *Anna Karenina* and, as mentioned earlier, Eisenstein's Soviet classic *Battleship Potemkin*. He assured the delegates that 'the new movement does not exhaust itself with parade-ground marches and blowing trumpets'. Such 'authoritarian doctrinairism' was anathema to the Nazi-led government, 'which in its heart of hearts is kindly disposed towards the film industry'. His avowed aim was not to 'put the film industry in a straitjacket', but rather to encourage certain outlooks that would offer 'an ample amount of scope for all kinds of artistic talent to roam freely'.[15] The fact that the full text of this speech was not published at the time gave it the aura of a heart-to-heart discussion with industry representatives, an expression of genuine views that the minister could not divulge to his less sophisticated supporters. This was all too understandable in view of the rioting SA troops and students angered by the failure to revolutionize the popular cinema along 'national' lines.[16] Since Goebbels could not afford to alienate the rank-and-file either, the *VB* published an abridged version of his speech that cynically omitted all talk of artistic freedom.[17]

The verbal reassurances given to filmmakers were flanked by more concrete measures to overcome industry unease. On 1 June the government announced, to general applause, the creation of the Filmkreditbank as a source of low-interest loans that would enable producers to offload much of the risk in the highly volatile market. Naturally, the loans came with strings attached. Applicants not only had to sign over ownership of a film until the loan was repaid, but also had to convince the bank of its profitability in the first place. The Filmkreditbank therefore gave officials considerable influence over film content through the selective opening of the financial tap at the pre-production stage—all the more so after its shares were transferred to the Reich Film Chamber in 1934. But apparently the film industry deemed such political interference a price worth paying, for within only a few years the Filmkreditbank was financing around three-quarters of all feature-length productions.

---

[15] Quoted from Welch, *Third Reich*, 185, 186, 188.
[16] G. Stahr, *Volksgemeinschaft vor der Leinwand?* (Berlin, 2001), 122–30.
[17] D. Welch, *Propaganda and the German Cinema 1933–45* (Oxford, 1983), 17.

It was undoubtedly the big corporations that profited most from the new arrangements. They not only received the bulk of credit from the bank, but also benefited from a series of new regulations on exhibitors.[18] In September 1933 the Propaganda Ministry issued a general ban on the 'two-hit' programme, which for years had effectively halved profits per film and thus starved the industry of much-needed investment capital.[19] Thenceforth the typical cinema programme was to consist of a feature, newsreel, and a handful of short films of no more than 127 minutes in total. In October 1933 the RMVP also issued new regulations on admission fees to prevent price wars and maximize profits, followed by new licensing requirements the following April. A few months later, in September 1934, the Reich Film Chamber finally grasped the nettle of Germany's perennial overcapacity problem by forbidding the construction of new cinemas without special permission.[20]

For all that the big producers cheered this 'clean-up' of the exhibition branch, whatever advantages it brought them came with an ever-greater erosion of artistic autonomy. A new Film Law in February 1934 vastly extended the government's censorship powers. Whereas the original law of 1920 gave censors the power to proscribe individual scenes or entire films in cases of indecency or a threat to public order, the new law widened the definition of suppressible material and provided for a new framework of vetting throughout the production process. The crucial job of pre-censorship was given to a new 'Reich film director' (*Reichsfilmdramaturg*), appointed by the propaganda minister, to whom synopses of scripts were submitted for approval before any filming could begin. At this and each subsequent stage in the production process the Reich film director could suggest alterations to ensure that a film conformed to the regime's political interests. The new Film Law also expanded the existing rating system as an incentive for filmmakers to tailor their productions to what the censors deemed 'educational' or 'politically and artistically valuable'. Between the Reich film director, the rating system, and the Filmkreditbank, there was effectively no way a film could be produced without the express approval of the Propaganda Ministry.

But the restructuring of the film industry in the 1930s reflected more than just the Nazi politicization of cultural life, for it was driven in large part by commercial imperatives. There was a dovetailing of interests at work. As the SPIO had argued in 1932, commercial concentration and tighter regulation was necessary to keep the German film industry profitable. Given the pressures of a highly competitive international market, it was vital to funnel investment to a handful of big firms rather than frittering it away on small production outfits. In addition, a greater share of profits needed to be ploughed back into production instead of seeping into the pockets of cinema operators. This cartel-like vision resonated

---

[18] Welch, *Propaganda*, 14–15.   [19] Stahr, *Volksgemeinschaft*, 61.
[20] Jason (ed.), *Handbuch 1935/36*, 116; K. Wolf, *Entwicklung und Neugestaltung der deutschen Filmwirtschaft seit 1933*, Ph.D thesis, Heidelberg (1938), 47.

with regime aims at a number of levels. A flourishing film industry not only promised healthy tax revenues at home, but also helped ameliorate Germany's crippling balance-of-payment problems through export earnings. High-quality films kept cinema audiences happy and at the same time demonstrated the government's support for German cultural production against foreign influence. Internationally successful films affirmed for Germans their status as a leading *Kulturvolk*, and also enhanced the image of the regime abroad. And of course, at a purely practical level, a more centralized organizational framework also made it easier to control production.

Among this mixture of incentives, perhaps the most important were the heightened commercial pressures within the film industry at large.[21] At the level of film production they greatly accelerated the ongoing process of commercial concentration that was already well under way before 1933, in Germany as elsewhere. The transition from silent to sound film signalled a dramatic increase in production costs and financial risk. Whereas the average film in 1932–3 required RM 250,000 and from twelve to twenty-five days to produce, by 1936–7 this had roughly doubled to RM 500,000 and from twenty to forty days.[22] Financial transactions of this magnitude quickly snuffed out the smaller independent producers (those making one or two films per year), who as late as 1929 still accounted for 80 per cent of film production in Germany. The extinction of small producers was further boosted by Nazi discrimination against Jews, since many of these smaller companies were in Jewish hands.[23] Of the 400 production firms in Germany at the end of the 1920s, only forty-nine were left in 1934, thirty-five of which were effectively subsidiaries of the three largest concerns (UFA, Tobis, and Terra). Barely 10 per cent of the independent producers could operate without the financial backing of one of the big companies.[24] By 1936 'the formally independent film producer', as the *Frankfurter Zeitung* bluntly put it, 'is nowadays little more than an occasionally enlisted production director'.[25] The end-result, as in other countries, was a dramatic drop in supply that had significant effects on the wider social role of film in Nazi Germany (to which we will return in the next chapter).

The distribution sector experienced much the same fate. In 1932 small and mid-sized distributors still handled 60 per cent of German-made films and a large proportion of foreign productions. By 1935 their market share had dropped to only 25 per cent of domestic films and a small handful of imports, with the four largest distributors accounting for nearly all the rest. Of the 112 films made in Germany in 1935, Tobis and UFA distributed 55 per cent, Terra and Bavaria a further 20 per cent. By 1937 the triad of Tobis, UFA, and Terra dominated almost entirely, their only competition coming from small firms with

---

[21] The following paragraphs are based on Ross, 'Mass Culture and Divided Audiences'.
[22] Bächlin, *Film*, 78.   [23] Wolf, *Entwicklung*, 39; Jason (ed.), *Handbuch 1935/36*, 123.
[24] Spiker, *Film*, 58; Wolf, *Entwicklung*, 41–2.   [25] Quoted from Bächlin, *Film*, 78.

at best a regional remit.[26] Again, similar processes of concentration and vertical integration were observable elsewhere, especially in the United States, Britain, and France.

The situation in the exhibition branch was more ambiguous. On the one hand, cinema owners undoubtedly felt the pinch from the (deliberate) under-supply of films, the demise of most small-scale producers, and concentration within the distribution sector, which significantly weakened their bargaining power in relation to the remaining film companies. In the face of these vertically integrated mega-concerns, cinema owners had little choice but to accept—however grudgingly—the higher rental fees and hated practice of blind- and block-booking, whereby whole blocks of films were reserved without prior viewing and often before they were even completed.[27] This was especially hard on the smallest cinemas, whose already thin profit margins were further squeezed by the 35 per cent rise in distribution fees (which more than doubled for some big films).[28] But on the other hand, and in stark contrast to the production and distribution sectors, there was very little commercial concentration among exhibitors in the 1930s. Unlike in the United States and Britain, where buy-outs and large-scale chaining were fast becoming the rule, the German exhibition branch was still dominated by single, independent cinemas. In 1936 82.3 per cent of cinemas were still owned by individual proprietors, the rest by joint-stock companies. That same year only 6.1 per cent were owned by entities running more than four cinemas (though such chained cinemas tended to be larger than average, and accounted for 13.6 per cent of seats).[29] This independence was admittedly somewhat nominal in view of the predominance of a handful of large distributors. But the entire cinema landscape in 1930s Germany nonetheless remained remarkably variegated in international comparison. Indeed, the Reich Film Chamber, despite its centralizing predilections, actually *discouraged* the growth of cinema chains on the grounds that it would strengthen their commercial position and therefore reduce the amount of capital flowing back into production.[30]

All of these policies paid dividends during the economic recovery of the mid-1930s. Underpinning the resurgence of profitability was a sharp rise in admissions, from 239 million in 1932 to 375 million in 1937, itself a reflection of rising disposable income. A comparison of household entertainment budgets in 1927/8 and 1937 shows that average yearly cinema expenditure among lower-income households (earning not more than RM 3,000/year) roughly doubled from RM 2.63 to RM 5.21, and that the number of households spending anything at all on the cinema also rose from around one-half to

---

[26] Spiker, *Film*, 140.
[27] 'Die Programme der Kleinen', *FK* (20 Nov. 1937), 1–2; 'Die Not der Kleinen', *FK* (23 Sept. 1935), 4; *Deutschland-Berichte der Sozialdemokratische Partei Deutschlands (Sopade), 1934–1940* (hereafter *Deutschland-Berichte*), vol. 4 (Frankfurt a. M., 1980), 903–4.
[28] 'Die Not der Kleinen', 4.   [29] Spiker, *Film*, 137–8.   [30] Ibid. 139.

two-thirds.[31] Other factors reinforced the trend, above all the popular attraction of sound films and, to a lesser extent, Nazi efforts to promote film among rural and working-class audiences. Latching on to the earlier efforts of rural-welfare associations, the Nazis established thirty-two Gaufilmstellen (regional film offices) that arranged regular screenings in some 48,000 villages. Employing a fleet of 'sound film lorries', the Gaufilmstellen organized 121,345 such events in 1935, attracting around 21 million visitors. In the cities and smaller towns too, the subsidized cinema offerings of 'Strength through Joy' also drew in additional spectators.[32]

But it is important to keep the growth in perspective, since Germany still lagged far behind most other comparably developed countries. In 1934 the number of weekly admissions per thousand inhabitants in Germany was only 86, compared to 160 for France, 342 for the United States, and 413 for Britain.[33] It was this relative weakness of the domestic market that made it so difficult for German filmmakers to amortize the costs of high-quality films at home and made them so heavily reliant on export profits. And in this respect the Nazi government was a clear liability, for the widespread international aversion to the regime manifested itself in limited demand for German films abroad, which many Jewish distributors in other countries flatly refused to carry.

Thus, despite the improvement in admissions figures and the clear privileges they enjoyed, German film producers continued to suffer financial difficulties. The combination of spiralling costs, a weak domestic market, and limited export opportunities furnished Goebbels with a plausible reason to extend state control yet further. Once again, political and commercial aims intermingled: further rationalization of film production promised both a better use of resources and greater responsiveness to the wishes of the Propaganda Ministry. Throughout the mid-1930s this agenda was pursued slowly but surely, with few in the industry, let alone the public, taking much notice. It started in 1934, when Goebbels commissioned the trustee Max Winkler to begin buying up company shares on behalf of the Reich, much as he was already doing with the German press (see below). In 1936 he established the Kautio Treuhand GmbH as a holding company for administering majority shares on behalf of the government without taking the controversial step of open national-ization. By 1937 Winkler had quietly acquired control of Tobis, Terra, and UFA, adding Bavaria and (after the annexation of Austria) Wien Film to the list in 1938. By the outbreak of the war, all of the major production com-panies were under indirect (*staatsmittelbar*) state control through the Kautio Treuhand.[34]

---

[31] Statistisches Reichsamt, *Lebenshaltung*, 57; Arbeitswissenschaftliches Institut der Deutschen Arbeitsfront, 'Erhebung', vol. 3.2, p. 347.

[32] 'Theaterbesitzer vor neuen Aufgaben', *FK* (23 Sept. 1935), 3–4.

[33] Jason (ed.), *Handbuch 1935/36*, 163.   [34] Welch, *German Cinema*, 32–4.

By the end of the 1930s the overall management of the German cinema was thus largely in the hands of the Propaganda Ministry. Among the various groups and institutions involved in the film business, Goebbels and his administrative apparatus were certainly the most powerful elements in the equation. But production was still not totally centralized, and the many divergent views within the Nazi hierarchy afforded considerable room for manoeuvre. The bulk of cinemas too remained in private hands, which also afforded some latitude for individual initiative in spite of the requirement to abide by Reich Film Chamber directives.

Most importantly, German films did not enjoy a monopoly over the domestic audience in any event. Of the 150 to 200 films that were annually distributed in the Reich from 1933 to 1939, a little over half were German, with roughly 20 per cent imported from the United States and a further 20 per cent from other countries. In 1933 almost a third (64 out of 206) were of American origin, and in 1935 over half of all feature films (96 out of 188) came from abroad. It was only in 1939 that imports significantly tailed off, falling to under a quarter in 1940 as imports from Hollywood were stopped.[35] The Propaganda Ministry could exert little direct influence over foreign-made productions, though German authorities possessed some measure of control via import regulations and censorship. Between 1933 and 1940 over 150 American films were banned in Germany, and many of those that passed the censors only did so after alterations.[36] But international trade agreements and, more importantly, the need to meet the demand for big-budget films meant that American productions ranging from Mickey Mouse to Buck Rogers could be seen all over pre-war Germany. In fact, the actual market share of Hollywood films far exceeded their proportion of titles. In 1933 seven of the ten most successful films in Germany (according to running times in Berlin premiere cinemas) came from the United States; in each of the years from 1935 to 1937 Hollywood accounted for four of the top ten, including the top two in 1936, *Broadway Melody of 1936* and *Our Daily Bread*.[37]

As in so many areas, the outbreak of the Second World War brought a number of far-reaching changes to the German cinema. The period from 1939 to 1942 witnessed not only a dramatic tightening of import regulations, but also a thoroughgoing centralization of domestic production as part of the Nazi bid to create a pan-European counterweight to Hollywood.[38] Yet, as we will see in the next chapter, this transformation was not especially evident in the actual content of films, where light entertainment and classical narrative continued to dominate much as before. Arguably the greatest changes under the Nazis were not to be found on the silver screen, but rather in how films were produced and the patterns of their appropriation by an ever-expanding audience.

[35] Calculated from M. Spieker, *Hollywood unterm Hakenkreuz* (Trier, 1999), 337.
[36] Ibid. 344–7; K. C. Führer, 'Two-fold Admiration', in Führer and Ross (eds.), *Media*, 99–102.
[37] Spieker, *Hollywood*, 340–1.
[38] See de Grazia, *Irresistible*, 319–35; generally, R. Vande Winkel and D. Welch (eds.), *Cinema and the Swastika: The International Expansion of Third Reich Cinema* (Houndmills, 2007).

TABLE 6. *Feature films distributed in Germany, 1923–1940* (by country of origin)

Year	Germany	USA	Other
1923	253	102	62
1924	220	186	154
1925	212	216	90
1926	185	216	86
1927	242	190	94
1928	224	199	94
1929	183	142	91
1930	146	79	59
1931	144	85	49
1932	132	55	26
1933	114	64	28
1934	129	41	40
1935	92	41	55
1936	112	28	36
1937	94	39	39
1938	100	35	27
1939	111	20	13
1940	85	5	13

Source: Spieker, *Hollywood*, 337.

RADIO AND RECORDING: STATE CONTROL AND MEDIA CONVERGENCE

It is an unfortunate irony that one of the principal advantages of state regulation over broadcasting during the Weimar Republic—namely, keeping the airwaves free from Nazi political agitation—should facilitate its takeover for precisely this purpose after the formation of Hitler's government. Compared to the complexity of coordinating the sprawling, highly competitive, and internationally oriented film industry, gaining control over the quasi-state-run German radio system was far more straightforward. There was, however, one striking similarity. Just as the Nazis' film policies were largely prefigured in the SPIO-plan of 1932, their conquest of the radio was also semi-complete by the time Hitler took office.

Once again, many of the key changes occurred in 1932 under the government of Franz von Papen, whose almost complete lack of popular or parliamentary support made his ultra-conservative cabinet eager to compensate by means of media publicity. The radio was by far the most promising avenue for disseminating government-friendly material, given the fragmented nature of the press and the prohibitive costs of film propaganda. Papen's interior minister, Wilhelm von Gayl, wasted little time in taking the necessary steps. On 11 June 1932, less than two weeks after the new cabinet had taken shape, he issued a decree requiring all German broadcasters to reserve at least half-an-hour every day between 18:30 and 19:30 for special government broadcasts in which ministers could explain their policies to the public. On the same day he also allowed political parties (including the NSDAP, but not the communists) to use the radio for the upcoming Reichstag elections in July. On 15 June he opened the so-called 'Government Hour' himself by justifying the move through a clear contrast between a 'party address' and a 'ministerial address'—a fuzzy distinction at the best of times, and in the current circumstances a ludicrous one, given the arch-conservative political composition of the cabinet. The novelty of these addresses, as he put it, was that 'we do not present ourselves as partisans for a governing majority and its individual groupings, nor for a particular occupational group or class, but rather solely as Reich ministers who were called to their difficult posts through the confidence of our universally revered President von Hindenburg'.[39] Just as the government could bypass parliament by using the president's emergency powers, so could it appeal over its head to the German electorate.

The ensuing state takeover of German radio was remarkably swift. By the end of July all of the corporations' private investors were bought out by the Reich Postal Ministry and the federal states. In the meantime, the influence of the Länder governments was also curtailed by the arrogation of new programming and personnel responsibilities by the Reich Interior Ministry. How was the government able to make such sweeping reforms so quickly? The answer was that it already had a ready-made blueprint in hand, previously drawn up by an ambitious official in the Interior Ministry, Erich Scholz. A DNVP man who drifted further and further to the radical Right over the early 1930s, Scholz had long sought an opportunity to bring radio broadcasting more firmly under the control of the Interior Ministry. When he first showed his plans to Interior Minister Wirth in March 1931, the liberal-leaning Centre Party politician was distinctly unimpressed. Scholz got much the same response from Wirth's successor Groener.[40] But with von Gayl he found himself preaching to the converted. On 10 August 1932 von Gayl appointed him as the ministry's new radio commissar (Bredow remained the radio commissar within the Postal Ministry), and Scholz quickly went to work with a wave of dismissals starting with the director of the republican-sympathizing Berliner Funkstunde, Hans Flesch. In September he reorganized the Dradag wireless news agency and dismissed its chief editor Josef Räuscher, thereby enhancing Interior Ministry influence over it as well. The alterations were so rapid that the legal framework had to catch up after the fact. Ironically, they only officially came into effect with the promulgation of a radio reform bill on 18 November, the day after the von Papen government fell.[41]

[39] Quoted from Lerg, *Rundfunkpolitik*, 450.   [40] Ibid. 446–50.
[41] Ibid. 473–8; Dussel, *Rundfunkgeschichte*, 75–7.

As it turned out, the changes of 1932 paved the way for the Nazi takeover of broadcasting. Indeed, for some weeks after Hitler's appointment they rendered any further alterations superfluous. Nazi propagandists found the radio a handy tool during the election campaign of February and March 1933, for the reforms under von Papen had set a clear precedent for the government's privileged use of radio. This was made all the easier by the fact that the interior minister, who was now largely responsible for radio content, was Wilhelm Frick, one of only three Nazis in the cabinet. Following directly in the footsteps of von Gayl, Frick proposed a disingenuously statesmanlike ban on all party-political broadcasts. Naturally, this did not include ministerial broadcasts or certain bulletins geared to 'clarify' the major issues to voters.[42] The perverse result was that during the course of the campaign there were no fewer than forty-five government broadcasts and none whatsoever for the opposition parties.

Goebbels, one of the chief architects of the Nazi election campaign, held a special interest in the propaganda value of broadcasting, and was especially eager to acquire control over it once the Propaganda Ministry was set up. As he told a gathering of executives on 25 March 1933, radio was the 'most modern and the most important instrument of mass influence that exists anywhere'. Yet, in contrast to his reassuring comments to filmmakers, Goebbels was remarkably forthright about the political constraints that would govern broadcasting: 'The radio will also need to be brought into the national movement . . . We make no bones about the fact that the radio belongs to us and to no one else. And we will place the radio in the service of our ideology, and no other ideology will find expression here.'[43]

No other ministry would find expression on the radio either, if Goebbels had his way. From the moment the Propaganda Ministry was established he quickly tried to poach responsibilities from other agencies. On 16 March, only three days into the job, he wrested control over personnel and programme supervision from the Interior Ministry, and soon forced the Postal Ministry to cede responsibility for certain economic and technical matters. The ensuing bureaucratic struggle with the Länder governments proved far more difficult, especially with Prussia and its power-hungry minister president Göring. It was only through Hitler's intervention on 30 June and 6 July that the dispute was finally resolved in Goebbels's favour. Shortly thereafter, the regional broadcasters were forced to sell their shares in the Reich Broadcasting Corporation to the Propaganda Ministry, which thenceforth owned the corporation outright. The final step came in early 1934, when the Länder governments formally transferred their shares in the regional companies to the Reich Broadcasting Corporation. After 1 April 1934 the nine regional stations, once the cornerstones of Germany's federalized broadcasting system, were no more than branches of the Reich Broadcasting Corporation, as was clearly reflected in their change of name to 'Reich Broadcasters' (*Reichssender*).

[42] Diller, *Rundfunkpolitik*, 65. [43] Quoted from Welch, *Third Reich*, 183–4.

In legal terms, the sole control over German radio thus fell to the Propaganda Ministry, more specifically to its Radio Department, directed after June 1933 by the 34-year-old Horst Dreßler-Andreß, an old associate of Goebbels who had earlier helped the Nazis infiltrate the right-wing Reichsverband Deutscher Rundfunkhörer. From the beginning, the aim of the Radio Department was to unify all aspects of broadcasting—economic, programming, technical—under a single roof in order to make the most of resources. The fact that it consisted of barely a dozen officials shows, however, that it was only capable of setting the broad guidelines of policy, not handling day-to-day management issues. One of its most important tasks was therefore to ensure that the key positions were filled by reliable figures. Goebbels made this crystal clear in his address to radio executives on 25 March: 'If I am responsible for the spiritual guidance of the radio, then I am also responsible for personnel appointments... Radio... is being cleaned up, just as the entire Prussian and German administration is being cleaned up. I would greatly prefer it, and would be very grateful to you, if you would carry out this act of purification yourselves. If you do not, or do not wish to, then we will carry it out ourselves.'[44] No one could dismiss this as an empty threat in view of the changes taking place. Hans Bredow himself, long a target of National Socialist scorn, resigned the moment Hitler became chancellor, and was subsequently hauled off to Oranienburg concentration camp. By the summer of 1933 all but one of the regional broadcasting executives (the comparatively populist Stuttgart director Alfred Bofinger, a Nazi sympathizer before 1933) had been newly appointed by the Propaganda Ministry.[45]

The most important position within the new broadcasting regime was the executive directorship of the Reich Broadcasting Corporation, a new post created in July 1933 as part of a wider management reorganization. This job was given to the 29-year-old former auto mechanic Eugen Hadamovsky, who, like Dreßler-Andreß, had been involved with the Reichsverband Deutscher Rundfunkhörer before 1933. In spite of his tender years, Hadamovsky soon became the primary spokesman of the NSDAP on all matters of broadcasting policy, and played a key role in the coordination of the radio system by virtue of his power over personnel matters.[46] It is estimated that around 270 radio employees (13 per cent) were dismissed in the first six months of the regime, a significantly higher proportion than in most state institutions.[47] The Reich Broadcasting Corporation thus functioned much as the Reich Chambers of Culture did for the other media: it ensured adherence to the party line through its control over

---

[44] H. Heiber (ed.), *Goebbels-Reden*, 2 vols (Düsseldorf, 1971), i. 100, 103.

[45] In November 1934 Bredow, Flesch, and other representatives of Weimar radio were subjected to a show trial, though the court eventually dropped most of the charges: J. Wulf, *Presse und Funk im Dritten Reich* (Gütersloh, 1964), 280–4.

[46] Diller, *Rundfunkpolitik*, 104.

[47] D. Münkel, 'Produktionssphäre', in I. Marßolek and A. v. Saldern (eds.), *Zuhören und Gehörtwerden 1* (Tübingen, 1998), 53.

employment opportunities. Indeed, lacking any other significant purpose, the Reich Radio Chamber was eventually dissolved in 1939, the only chamber to meet this fate.

Overall, by the spring of 1934 Goebbels could regard the situation of broadcasting with some satisfaction. Although full legal control did not always work in practice, he was largely able to realize his aims by means of personnel appointments. The two remaining blemishes were the limited central control over the actual programme, which was still a matter for the regional executives, and the significant financial difficulties of the Reich Broadcasting Corporation. Although Goebbels tried to blame the previous management for the deficits, they were in reality due to the effects of mass unemployment, and above all the inherited income allocation model that directed the lion's share of licence revenue to the Postal Ministry.[48] As always, the simplest means of cutting costs was to reduce personnel, but the purge of early 1933 left few obvious targets. A second alternative was to cut production costs through programme-sharing, which would kill two birds with one stone by centralizing control over content. Throughout the winter of 1933–4 the Propaganda Ministry tried in vain to assemble the regional broadcasters into larger groups that would transmit standard programming during the evening prime-time. But despite administrative and legal centralization, the actual programme still retained an echo of the regionalism that had pertained during the Weimar period.

Thus, broadcasting too was shaped by a combination of economic and political factors. The introduction of the legendary *Volksempfänger* (People's Receiver) was indeed a classic example of overlapping commercial and political interests. Despite being remembered as the 'everyday embodiment' of National Socialism, the Volksempfänger in fact grew out of existing industry efforts to standardize production as a means of lowering retail prices.[49] During the early part of 1933 the RMVP and radio manufacturers devised a plan to regulate production quotas and pricing for the new, low-priced 'VE 301' (the number commemorated Hitler's appointment on 30 January), which began production in May as one of the cheapest radio sets in Europe, set to retail at RM 76. Though the agreement entailed certain sacrifices on the part of manufacturers—namely, a final price near cost and a pledge not to undercut it with a less expensive set—it had advantages for both sides. For the regime, it represented an additional conduit for communicating with the populace and a prestigious piece of social policy for which it could claim the credit. For producers and retailers, at least the 'Aryan' ones not excluded from the scheme, it promised additional earnings in spite of the narrow profit margin.[50]

---

[48] Führer, *Wirtschaftsgeschichte*, 105.
[49] Quote from U. C. Schmidt, 'Radioaneignung', in Marßolek and v. Saldern (eds.), *Zuhören*, 286; see also W. König, *Volkswagen, Volksempfänger, Volksgemeinschaft* (Paderborn, 2004), 32–4.
[50] König, *Volkswagen*, 25–99; Schmidt, 'Radioaneignung', 283–98.

From the beginning the Volksempfänger was conceived as the key to expanding radio use. Under the slogan 'Every national comrade a radio listener', Goebbels's stated intention was to double the number of listeners within a few years.[51] The focus naturally fell on groups with the lowest listening rates, especially rural labourers and unskilled workers. But it was not enough simply to make an affordable receiver; what was needed, as one retailer put it, was 'to win over every last national comrade for the idea of radio'.[52] For this purpose the Reich Broadcasting Corporation expanded its fleet of advertising lorries and organized thousands of radio displays, concerts, and prize raffles. In 1936 alone the travelling exhibitions covered 60,000 km and visited 3,700 localities, where they reached an audience of over 1 million people.[53] Meanwhile 'Strength through Joy' courted industrial workers with special 'After Work' programmes designed to demonstrate radio's 'ardent solidarity with the German worker'.[54]

By making radio ownership affordable for such groups, the Volksempfänger undoubtedly helped popularize radio use in Germany. Although undemanding listeners could still satisfy themselves with a cheaper Detektor or Röhrenortsempfänger, it was impossible to find a receiver of comparable quality for less than around RM 100. In 1933 the VE 301 accounted for around half of all radios sold in Germany, rising to two-thirds in 1934. It has been estimated that without it the number of registered radios at the end of 1937 would have numbered only 6½ million instead of 9 million.[55] And in 1937 the Volksempfänger became even cheaper, dropping from RM 76 to RM 59. The following year saw the launch of the German Mini-Receiver (*Deutscher Kleinempfänger*), which at only RM 35 made radio listening affordable even for low-earners who had struggled to find the RM 59 for a VE 301. In order to ensure that the monthly fee did not pose a hindrance for needy households, the Propaganda Ministry also introduced exemptions for around 10 per cent of all 'Aryan' licence-holders over the course of the 1930s.[56]

Yet customers only got what they paid for. The performance of the VE 301 and especially the mini-receiver was limited. For most listeners clear reception was restricted to the closest medium-wave regional stations and the long-wave 'Deutschlandsender' (as the Deutsche Welle was renamed in January 1933). Although this has often been interpreted as a deliberate measure to prevent Germans from listening to foreign broadcasts, in reality it was nothing more than a practical price–performance decision. Indeed, long-distance reception,

[51] 'Neugestaltung der Funkwerbung', *RZ* 11 (5 Aug. 1933), 369–71.
[52] 'Rundfunkwerbung auf dem Lande', *RH* 12 (20 Mar. 1935), 269.
[53] 'Vorbildliche Rundfunkwerbung', *RH* 12 (17 Apr. 1935), 354; *RH* 12 (6 Feb. 1935), 95; 'Rundfunkpropaganda 1936–1937', *RH* 14 (17 Feb. 1937), 101. On rural programming F. Cebulla, *Rundfunk und ländliche Gesellschaft 1924–1945* (Göttingen, 2004), 247–63.
[54] 'Tag des Rundfunks', *RH* 11 (24 Jan. 1934), 64; *RH* 11 (21 Feb. 1934), 159.
[55] Schmidt, 'Radioaneignung', 291.
[56] Ibid. 292, 299; also R. Weisflog, 'Rundfunk und Einkommen', *RH* 16 (30 Aug. 1939), 863–6.

Fig. 11. 'All Germany listens to the Führer': advertisement for the *Volksempfänger* at the 1936 Radio Exhibition. bpk Berlin.

including foreign broadcasts, remained possible for millions of listeners. Not only did many Germans possess a more powerful receiver, but the Volksempfänger was itself perfectly capable of picking up foreign broadcasts, especially with the use of available upgrades.[57] As we saw in Chapter 4, the vast technical improvements of the early 1930s had greatly improved reception for all. By the time the Nazis were in power the Deutschlandsender could be received across the entire Reich, and the vast majority of Germans, including those with inexpensive sets, could choose from at least two stations. These technical improvements were crucial for the spread of radio use in rural areas far from transmitters. Moreover, as reception gradually improved there was also more radio to listen to. Whereas the average broadcast day in 1933 was around fourteen hours long, by 1938 it had increased to twenty hours.[58]

In sum, radio was becoming cheaper, easier to use, and more readily available over the 1930s. Among all of the media, broadcasting alone managed to escape the sales slump that hit nearly every other segment of the entire economy. From April 1933 to April 1938 the number of registered sets more than doubled, from 4.6 million to 9.6 million (though it should be noted that this growth was more or less in line with international trends). It is thus little wonder that radio was regarded by the regime as the single most important means of mass communication. The entire sphere of broadcasting, from production to sales, was kept under exceedingly close control, more so than any other medium.

But if the tight control over radio marked one end of the spectrum, the closely related recording industry marked the other. In spite of the increasing overlap between the two industries, their treatment by the regime could hardly have been more different. This was not immediately apparent over the first few months of Hitler's chancellorship, which witnessed the usual 'coordination' of the various recording organizations.[59] Typically, the Nazis promised to safeguard the interests of the industry against 'unhealthy competition' through the introduction of new licensing regulations and corporatist structures.[60] In autumn 1933 a new 'Phonographic Industry Contract' came into force, whereby companies belonging to the official manufacturers' organization (Verband der Deutschen Phonographischen Industrien) were only allowed to trade with members of the wholesale and retail organizations (Verband Deutscher Musikwaren-Großhändler, Reichsverband des Deutschen Phono- und Radio-Handels).[61] But as things turned out, the formal 'coordination' of spring 1933 had little practical effect, and subsequent plans

---

[57] König, *Volkswagen*, 39.
[58] H. Pohle, *Der Rundfunk als Instrument der Politik* (Hamburg, 1955), 330.
[59] 'Gleichschaltung im Reichsverband des Deutschen Phono- und Radio-Handels E.V.', *PZ* 34 (8 Apr. 1933), 179.
[60] F. Taube, 'Heraus mit der Markenschallplatte und dem Markensprechapparat aus dem Waren- und Kaufhaus!', *PZ* 34 (20 May 1933), 251–2; E. Kühl, 'Wer ist noch Phonohändler?', *PZ* 34 (3 June 1933), 278.
[61] 'Neuregelung im Schallplattenhandel' *PRZ* 34 (1 Oct. 1933), 527.

TABLE 7. *Radio use in German Reich, 1929–1941*
(excluding annexations, survey date 1 April)

Year	Registered sets × 1,000	Households with set (%)	Growth per annum (%)
1929	2,843	17.0	27.3
1930	3,244	19.0	14.1
1931	3,742	21.6	15.3
1932	4,185	23.7	11.8
1933	4,555	25.4	8.8
1934	5,453	29.8	19.7
1935	6,725	36.2	23.3
1936	7,584	40.2	12.8
1937	8,512	44.3	12.2
1938	9,598	49.2	12.7
1939	11,324	57.1	18.0
1940	12,615	62.7	11.4
1941	13,309	65.1	5.5

Source: *Rundfunkarchiv*, 14 (1941), 413.

to subsume the recording industry into the 'musical-instrument branch' of the Reich Music Chamber came to nothing. This was probably just as well, for as the *Phonographische Zeitschrift* explained in March 1933, the attitude of the industry towards state interference was less than enthusiastic: 'The position adopted by the recording branch should be clear: we must explain to the authorities that a medium that has hitherto functioned above all as a means of entertainment of the broad masses . . . must continue to serve this primary purpose. We must also ensure that this new agency's responsibilities for cultural supervision do not turn into a restriction on normal business.'[62] Exceptionally, the Nazi authorities seemed to agree with this assessment, for their efforts to control the recording industry remained remarkably tentative and half-hearted throughout the 1930s.

What accounts for this markedly different treatment in comparison to radio and film? There were two primary reasons: the precarious commercial situation of recording firms, and the specific nature of the medium. The recording industry was hit harder by the economic crisis than any other branch of the media. After peaking at the end of the 1920s, German record production went into freefall for a full half-decade, dropping from 30 million in 1929 to 10 million in 1933, before bottoming out at only 5 million in 1935.[63] By the time the Nazis were brought into government the entire branch was in deep trouble, and there was little appetite to make matters worse. Moreover, the international structure of the recording industry also set limits on political interference. Of the four biggest

[62] ' ". . .bindet den Helm fester!" ', *PZ* 34 (11 Mar. 1933), 125–6.
[63] D. Schulz-Köhn, *Die Schallplatte auf dem Weltmarkt*, Ph.D thesis, Königsberg (1940), 113.

recording firms in Germany, two were largely in foreign hands.[64] Recording was thus difficult to control in accordance with Nazi cultural policies without simply losing production firms, markets, and German jobs. Although a number of hard-line Nazi publications like *Das kulturpolitische Archiv* and *Das Schwarze Korps* argued for a purge of Jewish and other 'undesirable' musicians from the manufacturers' repertoires, even this was largely couched in terms of 'tactfulness'. And since such calls emanated not from the Propaganda Ministry, but from the increasingly marginalized ideological purists around Rosenberg, they had little practical impact.

Though the avoidance of intense political scrutiny was welcomed by the recording industry, the flip-side was a lack of state support. In this respect government efforts to expand radio use actually made the situation even worse. Although broadcasting was by this time perceived more as an ally than a competitor, government schemes to encourage people to focus their limited spending power on the radio were detrimental to record and player sales.[65] Tellingly, when the industry called for the creation of a 'People's Gramophone' (*Volksplattenspieler*), an affordable phonographic counterpart to the Volksempfänger, the plea fell on deaf ears.[66] The development of cheaper portable record-players in the mid-1930s thus came solely from within the industry, without government support. The simple fact was that the regime had no strategic interest in such plans, and the primary reason lay in the specific character of recorded sound. The very nature of the technology made controlling it far more difficult than in the case of radio or film. People could largely listen to what they wanted when they wanted to, and this lack of any sense of 'live broadcast'—quite apart from the fact that far fewer people owned gramophones than radios in the first place—severely restricted its propaganda value.[67]

The fortunes of the industry started turning towards the middle of the decade. A much-needed morale boost came in February 1936 with its victory in the ongoing legal battle with the Reich Broadcasting Corporation. The Reich Supreme Court ruled that radio companies could play as many records as they wanted but had to pay RM 300,000 for up to 25,000 records per year, and RM 60,000 for each additional quota of 5,000 records.[68] Although the judgement was in line with settlements elsewhere, its significance was highlighted in Germany by the fact that radio was directly state-owned: that is, the lawsuits were ultimately directed against the Propaganda Ministry, which drew the bulk of its revenue from the administration of the radio system.[69] Even more important

---

[64] Deutsche Grammophon and Telefunken were German-owned, Electrola and Carl Lindström were subsidiaries of UK-based companies.
[65] R. Albert, 'Die Auferstehung der Schallplatte', *PRZ* 37 (1 Jan. 1936), 6–7.
[66] *PRZ* 36 (1 Jan. 1935), 8.   [67] Fetthauer, *Deutsche Grammophon*, 43–4.
[68] *PRZ* 36 (15 June 1935), 241; *PRZ* 37 (14 Feb. 1936), 58.
[69] Fetthauer, *Deutsche Grammophon*, 20–3; Riess, *Knaurs*, 276–80; D. Mühlenfeld, 'Joseph Goebbels und die Grundlagen der NS-Rundfunkpolitik, *ZfG* 54 (2006), 442–67.

for the industry was the general economic upswing that gradually registered in rising sales, especially for the electric turntables capable of plugging into a radio loudspeaker. In 1937 domestic record sales had almost doubled from the low point of 1935, reaching 10 million by the end of the year and rising to 12 million in 1938, with a parallel rise in exports.[70]

The industry's gradual recovery after the nadir of the mid-1930s owed much to the ruthless commercial concentration over the intervening period. As was also the case in the film industry, the bulk of smaller firms did not survive the economic crisis, and the large corporations accordingly went on a buying spree. The frenzy of mergers and buy-outs was such that by the end of the 1930s the German market was almost completely divided between two large groups: on one side Carl Lindström along with Electrola and Kristall, and on the other Telefunken allied with Deutsche Grammophon. By 1937 there were only two smaller firms left sandwiched between these blocs: Tempo-Special, which produced cheap entertainment records, and Clangor, a reformist-affiliated firm specializing in 'valuable' recordings. Again, this process paid little attention to national borders. By 1940 there were, strictly speaking, no German-owned recording firms at all, only subsidiaries of multinationals. But international concentration proved highly beneficial to German producers, since the sharing of sound matrices between different countries allowed them to manufacture a wide international repertoire—an absolute necessity for any reputable recording firm in the 1930s—*within* Germany, thus forgoing the need to import actual records, which the Nazis' strict currency controls would almost certainly have prevented.[71]

This concentration into fewer, larger firms was furthermore accompanied by an interweaving of technical and financial interests with a variety of electrical concerns and other communications media. The ongoing technical integration of broadcasting and recording took on a whole new dimension in the 1930s. Prices for combination sets dropped substantially, and the inexpensive new electric turntables that relied on an external loudspeaker could be connected to all but the most outdated radio devices. At the same time, many of the large recording firms had effectively become subsidiaries of the mammoth electrical conglomerates in Germany, whose interests increasingly extended across recording, radio, and sound film. Telefunken, for instance, was itself a subsidiary of the two leading electrical concerns AEG and Siemens & Halske, as was the film company Klangfilm GmbH.[72]

Such shared ownership structures further encouraged the increasing inter-connection between the recording and film industries, above all in the form

---

[70] 'Schallplatten-Renaissance', *Die Deutsche Volkswirtschaft* 7 (1938), 1372; 'Schallplatten-Aufstieg', *PRZ* 38 (1 Sept. 1937), 261; 'Vom Aufstieg im Schallplattenfach', *PRZ* 38 (1 Nov. 1937), 324.
[71] Schulz-Köhn, *Schallplatte*, 17, 34–5, 43, 80–1.   [72] Ibid. 77–9.

of commodity tie-ins. Ever since the advent of the talkie, popular tunes were increasingly drawn from the ranks of sound film hits (*Tonfilmschlager*). An early example were the songs of Richard Tauber, a favourite tenor in the inter-war years, who sang the title song for the 1930 film *Ich glaub' nie mehr an eine Frau*. Likewise, his 1931 recording 'Das gibt's nur einmal' from the hit film *Der Kongreß tanzt* sold 120,000 copies.[73] By the middle of the 1930s the majority of hit tunes were sound-film hits, the film functioning as advertisement for the record, the record for the film, and the radio publicizing both. It is worth emphasizing that this technological and commercial convergence also affected the very nature of hit music itself. By creating an inseparable bond between song, singer, and film, the sound-film hit tended to immortalize and personalize a single performance of a given tune. For example, hits like Zarah Leander's 'Kann denn Liebe Sünde sein' from the UFA-film *Der Blaufuchs*, Hans Albers's 'La Paloma' from *Große Freiheit Nr. 7* or 'Good bye, Jonny' from *Wasser für Canitoga*, became one-offs in the sense that no one else could perform them to an audience's satisfaction. Only the 'original' version would do, and in many cases songs were specifically written for individual performers. This undoubtedly exerted a standardizing effect on popular music, for instead of audiences hearing various renditions of a tune, the personalization of the sound-film hit meant that they tended to hear a single standard performance.[74]

Although there is no way to quantify the growing synergy between film, radio, and recording, there is every reason to assume that it was beneficial to the recording industry. As the tellingly renamed *Phonographische und Radio Zeitschrift* remarked in early 1938: 'The record alone is not able to catapult a musical piece into notoriety. . . . The primary pacesetter for recording is the sound film.'[75] Yet if recording firms profited from a closer association with film producers, they could expect no such cooperation from the Propaganda Ministry, which in 1937 sought once again to enhance its control over the realm of recorded sound. Whether the renewed attacks were part of the wider anti-Semitic campaign after 1936 or rather motivated by the aforementioned Supreme Court ruling is difficult to say. Certainly the court's verdict did not help relations with the Propaganda Ministry, nor did the fact that the main lawyer for the records industry, Alfred Baum, was Jewish. But whatever the motives, in December 1937 the RMVP declared a crackdown against 'Jewish music and records' and established a new Reich Musical Inspection Office (Reichsmusikprüfstelle) to administer the ban on 'non-Aryan' musicians.[76] In May 1938 Hans Severus Ziegler, general director of the Weimar National Theater, organized the notorious exhibition 'Degenerate Music' (*Entartete Musik*) in Düsseldorf's Kunstpalast, which latched on to the 'degenerate art' exhibition opened in Munich the previous year. In

---

[73] Mühl-Benninghaus, *Ringen*, 270.
[74] Wicke, *Mozart*, 182; generally, Currid, *Acoustics*, 100–18.
[75] *PRZ* 39 (1 Jan. 1938), 3.   [76] See *PRZ* 39 (1 Jan. 1938), 2–3.

specially constructed listening-booths visitors could choose from some seventy condemned recordings, including the works of modern composers such as Alban Berg, Paul Hindemith, Arnold Schönberg, and Kurt Weill.[77]

But once again, the envisaged purge of 'undesirable' music was not very thorough, and the recording industry, for its part, was not very responsive. For one thing, such recordings represented sizeable investments for the companies concerned. As industry representatives pointed out, it was inconceivable 'simply to throw away the—let's say it for the sake of simplicity—"Jewish" records since they represented very significant capital investments, namely in the form of royalties'.[78] Furthermore, Nazi authorities found it no easier than the recording firms to define 'Jewish' or 'degenerate' records, since many musicians had been labelled as such by right-wing critics simply because they played modern music.[79] Many of these recordings were quite profitable. Telefunken, for instance, was loath to forfeit the proceeds from its recordings of Richard Tauber, whose Jewish ancestry alone was enough to blacklist him.[80] On a more general level, the entire category of modern dance music was simply too popular to ban completely. Worse still, the swelling repertoire of sound-film hits also raised the problem of shared ownership, since the rights and profits relating to these songs were regulated by contractual agreements between various firms. This placed additional limits on state intervention, insofar as banning a song affected not only the recording company but also a film producer and its investors. This was a particularly glaring instance of the ambivalent political implications of media convergence. While such overlap could in some ways ease the central coordination of mass communication, in other ways it could thwart it.

There were, then, a variety of reasons why the recording industry avoided the same degree of political control that governed the other media. But it is important to view this for what it was, for it did not reflect a principled or moral stance against National Socialism but rather a hard-boiled defence of business interests. While profitable jazz and 'Jewish' recordings were vigorously defended, Jewish colleagues in the recording firms were given little protection, and records of Nazi marching songs also swelled most firms' catalogues from spring 1933 onwards.[81] The same sense of bottom-line necessity also shaped the regime's views on the industry, for in the end the Nazis largely catered to popular tastes in the realm of recorded music, even more so than with film and radio. In spite of the rhetorical attacks on musical 'asphalt culture', the commercial imperative that so irritated conservative critics during the Weimar era remained paramount

---

[77] Generally, A. Dümling, P. Girth, and P. Schimmelpfennig (eds.), *Entartete Musik*, 3rd edn. (Düsseldorf, 1993); M. H. Kater, *The Twisted Muse* (Oxford, 1997).

[78] *PRZ* 39 (1 Jan. 1938), 4.

[79] 'Wie steht es mit der Ausmerzung der "jüdischen" Schallplatten?', *PRZ* 39 (1 Mar. 1938), 69–70.

[80] E. Levi, *Music in the Third Reich* (Basingstoke, 1994), 141.

[81] Fetthauer, *Deutsche Grammophon*, 33.

throughout the 1930s and continued to mould policy towards the recording industry even during the war.

THE PRINT MEDIA: ABOLITION, STEERING, AND STANDARDIZATION

In many respects the fate of the print media lay somewhere between that of the radio and recording industries. Like the radio, it was regarded as an essential means of communication in the 1930s. For all the fascination with film and broadcasting, it was indeed the most widely used medium of all.[82] Yet, like the recording industry, the complex commercial structure and ongoing financial problems of the German press also made it difficult to control. While the prospects of individual newspapers and journalists varied dramatically according to their political affiliation and commercial situation, the interests of local Nazi bosses and the simmering rivalries between various state and party institutions further complicated the restructuring of the print media.

Given the immense variety of the German press, the process of political coordination was necessarily multifaceted. It is helpful to conceive of it as three overlapping sets of changes: the rapid elimination of opposing journalists and publications, establishing a system of political and commercial control over the remaining papers, and steering their actual content in the government's interest.[83] It is also important to recognize that the timing and scope of change differed considerably between these three processes, and that the German press never became the well-oiled manipulative machine that the Nazi leadership desired. Yet this does not change the fact that by the mid-1930s the landscape of newspaper publishing had been fundamentally altered, never again to return to its pre-1933 incarnation. Although the Nazis were the primary driving-force, the changes they sought to bring about were often aided by the acquiescence or outright support of a majority of journalists and publishers.

This was quite clearly the case during the campaign to stifle oppositional voices in early 1933. As we saw above, one of the first acts of Hitler's cabinet was to curb the constitutional freedom of the press. The Reichstag Fire Decree led to the closure of some 200 SPD papers and thirty-five KPD papers, with a combined circulation of around 2 million copies; during the following weeks over 100 printing presses were confiscated. Although the limitations on press freedom were binding on all newspapers, the fact that they were focused on the 'Marxist press' (in particular, the communists) made them far more palatable. After all, many journalists perceived the communists as a threat, and had long since become inured to the practice of press bans on the basis of emergency

---

[82] Führer, 'Tageszeitung', 411–13.
[83] This follows Dussel, *Tagespresse*, 159; Koszyk, *Deutsche Presse 1914–1945*, 354–69.

decrees and the Laws to Protect the Republic.[84] It was by no means merely fear or opportunism that prompted the editor of the conservative *DAZ* to remark on 1 March that 'all honest and upstanding Germans will gratefully affirm the draconian measures that Reich Minister Göring has introduced against the communists'.[85]

Since the Nazis could not afford to alienate conservative opinion, the many 'bourgeois' journalists and newspapers of more traditional right-wing coloration had to be handled gently for the time being. So too did the bulk of moderate writers and publishers who had previously dominated the newspaper market. This selective circumspection helps to explain why the Nazis found it so easy to subsume the major press associations. The bulk of journalists and publishers coordinated themselves quite willingly. The Association of German Newspaper Publishers tellingly refrained from criticizing the brutal treatment of the SPD press, and indeed was eager to show its willingness to cooperate with the government in a spirit of 'national discipline'. It soon began excluding leftists from its membership, and in June appointed Max Amann, director of the Franz Eher Verlag, as chairman. The main journalists' organization, the German Press Association, was even more accommodating. On 30 April 1933 it handed its chairmanship to Otto Dietrich, Hitler's press chief, and immediately drafted a new set of statutes that excluded any racially or politically undesirable members.[86]

The ensuing purge of newspaper personnel proceeded in a far more bureaucratic manner than the initial, often violent, attacks on communists and socialists. Instead of midnight arrests and blanket round-ups, there came a series of legal and administrative decrees that were all the more insidious for their apparent orderliness. From September 1933 onwards the Reich Press Chamber, also chaired by Max Amann, effectively functioned as a professional guild. Membership was an absolute requirement for anyone working in the newspaper business, with the sole exception of the ghettoized Jewish press. The legal basis for these prohibitions was underpinned by the so-called Editor's Law (Schriftleitergesetz) of 4 October 1933. Like so many of the Nazis' early coordination measures, this law essentially amounted to a trade-off of state protection and enhanced professional status in exchange for certain restrictions. The principal advantage for journalists was a legal guarantee against political interference on the part of publishers—a long-standing professional goal. The Editor's Law also provided a new framework of regulation for entry into the profession, including a minimum one-year apprenticeship. The Reich Press Chamber's chief responsibility was to administer the all-important occupational register (*Berufsliste*), and it was here that journalists paid the price. To be included on the register one had to be a

[84] Generally, C. Dams, *Staatsschutz in der Weimarer Republik* (Marburg, 2002); N. Frei, *Nationalsozialistische Eroberung der Provinzpresse* (Stuttgart, 1980), 35–41.
[85] Quoted from Frei, Schmitz, *Journalismus*, 16, above figs. 22–3.
[86] Ibid. 26; Dussel, *Tagespresse*, 164.

German citizen, at least 21 years of age, of 'Aryan' background and not married to a non-Aryan, and also 'have the qualities which the task of exerting intellectual influence on the public requires'. What this meant more concretely was spelled out in paragraph 14 of the Editor's Law: namely, to avoid printing anything 'that is calculated to weaken the strength of the German Reich abroad or at home, the community will of the German people, German defence, culture, or the economy'.[87] As one might expect, these vague categories could be, and were, interpreted rather broadly.

There are no precise figures on the number of journalists affected by the purges. For what it is worth, Wilhelm Weiß, deputy editor of the *VB* and Berlin district chief of the German Press Association, estimated that by the end of 1934 at least 1,300 'Marxist' and 'Jewish' journalists had been banned. Given that there were approximately 13,000 registered in 1935, this represents a purge rate of around 10 per cent, or slightly higher if Weiß's figures did not include those already affected by the destruction of the socialist and communist press in early 1933.[88] The prospects for banned journalists were singularly grim. Most ended up either out of work or in concentration camps. For a handful of 'non-Aryans' the officially permitted Jewish press offered further employment. Under the umbrella of the Cultural League of German Jews, a total of 146 Jewish newspapers with a combined circulation of around 1 million copies continued to appear, until their closure in the wake of the 'Night of Broken Glass' in November 1938. Seventy per cent of these papers were based in Berlin, with Frankfurt and Hamburg accounting for much of the rest. Around a third were effectively parish papers, though a small number had a broader readership, most notably the *Jüdische Rundschau, CV-Zeitung* (published by the Centralverein deutscher Staatsbürger jüdischen Glaubens), and *Der Schild*. After the pogrom of 1938 the only Jewish paper permitted in Germany was the newly founded *Jüdisches Nachrichtenblatt*, established on the express orders of Goebbels, with an initial circulation of around 72,000.[89] Despite the best efforts of its editors, the *Jüdisches Nachrichtenblatt* could only employ a small number of those who were put out of work. The rest could count on little sympathy from their peers. Indeed, it was precisely the focus of repression onto a clearly defined minority that enabled the Nazi coordination measures to proceed as smoothly as they did. As in the film and broadcasting industries, the acquiescence of the majority was predicated on the confinement of the threat.

The ultimate purpose of all the personnel purges, legal decrees, and organizational changes was naturally to enhance the government's control over the content of the press. And certainly, the pressures of self-censorship they generated were generally sufficient to preclude the publication of undesirable material. But

---

[87] Repr. in Welch, *Third Reich*, 192.   [88] Frei and Schmitz, *Journalismus*, 28.
[89] K. Diehl, *Die jüdische Presse im Dritten Reich* (Tübingen, 1997), 141–4; see also R. Burger, *Von Goebbels Gnaden* (Münster, 2001).

the Nazis were hardly content to leave matters there. The overarching aim of the RMVP press department was actively to supply the press with a continual stream of news and views designed to quell discontent and win over support for the National Socialist cause. The primary conduits for this were the revamped Reich Press Conference and the flood of daily press instructions (*Presseanweisungen*) issued to editors.

At the first of his press conferences on 15 March 1933, the newly appointed propaganda minister Goebbels made perfectly clear his intentions to recast government press relations. The notion that the press should serve as a check to government power was obviously out of place. Quite the opposite: Goebbels presented his own ideal as 'a situation in which the press is so finely tuned that it is, as it were, like a piano in the hands of the Government on which the Government can play'. As a result, the very forum in which he was addressing the assembled journalists would have to undergo some changes. 'I view the purpose of the press conference that takes place here every day somewhat differently from what has gone on here before. You should obviously get your information here, but you should also get your instructions.'[90] Just after the press conference Goebbels menacingly commented in his diary that 'here, too, things will have to be thoroughly cleaned up. Many of those sitting here for the purpose of making public opinion are totally unsuited to the task. I will eradicate them very soon.'[91] But in the event this proved unnecessary, since most journalists did his bidding quite willingly. It took only a few months for the shift in government press relations to take institutional form. In late June the customary Reich Press Conference arrangement was turned on its head: instead of government spokesmen being invited to speak to the press, it was now ministry officials who issued the invitations, and indeed only to selected journalists who attended daily noon-time briefings at the Propaganda Ministry where they were told what they should and should not print.

The instructions issued by the Propaganda Ministry were strictly classified. Anyone who failed to destroy them immediately after use could be charged with treason.[92] Yet, in spite of the dangers involved, thousands have survived to reveal the RMVP's meticulous attempts to steer newspaper content. The instructions covered all manner of topics, from the suppression of unwanted reports to the preferred presentation of public figures to arcane linguistic conventions. Most dealt with minor issues: for instance, burying reports about 'symptoms of toxicity among German cows due to the effects of German potash on feed' (21 August 1935) or that 'amidst the boycott of the boxer Max Schmeling in the USA, the negroes support Schmeling' (13 January 1937). Only occasionally were the instructions more far-reaching, such as the 7 March 1936 directive

[90] Quoted from Welch, *Third Reich*, 179–80.
[91] Reuth (ed.), *Tagebücher*, ii. 780 (15 Mar. 1933).
[92] e.g. the journalist Walter Schwerdtfeger, who was sentenced to life imprisonment for handing the material to a foreign news service: Frei, Schmitz, *Journalismus*, 31.

issued just before the remilitarization of the Rhineland: 'the images from the Rhine should not be paraded in a "martial" manner . . . The happy, festive atmosphere of the Rhineland over the long-awaited liberation from a nightmare should stand in the foreground.' They also reached well beyond the realm of conventional politics. Whereas 'publicity for Charlie Chaplin in any form is absolutely undesirable' (13 February 1936), 'friendly reports on Greta Garbo are permitted' (20 November 1937). And sometimes they strayed into the absurd, such as the mysterious injunction on 9 September 1937 that, 'with immediate effect, the SA, SS and NSKK [Nazi Drivers' Association] are not to be spoken of as "chaps" (*Kerle*), for instance in the sense that "the SA men are real chaps". The expression "chap" is not to be used in this context.'[93]

Although the instructions were not binding in a word-for-word sense, they undoubtedly shaped the content of all the major newspapers. Granted, there were occasions on which individual editors might go their own way, especially in prestigious titles such as the *Frankfurter Zeitung* and *Berliner Tageblatt*. But by and large the bewildering variety and rival communicative networks that had shaped the Weimar press were either destroyed (as with the left-wing papers) or subsumed into a safe, government-friendly system of communication that, while not universally trumpeting the regime's accomplishments, at the very least did not undermine it.

What the Reich Press Conference achieved among leading periodicals, the centralization of the wire services brought to the thousands of small, provincial papers. As we have seen, the Reich government had already acquired majority ownership of the WTB in 1931. After the remainder of its shares were bought up by a front company in summer 1933, Hugenberg too was pressured to sell his Telegraphen-Union to the Reich-owned Kautio Treuhand. In December the two services were fused into the Deutsches Nachrichtenbüro GmbH, or DNB, which thenceforth monopolized the German market. Needless to say, the DNB operated under the close scrutiny of the Propaganda Ministry, filtering material as it came in before conveying a selected fraction to subscribers under a colour-coded system indicating how it should be used. It was not long before the DNB popularly stood for 'Darf Nichts Bringen', or 'can't report anything'.[94] Indeed, complaints about the uniformity of the German press were rife among both readers and journalists alike. By the end of the 1930s the regime's own information service remarked on the 'elimination of almost all independent work' among provincial editors 'through the mere printing of outside material, mostly in the form of matrix reports'.[95]

---

[93] H. Bohrmann and G. Toepser-Ziegert (eds.), *NS-Presseanweisungen der Vorkriegszeit* (Munich, 1984–2001), quotes from iii. 519; iv. 159, 252; v. 36–7, 732, 938.

[94] Basse, *Wolff's*, 247–53; Dussel, *Tagespresse*, 166–70; Frei, Schmitz, *Journalismus*, 33.

[95] '1. Vierteljahreslagebericht 1939', in H. Boberach (ed.), *Meldungen aus dem Reich* (hereafter *Meldungen*), vol. 2 (Herrsching, 1984), 290; also 'Jahreslagebericht 1938', ibid. 152.

The forced buy-out and amalgamation of the WTB and Telegraphen-Union represented only the tip of the iceberg of commercial concentration. This process of economic *Gleichschaltung*, though less dramatic than the wave of political purges and legal measures, was just as important for the extension of Nazi control. But here too, the economic transformation of the press was based not merely on force but also on the promise of commercial recovery and professional opportunity. Like the government's film policies, Nazi designs for the press were largely presented—and perceived—as a way out of structural crisis.

In the early 1930s much of the newspaper branch was in a parlous state. While cut-throat competition and high paper prices posed a challenge to even the most successful big-city periodicals, the vast majority of small-town 'Heimatblätter' were neither commercially profitable nor journalistically proficient. In 1932 around two-thirds of all papers had a circulation under 5,000, and even half of these were under 2,000.[96] Many consisted of only four pages, with any political news simply reprinted from wire services. Generally speaking, their journalistic standards were extremely poor in terms of topical coverage and editorial bias. Publishing such papers was in many cases literally a one-man job, with the editor doing both the writing and printing himself. Modern machinery, such as rotating presses, were well beyond their financial reach, and given their small circulations were unnecessary in any event. These Heimatblatt enterprises were thus woefully cost-ineffective, and their ubiquity throughout the countryside and small towns represented a huge structural block to the modernization of the entire publishing industry, which was becoming more vital than ever during the Depression.[97]

Against this background, Nazi remedies of commercial concentration and state regulation were pushing on an open door. The structural weaknesses of the German press presented a handy point of departure. The Kautio Treuhand quickly set about buying up newspapers with varying degrees of compulsion. In 1934 the Ullstein Verlag, the largest publishing house in Europe, was forcibly bought out in its entirety for only RM 6 million, around one-tenth of its real value. The Eher-Verlag also bought up many of its competitors' papers in order to capture the army of readers left 'paperless', as it were, by the banning of over 200 SPD and KPD papers in early 1933. The expansion of the party press often involved the abuse of its political power. SPD agents in Germany reported how civil servants were frequently coerced into subscribing to Nazi newspapers as a sign of political suitability. Likewise, the Eher-Verlag ruthlessly exploited its political advantage to get the jump on the competition, sending salesmen house to house with classified lists of subscribers to recently banned newspapers.[98]

By early 1935 this mixture of closures, takeovers, and sharp sales tactics had claimed around one-quarter of all the papers in print at the beginning of 1933,

---

[96] Deutsches Institut für Zeitungskunde, *Handbuch der deutschen Tagespresse*, 4th edn. (Berlin, 1932), 25*.

[97] Frei, Schmitz, *Journalismus*, 23–5.   [98] *Deutschland-Berichte*, ii. 720–2; also i. 318.

TABLE 8. *Concentration of newspaper readership,*
1932–1942

Year	Overall circulation (in millions)	Number of newspapers
1932	15.8	4,703
1934 (1st quarter)	16.4	—
1938 (4th quarter)	16.4	2,000–2,500
1939 (2nd quarter)	18.1	—
1942 (1 Jan.)	22.3	1,246

Source: Deutsches Institut für Zeitungskunde, *Handbuch der deutschen Tagespresse* (Berlin, 1932), 19*, 27*; Meier, *Zwischen Milieu und Markt*, ii; Institut für Zeitungswissenschaft, *Handbuch der deutschen Tagespresse* (Leipzig, 1944), xxviii, xxix, xxxxiii.

the vast majority of them small enterprises squeezed out by the huge growth of the Nazi regional press. From 1932 to 1935 the number of newspapers in party hands ballooned by around 250 per cent, their combined circulation by 150 per cent. Put differently, whereas the Nazi press in 1932 accounted for one paper in thirty-five and one reader in twenty, by 1935 it included one-eighth of all titles and one-fifth of all readers.[99] This actually fell some way short of Nazi aims, for available figures suggest that overall circulation in Germany stagnated and that their papers failed to absorb all of the demand released by the closures. But given the common misperception that circulation dropped sharply after the Nazi takeover, it is worth emphasizing that any statistical decline was largely due to the introduction of new regulations in early 1934 that finally put an end to the gross inflation of circulation figures by publishers. Despite all the contemporary talk of a 'crisis' in the newspaper branch (which has coloured many historical accounts), this stagnation can in fact be seen as a sign of the very success of the German press: with around 80 per cent of households receiving a newspaper, the market was essentially saturated.[100] One must not, therefore, overestimate the alleged aversion of readers to Nazi newspapers. But equally, it seems clear that many readers were unwilling to purchase one after their old stand-by had disappeared, preferring other periodicals instead.

The problem for Nazi press officials was not merely one of consumer habit or market inertia, but also the widespread perception that their papers were uniform and dull. The honeymoon period was plainly over by the middle of 1934, as the party press slipped into a steady decline vis-à-vis the old established

[99] Figures from ibid. iii. 825.
[100] See the corrective figures in Führer, 'Tageszeitung', 415–22. *Sopade* claims (*Deutschland-Berichte*, iii. 825) that overall circulation was down by *c*. 45% from 1932–5 are simply untenable. See also G. Kammann, 'Die Auflage der deutschen Zeitungen', *ZV* 37 (4 Jan. 1936), 3–5; 'Zur Auflagenentwicklung der deutschen Tagespresse', *ZV* 37 (15 Feb. 1936), 45–6.

'bourgeois' dailies. According to SPD reports from western Germany, papers like the *Dortmunder Zeitung, Düsseldorfer Nachrichten,* and *Kölner Stadtanzeiger* were all rebounding after initial losses to the Nazi *Düsseldorfer Volksparole* and *Westdeutscher Beobachter,* which by 1935 had to halve their length in order to stay afloat. The *Düsseldorfer Volksparole* even resorted to changing its name to *Rheinische Landeszeitung* in order to sound less partisan. In Berlin, the combined circulation of the *VB, Angriff,* and *Der Deutsche* stagnated over the course of 1934, while that of the *Berliner Morgenpost, BZ am Mittag, Berliner-Lokal-Anzeiger,* and *Berliner Nachtausgabe* rose by around 10 per cent. Over the same period many of the provincial NSDAP papers were also losing subscriptions fast.[101] Clearly, there were limits to the Nazification of the German press. The more overt the process became, the less attractive was the result for readers. The traditional Generalanzeiger dailies still had a very different look and feel from the party press, and indeed were intended to, in order to appeal to people who were unlikely to buy a National Socialist paper. Despite the plethora of press controls, these non-party newspapers still represented commercial and (to some extent) political competitors that were, moreover, showing signs of revival.

In April 1935 Nazi press officials responded with a trio of ordinances that systematized the ad hoc nature of economic coordination up to that point. The first of these so-called 'Amann decrees', on the 'Protection of the Independence of Newspaper Publishing', placed tight restrictions on the commercial structure of newspaper enterprises, including a prohibition against publishers owning more than one paper. It also barred newspapers aimed at particular confessional or occupational groups, which officially spelled the end of the Catholic press in the Third Reich.[102] The second decree, on the 'Closure of Newspaper Publishers for the Purpose of Eliminating Unhealthy Competition', made it possible to shut down any periodicals that, in the view of the Association of German Newspaper Publishers, were not profitable within their local market. As one might expect, this regulation was ruthlessly wielded against non-Nazi papers wherever such overcrowding existed, all under the guise of beneficial structural modernization.[103] The third decree, on the 'Elimination of the Scandal Press', furnished officials with a rubber paragraph to close down any publications that might 'cause offence or damage the dignity of the press'.[104]

Predictably, the resulting wave of takeovers and closures was of great commercial benefit to the Nazi press and party coffers. With the help of the Amann decrees, the Eher-Verlag and Reich government bought up scores of papers through a highly complex set of financial transactions. The mastermind behind it all was once again Max Winkler, the same man who had managed the

---

[101] *Deutschland-Berichte,* ii. 229–30, 232, 719.
[102] J. Krumbach, 'Das Ende der konfessionellen Tagespresse in Deutschland', *ZV* 36 (15 June 1935), 415–17.
[103] *Deutschland-Berichte,* iii. 782–3.
[104] The decrees are repr. in *ZV* 36 (27 Apr. 1935), 280–2.

sale of the WTB and Telegraphen-Union in 1933, and whom Goebbels had
entrusted with the commercial centralization of the film industry. Winkler used
several holding companies to camouflage the transfer of ownership: Hugenberg's
Vera-Verlagsanstalt for the Generalanzeiger dailies, the Herold Verlagsanstalt
for the secular political broadsheets, the Phönix GmbH for confessional papers,
and the Standarte GmbH for the often self-willed Nazi provincial press. By
1939 the Eher-Verlag had acquired direct or indirect control of around 150
publishers and saw its profits rise from around RM 4 million in 1936 to over
RM 35 million.[105] Although many of the affected papers continued to operate
much as before, the buy-outs of 1935–6 ultimately claimed a further 500–600
papers, bringing the total number of closures to around 1,500–1,600 titles,
over one-third of all papers published in Germany in 1933.[106] Throughout this
process most owners did little or nothing to salvage the independence of their
papers or to protect their vulnerable employees from Nazi persecution. The
fact that even the powerful *Münchner Neuesten Nachrichten*, the largest paper in
southern Germany, was purchased at rock-bottom price in 1935 with scarcely
a complaint from its owners testifies to the pressures involved.[107] It was no
longer just a small minority of leftists and 'non-Aryans' who saw their interests
threatened. By now, however, the opportunities for effective opposition had
dwindled dramatically.

By the later 1930s the Nazi restructuring of the press had brought about
fundamental changes on a variety of levels. The attacks against the Left had
silenced an entire segment of German political journalism. Other dissident
voices were subsequently eliminated by the new censorship regulations and press
instructions, which produced greater uniformity of coverage and commentary.
The process of commercial concentration greatly aided the consolidation of
political control and generally benefited the larger papers—Nazi and non-
Nazi alike—at the expense of the small Heimatblätter. Whereas papers with
circulations below 5,000 accounted for two-thirds of overall circulation in 1932,
by 1937 their share had fallen to around one-quarter. Over the same period,
papers selling over 50,000 copies saw their share of overall circulation rise from
8 to 44 per cent.[108] Although the aim of achieving total control over the press
was intrinsically chimerical, these changes nonetheless meant that the publishing
landscape was incomparably less fragmented along geographic, political, and
social divides than ever before. The competing networks of communication
that characterized the German press before 1933 were by and large abrogated
or overlaid by an unprecedented layer of political and economic centralization.
Granted, the result fell well short of the idealized nation of readers 'encompassing

---

[105] Dussel, *Tagespresse*, 174–5, Stöber, *Pressegeschichte*, 254.
[106] *Deutschland-Berichte*, iii. 824.
[107] P. Langer, 'Paul Reusch und die Gleichschaltung der "Münchner Neuesten Nachrichten"
1933 bis 1936', *VfZ* 53 (2005), 203–40.
[108] Figures from Meier, *Zwischen*, 160.

all classes, ranks, and walks of life'.[109] Yet the Nazi-driven restructuring of the 1930s nonetheless marked a clear departure from the traditional segmentation of the German press and a significant step towards a more socially integrated readership.

In this respect the transformation of the press under the Nazis showed a number of important parallels to the other media. Whether one looks at newspapers, film, radio, or the recording industry, many of the changes ran in a similar direction. The interrelated processes of commercial concentration, political centralization, and technological convergence were observable—albeit to differing degrees—across the entire span of communications. As a rule, enterprises became fewer and larger while Nazi political restrictions simultaneously circumscribed their content. At the same time, the aural media—including sound film—became more closely intertwined in terms of both their commercial structure and end-product; even the press became involved in this synergy through its coverage of cinema, radio programmes, music, and more generally through the promotion of media celebrity.

By no means was all of this a specific result of National Socialist intervention and political control. It was part of a broader international trend during the 1930s in which commercial rationalization and technical innovations made the media more accessible and cheaper to use everywhere. Although scholarly attention has understandably tended to focus on Nazi political controls, these other factors—along with the gradual expansion of household leisure budgets—also powerfully moulded the evolution of mass culture in the Third Reich.

Looking ahead to the next chapter, it is worth emphasizing that changes in the production of the media had far-reaching effects on their consumption as well. In many ways their commercial and technological merger encouraged a simultaneous convergence of audiences. The pressures of economic depression and sound conversion led to a dramatic decrease in the number of films from which audiences could choose; the expansion and improvement of radio brought shared aural experiences to a more variegated audience; the multitude of newspaper bans and takeovers further diluted political affiliation between readers and papers; and all the while, the effects of Nazi censorship reinforced the overall trend. By the end of the 1930s Germans were more likely to see or hear the same thing in a more similar fashion than ever before. But this opens up a whole new set of questions to which we must now turn: namely, how the extensive structural changes of the media were related to their actual content, their appropriation by audiences, and the emergence of new cultural formations in the 1930s and 1940s.

---

[109] W. Klutentreter, *Presse und Volksgemeinschaft*, Ph.D thesis, Cologne (1937), 51.

10

Entertaining the National Community

From the very beginning of the Nazi regime, the mass media played a central role in the attempt to replace the competing class, regional, and religious loyalties in Germany with a new sense of 'national community'. Purging them of the alleged decadence, individualism, and 'alien' influences of the Weimar years was only one step in the process. Once the ground was cleared, the Nazis also had to extend the availability of the media and ensure their popular attraction. There were, of course, various conceptions as to what most Germans could or should find appealing. Yet it was clear that the vision of a 'wholesome' and integrative national culture would have to straddle the poles of elitism and frivolous amusement. In this sense, the aims of Nazi cultural administrators showed some striking parallels to the reformist efforts of previous decades—though the Nazi Volk was conceived very differently from the socially underprivileged 'masses' that liberal and left-wing reformers had in mind. Common to both viewpoints was a desire to forge a 'universal art' characterized by popular appeal and minimum standards of aesthetic merit. As Goebbels proclaimed in 1936, the goal was to develop genres that 'are interesting to more discriminating tastes yet still appealing and comprehensible for the less demanding.' While this would necessarily entail a lifting of popular expectations, 'any posture of intellectual condescension or looking down one's nose at those with a lower level of education is reprehensible'. The effort to forge a national culture must therefore 'not take place in the stuffy atmosphere of an overwrought and elitist educational idealism, but rather must raise its tent in the very heart of the people, systematically edifying their tastes and raising their educational standards with care and devotion, not arrogantly poking fun at them'.[1]

The curiously progressive ring of such rhetoric should not obscure the fact that the Nazi cultivation of a popular national culture was never pursued for its own sake. Historians have often regarded it as a deliberate attempt to depoliticize public life by encouraging a cheery, consumer-oriented veneer of 'normality' or to distract audiences with escapist fare that indirectly reinforced National Socialist sensibilities. Although recent research has shown that Nazi repression

---

[1] Quoted from Dussel and Lersch (eds.), *Quellen*, 136–7.

was portrayed more openly in the media than is often assumed, most would agree that the deceptively 'beautiful sheen' (Reichel) of the Third Reich ultimately helped camouflage the murderous brutality at its core.[2]

But this interpretation, though plausible in itself, fails to capture the multi-faceted role of the mass media in the Third Reich. For one thing, the Nazis quite obviously could not have everything their own way. The strategy of mobilizing the populace through diversion was something of a paradox. As often as not, these two different imperatives worked at cross-purposes rather than in tandem. Intention and effect were thus difficult to harmonize, for even under such a control-obsessed dictatorship German audiences were still active, critical users of mass culture who could largely take what they wanted from what was on offer. More importantly, the idea that Nazi mass culture served primarily to distract audiences from 'social reality' ironically tells us little about the actual social role of the mass media and the entertainments they conveyed. Certainly, the question of how far the regime's social propaganda eroded older sectional loyalties has been vigorously debated.[3] Despite all of the Nazis' egalitarian rhetoric, it seems clear that they were ultimately rather indifferent to social inequality. The social myth of the 'Volksgemeinschaft' was never powerful enough to break down real social differences or, for that matter, continued perceptions of these differences. Given the mere twelve-year life-span of the regime it would be surprising if it did.

Yet if we view the Nazi period within a longer-term context, what is most striking is not the failure of the Volksgemeinschaft rhetoric, but rather how far the decades-old goal of creating a shared 'middlebrow' culture advanced over these years. While this was at one level part of a much wider trend across the industrialized world in the 1930s, it received a peculiar boost under the Nazis through the far-reaching concentration of the media and the deliberate efforts to forge a culture befitting the 'national community'. Typically, these efforts were not well coordinated but emerged over time as rival factions vied for predominance. Nor were they remotely 'progressive' in the sense that Weimar reforms were intended to be, for the Nazis' distinctive brand of cultural inclusion was fundamentally predicated on racial and political exclusion. And they certainly did not smother all regional and social diversity: popular culture in the Third Reich was no more monolithic or undifferentiated than the legendarily motley regime itself.[4] Yet during the 1930s a confluence of technical, commercial, and political developments encouraged the emergence of a more widely shared culture of entertainment that, for all its diversity, clearly dovetailed with Nazi visions of national unity.

---

[2] Reichel, *Der schöne Schein*; Maase, *Grenzenloses*, 233; Grunberger, *Social History*; Dröge, Müller, *Macht*. On coverage of Nazi coercion, Gellately, *Backing Hitler*, chap. 3.

[3] For an overview: Kershaw, *Dictatorship*, chap. 7.

[4] V. Dahm, 'Nationale Einheit und partikulare Vielfalt', *VfZ* 43 (1995), 221–65.

FROM AGITATION TO 'STATE PROPAGANDA': POLITICS, MARKETING, AND ENTERTAINMENT

The idea of harnessing the media for the goal of national unity was by no means a Nazi invention. As we have seen, it had long been championed by an assortment of cultural reformers and publicity experts keen to mitigate the fragmentation of modern society. There was an overriding sense in the inter-war period that political stabilization could not be achieved simply by forging compromises between competing material interests. Rather, it required a more far-reaching harmonization of experiences, outlooks, and values. During the depths of the crisis in the early 1930s the increasingly dire prospects for material conciliation made this communicative harmonization seem all the more important. This was certainly the view among the leading figures in the German Advertising Association, who in early January 1933 founded a non-governmental Reichs-Werbe-Zentrale for the purpose of 'awakening and sustaining within the Volk and nation the consciousness of the idea of a community'. Now, in the nation's hour of despair, it was more important than ever to overcome 'the chaos of party-political strife' through the promotion of 'that which is held in common, that which unites, that for which all can strive'.[5]

In many ways the Nazi propaganda strategy after January 1933 built on these very same sentiments. As we saw at the close of Chapter 8, Hitler's appointment as chancellor came just in the nick of time. The deep-seated republican doubts about the efficacy of quick-fix emotional agitation were just being realized when the Nazis were brought into government. Among Nazi propaganda officials and party activists alike there was a tangible sense that their agitation bubble was deflating, and that tactics would have to change.

And change they did, for the transition from opposition to government brought about a marked shift in the tone and character of National Socialist publicity. The acquisition of power put the Nazi propaganda effort on a fundamentally different footing. For one thing, it placed incomparably greater resources and media outlets at their disposal. As Goebbels gloatingly remarked on 21 February, 'both the domestic and foreign press view our propaganda as exemplary and unprecedented . . . Now we are showing them what one can do with the state apparatus when one knows how to use it'.[6] Unlike the preceding republican governments, the Nazis needed no persuading to use this apparatus to the fullest, including police bans and harassment of opponents. Yet, just as important was the fact that exercising power as opposed to acquiring it also called for different tools. As the Nazis consolidated their grip on government, the shrill, insurrectionary propaganda of the 'period of struggle' was increasingly out of

[5] *DR* 26 (Jan. 1933), 6.　　[6] Reuth (ed.), *Tagebücher*, ii. 767 (21 Feb. 1933).

place. What was needed was not the divisive techniques of electioneering but a more consensual form of 'state publicity'. This was all part of the general shift from 'revolution' to 'evolution', as Hitler repeatedly put it. The hoards of marching and leafleting brownshirts who had previously fuelled the Nazi publicity machine were becoming increasingly superfluous—even counterproductive—given the media now at their disposal. The shift from electioneering to 'integration propaganda' meant that provocation gave way to harmony, agitation to entertainment, anger to pleasure, fundamental opposition to the positive pathos of regeneration.[7] And as we will see, it often meant that ideological orthodoxy gave way to pragmatism.

Despite all the adjustments this entailed, there was one important element of continuity: Nazi 'state publicity' was still centred on emotional appeal. Hitler and Goebbels were in complete agreement on this. Because the broad masses of the populace were, in Hitler's view, governed by primitive impulses and emotions and prone to 'feminine' irrationality and hysteria, government publicity under the Nazis was to be wholly different from that of the republican RfH. According to Goebbels, the RfH's complex and cerebral messages were largely self-defeating: 'during the time we were in opposition . . . we were always pleased when the Reichszentrale für Heimatdienst issued a new leaflet. These leaflets were enormously useful to us; indeed we were sometimes tempted to distribute them ourselves.'[8] Where the two differed was over how best to harness popular emotions for political ends. For Hitler, as for most Nazi campaigners, this was largely a matter of distilling complex political ideas into catchy, memorable slogans. For Goebbels it was more a matter of style, of forging a subtle union of politics with sensory experience. As one commentator has neatly put it, in Goebbels's view 'the politics of representation was more important than the representation of politics'.[9] Nowhere was this more clearly expressed than in his address to radio executives on 25 March 1933: 'The correct political attitudes must be conveyed, but this need not be boring . . . You must use your imagination, an imagination that is based on firm foundations and that employs every means available to bring to the masses the new way of thinking in a modern, up to date, interesting, and appealing manner . . . *That* is the secret of propaganda; *completely* to imbue the targeted person with the ideas of your propaganda without him even realizing it.'[10]

As this statement makes clear, the boundary between 'entertainment' and 'politics' in Nazi Germany was deliberately blurred, indeed from *both* directions. It was not simply a matter of politicizing entertainment but also of making 'politics' more entertaining. The mass rallies, with their sea of flags and standards,

---

[7] T. Bussemer, *Propaganda und Populärkultur* (Wiesbaden, 2000), 15; also Paul, *Aufstand*, 263.
[8] Hitler, *Mein Kampf*, 167; Welch, *The Third Reich*, 180. Goebbels accepted few RfH personnel into the Propaganda Ministry: BAB R43/I/2515, fos. 184–98; R43/I/2523, fos. 178–219 *passim*.
[9] Hake, *German*, 77.
[10] Quoted from Heiber (ed.), *Goebbels-Reden*, i. 95, emphasis in the original.

were more akin to a royal jubilee celebration than a party conference. The light-shows, music, and gargantuan stage backdrops designed by Albert Speer seem to twenty-first-century eyes more like a rock concert than a political event.[11] Even the use of the spoken word was consciously designed to be entertaining: the fist-waving, pulpit-thumping style—interspersed with plenty of opportunities for 'Sieg Heil' audience participation—said at least as much as the actual text. And for the vast majority of Germans who did not witness all of this in person, teams of filmmakers, photographers, and radio announcers brought it to them. The Nazis were firmly convinced about the importance of, to use Domizlaff's terminology, 'style devices of the state as psychological supports'.[12] As a movement whose very essence was rooted in Germany's defeat in 1918, the Nazi Party fervently believed it had learned the lessons of the war: 'we did not lose the war because our artillery gave out but because the weapons of our minds did not fire.' This meant that 'the mobilisation of the mind is as necessary as, possibly even more important than, the material mobilisation of the nation'.[13] The goal was quite literally to rekindle the mythical 'spirit of 1914' as the basis of an organic 'national community'.[14]

This racially defined community was the cornerstone of the Nazi publicity effort once in power. It served as both a means and an end, at once a policy aim and a principal theme of social propaganda. It was a multimedia phenomenon in which the cinema, radio, and press constantly paraded the Nazis' social 'achievements', from charity appeals to 'Strength through Joy' leisure schemes. Many of these efforts were specifically designed to wean the industrial working class from socialism and facilitate its integration into the 'national community'. Whether by valorizing workers' skill or promising the 'good life' for all, Nazi social propaganda latched onto potent desires for social recognition, upward mobility, and equal opportunity that had swelled during the post-war years. Although the underlying aim remained unambiguously productivist, the manner of presentation was unabashedly consumer-oriented.[15]

National Socialist 'integration propaganda' (Bussemer) was thus characterized not only by calls for common sacrifice but also by the promise of consumption and pleasure. And since the voracious material needs of rearmament dictated an emphasis on cultural consumption, the media played a central role in generating the desired sense of social solidarity and reform, along with tourism, sport, and other leisure opportunities. Pleasure and gratification were of the utmost importance, for simply proclaiming these ideas from on high would never suffice.

---

[11] See generally M. Urban, *Die Konsensfabrik* (Göttingen, 2007).
[12] Domizlaff, *Propagandamittel*, 95.
[13] Goebbels to radio executives, 24 Mar. 1933: Welch, *The Third Reich*, 183.
[14] A connection analysed by Verhey, *Spirit*.
[15] S. Baranowski, *Strength through Joy* (Cambridge, 2004); W. Buchholz, *Die nationalsozialistische Gemeinschaft 'Kraft durch Freude'*, Ph.D thesis, Munich (1976); A. Lüdtke, '"Ehre der Arbeit"', in K. Tenfelde (ed.), *Arbeiter im. 20. Jahrhundert* (Stuttgart, 1991), 343–92.

As Goebbels in particular recognized, manufacturing a sense of racial belonging and social progress required a degree of internalization on the part of spectators, a positive inner experience that corresponded with Nazi sensibilities. And the key to merging this inner experience with a particular set of political views was to make it enjoyable. This is the fundamental reason why popular culture in the Third Reich often looked so disconcertingly similar to the culture of other times and places. It, too, was based on the tried-and-tested formats of linear narrative, human interest, and storytelling. In order to draw an audience it had to be, for otherwise the state incorporation of popular culture would be a Pyrrhic victory.

Yet the strategy of appealing to pleasure and desire came at a price. It inevitably diluted the political message and left much of the meaning in the eye of the beholder. For many Germans, the regime's amusement and leisure offerings were just that and little more. Even committed socialists often struggled to find any hints of Nazism per se in the 'Strength through Joy' activities. As one former Workers' Sport member put it: 'At first I had misgivings about taking part in a KdF event, but after all there are no other alternatives. So I was all the more pleasantly surprised to find nothing specifically National Socialist at all about the make-up and operation of the course.'[16] Even when there was a more obvious political gloss, it was often little more than pious window-dressing, and indeed was perceived as such by participants and officials alike. When, for instance, a group of KdF vacationers from Nuremberg arrived at their destination in the Allgäu, they were initially treated to a brief address from the local party leader and were summoned to sing the Horst Wessel Song. Then, as Julius Streicher's own *Fränkische Tageszeitung* reported it: 'After three salutes to the Führer Adolf Hitler and singing the national anthem they proceeded to the enjoyable part (*ging man zum gemütlichen Teil über*).'[17]

As these examples suggest, people could often get what they wanted out of the popular-culture offerings of the Third Reich, gladly 'plundering' them without necessarily taking the intended political messages on board.[18] In this sense, acceptance and rejection of Nazi propaganda could readily coexist within a single individual, indeed within a single experience; users could ascribe a range of different meanings to what they saw and heard. Although this ambiguity irritated Nazi purists, it was more an asset than a liability. For it meant that the regime's social propaganda did not need to bring about a radical change of consciousness in order to help stabilize the regime. Even if the vaunted 'national community' remained an illusion, the rhetoric and imagery nonetheless tapped widely held desires for social inclusion and renewal.[19]

[16] Quoted from Bussemer, *Propaganda und Populärkultur*, 81.
[17] Quoted from M. Maaß, *Freizeitgestaltung und kulturelles Leben in Nürnberg 1930–1945* (Nürnberg, 1994), 321.
[18] Bussemer, *Propaganda und Populärkultur*, 2, 149.
[19] See P. Fritzsche, *Germans into Nazis* (Cambridge, Mass., 1998), esp. 227–35.

By playing on desires for upward mobility and acceptance, Nazi publicity once again showed some striking parallels to contemporary developments in commercial advertising. In some respects it was remarkably similar to the new mass-marketing techniques emanating from the United States. By the early 1930s the primary purpose of modern advertising was not merely to shout a product's name into the world, but to create new needs and open up new markets among hitherto ignored social groups. By overcoming geographical barriers and traditional hierarchies of taste, modern advertising sought to construct new consumer identities centred on participation in the burgeoning world of commodities. As a self-declared 'People's Party' that claimed to rise above sectional interests, the Nazis similarly sought to open up new constituencies by breaking down older class- and regionally-based allegiances and constructing new political identities revolving around social entitlement based on nation and race. In this sense, T. J. Jackson Lears's description of American ad agencies in the early twentieth century is remarkably applicable to the social propaganda of the Third Reich: 'the fables they fashioned merged personal and social health, individual and nation, creating narratives of adjustment to a single, efficient system.'[20] Just as advertisers were recognizing how better to tap the human craving for acceptance, Nazi propagandists similarly sought to harness the yearning for social harmony and belonging.

Nowhere was this more strikingly manifested than in the cult of the Führer, the most powerful integrative symbol in the Third Reich. The figure of the Führer, rooted in *völkisch* notions of a mystical hero embodying the nation's will, functioned as the glue that held the administrative apparatus together and as a vital icon of unity and trust in the government.[21] Hitler himself was by far the most popular figure of the regime, hovering above the day-to-day mishaps of government and providing it with a crucial symbol of legitimacy amidst the growing scepticism towards the Nazi Party itself. Although his charismatic authority derived in large part from his achievements as chancellor (in particular the reduction of unemployment and his stunning string of foreign-policy successes), the packaging—the skilful manipulation of his public image—was just as important as the contents. In many ways Hitler served as a political brand-name, invoking a sense of loyalty, continuity, and trust among a highly diverse 'market' of constituents.

Indeed, Hitler's image was quite deliberately constructed along the lines of a commercial brand. He had long served as a rallying figure within the Nazi movement itself, and in the presidential elections of spring 1932 the Nazis campaigned for the first time with the image of Hitler's face (though not yet with the signature hair falling diagonally across forehead).[22] These elections also witnessed Hitler's 'Germany flights' that cast him as a modern, impelling figure

---

[20] Lears, *Fables*, 12.   [21] I. Kershaw, *The 'Hitler Myth'* (Oxford, 1987).
[22] R. Herz, *Hoffmann & Hitler* (Munich, 1994), 107.

metaphorically above the wrangling of day-to-day politics. After his appointment as chancellor, the image of Hitler as a dynamic personality was tempered by a new emphasis on his responsible statesmanship. The 'Day of Potsdam' on 21 March 1933, carefully choreographed to symbolize the union of the revolutionary Nazi movement with the traditional Prussian virtues, was one of the Nazis' most successful pieces of stage management, spawning innumerable special newspaper editions and broadcast in its entirety on radio. From this point onwards Hitler was presented as a leader who was forceful yet moderate, dynamic yet trustworthy—an image that was cemented with his ruthless (and loudly publicized) purge of the SA leadership on 30 June 1934.[23]

After Hindenburg's death the 'Hitler' brand was rapidly recast into the Führer. In the run-up to the plebiscite of 19 August 1934 (on whether the positions of Reich president and chancellor should be amalgamated), images of the would-be supreme leader were 'hanging from every window, every car', as an SPD agent put it.[24] Interestingly, however, the countless portraits were drawn from a limited number of motifs taken by his personal photographer Heinrich Hoffmann.[25] This was crucial insofar as it guaranteed a high degree of recognition and consistency, two key elements of branding technique. One of the posters for the plebiscite neatly illustrates the approach (see Fig. 12). It was based on a portrait of Hitler staring at the onlooker, selected from a series taken by Hoffmann in early 1933, and was completely devoid of any text apart from one word: 'Ja!' This complete lack of textual exposition demonstrates the degree to which Hitler had already become a brand-name: he so obviously stood for a movement and a particular set of policies that no further elaboration was needed. The poster's composition of sixteen identical images was also geared to enhance brand recognition, based as it was on the principle of spatial repetition, whose effectiveness was highly prized by advertisers.[26]

After summer 1934, with the popular Hindenburg and intra-party rivals Gregor Strasser and Ernst Röhm literally out of the picture, the political brand Führer effectively held a market monopoly. But, like any successful brand, it still needed protection from the threats of piracy and overuse. Exclusivity, the third key element alongside recognizability and consistency, was an absolute requirement for continued effectiveness. The Propaganda Ministry regularly issued press instructions on the use of Hitler photographs in the newspapers, and only officially approved portraits were allowed for sale or display. Even the use of the term 'Führer' was tightly circumscribed for fear that the proliferation of titles such as 'Factory Führer' would dilute its brand value. Once the 'Führer' *qua* brand-name was firmly established, its usage was closely regulated through various speech conventions. Hitler himself insisted wherever possible on being

[23] Behrenbeck, 'Der Führer', 56–61; Voigt, 'Goebbels'.
[24] *Deutschland-Berichte*, i. 347.   [25] Herz, *Hoffmann*, 92–107.
[26] Behrenbeck, 'Führer', 65; Herz, *Hoffmann*, 107.

Fig. 12. The Führer as brand: poster for the plebiscite of 19 August 1934. Bundesarchiv, Plakat 003-002-055.

referred to only as 'Führer', so as to avoid associating his image with terms such as 'Reich chancellor' or 'commander-in-chief'.[27]

The Führer was not the only National Socialist symbol in need of protection. As we have seen, manufacturers and retailers keen to associate themselves with (and profit from) the movement had already made use of Nazi slogans and emblems to embellish their products before 1933. The swastika was especially vulnerable to such commercial exploitation, and indeed could be found on everyday items ranging from shoehorns to butter patties. In the wake of the Nazi takeover this phenomenon mushroomed out of all control. By the spring of 1933 bakers were kneading swastika-shaped loaves of bread, and one enterprising

[27] Behrenbeck, 'Führer', 67.

butcher even decorated his display window with a bust of Hitler sculpted out of lard. In order to prevent a wholesale trivialization of the party's symbols, the government quickly forbade 'the use of emblems as well as names and symbols of the movement for the purposes of commercial advertising'. Since this proved inadequate, it soon passed a 'Law for the Protection of National Symbols' on 19 May, which subsequently had to be sharpened several times before achieving the desired effect. The extended versions of the law expressly prohibited, among other things, the use of Hitler portraits and swastikas for all advertising purposes, effectively copyrighting them on behalf of the party.[28] Incidentally, Nazi leaders were not the only ones playing this game. According to Goebbels's diaries, the mother of Horst Wessel, the Nazi martyr who had written the lyrics for the party anthem 'Die Fahne hoch', also tried to claim proprietary rights over the song shortly after it was recognized as a national symbol under the law of 19 May.[29] But to return to the main point, the problems of brand protection showed that the relationship between Nazi propaganda and commercial advertising had to be managed carefully. The party might borrow as much as it wanted from the advertising industry, even arranging cabinet-level meetings with the American public-relations guru Ivy Lee, but commercial businesses were strictly prohibited from using Nazi brands.[30]

As with all forms of commercial or political publicity, the key for Nazi integration propaganda was to stir people's desires while simultaneously channelling them in a particular direction. Put differently, the challenge was to strike a balance between release and control. In the context of 1930s Germany this elusive equilibrium was no more attainable via heavy-handed indoctrination than through the insistent didacticism of decades past. Although a more ideologically adamant approach might be practicable for the representative arts, when it came to the mass media the forms and messages needed to be more subtle, more consensual, more appealing. Although not everyone in the party leadership liked it, pleasure and entertainment formed the bedrock of popular culture in the Third Reich.

'FILM FOR ALL': CINEMA AND SOCIETY IN THE 1930s

Given the far-reaching government control over the film industry, what is most remarkable about German cinema of the 1930s was not the appearance of obviously pro-Nazi dramas like *Hitlerjunge Quex* and *Hans Westmar* (1933), or monumental propaganda films such as Leni Riefenstahl's *Triumph des Willens*

---

[28] Reinhardt, *Reklame*, 423–4; H. Berghoff, 'Von der "Reklame" zur Verbrauchslenkung', in H. Berghoff (ed.), *Konsumpolitik* (Göttingen, 1999), 93–4.
[29] Reuth (ed.), *Tagebücher*, ii. 811 (10 June 1933).
[30] On Lee, see Sproule, *Propaganda*, 55–6.

(1935) and *Olympia* (1938), but rather how *little* the bulk of film production seemed to change. As Richard Grunberger put it long ago, 'had a cinema-going Rip van Winkel dozed off in the Depression and woken in the Third Reich he would have found the screen filled with the self-same images: spike-helmeted, hollow-eyed soldiers "going over the top", bewigged courtiers posturing before rococo backdrops, poachers and milkmaids tangling among ears of golden corn, and ganglia-flexing mountaineers scaling cloud-wreathed pinnacles.'[31] At first sight one is tempted to interpret these continuities as evidence of proto-fascist tendencies before 1933. But the more convincing explanation is that film in the Third Reich did not significantly diverge from previous trends or international norms. Amidst the many continuities there were, of course, certain changes from the Weimar era. The film images confronting Grunberger's Rip van Winkel had indeed been around for years, but on closer inspection he might have noticed that certain things were no longer so common on the silver screen in the 1930s, such as the trickle of social critique and the ambivalent prognoses of modern society that were also part of Weimar's cinema culture. In addition, he may have discerned a marked decline in low-budget films and a greater emphasis on the production of lavish melodramas and star-studded comedies capable of achieving cross-class appeal. Yet this does not change the fact that the cinema under the Nazis largely remained what it had always been: a commercial form of entertainment that, while unavoidably conveying certain political messages, was primarily geared towards enjoyment.

The vast majority of feature films made in Nazi Germany thus followed the conventional format of love stories, dramas, and comedies that had pulled in the crowds for decades and were simultaneously being churned out in Hollywood, Paris, and London. Insofar as there was anything distinctive about them, it was the degree to which they fused personal happiness with social harmony. These themes lay at the core of some of the most successful German films of the 1930s, whose obligatory happy ends generally involved the parallel resolution of social conflicts and personal problems. An example was Willi Forst's *Maskerade* (1934), in which the heroine, played by Paula Wessely, finally resolves an ongoing dispute over a nude painting by appealing to the compassion of her jealous physician husband Peter Peterson to save the life of the offending artist, Adolf Wohlbruck. In a somewhat similar vein, Paul Martin's box-office hit *Glückskinder* (1936) ends with Lilian Harvey and Willy Fritsch finding true love after initially pretending to be married in order to avoid jail, in the process reacquiring Fritsch's lost job and clarifying Harvey's family identity. Both of these films demonstrate the common recipe of interweaving a central love story with a wider set of social relations, in which the resolution of group tensions goes hand in hand with the fulfilment of individual desires. In this formula, the social and the personal suggestively converge into a wider community of fate. Finding love coincides with the

---

[31] Grunberger, *Social History*, 475.

attainment of justice and understanding, and individual happiness derives not from resisting the external pressures of society (as Romeo and Juliet), but rather is predicated upon harmonious social relations and the alleviation of tensions.[32]

Most feature films of the 1930s followed the typical conventions of dramas, adventures, thrillers, musicals, or comedies. Overtly 'political' films were rare, and remained so even during the war. Even many of the productions commissioned directly by the state (which amounted to less than 10 per cent of all films made) were for all intents and purposes entertainment films.[33] Although German film companies proved more than willing to cooperate with the regime, there were commercial and artistic limits to churning out overt propaganda. The fact that even so skilful a propaganda film as *Triumph des Willens* ran only three days in Berlin and, according to SPD agents, 'exerted only a very slight attraction', clearly showed the risks involved.[34] Ultimately, neither the industry nor the government had any interest in compromising the entertainment value of the cinema. Personnel factors might also have played a role, for despite the purges of 1933 the film world was probably the least Nazified segment of the cultural elite. Axel Eggebrecht, a former communist who was eventually allowed to work as a scriptwriter after his arrest in 1933, recalled that 'nowhere, in no other surroundings . . . did I feel as safe as among film people. Anyone who was a National Socialist there was so well known that one simply avoided them.'[35]

Although the cinema was certainly not a politics-free zone within the Third Reich, it is nonetheless striking how 'normal' it appeared to many contemporaries. 'One has to look a long time before one finds a cinema programme announcing a film with an obvious political slant,' remarked the party's youth journal *Wille und Macht* in 1937. 'Even the most suspicious film-goers cannot claim that German films seek to hit them over the head with politics or to impose a world-view. Except for portions of the newsreels, cinema in a newly politicised Germany amounts to an unpolitical oasis.' The SPD's informants largely concurred, noting that 'anything one could speak of as a new world-view is entirely absent'.[36] Interestingly enough, this assessment was even shared by many who suffered grievously at the hands of the regime. The Jewish Filmbühne, a cinematic ghetto established after Jews were banned from mainstream cinemas in November 1938, found nothing wrong with the bulk of German film productions; indeed they constituted well over two-thirds of its entire repertoire (alongside mainly US films).[37] Understandably, its audiences tended to prefer films that were set

---

[32] See esp. L. Schulte-Sasse, *Entertaining the Third Reich* (Durham, NC, 1996); Rentschler, *Ministry*; Kreimeier, *Ufa Story*, 236–46.

[33] Welch, *German Cinema*, 42–3.   [34] *Deutschland-Berichte*, ii. 714.

[35] E. Offermanns, *Internationalität und europäischer Hegemonialanspruch des Spielfilms der NS-Zeit* (Hamburg, 2001), 60.

[36] Quotes from Rentschler, *Ministry*, 19; *Deutschland-Berichte*, iv. 911–12.

[37] E. Offermanns, *Die deutschen Juden und der Spielfilm der NS-Zeit* (Frankfurt a. M., 2005), 67–70.

abroad or in the past rather than in current-day Germany. But as it happened this excluded only a small proportion of available pictures. So-called 'Auslandsfilme', that is, those set and filmed abroad, constituted an unusually large proportion of German productions. From 1933 to 1939 some twenty-four German-made features were set in Britain, eighteen in France, nine in Hungary, six in the United States, and eight in Italy. By 1937 Reich Film Chamber president Oswald Lehnich openly complained that 'people look abroad for material instead of mobilizing the spiritual forces of the German people. . . . One almost has the impression that German film is still wrestling with a spirit that should have disappeared long ago with the purge of the Jews.' Moreover, a high proportion of movie stars in Nazi Germany (noticeably more than in Hollywood) were foreigners, including Anny Ondra (Czech), Käthe von Nagy (Hungarian), Jan Kiepura (Polish), Iwan Petrovich (Yugoslavian), and Jack Trevor and Lilian Harvey (British). Indeed, among the top sound-film songsters an outright majority was foreign: Marika Rökk (Hungarian), Zarah Leander (Swedish), Rosita Serrano (Chilean), Louis Graveure (British), and Johannes Heesters (Dutch).[38]

These foreign settings and stars lent an air of trendy cosmopolitanism to what might otherwise have seemed a rather parochial 'national community'. The sense of cinematic 'normality' they sustained was also reinforced by the willingness of Nazi authorities to allow a significant number of foreign films into Germany. Much to the frustration of xenophobic party zealots, the glamour of the wider world and the latest international fashions remained central elements of the Third Reich's film culture. The modern, consumer-oriented lifestyle on display in hit comedies like Carl Froehlich's *Die Vier Gesellen* (1938, starring Swedish actress Ingrid Bergmann), Willi Forst's *Allotria* (1936), or the aforementioned *Glückskinder* (1936, an unconcealed remake of Frank Capra's *It Happened One Night*, set in New York City) exuded an almost hedonistic attraction amidst the constant appeals to discipline and heroic self-sacrifice that otherwise characterized the National Socialist way of life.[39] In the cinema, German audiences found not only the subtle convergence of personal happiness and social harmony, but also the stimulation and fulfilment of quintessentially private dreams and desires.

The fact that so many successful German films of the 1930s owed a visible debt to Hollywood underscores the numerous parallels between the cinematic aims of the Nazis and the strategy of the big American studios: to create popular, class-transcending forms of entertainment that combined artistic and commercial success. Irksome though it may seem, it was first under the Nazis that the long-standing calls to create the 'film for all' finally became a political imperative. Viewed in a long-term context, such films were a prime example of the 'refined entertainment' that German cultural reformers had long strived for. Unlike the demanding artistic films of classic Weimar cinema, gripping dramas such as

[38] Offermanns, *Internationalität*, 17–19, 29, 36.
[39] On comedies, K. Witte, *Lachende Erben, Toller Tag* (Berlin, 1995).

Schwarze Rosen (1935) or screwball comedies like *Paradies der Junggesellen* (1939) could satisfy both the distracted pleasure-seeker as well as the discriminating viewer. The fact that Hollywood furnished the mould for such films was openly recognized by producers and state officials alike. Ever since the late 1920s UFA had resolved itself to compete with Hollywood toe to toe, which unavoidably involved imitating its techniques and narrative structures. Despite the racially motivated dismissal of the producer Erich Pommer, the most outspoken advocate of this strategy before 1933, the company made no secret of its admiration for the creative skill and popular touch of the Hollywood majors. Germany's leading actors and film critics generally regarded Hollywood as the principal yardstick for comparison. As the journal *Film-Kurier* curtly advised German filmmakers after the premiere of MGM's *San Francisco* in 1937: 'go, see, and imitate.'[40] German audiences also admired Hollywood films—though, to be fair, they were treated to only a small and carefully censored selection of high-quality productions, and were thus spared the countless B-films churned out by the studio system. For this reason any talk of a straightforward 'Americanization' of German cinema is off the mark. But despite the import restrictions, German audiences could see enough Hollywood films for celebrities from Laurel and Hardy to Joan Crawford to achieve remarkable notoriety among German cinemagoers, including the very pinnacle of the Nazi hierarchy. Goebbels's Christmas gift to Hitler in 1937 consisted of thirty-two 'classics' and twelve Mickey Mouse films: 'He is very pleased about it, delighted with this treasure.'[41]

This admiration of Hollywood film was not confined to an appreciation of cinematic techniques. The esteem among Babelsberg's producers for the craftsmanship of their American rivals (often mutually felt) was part of a much wider fascination with what many Germans saw as the unique cultural populism of the United States—the unproblematic attitude towards art and entertainment that had intrigued critics since the 1920s, and whose social inclusivity resonated with the Nazi vision of a politically and culturally unified Volksgemeinschaft. Nowhere was the assimilative character of American popular culture more plainly manifested than in the images and narrative strategies of Hollywood film. The stories they fashioned possessed an uncanny ability to transcend social boundaries, flatten cultural hierarchies, and appeal to an extraordinarily diverse audience of different faiths, colours, and creeds. For Nazi officials and German producers alike, the key was to harness these techniques for their own ends. At base, the high-quality 'film for all' was modelled on the big-budget Hollywood feature.

This situation was more than a little ironic, for it meant that the officially endorsed 'national blockbuster' drew its primary inspiration from a foreign film industry marked by a conspicuous presence of Jewish talent and based in a

---

[40] Quoted from Spieker, 'Hollywood', 151.
[41] From E. Fröhlich (ed.), *Die Tagebücher von Joseph Goebbels*, 1: 5 (Munich: Saur, 2000), 64 (22 Dec. 1937).

country that German nationalists instinctively regarded as a cultural wasteland.[42] It also meant that the old progressive goal of using the cinema as a vehicle for shared experience found its most powerful political champion in the Nazi Propaganda Ministry.

But this raises the crucial question of the extent to which German cinema in the 1930s was actually capable of transcending social boundaries. When approaching this question it is important to recognize that any such potential not only derived from the aesthetic qualities of the films themselves but was also related to the bundle of commercial and technological developments discussed in previous chapters. Reaching a 'mass' cinema audience required more than just making the right films; it was also based on the changing context within which they were produced and consumed.

As we have seen, the conversion to sound film had already rendered the nature of cinematic presentation and audience uptake far more uniform than during the silent era. Although a gaping chasm still separated the comfortable premiere cinemas from the thousands of neighbourhood fleapits, the standardization of sound and projection speeds somewhat evened out the actual cinematic experience. These trends were further reinforced after 1933 by Nazi efforts to standardize cinema programmes into one feature, a newsreel, and several short films. The Reich Film Chamber also tried—with only limited success—to crack down on the old convention of open admissions, whereby visitors came and went whenever they pleased.[43] Although partly motivated by a desire to enhance the propaganda value of the newsreels, the attempt to introduce closed viewings was also a means of gentrifying the cinema experience for a bourgeois clientele.

At the same time, the spiralling production costs for sound film also resulted in a dramatic decrease in the number and types of films on the market. By and large it was small- and medium-budget productions that took the brunt of the pressure. These inexpensive films, whose costs could be amortized within a regional market and which could therefore cater to regional interests, all but disappeared from the screen with the demise of the silent film over the early 1930s. As we saw in Chapter 5, their decline was so sudden that UFA considered proposals that cinema directors continue making them. But such efforts were no more than drops in the ocean, for continually rising costs forced filmmakers to concentrate on producing fewer, better films that could satisfy international tastes as well as an increasingly demanding domestic audience. The end-result was a dramatic narrowing of offerings in the cinemas, which increasingly had to choose from a smaller and less variegated palette of films.

---

[42] Führer, 'Two-fold', 106–9; generally, L. P. Koepnick, *The Dark Mirror* (Berkeley, 2002).

[43] 'Auch ein Doppelprogramm', *FK* (21 Aug. 1934), 3; 'Gegen die Unpünktlichen', *FK* (1 Feb. 1937), 4; C. Hoffmann, 'Geschlossene Vorstellungen und numerierte Plätze', *FK* (21 Nov. 1938), 1–2.

While the supply of films and the range of presentation styles were rapidly shrinking, the sociological make-up of cinema audiences was significantly expanding.[44] Although we lack detailed survey data on audiences, the available statistics show that households with modest incomes were spending roughly twice as much on the cinema in 1937 as they had a decade earlier (see Chapter 9). This not only suggests that the cinema was drawing in new spectators, but also that previous movie-goers were attending more often. Although Nazi efforts to promote film may have helped matters, by and large this expansion reflected the tapping of new audiences in the context of economic recovery.[45] An interesting picture emerges if one considers these findings against the backdrop of overall cinema attendance. While the number of annual admissions rose from roughly 330 million in 1927 to 375 million in 1937, or around 14 per cent, there was, according to these statistics, an increase of around 100 per cent among lower-income households. Given stable ticket prices over this period,[46] this translated into roughly a doubling of actual attendance. Whatever the shortcomings of these surveys and however approximate their figures may be, it seems clear that the sharp rise in cinema-going after the most acute phase of economic depression (from 239 million in 1932 to 375 million in 1937) reflected an increase above all among low-income households.

At the same time that rising disposable income was bringing in more working-class viewers, the inexorable process of generational change was slowly but surely eroding the edifice of film snobbery among educated elites. Doubtless the traditional aversion towards film among the Bildungsbürgertum remained strong, at least in publicly expressed attitudes. As a 1938 survey of 'cinema abstainers' concluded, 'the opinions of the so-called better sort exert an after-effect here. Film is still not considered "legitimate".'[47] Just like their spiritual ancestors a generation earlier, conservative critics still lined up to denounce the 'tasteless and brainless and at times obscene performances', and still despised the notion that it was all nothing more than 'a purely mechanical process of reproduction'. Yet even among the highly educated it was difficult to find young people who shared these sentiments, 'for it is only in very isolated cases that a pronounced aversion to film can be discerned among persons under 30'.[48] Moreover, many cultural snobs were reported to 'go to cinemas where no one knows them. That way they can guard their reputations. . . . One might think that such people do not exist—more than one thinks.'[49] The heightened popular appeal of sound film undoubtedly played a role here, as did the producers' focus on widely marketable blockbusters and the corresponding decline of woeful 'quota quickies' that were

[44] The following is drawn in part from Ross, 'Mass Culture'.
[45] 'Theaterbesitzer vor neuen Aufgaben. Wie fülle ich mein Kino?', *FK* (23 Sept. 1935), 3–4.
[46] Averaging around RM 0.72: Jason, *Handbuch 1935/36*, 146.
[47] H. Meyer, 'Film und Seele', *FK* (1 Dec. 1938), 4.
[48] 'Die noch immer nicht ins Filmtheater gehen', *FK* (10 Jan. 1939), 1–2.
[49] Meyer, 'Film und Seele'.

previously churned out simply in order to obtain import licences for foreign films.[50] The many technical and architectural improvements to cinemas in the 1930s (better sound, projection, ventilation) and the new controls against particularly audacious film advertisements also helped the cinema to shed some of its unsavoury image.[51] In this sense it was, ironically, the very process of cultural 'massification' (the narrowing of film offerings and greater uniformity of presentation) so decried by bourgeois commentators that encouraged a further penetration of the Bildungsbürgertum.

German movie-goers of the later 1930s were thus far more likely to share the experience of the same film in roughly the same acoustic and visual presentation with a wider range of social groups than was the case a decade earlier. It is highly revealing in this respect that so few German films of the silent era managed to achieve both artistic recognition and commercial success. Though we can do little more than speculate why, one possible explanation is that audiences were simply too fragmented before the 1930s for a film to achieve universal admiration. Put differently, the main factor behind the successful cross-class appeal of the 'national blockbuster' was not the character of the films themselves, but rather the new commercial and technological structures through which they were created and viewed. As we have seen in some detail, cinema audiences in the 1920s were deeply divided in terms of attendance patterns, film preferences, and modes of reception. After the transition to sound and the standardizing effects this had on film supply and consumption, it became far more common for individual films to enjoy both popular and critical acclaim, starting with the earliest sound blockbusters *Die drei von der Tankstelle* (1930) and *Der Kongress tanzt* (1931), and continuing from there.[52] To this extent, the advent of the talking film represented a key moment in the emergence of a more widely shared media culture in the inter-war period.

To avoid any misunderstanding, this is *not* to suggest that German cinema had become a thoroughly undifferentiated purveyor of homogenized 'mass culture'. It is rather to say that the 1930s witnessed the emergence of a new constellation of artistic genres, production techniques, and viewing practices that made individual films more accessible and appealing to a wider range of spectators than ever before. The cinema in Nazi Germany was still characterized by a mixture of integrative *and* divisive tendencies, much as it had always been. What happened in the 1930s was not a wholesale triumph of the former over the latter, but a shift in their balance. For in spite of the unprecedented distribution and popularity of certain films, the cinema audiences of the Third Reich were still visibly divided by social and economic discrepancies.

---

[50] This was the common means of circumventing protective legislation from the 1920s which stipulated that German companies could only import as many films as they produced domestically.

[51] '1938—ein Jahr der Theater-Erneuerungen', *FK* (30 Dec. 1938), 1.

[52] See Chap. 3. This argument follows a suggestion by Karl Christian Führer. Both films were the biggest commercial successes of the year.

At the most fundamental level, there remained huge disparities between city and countryside. In 1935 only 2,470 of the 50,881 *Gemeinden* (municipalities ranging from small rural communities to large cities) in Germany had a cinema.[53] Although the vast majority of towns with populations over 10,000 had at least one by the mid–1930s, they were often open only two or three nights a week.[54] Movie-going opportunities remained few and far between in the countryside, and the primitive nature of many rural cinemas greatly diminished their appeal. As one Bavarian farmer complained, 'a proper film simply calls for a proper cinema too'.[55] The efforts of the Nazi Gaufilmstellen only marginally improved matters. As a rule, the venues for their 'village film events' (*Dorf-Filmfeierstunden*) bore precious little resemblance to the 'dream-like' experience of urban cinema. Most screenings took place in the local pub, sometimes in barns, and were often marred by a dim picture on a small screen, poor acoustics, and uncomfortable makeshift seating.[56] As for the films themselves, Nazi reluctance to screen anything that could make urban life look attractive (and therefore compound the problem of migration to the cities) meant that the Gaufilmstellen showed mostly out-of-date, 'culturally valuable' films that had long since disappeared from urban cinemas.[57] Even the newsreels were usually so old as to have little or no information value. It is therefore hardly surprising that film attendance remained low in rural areas. In the small village of Thürungen in Saxony, a detailed survey from the late 1930s found that only 191 of the village's 335 inhabitants went to the movies at all, and only eighty of these 'regularly' (more than six times per year), in spite of the existence of two small cinemas within only a few kilometres.[58] As in the 1920s, the large cities with populations over 100,000 remained the primary pillars of the film market. Yet even here, the density of cinemas and average attendance rates still varied dramatically: from 1932 to 1934 per capita admissions were twice as high in Berlin, Hamburg, and Düsseldorf as in Stuttgart, Bochum, and Nuremberg.[59]

The entire cinema landscape in 1930s Germany also remained unusually heterogeneous by international standards, given the lack of large-scale 'chaining' and the survival of thousands of independent neighbourhood theatres. As a 1937 study by the Institut für Filmforschung noted, 'the entire secret to success' still lay in pitching to a very local clientele.[60] The differences between Berlin's East and West End, for example, remained blindingly obvious, and it was still common for films slated by Berlin critics to do very well in the provinces.[61] In

[53] Jason, *Handbuch 1935/36*, 135.   [54] Ibid. 141.

[55] 'Die noch immer nicht ins Filmtheater gehen', 2.

[56] C. Zimmermann, 'Landkino im Nationalsozialismus', *AfS* 41 (2001), 238–42.

[57] 'Dorfkino', *FK* (4 June 1935), 3; also Zimmermann, 'Landkino', 238.

[58] A. Schmidt, *Publizistik im Dorf*, (Dresden, 1939), 165, 171, 174–5.

[59] Jason, *Handbuch 1935/36*, 158; also 'Der Kinobesuch im 3. Vierteljahr 1938', *FK* (19 Dec. 1938), 1.

[60] H. Meyer, 'Die verbrauchspsychologischen Grundlagen des Filmtheaterbesuchs', *FK* (6 Oct. 1937), 4.

[61] 'Des Volkes Stimme', *FK* (4 Sept. 1935), 2.

addition, the fact that movie-going continued to take place in groups, and not just by anonymous individuals within a 'mass' audience, ensured that film was mediated through other social structures outside of the cinema. This affected not only the reception of a film and the ascription of cultural meanings to it (by facilitating discussion about it after the viewing), but also the selection of films in the first place. 'Group visits often entail a degree of prior squabbling about which film and cinema,' explained one researcher from the Institut für Forschung. 'A parliamentary resolution rarely materializes. In most cases the most enthusiastic or experienced cinema-goer decides, and that is, as one would hardly expect otherwise, frequently the woman.'[62] Such assumptions explain why women were the primary targets of film advertisement: they were the best 'word-of-mouth propagandists' (*Mundpropagandisten*). Yet even here the social divisions of the film public were clearly visible, for such 'word-of-mouth propaganda' operated more *within* than *across* different social strata, and thus reinforced the differences between audiences and cinemas.[63]

Not surprisingly, there were still determined attempts to match particular films with particular cinemas, despite the imposition of blind- and block-booking by the big production conglomerates. As cinema owners continually complained, 'the timing and appropriate selection of venue are more decisive for the success of a film than those responsible for these matters, judging by their actions, seem to believe'.[64] If a cinema's 'regular crowd' saw too many ill-suited films that the proprietor was forced to show, it was bad for the entire industry. This problem was particularly acute in small towns that received only a portion of the year's films anyway.[65] Groups of cinemas with differing audiences would thus often share a 'block' of films and distribute them among themselves—one getting the bulk of sensational films, the other taking the dramas, and so on.[66] As a result, cinemas still managed to tailor their programmes to their particular audience expectations. As a 1938 newspaper report explained, even in a (unnamed) mid-sized town of 40,000 inhabitants the three local cinemas were still able to retain their distinctive profiles: the *Capitol* favouring the 'refined feature film', the *Zentraltheater* screening mostly comedies and operettas, and the *Eden* specializing in foreign and adventure films.[67]

The divergent programmes and 'regular crowds' in different cinemas continued to reflect the social make-up of the neighbourhoods in which they were located. Such mixing of audiences as occurred in the city-centre cinema palaces remained

---

[62] Quote from Meyer, 'Die verbrauchspsychologischen Grundlagen', 4. In 1932 only 17% of boys and 6% of girls went to the cinema alone: Funk, *Film und Jugend*, 60.
[63] 'Mundpropaganda und Film', *FK* (20 Feb. 1937), 3.
[64] 'Gedanken eines Theaterbesitzers', *FK* (19 June 1937), 1.
[65] 'Die Programme der Kleinen', *FK* (20 Nov. 1937), 1.
[66] Paschke, *Tonfilmmarkt*, 142, 147.
[67] J. Schüddekopf, 'Ein Brief aus der Provinz', *DAZ* (17 Sept. 1938). My thanks to Christian Führer for alerting me to this article.

the exception rather than the rule, and was still limited by ticket pricing, travel costs, and the social inhibitions erected by their theatre-like customs of comportment and attire. As one factory-worker explained to a 1938 survey: 'It feels awkward for me to go into the big cinemas in the city centre, so I satisfy myself with the local cinemas.'[68] Despite the sound film's silencing of the noisy, participatory audiences of the silent era, norms of behaviour in the thousands of local cinemas still differed markedly from the bourgeois ambience in the posh premiere movie-houses. 'Film has not struggled its way up from slapstick and hullabaloo to a recognized art form,' so ran the complaint of many a 1930s cinema reformer, 'in order to continue being flouted and run down as *Kintopp* by the audience. Just as film has had to learn much from the theatre in its development, so too must the cinema public learn much from theatre audiences.'[69]

But in spite of such pleas, there was little appetite in the Propaganda Ministry to make the cinema more like the classical theatre. Quite the opposite: popular appeal and user-friendliness remained paramount. The primary aim was to make the cinema attractive for the masses, even if this entailed a dilution of its direct political utility and a continuing degree of suspicion among cultural elites. For a medium that was held in such high esteem by a movement ostensibly bent on a national cultural revolution, film under the Nazis was in fact remarkably un-revolutionary. Conventional entertainment genres and a thoroughly populist commercial orientation remained the bedrock of the Third Reich's cinema culture. But given that the primary aim was to create a more socially inclusive culture for the 'national community' there was in fact little need for radical intervention, considering the direction things were moving. Although cinema audiences were still shaped by age, class, education, and income, the changes of the 1930s nonetheless meant that they shared more in common than ever before.

BETWEEN INSTRUMENTALIZATION AND AMERICANIZATION: PRESS AND ADVERTISING

Compared to the populist impetus of the cinema, the press in Nazi Germany is generally regarded as a more crude purveyor of political propaganda. After all, the stated aim of press officials was to use the print media as a means of political leadership. 'Why do we create newspapers?', asked Dietrich's assistant Helmut Sündermann. 'Above all to achieve political aims! Political utility is the sole, decisive criterion, behind which all other arguments recede.'[70] But as others were quick to retort, in order to have any political utility a newspaper or magazine still

[68] 'Die noch immer nicht ins Filmtheater gehen', 2.
[69] R. Bergenau, 'Das Publikum will erzogen werden—es werde erzogen!', *FK* (3 Sept. 1938), 7.
[70] Sündermann in *ZV* (15 July 1939), quoted from Wulf, *Presse*, 70.

had to be attractive enough for people to buy it. As one of the many press studies of the 1930s concluded, newspaper editors must ultimately 'produce a paper that fulfils its aim—to be read—by making its contents palatable to readers. This means that the reader is in all events, either consciously or unconsciously, the decisive factor in the production of a newspaper.'[71]

At first glance these divergent statements read like a rehearsal of the decades-old clash between the 'conviction' and 'commercial' press. Certainly, the tension between politics and entertainment was anything but new. Yet in the 1930s their relationship was significantly altered by the totalitarian ambitions of the regime. If the Weimar years witnessed a creeping overlap between the commercial and political press, the new structures of Nazi political control rendered the distinction essentially meaningless. Henceforth the entire press was to perform a 'political' function, which naturally required meeting readers' tastes and expectations.

The difficulty lay in striking the right balance, and the challenge this posed looked quite different from paper to paper. For the big commercial dailies it was largely a matter of adapting their tried-and-tested formulas to the new political constraints. The more 'unpolitical' or conservative the periodical, the easier this would be. Although the established dailies lost a sizeable share of their market to National Socialist papers in 1933–4, most were able to weather the storm and recover or even expand their readerships over the following years. The overriding challenge for Nazi papers was thus somewhat different: namely, to make themselves attractive over the long term. Officials in the Office for the NSDAP Press therefore continually suggested improvements to the format and presentation of party periodicals. The remedies they prescribed differed little from those with which other political parties had tried to improve their publicist fortunes in the 1920s.

First on the list was the importance of local news and advertisements. The aforementioned media survey in the Saxon village of Thürungen found that among regular newspaper readers (over three-quarters of the village population, most of whom subscribed to the local *Sangerhäuser Zeitung*) the local sections and advertisements were read by nearly everyone. By comparison, under half read the political section, and only one-tenth browsed the economics pages. Too much focus on politics had long been recognized as detrimental to sales, and it is likely that the Nazis' elimination of dissent made it even less interesting to the average reader than before. This led some observers to conclude that the local section was actually the most important vehicle of state propaganda, for 'if propaganda is confined to the political section of the paper there is a danger that a large portion of the populace will know nothing about it'.[72] Editors were thus encouraged to enliven their local sections by borrowing from the reportage style

---

[71] Klutentreter, *Presse*, 30.
[72] Schmidt, *Publizistik*, 65, 89–90. Rural subscription rates were significantly lower in many villages: cf. Josef Müller, *Ein deutsches Bauerndorf im Umbruch der Zeit* (Würzburg, 1939), 118–19.

of the 1920s, though without the alleged superficiality of the celebrated 'racing reporter' of the Weimar era, Egon Erwin Kisch. Nazi officials also pushed for an expansion of local news in the party press, which indeed grew in relation to other sections after 1933.[73]

A broad variety of stories and an entertaining mode of presentation also remained a must for commercial success, for reading habits still differed significantly according to age, education, and especially gender. Although the elimination of the left-wing press meant that readerships were less divided along class lines than in the 1920s, the scant evidence available for the mid–1930s suggests that little else had changed over the previous decade. Sport was still read predominately by the young, and men were still far more likely than women to read the political and economic sections. Although most female readers apparently browsed the political headlines (not articles), their attention was reportedly focused on local news and ads, household tips, and to a lesser extent the cultural sections and serialized novels. Practicality, user-friendliness, and time economy were considered the key to appealing to women; a brief and simple listing of upcoming local events was a necessity for any paper.[74] Topical breadth was more important than ever, given the distinct lack of political diversity. 'The German press and its creators have been accused of uniformity, tedium, even dullness,' noted one commentator in 1936, 'and not only by its enemies abroad, but also by foes and even friends within Germany.'[75] The best antidote was to print a variety of stories that were easy to read, presumed no prior knowledge, transported readers across their daily horizons, and fired their imaginations. According to the Thüringen study, reports of criminal activity, accidents, and natural catastrophes were the most popular of all, especially among school-age readers, over three-quarters of whom regularly read the entertainment section.[76] 'Sensation', though often decried as the dishonest gimmickry of the Weimar era, was still an integral part of the press in the Third Reich. Despite concerns that overcooked stories and screaming headlines could undermine the credibility (and therefore political utility) of newspapers, they were generally tolerated so long as the content was not subversive. 'Sensationalism has its value and its limits', proclaimed the leading publishers' journal in 1936. 'Dispense with sensation in the daily press? We cannot if we want to fulfil our current tasks.'[77]

Apart from the obvious constraints on political coverage, the overall presentation and content of the daily press changed little after the Nazi seizure of power. And such changes as did occur largely represented the continuation of longer-term trends, above all the search for more entertaining formats and the

---

[73] F. Rauch, 'Soll der Reporter "rasen"?', *ZV* (26 Oct. 1935), 735–6; 'Der Wert eines guten Heimatteils', *ZV* (13 June 1936), 1; Meier, *Zwischen*, 287.
[74] S. Teubner, 'Die Zeitungsleserin hat das Wort!', *ZV* (15 Feb. 1936), 104–5.
[75] 'Ist die deutsche Presse volkstümlich?', *ZV* (14 Nov. 1936), 705.
[76] Schmidt, *Publizistik*, 70–1.
[77] F. Hirschner, 'Die Sensation hat ihren Wert und ihre Grenzen', *ZV* (18 Jan 1936), 41.

swelling interest in photographic illustration, for which the American press still provided much of the inspiration.[78] Nazi officials were indeed especially keen to expand the use of photography in newspapers as a remedy against the scepticism generated by political censorship. By supposedly only showing what was 'really there', photographs were, it was thought, uniquely capable of overcoming critical reservations.[79]

Illustrated magazines remained the primary medium of photographic journalism. Here too, the continuities greatly outweighed the changes after 1933—perhaps unsurprising given the leading international position of German photojournalism at the time.[80] Admittedly, the most prominent NS weeklies, the *Illustrierter Beobachter* and *NS-Frauenwarte*, did make a significant impact after early 1933. But one certainly cannot speak of a thorough Nazification of the illustrated periodical market. Indeed, as the Reich Association of German Magazine Publishers complained in 1935, 'unfortunately we can still find entertainment magazines or at least advertisements within them that can only be appealing to those circles of people who, due to racial reasons or a lack of taste, have learned nothing from the new spirit of the age'.[81] Two years later the situation was essentially unchanged: countless women's and fashion magazines still clung to the habit of portraying women as 'flappers and creatures of luxury . . . who could hardly differ more from the hard-working, loveable, and reliable women we know as wives, mothers and colleagues'. The problem in a nutshell was that many magazines 'still look like they could have looked ten or twenty years ago'.[82]

The reason for this was quite simple: the vast majority of illustrated magazines were, regardless of the political affiliations of their publishers, wholly non-partisan in character before 1933, and could by and large stay that way. While the tiny handful of consciously political magazines (such as the *Arbeiter-Illustrierte-Zeitung*) were immediately banned in early 1933, most were able to continue in much the same vein as before. In the realm of women's magazines, Ullstein's *Die Dame* and *Blatt der Hausfrau* stuck very much with their old formulas, despite the forced buy-out of the publisher in early 1934: the former chic, cosmopolitan, and style-conscious, the latter carrying household tips, fashion, crafts, and puzzles in its intimate 'woman to woman' tone. Most of the other women's weeklies also managed to survive with little alteration. Despite the rapid growth of the *NS-Frauenwarte*, which became the single largest women's magazine with a

---

[78] As examples: *ZV* (18 Apr. 1936), 245; (19 May 1936), 295; (18 July 1936), 438; (26 Sept. 1936), 598. On 'Americanization' generally: P. Gassert, *Amerika im Dritten Reich* (Stuttgart, 1997); de Grazia, *Irresistible*.

[79] W. Stiewe, *Das Pressephoto als publizistisches Mittel* (Leipzig, 1936), 126; 'Und Bilder helfen mit', *ZV* (2 Apr. 1938), 209; 'Das Bild setzt sich durch', *ZV* (19 May 1936), 295.

[80] Knoch, 'Living Pictures', 226–30.

[81] A. Hoffmann, 'Zeitschrift und Volk' (1935), quoted from Wulf, *Presse*, 211.

[82] *Der Zeitschriften-Verleger* (21 Apr. 1937), quoted from Frei, Schmitz, *Journalismus*, 71.

circulation of 1.4 million by 1939, the 'unpolitical' women's magazines still accounted for the bulk of overall circulation.[83]

Much the same could be said of the general illustrated weeklies such as the *Hamburger Illustrierte, Kölnische Illustrierte Zeitung, Münchner Illustrierte Presse,* and the market-leading *BIZ.* For the *BIZ,* which had always kept a safe distance from political partisanship, the upheavals of 1933 seemed to make no visible difference at all. The huge personnel turnover at Ullstein made no difference to its established formula of eye-catching photos and illustrations that spoke for themselves with little explanatory text. In terms of subject-matter, the *BIZ* continued to serve up the same diet of celebrity portraits, fashion, high society, royals, serialized novels, recent inventions, natural catastrophes, and all manner of human-interest stories that had packed its pages for decades. Measured against the *Illustrierter Beobachter,* which specialized in the visual portrayal of the Führer and Nazi movement, the *BIZ* was noticeably more sober and tended to depict prominent figures in a personal rather than iconic manner, for instance Hitler walking his dog in the Alps, or Goebbels on holiday with his children.[84] Tellingly, the intense anti-Semitic newspaper campaign in the wake of the 'Night of Broken Glass' in November 1938 was conspicuously muted in the *BIZ,* as in the bulk of general-interest magazines. This is not to say that the big illustrated weeklies were wholly impervious to the changed political context. Like the *Illustrierter Beobachter,* the *BIZ* also showed a highly sanitized version of the early concentration camps (emphasizing their supposedly 'correctional' attributes), and enthusiastically hailed the 'unification' of Germany amidst the foreign-policy triumphs of 1938.[85] The point is rather that, like the popular cinema, their political utility lay not in shouting the virtues of a Nazi-led Germany from the rooftops but in conveying a reassuring sense of cosmopolitanism and social harmony by means of visual pleasure, thus teaching readers to look away from the brutality of the regime.[86]

In the meantime, the advertisements that provided much of their revenue were also shaped by stubborn continuities stretching across the political caesura of 1933. Given the inextricable links between the publishing and advertising industries, the persistence of previous marketing trends will by now come as little surprise. Somewhat more surprising is the fact that a number of these trends actually *accelerated* during the Nazi years, above all the adoption of advertising methods from the United States.

[83] Frei, Schmitz, *Journalismus,* 72. For magazine circulation, see K. C. Führer, 'Praktischer Nutzen und Propaganda. Populäre Zeitschriften im nationalsozialistischen Deutschland 1933–1939', unpubl. ms, 2007.
[84] Frei, Schmitz, *Journalismus,* 75–6; Herz, *Hoffmann,* 242–59.
[85] Gellately, *Backing Hitler,* 55–6; Führer, 'Praktischer Nutzen', 25–8.
[86] R. Sachsse, *Die Erziehung zum Wegsehen* (Dresden, 2003); Frei, Schmitz, *Journalismus,* 77–8; Knoch, 'Living Pictures', 229–30.

In many respects the pre-war years of the Third Reich witnessed the most rapid and far-reaching 'Americanization' of the German advertising scene to date.[87] This was true not least of the new regulatory framework. The Nazi government wasted little time in introducing a raft of new measures geared to 'clean up' and modernize the advertising industry, starting with the Law on Commercial Advertisement in September 1933 and the creation of a central Advertising Council (Werberat der deutschen Wirtschaft) the following month.[88] As with government press controls more generally, these measures were motivated by a mixture of commercial considerations (the regulation of competition) and political interests (ensuring the credibility and thus efficacy of advertising as a tool for steering consumption). But unlike the harsh treatment meted out to the left-wing press, they involved almost no coercion. Apart from the usual institutional coordination into the Reich Association of German Advertisers, the reforms were indeed applauded both within and beyond the profession. The establishment of reliable circulation figures and precise size and format standards fulfilled a long-standing professional demand for an American-style audit bureau. The new regulations against misleading advertisements also mirrored the 'Truth in Advertising' campaign with which reformers in the United States had previously sought to raise industry standards and credibility. American techniques of market research also became mainstream after 1933, as evidenced in the creation of the Institute for Market Research, Society for Consumer Research, and Institute for Economic Research. That said, some of the Nazis' advertising reforms were anything but forward-looking. The discrimination against foreign competition and the clear distinction between advertising consultants (*Werbeberater*) and brokers (*Werbevermittler*) meant that the American full-service agency model never had a chance to develop in Germany, unlike the rest of Europe. Certain new 1930s genres like the comic strip ad also remained marginal, and there was a complete ban on radio advertising after December 1935. Yet, from the standpoint of practitioners, the reforms represented on balance a salutary modernization of professional structures. Even the Americans thought so: in 1938 a McCann executive remarked that it was the Nazis who had at last restructured the German advertising trade along American lines.[89]

In stylistic terms too, the 1930s witnessed the breakthrough of the quintessentially 'American-style' editorializing ad that had first taken root in Germany a decade earlier (see Chapter 7). There were a number of reasons for this. At the most basic level, technical advances in photography and colour printing significantly enhanced the visual appearance and cost-effectiveness of text-based ads. In addition, the sheer length of exposure to American marketing styles was reinforced through the first-hand experience of German advertisers who had

---

[87] For a more detailed discussion on which the following is based: C. Ross, 'Visions of Prosperity', in Swett, Wiesen, and Zatlin (eds.), *Selling*, 52–77.

[88] M. Rücker, *Wirtschaftswerbung unter dem Nationalsozialismus* (Frankfurt a. M., 2000), 175–241.

[89] de Grazia, 'Arts', 249–50, 257; Reinhardt, *Reklame*, 128; Berghoff, 'Reklame', 96.

worked in the branch offices of US agencies during the late 1920s and early 1930s. By this time there was also a recognition that the future of marketing lay in selling branded products to an increasingly national and socially diverse market, as had already emerged in the United States. It thus no longer made sense to focus advertising budgets on urban centres, to the exclusion of millions of new consumers in the small towns and countryside. Nor would merely displaying the product and its name, however eye-catching the imagery, suffice to persuade such first-generation consumers to buy unfamiliar goods. The traditional poster-style advertisement, with its limited spatial reach and concern for aesthetic effect rather than 'reason why' explanation, was singularly unsuited to this task. By contrast, American-style 'salesmanship in print' was specifically designed to awaken new expectations among a far-flung market of first-generation consumers. It was also becoming far easier to deploy, now that the new regulatory regime had removed many of the previous obstacles. Solid circulation figures and the standardization of formats greatly enhanced the transparency and profitability of print advertising, and new regulations requiring written authorization to quote or cite public personalities also removed some of the suspicion and odium attached to the much-abused genre of testimonial ads. These measures, in conjunction with a new set of restrictions on postering, contributed to the far-reaching eclipse of the poster by newspaper advertisements over the course of the 1930s (though the poster remained a standby for political propaganda).[90]

Practical issues aside, the most intriguing aspect of the expansion of American-style marketing techniques in the mid–1930s was their affinity with many of the Nazis' own ideas about advertising. This kinship was not—to put it mildly—immediately apparent in 1933. On the contrary, the newly coordinated advertising organizations initially went out of their way to denounce the 'vacuous imitation of foreign advertising that does not correspond to the German character' and to declare an end to 'the era of uncritical adulation of American "models"'.[91] There was a sudden chorus of calls to replace foreign methods with a truly 'German' form of advertising, whatever that meant. Among the plethora of gripes and suggestions were the replacement of the seductive vamp with the wholesome blond-braided peasant girl and Latin script with Gothic *Fraktur*.[92] But such chauvinistic bluster had little impact on mainstream advertising, and it certainly did not stop Germans from studying and increasingly adopting American advertising methods.[93]

---

[90] Reinhardt, *Reklame*, 188–9, 201, 256–7; de Grazia, 'Arts', 257.

[91] 'Deutsche Werbung für deutsche Arbeit!', *SR* 17 (1933), 145; W. Lüders, 'Sünde wider die Natur!', *SR* 17 (1933), 194.

[92] Ibid.; also 'Deutsche Werbung', *DR* 26 (Apr. 1933), 235; H. Wolf, 'Deutsche Werbung', *DW* 27 (Jan. 1934), 11; W. Brauns, 'Wie soll die deutsche Werbung aussehen?', *DW* 27 (May 1934), 284–5.

[93] See 'Originelle Muster amerikanischer Werbung', *DW* 27 (1934), 628–9; O. v. Halem, 'Amerikanische Werbung', *SR* 18 (1934), 258–60.

Despite the clear prioritization of rearmament over living standards, the Fordist vision of a mass consumer society plainly resonated with National Socialist dreams of social integration and material entitlement for all 'national comrades'. As the journal *Die Reklame* put it in July 1933: 'It is precisely the new Volksgemeinschaft . . . which, by bridging class differences and therefore also distinctions of taste, works towards a grand appreciation of authenticity, beauty, and propriety that is held in common by all Germans.'[94] Although this consumer Volksgemeinschaft remained a mirage, the myth of a community of interests between producers and consumers nonetheless shaped perceptions about the very nature and function of advertising, and in the process encouraged a more 'American' look and feel to press advertisements. The aim was no longer to flog a product regardless of the wider implications. While there was nothing wrong with increasing sales per se, this was justified only insofar as it brought a real benefit to consumers and served the higher aim of strengthening the German economy. The cynical manipulation of the consumer was to have no place in the 'national community'. Henceforth the emphasis was to be placed on factual persuasion and consumer wishes, the desire for beauty, health, and social acceptance.[95] Accordingly, the ideal role of advertisers was not merely to sell goods on behalf of producers, but to act as an honest broker and consumer educator. In the words of Ludwig Erhard, assistant at the Society for Consumer Research and future West German chancellor, the point of advertising was 'to lead, not mislead' consumers.[96]

This shift in the understanding of advertising necessarily entailed the adoption of new methods. As *Die Reklame* programmatically put it, 'the millions that are spent in Germany on advertisements that merely scream a name into the world could all be spent much more successfully on a truly matter-of-fact method that awakens new consumer needs'.[97] What this meant more concretely was spelled out in 1934 in a series of articles by the prominent advertiser Hanns Kropff, which read as nothing less than a full-blown argument for imitating American practices, repeatedly juxtaposing a poorly conceived German announcement against a 'persuasive' editorializing ad drawn from an American periodical.[98] Though based on fundamentally different ideological premises, the National Socialist conception of good marketing practice and the American 'capitalist realist' style displayed a number of unmistakeable parallels. Apart from the pious calls for responsibility towards both consumer and producer, the overall recommendations could just

[94] E. Endres, 'Die neue Gesinnung in der Werbung', *DR* 26 (1933), 382.
[95] Influential along these lines was H. Kropff, *Psychologie in der Reklame als Hilfe zur Bestgestaltung des Entwurfs* (Stuttgart, 1934).
[96] Quoted from S. Schwarzkopf, 'Kontrolle statt Rausch?', in A. von Klimo and M. Rolf (eds.), *Rausch und Diktatur* (Frankfurt a. M., 2006), 204.
[97] 'Setzt sich eine neue Werbeauffassung durch?', *DR* 27 (1934), 296.
[98] H. Kropff, 'Suggestion, Glaube und Überzeugung in der Reklame', *SR* 18 (1934), 227–30, 263–6, 302–4, 355–7, 393–5.

Fig. 13. The adoption of 'reason why' advertising: comparison of two Kaloderma soap ads from *Die Woche*. Above: vol. 28(1926). Below: vol. 38(1936). Note the expanded use of text, the employment of scientific data and the prescription-like recommendation. By permission of Berlin Cosmetics GmbH and Henkel KGaA.

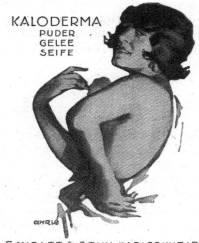

KALODERMA
PUDER
GELEE
SEIFE

F. WOLFF & SOHN KARLSRUHE i.B

Kaloderma-Seife eine hochwertige Toilette-Seife von angenehm erfrischender Parfümierung. Preis: Das Stück Mk. —.70, die Schachtel zu 3 Stück Mk. 2.—.

Kaloderma-Gelee zur Erhaltung einer jugendlich straffen u. gegen Witterungseinflüsse widerstandsfähigen Haut. Preis: Die Tube Mk. —.25, —.50 und 1.—.

Kaloderma-Reispuder schmiegt sich der Haut vollkommen an und verleiht ihr einen diskret matten Schimmer. Preis: Die Schachtel Mk. —.65 und 1.25.

Kaloderma-Talkpuder feinster antiseptischer Toilette-Puder in ovalflacher Metall-Streudose. Preis: Die Dose Mk. 1.—.

Machen Sie einmal folgenden Versuch: Waschen Sie morgens und abends Ihre Haut gründlich mit Kaloderma-Seife und warmem Wasser und spülen Sie mehrmals abwechselnd warm und kalt nach. Augenblicklich werden Sie die erfrischende Wirkung dieser einfachen Behandlung spüren. Setzen Sie sie consequent mehrere Wochen lang fort und beachten Sie die auffallende Verschönerung Ihrer Haut und Ihres Teints.

Rezept FÜR
EINE REINE UND ZARTE HAUT

Unzählige Frauen haben die verblüffende Wirkung einer Kaloderma-Kur von wenigen Wochen aus eigener Erfahrung erlebt. Fahler Teint und unreine Gesichtshaut haben ihre Ursache fast immer in dem allmählichen Verstopfen der Hautporen und der dadurch bedingten Behinderung der Hautatmung. Die auf physiologischer Basis zusammengestellte Kaloderma-Seife erwirkt eine gründliche und tiefgehende Reinigung dieser Hautporen. Ihr sahniger, milder Schaum belebt die Hautatmung und führt dem Gewebe die einzigartigen Kaloderma-Bestandteile zu, die Ihren Teint zart, rein und durchsichtig machen und die Ihrer Haut Transparenz und Frische geben.

KALODERMA
DIE *Seife* NACH DER IHRE HAUT VERLANGT
Stück RM —.55

F · WOLFF & SOHN · KARLSRUHE

as easily have originated from a leading firm on Madison Avenue: 'Do not just propagate the name, but also the product—do not merely place an ad for the producer, but also for the consumer—do not simply write, but also explain and convince.'[99] The American 'reason why' approach was not only more ideologically palatable than the manipulative impulse of the poster-style ad, it was also more effective at steering consumption in the interests of the national economy and integrating the masses into a new community of needs and goods. By the mid–1930s American-inspired 'salesmanship in print' had become an integral element of the consumer Volksgemeinschaft.

'JUST DON'T BE BORING': NAZI RADIO

Among all of the media at its disposal, the Nazi leadership pinned the greatest hopes on radio. Its novelty, centralized organizational structure, and unique capacity for simultaneous communication made it a 'means of leadership' (*Führungsmittel*) par excellence. The RMVP indeed regarded listening as a 'national duty', quite literally a prerequisite for participation in public life. The dream of Nazi programmers was to create a kind of Volksgemeinschaft on the airwaves, a national community of listeners united across time and space. Radio would help ensure that there could be, as Goebbels put it, 'no events of political and historic importance in the future in which the people do not take part'.[100] If making the wireless more affordable was the first step towards this goal, the second was ensuring that people would willingly listen to what was offered.

Tailoring the programme towards this end took some time, and it was not clear at first what course would be steered. Historians generally agree that there were several distinct phases to the development of radio under the Nazis, and that the first of these, roughly covering 1933, was decidedly ill-suited to increasing the number of listeners.[101] The initial tactic was to broadcast a blitz of propaganda. As the Reich broadcasting director Eugen Hadamovsky later recalled, 'our radio work began with a fantastic wave of political influence, agitation, and propaganda in every form. From 10 February to 4 March speeches by the Reich chancellor went out almost every evening on some or all German broadcasters.'[102] Although such zealous campaigning tailed off somewhat after the March elections, the surge of political broadcasts did not stop there. Over the following months there was an unremitting series of political programmes, stretching from the 'Day of Potsdam' on 21 March to the Harvest Festival in early October. Something

---

[99] 'Setzt sich eine neue Werbeauffassung durch?', 297.
[100] Heiber (ed.), *Goebbels-Reden*, 93.
[101] See Dussel, *Rundfunkgeschichte*, 91; Pohle, *Rundfunk*, 275–83; N. Dreschler, *Die Funktion der Musik im deutschen Rundfunk 1933–1945* (Pfaffenweiler, 1988), 34.
[102] From Dussel and Lersch (eds.), *Quellen*, 120.

of the flavour of such broadcasts can be deduced from the coverage of the 'Day of National Labour' on 1 May. Carefully choreographed as a means of charming industrial workers, the celebrations were intended to be an event that no one could miss. While crowds of SA men gathered before loudspeakers in squares all across Germany, radio owners were explicitly encouraged to place their sets in windows so that others could hear. What the millions of listeners were offered, however, was a relentless sequence of speeches and commentary devoid of musical interlude, apart from the songs chanted by thousands of marchers. After nearly twelve hours of such coverage the long-awaited climax finally came at 19:40, when Hitler spoke without interruption for nearly two hours, his speech capped off by fireworks, endless salutes to victory, and a performance of the national anthem.[103] To say the very least, such broadcasting indicates a distinct lack of imagination as to the unique potential of the radio as a conduit into the private sphere (Roosevelt's homey 'fireside chats' showed how it should be done), not to mention a blatant disregard for the interests of listeners. To make matters worse, such big events marked only the highlights of a steady stream of mundane political broadcasts, such as the daily 'National Hour' (*Stunde der Nation*) launched in April and the many irregular broadcasts by an army of lesser regime functionaries keen to have their voices heard.[104]

Predictably, such programming was not popular among listeners. As if long-winded political lectures were not wearisome enough, the changes they caused to the published programme only added to the irritation. Goebbels, for his part, was opposed to this approach from the beginning. As he explicitly told radio executives on 25 March: 'The primary rule is: just don't be boring. I prioritize this above *everything* else. Whatever you do, do not broadcast tedium, do not present the desired attitude on a silver platter, do not think that one can best serve the national government by playing thunderous military marches every evening. . . . Rather, you must help to cultivate a nationalistic art and culture that also genuinely matches the modern pace of life and modern sensibilities.'[105] Although it took some time to push this policy through, by the end of the year there was a dramatic decrease in the number of such overt political broadcasts.[106]

Yet the advocates of a more popular programme did not immediately have things all their way. Many leading Nazis were determined to prove their cultural credentials to the German Bildungsbürgertum and the rest of the world. Over spring and summer 1934 broadcasters launched a series of highbrow programmes, under the slogan 'radio as a cultural and artistic instrument', that recalled the most pedagogically minded efforts of their Weimar predecessors. In February

---

[103] I. Marßolek, ' "Aus dem Volke für das Volk" ', in Marßolek and v. Saldern (eds.), *Radiozeiten*, 122–8.

[104] Dussel, *Rundfunkgeschichte*, 92; Levi, *Music*, 132. On Roosevelt's 'fireside chats', L. W. Levine, *The People and the President* (Boston, 2002).

[105] Heiber (ed.), *Goebbels-Reden*, 94–5, emphasis in the original.

[106] Dröge and Müller, *Macht*, 296; Marßolek, 'Aus dem Volke', 128.

Fig. 14. Ensuring that no one misses out: passers-by listening to a public Hitler broadcast in front of a radio store, 1936. bpk Berlin. Photo: Josef Donderer.

a two-week-long Beethoven cycle celebrated the great composer for his clear and harmonious tones, which were portrayed as the antithesis of the degenerate anarchy pervading modern music. But since Beethoven was a less-than-convincing spiritual forebear of National Socialism, Nazi programmers subsequently aired a series of summer broadcasts on the far more plausible ancestors Richard Wagner and Houston Stewart Chamberlain. Comprising a mixture of music and lectures, this 'Wagner-Schiller-Chamberlain-Cycle' (Friedrich Schiller was included to lend credibility to the broadcasts, as it was the 175th anniversary of his birth) was deemed a great propaganda triumph.[107] The fact that a large number of foreign broadcasters transmitted the performances of Wagner's *Ring der Nibelungen* direct from Bayreuth was paraded as proof of international cooperation and Germany's continued cultural leadership. On the back of this success there followed a handful of similar broadcasts in 1935, most notably on the 250th anniversary of the births of Bach and Handel.[108]

[107] N. Martin, 'Images of Schiller in National Socialist Germany', in N. Martin (ed.), *Schiller: National Poet—Poet of Nations* (Amsterdam, 2006), 275–99.
[108] Pohle, *Rundfunk*, 280–1; Levi, *Music*, 133–5.

But in the meantime the misgivings about such programming continued to mount among radio functionaries. It was clear to all that even the most beloved Beethoven or Wagner pieces drew only a meagre audience. By January 1935 Hadamovsky openly announced that 'the relaxation of listeners through light-entertainment broadcasts in the most suitable time slots' was henceforth an 'essential basis of programming'.[109] This statement, backed by similar proclamations from the Propaganda Ministry, marked an important watershed. By legitimating 'light entertainment' as a key priority, and implying that it should be given pride of place in the broadcasting schedule, it represented an unambiguous shift from the understanding of radio as a 'cultural factor' towards a new emphasis on consumer wishes. Goebbels made the point eminently clear in 1936: 'Special emphasis should be placed on relaxation and entertainment, for the vast majority of radio listeners lead lives of unceasing toil and therefore have a right to genuine relaxation and recuperation in their few hours of leisure. In contrast, the small minority who want to subsist on Kant and Hegel are hardly of consequence.'[110]

This revaluation of entertainment was quickly translated into the radio programme. One indication was the sharp rise in music broadcasts, from 61.6 per cent of airtime in 1935 to 69.3 per cent only two years later. Another was the fact that it came largely at the expense of spoken broadcasts, especially lectures, whose gradual reduction since the mid–1920s was accelerated after 1935, tallying under 6 per cent by 1937.[111] Naturally, not all music on the radio was popular nor all spoken broadcasts rigidly elitist. Classical music still accounted for a sizeable, albeit shrinking, percentage of airtime, and some of the most popular shows of the 1930s consisted of a mixture of music and spoken word. But the scheduling of these broadcasts was another indication of the changes underway. Whereas programmers had hitherto reserved the key slot of 20:00–22:00 for demanding material, after the mid–1930s light entertainment increasingly displaced 'opus music' during prime time. In order to dispel any doubts about such programming heresy, in March 1936 Hadamovsky issued a clear directive that 'the entertainment previously transmitted from 18:00 to 19:45 is to be transferred to the period from 20:10 to 22:00. Besides purely entertaining concerts, only variety shows and dance music should occupy the slot from 20:10 to 22:00.'[112] Although the regional broadcasters occasionally ignored this injunction, the overall shift of emphasis was cemented by the reorganization of the Reich Broadcasting Company management in early 1937, which created a more hierarchical structure under the new position of Reichsintendant, or director-general. As Heinrich Glasmeier, the first director-general, made clear to the regional executives now under his direct supervision: 'In the future the programmes of the regional broadcasters will be

[109] Quoted from Dussel and Lersch (eds), *Quellen*, 131–3.   [110] Ibid. 136.
[111] Münkel, 'Produktionssphäre', 101; Dussel, *Rundfunkgeschichte*, 94.
[112] Dussel, 'Deutsches Radio', 125–6.

relaxed to the greatest possible extent and will renounce all forms of intellectual arrogance.'[113]

In many respects this populist reorientation of German broadcasting was nothing more than a practical acceptance of reality. It was obvious that the best way to expand the audience was to make the programme more attractive to the average time-strapped 'incidental listener'. Instead of wilfully imagining that audiences listened in rapt concentration to carefully selected portions of the programme, the Nazis accepted that most people were simply in search of a little relaxation and wanted to know when they could expect it, preferably between 20:00 and 22:00. This acknowledgment not only encouraged a 'lighter' programme but also helped to establish the principle of the regular broadcast slot. Transmitting the same programme at the same time every day allowed listeners to dispense with prior consultation of a guide or newspaper, and had the added benefit of generating a strong sense of familiarity, even intimacy, between radio and listeners by ensuring that it consistently fulfilled their expectations. The adherence to a regular broadcast slot both capitalized on and further reinforced the growing tendency in the 1930s to plan one's leisure time around favourite radio programmes.[114] Such considerations were of central importance for Nazi broadcasting officials, for once again the underlying goal was to 'bind' listeners to the radio and thereby make them more receptive to political messages. As one contemporary put it, the fundamental idea was that 'political broadcasts, always accounting for only a small portion of broadcasting time, first acquire their value through the existence of entertaining broadcasts that lead listeners to the receiver'.[115]

Even so, the main beneficiary of the programme reforms was undoubtedly popular music. Although most officials favoured folk tunes and operetta melodies as 'edifying' forms of entertainment, commercially oriented hit songs and dance music also became more prominent than before. It is worth highlighting the double paradox here, for it boiled down to filling the programme with the very music that the Nazis had previously attacked as rootless, anonymous 'asphalt culture', and that the supposedly 'liberal' Weimar programmers had assiduously kept off the airwaves in favour of the classics and the promotion of Volk and Heimat culture. At any rate, the enhanced status of modern hits and dance music marked a clear victory of pragmatism over ideology, as well as a shift in the relationship between radio and recorded sound. Shortly after the programme alterations were introduced, record companies discerned a marked increase in demand for 'good music' recordings (by which they meant classical, opera, operetta, and folk music). Whereas the previous sales ratio between hits and 'good music' was around 9 : 1, by autumn 1936 it had reportedly dropped to around 4 : 1 and continued to fall throughout the following years. By the middle

---

[113] Speech of May 1937, quoted from Pohle, *Rundfunk*, 282.
[114] G. Eckert, *Der Rundfunk als Führungsmittel*, (Berlin, 1941), 161.   [115] Ibid. 179.

of 1939 the proportion of 'good' to 'hit' record sales had nearly levelled out at 40 : 60, a fourfold increase from the 10 per cent share it had possessed only three years earlier.[116] Although these figures may be partly attributable to the fuzzy boundaries between the categories, it nonetheless seems clear that the new radio programme had a sizeable impact on record sales and gramophone use.

As one might expect, the promotion of popular music from the late-evening slots to prime time was not greeted with universal enthusiasm. For conservatives such as Reich Music Chamber president Peter Raabe, the search for truly 'German music' meant above all a turn towards the classics. Like the majority of tradition-minded musicologists, he was dismayed by the aura of legitimacy such changes bestowed to music he regarded as essentially worthless. Yet for most Nazi cultural officials, the bulk of whom were a generation younger than Raabe, the idea that radio should chiefly serve the interests of cultural elites was hopelessly out of date. Indeed, Goebbels—a failed writer himself—had little patience for the self-importance of elite artists. On one occasion he reportedly sneered to the composer Richard Strauss that 'Lehar [Franz Lehar, a popular operetta composer] has the masses, not you! When will you finally stop with this prattle about the importance of serious music!' He also seemed relatively unconcerned when the renowned conductor Wilhelm Furtwängler resigned from his post at the Berlin Philharmonic: 'What does this Furtwängler want with his pitiful 2,000 listeners in the Philharmonic? What we need are the millions, and we have them with the radio.'[117]

Yet if the Nazis insisted on the value of popular music in general, they were less sure when it came to modern dance music, especially jazz.[118] Despite being tamed down by European bands, jazz of all shades had long been attacked by traditionalists and nationalists as a repulsive outgrowth of cultural degeneration. Before 1933 the Nazi Combat League for German Culture numbered among its most vociferous critics, and shortly after Wilhelm Frick became education minister in Thuringia in 1930 he banned the public performance of jazz outright. As it happened, however, the Nazi takeover by no means spelled the end of jazz in Germany. As one contemporary remarked in 1937, the visitor to many a dance hall still 'cannot avoid the feeling that one is in America in the year 1930! The band reels off one foreign dance tune after another, and it never stops!'[119] In the absence of laws specifically banning such music, officials were often powerless to halt live performances. The radio was a different matter. In October 1935 Hadamovsky tried to clarify the situation by issuing a 'definitive prohibition of negro-jazz for the entire German broadcasting system'.[120] But in the event

[116] 'Schlagerdämmerung?', *PRZ* 37 (15 Oct. 1936), 347–9; 'Schlager und "gute" Musik', *RH* 16 (24 May 1939), 428–9.

[117] Quotes from H.-J. Koch, *Das Wunschkonzert im NS-Rundfunk* (Cologne, 2003), 83, 101–2.

[118] Generally, Kater, *Different*; B. Polster (ed.), *'Swing Heil'* (Berlin, 1989).

[119] Quoted from Bollenbeck, *Tradition*, 336.

[120] Reprinted in Dussel and Lersch (eds.), *Quellen*, 134–5.

this raised more questions than answers. Where should programmers draw the line between acceptable dance music and frivolous 'Niggerei'? And given the emphasis on satisfying popular tastes, what could replace the music deemed unfit to broadcast?[121]

As for the first question, the newly established 'Inspection Committee for German Dance Music' could only fumble for answers. The ill-advised attempt to 'educate' listeners by airing a series of anti-jazz programmes (entitled 'From the Cakewalk to Hot') was a spectacular own goal; if anything they generated more interest than aversion, at least among the young.[122] The solution to the second problem was similarly inept. In order to encourage native dance music that could replace 'negro jazz,' officials organized a national dance-band contest that was partially broadcast on the radio. After multiple rounds of competition the contest unearthed precious little talent, and listeners were less than enthusiastic. Ultimately the advocates of 'German dance music' were fighting an uphill battle, given the continued availability of American-style jazz in dance locales, record catalogues, and the cinemas, where audiences could hear catchy Cole Porter tunes in the hit film *Broadway Melody of 1936* and Louis Armstrong singing in the 1937 musical *Swing High, Swing Low*.[123]

But despite the flop with 'German jazz', the new programme was largely popular with audiences—and with radio retailers.[124] It seems reasonable to assume that it aided the expansion of the listening public, which more than doubled from 4.5 million registered sets in 1933 to 9.6 million in 1938. Yet it is important to recognize that even at the end of the 1930s the radio was still far from an indispensable element of everyday life. As late as 1938 there were still more German households without a radio than with one.[125] Certainly the audience had widened since the 1920s, but its social profile was still disproportionately middle class and urban. Survey results from the mid-1930s show that civil servants were nearly four times more likely to listen to the radio than manual workers, and white-collar workers nearly twice as likely. Radio ownership was also 2.5 times higher in cities with a population of over 100,000 than in rural areas. The situation in the village of Sulzthal in Mainfranken, where only thirty of 176 households had a radio in the later 1930s—with none at all among 'purely peasant families'—was not uncommon. Most of this discrepancy was still attributable to uneven purchasing power, for the costs of even the simplest Volksempfänger bought on instalment still amounted to nearly RM 10 per month including the licence fee, a sum that stretched the means of many low-income groups.[126] Indeed, the same applied to working-class households,

---

[121] See H. Gerigk, 'Was ist mit der Jazzmusik?', *Die Musik*, 30 (July 1938), 686.

[122] Polster (ed.), *'Swing Heil'*, 25.   [123] Kater, *Different*, 52–6; Wicke, *Mozart*, 170.

[124] 'Programmwandel im deutschen Rundfunk', *RH* 14 (7 July 1937), 440.

[125] Figures from *Rundfunkarchiv*, 14 (Oct. 1941), 413.

[126] Müller, *Bauerndorf*, 121; Eckert, *Rundfunk*, 207–12; Schmidt, 'Radioaneignung', 262–3, 266–7; R. Weisflog, 'Rundfunk und Einkommen', *RH* 16 (30 Aug. 1939), 863–6.

whose narrow entertainment budgets largely explain why listening rates at the end of the 1930s were still far lower in some cities than others, especially the industrial hubs of the Ruhr and Upper Silesia. There were similar disparities between different rural areas, with the relatively cash-poor and sparsely populated regions of East Prussia, Silesia, Bavaria, and Austria still registering the lowest listening rates.[127]

Such social and economic divisions were also clearly visible *within* the audience. According to a 1939 survey, there were still vast discrepancies between working-class and middle-class listening preferences, particularly with regard to music. Symphony concerts, for example, were listened to by 40.6 per cent of professionals but only 1.8 per cent of manual labourers; radio lectures by 34.8 per cent and 11.9 per cent, respectively. By contrast, traditional dance music was extremely popular among industrial workers (93.1 per cent) and farmers (90.4 per cent), but only moderately so among professionals (46.4 per cent). These class and educational divides were further overlaid by differences of age and gender, especially when it came to sport and dance music. The average sport listener was, unsurprisingly, a young male: men under 20 years of age listened twice as much as men over 55, and men of all ages roughly twice as much as women. In the case of dance music, the gender preference was reversed and the generation difference greatly magnified: it was 50 per cent more popular among women than men (though roughly equal among the younger generation), and almost six times more popular among women under 20 than over 55.[128] One should take care not to overemphasize the differences, for several elements of the programme were popular among men and women of all ages and social groups: radio plays were listened to by roughly half of respondents in all categories, and operettas by just under a third. Yet by and large the radio audience was still deeply divided, and was in all events a far cry from the unified listening public envisaged by broadcasting officials.

Thus the challenge was not merely to appeal to the German 'national public' but indeed to create it in the first place, at least for short periods of time. The first attempts to do so came with the aforementioned series of political broadcasts in 1933, which, for all their shortcomings, achieved an unusually high listening quota. Live broadcasts of the Olympic Games in 1936 were more successful still, and contemporaries estimated that some of Hitler's speeches were heard by the vast majority of the adult population, thanks to the use of public loudspeakers.[129] On these occasions Nazi programmers probably achieved some semblance of the radio Volksgemeinschaft to which they aspired, not only in the size of the audience but also in generating a sense of the individual listener being a 'part of a larger whole, of the unity of the nation'.[130] But such instances remained few and

---

[127] See *Rundfunkarchiv*, 14 (Oct. 1941), 416–17.
[128] Eckert, *Rundfunk*, 195, 197, 198, 201–4.
[129] Ibid. 182; Marßolek, 'Aus dem Volke', 133–4. [130] Eckert, *Rundfunk*, 245.

far between, and their exceptional nature could not, by definition, be replicated on a weekly basis. It is also highly questionable how closely people actually listened to the long-winded political expositions that usually characterized such broadcasts, however well suited they were for invoking the existence of a 'national community' of listeners.

The most promising opportunity for creating a regular national public was clearly the prime-time slot of 20:00–22:00, when around 80 per cent of listeners in the 1930s had their sets switched on.[131] But the main problem was how to please the wide range of tastes we have just encountered. One possible solution was to broadcast a wide variety of material that could offer something for everyone, though the disadvantage of such a grab-bag programme was that it risked satisfying no one. So instead of catering to diversity, the more promising approach lay in devising new forms of commonality, the most successful of which was the *Bunte Stunde* or variety show, which became a staple feature of the radio programme after the overhaul of 1934/5.

As with most successful entertainment genres, these highly popular shows were based on a mixture of tradition and innovation. Their structure essentially followed the traditional Varieté format of a series of different numbers introduced by a moderator who held the programme together with a thin leitmotif. They also borrowed from the more recent innovations of Weimar reformers, whose interest in the development of a popular radio art had already led to the first such programmes (see Chapter 3). The succession of music and short comic sketches usually revolved around the conventional themes of private life, from leisure activities and holidays to gender relations and family tribulations. Although this easily allowed for a sprinkling of political commentary, the shows largely refrained from it, especially after Goebbels declared all references to politics, religion, and state authorities out of bounds in 1937.[132] After all, the aim was relaxation not agitation. And it worked. According to survey results from 1939, variety shows were by far the most popular element of the entire radio programme. They were listened to by no fewer than 87 per cent of all respondents, regardless of age or gender. They even managed, more than any other segment of the programme, to bridge the divides of class and education. Although their popularity was lowest among the well educated, they were still listened to by 64 per cent of professionals and 72 per cent of intellectuals—more than listened to lectures, operas, symphonies, or chamber music.[133]

A handful of regular variety shows achieved special notoriety. Several target broadcasts aimed specifically at housewives (such as *Guten Morgen, liebe Hörer* and *Ständchen für die Hausfrau*) were perennial favourites. More successful still were the evening programmes geared for a general audience, especially

131 Schmidt, 'Radioaneignung', 340.
132 M. Pater, 'Rundfunkangebote', in Marßolek and v. Saldern (eds.), *Zuhören*, 212–15.
133 Eckert, *Rundfunk*, 195–204.

the *Blauer Montag* show launched from Breslau in late 1935 and broadcast every Monday from 20:10 to 22:00. Most popular of all, however, was *Der frohe Samstagnachmittag*, the Saturday afternoon show from Cologne. Broadcast nearly every week from the end of 1934 to 1939, this programme was one of the first 'street sweepers' in the history of the German media. After its launch in the Rhineland it was quickly picked up by the other broadcasters and transmitted across the entire Reich every Saturday from 16:00 to 18:00, the traditional time for coffee and cake and the single best slot of the week. The anchor of the programme was a trio of characters called the 'three jolly bachelors', Hans, Rudi, and Karl, who embodied the stereotypical characteristics of their different regional backgrounds. The trio functioned as both performers and moderators, introducing the different numbers and interspersing them with their own comic sketches. Invited guests provided the week-to-week variety, and the music consisted entirely of cheery folk tunes, marches, and the like. Each show was capped off, in true Varieté tradition, with a 'big number': the 'magic lantern' that dredged up a new curiosity every week.[134]

As a regular and highly popular series, *Der frohe Samstagnachmittag* embodied much of what Nazi radio officials sought to achieve. It was, first of all, pure entertainment, and moreover entertainment in which listeners could take part by singing along or laughing with the studio audience. In addition, its serialization generated a sense of consistency and familiarity that enabled it, unlike the many one-off entertainment shows, to become more than the sum of its disparate parts. The same format and characters broadcast at the same time every week combined the necessary dose of variety with a comforting sense of reliability. It was an ideal recipe for 'binding' listeners to their sets. Yet in many respects these shows also embodied much of what cultural reformers of all stripes had long sought to achieve. Though not necessarily loved by all—or even universally available, given the uneven distribution of radio in the 1930s—they were archetypal examples of a 'universal art' capable of transcending the wide disparities of taste that otherwise segregated the audience. Of course, their widespread popularity could not of itself erode these audience divides, which were based on fundamental educational and economic discrepancies. But they nevertheless represented a new cultural space in which different milieu could more readily find something in common. It was above all through such radio programming that the Nazis created the 'national public' they desired.

But what about the Nazis' avowed political aims? Did the development of such well-liked but essentially non-political programmes really mark the extent of their popular-culture ambitions? Disconcerting though it may seem, it is extremely difficult to discern any specifically 'Nazi' characteristics among the bulk of entertainments in this period. Of course, the centralized system of

---

[134] This paragraph is based on Pater, 'Rundfunkangebote', 190–204.

political control gave the media landscape in the Third Reich its own peculiar topography, as did the forcible exclusion of Jews and other 'outsiders' from most spheres of production—and eventually from mainstream consumption as well. But these were matters of structure. As for the content, one might perceive traces of National Socialist ideology in, for example, the emphasis on collective media events, the use of light entertainment to buoy morale, or the desire to create a more socially inclusive culture for the Volk. But these tendencies were hardly original or unique. Conjuring a sense of 'being there' at big events was a staple feature of the media across the industrialized world, and the desire to integrate diverse audiences through 'middlebrow' entertainment was by no means a Nazi innovation.

Whereas news and information in the Third Reich was blatantly biased, it is impossible to make blanket judgements about the political or ideological status of popular amusements. In Nazi Germany, as elsewhere, entertainment was too multifarious and politically ambivalent to allow any straightforward exploitation. Thus the key question is not whether a given film, radio programme, or press advertisement exhibited 'National Socialist' characteristics, but rather the specific aims of the producers and censoring agencies that created it, and above all the relationship of these cultural artefacts to the wider social and political context. Put differently, the issue is not so much *what* the entertainments supposedly conveyed as *how* they were used. And as we have seen, the answer to this depends very much on which users one is talking about, for the immense social diversity of audiences and the ability of ordinary people to 'plunder' cultural offerings meant that media-based entertainments could be appropriated in a variety of ways well beyond the intentions of producers. Insofar as one can generalize about their political impact, it seems that commercial culture under the Nazis neither seduced Germans through the charms of manipulative indoctrination nor, as the Frankfurt School theorists postulated, demobilized them into a mass of apathetic consumers, but rather invited mass participation within a socially expansive yet politically circumscribed culture of entertainment.

But before moving on, it is worth reiterating that whatever pleasure, relaxation, and diversion the millions of spectators got for their money, the Nazi leadership, for its part, never regarded entertainment as an end in itself. Amusement was conceived as a lure to political programming, just as recreation in general was regarded as a means of boosting productivity and quelling political discontent. Entertainment, in short, was a means of achieving political goals. And among these political goals was not just the maintenance of morale or the cultural integration of the 'national community', but also the brutal exclusion of outsiders and eventually the waging of the most destructive war the world had ever seen. Although the bulk of hit songs, films, and variety shows were themselves little more than fun and games, entertaining the Volk was ultimately a deadly business.

11

The Media and the Second World War:
From Integration to Disintegration

The Second World War was in many respects the pivotal event of the twentieth century. The unprecedented ferocity of the conflict and the seismic political and economic shifts it unleashed still cast a palpable shadow over Europe decades after the event. Even more than in the war of 1914–18, the extraordinary pressures of industrial-scale military conflict proved uniquely capable of magnifying previous contradictions and accelerating ongoing trends, nowhere more so than in Nazi Germany. Whether one looks at its surveillance practices, rapacious economic plundering, or murderous biological crusade, the outbreak of the Second World War is generally regarded as a fundamental turning-point in the radicalization of the Nazi regime. Although the media and popular culture may seem an almost frivolous subject of study amidst the human catastrophe of these years, they nonetheless formed an integral part of the social fabric that gave rise to the horrors of Nazism. As such, the same wartime watershed is observable here as well: they too were marked by an extraordinary intensification of pre-existing problems and developments.

One set of ongoing tensions was between the twin media functions of political mobilization and consumer-centred entertainment. The inbuilt dissonance between the desire to steer popular views and the need to provide amusement and distraction increased considerably under the strains of war. Of course, these two imperatives are not mutually exclusive; entertainment can certainly function as political propaganda, indeed quite effectively. But ultimately they are based on different premises and, despite their overlap, tend to pull in different directions.

A more fundamental set of tensions was, once again, between the unifying and divisive social effects of the mass media. On the one hand, the emergence of a more widely shared media culture in the 1930s in many ways reached its apogee during the early years of the war, as audiences mushroomed and supply became more standardized than ever. But on the other hand, the potential of the media to reinforce distinctions and divide audiences increasingly came to the fore the longer the war dragged on. The unsteady balance between these two forces closely reflected the changing nature of everyday life on the home front, of which the media were themselves an integral part. Over the course of the war we thus see yet again that the shifting context of media production and consumption crucially shaped their overall social and cultural impact. This chapter will examine how the wartime media helped to integrate and mobilize German audiences as well as their relationship to the multiplying signs of social breakdown during the second half of the war.

DEFENDING THE ATTACK: NAZI REMILITARIZATION AND THE MEDIA

First, however, the Nazi leadership needed to prepare the German populace for the upcoming struggle. Entertainment itself was hardly sufficient for this task; more direct forms of propaganda would also be necessary. This became abundantly clear during the Sudeten Crisis of autumn 1938, as internal reports recorded a complete lack of popular enthusiasm for the prospect of war: 'Among broad segments of the population the ruthless defence of the rights and honour of the German nation was replaced by the wish for maintaining peace at any price.' While nearly all Germans despised the Versailles Treaty, 'nobody wants to contemplate a war with England and France. The education of the whole nation in the tasks required by a total war with all its burdens of various kinds is by no means adequate.'[1] When, on the evening of 27 September 1938, the Nazi leadership sent a huge procession of motorized columns through Berlin in an attempt to whip up a show of war enthusiasm, they were greeted not with cheering crowds but anxious silence. The American journalist William Shirer described the event as 'the most striking demonstration against war I've ever seen'.[2] And when Hitler heard about it he angrily remarked that 'I cannot yet fight a war with this people'.[3] Yet the obvious failure to rouse German fighting spirit also stirred a new determination to tackle the issue. As Hitler put it to an assembly of journalists on 10 November 1938, the evening after the pogrom of 'Kristallnacht', their duty from that day forward was 'to transform the psychology of the German people and make it clear that there are things that must be achieved by force if they cannot be realized by peaceful means'.[4] Henceforth the media were to be fully conscripted to the war effort.

As it happened, this journalistic call to arms was part of an ongoing process that had started years earlier. From the very beginning of Hitler's government a broad network of organizations busily sought to restore German military capacity, most notably the party's Defence Policy Office (Wehrpolitisches Amt),

---

[1] Quotes from *Meldungen*, ii. 151; Noakes and Pridham (eds.), *Nazism*, ii. 597.

[2] W. L. Shirer, *The Rise and Fall of the Third Reich* (New York, 1960), 399; generally, Kershaw, '*Hitler Myth*', 137.

[3] J. Sywottek, *Mobilmachung für den totalen Krieg* (Opladen, 1976), 159.

[4] 'Rede Hitlers vor der deutschen Presse (10. November 1938)', ed. Wilhelm Treue, *VfZ* 6 (1958), 182; generally, E. Schwarzenbeck, *Nationalsozialistische Pressepolitik und die Sudetenkrise 1938* (Munich, 1979).

the Association for Defence Policy and Studies (Gesellschaft für Wehrpolitik und Wehrwissenschaften), and the War Ministry's Psychological Laboratory, which had long been working in secret on methods of psychological warfare. Only four days after his appointment as chancellor, Hitler openly told a gathering of military officers that his ultimate goal was the 'conquest and ruthless Germanization of new living space in the East'. A top priority would therefore be to 'strengthen the will to fight by all means possible', and to 'convince young people and the entire nation that only fighting will save us'.[5]

Mobilizing the nation for war was in fact one of the primary motivations behind the Nazi coordination of the media. As publicity experts had been arguing since the First World War, centralized control over the press, film, and radio was an optimal precondition for successfully deploying 'propaganda as a weapon'. From 1933 onwards, any book, article, or film deemed to undermine the German people's 'will to fight' was a prime candidate for the censor's scissors, while anything that glorified the heroic sacrifices of the soldier was extolled for its virtuous martial spirit. Thus, whereas G. W. Pabst's internationally acclaimed film *Westfront 1918* (1930) was immediately banned in 1933 for its grimly realistic depiction of trench warfare, Hans Zöberlein's egregious romanticization of war and death in *Stoßtrupp 1917* (1933) was awarded a rating of 'especially valuable'.[6] The positive image of the armed forces was systematically cultivated through events such as Heroes' Memorial Day ('Heldengedenktag', as the National Day of Mourning was renamed on 25 February 1934) and special party rallies dedicated to the navy, air force, and army, all of which were extensively covered by the media.[7] Public interest in military matters swelled following the 1935 publication of Erich Ludendorff's book *Total War*. Although largely a rehash of ideas he had long put forward, the book's appearance triggered a public engagement with the notion of psychological warfare well beyond the military and scholarly circles to which it had previously been confined.[8]

During the early years of the Nazi regime Germany's precarious international position placed certain limits on the glorification of the army. Given the need to avoid antagonizing other powers, the initial propaganda tactic was to insist on international reconciliation as a means of camouflaging the rapid military build-up. As Hitler remarked in November 1938: 'For years, the situation forced me to speak almost exclusively of peace. Only by emphasizing our peaceful intentions was it possible for me to achieve the liberation of the German nation piece by piece and to give it the arms that were the necessary precondition for the next step.'[9] This all began to change around the middle of the 1930s, first with the

[5] Sywottek, *Mobilmachung*, 22, also 41–3; on the Psychological Laboratory, A. Blau, *Propaganda als Waffe* (Berlin, 1935).
[6] Ibid. 54–5.   [7] Ibid. 58.
[8] E. Ludendorff, *Der totale Krieg* (Munich, 1935); see also Scherke and Vitzthum (eds.), *Bibliographie*; Sywottek, *Mobilmachung*, 67.
[9] 'Rede Hitlers', 182.

double breach of the Versailles Treaty in March 1935 (disclosure of the Luftwaffe and the introduction of conscription) and then with the remilitarization of the Rhineland on 7 March 1936. Both of these incidents were used to highlight the soldier as a symbol of Germany's national revival—all the while insisting that the government was pursuing nothing more than a peaceful and justifiable case of equal rights.[10] The usual tactic was to blame other countries while simultaneously making ostentatious peace gestures to reassure people at home and abroad. This was especially crass during the remilitarization of the Rhineland, which was presented as a purely defensive measure and accompanied by a loudly publicized offer of a twenty-five-year non-aggression pact with France and Belgium.

Following the success of this audacious foreign-policy gamble, the promotion of military themes was noticeably intensified. First of all, the Propaganda Ministry commissioned a whole string of militaristic feature films (so-called 'Zeitfilme'), many of them directed by long-term NSDAP member Karl Ritter, who thereby cemented his status as the Third Reich's leading film propagandist: *Verräter* (1936), *Unternehmen Michael* (1937), *Urlaub auf Ehrenwort* (1937), *Patrioten* (1937) and *Pour le Mérite* (1938). Although Ritter scooped up most of the acclaim, other directors were involved as well: Herbert Maisch with *Menschen ohne Vaterland* (1937), Johannes Meyer in *Dreizehn Mann und eine Kanone* (1938), and Heinz Paul in *Kamaraden auf See* (1938).[11] Meanwhile, broadcasting stations also began transmitting regular radio programmes—some jointly produced by the Hitler Youth and the Wehrmacht—designed to glorify the armed forces and give an exciting gloss to the life of the soldier, frequently playing on young men's desire for adventure and camaraderie: 'O What Joy to Be a Soldier', 'A Soldier's Life is a Jolly Life'.[12] For Willi Münzenberg, writing from his Parisian exile in 1937, it all amounted to an 'immense war propaganda campaign that operates with huge sums of money and that utilizes, far more than elsewhere, all of the propaganda experiences of the World War'. As he saw it, what the Nazis recognized more clearly than their rivals was not only that 'the rotation press and the radio will be even more important in the coming war than guns and tanks', but also that 'the war does not begin with the firing of the first shots, but rather years earlier with the political encirclement and propagandistic subversion of the enemy'.[13]

Returning to autumn 1938, however, it was clear that these efforts had failed to generate much fighting spirit. Shortly after the diplomatic crisis had blown over, the Military Economic Inspectorate bluntly concluded that 'political indoctrination and education, particularly to prepare the people for war, is still completely inadequate. . . . One can only regard it as an almost total failure.'[14] If the German populace were to support the upcoming war, it was absolutely

---

[10] Sywottek, *Mobilmachung*, 60–3.   [11] Welch, *German Cinema*, 319–20.
[12] Sywottek, *Mobilmachung*, 89–91.   [13] Münzenberg, *Propaganda*, 25.
[14] From Noakes and Pridham (eds.), *Nazism*, ii. 598.

necessary to justify the use of military force. The problem was twofold. First, the experience of the Sudeten Crisis had heightened popular suspicion of the official news. As the Security Service reported, the huge appetite for information was left totally unsatisfied by the German press and radio service, which released information solely 'on the basis of diplomatic negotiating tactics'. The result was that 'millions of national comrades turned to foreign sources of news', especially the German-language services of the French and British broadcasting systems.[15] The second problem was that openly arguing for the necessity of war would directly contradict one of the key themes of government propaganda to date, namely the systematic cultivation of Hitler as a man of peace. Such a volte-face would not only seem unconvincing but also risked undermining the popularity of the Führer himself, for the pervasive admiration of Hitler's foreign-policy accomplishments was predicated precisely on their bloodlessness.[16]

This latter problem came to a head with the invasion of Czechoslovakia in March 1939, after which the notion that Hitler was merely pursuing an irredentist agenda was no longer credible. The Propaganda Ministry therefore undertook a subtle change of tack. The standard refrain that Germany should regain her rightful place after the injustice of Versailles was now flanked by the idea that the country was actually being forced into a war. Soon after the Munich agreement, the old idea of Germany's 'encirclement' was dusted off and rolled out much as during the First World War. The Western powers, in league with their Polish clients and the Bolsheviks (all allegedly in tow to a worldwide Jewish conspiracy bent on Germany's destruction), were trying to squeeze the Third Reich into submission. By summer 1939 these vague apparitions were supplemented with lurid tales of Polish brutality. During the final month before the war the press circulated all manner of atrocity stories about the maltreatment of ethnic Germans in Poland, which the newsreels then translated into emotive images of traumatized refugees. From the ingrained hostility of Polish authorities to alleged acts of violence by anti-German vigilante groups, the media furore surrounding these stories was intended to suggest that Hitler's steadfast desire for peace—which was never disavowed—might not in itself be a sufficient foreign-policy response to the injustices perpetrated against Germany and her people.[17]

When the war came, it was thus unequivocally presented as a defensive measure. Indeed, there is evidence that the Nazi leadership actually believed that a 'Jewish conspiracy' was behind the war and that Germany's attack was nothing other than self-protection.[18] Against the backdrop of Versailles and the devious conspiracies masterminded by the British 'plutocracy', the attacks

---

[15] *Meldungen*, ii. 151; similar: *Deutschland-Berichte*, v. 1327–8.
[16] Kershaw, *'Hitler Myth'*, 124–32, 137–9.
[17] Generally, Kallis, *Nazi Propaganda*, 95–8; Sywottek, *Mobilmachung*, 194–201, 209–33.
[18] J. Herf, *The Jewish Enemy* (Cambridge, Mass., 2006).

on ethnic Germans were perceived and portrayed as the final straw. German propaganda never disowned the peaceful intentions of the government. As Hitler told the Reichstag on 1 September, the day German troops marched into Poland: 'As always, I sought to bring about a change by peaceful means, by offering proposals to remedy this situation which meanwhile had become unbearable.'[19] His armistice offer to Britain and France on 6 October (the official end of the victorious Polish campaign) was clearly designed to confirm Hitler's status as peace-seeker—and not without effect, both at home and abroad.[20] But the very success of this gesture as a publicity exercise also suggested a broader propaganda failure, for it simultaneously revealed the widespread anxieties surrounding the prospect of a war against the Allies. Whereas initial reports of the peace offer triggered a wave of hopeful rumours that hostilities were over, once it became clear that the fighting would continue there emerged a 'deep despondency' and a 'strong *wish for peace* among the populace'.[21]

After the Allied rejection of Hitler's overture there was no longer much to gain from declarations of peaceful intentions. Henceforth the most promising approach was not to distract Germans from their apprehensions but rather to tackle their fears head-on. And the best means of overcoming these fears was to generate a sense of invincibility through a steady depiction of triumphs. As Aristotle Kallis has put it, in autumn 1939 'the real trade-off from a propaganda point of view was between the fear of war and the appeal of victory'.[22] If the government could convince the millions of newspaper readers, cinema-goers, and radio listeners that German arms would prevail, the resulting sense of confidence would galvanize popular opinion behind the war effort. Fortunately for Goebbels, this was relatively easy so long as there were plenty of victories to boast about.

A VIRTUAL *VOLKSGEMEINSCHAFT*

The period immediately following the outbreak of the Second World War was one of the most extraordinary episodes in media history. Never before had war been so extensively communicated to civilian audiences. While the press carried thousands of combat photos and the radio kept listeners continually up to date, the newsreels conveyed the sights and sounds of battle more vividly than anything that preceded them. At the same time, never before were the media used so

---

[19] M. Domarus (ed.), *Hitler: Speeches and Proclamations 1932–1945*, vol. 3 (Würzburg, 1997), 1751.

[20] Kershaw, 'Hitler Myth', 144–5.

[21] *Meldungen*, ii. 339, 347, 356, 364, emphasis in the original. Recent research suggests that popular support for the regime actually plummeted after the invasion of Poland, with the supposed 'high' of summer 1940 only temporarily halting the decline: G. Aly (ed.), *Volkes Stimme* (Frankfurt a. M., 2006).

[22] Kallis, *Propaganda*, 99.

intensively in Germany. Once the fighting started, newspapers literally flew off kiosk stands, cinemas were regularly packed to overflowing, and demand for new wireless sets exceeded the most optimistic expectations of the radio industry.

At one level this is not all that remarkable. After months of uncertainty surrounding Hitler's international brinksmanship, people simply wanted to know what was happening. Whether or not they had loved ones at the front, there was an immense hunger for information about the fighting. Entertainment was also in high demand, for the occasional dose of distraction furnished a welcome respite from the anxieties caused by the onset of hostilities. And since most of the German military news was good throughout the early phases of the war, it is understandable that audiences should want to revel in the Wehrmacht's victories. From a twenty-first-century vantage-point, the synergies between the Nazi war machine and the mass media seem anything but surprising.

Yet in other respects the early war years also marked a pivotal phase in the history of media culture. First and foremost, they witnessed the most explosive growth of media use ever seen in Germany. There were a number of reasons for this, not least the shortage of consumer goods and the resulting surplus of purchasing power that greatly favoured investment in entertainment. But there was more to it than household economics, for this period also produced some of the most popular films and radio shows of the twentieth century. If there was ever a 'golden age' of mass culture in Germany, it was not the heady era of Weimar experimentation but rather the very years in which the Nazis launched the most lethal war in human history. Perceptions of the media could hardly contrast more starkly with what happened at the outbreak of the First World War. Instead of radically curtailing amusements, Germany's leaders (like their opponents) now saw even 'frivolous' entertainment as a vital factor for maintaining morale and mobilizing popular opinion. As Goebbels put it, 'entertainment is nowadays politically crucial, perhaps even decisive for the war (*kriegsentscheidend*)'.[23] And in terms of their social impact, wartime films and programmes were shared by more Germans from more different backgrounds than ever before. In many respects the emergence of a more socially integrated, media-based popular culture in Germany reached an interim apex from around 1940 to 1942.

This was most apparent in the cinemas, where admissions skyrocketed during the first weeks of the war. Reports in the film press spoke of an 'onslaught that recalled the best periods of high season. . . . From big cities and small towns come the same success stories: everywhere crowds of people are thronging the ticket counters.'[24] This was no mere flash in the pan, for admissions continued to rise over the following months. In Frankfurt am Main, for instance, ticket sales for the fourth quarter of 1939 were up by 28 per cent, by far the highest

---

[23] Fröhlich (ed.), *Tagebücher* 2: 3, p. 274 (8 Feb. 1942).
[24] 'Die Westdeutschen Filmtheater sind stark besucht', *FK* (2 Oct. 1939), 2; see also 'Ueberall im Reich starker Filmtheaterbesuch', *FK* (5 Oct. 1939), 1.

growth to date over such a short period.[25] Such results surpassed even the wildest hopes of Goebbels, who in October 1939 confided to his diary that 'the financial success of our films is downright amazing. We're making real war profits.'[26]

The unique appeal of the newsreels was undoubtedly an important factor behind the rush on the cinemas.[27] More than any other medium, they were capable of conveying a visual and acoustic impression of the fighting that was all the more gripping for its seeming authenticity. By the last week of September 1939 cinemas were reporting that the newsreels 'have become popular with astonishing speed' among almost all segments of the populace.[28] In early October the Security Service in Munich noted that 'it is striking how farmers, whom one never used to see in the cinemas, come into the city just to see the newsreels and the supporting programme of political and military films. The title of the feature film is of no interest to them.' Even well after the Polish campaign there remained 'a burning interest in the newsreels', which prompted cinema operators to offer special programmes consisting solely of them.[29] For many movie-goers the newsreels had become the main attraction.

As one would expect, the upsurge in newsreel demand was quickly met by an increase in supply. In autumn 1939 UFA more than quadrupled the number of its newsreel copies, from 400 to 1,700, thereby shortening their circulation period from sixteen to four weeks to ensure they remained up-to-date. Over the following year the supply of newsreel footage was expanded yet further, thanks to the millions of metres of film shot by the Wehrmacht's propaganda units. In May 1940 their length was doubled from twenty to forty minutes, and in November the four existing newsreels (*Ufa-Tonwoche, Deulig-Tonwoche, Tobis-Woche, Fox Tönende Wochenschau*) were amalgamated into a single 'Deutsche Wochenschau', whose contents were supervised by a central newsreel office (*Wochenschauzentrale*) directed by Fritz Hippler.[30]

The extraordinary popularity of the wartime newsreels soon spawned a series of feature-length military documentaries. The first of these, *Feldzug in Polen* (released in early 1940), was reportedly viewed 'with the utmost interest of the populace'. A visual eulogy to the crushing Blitzkrieg victory over Poland, most of its early screenings were sold out, and in many instances spectators broke into spontaneous applause at the most dramatic scenes. According to internal reports, interest was especially high in the border regions and the countryside, where screenings were 'downright stormed'. Yet everywhere the film

---

[25] Stahr, *Volksgemeinschaft*, 174.   [26] Fröhlich (ed.), *Tagebücher* 1:7, p. 162 (21 Oct. 1939).
[27] On the NS-era newsreels generally: U. Bartels, *Die Wochenschau im Dritten Reich* (Frankfurt a. M., 2004).
[28] 'Wochenschau-Vorstellungen stark besucht', *FK* (26 Sept. 1939), 1.
[29] *Meldungen*, ii. 384; iii. 527; 'Die Abrechnung bei Sonderveranstaltungen', *FK* (5 Oct. 1939), 1.
[30] Barkhausen, *Filmpropaganda*, 214; Bartels, *Wochenschau*, 162–204; Welch, *German Cinema*, 192–7.

had an 'extraordinarily favourable' effect on morale, the only minor criticisms stemming from jaded big-city audiences who quickly spotted that it had been pieced together from old newsreel footage.[31] Much the same can be said of the subsequent documentary *Feuertaufe* (1940), a tribute to the role of the Luftwaffe released shortly after *Feldzug in Polen* and 'enthusiastically watched by all segments of the populace'.[32]

Yet the pinnacle of the newsreel craze came with the western offensive of May and June 1940, during which 'the cinemas in many cases simply could not cope with the crush of patrons'.[33] In late May popular interest in the newsreel covering the siege of Calais and the battle for Narvik was described by internal reports as 'hardly surpassable', especially the images of destroyed cities and the grossly racist portrayal of captured Afro-French troops.[34] A number of newly founded newsreel theatres offered up to ten hour-long shows per day, attracting a predominately male audience.[35] And by the end of May there were reports of people leaving the cinema immediately after the newsreel, whether from lack of interest in the feature or, as the SD suggested, to avoid the sense of dissonance that a 'shallow feature film' might cause after such momentous fare. For those who decided to stay, most cinemas observed the Reich Film Chamber directive requiring several minutes' hiatus to digest the 'rousing experience of the newsreel' before the feature.[36] Eventually, the miles of film footage from the western offensive were compiled into the most successful of all the feature-length military documentaries, *Sieg im Westen* (1941), a stunning military spectacle that invited audiences to bask in the Wehrmacht's apparent invincibility without drawing attention to the dangers and loss of life that the continuing war with Britain promised to bring.[37]

Yet, even as the newsreels reached the peak of popularity, they were already losing some of their credibility. A sense of popular scepticism set in earlier than many accounts suggest, and certainly well before the attack on the Soviet Union.[38] Although at one level this reflected little more than the novelty wearing off, it also expressed the growing sense that the newsreels were far less authentic than they appeared. In February 1940 a newsreel depicting a scouting expedition in Spichern, just across the border in French Lorraine, was widely regarded as staged. The fact that the camera was placed in advance of a reconnaisance patrol prompted one group of soldiers in Dresden 'to burst out in loud laughter'.

---

[31] *Meldungen*, iii. 759, 846. [32] Ibid. iv. 1131.

[33] 'Millionen sahen bereits die neue Wochenschau', *FK* (27 May 1940), 1.

[34] Many of whom were murdered in captivity: R. Scheck, *Hitler's African Victims* (Cambridge, 2006); *Meldungen*, iv. 1221–2.

[35] F. Henseleit, 'Das Wochenschautheater', *FK* (20 June 1941), 1.

[36] 'Millionen sahen', 1; *Meldungen*, iv. 1222–3.

[37] Generally, T. Sakmyster, 'Nazi Documentaries of Intimidation', *Historical Journal of Film, Radio and Television*, 16 (1996), 485–514.

[38] Cf. Welch, *German Cinema*, 199–203; Kallis, *Propaganda*, 191–2; more convincing is Stahr, *Volksgemeinschaft*, 180–5.

Indeed, 'even the women present also made fun of the film and regarded it as thoroughly implausible'.[39]

Why, then, did subsequent reports insist that the newsreels 'still constitute the main attraction of the film programme for a large portion of the film audience'?[40] It is possible that some audiences were simply more discerning than others. But a more helpful explanation is that the newsreels performed both an entertainment and information function for viewers—that is, audiences were attracted to them without believing everything they saw. The war newsreels managed more than anything else to unite the functions of information and entertainment, wrapping their dramatic imagery within an aura of documentary-style accuracy. This was clearly a potent propaganda formula, but the symbiosis of entertainment and information was inherently unstable. As the Security Service in Chemnitz complained at the height of the western campaign, 'it occasionally appears that the narrow-minded philistine (*Spießer*) forgets, in the safety of the cinema, that the war newsreels are not meant for entertainment or giving viewers the creeps, but rather are an experience of a very special kind that obliges people to regard them with reverence'.[41] Such objections were nonsense, for the sensationalist character of the newsreels was deliberately intended to enthrall viewers, and officials should hardly have been surprised if audiences took up the offer. Indeed, the problem was not just confined to the newsreels. Around the same time, the popular series of 'Tran und Helle' films—short comic sketches about the correct behaviour to adopt in everyday home-front situations (blackouts, encountering illegal trading)—faced the same dilemma. Despite their notable success, Goebbels brought them to a halt in September 1940 after concluding that they threatened to descend into mere comedy and thereby surrender all propaganda value.[42]

Although the newsreels undoubtedly helped draw Germans to the cinema in 1939–40, their sinking credibility over the following years did not lead to a drop in attendance. Quite the opposite: admissions continued at record levels throughout the war (see Table 9, below). Territorial expansion accounted for only a small part of the absolute increase, as per capita admissions more than doubled from 1936 (6.9) to 1941 (14.3).[43] Moreover, this increase transcended many of the social barriers that had hitherto structured the German film audience, encompassing young and old (though still disproportionately young), rich and poor, and even eroding the stubborn urban–rural divide. In 1940 alone the party deployed some 1,000 film vehicles at 243,000 village screenings, reaching an audience of 50 million, and even this was estimated to cover only half of the demand.[44] As a report from September 1940 put it, 'across the entire Reich *the desire of the rural populace for cultural events during the war has not diminished but*

[39] *Meldungen*, iii. 741.   [40] Ibid. iv. 979.   [41] Ibid. 1266.
[42] Ibid. 1222, 1267, 1438, 1578; Stahr, *Volksgemeinschaft*, 178–80.   [43] Spiker, *Film*, 197.
[44] 'Die Filmarbeit der NSDAP', *FK* (29 May 1941), 1; *Meldungen*, iv. 986.

rather steadily increased. Undoubtedly this general interest is focused largely on film screenings.'[45]

During the early phase of the war the widespread desire to 'be part of it all' generated a slingshot effect in those regions and milieux where media use had traditionally been lowest. This was not just the case in the countryside but also in previously 'film-unfriendly' cities. Although Berlin still topped the list with 20.8 admissions per capita in 1940, its growth rate over the period 1939–40 was actually one of the lowest, at 21.9 per cent. By contrast, Würzburg, which had perennially propped up the bottom of the admissions table, now topped the growth list with an increase of 47 per cent, and other perennial cinema laggards such as Nuremberg and Wuppertal likewise witnessed exceptionally high growth over 1939–40 (37.5 and 38.1 per cent respectively).[46] The surge in film demand was also more consistent than in the past, levelling out seasonal fluctuations and prompting many cinemas to abandon the traditional summer closure. The fact that a newly released blockbuster could achieve record admissions even during a summer month represented 'a complete transformation during the war'.[47] All in all, film audiences had become larger, more regular, and more socially and regionally inclusive than ever before. As Gerhard Stahr has neatly put it, 'it was not the cinema that mobilized the populace for the war, but the war that mobilized the populace for the cinema'.[48]

If the wartime newsreels were an unexpected boon to the film industry, the tried-and-tested genres of light entertainment always played a central role. According to Gerd Albrecht's calculations, 'manifestly propaganda films' accounted for a mere 14 per cent of production throughout the entire period of the Third Reich, which left the vast bulk of the programme to be filled by relatively 'unpolitical' entertainment (and even 'manifest propaganda' could be entertaining).[49] Sheer pleasure-seeking never went ignored. Goebbels's 'orchestra principle', whereby different media played different communicative roles, meant that feature films could largely leave the burden of political propaganda to the newsreels and documentary films. Yet, as Albrecht's calculations also suggest, it was precisely during the first half of the war—as the cinema audience underwent its most rapid growth—that the proportion of overtly 'political' films was highest, peaking at 34 per cent in 1941 (against a low of only 7 per cent in 1936). While this might at first glance be read as evidence of a popular taste for propaganda, what it actually reflects is the rising demand for films of any sort and the genuine concern among Nazi filmmakers to make their 'political' films as entertaining as possible.

The determination to fuse popular appeal and political commitment was clearly visible in the string of big-budget state-commissioned features during the

[45] *Meldungen*, v. 1553.
[46] 'Bisher Jahreserbegnisse aus 27 Großstädten', *FK* (7 Mar. 1941), 1. See also Chap. 4, n. 12.
[47] G. H., 'Unsere Filmtheater spielen ohne Sommerpause', *FK* (14 July 1942), 1.
[48] Stahr, *Volksgemeinschaft*, 284.
[49] G. Albrecht, *Nationalsozialistische Filmpolitik* (Stuttgart, 1969), 110.

early war years. Historical dramas lent themselves especially well to straddling the divide between fiction and non-fiction, propaganda and entertainment. Over 1940–2 many focused on 'great Germans' and sought to draw a none-too-subtle connection between the genius of Germany's leaders past and present: for instance, *Bismarck* (1940), *Friedrich Schiller* (1940), and *Der große König* (1942, yet another biopic of Frederick the Great).[50] A whole other category of dramas was focused on Germany's sworn enemies. While *Carl Peters* (1941, on the founding of Deutsch-Ostafrika) and *Ohm Krüger* (1941, on the Boer War) drove home the anti-British and anti-'plutocracy' theme, and *GPU* (1942) railed against the Bolsheviks, *Jud Süß* (1940) and *Die Rothschilds* (1940) focused on the most hated foe of all, 'international Jewry'.

Many of these relatively 'political' dramas numbered among the greatest commercial successes of the period, in particular *Der große König, Ohm Krüger*, and *Jud Süß*, the latter of which drew over 20 million viewers (or around one-third of the adult population).[51] Yet these films also demonstrated the limits of such entertainment-oriented propaganda, for their success depended in part on the audience's ability to read them in different ways. For instance, according to internal reports *Jud Süß* enjoyed almost unanimous praise (mostly for the fine acting performances), but nonetheless elicited varying interpretations. Among most viewers the intended message that Jews were criminals and parasites was clear enough, given the wilful distortion of Leon Feucht-wanger's original novel about Joseph Süß Oppenheimer, financier and adviser to the ambitious but weak-willed eighteenth-century Duke Karl Alexander of Württemberg. In some cases the depictions of backroom dealings and the rape of a Christian girl prompted spontaneous anti-Semitic outbursts: 'Drive the Jews off the Kurfürstendamm! Throw the last Jews out of Germany!' Yet other viewers saw the film quite differently, and despite the general loathing of Süß Oppenheimer, many seemed to think 'that the duke was just as worthy of condemnation as Jud Süß and that his death was a just punishment'.[52] The need to tell an interesting story inevitably left some of the meaning up to the audience.

The contemporary revue films of the period were even more successful. Understandably, anything that enabled spectators to bask in Germany's present triumphs was highly popular around 1940–1. As the director Fritz Hippler remarked, there was a general desire at the time for 'proximity to the present'.[53] Two films deserve special mention here: *Wunschkonzert* (1940) and *Die große Liebe* (1942), the two most popular movies of the Nazi years. Both were very much films of their time, revolving around the relationship between the war and

[50] H. Segeberg, 'Die großen Deutschen', in H. Segeberg (ed.), *Mediale Mobilmachung* (Munich, 2004), 267–91.

[51] S. Lowry, *Pathos und Politik* (Tübingen, 1991), 269–70; Segeberg, 'Die großen', 275.

[52] *Meldungen*, vi. 6, 1811; see also Welch, *German Cinema*, 284–92.

[53] F. Hippler, *Betrachtungen zum Filmschaffen* (Berlin, 1942), 80; *Meldungen*, v. 1655–6.

the home front, personal fate and forces beyond one's control. As stories about love, loyalty, and duty, they also carried a distinct political message.

Premiering in December 1940, *Wunschkonzert* offered a highly personalized perspective on the major events of recent years. The young couple Inge Wagner (Ilse Werner) and Herbert Koch (Carl Raddatz) fall in love at the Berlin Olympics, only to lose contact shortly thereafter when Herbert, a pilot in the Condor Legion, is posted to Spain during the civil war. Three years later, after the attack on Poland, they finally regain contact when Herbert, still dreaming of Inge, places a nostalgic request for Olympia music with the popular radio programme *Wunschkonzert für die Wehrmacht* (see below). Their planned reunion in Hamburg is foiled, however, when Herbert dutifully answers the call to fly a mission where he is shot down with his friend Helmut, who, unbeknownst to Herbert, is also a childhood friend of Inge. After years of waiting, the lovers are finally reunited at Helmut's hospital bedside. According to internal reports, the immense popularity of *Wunschkonzert* rested not only on its successful combination of contemporary events with a dramatic plot, but also the authentic feel it generated through its references to recent events and its use of original documentary footage.[54] Moreover, the overarching message was exactly what many Germans wanted to hear at the time: duty and patience ultimately pay off in personal happiness; the needs of the battlefront and the desires of the home front are harmoniously united.

It is thus no coincidence that the very same theme lies at the heart of *Die große Liebe*, in which pilot Paul Wendlandt (Viktor Staal) falls in love with cabaret singer Hanna Holberg (Zarah Leander) during a short trip to Berlin. Once again the front calls the man away from his lover, and once again their happiness is threatened by a series of misunderstandings and sheer bad luck. Only after Paul firmly places his sense of duty over his personal wishes, eventually getting injured on the eastern front, are the two reunited. Even more explicitly than *Wunschkonzert*, *Die große Liebe* melds the fulfillment of personal desires with sacrifice for the national cause. Released on 12 June 1942, less than two weeks after the RAF's first 1,000-bomber raids had levelled much of Cologne and Essen, its appeal to a sense of duty and loyalty was more timely than the RMVP could possibly have wished for.

Both of these films drew audiences of unprecedented size. By the end of the war *Wunschkonzert* drew 26.5 million admissions worth RM 7.6 million, *Die große Liebe* 28 million admissions worth over RM 9 million.[55] But if these films were clearly exceptional, they were not in a league of their own. A significant number of concurrent films were not far behind, including *Frauen sind doch die bessere Diplomaten* (1941), *Ohm Krüger* (1941), *Die Entlassung* (1942), and *Die goldene Stadt* (1942), not to mention the hit films of the following years such as *Der weiße Traum* (1943), *Die Frau meiner Träume* (1944), and *Die*

[54] *Meldungen*, vi. 2007.   [55] Kreimeier, *Ufa Story*, 316.

Feuerzangenbowle (1944).[56] The point is that all of these wartime blockbusters achieved audience figures that pre-war filmmakers could scarcely dream of. As *Film-Kurier* giddily put it in autumn 1940, demand for moving pictures 'leaves everything we have previously seen in the shade'. The cinema was becoming a primary social habit, far more prominent in popular consciousness than before the war: 'Never before has German film production been discussed so vigorously as it is today.'[57]

Although the effects of excess purchasing power undoubtedly played a role in this, it was generally agreed that the superior quality of films was also crucial. The strategic decision to prioritize big-budget blockbusters appears to have paid off. Audience tastes were, it seems, better than many filmmakers had previously thought. 'Nowadays it is highly unusual for an artistically superior film to find no resonance among the people,' remarked one film journalist in 1942. 'Our best films, made highly visible through the award of prizes, now generate the highest box office revenues.'[58] The high-quality 'film for all' truly came into its own by the early 1940s. And as a result, there emerged the outlines of a virtuous circle whereby the limited supply of good films generated higher profits that could in turn be ploughed back into the making of even better films, and so on. For many observers it seemed as if the German cinema was entering a kind of 'golden era', both commercially and artistically. This was certainly the view of Fritz Hippler, for whom such rhetoric was 'not just an empty assertion but rather a sober assessment of the gratifying facts, which are incidentally confirmed by the broad majority of the German people through a mass attendance at the cinema that was hardly considered possible before'.[59]

Yet it is important to recognize that the huge audiences for individual films reflected not only a rise in demand but also a sharp reduction in supply. This too represented an acceleration of a longer-term process rather than a wholly new departure. As noted in Chapter 10, the production of German features had already declined in the 1930s as a result of sound conversion. But the war ushered in a new order of magnitude. From 1939 to 1942 the number of productions almost halved, rebounding only slightly over 1943–4 before collapsing at the end of the war. Furthermore, the shortage was notably exacerbated by the ban on US films after summer 1940, which, as we have seen, had previously accounted for around a fifth of all films on the German market and an even larger share of admissions.[60]

Quite obviously, dwindling supply and audience growth meant that far more people were seeing the same films. For filmmakers, this represented a beneficial rationalization of resources that vastly increased their profits. Yet for other

[56] Lowry, *Pathos*, 269–70.
[57] 'Neue Spielzeit begann mit ungewöhnlichen Erfolgen', *FK* (26 Oct. 1940), 1.
[58] G. H., 'Filmschaffende sollen aus Besucherzahlen lernen', *FK* (10 Mar. 1942), 1.
[59] Hippler, *Betrachtungen*, 28.   [60] Spieker, *Hollywood*, 337.

TABLE 9. *German film productions, 1933–1945* (SPIO figures)

1933	1934	1935	1936	1937	1938	1939	1940	1941	1942	1943	1944	1945
114	129	92	112	94	93	111	85	67	57	78	64	—

Source: Albrecht, *Nationalsozialistische Filmpolitik*, 100.

observers the effects were primarily qualitative, namely a vague yet undeniable transformation in public attitudes towards cinema. As *Film-Kurier* remarked, 'whereas even zealous film fans used to see only a fraction of film production in the past, nowadays millions of film-loving compatriots are familiar with nearly all of the major cinematic works'.[61] Just as going to the movies was becoming a more universal experience, so popular attention was focused on fewer objects of discussion. Before the war it was difficult for a group of ten people to discuss films, since only two or three of them would usually have seen any given picture. 'Today, however, one can assume with a degree of certainty that our top films become the common spiritual property of the entire nation fairly soon after their release.'[62]

Indeed, Germans were also increasingly likely to see the same films in the same cinemas. As wartime price regulations flattened the cost differences between the premiere and second-run theatres, more and more people began to visit the plush cinema palaces instead of waiting for a film to come to their *Stammkino*. This tendency was further reinforced by the longer running times of individual films caused by the shortage of supply, which gave movie-goers more opportunity to see a new release in a premiere theatre and also meant a longer wait before it was cascaded down the cinema hierarchy.[63]

Overall, the shrinking supply of films was being appropriated in a more standardized manner by a far larger and more socially inclusive audience than ever before. If there was ever a 'Volksgemeinschaft in the cinema', its heyday was the early years of the war.

Much the same argument applies to the radio, demand for which soared after the outbreak of the war. From 1 September to 1 December 1939 the number of registered listeners leapt from 12,677,328 to 13,435,301, the largest increase ever recorded for one quarter.[64] September 1939 was a record month

[61] G. H., 'Das Publikum ist heute sachverständiger als früher', *FK* (14 May 1942), 1–2.
[62] G. Herzberg, 'Der Film gehört heute zu den beliebtesten Gesprächsthemen', *FK* (27 Jan. 1942), 3.
[63] G. Herzberg, 'Die Ausdehnung der Spielzeiten', *FK* (8 Apr. 1940), 1–2; 'Dieswöchige Dispositionen der Berliner Filmtheater', *FK* (16 Apr. 1940), 1; 'Die Erstaufführungstheater werden bevorzugt', *FK* (20 Mar. 1943), 1; 'Die langen Laufzeiten in den Erstaufführungstheatern', *FK* (8 Apr. 1943), 1.
[64] Apart from the inclusion of 50,000 listeners in Danzig, these figures did not reflect Germany's territorial expansion: *RH* 17 (3 Jan. 1940), 8.

for sales, chalking up a 75 per-cent increase over the previous year.[65] Although popular trust in the news had been severely shaken during the crisis of autumn 1938, there was an immense appetite for up-to-date information once the fighting actually broke out. Internal reports repeatedly noted that the news was 'generally received very positively and considerably more favourably than before 1 September'.[66] Interest rose even further with the launch of the western offensive, during which the populace was 'literally clinging to the loudspeakers'. Above all, the daily OKW (Supreme Army Command) reports 'were listened to by almost everyone who could somehow make their way to a loudspeaker'.[67]

In these circumstances, simply reporting the Wehrmacht's victories was itself ideal advertising for radio ownership, just as it made for powerful political propaganda. German victory on the battlefield made it unnecessary to lay it on thick. Although broadcasting could hardly match the newsreels for conveying a 'total' audio-visual impression of the fighting, its unique ability to transcend space in real time generated an even stronger sense of listeners actually taking part in events. As a report during the western campaign put it, 'the topicality of the news coverage via the available technology creates an *inner unity* between front and home front *as never before*'.[68]

This sense of unity was, of course, precisely what Nazi programmers were striving for. And as with news coverage, so with entertainment. Without a doubt, the aforementioned *Wunschkonzert für die Wehrmacht*, the most popular programme of the war era, represented the pinnacle of the envisioned 'national community on the airwaves'.[69] The request-show format was by this time a well-established genre, first introduced during the Weimar years and further popularized by the Winter Aid programme in 1936. Yet the first wartime *Wunschkonzert*, held on 1 October 1939, made an extraordinary impact. The day after its debut the producers received 23,117 requests for the next episode, and were soon inundated by a 'maelstrom' of correspondence that officials in the Haus des Rundfunks no longer bothered to count.[70] Within a couple of months it is estimated that around half of the entire population tuned in.[71] Touted as a 'megaphone between front and home front', the show was carried by all of Germany's regional broadcasters and gave soldiers the opportunity to request songs and convey brief messages back home. Under the motto: 'The front holds out its hands to the homeland', the sense of 'togetherness' that it conjured was repeatedly reinforced by programming content that played with the bridging of space: for instance, soldiers on the Westwall requesting that the moderator,

[65] 'Die Einzelhandelsumsätze 1939', *RH* 17 (14 Aug. 1940), 352–3.
[66] *Meldungen*, ii. 334, 382.   [67] Ibid. iv. 1154, 1165.
[68] Ibid. 1165, emphasis in the original.   [69] Generally, Koch, *Wunschkonzert*, 168–223.
[70] H. Goedecke and W. Krug, *Wir beginnen das Wunschkonzert für die Wehrmacht* (Berlin, 1940), 36, 39.
[71] Dreschler, *Funktion*, 131.

Fig. 15. Entertaining the wartime 'national community': title cover of the book for the 'Request Show for the Wehrmacht', 1940. bpk Berlin.

sitting some 600 km away in Berlin, simultaneously drink a bottle of beer with them.[72]

So beloved was the *Wunschkonzert* that it quickly evolved into a multimedia cultural institution, raising over RM 15 million and spawning both the blockbuster film and a best-selling compilation of the show's highlights.[73] As such, it was probably the single most successful piece of 'integration propaganda' the regime ever devised. In the words of its moderator, Heinz Goedecke: 'Whoever heard one of the request shows knows how the nation and army felt bound together into a single great family during those hours. He clearly understands the immense importance of the radio as the only medium which is currently able to bring together eighty million people for a single communal experience.'[74] While much of this 'communal experience' consisted of the usual comic sketches, hit songs, and guest appearances by popular stars, what distinguished the *Wunschkonzert* was its deliberate emphasis on a sense of national togetherness. At its seventy-fifth broadcast on 25 May 1941 (the last one as it turned out), the *Wunschkonzert* was triumphantly presented as 'a golden bridge . . . from the North Cape (of Norway) to the extreme South, from the furthest East to the West', enabling 'millions of hearts to find each other through the miracle of radio'.[75] For its producers and many of its listeners, the *Wunschkonzert* was the epitome of a virtual 'national community'.

Why such a successful programme was discontinued after May 1941 is not entirely clear. It seems likely that radio officials, notably Goebbels, thought it had peaked and could only go downhill with the launch of the war in the east. In all probability the decision was also related to the mounting practical difficulty of producing such a programme, as more and more technicians and entertainers were conscripted into the armed forces.[76] But whatever the specific reason, the discontinuation of the *Wunschkonzert* was part of a wider trend. Just as the supply of films shrank during the war, so too did the variety of programmes on the radio.

It was clear from the outbreak of fighting that programming structures would need to change. Given the inefficiencies of a broadcasting system in which around half of airtime was still filled by individual regional companies, a further centralization of the programme was now inevitable. The first major change came on 9 July 1940, as the broadcasting system was amalgamated into a single Reich-wide programme. But if the advantage of such an arrangement was an efficiency gain and a less fragmented listening public, the disadvantage was a highly unpopular reduction in choice. There were soon widespread complaints that

---

[72] Goedecke and Krug, *Wunschkonzert*, 93–4, 161.
[73] Namely, Goedecke and Krug, *Wunschkonzert*. Figure from Koch, *Wunschkonzert*, 211.
[74] Goedecke and Krug, *Wunschkonzert*, 8.
[75] Koch, *Wunschkonzert*, 220.   [76] Ibid. 222–3.

'listeners are no longer able to switch to another broadcaster when the programme of his local station does not appeal to him'—an annoyance compounded by the collapsing availability of records after 1939, for which demand outstripped supply at least fourfold.[77] Since the lack of choice threatened to undermine the popularity of radio-listening itself, officials moved in early 1941 to a dual broadcasting system (for at least part of the day) between a popular Reich programme and the more 'serious' Deutschlandsender.[78] But this concession only partially compensated for the dramatic reduction of regional variety.

Altogether, the standardization of programming and the importance attached to radio as a means of boosting home-front morale put broadcasters under more pressure than ever to cater to majority tastes. And what this entailed in practice was a further shift towards light entertainment and popular music. These issues were very much on Goebbels's mind ever since the switch to a single programme in summer 1940. Within months, the military leadership candidly warned that the popularity of British radio among German soldiers threatened to undermine fighting morale. The Reich's ace pilot (and avid jazz fan) Werner Mölders also pleaded for a more vibrant programme if the young men in the armed forces were to be weaned off the BBC.[79] The problem was that modern dance music had many enemies within the Nazi leadership, and jazz was still formally banned from German radio.

The dilemma came to a head in April 1941, when German forces took over Radio Belgrade and turned it into a popular soldiers' station capable of competing with foreign broadcasters. Within a couple of weeks German civilians were also tuning into its 'superb, lively' programme composed 'almost exclusively of cheerful dance, operetta, and march music'.[80] The launch of Radio Belgrade immediately stirred up disagreements over whether such music should be allowed for civilians, though there was no practical way to stop it, since this was hardly a foreign-run station. But as far as soldiers' entertainment was concerned, pragmatism clearly outweighed ideology. And as far as Goebbels was concerned, soldiers' tastes took priority over those of civilians, let alone tradition-minded officials. On 14 June 1941, a week before the invasion of the Soviet Union, he openly called for a lighter and more cheerful programme in a lead article in *Das Reich* (on which more below), parts of which were broadcast that same evening, to general approval. What was good for the morale of soldiers was presumably good for civilians, especially in western areas plagued by frequent air raids, where 'the receptivity for amusing and distracting entertainment is especially great'.[81]

The mounting chorus in favour of lighter programming was motivated by two chief concerns: to maintain fighting morale and to maximize radio use as a

---

[77] *Meldungen*, v. 1494; 'Rückblick und Ausblick im Schallplattengeschäft', *RH* 17 (3 Jan. 1940), 15.

[78] Dussel, *Rundfunkgeschichte*, 104, 113

[79] Kater, *Different*, 124–7.   [80] *Meldungen*, vii. 2290.

[81] Ibid. 2419. The text is repr. in *Rundfunkarchiv*, 14 (June 1941), 211–14.

means of distributing information. Both concerns grew increasingly acute over summer 1941 as Operation Barbarossa unleashed a new wave of popular anxiety that once again threatened popular trust in the news. Hitler and Otto Dietrich only made matters worse when they optimistically proclaimed at the beginning of October that the Soviets were as good as finished. By the end of the month the continuing reports of determined resistance had led to 'a certain scepticism towards the propaganda of recent weeks among broad segments of the populace. . . . Many national comrades are amazed that the Soviet Union has not collapsed, that the "Russians" are so tough.' This scepticism swelled over the following months, due to 'the feeling of unclear and incomplete information about the military situation on the eastern front and North Africa'.[82]

It was thus no coincidence that the definitive step towards a more entertaining radio format came in autumn 1941. As news of another victory seemed increasingly remote, the task of 'binding' listeners to the radio would increasingly fall to light entertainment. From early October the programme was put on a whole new footing, and the popular response was immediate. Within weeks it was reported that 'the new programme since the beginning of the month is met with almost universal approval. The shift of the programme towards almost exclusively cheerful and light broadcasts is highly conspicuous. The programme has a "peacetime" feel to it.'[83] In February 1942 the changes were underpinned with the restructuring of the RRG into ten different programme sections, under the overall control of Hans Hinkel. Unsurprisingly, groups A through C, responsible for light music and entertainment genres, dominated the prime-time slots.

Nor was it a coincidence that the officially approved 'German Dance and Entertainment Orchestra' was established in autumn 1941.[84] The job of putting the band together was handed to Georg Haentzschel and Franz Grothe, the directors of the newly formed RRG sections A ('light dance and entertainment music') and B ('refined entertainment music'), which ensured that by the time the orchestra was up and running in spring 1942 it was already integrated into programme planning. Crucially, its official status allowed it to play music that might otherwise have fallen foul of the ban on 'negro-jazz'. But while this proved popular with soldiers and young people, many listeners who otherwise approved of the light radio programme felt a specific aversion towards such 'trumpet and saxophone racket'.[85] The long-standing dispute over jazz and modern dance music still showed no signs of abating.

Yet, in the context of the war, the time-honoured objections of musical conservatives cut little ice. As Goebbels remarked in spring 1942, 'impassioned letters and petitions from classical music lovers tell us that the emphasis on light and entertaining music is gradually going too far. Some even see in this the signs of a general cultural degeneration that must be averted at all costs. *Soldiers at the*

---

[82] *Meldungen*, viii. 2929; ix. 3164.   [83] Ibid. viii. 2931.
[84] This discussion is based on Kater, *Different*, 124–7.   [85] *Meldungen*, xi. 4333.

front, however, tell us how gratifying it is to hear some, as they put it, decent—that is, entertaining and light—music in their cold and uncomfortable barracks after a hard day's duty.' By maintaining the nation's morale, jazz-inspired dance music and light entertainment were deemed crucial to the war effort: 'There can be no doubt that the vast majority of our people, on the front and at home, are so burdened by the pressures of the war that they simply cannot concentrate long enough in the evenings to take in two hours of demanding programming.'[86]

In short, Nazi radio had become unabashedly populist by late 1941. Just as the regime became more brutal and prescriptive than ever, it also catered more sensitively to listener tastes. In terms of both audience size and programme content, the early 1940s were in fact a kind of heyday for 'popular radio' in Germany. Within a short period of time the tenacious—if gradually eroding—pedagogical orientation of German radio was quickly consigned to the margins under the pressures of the war. It would take at least two decades for light entertainment in general, and pop music in particular, to regain such prominence on German airwaves.

In many respects the war marked an equally important watershed for the German press, indeed for many of the same reasons as for the other media. Here too, demand rose while the variety of supply decreased. The immense desire for information after the fighting began meant that, as the journal *Zeitungs-Verlag* put it, 'newspapers are nowadays often read from front to back, not just skimmed through. . . . We are presently experiencing a huge enthusiasm for reading and newspapers.'[87] At the same time, the overall number of titles dropped rapidly throughout the war, from just under 2,500 in 1939 to 1,300 in 1942 and only 700 in early 1945. Once again it was primarily small, independent (non-NSDAP owned) papers that were shut down. Whereas in 1937 papers selling over 50,000 copies accounted for only 5 per cent of titles and 44 per cent of overall circulation, by 1942 they accounted for 15 per cent of titles and over 70 per cent of circulation.[88]

This latest bout of commercial concentration meant that people were far more likely to read the same paper during the war than before it. They were also more likely to read the same sections, since wartime restrictions immediately halved average newspaper length. But here we come to the key difference between the press and the other media, for unlike cinema and radio, it was entertainment that bore the brunt of the cuts. In order to make room for expanded war coverage, most newspapers radically reduced their human-interest stories, celebrity chitchat, and hobby supplements. 'Sensational' forms of presentation were another victim of the paper shortage, which furnished a powerful incentive to scale down the

---

[86] J. Goebbels, 'Der treue Helfer', repr. in *Rundfunkarchiv*, 15 (Mar. 1942), 97–100, emphasis in the original.
[87] 'Das neue Gesicht der deutschen Presse', *ZV* (23 Sept. 1939), 571.
[88] Meier, *Zwischen*, ii. 160–1.

use of white space and non-essential text in newspaper layout. This primarily meant cutting down on large headlines—less of a sacrifice than it sounds, since the real 'sensation' of combat made sensational presentation somewhat superfluous.[89] Advertisements too dropped sharply after September 1939, as many businesses felt little need to promote scarce products. And as the consumer situation worsened over 1941 and 1942, the Advertising Council prohibited all advertisement for shortage goods as well as ads that suggested a sense of abundance.[90]

The outbreak of the war also brought changes to the system of press controls. For one thing, it added a layer of filtering in the form of military censors, who initially tailored all information from the front before passing it on. The subsequent management of this material was further complicated by the growing influence of Reich press chief Otto Dietrich, who ruthlessly used his close personal contact with Hitler to encroach on Goebbels's press competences, eventually issuing his own daily directives alongside those of the Propaganda Ministry.[91] Control over magazine content was likewise tightened in 1939 with the establishment of a centralized Periodical Service (*Zeitschriften-Dienst*, a weekly bulletin for magazine editors), the German Weekly Service (*Deutscher Wochendienst*, which supplied pictures and other information), and a new system of instructions similar to those issued to newspapers. The effects were soon visible in the main illustrated weeklies. While Scherl's *Die Woche* focused almost entirely on war-related stories, the previously 'non-political' *BIZ* also ceaselessly glorified the armed forces with dramatic images of forward movement and victory. Women's magazines too were enlisted for the war effort, through publicizing savings measures, household substitutes, blackout procedures, and first-aid instructions.[92]

Press officials, like their counterparts in the film and radio sectors, had a fairly easy time over the first two years of the war, since the news from the front largely sold itself. Yet unlike these other media, newspapers never quite overcame the lingering sense of blandness, uniformity, and close political control that had undermined their standing before the war.[93] As an antidote, officials quickly set about 'modernizing' the image of the German press. The single greatest innovation was the launch of the weekly newspaper *Das Reich* in May 1940, a highbrow periodical that almost immediately became the leading organ of German journalism and commentary. Consciously modelled on the *Observer*, it was printed in Latin script, featured a modern and 'serious' layout, and was couched in a more sober tone than any of the leading dailies. From its inception it enjoyed a unique degree of political latitude, even to the point of voicing limited

---

[89] F. Gottinger, 'Aufmachungsindex bis zu 38%', *ZV* (16 Dec. 1939), 667.
[90] Rücker, *Wirtschaftswerbung*, 269–72.
[91] Generally, D. Kohlmann-Viand, *NS-Pressepolitik im Zweiten Weltkrieg* (Munich, 1991).
[92] Koszyk, *Deutsche Presse 1914–1945*, 413–18; Frei and Schmitz, *Journalismus*, 78–81.
[93] *Meldungen*, ii. 152.

criticism (which nonetheless cost some writers their jobs). Its editorial staff read like a who's who of German journalism, and its feuilleton pages were graced by the likes of Theodor Heuss (future president of the FRG), the physicist Max Planck, and the philosopher Eduard Spranger. First conceived by Max Amann and his associates, Goebbels was quickly won over to the project and often wrote the lead article, pocketing a cool RM 2,000 every time he did so. It also won over plenty of readers, reaching a circulation of 1.4 million by 1944.[94] But *Das Reich* was only the most conspicuous manifestation of this wider 'modernizing' impulse. In order to save space and make German newspapers more accessible to other (conquered) peoples, there was a general push to replace traditional Gothic with Latin script. There were also attempts to modernize the look of mastheads through the replacement of 'poster-like presentation' with a 'calm appearance'. The logic was simple: sober form suggested sober content. As one journalist remarked in 1942, 'trust among readers cannot be achieved through placard-like agitation, but through a clear and balanced appearance that automatically suggests that the reports and articles possess the same inner quality'.[95] Judging from internal reports, Nazi press modernizers had their work cut out. Many wartime readers regarded the abbreviated newspapers as 'primitive', and their tightly controlled content was also viewed with considerable scepticism.[96]

By the end of 1941 this issue of popular trust became a major concern, as the credibility of official news rapidly eroded. The feeling of being *verschaukelt*, or 'taken for a ride', became more and more widespread the longer one had to wait for the 'final victory'. Although this rising tide of distrust rarely spilled over into outright dissent—it is clear that the majority of Germans exhibited an overall attitude of loyalty, however 'reluctant', right up to the end[97]—it nonetheless signalled an important sea change. Under the auspicious circumstances of the early war years the mass media undoubtedly helped to galvanize public opinion behind the Nazi leadership. But as we will now see, all of this changed as the situation worsened. Once the news turned bad, and once the war came home to Germany, the increasingly desperate attempt to maintain morale through escapist entertainment could hardly halt the unravelling of whatever sense of national unity and common purpose that the media had nourished in the first place.

INTO THE COLLAPSE

The rising strain on the German home front after the stalled Russian campaign and the intensification of Allied bombing dramatically altered the societal terrain

---

[94] This discussion is based on Frei and Schmitz, *Journalismus*, 108–20.
[95] E. Hornig, 'Die Wandlung zum ruhigen Zeitungsbild', *ZV* (31 Oct. 1942), 346; 'Der Zeitungskopf geht mit der Zeit', *ZV* (23 May 1942), 161–2.
[96] *Meldungen*, viii. 2798, 2851.
[97] K.-M. Mallmann, G. Paul, *Herrschaft und Alltag* (Bonn, 1991).

on which the media, their producers, and their users operated. As ever, these changes also altered the social and political role of mass communications. The transformation was neither precipitate nor clear-cut: circumstances on the home front deteriorated over several years, and the oscillating military fortunes of the Wehrmacht during 1942 still provided the regime with a supply of successes to put on display. Yet, as the destruction mounted and hopes for final victory dwindled, the relationship between mobilization and distraction underwent a significant shift. After 1941 the potent amalgamation of propaganda and populist entertainment epitomized by the contemporary revue films and *Wunschkonzert für die Wehrmacht* gradually disintegrated into its constituent parts. To a large extent, entertainment became just that, and overt political propaganda became an increasingly hard sell.

One of the main reasons for this was the transparent suppression of more and more unwelcome news from the front. Throughout 1942–3 the stories and images conveyed by press, radio, and cinema made strikingly little reference to the mounting setbacks and losses. The coverage of the illustrated magazines typified the process: whereas the *BIZ* provided a spectacular visual reportage of the victories over Poland and France, images of the defeat at Stalingrad were wholly absent.[98] The newsreels painted a similar picture: in early 1943 audiences complained that they 'do not go into the current situation in any way, especially the struggle around Stalingrad', and instead conveyed a 'harmless' and 'peaceful' impression.[99] This blatant glossing over of what many Germans already knew from other sources led to an almost wholesale collapse of popular trust in the official news. Staying informed soon became a do-it-yourself activity. As the Security Service noted in October 1943, 'it is generally noticed that the populace is forming its view of the situation from the "facts" available to them, independent of the official sources of information'.[100]

Intriguingly, however, this collapse of credibility did not cause a noticeable drop in demand for official news. The sheer appetite for information of any kind buoyed newspaper circulation at around 25 million all the way through late 1944, and also sustained a keen interest in the daily OKW broadcasts until the very end of the war.[101] The difference was that official news was now merely one source of information among many. Millions of Germans turned to foreign broadcasters, in spite of the draconian punishments handed out for this 'crime'.[102] And as more men were called up, more families acquired second-hand information about the fighting. From the beginning of 1943 the rumour mill effectively ran out of control, fed by a torrent of snippets from news sources, eyewitness accounts, and letters from the front which people tried to assemble into an understanding of the

---

[98] Frei and Schmitz, *Journalismus*, 78.
[99] *Meldungen*, xii. 4722.   [100] Ibid. xv. 5904.
[101] Koszyk, *Deutsche Presse 1914–1945*, 369; Meier, *Zwischen*, ii.
[102] Generally, M. Hensle, *Rundfunkverbrechen* (Berlin, 2003).

TABLE 10. *Registered wireless sets in the German Reich, 1933–1944*

Year	Registered sets × 1,000	Sets per 1,000 inhabitants
1933	4,533	70
1934	5,245	83
1935	6,725	102
1936	—	—
1937	9,575	126
1938	10,575	141
1939	12,415	157
1940	14,152	166
1941	16,178	179
1942	16,004	188
1943	16,179	190
1944	15,264	179

Source: Koch, *Wunschkonzert*, 53–4.

TABLE 11. *Cinema admissions in the German Reich, 1928–1944* (including annexations)

Year	Admissions (in millions)	Annual admissions per person	Gross ticket sales (million RM)
1928	352.5	—	274.9
1930	290.3	—	243.9
1932/3	238.4	4.6	176.4
1933/4	244.9	4.8	176.3
1934/5	259.4	5.0	194.6
1935/6	303.3	5.9	230.9
1936/7	361.6	6.9	282.1
1937/8	396.4	7.6	309.2
1938/9	441.6	8.4	353.3
1939	623.7	10.5	476.9
1940	834.1	13.3	650.0
1941	892.3	14.3	725.7
1942	1,062.1	14.3	894.2
1943	1,116.5	14.4	958.6
1944	1,101.7	14.4	951.3

Source: Spiker, *Film*, 136, 197, 231.

situation. The continually high demand for newspapers and radio reports must not be confused with undiminished interpretive control. In spite of the healthy circulation figures, by early 1944 it was reportedly 'difficult for the official means of communication . . . to have any influence on the people'.[103]

As popular trust in the news plummeted, the allure of light entertainment was never higher. The sheer size of radio and film audiences leaves little doubt about this. According to Postal Ministry figures, radio distribution peaked in 1943 with 16,179,000 registered sets, or 190 sets per 1,000 inhabitants. Although there are indications that the number of actually functioning sets had fallen since 1941 due to the shortage of spare parts, the fact that applications for new and used receivers—many of them plundered from occupied territories—vastly outstripped supply testifies to the high demand.[104] Even more remarkable was the continuing boom in cinema admissions, which likewise peaked in 1943 at over 1.1 billion, or 14.4 annual admissions per person, remaining essentially unchanged through 1944. This meant that the average German went to the cinema around 40 per cent more in 1943–4 than in 1939 and three times more than in 1933—a similar rate of wartime growth as in Britain, though still well below per-capita admissions there or in the United States.[105] Although in one sense good news for the regime, this turned out to be an embarrassment of riches, in that the popularity of the cinema became a problem. As the demand for seats exceeded supply there were numerous reports of 'unpleasant side-effects', audiences that were 'difficult to deal with', and even 'turbulent scenes in the foyer or on the street'.[106] Ticket-scalping also became increasingly common; the fact that theatres were frequently sold out meant fat profits for minimal financial risk (though the punitive hazards were substantial, given the treatment of scalping as a form of war profiteering).[107]

But it is not entirely clear how to interpret the high audience figures. Did the millions of cinema-goers and radio listeners find their fighting spirit bolstered by what they saw and heard? Or did they rather use the media as an individualistic means of fleeing the demands of the regime and the growing stresses of everyday life? The fact that the media continued to profit from a wartime boom does not mean that the underlying reasons remained the same. If the swelling audiences of 1939–41 were at least partially drawn by the vicarious experience of victory, it seems likely that the even larger audiences of 1942–4 were motivated primarily by a yearning for diversion. Although difficult to pin down, there are a number of indices that point in this direction. The reception

---

[103] *Meldungen*, xvi. 6416; on rumours: F. Dröge, *Der zerredete Widerstand* (Düsseldorf, 1970).
[104] *Meldungen*, xvi. 6195; on unusable sets: König, *Volkswagen*, 97–9.
[105] Cf. figures in Spiker, *Film*, 197, 231; J. Richards and D. Sheridan (eds.), *Mass-Observation at the Movies* (London, 1987), 12; T. Schatz, *Boom and Bust* (Berkeley, 1997), 153.
[106] G. H., 'Die Placierung der Besucher', *FK* (1 Dec. 1941), 1.
[107] G. H., 'Kampf den Billetthändlern', *FK* (15 July 1942), 2.

Fig. 16. Sold out: queueing for cinema tickets, 1942. bpk Berlin. Photo: Arthur Grimm.

of the film *Der große König*, a high-budget biopic of Frederick the Great released in spring 1942, can serve as an illustration. Like the big historical dramas of 1940–1, the film scored remarkably well at the box-office and was reportedly viewed, as intended, as a 'reflection of our own times'; if anything, the parallels between Hitler and Frederick were 'laid on a bit thick'. But in contrast to the audience mood in 1940 there was little desire to see so many battle scenes amidst the current setbacks in Russia and the bombing in western areas. Women in particular thought there was 'too much about war' in the film, which put a 'powerful strain on their nerves' and even set off underground rumours in some areas.[108]

It seems that the reluctance of propaganda officials to dwell on unpleasant realities was thus paralleled by a growing desire among audiences to forget them as well, at least for a few hours. The continuing demand for newspapers, radios, and cinema tickets did not necessarily reflect the mobilization of the populace, but on the contrary a widespread attempt to *avoid* being mobilized, to retreat temporarily into a private world of thoughts and dreams.[109] Indeed, the swelling anxiety and loss of life seemed only to increase the hunger for entertainment over the second half of the war. By the end of 1943 cinema and radio figures were at a historic peak, and even the serialized newspaper novel was making a comeback after years of neglect. Here too, the last thing readers wanted was more about the war, which they could already read about in the rest of the paper.[110]

The Propaganda Ministry willingly obliged such wishes, avoiding war references in popular amusements and generally prioritizing the maintenance of morale through light entertainment. As Goebbels remarked in his diary in early 1942: 'Optimism is now an integral part of warfare. . . . The seriousness of war is approaching us without our summoning it; it therefore does not need to be constantly conjured up anew.'[111] The ambitious attempt to rally the nation behind the war thus largely gave way to the more limited aim of defusing dissatisfaction.[112] This was typified by the Propaganda Ministry's musical efforts, which owed far more to Glenn Miller than to Richard Wagner. In 1941–2 the RMVP commissioned a series of 'optimistic hit songs' specially designed to lift morale, even launching a competition just as the Stalingrad defeat unfolded. Although it involved some of the most successful songwriters of the time (Franz Grothe, Michael Jary, Peter Kreuder), the campaign produced only a handful of actual 'hits': for instance, Grothe's 'Wir werden das Kind schon richtig schaukeln' ('We'll manage it all right') and Albert Vossen's 'So sind wir, wir pfeifen auf die Sorgen' ('We could care less about our worries'). But this hardly mattered, given the string of highly successful 'optimistic' sound-film hits around at the time, most notably Zarah Leander's 'Davon geht die Welt nicht unter' ('It's not the end of the world') and 'Ich weiß, es wird einmal ein Wunder geschehen' ('I know a miracle will happen someday'), both from the box-office smash *Die große Liebe*. And no wartime song could match the popularity of the schmaltzy 'Lili Marleen', ritually broadcast every evening from 21:56 to 22:00 by the Wehrmacht station in Belgrade to the delight of soldiers and civilians on all sides.[113]

This cheerful and entertaining tone dominated German radio programming after the reforms of autumn 1941. Among the biggest hit songs of the day

---

[108] *Meldungen*, x. 3759.   [109] See also Stahr, *Volksgemeinschaft*, 292.
[110] *Meldungen*, xv. 5860.   [111] Fröhlich (ed.), *Tagebücher* 2:3, p. 383 (27 Feb. 1942).
[112] B. Kundrus, 'Totale Unterhaltung?', in J. Echternkamp (ed.), *Die deutsche Kriegsgesellschaft 1939 bis 1945* (Munich, 2005), 97–8.
[113] Koch, *Wunschkonzert*, 296–306.

there was precious little reference to war, absence, and loss. Titles such as 'Mit Musik geht alles besser' ('Music makes everything better'), 'Mein Herz hat heut' Premiere' ('My heart debuts today'), and 'Kauf dir einen bunten Luftballon' ('Buy yourself a bright balloon') characterized the overall tone.[114] But there were limits to how far this emphasis could go, for it sometimes came across as 'strained joviality'.[115] Occasionally people regarded such programming as inappropriate, even offensive, in view of the increasing destruction and hardship. In summer 1942 listeners were incensed at the broadcast of a cheery polka directly after an announcement of a bomb attack on Cologne that claimed 200 lives. Similarly, in spring 1943 the lyrics of the hit song 'Ich tanze mit Dir in den Himmel hinein' ('I'll dance with you into the sky') were deemed downright perverse amidst the huge bombing raids in the Ruhr.[116] Radio officials were acutely sensitive to such problems. In January 1943, as the Sixth Army faced defeat at Stalingrad, Hans Hinkel warned programmers to avoid overly cheerful hits for the time being. But although Goebbels agreed with the temporary elimination of all 'silly lyrics and titles', he nonetheless insisted on the retention of light, upbeat music as far as possible, firmly convinced that most people would welcome a diversion from their worries. And it seems he was right, for as the Security Service reported two months later, 'the structure of the music programme meets with approval. The transition to lighter broadcast content has been "tactically" carried out and is welcomed.'[117]

This same tactical calculation was applied even more directly to the cinema. Although 1941–2 marked the peak of overtly 'propaganda' films, this reflected production decisions taken at an earlier stage in the war, when confidence was high and matters seemed under control. According to Gerd Albrecht's calculations (which, though inevitably somewhat arbitrary, are indicative of trends), while manifestly political films accounted for 34 per cent of the features released in 1941 and 25 per cent in 1942 (against an average of 14 per cent over 1933–45 as a whole), the proportion of comedies sank to 38 per cent in 1941 and 35 per cent in 1942 (well below the average of 48 per cent). But in 1943 the pendulum swung back with a vengeance, as the quota of comedies rose to over 55 per cent while propaganda films slumped to 8 per cent.[118] This abrupt quantitative shift can be traced qualitatively as well. It was indicative that the twenty-fifth anniversary of UFA was celebrated with the release of *Münchhausen* (1942/3), a light costume drama loaded with special effects. Even more tellingly, whereas several of the most popular films of 1942 featured the war as the essential backdrop (*Die große Liebe, Fronttheater*), the leading box-office hits of the following years made little reference to it whatsoever. In fact, many were pure distraction, from the circus film *Zirkus Renz* (1943) to the beloved comedy

---

[114] Ibid. 129; Dussel, *Rundfunkgeschichte*, 113–14. [115] *Meldungen*, ix. 3199.
[116] Dreschler, *Funktion*, 139; *Meldungen*, xiii. 4970.
[117] *Meldungen*, xiii. 4873; Koch, *Wunschkonzert*, 129, 132. [118] Albrecht, *Filmpolitik*, 110.

Feuerzangenbowle (1944, still occasionally shown on German television) to the ice-dance revue *Der weiße Traum* (1943), whose popular hit song 'Kauf dir einen bunten Luftballon' was the very epitome of wartime escapism: 'Buy yourself a bright balloon | Take it firmly in your hand | Imagine that you fly away | To a far-off fairyland.'[119]

This façade of civilian normality in the midst of appalling destruction clearly struck a chord with German audiences. Indeed, for many people it seems that the continuing supply of entertainment gradually became equated with the maintenance of 'normality' itself, both as a comforting symbol of pre-war certainties and an alluring taste of the good life that would hopefully follow the fighting. One can perhaps draw a connection to the experience of the First World War, as the post-war boom in amusements was widely seen as a symbol of the return to normality after a four-year state of emergency. In any event, the ongoing efforts to keep bomb-damaged cinemas open were greatly appreciated by a populace that knew what it felt like to crawl out of an air-raid shelter in the morning and start to repair things. 'They understood what it meant to make a cinema operational again,' noted one film journalist in late 1942. 'For them it meant a further step towards *normal life* when the screen in their cinema was lit up and the speakers resounded once again.'[120] The maintenance of cinema capacity was deemed so crucial for morale that building regulations were substantially loosened in 1942 to allow damaged theatres to reopen with only makeshift repairs. And in many cities there were concerted efforts to keep outlying suburban cinemas running in order to take the pressure off the most at-risk central premiere theatres, which were allowed to open as early as 10:00 to cope with demand.[121]

Wartime entertainment and the sense of normality that it generated were so coveted that many came to regard them as a kind of social entitlement. For some the radio was the primary concern. Given the scarcity of gramophone records and the time required to queue for a cinema ticket, in many cases the wireless represented the only regular source of amusement and was increasingly viewed as a right. By 1943 the authorities were deeply worried that the lack of new sets and spare parts would damage morale.[122] But it was undoubtedly the shortage of cinema tickets that caused the most tension. The scarcer they became, the more they mutated from a taken-for-granted passport to relaxation into a token of social privilege. In the context of rationing and absence of luxury goods, access to the cinema was a remarkably important form of social currency. In the eastern occupied territories, where the imbalance between supply and demand was especially acute, there had long been complaints from ethnic Germans that

---

[119] Lowry, *Pathos*, 120, 236–7, 270.
[120] G. H., 'Filmtheaterbesitzer haben sich bewährt', *FK* (27 Nov. 1942), 1, my emphasis.
[121] 'Wiederaufbau kriegszerstörter Filmtheater', *FK* (7 Oct. 1942), insert; 'Spielergebnisse der Filmtheater', *FK* (29 Feb. 1944), 1; generally, Stahr, *Volksgemeinschaft*, 258–61.
[122] *Meldungen*, xiii. 4929; xvi. 6195.

Poles were allowed to visit the premiere cinemas at all. In Posen, Krakow, Bromberg, and other cities, 'the German population is increasingly demanding a regulation that the leading cinemas . . . be reserved for German viewers and for German high-quality films and that the smaller cinemas be reserved for Poles and films suited to them'.[123] Nor was this cinematic apartheid new within the Reich itself. It had already been applied to Polish labourers in 1940 and was eventually extended in gradational form to POWs and labourers from all across western Europe.[124] And of course German Jews had already been banned from mainstream cinemas and from owning radio sets ever since the later 1930s.

But if these media-based social stratifications initially distinguished Germans from their alleged racial inferiors, they eventually began to divide the 'national community' as well. The widespread anger among those who felt unfairly disadvantaged prompted cultural authorities to introduce a raft of measures for rationing the availability of amusement. Radios and gramophone records were distributed according to need, with bombing victims and refugees at the top of the list (though this was continually undermined by the flourishing black market).[125] Yet again, the cinema posed the greatest problem, for the constant overfilling of theatres confronted operators with difficult choices. Like anyone controlling access to a scarce commodity, they found it impossible to satisfy everyone. Selling tickets in advance was one way to avoid 'unpleasant occurrences' at the ticket-counter, but this led to complaints that 'cinema visits have become a privilege for those compatriots who have time in the morning to buy tickets'. Limiting sales to two per person was commonly employed to reduce scalping, but this led to objections from people who were unable to get others to queue for them. To remedy the situation the Reich Film Chamber eventually banned under-eighteens from most evening and weekend screenings, since they could more easily attend weekday matinees. Most operators also reserved a small number of tickets for soldiers on leave, who felt particularly aggrieved if they were unable to see a film during furlough because a cinema was crammed with civilians who had regular access to it. As the *Film-Kurier* revealingly put it, 'there is no shortage of attempts to help every national comrade *get his rights*'. The cinema had become an essential social entitlement on the increasingly grim home front, and as such the just distribution of tickets represented nothing less than a 'service to the national community'.[126]

---

[123] Ibid. vii. 2241.
[124] 'Filmische Betreuung französischer u. belgischer Kriegsgefangener in den Filmtheatern', *FK* (30 Apr. 1942), insert; Stahr, *Volksgemeinschaft*, 238–40.
[125] 'Schallplattenfragen', *RH* 19 (30 Dec. 1942), 546–7; R. Albert, 'Schallplatte und Heimatfront', *RH* 21 (Apr. 1944), 125–6.
[126] Quotes from G. H., 'Wenn Eintrittskarten Mangelware werden', *FK* (13 Oct. 1942), 1–2, my emphasis; see also G. H., 'Fronturlauber sind Ehrengäste der Filmtheater. Bevorzugte Kartenzuteilung bei starkem Andrang', *FK* (19 Nov. 1942), 1; 'Maßnahmen zur Steuerung des Filmtheater-Besuchs', *FK* (22 Feb. 1943), 1; 'Aktuelle Fragen des Filmtheaterbesuchs', *FK* (25 July 1944), 1.

Taken together, the insatiable desire for entertainment, the effort required to allocate it, and the ever-dwindling supply of good news left precious little scope for direct political mobilization. As it turned out, the last credible chapter of mobilization propaganda came with the spate of German victories during summer 1942. For the cinema, the film *Die große Liebe* and the hit songs it popularized were, as mentioned above, clearly geared to stabilize morale and did not shy away from direct reference to the war. But after the debacle at Stalingrad, the central message that commitment to the war effort represented the surest road to personal happiness was no longer convincing.[127] The newsreels also became more of a current-events reportage than a military documentation. As the Security Service reported in autumn 1943, it was obvious why the newsreels focused so heavily on sport and trivia: the shift towards 'peace-time matters' was a by-product of 'suppression of material about the front'.[128] As for the radio, broadcasting officials tried one last time to conjure a virtual Volksgemeinschaft in grand style on Christmas Day 1942. Thirty transmitting stations were set up all the way from Stalingrad to the Atlantic coast and from Norway to North Africa, to demonstrate once again the extent of German conquest. After all of the stations had reported in, listeners were enjoined to sing 'Silent Night' in unison as a kind of national blessing shared through state-of-the-art technology.[129] But by now such programming was wholly exceptional, and the subsequent military reversals further reinforced the entertainment focus of broadcasting. This steady displacement of mobilization propaganda by light entertainment paralleled the withdrawal of the Führer himself from public light, the regime's central propaganda figure. Having graced the front cover of the *Illustrierter Beobachter* fourteen times in 1940 (already down from around thirty times per year in the mid-1930s), Hitler appeared there only five times in 1943 and twice in 1944.[130] The mixture and tone of media content changed markedly as the war effort foundered, above all in autumn 1941 and over the winter of 1942–3. Making audiences receptive to political messages subsequently required so much 'bait' (that is, entertainment) that soon there was little else left.

That said, the regime's propaganda conduits were never totally severed, and some of its messages appear to have got through in spite of the seeming capitulation to amusement. Stories of Russian barbarity clearly stirred up anxieties about what would happen to anyone who surrendered to them, and constant tirades against the 'terrorist' bombings of historic city centres by uncultured Anglo-American bandits also successfully built on anti-western prejudices.[131] Although it is impossible to know what the majority of Germans made of the regime's anti-Semitic propaganda, the huge outpouring of bluntly annihilatory rhetoric

---

127 Kundrus, 'Totale', 154.   128 *Meldungen*, xiv. 5726–7.
129 Marßolek, 'Aus dem Volke', 134–5; Kundrus, 'Totale', 138.
130 Herz, *Hoffmann*, 339–47.   131 Kundrus, 'Totale', 126–9.

from summer 1941 onwards cannot have washed over the populace without effect.[132] For the time being, the daily OKW broadcast reports maintained a degree of credibility that other official sources of information had long since forfeited, providing a communication link between the military leadership and the populace right up through early 1945.[133] The detailed Wehrmacht information supplied to the press also helped to sustain a buoyant demand for newspapers and magazines, which eventually became scarce commodities alongside cinema tickets. Magazines were the hardest to find; by 1944 only around one-tenth of 1939 titles were still in print and overall circulation had dropped to one-fifth of pre-war levels.[134] Newspapers were also frequently sold out by early evening, which led some newsagents to sell only to 'regular customers'. At a U-Bahn station in south-west Berlin, for instance, such favouritism reportedly caused 'great irritation, quite apart from the snottiness of the salesgirl'.[135]

But as the military situation went from bad to worse, the constant appeals to resist and 'hold out' rang increasingly hollow. Given the overall mood, the RMVP was probably correct to conclude that the maintenance of morale was best served by avoiding unpleasant truths. Goebbels's famous 'orchestra' metaphor now took on a wholly different meaning: the regime's propaganda was, as one contemporary put it, 'like a band eagerly playing on board a sinking ship'.[136] For some Germans the jarring incongruence between escapist fantasies and the dire military predicament aroused a deep sense of scorn. Echoing the old refrain of the 'seriousness of the times', there were numerous calls for a ban on all public amusements, especially after the clampdown on unnecessary travel in summer 1944. 'The closure of all theatres, cinemas and pubs is the minimum demand made by broad segments of the populace,' reported the Security Service in July 1944. 'Why can the Japanese cope with these restrictions and we Germans cannot, especially now that there can be no doubt that we are in a fight for survival?'[137] These demands were in fact partially met on 1 September 1944, as all theatres, cabarets, and concert halls were closed indefinitely, leaving film and radio as the sole sources of entertainment.[138] Yet there were still complaints about the screening of lavish films and the existence of sizeable radio orchestras amidst the increasingly desperate mobilization for 'total war'. In early 1945 Berliners were complaining that 'there are supposedly "hundreds of men" walking around the Broadcasting House who could just as easily be soldiers. Why can't people satisfy themselves with records for the time being?'[139]

---

[132] Though interesting on this point, Herf, *Jewish Enemy*, overstates the case.

[133] Report from Nürnberg, 13 Mar. 1945, in W. Wette, R. Bremer, and D. Vogel (eds.), *Das letzte halbe Jahr* (hereafter *Das letzte halbe Jahr*) (Essen, 2001), 381.

[134] Frei, Schmitz, *Journalismus*, 82.

[135] *Das letzte halbe Jahr*, 196–7; see also 156, 179–80, 225, 360.

[136] Ibid., 310.   [137] *Meldungen*, xvii. 6657.

[138] 'Die neuen Maßnahmen für den totalen Kriegseinsatz', *FK* (25 Aug. 1944), 1.

[139] *Das letzte halbe Jahr*, 234.

Yet in spite of—or perhaps because of—the unfolding catastrophe, the cheerful tone of popular amusements lost little of its attraction. When, in the final months of the war, broadcasters temporarily deviated from the cheery prime-time format, it triggered widespread grumbling that 'too little light and entertainment music is being broadcast. Instead one hears some "Opus 296" or the like that would be better placed in the late-night slot.' After a hard days' work and an air-raid alarm most people wanted to hear 'cheerful and exhilarating music', not 'heavy music like Bach, Bruckner, Wagner, etc.'.[140] The danger was, as the Wehrmacht Propaganda Section warned, that 'when one tries to find other music on the radio it is not uncommon that one unintentionally listens to enemy broadcasters', thus counteracting the entire aim of keeping listeners tuned into German broadcasts.[141] Meanwhile, the fantasies and dramas in the cinema were also more sought-after than ever. As the struggle for seats intensified, so too did the scuffles in the queues and at the ticket-counters. Germans frequently took exception to the admission of foreigners, and soldiers sometimes resented the admission of civilians. In some cases, not even the police were able to bring the trouble under control. Once inside, customers understandably insisted on getting their money's worth. When, for instance, operators tried to close their cinemas after lengthy interruptions by air-raid alarms, this often led to 'tumultuous scenes, in the course of which there was no shortage of blunt remarks'.[142]

In these closing stages of the war there was precious little sense of 'national community' in the cinemas or on the airwaves. The continuing popularity of film and radio was hardly an expression of national resolve, but rather of the chaotic, individualized, dog-eat-dog 'society of collapse' in which survival, both physical and psychological, was paramount. What radio listeners demanded and what cinema-goers fought over was a brief respite from the grim realities of destruction and defeat, an individual refuge rather than a site of collective solidarity. This is not to argue that the regime's indulgence of such wishes was wholly counter-productive, for the sense of peacetime ordinariness and civilian familiarity this induced could have powerful stabilizing effects. What is so remarkable about the latter stages of the war is the extent to which German society held together at all. Among the multitude of factors behind this, it seems likely that entertainments played a significant role—not through indoctrination or aiding popular mobilization, but rather by invoking that desirable sense of 'normality' that helped people to soldier on in spite of the swelling chaos. The underlying message of the cheery tunes and upbeat films was not just 'enjoy yourself while you can', but also 'life goes on'.

Yet even so, media use over 1944–5 increasingly reflected the wider process of social breakdown under the pressures of 'total war'. As far as the information function of the media was concerned, the material they conveyed had become an

---

[140] *Das letzte halbe Jahr*, 145, 208.　　　[141] Ibid. 224; also Koch, *Wunschkonzert*, 137, 141.
[142] *Das letzte halbe Jahr*, 142; see also 172, 209.

essential part of the pulsating network of rumours and informal communication through which ordinary Germans sought to piece together a picture of events.[143] Despite their 'mass' distribution, the actual use and interpretation of media artefacts was thus increasingly shaped by the socially and spatially bounded channels of primary communication that gradually filled the vacuum left by the obvious omissions of official news sources. And as for their entertainment function, the media not only furnished an attractive opportunity for individual escapism but also, as we have just seen, new forms of social privilege and conflict. These new audience divides were noticeably different from the older lines of class, milieu, gender, and generation that shaped media use in the 1920s or 1930s. They were far more random, and had as much to do with circumstance and luck—the need to evacuate one's home, the vagaries of bomb damage, the time to wait in a queue—as with anything else. Nevertheless, they reflected a change in the social role of mass communications since the early years of the war. If the media initially helped to unify Germans by bringing common experiences and a shared sense of victory to a wider and more socially diverse audience, they were also part of the disintegration of the social fabric during the latter stages of the fighting. To make the point again, the context of media production and consumption was crucial.

Goebbels was thus quite wrong to interpret what he called the 'astounding' level of cinema admissions in early 1945 as evidence that 'in some respects the German people demonstrates a vitality and positive attitude to life that is absolutely astonishing; proof that we haven't the slightest reason to doubt them. They will follow us through thick and thin.'[144] A far more convincing explanation was provided by an internal morale report compiled a few weeks later: 'A large portion of the population has got used to living merely day by day. Every available source of pleasure is exploited. An otherwise trivial occasion is seized upon to drink the last bottle that was initially set aside for the victory celebration, for the end of blackouts, and the return of husbands and sons.'[145]

The correlate of this zealous search for enjoyment was a hypersensitivity against anything that reeked of 'propaganda'. Attempts to counteract the growing signs of disintegration with yet more appeals to resist were largely futile, and quite commonly counterproductive. This was particularly apparent in the cinema, which, unlike the radio or print press, had long been cherished as a source of entertainment rather than information and thus as a refuge from the regime. The newsreels and documentaries that had long carried the bulk of the propaganda burden were increasingly viewed with derision, eliciting widespread foot-stamping and artificial coughing. According to a report from Berlin, during a newsreel screening in November 1944 the bulk of the audience 'chatted as if in a

---

[143] Generally, Dröge, *Widerstand*.
[144] Fröhlich (ed.), *Tagebücher* 2:15, p. 190 (23 Jan. 1945).
[145] *Meldungen*, xvii. 6737; see also Stahr, *Volksgemeinschaft*, 258–67.

pub, with some people leaving while others arrived. References to the seriousness of the newsreel were answered with laughter.'[146] By early 1945 many towns were no longer getting the latest newsreels at all, which inevitably prompted suspicions 'that they cannot offer anything suitable at the moment. The people are not allowed to know what is happening at the front.' Even when the latest newsreel arrived, many viewers suspected—not entirely incorrectly—that they were staged.[147] In March 1945 viewers at the 'Onkel Tom' cinema in Berlin-Zehlendorf had grown sick and tired of the feature being interrupted by the daily air-raid alarms and demanded that it be screened before the newsreel: 'A number of visitors forced a change of programme through thoroughly vulgar behaviour such as stamping, whistling, bellowing etc. People wanted to see the main film . . . first. Who was still interested in the newsreel, it is all fraud, propaganda, etc.' Sure enough, after the operator assented to their wishes the newsreel was interrupted by the usual sirens.[148]

If ordinary civilians sought a temporary escape from reality during the closing months of the war, the regime's propaganda demonstrated little grasp of reality at all. Granted, hyperbole is an integral part of the publicity game, and the point at which it strays into absurdity is a matter of opinion. But the use of hopelessly exaggerated slogans such as 'Every *Volkssturm*-man has the fighting power of a whole company!' eventually brought even the valued OKW reports into disrepute. After all, most of the promises had proven empty: there was no secret weapon, there were no adequate air defences, and there was no point in pretending otherwise.[149] 'The people have no trust in the leadership anymore,' concluded an internal report from March 1945. 'They sharply criticize the party, certain leading figures, and official propaganda. . . . An attitude is spreading in which the means of propaganda can hardly even reach the people anymore.'[150] This inaccessibility of would-be recipients was thoroughly unsurprising, given how out of touch the propaganda had become. To offer merely one illustration, the final 'slogan of the week' issued by the Periodical Service on 9 March 1945 still enjoined magazine editors to spread the message 'Resist! Attack!' Though farcical enough in itself, the slogan takes on an almost surreal quality when considered alongside the accompanying letter explaining that the entire edition of 3 February had been destroyed by the Allied bombers' 'terror attack' on Berlin that day, and therefore would not be delivered.[151]

Nowhere were these propaganda delusions so manifest as in the bombastic Veit Harlan film *Kolberg*, the swansong of Nazi cinema that symbolically premiered on 30 January 1945, the twelfth anniversary of the Nazi takeover. Filmed between summer 1943 and summer 1944, it was the single most expensive production of the Third Reich, costing a mammoth RM 8.8 million. The story revolves around

---

[146] *Das letzte halbe Jahr*, 163, 246.   [147] *Das letzte halbe Jahr*, 365.
[148] Ibid. 332.   [149] Ibid. 246, 335.   [150] *Meldungen*, xvii. 6738–9.
[151] Koszyk, *Deutsche Presse 1914–1945*, 423–4.

the defence of the Pomeranian fortress town of Kolberg (Kołobrzeg) in 1807, where retreating Prussian forces under Count Neidhardt von Gneisenau and the local militia under never-say-die city councillor Joachim Nettelbeck heroically hold out against French troops and doubters within their own ranks. This was the Nazis' definitive *Durchhaltefilm*, unabashedly geared to steel resolve and spur resistance. No expense was spared, whether financial, material, or logistical. As Berlin was being pounded into rubble, large sections of historic Kolberg were replicated nearby, only to be blown up by a team of thirty pyrotechnicians. As Soviet troops were crossing into East Prussia, some 5,000 troops and 3,000 horses were temporarily diverted from the front for the monumental battle scenes. As the Wehrmacht was plagued by transportation difficulties, around 100 railway wagons full of salt were hauled in to film snow scenes during the summer.[152]

Yet, in spite of all the resources poured into the film, by the time it was released it gained only a limited screening. In early 1945 many of Germany's cinemas had been destroyed, and transport bottlenecks made the film impossible to distribute to more than a handful of cities. Bizarrely, it was first screened to German troops surrounded by Allied forces in La Rochelle, after allegedly being parachuted in by a daring behind-the-lines operation. Following its simultaneous premiere in Berlin, copies of the film were specially dispatched to beleaguered cities such as Breslau, Danzig, and Königsberg in the hope that viewers would follow Nettelbeck's example and ward off the invaders.[153] But *Kolberg* came too late to reach more than a tiny portion of the population, and had it done so it is doubtful that the film would have fulfilled even a fraction of the high expectations Goebbels placed on it. In mid-March the actual town of Kolberg was captured by the Red Army, and no amount of dramatized heroism would change this. The tens of thousands of soldiers, residents, and refugees who fled the destroyed 'fortress city' of Kolberg were, like the millions of others on the move to escape the fighting, hardly likely to take much courage from the film, or even to see it for that matter. Even the handful of guests invited to the premiere at Berlin's Tauentzien-Palast (the flagship UFA-Palast am Zoo had already been destroyed) were more worried about getting home before the next air raid than pointlessly resisting the Soviet forces encamped barely 80 kilometres away on the Oder river.[154]

Tellingly, by the closing stages of the war it seems that the propaganda minister genuinely deemed the fictional defence of *Kolberg* more important than the actual fall of the city. In late March he tried to 'ensure that the evacuation of

---

[152] See R. Giesen, *Nazi Propaganda Films* (Jefferson, NC, 2003), 169–72. As Giesen correctly points out, Harlan's oft-cited claim of deploying 187,000 troops and 6,000 horses as film extras is hugely exaggerated, and has unfortunately been passed on by nearly every study on Nazi film: V. Harlan, *Im Schatten meiner Filme. Selbstbiographie* (Gütersloh, 1966), 262–3.

[153] Giesen, *Nazi Propaganda Films*, 174–5, which expresses well-founded scepticism about Goebbels' parachuting claim.

[154] Ibid. 176–7.

Fig. 17. Ruins of the flagship Ufa-Palast am Zoo, 1945. bpk Berlin.

Kolberg is not mentioned in the OKW report. We could do without that at the moment in view of the dire psychological repercussions for the Kolberg film.'[155] No inopportune facts were to detract from its carefully staged images of heroic loyalty and self-sacrifice. A few weeks later, on 17 April, this obsession with appearance, this confusion of art and reality, was even more blatantly revealed at the last of the daily 11 o'clock briefings in the Propaganda Ministry. Surrounded by fifty of his closest associates, most of whom were desperate to get out of the capital before the Soviets came, Goebbels issued one final appeal: 'Gentlemen, in a hundred years someone will make a fine colour film about the terrible days we are living through. Wouldn't you like to play a role in this film? Hold out now so that the spectators don't boo and whistle when you appear on the screen.'[156]

[155] Fröhlich (ed.), *Tagebücher*, 2:15, 542 (20 Mar. 1945).
[156] Quoted from B. Kleinhans, *Ein Volk, ein Reich, ein Kino* (Cologne, 2003), 7.

Futile resistance as big-budget film epic; Germany's defeat and devastation in splendid Agfa colour. This perverse choice of metaphor testifies not only to the Nazi predilection for melodramatic *Götterdämmerung*, but also to the unshakeable belief in the power of propaganda among much of the leadership. It demonstrates the extraordinary extent to which the 'realities' conveyed by the media were gradually conflated with reality per se. The Nazis always prioritized appearance over substance, and once the regime had disintegrated, appearances were all that was left. From this perspective Goebbels' final appeal to ministry officials was, like Hitler's notorious 'scorched earth' order that consigned the German populace to its fate, more than just a call to die a noble death at the side of the Führer. It was above all a gesture to posterity, a conscious aesthetic pose for the sake of remembrance as a tragically heroic movement. True to Nazi priorities, starring in this 'final film' was not a point of honour but a matter of image.

Conclusion

It seems only fair at the end of this book to offer some thoughts about the place of mass culture in German life during the period covered here. And as a starting-point it is worth reiterating that the expansion of mass communications and the cultural changes it entailed were a fundamental part of the industrial era. Some of the most elemental aspects of modern society have been decisively shaped by the media, and indeed developed in conjunction with them. A sense of nationhood and shared history, the exchange of mutually relevant information, the formation and reproduction of societal cohesion and commonly held cultural values—all are rooted in 'mass' forms of communication. Throughout most of Europe, and quite clearly in the case of Germany, the nation-state itself coalesced into a stable political entity in the age of mass communications. By transcending the older social and regional structures in which primary, inter-personal communications were firmly embedded, the mass media helped create a more open and accessible public space in which common political concerns could be discussed and common cultural interests satisfied—in short, a forum for 'mass politics' and 'mass culture'.

It is thus often said that the overall impetus of mass culture is fundamentally democratic. Viewed over the long run, it represented the displacement of bourgeois cultural predominance by the supremacy of popular culture. As such, it was the cultural correlate of democratic suffrage: it embodied the ability of the uncultivated masses to choose what they wanted rather than accept what others chose for them. Although the primary interest of entertainers and media magnates was to make money, they nonetheless aided this transformation by trying to meet the demands of the majority, who for their part enjoyed higher incomes and shorter working hours than ever before. The commercial market for entertainments meant that much of cultural life was no longer under the control of traditional elites. At base, mass culture was about ordinary people doing what they liked with the spare time and money that they justly demanded from their labour.[1]

Viewed from the perspective of the early twenty-first century, this basic narrative seems plausible enough—allowing, of course, for the various problems

---

[1] Maase, *Grenzenloses*, 16–20, makes a concise case; also K. H. Jarausch and M. Geyer, *Shattered Past* (Princeton, 2003), 286–90; E. Hobsbawm, *The Age of Empire* (London, 1994), 219–42.

and drawbacks that inevitably arose. But when applied to the period under investigation here, it is clear that this argument should not be taken too far. As this book has shown at length, Germany of all countries demonstrates not the intrinsic affinity between medialization and democratization, but rather its political ambivalence.[2] Yes, mass culture and communications clearly resonate with ideas about equality, popular sovereignty, and democratic choice, but they can just as easily serve to undermine this project and indeed uphold the most vicious anti-democratic dictatorship. Looking back on the preceding chapters, the story told here is thus not a celebration of popular emancipation or cultural democratization. But even less is it a tale of social atomization and elite manipulation. Historical research on twentieth-century Germany emphasized for too long the anti-democratic potential of the mass media, which is why studies of communications have largely focused on the Nazi period or the years leading up to it. Although the media have at times certainly misled the public and suppressed the truth, it is nonetheless impossible to imagine a broadly based democratic order without them. One thing we have learned over the last two decades is that the sphere of modern consumption and leisure was (and is) a point of access and an arena for political participation, in terms of both the 'big politics' of state affairs as well as the 'small politics' of everyday life. The rise of mass culture symbolized the legitimacy of popular tastes and the importance of attending to the interests of 'the people'. In this sense the media were a fundamental prerequisite for both the mass-mobilizing 'totalitarian' movements of the twentieth century as well as the creation of a more open and democratic society.

Of course, the idea that the media played an ambiguous role in twentieth-century politics is not much of an insight. Far less obvious is their impact on patterns of social and cultural change. As Part III in particular demonstrated, the common assumption that the rise of mass communications replaced traditional patterns of leisure with a more classless, standardized, and international 'mass culture' assumes too much. Over the long term there can be little doubt that the media helped to erode traditional socio-cultural hierarchies. But as we have seen in some detail, this was neither straightforward nor inevitable, for their impact was continually mediated through the social and political structures in which audiences lived. In order to understand the social role or 'life' of mass culture, it is thus crucial to abandon notions of a thoroughly standardized cultural product consumed by an increasingly uniform 'mass' or even 'national' audience. Although early twentieth-century audiences often transcended class, regional, generational, and gender boundaries (less so for the press than for radio and film), their sociological make-up was highly uneven, and many social divisions were reproduced or even accentuated by the expansion of media-borne entertainments. Moreover, even when different social groups read the same

---

[2] The central theme of Bösch and Frei (eds.), *Medialisierung*.

newspaper or saw the same film, this did not mean that the actual reception and effects of these cultural artefacts were in any sense 'homogenizing'. Users not only actively chose from what was on offer, but also imbued it with their own meanings—which is why mass entertainments have ultimately proved more compatible with pluralism than with totalitarian claims to absolute truth.[3]

The point is not that the linear assumptions about the rise of 'mass culture' are totally wrong, since the gradual transcendence of geographical and social boundaries by the media obviously denoted far-reaching cultural changes. Nor is it to posit a reverse chain of causality, whereby social transformation drives the media instead of the other way around. The tired old debates about whether the media function as a 'motor' or 'mirror' of social change are based on a false dichotomy. A more useful way to conceive of this relationship is to recognize that the media can actively promote change by enabling more open communication between different groups, while at the same time reflecting in crucial respects the immediate social contexts in which they operate. Put differently, the point is—once again—that the media could both unite *and* divide audiences, and that the particular outcome depended very much on the circumstances of any given time and place. All the talk of social and cultural 'levelling' is easily understandable from the perspective of contemporaries. What struck most observers during the first third of the twentieth century was the apparent decline of older structures of distinction. Among educated elites in particular, this sense of upheaval was no doubt magnified after 1918 by the fact that it coincided with far-reaching changes to the structures of political sovereignty and economic power (suffrage and welfare expansion, the effects of inflation). By contrast, the simultaneous emergence of new differences, or rather the shifting ways in which social differences were expressed via new cultural practices, seems to have been far less obvious to most contemporaries. The demise of the conventional is perhaps always more recognizable than the emergence of the unfamiliar. When historians adopt this rhetoric of socio-cultural 'levelling' they are, to a certain extent, taking contemporaries' word for it.

The question we are then confronted with is not whether the rise of mass culture undercuts or reinforces social and cultural difference, but rather its role within an ever-shifting structure of differentiation. Bourdieu's concept of cultural 'habitus', which stresses how social distinction is produced (both consciously and unconsciously) in everyday behaviour and matters of 'taste', can be fruitfully applied here.[4] Viewing the new media not through the lens of the stark class divides of the nineteenth century but rather the 'subtle distinctions' of the age of mass culture seems the most promising way to make sense of these changes.[5]

---

[3] On this thought, see T. Lindenberger (ed.), *Massenmedien im Kalten Krieg* (Cologne, 2006), 14–17.

[4] Bourdieu, *Distinction*; id., 'Structures'.

[5] One can, furthermore, overestimate the class character of the media in the 19th century: e.g. W. Faulstich, *Medienwandel im Industrie- und Massenzeitalter (1830–1900)* (Göttingen, 2004), 257–8.

Put differently, insofar as the media helped to create a more universally shared cultural space held in common by a wide spectrum of social groups, it was their variegated appropriation by these different groups that holds the key to understanding their social impact.

How the media were appropriated was—though inherently difficult to analyse—clearly based on a wide range of social, economic, and political factors. At the most basic level, the audiences of this period were decisively shaped by cost and availability. In our current age of media saturation it is easy to lose sight of the many material limitations within which mass culture developed over the first half of the century. Moreover, the effects of the various media also differed according to the character of their regulation, their relationship to established customs, and how they were mediated to actual audiences. As always, the precise nature of production and consumption was paramount. As we have seen at length, state-sponsored radio could either prioritize the interests of educated elites or seek to overturn such hierarchies, depending on the intentions of producers and make-up of the audience. And commercial cinema could either reinforce socio-cultural divides or efface them, depending on the diversity of supply and nature of reception. Only when we look at the media within their wider historical context can we adequately understand their social uses and meanings.

Approaching the question in this way helps us to understand not only the situation within Germany but also what, if anything, was unique about the story there, for the rise of mass culture always included a global and local dimension. Many of the underlying changes were universal, from the medialization of politics to the 'democratizing' effects of commercial entertainments. What was distinctive in the German case was a particular set of circumstances that profoundly shaped these common elemental trends: the peculiar self-understanding and cultural fixations of the educated elite, the remarkably deep social and political divisions in Germany, the curious compensatory faith in the power of propaganda and 'fighting spirit' (further magnified by the loss of the First World War), the extraordinary degree of economic upheaval and political polarization, and, of course, the sheer ruthlessness of the Nazi movement in controlling cultural life and excluding racial 'outsiders'. In Germany as elsewhere, the mass media became an integral part of the social, cultural, and political fabric during this period. But as this book has sought to show, their specific role in Germany's turbulent history was decisively shaped by local conditions.

Likewise, only by considering these issues over a lengthy stretch of time can we appreciate how the societal context of mass culture changed. When we do so, an interesting pattern emerges. By and large, the most formative episodes were not the 'good times' of relative stability and prosperity but rather periods of economic upheaval and social disorientation. For both the cinema and the print press, the First World War witnessed as much change as the preceding decade-and-a-half since 1900. Under the Weimar Republic it was not the (relatively) 'golden years' of the later 1920s but the ordeals of revolution and inflation during which popular entertainments made their most rapid strides.[6] Most significant of all was the Depression of the early 1930s. During these years a combination of commercial and technological changes transformed the media ensemble from within, while immense social and political upheavals transformed the overall context from without. The Second World War had a huge impact as well, though many of the changes after 1939 represented an intensification of trends and patterns that had already emerged from the fundamental shifts of the early 1930s. Although the breakthrough of a new, commercial 'mass culture' in Germany is often associated with the rising prosperity of the turn of the century or the cultural fermentation of the 1920s, it was in fact the traumas of war and Depression that marked the most important turning-points.

One of the conclusions we can draw from this is that the increasingly media-oriented culture of the Weimar Republic was, for all its vaunted 'modernity', very much embedded in existing social and cultural structures. If film, recording, broadcasting, and the press partly overlaid existing social boundaries, on balance they reflected and even reinforced them.[7] In large part this was due to the practical problems of distribution and availability, which were themselves based on cost and technical constraints. It also mirrored the diverse expectations among different social groups whose very access to the media varied greatly. And not least, it reflected the predominantly conservative and paternalist orientation of most Weimar cultural elites. Whether this took the form of a rearguard action against the profanity of the masses or a well-meaning attempt to counter the down-draughts of commercialization, neither response did much to advance the development of a 'universal art'. Yes, the tabloid headlines, gaudy film advertisements, six-day cycle races, and Marlene Dietrich were all part of Weimar's exciting new visual culture—arguably 'the visual embodiment of the modern *per se*'.[8] But they represented only a tiny part of the cultural puzzle in inter-war Germany, and even among people familiar with them their impact was still filtered through older structures. When we consider the social role of mass culture in 1920s Germany, what is most striking is not the tradition-smashing novelty of Weimar's cultural 'modernity', but rather how closely it was still tied to class, region, and milieu.

Under the Nazis this looked rather different. As an avowedly populist move-ment, National Socialism deliberately sought to promote the emergence of a widely shared popular culture. Insofar as they succeeded, the Nazis certainly could not claim all of the credit. Over the course of the 1930s their endeavours were abetted by a series of commercial, technological, and economic developments

---

[6] See esp. Geyer, *Verkehrte*, 387.

[7] One need not make an exception for 'Weimar culture' when arguing that patterns of consumption in this period reinforced social boundaries more than undermined them: Jarausch and Geyer, *Shattered*, 308.

[8] Ward, *Weimar*, 2.

over which they had limited control at best. But in the sphere of popular culture the Nazis nonetheless realized many of the goals held by reformist groups throughout the first third of the century. Of course, their aim of tying a shared popular culture to the construction of a violently exclusive racial community was quite different from that of their left-leaning predecessors. But neither did it mirror the paternalistic tenets of the conservative Bildungsbürgertum. It was not Rosenberg and the *Kultur*-fanatics in the Combat League who won the day, but Goebbels the entertainer. Just as established political elites were increasingly marginalized in the affairs of state, so too were cultural elites increasingly disregarded in the Nazi administration of the mass media. What mattered was the creation of a popular national culture that could be shared by the entire Volk, and toward this end the regime achieved some notable successes. Ironically, the road to Nazi mass culture was paved in large part by the very 'asphalt culture' of Hollywood-style films and jazz-inspired hit songs that the movement had so noisily railed against before 1933.

For the more puritanical *völkisch* elements in the party, this fell well short of the grand cultural revolution they envisaged. Clearly, there can be no talk of a thorough homogenization or *Gleichschaltung* of popular culture under the Nazis. But the emphasis that is often placed on the lack of a decisive break during the Third Reich expects a lot from such a short period of time.[9] If we dispense with such expectations and place these years within a longer-term context, what becomes most striking is not the inevitable continuities but rather the unusual scope and pace of change. Mass culture under the Nazis did not and could not destroy the multitude of class, confessional, or regional differences that shaped German cultural life, nor could it completely stifle the continuing perception of these differences. But the particular constellation of the Third Reich did promote a popular set of cultural artefacts and practices that were significantly more widely shared than before—an 'alternative public sphere in which Germans identified themselves increasingly as *Volksgenossen*'.[10] Disturbing though it may seem, the Nazi years were in many respects the heyday of 'mass culture' in Germany—not just of politically coordinated uniformity and standardization, but also of a broadly accessible cultural space in which different social groups could readily find something in common.

From this perspective, viewing the growth of the media as part of the 'modernizing' impact of the Third Reich has its merits. Indeed, it is arguably in the realm of popular culture that this ostensible phenomenon was most apparent.[11] Nazi cultural officials did far more to legitimate 'mere entertainment' than most of their predecessors. Furthermore, for the many millions of Germans

---

[9] Cf. the basic thrust of Reichel, *Der schöne Schein*; Grunberger, *Social History*.
[10] P. Fritzsche, 'Nazi Modern', *Modernism/modernity*, 3 (1996), 7.
[11] Bavaj, *Ambivalenz*, 158–63; C. Zimmermann, 'From Propaganda to Modernization', *GH* 24 (2006), 443–5.

living in small towns and villages, it was first under the Nazis that the glitz and glamour of media hype and celebrity arrived in full force. By the end of the 1930s the media had become an essential part of the popular cultural infrastructure, not just for entertainments narrowly definexe but for everything from sport to cooking. Indeed, the 'modernity' of National Socialist Germany was itself a primary theme in much of what they conveyed, from idolized racing-drivers to women's fashions.[12] If one of the defining characteristics of modernization is a break with tradition and an acceleration of change, then National Socialism had a sizeable modernizing effect in the realm of mass communications and popular culture, especially during the war. And if the last generation of scholarship on Imperial and Weimar Germany has taught us anything, it is to avoid rigid dualities that pit the modern and emancipatory against the anti-modern and illiberal.

Yet the preceding chapters nonetheless show that any benefits of viewing these changes through the lens of 'modernization' must not obscure the very substantial drawbacks. The disadvantages are related not only to the normative connotations of the term 'modern', but also to questions of substance. Despite persistent myths to the contrary, the Nazis were not especially advanced in the advocacy of media use and popular entertainments. Clearly they adopted a more modern approach than most Weimar or Imperial elites, but as was just pointed out, this is not saying much. Much of what the Nazis 'accomplished' within the media landscape was essentially destructive, not creative. In contrast to developments elsewhere in the 1930s and 1940s, the emergence of a more universal and socially inclusive 'mass culture' in the Third Reich resulted not only from the overlapping and amalgamation of different regional or milieu-based networks of communication, but also from the forceful repression of opposing views and the brutal amputation of public spheres deemed undesirable by the regime.[13] Reducing the fragmentation of the press involved the violent suppression of political rivals and the ruthless commercial exploitation of state pressure. Transforming the radio into an instrument of popular entertainment was a tactic to lure audiences towards a tightly controlled flow of news and views. Granted, the popularity of the 'national *Großfilm*' was rooted in much the same formula as the Hollywood blockbusters on which it was modelled; but even here the messages it conveyed were constrained by Nazi censorship, and 'racial outsiders' were expressly forbidden from taking part.

In other words, the remarkable ability of the mass media to integrate audiences in the Third Reich was predicated not only on social assimilation but also on exclusion and repression. And what started out as the suppression of rival

---

[12] See generally E. Schütz and G. Streim (eds), *Reflexe und Reflexionen von Modernität 1933–1945* (Bern, 2002), esp. U. Day, 'Das dritte Reich dreht auf. Rennsport in den NS-Medien und die Modernisierung der Sinne', 61–81; J. Bertschik, 'Zopf mit Bubikopf', 273–92.

[13] For Britain and the USA: LeMahieu, *Culture*; Cohen, *Making*.

networks of communication grew over time into a carefully constructed edifice of social isolation and racial discrimination. After the personnel purges and newspaper closures of the early years came the banning of Jews from mainstream cinemas and the confiscation of their radios, followed by the wartime exclusion of foreign labour conscripts and POWs from the cultural life of the Volk. For all its seemingly apolitical stress on personal pleasure, Nazi mass culture in practice thus forged subtle but powerful links between individual enjoyment and racial hierarchy, and ultimately between racial hierarchy and conquest.

Indeed, Goebbels underscored these connections with remarkable frankness in a lead article for *Das Reich* on 31 May 1942, as Cologne still literally burned from the RAF's largest bombing attack to date. In response to the question 'What's it all for?', he argued that this was not a war for throne and altar but rather 'to secure the preconditions for a national prosperity which will give our people the amount of earthly happiness they deserve'. At base it was a struggle for the good life: for a well-stocked table, pretty villages, plentiful raw materials, adequate housing and—yes—'for theatres and cinemas' too. Although such pronouncements were obviously intended to boost morale, there is something eerily candid about the assertion that 'We as a nation want at last to cash in (*einkassieren*) . . . to enjoy the fruits of our endless working and fighting, of all our efforts and our patience'. In essence, this declaration took the implicit message of films like *Wunschkonzert* and *Die große Liebe* to its logical conclusion. Not only was performing one's duty the surest road to personal fulfilment, but fighting for the national cause was the key to a better future, a future 'marked by a joy in life' in which 'the theatres and music halls, the cinemas and community halls will fill up every evening with happy people. Art will go to the people and the people will go to art.'[14] In short, the wages of conquest would be pleasure.[15] The 'beautiful sheen' created by the media did not furnish a curtain behind which the violence, aggression, and murder could take place, but rather integrated this project into the everyday lives of ordinary people. These underlying connections between cultural integration and violent exclusion, between light-hearted amusement and racial warfare, were what most clearly distinguished mass culture in the Third Reich from parallel developments elsewhere. Certainly there were many innovations and forward-looking changes along the way, and the barbaric ends to which they were put does not mean that we should ignore them. But against this backdrop, viewing the Nazi-controlled media as a 'modernizing' force per se only seems appropriate if we adopt an extraordinarily gloomy and inhumane assessment of 'modernity'.

There is also the question of how far the changes under the Nazis were actually caused by the regime or merely coincided with it. As noted above, many of

---

[14] Repr. in Noakes (ed.), *Nazism*, iv. 486–7.
[15] For a fuller, if overstated, elaboration of this idea: G. Aly, *Hitler's Beneficiaries* (New York, 2006).

the basic trends were readily observable across Europe and North America. The process of commercial concentration and technological convergence between the different media was a global phenomenon, and if anything went farther in some other countries, notably the United States. In terms of content, the constant appeals to upward mobility and social harmony were by no means exceptional. It is often suggested that Nazi mass culture was distinguished above all by its productivist thrust and its emphasis on collective experience, both of which were undoubtedly very prominent.[16] Prominent, but not unique, for again we can see numerous parallels elsewhere. The leisure agency 'Strength through Joy' was part of a much wider pattern of 'rational recreation' in the 1930s, consciously modelled on the Italian 'Dopolavoro' and, despite its considerable popularity, clearly outstripped by the mass leisure efforts of the Popular Front government in France. Furthermore, utilizing the media for the purpose of national integration was hardly peculiar to Germany, especially during the Depression. King George V's first Christmas radio address in 1932, listened to by some 20 million people around the world, was specially crafted by Rudyard Kipling to evoke the sense of a virtual community, in this case a global Commonwealth family: 'I speak now from my home and from my heart to you all.'

When one considers developments in other countries in the 1930s and 1940s, it is difficult to escape the conclusion that much of what constituted 'Nazi mass culture' would have come about anyway.[17] Indeed, apart from the explicit racism on display (which itself was not wholly without parallel elsewhere), probably the most unique characteristic of the Third Reich was the extent to which government policies actually *hindered* rather than helped the growth of a media-based popular culture. For all the efforts to promote radio, cinema, and the press, the forced rearmament drive of the 1930s and the deliberate suppression of real wages effectively stifled audience expansion. Although this changed markedly with the wartime glut of purchasing power, even during the boom years of 1939–44, media uptake was more or less in line with similarly developed countries—at least those that did not have their radios and paper supplies plundered by German occupying forces.

At this point one might object that there was one area in which the Nazis clearly excelled, namely the use of modern propaganda techniques. As a movement led largely by failed artists, National Socialism always exhibited a certain penchant for publicity. Its successful bid to become the first broad-based 'people's party' in Germany owed much to its ability to tailor a new, cross-class message to the socially diverse media public that had emerged over the 1910s and 1920s; to some extent the rise of the mass media furnished the basic conditions for building such a multifarious movement. Undoubtedly, Goebbels and his associates were

---

[16] e.g. G. Brockhaus, *Schauder und Idylle* (Munich, 1997); Kundrus, 'Totale'; Baranowski, *Strength*; Jarausch, Geyer, *Shattered*, 294–5.

[17] For more general comparisons: W. Schivelbusch, *Entfernte Verwandtschaft* (Munich, 2005).

far better at this than their electoral opponents before 1933. And once in power, the Nazis were unquestionably pioneers of 'politainment'. By the end of the war their propaganda skills were already the stuff of legend. To this day, popular perceptions differ little from Albert Speer's self-exculpatory depiction of the Third Reich as 'a dictatorship which made complete use of all technical means in a perfect manner for the domination of its own nation. Through technical devices such as radio and loudspeaker 80 million people were deprived of independent thought. It was thereby possible to subject them to the will of one man.'[18]

But here too we must take care not to exaggerate, for despite their undoubted supremacy within Germany, Nazi publicists were hardly in a league of their own. When it came to overseas propaganda it was arguably the French who led the way, with their emphasis on subtle cultural diplomacy. In many countries, and certainly the United States, the Nazis' aggressive agitation proved counterproductive.[19] And when it came to merging political appeals with entertainment and utilizing the insights of modern marketing, the National Publicity Bureau in Britain, a Tory-run agency that made propaganda for the National Government, was every bit as clever as the RMVP. From the use of cinema vans to the launch of slick journals to the involvement of professional advertisers, its behind-the-scenes activities were all the more effective for their concealment.[20] In the United States, 'public relations' was already an integral part of politics by the 1930s. As noted earlier, President Roosevelt's personalized fireside chats, which were specially designed to exploit the distinctive characteristics of broadcasting, made Hitler's long-winded radio sermons look positively amateurish.[21]

Why, then, did the Nazis, the most renowned propagandists of the twentieth century, get some aspects of their propaganda so visibly wrong? The comparison with Roosevelt is instructive, for it highlights the often-overlooked self-limitations of National Socialist propaganda. Even after taking power, the Nazis were still bound by the particular political style they had developed. Although their brash and dynamic image proved highly effective at drumming up electoral support in the early 1930s, to some extent it became an encumbrance thereafter. Try as one might, no individual or movement can totally change its public image once it is established. The strident and aggressive manner that Hitler had rehearsed before 1933 meant that he could not convincingly strike a personal tone like George V, let alone hold a 'fireside chat' like Roosevelt, whose wise, grandfatherly image was also cultivated for years. Furthermore, the difference between Roosevelt's

[18] Testimony at Nuremberg, available at http://www.yale.edu/lawweb/avalon/imt/proc/08-31-46.htm.

[19] R. J. Young, *Marketing Marianne* (Piscataway, NJ, 2004), 119–21, 175–6; also P. Taylor, *The Projection of Britain* (Cambridge, 1981).

[20] R. Cockett, *Twilight of Truth* (London, 1989); T. J. Hollins, 'The Conservative Party and Film Propaganda Between the Wars', *English Historical Review*, 96 (1981), 359–69.

[21] Levine, *People and the President*.

homespun tête-à-têtes and Hitler's pulpit-thumping monologues was not only a matter of personal styles but also of fundamental differences in political culture. Obvious though it seems, it is worth remembering in this context that a dictatorship can ultimately fall back on coercion, whereas a democracy cannot. For Hitler, unlike Roosevelt, swaying the crowd was desirable but not absolutely essential. True, popular adulation and personal prestige were crucial in both cases. But the sovereign Führer could indulge in a measure of narcissistic self-importance, the elected president could not. The Nazis' propaganda shortcomings become less puzzling when we recognize that, in the final instance, democrats have a greater need for effective persuasion.

Be that as it may, German elites from the Empire to the Third Reich clearly recognized that the rise of the mass media brought obvious political advantages. Not only did they furnish a powerful communicative conduit to the masses, but in a deeply divided society they also promised to ameliorate social antagonisms and thereby contribute to political stability. By the First World War at the latest, and especially in its aftermath, the political significance of modern communications was taken for granted. Astute observers recognized the close interrelationship between the development of commercialized mass culture and patterns of political mobilization, in terms of both adapting political appeals to the new communicative terrain as well as ensuring that entertainments conformed to certain rules. But what German elites (like most of their counterparts elsewhere) tended to misunderstand was why such entertainments were so popular in the first place. Most of what the mass media conveyed seemed primitive or tasteless by the standards of educated observers, but it played on much more than the 'base instincts' or 'false consciousness' of the crowd. As cultural snobs themselves discovered when they slunk into a cinema or furtively browsed through the sports pages, commercial amusements appealed to the universal longing for 'fun' and simple pleasure. Of course, what different groups might regard as 'fun' can vary immensely, but all the same, this was much more than an opiate substitute for 'real' fulfilment. Comic sketches, human-interest stories, Westerns, and dance tunes were popular not only because they offered a temporary flight from life's disappointments, but above all for providing a genuine aesthetic experience for ordinary people. They afforded some distance from the given routines and horizons of daily life. They were, in short, 'art', and indeed an art form that was specifically designed for the modern division between work and free time, for temporary distraction and relaxed absorption in the midst of a busy schedule.[22] And it was in part this very user-centredness that led most German elites, steeped as they were in the veneration of *demanding* art, to overlook their aesthetic appeal.

As we try to account for the huge expansion of the media throughout this period, it is thus crucial to remember that their growth was driven not only by far-reaching technological, social, and cultural changes but also by eminently

---

[22] Maase, *Grenzenloses*, 27–31.

quotidian concerns about the pursuit of happiness and self-fulfilment. This is, perhaps, of special importance in the German case, for the fact that these concerns could resonate with the various social visions on offer during the early twentieth century helps to explain why mass culture continued to thrive under such vastly different political orders. Pleasure and fun were always a decisive element in the equation, from the growth of the Wilhelmine press to the dance craze of the Weimar years to the escapist fantasies of Nazi cinema. And this was also why the tried-and-tested formats of popular amusements constituted such a persistent thread of continuity throughout a period characterized by the most immense and catastrophic ruptures, running well into the age of tranquil prosperity that followed. Fritz Hippler was quite right when he remarked in 1940 that: 'I am convinced that the great Sunday mass-experience of the *Wunschkonzert* will still be in demand among tens of thousands of future peacetime listeners long after the wartime premises no longer apply.'[23] Although he undoubtedly had a very different post-war order in mind than what actually came, there was every reason to assume that the highly popular wartime request shows and contemporary revues—themselves successful adaptations of long-established entertainment genres—would shape cultural expectations for years, even decades, after 1945.

Indeed, the mass cultural experiences of the first half of the twentieth century not only shaped expectations but also significantly informed post-war memories in Germany. Even—perhaps especially—during the catastrophic years of the Second World War, the bulk of films, operetta tunes, and radio shows still revolved around the joys and misfortunes of private life, without leaders, without the horrors of the war, without victims—that is to say, without context. In many ways these disembodied dream worlds fitted perfectly into the decontextualized memories of the Nazi years as a whole, where the life stories of civilians and soldiers alike were often recalled as narratives of victimhood and primary group survival against powerful forces beyond one's control.[24] Although this tendency was obviously based on the reluctance to face painful questions of responsibility and blame, it was also encouraged by the fact that so much of popular culture under National Socialism was set at a safe distance from the wider world of war and politics. Even amidst the all-out mobilization for 'total war', mass entertainments still principally catered to the private search for pleasure. As other leisure alternatives dried up, the media of radio and especially cinema could be used as a haven of 'non-political' enjoyment amidst the increasingly harsh and threatening landscape of the Third Reich. Devoid of the destruction, murder, and complicity that surrounded them, most of the entertainments from the Nazi era could thus be easily integrated into the cultural fabric of the post-war period, which for many years refrained from drawing unsettling connections between the

---

[23] F. Hippler, 'Politischer Film oder Unterhaltungsfilm?', *FK* (26 Sept. 1940), 2.
[24] R. G. Moeller, *War Stories* (Berkeley, 2001); U. Herbert, 'Good Times, Bad Times', in R. Bessel (ed.), *Life in the Third Reich* (Oxford, 1987), 97–110.

wider context and the immediate life-worlds of ordinary people. After the war, as before, the reception and impact of the media was determined not so much by their specific content as by the ways in which audiences used them within the particular historical context. But this complex process of integrating different, and often problematic, cultural remnants into a new mosaic of post-fascist civility is another story, and one that historians have only recently begun to tell.

Bibliography

PUBLISHED PRIMARY WORKS

ACKERKNECHT, E., *Bildungspflege und Schallplatte* (Stettin, 1930).

ADAMS, M., *Ausnutzung der Freizeit des Arbeiters*, Ph.D thesis, Cologne (1929).

ALTENLOH, E., *Zur Soziologie des Kino. Die Kino-Unternehmung und die sozialen Schichten ihrer Besucher* (Jena, 1914).

Arbeitswissenschaftliches Institut der Deutschen Arbeitsfront, 'Erhebung von Wirtschaftsrechnungen für das Jahr 1937', in id., *Jahrbuch 1938*, vol. 2, (Berlin, 1938), repr. in M. Hepp and K. H. Roth (eds.), *Sozialstrategien der Deutschen Arbeitsfront*, vol. 3.2 (Munich, 1986).

BERNHARD, G., 'Die Deutsche Presse', in *Der Verlag Ullstein zum Welt-Reklame-Kongress Berlin 1929* (Berlin, 1929).

BERNSTEIN, A., 'Wie die "Berliner Morgenpost" wurde', in *50 Jahre Ullstein*.

BESTLER, M., *Das Absinken der parteipolitischen Führungstätigkeit der deutschen Tageszeitungen*, Ph.D thesis, Berlin (1941).

BLAU, A., *Propaganda als Waffe* (Berlin, 1935).

BRAUNE, G., *Der Einfluß von Schallplatte und Rundfunk auf die deutsche Musikinstrumentenindustrie* (Berlin, 1934).

BREDOW, H. (ed.), *Aus meinem Archiv. Probleme des Rundfunks* (Heidelberg, 1950).

BRUNNER, K., *Der Kinematograph von heute—eine Volksgefahr* (Berlin, 1913).

—— and GAUPP, R., *Der Kinematograph als Volksunterhaltungsmittel* (Munich, 1912).

DE MAN, H., *Sozialismus und Nationalfascismus* (Potsdam, 1931).

DEHN, G., *Proletarische Jugend. Lebensgestaltung und Gedankenwelt der großstädtischen Proletarierjugend*, 2nd edn. (Berlin, 1930).

Deutscher Textilarbeiterverband, *Mein Arbeitstag—Mein Wochenende. 150 Berichte von Textilarbeiterinnen* (Berlin, 1930).

Deutsches Institut für Zeitungskunde, *Handbuch der deutschen Tagespresse*, 4th edn. (Berlin, 1932).

DIERICHS, P., *Der Zeitungsmarkt in Deutschland: unter besonderer Berücksichtigung der Verhältnisse in Westfalen und am Niederrhein in den zwanziger Jahren*, Ph.D thesis, Munich (1928).

DINSE, R., *Das Freizeitleben der Großstadtjugend. 5000 Jungen und Mädchen berichten* (Eberswalde, 1932).

DOMIZLAFF, H., *Typische Denkfehler der Reklamekritik* (Leipzig, 1929).

—— *Propagandamittel der Staatsidee* (Leipzig, 1932).

ECKERT, G., *Der Rundfunk als Führungsmittel* (Berlin, 1941).

ERZBERGER, M., *Erlebnisse im Weltkrieg* (Stuttgart, 1920).

FROMM, E., *Arbeiter und Angestellte am Vorabend des Dritten Reiches. Eine sozialpsychologische Untersuchung*, ed. W. Bonß (Stuttgart, 1980).

FUNK, A., *Film und Jugend. Eine Untersuchung über die psychischen Wirkungen des Films im Leben der Jugendlichen* (Munich, 1934).

GOEDECKE, H. and KRUG, W., *Wir beginnen das Wunschkonzert für die Wehrmacht* (Berlin, 1940).

HÄFKER, H., *Der Kino und die Gebildeten. Wege zur Hebung des Kinowesens* (Mönchen-Gladbach, 1915).

HEENEMANN, H., *Die Auflagenhöhen der deutschen Zeitungen. Ihre Entwicklung und ihre Probleme*, Ph.D thesis, Leipzig (1930).

HENSEL, W. and KEßLER, E., *1000 Hörer antworten. Eine Marktstudie* (Berlin, 1935).

HEUSS, T., *Hitlers Weg. Eine historisch-politische Studie über den Nationalsozialismus* (Stuttgart, 1932).

HITLER, A., *Mein Kampf*, trans. R. Manheim (London, 1969).

HOFER, M. (ed.), *Die Lebenshaltung des Landarbeiters. Wirtschaftsrechnungen von 130 Landarbeiterfamilien. Eine Erhebung des Reichsverbandes ländlicher Arbeitnehmer* (Berlin, 1930).

Institut für Zeitungswissenschaft, *Handbuch der deutschen Tagespresse*, 7th edn. (Leipzig, 1944).

JASON, A., *Der Film in Ziffern und Zahlen (1895–1925)* (Berlin, 1925).

—— *Handbuch der Filmwirtschaft, Jahrgang 1930* (Berlin, 1930).

—— (ed.), *Handbuch des Films 1935/36* (Berlin, 1935).

JOLOWICZ, E., *Der Rundfunk. Eine psychologische Untersuchung* (Berlin, 1932).

KAUDER, G., ' "Bezett—Bezett am Mittag!" Die Geschichte eines neuen Zeitungstyps. Zeitgeist und Sportgeist', in *50 Jahre Ullstein*.

KLUTENTRETER, W., *Presse und Volksgemeinschaft. Eine soziologisch-zeitungswissenschaftliche Studie über das Verhältnis von Presse, Volk und Staat in Deutschland*, Ph.D thesis, Cologne (1937).

KNAPP, A., *Reklame, Propaganda, Werbung. Ihre Weltorganisation* (Berlin, 1929).

KÖNIG, T., *Die Psychologie der Reklame*, Ph.D thesis, Würzburg (1922).

KREBS, R., *Die phonographische Industrie in Deutschland unter besonderer Berücksichtigung ihres Exports*, Ph.D thesis, Greifswald (1925).

KROLZIG, G., *Der Jugendliche in der Großstadtfamilie. Auf Grund von Niederschriften Berliner Berufsschüler und -schülerinnen* (Berlin, 1930).

KULLMANN, M., *Die Entwicklung des deutschen Lichtspieltheaters*, Ph.D thesis, Nuremberg (1935).

LANGE, K., *Der Kinematograph vom ethischen und ästhetischen Standpunkt* (Munich, 1912).

LASSWELL, H., *Propaganda Technique in World War 1* (Cambridge, Mass. 1971), 34–5, originally published as *Propaganda Technique in the World War* (London, 1927).

LEMBKE, F., *Jedem Dorf sein Kino!* (Berlin, 1930).

LIPPMANN, W., *Public Opinion* (New York, 1922).

LUDENDORFF, E., *My War Memories, 1914–1918* (London, 1919).

—— *Der totale Krieg* (Munich, 1935).

LUEB, L., *Die Freizeit der Textilarbeiterinnen. Eine Untersuchung über die Verwendung der Freizeit der Arbeiterinnen des christlichen Textilarbeiterverbandes Bezirk Westfalen*, Ph.D thesis, Münster (1929).

MARSOP, P., *Öffentliche Unterhaltungsmusik in Deutschland* (Munich, 1915).

MATAJA, V., *Die Reklame. Eine Untersuchung über Ankündigungswesen und Werbetätigkeit im Geschäftsleben*, 4th edn. (Munich, 1926).

MORECK, C., *Sittengeschichte des Kinos* (Dresden, 1926).

—— *Führer durch das 'lasterhafte' Berlin* (Leipzig, 1931).

MÜLLER, J., *Ein deutsches Bauerndorf im Umbruch der Zeit. Sulzthal in Mainfranken. Eine bevölkerungspolitische, soziologische und kulturelle Untersuchung* (Würzburg, 1939).

MÜNZENBERG, W., *Propaganda als Waffe* (Paris, 1937).

MUSER, G., *Statistische Untersuchung über die Zeitungen Deutschlands, 1885–1914* (Leipzig, 1918).

NICKOL, H., *Kino und Jugendpflege* (Langensalza, 1919).

OSTWALD, H., *Das galante Berlin* (Berlin, 1905).

—— *Sittengeschichte der Inflation. Ein Kulturdokument aus den Jahren des Marktsturzes* (Berlin, 1931).

OTT, R., *Wie führe ich mein Kino?* (Berlin, 1922).

PASCHKE, G., *Der deutsche Tonfilmmarkt* (Berlin, 1935).

PETZET, W., *Verbotene Filme. Eine Streitschrift*, (Frankfurt a. M., 1931).

PLENGE, J., *Deutsche Propaganda. Die Lehre von der Propaganda als praktische Gesellschaftslehre*, (Bremen, 1922).

'Rede Hitlers vor der deutschen Presse (10 November 1938)', ed. Wilhelm Treue, *VfZ* 6 (1958), 175–91.

RICHTER, T., *Hinter roten Kulissen: Was ich in der KPD erlebte* (Berlin, 1932).

SCHERKE, F. and GRÄFIN VITZTHUM, U., *Bibliographie der geistigen Kriegsführung* (Berlin, 1938).

SCHMIDT, A., *Publizistik im Dorf* (Dresden, 1939).

SCHMITT, W., *Das Filmwesen und seine Wechselbeziehungen zur Gesellschaft. Versuch einer Soziologie des Filmwesens* (Freudenstadt, 1932).

SCHULTZE-PFAELZER, G., *Propaganda, Agitation, Reklame. Eine Theorie des gesamten Werbewesens* (Berlin, 1923).

SCHULZ-KÖHN, D., *Die Schallplatte auf dem Weltmarkt*, Ph.D thesis, Königsberg (1940).

SIMMEL, G., 'Die Großstädte und das Geistesleben' (1903), trans. in K. H. Wolff, *The Sociology of Georg Simmel* (Glencoe, 1950).

STARK, G., *Moderne politische Propaganda* (Munich, 1930).

Statistisches Reichsamt, *Die Lebenshaltung von 2000 Arbeiter-, Angestellten- und Beamtenhaushaltungen. Erhebungen von Wirtschaftsrechnungen im Deutschen Reich vom Jahre 1927/28*, in *Einzelschriften zur Statistik des Deutschen Reichs*, no. 22 (Berlin, 1932).

STERN-RUBARTH, E., *Die Propaganda als politisches Instrument* (Berlin, 1921).

SUHR, O., *Die Lebenshaltung der Angestellten. Untersuchungen auf Grund statistischer Erhebungen des Allgemeinen freien Angestelltenbundes* (Berlin, 1928).

SUHR, S., *Die weiblichen Angestellten. Arbeits- und Lebensverhältnisse* (Berlin, 1930).

THANN, G., 'Von der sozialen Bedeutung des Rundfunks', *Soziale Praxis*, 44 (1935), 377–82.

TSCHACHOTIN, S. and MIERENDORFF, C., *Grundlagen und Formen politischer Propaganda* (Magdeburg, 1932).

VON HARTUNGEN, C., *Psychologie der Reklame* (Stuttgart, 1921).

VERLAG ULLSTEIN, *50 Jahre Ullstein, 1877–1927* (Berlin, 1927).

WOLF, K., *Entwicklung und Neugestaltung der deutschen Filmwirtschaft seit 1933*, Ph.D thesis, Heidelberg (1938).

WOLGAST, H., *Das Elend unserer Jugendliteratur. Ein Beitrag zur künstlerischen Erziehung der Jugend* (Hamburg, 1896).

SECONDARY LITERATURE

ABRAMS, L., 'From Control to Commercialization: The Triumph of Mass Entertainment in Germany 1900–1925?', *GH* 8 (1990), 278–93.

—— *Workers' Culture in Imperial Germany: Leisure and Recreation in the Rhineland and Westphalia* (London, 1992).

ADAM, T., *Arbeitermilieu und Arbeiterbewegung in Leipzig 1871–1933* (Cologne, 1999).

AGAR, J., 'Medium Meets Message: Can Media History and History of Technology Communicate?', *JCH* 40 (2005), 793–803.

ALBRECHT, G., *Nationalsozialistische Filmpolitik. Eine soziologische Untersuchung über die Spielfilme des Dritten Reichs* (Stuttgart, 1969).

ALBRECHT, R., 'Symbolkampf in Deutschland 1932: Sergej Tschachotin und der "Symbolkrieg" der drei Pfeile gegen den Nationalsozialismus als Episode im Abwehrkampf der Arbeiterbewegung gegen den Faschismus in Deutschland', *IwKGA* 22 (1986), 498–533.

—— *Der militante Sozialdemokrat. Carlo Mierendorff 1897 bis 1943* (Bonn, 1987).

ALEXANDER, T., *Carl Severing—ein Demokrat und Sozialist in Weimar*, 2 vols. (Frankfurt a. M., 1996).

ALY, G. *Hitler's Beneficiaries: Plunder, Racial War, and the Nazi Welfare State*, trans. J. Chase (New York, 2006).

—— (ed.), *Volkes Stimme. Skepsis und Führervertrauen im Nationalsozialismus* (Frankfurt a. M., 2006).

ANDERSON, B., *Imagined Communities: Reflections on the Origin and Spread of Nationalism* (London, 1983).

ANDERSON, M. L., *Practicing Democracy: Elections and Political Culture in Imperial Germany* (Princeton, 2000).

ASMUSS, B., *Republik ohne Chance? Akzeptanz und Legitimation der Weimarer Republik in der deutschen Tagespresse zwischen 1918 und 1923* (Berlin, 1994).

BÄCHLIN, P., *Der Film als Ware* (Frankfurt a. M., 1975).

BACK, N., 'Zeitgemäßer Fortschritt'. Die Weimarer Republik in der Provinz. Moderniseriung im Widerstreit am Beispiel der Filder* (Frankfurt a. M., 1998).

BARANOWSKI, S., *Strength Through Joy: Consumerism and Mass Tourism in the Third Reich* (Cambridge, 2004).

BARCLAY, D. and WEITZ, E. (eds.), *Between Reform and Revolution: German Socialism and Communism from 1840 to 1990* (New York, 1998).

BARKHAUSEN, H., *Filmpropaganda für Deutschland im Ersten und Zweiten Weltkrieg* (Hildesheim, 1982).

BARTELS, K., 'Proto-kinematographische Effekte der Laterna magica in Literatur und Theater des achtzehnten Jahrhunderts', in Segeberg (ed.), *Mobilisierung*.

BARTELS, U., *Die Wochenschau im Dritten Reich. Entwicklung und Funktion eines Massenmediums unter besonderer Berücksichtigung völkisch-nationaler Inhalte* (Frankfurt a. M., 2004).

BARTH, B., *Dolchstoßlegenden und politische Desintegration. Das Trauma der deutschen Niederlage im ersten Welkrieg 1914–1933* (Düsseldorf, 2003).

BASSE, D., *Wolff's Telegraphisches Bureau 1849 bis 1933. Agenturpublizistik zwischen Politik und Wirtschaft* (Munich, 1991).

BAVAJ, R., *Die Ambivalenz der Moderne im Nationalsozialismus. Eine Bilanz der Forschung* (Munich, 2003).

BEHRENBECK, S., ' "Der Führer". Die Einführung eines politischen Markenartikels', in Diesener and Gries (eds.), *Propaganda*.

—— 'The Nation Honours the Dead: Remembrance Days for the Fallen in the Weimar Republic and the Third Reich', in K. Friedrich (ed.), *Festive Culture in Germany and Europe from the Sixteenth to the Twentieth Century* (Lampeter, 2000).

BENJAMIN, W., 'The Work of Art in the Age of Mechanical Reproduction' (1936), in id., *Illuminations* (London, 1973).

BERGER, A. A. (ed.), *Making Sense of Media: Key Texts in Media and Cultural Studies* (Malden, 2005).

BERGHOFF, H., 'Von der "Reklame" zur Verbrauchslenkung. Werbung im national-sozialistischen Deutschland', in H. Berghoff (ed.), *Konsumpolitik. Die Regulierung des privaten Verbrauchs im 20. Jahrhundert* (Göttingen, 1999).

BERKING, H., *Masse und Geist. Studien zur Soziologie in der Weimarer Republik* (Berlin, 1984).

BESSEL, R., *Political Violence and the Rise of Nazism: The Storm Troopers in Eastern Germany 1925–1934* (New Haven, 1984).

—— *Germany After the First World War* (Oxford, 1993).

BEßLICH, B., *Wege in den 'Kulturkrieg'. Zivilisationskritik in Deutschland 1890–1914* (Darmstadt, 2000).

BLAUKOPF, K., *Massenmedium Schallplatte* (Wiesbaden, 1977).

BOBERACH, H. (ed.), *Meldungen aus dem Reich. Die geheimen Lageberichte des Sicherheits-dienstes der SS 1938–1945*, 17 vols. (Herrsching, 1984).

BOEGER, P., *Architektur der Lichtspieltheater in Berlin: Bauten und Projekte 1919–1930* (Berlin, 1993).

BOHRMANN, H. and TOEPSER-ZIEGERT, G. (eds.), *NS-Presseanweisungen der Vorkriegszeit. Edition und Dokumentation*, 7 vols. (Munich, 1984–2001).

BOLLENBECK, G., *Bildung und Kultur. Glanz und Elend eines deutschen Deutungsmusters* (Frankfurt a. M., 1994).

—— *Tradition, Avant-Garde, Reaktion: Deutsche Kontroversen um die kulturelle Moderne* (Frankfurt a. M., 1999).

BÖSCH, F., 'Zeitungsberichte im Alltagsgespräch. Mediennutzung, Medienwirkung und Kommunikation im Kaiserreich', *Publizistik*, 49 (2004), 319–36.

—— 'Katalysator der Demokratisierung? Presse, Politik und Gesellschaft vor 1914', in Bösch and Frei (eds.), *Medialisierung*.

—— and BORUTTA, M. (eds.), *Die Massen bewegen. Medien und Emotionen in der Moderne* (Frankfurt a. M., 2006).

—— and Frei, N. (eds.), *Medialisierung und Demokratie im 20. Jahrhundert* (Göttingen, 2006).

BOURDIEU, P., *Distinction: A Social Critique of the Judgement of Taste* (London, 1984).

—— 'Structures, Habitus, Practices', in id., *The Logic of Practice* (Cambridge, 1990).

BRACHER, K. D., *Zeit der Ideologien. Eine Geschichte politischen Denkens im 20. Jahrhundert* (Stuttgart, 1982).

BROCKHAUS, G., *Schauder und Idylle. Faschismus als Erlebnisangebot* (Munich, 1997).

BRUFORD, W. H., *The German Tradition of Self-Cultivation: Bildung from Humboldt to Thomas Mann* (Cambridge, 1975).

BRY, G., *Wages in Germany, 1871–1945* (Princeton, 1960).

BUCHHOLZ, W., *Die nationalsozialistische Gemeinschaft 'Kraft durch Freude'. Freizeitgestaltung und Arbeiterschaft im Dritten Reich*, Ph.D thesis, Munich (1976).

BURGER, R., *Von Goebbels Gnaden. 'Jüdisches Nachrichtenblatt' (1938–1943)* (Münster, 2001).

BURKE, P. and BRIGGS, A., *A Social History of the Media: From Gutenberg to the Internet* (Cambridge, 2005).

BURLEIGH, M., *The Third Reich: A New History* (London, 2000).

BUSSEMER, T., *Propaganda und Populärkultur. Konstruierte Erlebniswelten im Nationalsozialismus* (Wiesbaden, 2000).

—— *Propaganda. Konzepte und Theorien* (Wiesbaden, 2005).

BYTWERK, R., 'Die nationalsozialistische Versammlungspraxis. Die Anfänge vor 1933', in Diesener and Gries (eds.), *Propaganda*.

CALHOUN, C. (ed.), *Habermas and the Public Sphere* (Cambridge, 1992).

CAMPBELL, J., *The German Werkbund: The Politics of Reform in the Applied Arts* (Princeton, 1978).

CEBULLA, F., *Rundfunk und ländliche Gesellschaft 1924–1945* (Göttingen, 2004).

CHARLTON, M. and SCHNEIDER, S. (eds.), *Rezeptionsforschung. Theorien und Untersuchungen zum Umgang mit Massenmedien* (Opladen, 1997).

CHICKERING, R., *We Men Who Feel Most German: A Cultural Sudy of the Pan-German League, 1886–1914* (London, 1984).

—— *Imperial Germany and the Great War, 1914–1918* (Cambridge, 1998).

CHILDERS, T., *The Nazi Voter: The Social Foundations of Fascism in Germany, 1919–1933* (Chapel Hill, NC, 1983).

COCKETT, R., *Twilight of Truth: Chamberlain, Appeasement, and the Manipulation of the Press* (London, 1989).

COETZEE, F. and SHEVIN-COETZEE, M. (eds.), *Authority, Identity and the Social History of the Great War* (Providence, RI, 1996).

COHEN, L., *Making a New Deal: Industrial Workers in Chicago, 1919–1939* (Cambridge, 1990).

CORNWALL, M., *The Undermining of Austria-Hungary: The Battle for Hearts and Minds* (Basingstoke, 2000).

CRAFTON, D., *The Talkies: American Cinema's Transition to Sound* (Berkeley, 1997).

CREUTZ, M., *Die Pressepolitik der kaiserlichen Regierung während des Ersten Weltkriegs: die Exekutive, die Journalisten und der Teufelskreis der Berichterstattung* (Frankfurt a. M., 1996).

CUOMO, G. (ed.), *National Socialist Cultural Policy* (London, 1995).

CURRID, B., *A National Acoustics: Music and Mass Publicity in Weimar and Nazi Germany* (Minneapolis, 2006).

DAHL, P., *Arbeitersender und Volksempfänger. Proletarische Radiobewegung und bürgerlicher Rundfunk* (Frankfurt a. M., 1978).

DAHM, V., 'Nationale Einheit und partikulare Vielfalt. Zur Frage der kulturpolitischen Gleichschaltung im Dritten Reich', *VfZ* 43 (1995), 221–65.

DAMS, C., *Staatsschutz in der Weimarer Republik. Die Überwachung und Bekämpfung der NSDAP durch die preußische politische Polizei von 1928 bis 1932* (Marburg, 2002).

DE CERTEAU, M., *The Practice of Everyday Life* (Berkeley, 1984).

DE GRAZIA, V., 'Mass Culture and Sovereignty: The American Challenge to European Cinemas', *JMH* 61 (1989), 53–87.

—— 'The Arts of Purchase: How American Publicity Subverted the European Poster, 1920–1940', in B. Kruger and P. Mariani (eds.), *Remaking History* (Seattle, 1989).

—— 'Introduction: Changing Consumption Regimes', in V. de Grazia and E. Furlough (eds.), *The Sex of Things* (Berkeley, 1996).

—— 'Changing Consumption Regimes in Europe, 1930–1970: Comparative Perspectives on the Distribution Problem', in S. Strasser, C. McGovern, and M. Judt (eds.), *Getting and Spending: European and American Consumer Societies in the Twentieth Century* (Cambridge, 1998).

—— *Irresistible Empire: America's Advance through Twentieth-century Europe* (Cambridge, Mass., 2005).

DE MENDELSSOHN, P., *Zeitungsstadt Berlin. Menschen und Mächte in der Geschichte der deutschen Presse* (Berlin, 1959).

DEIST, W., *Flottenpolitik und Flottenpropaganda. Das Nachrichtenbureau des Reichsmarineamtes 1897–1914* (Stuttgart, 1976).

Deutschland-Berichte der Sozialdemokratische Partei Deutschlands (Sopade), 1934–1940, 7 vols. (Frankfurt a. M., 1980).

DIEHL, K., *Die jüdische Presse im Dritten Reich. Zwischen Selbstbehauptung und Fremdbestimmung* (Tübingen, 1997).

DIESENER, G. and GRIES, R. (eds.), *Propaganda in Deutschland. Zur Geschichte der politischen Massenbeinflussung im 20. Jahrhundert* (Darmstadt, 1996).

DILLER, A., *Rundfunkpolitik im Dritten Reich* (Munich, 1980).

DOMARUS, M. (ed.), *Hitler: Speeches and Proclamations 1932–1945*, 4 vols. (Würzburg, 1997).

DRESCHLER, N., *Die Funktion der Musik im deutschen Rundfunk 1933–1945* (Pfaffenweiler, 1988).

DREßLER, R., *Von der Schaubühne zur Sittenschule. Das Theaterpublikum vor der vierten Wand* (Berlin, 1993).

DRÖGE, F., *Der zerredete Widerstand. Zur Soziologie und Publizistik des Gerüchts im 2. Weltkrieg* (Düsseldorf, 1970).

—— and MÜLLER, M., *Die Macht der Schönheit. Avantgarde und Faschismus oder die Geburt der Massenkultur* (Hamburg, 1995).

DÜMLING, A., GIRTH, P., and SCHIMMELPFENNIG, P. (eds.), *Entartete Musik. Dokumentation und Kommentar zur Düsseldorfer Ausstellung von 1938*, 3rd edn. (Düsseldorf, 1993).

DUSSEL, K., 'Deutsches Radio, deutsche Kultur. Hörfunkprogramme als Indikatoren kulturellen Wandels', *AfS* 41 (2001), 119–44.

—— *Deutsche Rundfunkgeschichte* (Konstanz, 2004).

—— *Deutsche Tagespresse im 19. und 20. Jahrhundert* (Münster, 2004).

—— and FRESE, M., *Freizeit in Weinheim. Studien zur Geschichte der Freizeit* (Weinheim, 1989).

—— and LERSCH, E. (eds.), *Quellen zur Programmgeschichte des deutschen Hörfunks und Fernsehens* (Göttingen, 1999).

EKSTEINS, M., *The Limits of Reason: The German Democratic Press and the Collapse of Weimar Democracy* (Oxford, 1975).

—— *The Rites of Spring: The Great War and the Birth of the Modern Age* (Boston, 1989).

ELEY, G., *Reshaping the German Right: Radical Nationalism and Political Change after Bismarck*, (1980; Ann Arbor, Mich., 1991).

—— 'Cultural Socialism, the Public Sphere, and the Mass Form', in Barclay and Weitz (eds.), *Between Reform*.

ERMAN, H., *August Scherl. Dämonie und Erfolg in Wilhelminischer Zeit* (Berlin, 1954).

ETLIN, R. (ed.), *Art, Culture, and Media Under the Third Reich* (Chicago, 2002).

EVANS, R. J., *The Coming of the Third Reich* (London, 2003).

EWEN, S., *PR! A Social History of Spin* (New York, 1996).

FALTER, J., *Hitlers Wähler* (Munich, 1991).

FAULSTICH, W., *Medienwandel im Industrie- und Massenzeitalter (1830–1900)* (Göttingen, 2004).

—— *Mediengeschichte 2. Von 1700 bis ins 3. Jahrtausend* (Konstanz, 2006).

FELDMAN, G., *The Great Disorder: Politics, Economics, and Society in the German Inflation, 1914–1924* (Oxford, 1993).

FETTHAUER, S., *Deutsche Grammophon: Geschichte eines Schallplattenunternehmens im 'Dritten Reich'* (Hamburg, 2000).

FIELDING, R. (ed.), *A Technological History of Motion Pictures and Television* (Berkeley, 1967).

FISCHER, C., *The Ruhr Crisis, 1923–1924* (Oxford, 2003).

FISKE, J., *Understanding Popular Culture* (London, 1991).

FOX, J., *Film Propaganda in Britain and Nazi Germany: World War II Cinema* (Oxford, 2007).

FRASER, N., 'Rethinking the Public Sphere: A Contribution to the Critique of Actually Existing Democracy', *Social Text*, 25/6 (1990), 56–80.

FREI, N., *Nationalsozialistische Eroberung der Provinzpresse. Gleichschaltung, Selbstanpassung und Resistenz in Bayern* (Stuttgart, 1980).

—— and SCHMITZ, J., *Journalismus im Dritten Reich*, 3rd edn. (Munich, 1999).

FRIEBE, H., 'Branding Germany: Hans Domizlaff's *Markentechnik* and its Ideological Impact', in Swett, Wiesen, and Zatlin (eds.), *Selling Modernity*.

FRITZSCHE, P., *Reading Berlin 1900* (Cambridge, Mass., 1996).

—— 'Did Weimar Fail?', *JMH* 68 (1996), 629–56.

—— 'Nazi Modern', *Modernism/modernity*, 3 (1996), 1–22.

—— *Germans into Nazis* (Cambridge, Mass., 1998).

FRÖHLICH, E. (ed.), *Die Tagebücher von Joseph Goebbels*, 2 parts (Munich, 1998-).

FÜHRER, K. C., 'Auf dem Weg zur "Massenkultur"? Kino und Rundfunk in der Weimarer Republik', *Historische Zeitschrift*, 262 (1996), 739–81.

—— 'A Medium of Modernity? Broadcasting in Weimar Germany, 1923–1932', *JMH* 69 (1997), 722–53.

—— *Wirtschaftsgeschichte des Rundfunks in der Weimarer Republik*, (Potsdam, 1997).

—— 'German Cultural Life and the Crisis of National Identity During the Depression, 1929–1933', *German Studies Review*, 24 (2001), 461–86.

—— 'Two-fold Admiration: American Movies as Popular Entertainment and Artistic Model in Nazi Germany, 1933–1939', in Führer and Ross (eds.), *Mass Media*.

—— 'Die Tageszeitung als wichtigstes Massenmedium der nationalsozialistischen Gesellschaft', *ZfG* 55 (2007), 411–34.

—— 'Praktischer Nutzen und Propaganda. Populäre Zeitschriften im nationalsozialistischen Deutschland 1933', (unpubl.) ms, 2007.

—— HICKETHIER, K., and SCHILDT, A., 'Öffentlichkeit—Medien—Geschichte. Konzepte der modernen Öffentlichkeit und Zugänge zu ihrer Erforschung', *AfS* 39 (2001), 1–38.

—— and Ross, C. (eds.), *Mass Media, Culture and Society in Twentieth-century Germany* (Basingstoke, 2006).

FULDA, B., *Press and Politics in Berlin, 1924–1939*, DPhil. thesis, Cambridge (2003).

—— 'Industries of Sensationalism: German Tabloids in Weimar Berlin', in Führer and Ross (eds.), *Mass Media*.

FULLERTON, R., 'Toward a Commercial Popular Culture in Germany: The Development of Pamphlet Fiction, 1871–1914', *Journal of Social History*, 12 (1979), 489–512.

GALL, L., *Bismarck: The White Revolutionary*. vol. 1 (London, 1986).

GALLE, H. J., *Groschenhefte: Die Geschichte der deutschen Trivialliteratur* (Frankfurt a. M., 1988).

GARNACZ, J., 'Hollywood in Germany. Die Rolle des amerikanischen Films in Deutschland: 1925–1990', in Jung (ed.), *Der deutsche Film*.

GASSERT, P., *Amerika im Dritten Reich. Ideologie, Propaganda und Volksmeinung 1933–1945* (Stuttgart, 1997).

GAY, P., *Weimar Culture: The Outsider as Insider* (London, 1969).

GEBHARDT, H., ' "Halb kriminalistisch, halb erotisch": Presse für die "niederen Instinkte". Annäherungen an ein unbekanntes kapitel deutscher Mediengeschichte', in Kaschuba and Maase (eds.), *Schund*.

GELLATELY, R., *Backing Hitler: Coercion and Consent in Nazi Germany* (Oxford, 2001).

GELLNER, E., *Nations and Nationalism* (Cornell, 1983).

GERSCH, W., *Chaplin in Berlin. Illustrierte Miniatur nach Berliner Zeitungen von 1931* (Berlin, 1989).

GERWARTH, R., 'The Past in Weimar History', *Contemporary European History*, 15 (2006), 1–22.

GEYER, M. H., *Verkehrte Welt. Revolution, Inflation und Moderne: München, 1914–1924* (Göttingen, 1998).

GIESEN, R., *Nazi Propaganda Films: A History and Filmography* (Jefferson, NC, 2003).

GLASER, H., *Bildungsbürgertum und Nationalismus: Politik und Kultur im wilhelminischen Deutschland* (Munich, 1993).

GOERGEN, J., 'Der pikante Film. Ein vergessenes Genre der Kaiserzeit', in T. Elsaesser and M. Wedel (eds.), *Kino der Kaiserzeit. Zwischen Tradition und Moderne* (Munich, 2002).

GÖPFERT, H. (ed.), *'Unmoralisch an sich . . .' Zensur im 18. und 19. Jahrhundert* (Wiesbaden, 1988).

GRUNBERGER, R., *A Social History of the Third Reich* (Harmondsworth, 1974).

GRZESINKI, A., *Im Kampf um die deutsche Republik. Erinnerungen eines Sozialdemokraten*, ed. E. Kolb (Munich, 2001).

GURATZSCH, D., *Macht durch Organisation. Die Grundlegung des Hugenbergschen Presseimperiums* (Düsseldorf, 1974).

GUTTSMAN, W. L., *Workers' Culture in Weimar Germany: Between Tradition and Commitment* (New York, 1990).

HAAS, W., *Das Jahrhundert der Schallplatte. Eine Geschichte der Phonographie* (Bielefeld, 1977).

HABERMAS, J., *The Structural Transformation of the Public Sphere: An Inquiry into a Category of Bourgeois Society* (Cambridge, Mass., 1989).

HACHMEISTER, L., *Theoretische Publizistik. Studien zur Geschichte der Kommunikationswissenschaft in Deutschland* (Berlin, 1987).

HAGENER, M. and Hans, J., 'Von Wilhelm zu Weimar. Der Aufklärungs- und Sittenfilm zwischen Zensur und Markt', in M. Hagener (ed.), *Geschlecht in Fesseln. Sexualität zwischen Aufklärung und Ausbeutung im Weimarer Kino, 1918–1933* (Munich, 2000).

HAKE, S., *German National Cinema* (London, 2002).

HALEFELDT, H., 'Ein Sender für acht Länder: Die NORAG. Regionaler Rundfunk in der Weimarer Republik', *AfS* 41 (2001), 145–70.

HALL, A., 'The War of Words: Anti-socialist Offensives and Counter-propaganda in Wilhelmine Germany', *JCH* 11 (1976), 11–42.

—— *Scandal, Sensation and Social Democracy: The SPD Press and Wilhelmine Germany, 1890–1914* (Cambridge, 1977).

HAMILTON, R., *Who Voted for Hitler?* (Princeton, 1982).

HANNA-DAOUD, T., *Die NSDAP und der Film bis zur Machtergreifung* (Cologne, 1996).

HÄNSEL, S., *Kinoarchitektur in Berlin 1895–1995* (Berlin, 1995).

HARSCH, D., *German Social Democracy and the Rise of Nazism* (Chapel Hill, NC, 1993).

—— 'The Iron Front: Weimar Social Democracy Between Tradition and Modernity', in Barclay and Weitz (eds.), *Between Reform*.

HARVEY, E., 'Culture and Society in Weimar Germany: The Impact of Modernism and Mass Culture', in M. Fulbrook (ed.), *Twentieth-Century Germany: Politics, Culture and Society 1918–1990* (London, 2001).

HEFFEN, A., *Der Reichskunstwart—Kunstpolitik in den Jahren 1920–1933* (Essen, 1986).

HEIBER, H. (ed.), *Goebbels-Reden*, 2 vols. (Düsseldorf, 1971).

HEINEMANN, U., *Die verdrängte Niederlage. Politische Öffentlichkeit und Kriegsschuldfrage in der Weimarer Republik* (Göttingen, 1983).

HELLER, H., *Literarische Intelligenz und Film. Zu Veränderungen der ästhetischen Theorie und Praxis unter dem Eindruck des Films 1910–1930 in Deutschland* (Tübingen, 1985).

HENSLE, M., *Rundfunkverbrechen: das Hören von 'Feindsendern' im Nationalsozialismus* (Berlin, 2003).

HERBERT, U., 'Good Times, Bad Times: Memories of the Third Reich', in R. Bessel (ed.), *Life in the Third Reich* (Oxford, 1987).

—— *Best. Biographische Studien über Radikalismus, Weltanschauung und Vernunft, 1903–1989* (Bonn, 1996).

HERF, J., *The Jewish Enemy: Nazi Propaganda During World War II and the Holocaust* (Cambridge, Mass., 2006).

HERMAND, J. and TROMMLER, F., *Die Kultur der Weimarer Republik* (Munich, 1978).

HERWIG, H., 'Clio Deceived: Patriotic Self-Censorship in Germany After the Great War', in K. Wilson (ed.), *Forging the Collective Memory: Government and International Historians Through Two World Wars* (Providence, RI, 1996).

HERZ, R., *Hoffmann & Hitler. Fotografie als Medium des Führer-Mythos* (Munich, 1994).

HEUSER, J., *Zeitungswissenschaft als Standespolitik. Martin Mohr und das 'Deutsche Institut für Zeitungskunde' in Berlin* (Münster, 1994).

HOBSBAWM, E., *The Age of Empire, 1875–1914* (London, 1994).

HOLLINS, T. J., 'The Conservative Party and Film Propaganda Between the Wars', *English Historical Review*, 96 (1981), 359–69.

HOLQUIST, P., '"Information is the Alpha and Omega of Our Work": Bolshevik Surveillance in its Pan-European Context', *JMH* 69 (1997), 415–50.

HOLZBACH, H., *Das 'System Hugenberg'. Die Organisation bürgerlicher Sammlungspolitik vor dem Aufstieg der NSDAP* (Stuttgart, 1981).

HORAK, J. C., 'Exilfilm, 1933–1945', in Jacobsen, Kaes, and Prinzler (eds.), *Geschichte*.

HÖRBURGER, C., *Das Hörspiel der Weimarer Republik. Versuch einer kritischen Analyse* (Stuttgart, 1975).

HORNE, J. and KRAMER, A., *German Atrocities, 1914: A History of Denial* (New Haven, 2001).

HOSER, P., *Die politischen, wirtschaftlichen und sozialen Hintergründe der Münchener Tagespresse zwischen 1914 und 1934*, 2 vols. (Frankfurt a.m., 1990).

JACKSON LEARS, T. J., *Fables of Abundance: A Cultural History of Advertising in America* (New York, 1994).

JACOBSEN, W., 'Frühgeschichte des deutschen Films. Licht am Ende des Tunnels', in Jacobsen, Kaes, and Prinzler (eds.), *Geschichte*.

—— KAES, A., and PRINZLER, H. H. (eds.), *Geschichte des deutschen Films* (Stuttgart, 1993).

JARAUSCH, K. H. and Geyer, M., *Shattered Past: Reconstructing German Histories* (Princeton, 2003).

JEFFERIES, M., *Imperial Culture in Germany, 1871–1918* (Basingstoke, 2003).

JELAVICH, P., *Berlin Cabaret* (Cambridge, Mass., 1993).

—— '"Darf ich mich hier amüsieren?" Bürgertum und früher Film', in M. Hettling and S.-L. Hoffmann (eds.), *Der bürgerliche Wertehimmel. Innenansichten des 19. Jahrhunderts* (Göttingen, 2000).

—— 'Paradoxes of Censorship in Modern Germany', in M. Micale and R. Dietle (eds.), *Enlightenment, Passion, Modernity: Historical Essays in European Thought and Culture* (Stanford, 2000).

—— *Berlin Alexanderplatz: Radio, Film and the Death of Weimar Culture* (Berkeley, 2006).

JUNG, U. (ed.), *Der deutsche Film. Aspekte seiner Geschichte von den Anfängen bis zur Gegenwart* (Trier, 1993).

—— and LOIPERDINGER, M. (eds.), *Geschichte des dokumentarischen Films in Deutschland*, vol. 1 (Stuttgart, 2005).

KAES, ANTON (ed.), *Kino-Debatte. Texte zum Verhältnis von Literatur und Film 1909–1929* (Tübingen, 1978).

—— JAY, M., and DIMENDBERG, E. (eds.), *The Weimar Republic Sourcebook* (Berkeley, 1994).

KALLIS, A. A., *Nazi Propaganda and the Second World War* (Basingstoke, 2005).

KASCHUBA, W. and MAASE, K. (eds.), *Schund und Schönheit. Populäre Kultur um 1900* (Cologne, 2001).

KATER, M. H., *Different Drummers: Jazz in the Culture of Nazi Germany* (New York, 1992).

—— *The Twisted Muse: Musicians and their Music in the Third Reich* (Oxford, 1997).

KERSHAW, I., *Popular Opinion and Political Dissent in the Third Reich: Bavaria 1933–1945* (Oxford, 1983).

—— *The 'Hitler Myth': Image and Reality in the Third Reich* (Oxford, 1987).

—— *The Nazi Dictatorship: Problems and Perspectives of Interpretation*, 4th edn. (London, 2000).

KESTLER, S., *Die deutsche Auslandsaufklärung und das Bild der Ententemächte im Spiegel zeitgenössischer Propagandaveröffentlichungen während des Ersten Weltkrieges* (Frankfurt a. M., 1994).

KINTER, J., *Arbeiterbewegung und Film (1895–1933)* (Hamburg, 1985).

KITTEL, M., *Provinz zwischen Reich und Republik. Politische Mentalitäten in Deutschland und Frankreich 1918–1933/36* (Munich, 2000).

KLÄR, K., *Film zwischen Wunsch und Wirklichkeit* (Wiesbaden, 1957).

KLEINHANS, B., *Ein Volk, ein Reich, ein Kino. Lichtspiel in der braunen Provinz* (Cologne, 2003).

KLEMPERER, V., *Leben sammeln, nicht fragen wozu und warum. Tagebücher 1918–1924* (Berlin, 1996).

KNOCH, H., 'Living Pictures: Photojournalism in Germany, 1900 to the 1930s', in Führer and Ross (eds.), *Mass Media*.

KOCH, H.-J., *Das Wunschkonzert im NS-Rundfunk* (Cologne, 2003).

KOEPNICK, L. P., *The Dark Mirror: German Cinema Between Hitler and Hollywood* (Berkeley, 2002).

KOHLMANN-VIAND, D., *NS-Pressepolitik im Zweiten Weltkrieg. Die 'vertraulichen Informationen' als Mittel der Presselenkung* (Munich, 1991).

KOHLRAUSCH, M., *Der Monarch im Skandal. Die Logik der Massenmedien und die Transformation der wilhelminischen Monarchie* (Berlin, 2005).

KOMBÜCHEN, S., *Von der Erlebnisgesellschaft zur Mediengesellschaft. Die Evolution der Kommunikation und ihre Folgen für den sozialen Wandel* (Münster, 1999).

KÖNIG, W., *Volkswagen, Volksempfänger, Volksgemeinschaft. 'Volksprodukte' im Dritten Reich. Vom Scheitern einer nationalsozialistischen Konsumgesellschaft* (Paderborn, 2004).

KORFF, G., 'Rote Fahnen und geballte Faust. Zur Symbolik der Arbeiterbewegung in der Weimarer Republik', in D. Petzina (ed.), *Fahnen, Fäuste, Körper. Symbolik und Kultur der Arbeiterbewegung* (Essen, 1986).

KORTE, H., *Der Spielfilm und das Ende der Weimarer Republik. Ein rezeptionshistorischer Versuch* (Göttingen, 1998).

KOSZYK, K., *Deutsche Presse im 19. Jahrhundert* (Berlin, 1966).

—— *Deutsche Pressepolitik im Ersten Weltkrieg* (Düsseldorf, 1968).

—— *Deutsche Presse 1914–1945* (Berlin, 1972).

KRACAUER, S., *Das Ornament der Masse* (Frankfurt a. M., 1977).

KRAUS, E., *Die Familie Mosse. Deutsch-jüdisches Bürgertum im 19. und 20. Jahrhundert* (Munich, 1999).

KRAUS, H.-C. (ed.), *Konservative Zeitschriften zwischen Kaiserreich und Diktatur. Fünf Fallstudien,* (Berlin, 2003).

KREIMEIER, K., *The Ufa-Story: A History of Germany's Greatest Film Company 1918–1945* (New York, 1996).

—— EHMANN, A., and GOERGEN, J. (eds.), *Geschichte des dokumentarischen Films*, vol. 2 (Stuttgart, 2005).

KRENZLIN, N. (ed.), *Zwischen Angstmetapher und Terminus. Theorien der Massenkultur seit Nietzsche* (Berlin, 1992).

KUNDRUS, B., 'Totale Unterhaltung? Die kulturelle Kriegführung 1939 bis 1945 in Film, Rundfunk und Theater', in J. Echternkamp (ed.), *Die deutsche Kriegsgesellschaft 1939 bis 1945. Zweiter Halbband. Ausbeutung, Deutungen, Ausgrenzung* (Munich, 2005).

LACEY, K., *Feminine Frequencies: Gender, German Radio and the Public Sphere* (Ann Arbor, Mich., 1996).

—— 'The Invention of a Listening Public: Radio and its Audiences', in Führer and Ross (eds.), *Mass Media*.

LAMBERTY, C., *Reklame in Deutschland 1890–1914* (Berlin, 2000).

LANGER, P., 'Paul Reusch und die Gleichschaltung der "Münchner Neuesten Nachrichten" 1933 bis 1936', *VfZ* 53 (2005), 203–40.

LAQUEUR, W., *Weimar: A Cultural History, 1918–1933* (London, 1974).

LEHNERT, D., 'Propaganda des Bürgerkriegs? Politische Feindbilder in der Novemberrevolution als mentale Destabilisierung der Weimarer Demokratie', in D. Lehnert and K. Megerle (eds.), *Politische Teilkulturen zwischen Integration und Polarisierung. Zur politischen Kultur in der Weimarer Republik* (Opladen, 1990).

LEMAHIEU, D. L., *A Culture for Democracy: Mass Communication and the Cultivated Mind in Britain Between the Wars*, (Oxford, 1988).

LEMMONS, R., *Goebbels and Der Angriff* (Lexington, 1994).

LENK, C., *Die Erscheinung des Rundfunks. Einführung und Nutzung eines neuen Mediums 1923–1932* (Opladen, 1997).

—— 'Medium der Privatheit? Über Rundfunk, Freizeit und Konsum in der Weimarer Republik', in Marßolek und von Saldern (eds.), *Radiozeiten*.

LENMAN, R., 'Art, Society and the Law in Wilhelmine Germany: The Lex Heinze', *Oxford German Studies*, 8 (1973), 86–113.

LEONHARD, J.-F. (ed.), *Programmgeschichte des Hörfunks in der Weimarer Republik*, 2 vols. (Munich, 1997).

LERG, W., *Rundfunkpolitik in der Weimarer Republik* (Munich, 1980).

LERSCH, E. and SCHANZE, H. (eds.), *Die Idee des Radios. Von den Anfängen in Europa und den USA bis 1933* (Konstanz, 2004).

LEVI, E., *Music in the Third Reich* (Basingstoke, 1994).

LEVINE, L. W., 'The Folklore of Industrial Society: Popular Culture and its Audience', *American Historical Review*, 97 (1992), 1369–99.

—— *The People and the President: America's Extraordinary Conversation with FDR* (Boston, 2002).

LINDENBERGER, T. (ed.), *Massenmedien im Kalten Krieg* (Cologne, 2006).

LINSMAYER, L., *Politische Kultur im Saargebiet 1920–1932. Symbolische Politik, verhinderte Demokratisierung, nationalisiertes Kulturleben in einer abgetrennten Region* (St Ingbert, 1992).

LINTON, D. S., *'Who Has the Youth, Has the Future': The Campaign to Save Young Workers in Imperial Germany* (Cambridge, 1991).

LIPP, A., *Meinungslenkung im Krieg. Kriegserfahrungen deutscher Soldaten und ihre Deutung, 1914–1918* (Göttingen, 2003).

LOIPERDINGER, M., 'Der frühe Kino der Kaiserzeit. Wilhelm II. und die "Flegeljahre" des Films', in Jung (ed.), *Der deutsche Film*.

—— 'The Beginnings of German Film Propaganda: The Navy League as Travelling Exhibitor, 1901–1907', *Historical Journal of Film, Radio and Television*, 22 (2002), 305–13.

LOWRY, S., *Pathos und Politik. Ideologie in Spielfilmen des Nationalsozialismus* (Tübingen, 1991).

LÜDTKE, A., ' "Ehre der Arbeit". Industriearbeit und Macht der Symbole. Zur Reichweite symbolischer Orientierungen im Nationalsozialismus', in K. Tenfelde (ed.), *Arbeiter im 20. Jahrhundert* (Stuttgart, 1991).

MAASE, K., *Grenzenloses Vergnügen. Der Aufstieg der Massenkultur 1850–1970* (Frankfurt a. M., 1997).

—— 'Krisenbewußtsein und Reformorientierung. Zum Deutungshorizont der Gegner der modernen Populärkünste 1880–1918', in Kaschuba and Maase (eds.), *Schund.*

—— 'Massenkunst und Volkserziehung. Die Regulierung von Film und Kino im deutschen Kaiserreich', *AfS* 41 (2001), 39–77.

MAAß, M., *Freizeitgestaltung und kulturelles Leben in Nürnberg 1930–1945. Eine Studie zu Alltag und Herrschaftsausübung im Nationalsozialismus* (Nürnberg, 1994).

MCKIBBIN, R., *Classes and Cultures: England 1918–1951* (Oxford, 1998).

MCMEEKIN, S., *The Red Millionaire: A Political Biography of Willy Münzenberg, Moscow's Secret Propaganda Tsar in the West, 1917–1940* (New Haven, 2003).

MAJOR, P., ' "Trash and Smut": Germany's Culture Wars against Pulp Fiction', in Führer and Ross (eds.), *Mass Media.*

MALLMANN, K.-M., *Kommunisten in der Weimarer Republik. Sozialgeschichte einer revolutionären Bewegung* (Darmstadt, 1996).

—— and PAUL, G., *Herrschaft und Alltag. Ein Industrierevier im Dritten Reich* (Bonn, 1991).

MARCHAND, R., *Advertising the American Dream: Making Way for Modernity, 1920–1940* (Berkeley, 1985).

MARCHAND, S. L. and LINDENFELD, D. F. (eds.), *Germany at the Fin de Siècle: Culture, Politics and Ideas* (Baton Rouge, 2004).

MARßOLEK, I., ' "Aus dem Volke für das Volk". Die Inszenierung der "Volksgemeinschaft" um und durch das Radio', in Marßolek and von Saldern (eds.), *Radiozeiten.*

—— and VON SALDERN, A. (eds.), *Zuhören und Gehörtwerden 1. Radio im Nationalsozialismus* (Tübingen, 1998).

—— —— (eds.), *Radiozeiten. Herrschaft, Alltag, Gesellschaft (1924–1960)* (Potsdam, 1999).

MARTIN, N., 'Images of Schiller in National Socialist Germany', in N. Martin (ed.), *Schiller: National Poet—Poet of Nations: A Birmingham Symposium* (Amsterdam, 2006).

MATYSIAK, S., 'Zwischen Traditionsbildung und Traditionsverweigerung. Zu den Konstruktionsmechanismen von Tageszeitungestradition durch die Verlage', *Jahrbuch für Kommunikationsgeschichte,* 7 (2005), 122–46.

MAY, R., 'Die Schallplatte als "Kult"-mittel', *MkF* 15 (1992), 182–225.

MEIER, G., *Zwischen Milieu und Markt. Tageszeitungen in Ostwestfalen 1920–1970* (Paderborn, 1999).

MENDE, M., *Sensationalismus als Produktgestaltungsmittel. Eine empirische Analyse über die verlegerische und journalistische Orientierung am Sensationsbedürfnis in der deutschen Presse zwischen 1914 und 1933* (Cologne, 1996).

MERGEL, T., 'Überlegungen zu einer Kulturgeschichte der Politik', *GG* 28 (2002), 574–606.

—— and WELSKOPP, T. (eds.), *Geschichte zwischen Kultur und Gesellschaft. Beiträge zur Theoriedebatte* (Munich, 1997).

MERKEL, F., *Rundfunk und Gewerkschaften in der Weimarer Republik und in der frühen Nachkriegszeit* (Potsdam, 1996).

MERLIO, G. and RAULET, G. (eds.), *Linke und rechte Kulturkritik. Interdiskursivität als Krisenbewußtsein* (Frankfurt a. M., 2005).

MEYEN, M., *Leipzigs bürgerliche Presse in der Weimarer Republik. Wechselbeziehungen zwischen gesellschaftlichem Wandel und Zeitungsentwicklung* (Leipzig, 1996).

MOELLER, R. G., *War Stories: The Search for a Usable Past in the Federal Republic of Germany* (Berkeley, 2001).

MÖLLER, F., 'Die sich selbst bewußte Massenbeeinflussung. Liberalismus und Propaganda', in Diesener and Gries (eds.), *Propaganda.*

MOMMSEN, W., *Bürgerliche Kultur und künstlerische Avantgarde, 1870–1918* (Berlin, 1994).

MONACO, P., *Cinema and Society: France and Germany During the Twenties* (New York, 1976).

MÜHL-BENNINGHAUS, W., *Das Ringen um den Tonfilm. Strategien der Elektro- und der Filmindustrie in den 20er und 30er Jahren* (Düsseldorf, 1999).

MÜHLBERGER, D., *Hitler's Voice: The Völkischer Beobachter, 1920–1933*, 2 vols. (Bern, 2004), i. 17–24.

MÜHLENFELD, D., 'Joseph Goebbels und die Grundlagen der NS-Rundfunkpolitik', *ZfG* 54 (2006), 442–67.

MÜLLER, C., *Frühe deutsche Kinematographie. Formale, wirtschaftliche und kulturelle Entwicklungen 1907–1912* (Stuttgart, 1994).

—— 'Anfänge der Filmgeschichte: Produktion, Foren und Rezeption', in Segeberg (ed.), *Mobilisierung.*

—— 'Das "andere" im Kino? Autorenfilme in der Vorkriegsära', in Müller and Segeberg (eds.), *Modellierung.*

—— 'Variationen des Kinoprogramms. Filmform und Filmgeschichte', in Müller and Segeberg (eds.), *Modellierung.*

—— 'Der frühe Film, das frühe Kino und seine Gegner und Befürworter', in Kaschuba and Maase (eds.), *Schund.*

—— and SEGEBERG, H. (eds.), *Die Modellierung des Kinofilms. Zur Geschichte des Kinoprogramms zwischen Kurzfilm und Langfilm (1905–1918)* (Munich, 1998).

MÜLLER, H. J., *Auswärtige Pressepolitik und Propaganda zwischen Ruhrkampf und Locarno (1923–1925)* (Frankfurt a. M., 1991).

MÜNKEL, D., 'Produktionssphäre', in Marßolek and von Saldern (eds.), *Zuhören.*

—— '"Der Rundfunk geht auf die Dörfer". Der Einzug der Massenmedien auf dem Lande von den zwanziger bis zu den sechziger Jahren', in id. (ed.), *Der lange Abschied vom Agrarland. Agrarpolitik, Landwirtschaft und ländliche Gesellschaft zwischen Weimar und Bonn* (Göttingen, 2000).

NOAKES, J. and PRIDHAM, G. (eds.), *Nazism 1919–1945: A Documentary Reader*, 4 vols. (Exeter, 1983–98).

OFFERMANNS, E., *Die deutschen Juden und der Spielfilm der NS-Zeit* (Frankfurt a. M., 2005).

—— *Internationalität und europäischer Hegemonialanspruch des Spielfilms der NS-Zeit* (Hamburg, 2001).

OPPELT, U., *Film und Propaganda im Ersten Weltkrieg: Propaganda als Medienrealität im Aktualitäten- und Dokumentarfilm* (Stuttgart, 2002).

PARK, R., BURGESS, E., and McKENZIE, R., *The City* (Chicago, 1967).

PATER, M., 'Rundfunkangebote', in Marßolek and von Saldern (eds.), *Zuhören*.

PAUL, G., *Aufstand der Bilder. Die NS-Propaganda vor 1933* (Bonn, 1990).

—— 'Krieg der Symbole. Formen und Inhalte des symbolpublizistischen Bürgerkrieges 1932', in D. Kerbs and H. Stahr (eds.), *Berlin 1932. Das letzte Jahr der ersten deutschen Republik* (Berlin, 1992).

PETERSEN, K., *Zensur in der Weimarer Republik* (Stuttgart, 1995).

PEUKERT, D., *Grenzen der Sozialdisziplinierung. Aufstieg und Krise der deutschen Jugendfürsorge von 1878 bis 1932* (Cologne, 1986).

—— *Inside Nazi Germany: Conformity, Opposition and Racism in Everyday Life* (London, 1987).

—— *The Weimar Republic: The Crisis of Classical Modernity* (London, 1991).

—— 'Das Mädchen mit dem "wahrlich metaphysikfreien Bubikopf". Jugend und Freizeit im Berlin der zwanziger Jahre', in P. Alter (ed.), *Im Banne der Metropolen. Berlin und London in den zwanziger Jahren* (Göttingen, 1993).

POHLE, H., *Der Rundfunk als Instrument der Politik. Zur Geschichte des deutschen Rundfunks von 1923–1938* (Hamburg, 1955).

POLSTER, B. (ed.), *'Swing Heil'. Jazz im Nationalsozialismus* (Berlin, 1989).

POTTER, P., *Most German of the Arts: Musicology and Society from the Weimar Republic to the End of Hitler's Reich* (New Haven, 1998).

QUATAERT, J., 'Demographic and Social Change', in R. Chickering (ed.), *Imperial Germany: A Historiographical Companion* (Westport, Conn., 1996).

RADEMACHER, H. (ed.), *Plakatkunst im Klassenkampf. 24 politische Plakate der Weimarer Republik* (Leipzig, 1974).

RASS, M., 'Arbeit, Helden, Straßenkämpfe: Krieg in Hugenbergs Medien', in W. Bialas and B. Stenzel (eds.), *Die Weimarer Republik zwischen Metropole und Provinz* (Cologne, 1996).

REDSLOB, E., *Von Weimar nach Europa. Erlebtes und Durchdachtes* (Berlin, 1972).

REICHEL, P., *Der schöne Schein des Dritten Reiches. Faszination und Gewalt des Faschismus* (Munich, 1991).

REINHARDT, D., *Von der Reklame zum Marketing. Geschichte der Wirtschaftswerbung in Deutschland* (Berlin, 1993).

RENTSCHLER, E., *The Ministry of Illusion: Nazi Cinema and its Afterlife*, (Cambridge, Mass., 1996).

REPP, K., *Reformers, Critics and the Paths of German Modernity: Anti-politics and the Search for Alternatives, 1890–1914*, (Cambridge, Mass., 2000).

REQUATE, J., *Journalismus als Beruf. Entstehung und Entwicklung des Journalistenberufs im 19. Jahrhundert. Deutschland im internationalen Vergleich* (Göttingen, 1995).

—— 'Öffentlichkeit und Medien als Gegenstände historischer Analyse', *GG* 25 (1999), 5–32.

—— 'Zwischen Profit und Politik. Deutsche Zeitungsverleger im ersten Drittel des 20. Jahrhunderts', in D. Ziegler (ed.), *Großbürger und Unternehmer. Die deutsche Wirtschaftselite im 20. Jahrhundert* (Göttingen, 2000).

—— 'Medienmacht und Politik. Die politischen Ambitionen großer Zeitungsunternehmer—Hearst, Northcliffe, Beaverbrook und Hugenberg im Vergleich', *AfS* 41 (2001), 79–95.

RETALLACK, J., *The German Right, 1860–1920: The Political Limits of the Authoritarian Imagination* (Toronto, 2006).

REULECKE, J., '"Veredelung der Volkserholung" und "edle Geselligkeit". Sozialreformerische Bestrebungen zur Gestaltung der arbeitsfreien Zeit im Kaiserreich', in G. Huck (ed.), *Sozialgeschichte der Freizeit*, 2nd edn. (Wuppertal, 1982).

—— *Soziale Friede durch Soziale Reform. Der Centralverein für das Wohl der arbeitenden Klassen in der Frühindustrialisierung* (Wuppertal, 1983).

REUTH, R. G. (ed.), *Joseph Goebbels Tagebücher*, 5 vols. (Munich, 1992).

—— 'Lesen und Konsum. Der Aufstieg der Konsumkultur in Presse und Werbung Deutschlands', *AfS* 41 (2001), 97–117.

—— 'The "Crisis of the Book" and German Society After the First World War', *GH* 20 (2002), 438–61.

—— *Reading Germany: Literature and Consumer Culture in Germany Before 1933*, trans. R. Morris (Oxford, 2006).

—— 'Reading, Advertising and Consumer Culture in the Weimar Period', in Führer and Ross (eds.), *Mass Media*.

RIBBE, W., 'Flaggenstreit und Heiliger Hain. Bemerkungen zur nationalen Symbolik in der Weimarer Republik', in D. Kurze (ed.), *Aus Theorie und Praxis der Geschichtswissenschaft. Festschrift für Hans Herzfeld zum 80. Geburtstag* (Berlin, 1972).

RICHARDS, J. and SHERIDAN, D. (eds.), *Mass-Observation at the Movies* (London, 1987).

RIESS, C., *Knaurs Weltgeschichte der Schallplatte* (Zurich, 1966).

RINGER, F., *The Decline of the German Mandarins: The German Academic Community, 1890–1933* (Cambridge, Mass., 1969).

RITZEL, F., '"Hätte der Kaiser Jazz getanzt . . ." US-Tanzmusik in Deutschland vor und nach dem Ersten Weltkrieg', in S. Schutte (ed.), *Ich will aber gerade vom Leben singen . . . Über populäre Musik vom ausgehenden 19. Jahrhundert bis zum Ende der Weimarer Republik* (Reinbek, 1987).

—— 'Synkopen-Tänze. Über Importe populärer Musik aus Amerika in der Zeit vor dem Ersten Weltkrieg', in Kaschuba and Maase (eds.), *Schund*.

ROSENBERGER, B., *Zeitungen als Kriegstreiber? Die Rolle der Presse im Vorfeld des Ersten Weltkrieges* (Cologne, 1998).

ROSENHAFT, E., *Beating the Fascists? The German Communists and Political Violence, 1929–1933* (Cambridge, 1983).

—— 'Restoring Moral Order on the Home Front: Compulsory Savings Plans for Young Workers in Germany, 1916–1919', in Coetzee and Shevin-Coetzee (eds.), *Authority*.

—— 'Lesewut, Kinosucht, Radiotismus. Zur (geschlechter-) politischen Relevanz neuer Massenmedien in den 1920er Jahren', in A. Lüdtke, I. Marßolek, and A. von Saldern (eds.), *Amerikanisierung. Traum und Alptraum im Deutschland des 20. Jahrhunderts* (Stuttgart, 1996).

ROSS, C., 'Mass Culture and Divided Audiences: Cinema and Social Change in Inter-war Germany', *Past & Present*, 193 (Nov. 2006), 157–95.

ROSS, C., 'Mass Politics and the Techniques of Leadership: The Promise and Perils of Propaganda in Weimar Germany', *GH* 24 (2006), 184–211.

Ross, C., 'Entertainment, Technology and Tradition: The Rise of Recorded Music from the Empire to the Third Reich', in Führer and Ross (eds.), *Mass Media*.

—— 'Visions of Prosperity: The Americanization of Advertising in Inter-war Germany', in Swett, Wiesen, and Zatlin (eds.), *Selling Modernity*.

—— 'Writing the Media into History: Recent Works on the History of Mass Communications in Germany', *GH* 26(2008).

Rücker, M., *Wirtschaftswerbung unter dem Nationalsozialismus. Rechtliche Ausgestaltung der Werbung und Tätigkeit des Werberats der deutschen Wirtschaft* (Frankfurt a. M., 2000).

Rügner, U., *Filmmusik in Deutschland zwischen 1924 und 1934* (Hildesheim, 1988).

Sachsse, R., *Die Erziehung zum Wegsehen. Fotografie im NS-Staat* (Dresden, 2003).

Sakmyster, T., 'Nazi Documentaries of Intimidation: "Feldzug in Polen" (1940), "Feuertaufe" (1940) and "Sieg im Westen" (1941)', *Historical Journal of Film, Radio and Television*, 16 (1996), 485–514.

Saunders, T., *Hollywood in Berlin: American Cinema and Weimar Germany* (Berkeley, 1994).

Schäfer, H.-D., *Das gespaltene Bewußtsein. Über deutsche Kultur und Lebenswirklichkeit, 1933–45* (Munich, 1981).

Schär, C., *Der Schlager und seine Tänze im Deutschland der 20er Jahre. Sozialgeschichtliche Aspekte zum Wandel in der Musik- und Tanzkultur während der Weimarer Republik* (Zurich, 1991).

Schatz, T., *Boom and Bust: American Cinema in the 1940s* (Berkeley, 1997).

Scheck, R., *Hitler's African Victims: The German Army Massacres of Black French Soldiers in 1940* (Cambridge, 2006).

Schellack, F., *Nationalfeiertage in Deutschland von 1871–1945* (Frankfurt a. M., 1990).

Schenda, R., *Volk ohne Buch. Studien zur Sozialgeschichte der populären Lesestoffe 1770–1910* (Frankfurt a. M., 1970).

—— *Die Lesestoffe der kleinen Leute. Studien zur populären Literatur im 19. und 20. Jahrhundert* (Munich, 1976).

Schildt, A., 'Ein konservativer Prophet moderner nationaler Integration. Biographische Skizze des streitbaren Soziologen Johann Plenge', *VfZ* 35 (1987), 523–70.

—— 'Von der Aufklärung zum Fernsehzeitalter. Neue Literatur zu Öffentlichkeit und Medien', *AfS* 40 (2000), 487–509.

—— 'Das Jahrhundert der Massenmedien. Ansichten zu einer künftigen Geschichte der Öffentlichkeit', *GG* 27 (2001), 177–206.

Schindelbeck, D., 'Stilgedanken zur Macht—"Lerne wirken ohne zu handeln": Hans Domizlaff, eines Werbeberaters Geschichte', in R. Gries, V. Ilgen, and D. Schindelbeck, *'Ins Gehirn der Masse kriechen!' Werbung und Mentalitätsgeschichte* (Darmstadt, 1995).

Schivelbusch, W., *Entfernte Verwandtschaft. Faschismus, Nationalsozialismus, New Deal 1933–1939* (Munich, 2005).

Schlingmann, S., *'Die Woche'—Illustrierte im Zeichen emanzipatorischen Aufbruchs? Frauenbild, Kultur- und Rollenmuster in Kaiserzeit, Republik und Diktatur (1899–1944)* (Hamburg, 2007).

Schlüpmann, H., *Unheimlichkeit des Blicks. Das Drama des frühen deutschen Kinos* (Basel, 1990).

SCHMIDT, A., *Belehrung—Propaganda—Vertrauensarbeit. Zum Wandel amtlicher Kommunikationspolitik in Deutschland 1914–1918* (Essen, 2006).

SCHMIDT, U. C., 'Radioaneignung', in Marßolek and von Saldern (eds.), *Zuhören.*

SCHMITT, C., *The Crisis of Parliamentary Democracy*, trans. E. Kennedy (Cambridge, Mass., 1985).

SCHNEIDER, B., *100 Jahre Koblenzer Filmtheater* (Koblenz, 1995).

SCHNEIDER, I. (ed.), *Radio-Kultur in der Weimarer Republik* (Tübingen, 1984).

SCHOCH, R. (ed.), *Politische Plakate der Weimarer Republik 1918–1933. Ausstellungskatalog* (Darmstadt, 1980).

SCHÖNERT, J., 'Zu den sozio-kulturellen Praktiken im Umgang mit Literatur(en) von 1770 bis 1930', in Kaschuba and Maase (eds.), *Schund.*

SCHRÖDER, H., *Tanz- und Unterhaltungsmusik in Deutschland 1918–1933* (Bonn, 1990).

SCHULTE-SASSE, L., *Entertaining the Third Reich: Illusions of Wholeness in Nazi Cinema* (Durham, NC, 1996).

SCHUMACHER, R., 'Programmstruktur und Tagesablauf der Hörer', in Leonhard (ed.), *Programmgeschichte.*

SCHÜTZ, E. and STREIM, G. (eds.), *Reflexe und Reflexionen von Modernität 1933–1945* (Bern, 2002).

SCHWARTZ, F., *The Werkbund: Design Theory and Mass Culture Before the First World War* (New Haven, 1996).

SCHWARTZ, V., *Spectacular Realities: Early Mass Culture in Fin-de-Siècle Paris* (Berkeley, 1998).

SCHWARZENBECK, E., *Nationalsozialistische Pressepolitik und die Sudetenkrise 1938* (Munich, 1979).

SCHWARZKOPF, S., 'Kontrolle statt Rausch? Marktforschung, Produktwerbung und Verbraucherlenkung im Nationalsozialismus zwischen Phantasien von Masse, Angst und Macht', in A. von Klimo and M. Rolf (eds.), *Rausch und Diktatur. Inszenierung, Mobilisierung und Kontrolle in totalitären Systemen* (Frankfurt a. M., 2006).

SCHWEINITZ, J. (ed.), *Prolog vor dem Film. Nachdenken über ein neues Medium 1909–1914* (Leipzig, 1992).

SEGEBERG, H. (ed.), *Die Mobilisierung des Sehens. Zur Vor- und Frühgeschichte des Films in Literatur und Kunst* (Munich, 1996).

—— 'Die großen Deutschen. Zur Renaissance des Propagandafilms um 1940', in H. Segeberg (ed.), *Mediale Mobilmachung. Das Dritte Reich und der Film* (Munich, 2004).

—— 'Literarische Kinoästhetik. Ansichten der Kinodebatte', in Müller and Segeberg (eds.), *Modellierung.*

SENNETT, R., *The Fall of Public Man* (London, 1986).

SHERAYKO, G., 'The Science of Selling: The Professionalization of Advertising and the Role of Education in Weimar Germany', unpublished paper, Nov. 2003.

SHIRER, W. L., *The Rise and Fall of the Third Reich* (New York, 1960).

SLING (SCHLESINGER, P.), *Die Nase der Sphinx oder: Wie wir Berliner so sind. Feuilletons aus den Jahren 1921 bis 1925* (Berlin, 1987).

SMAIL, D., *White-collar Workers, Mass Culture and Neue Sachlichkeit in Weimar Berlin* (Bern, 1999).

Sösemann, B., *Das Ende der Weimarer Republik in der Kritik demokratischer Publizisten* (Berlin, 1976).

—— 'Publizistik in staatlicher Regie. Die Presse- und Informationspolitik der Bismarck-Ära', in J. Kunisch (ed.), *Bismarck und seine Zeit* (Berlin, 1992).

—— (ed.), *Theodor Wolff. Der Journalist* (Düsseldorf, 1993).

Spieker, M., *Hollywood unterm Hakenkreuz. Der amerikanische Spielfilm im Dritten Reich* (Trier, 1999).

Spiker, J., *Film und Kapital. Der Weg der deutschen Filmwirtschaft zum nationalsozialistischen Einheitskonzern* (Berlin, 1975).

Sproule, J. M., *Propaganda and Democracy: The American Experience of Media and Mass Persuasion* (Cambridge, 1997).

Stahr, G., *Volksgemeinschaft vor der Leinwand? Der nationalsozialistische Film und sein Publikum* (Berlin, 2001).

Stark, G., 'Cinema, Society, and the State: Policing the Film Industry in Imperial Germany', in G. Stark and B. K. Lackner (eds.), *Essays on Culture and Society in Modern Germany* (College Station, 1982).

—— 'The Censorship of Literary Naturalism, 1885–1895: Prussia and Saxony', *CEH* 18 (1985), 326–43.

—— 'All Quiet on the Home Front: Popular Entertainments, Censorship, and Civilian Morale in Germany, 1914–1918', in Coetzee and Shevin-Coetzee (eds.), *Authority*.

Stein, P., *Die NS-Gaupresse, 1925–1933. Forschungsbericht, Quellenkritik, neue Bestandsaufnahme* (Munich, 1987).

Steiner, K., *Ortsempfänger, Volksfernseher und Optaphon. Die Entwicklung der deutschen Radio- und Fernsehindustrie und das Unternehmen Loewe, 1923–1962* (Essen, 2005).

Steinweis, A. E., *Art, Ideology, and Economics in Nazi Germany: The Reich Chambers of Music, Theater and the Visual Arts* (Chapel Hill, NC, 1993).

—— 'Cultural Eugenics: Social Policy, Economic Reform, and the Purge of Jews from German Cultural Life', in Cuomo (ed.), *Cultural Policy*.

Stern, F., *The Politics of Cultural Despair: A Study in the Rise of the Germanic Ideology* (Berkeley, 1961).

Stieg, M. F., 'The 1926 Law to Protect Youth Against Trash and Dirt: Moral Protectionism in a Democracy', *CEH* 23 (1990), 22–56.

Stöber, G., *Pressepolitik als Notwendigkeit. Zum Verhältnis von Staat und Öffentlichkeit im Wilhelminischen Deutschland 1890–1914* (Stuttgart, 2000).

Stöber, R., 'Der "Berliner Lokal-Anzeiger" und sein Blattmacher Hugo von Kupffer', *Publizistik* 39 (1994), 314–30.

—— 'Bismarcks geheime Presseorganisation von 1882', *HZ* 262 (1996), 423–51.

—— *Die erfolgverführte Nation. Deutschlands öffentliche Stimmungen 1866 bis 1945* (Stuttgart, 1998).

—— 'Emil Dovifat in der Weimarer Republik: Bemerkungen zu Pressefreiheit, Demokratie und Subsidiaritätsprinzip', in B. Sösemann (ed.), *Emil Dovifat. Studien und Dokumente zu Leben und Werk* (Berlin, 1998).

—— 'Die "Provinzial-Correspondenz" 1863–1884. Das größte politische "Wochenblatt" seiner Zeit', *Publizistik* 44 (1999), 165–84.

—— *Deutsche Pressegeschichte. Einführung, Systematik, Glossar*, 2nd edn. (Konstanz, 2005).

Stoffels, L., 'Kulturfaktor und Unterhaltungsrundfunk', in Leonhard (ed.), *Programmgeschichte*.

—— 'Rundfunk und die Kultur der Gegenwart', in Leonhard (ed.), *Programmgeschichte*.

Storim, M. '"Einer, der besser ist, als sein Ruf". Kolportageroman und Kolportagebuchhandel um 1900 und die Haltung der Buchbranche', in Kaschuba and Maase (eds.), *Schund*.

Strauss, H. A., 'The Movement of People in a Time of Crisis', in J. C. Jackman and C. M. Borden (eds.), *The Muses Flee Hitler: Cultural Transfer and Adaptation, 1930–1945* (Washington, DC, 1983).

Swett, P., 'Celebrating the Republic Without Republicans: The Reichsverfassungstag in Berlin, 1929–32', in K. Friedrich (ed.), *Festive Culture in Germany and Europe from the Sixteenth to the Twentieth Century* (Lampeter, 2000).

—— *Neighbors and Enemies: The Culture of Radicalism in Berlin, 1929–1933* (Cambridge, 2004).

—— Wiesen, J., and Zatlin, J. (eds.), *Selling Modernity: Advertising in Twentieth-Century Germany* (Durham, NC, 2007).

Sywottek, J., *Mobilmachung für den totalen Krieg. Die propagandistische Vorbereitung der deutschen Bevölkerung auf den Zweiten Weltkrieg* (Opladen, 1976).

Taylor, P., *The Projection of Britain: British Overseas Publicity and Propaganda 1919–1939* (Cambridge, 1981).

Toeplitz, J., *Geschichte des Films*, 5 vols. (Berlin, 1992).

Tooze, A., *The Wages of Destruction: The Making and Breaking of the Nazi Economy* (London, 2006).

Tournès, L., 'The Landscape of Sound in the Nineteenth and Twentieth Centuries', *Contemporary European History*, 13 (2004), 493–504.

Tye, L., *The Father of Spin: Edward L. Bernays and the Birth of Public Relations* (New York, 1998).

Ungern-Sternberg von Pürkel, J. and von Ungern-Sternberg, W., *Der Aufruf an die Kulturwelt. Das Manifest der 93 und die Anfänge der Kriegspropaganda im Ersten Weltkrieg* (Stuttgart, 1996).

Urban, M., *Die Konsensfabrik. Funktion und Wahrnehmung der NS-Reichsparteitage, 1933–1941* (Göttingen, 2007).

Usborne, C., *The Politics of the Body in Weimar Germany: Women's Reproductive Rights and Duties* (Basingstoke, 1992).

vom Bruch, R., *Wissenschaft, Politik und öffentliche Meinung. Gelehrtenpolitik im wilhelminischen Deutschland (1890–1914)* (Husum, 1980).

von Saldern, A. 'Massenfreizeitkultur im Visier. Ein Beitrag zu den Deutungs- und Einwirkungsversuchen während der Weimarer Republik', *AfS* 33 (1993), 21–58.

—— *Häuserleben. Zur Geschichte städtischen Arbeiterwohnens vom Kaiserreich bis heute* (Bonn, 1995).

—— '*Volk* and *Heimat* Culture in Radio Broadcasting During the Period of Transition from Weimar to Nazi Germany', *JMH* 76 (2004), 319–20.

Vande Winkel, R. and Welch, D. (eds.), *Cinema and the Swastika: The International Expansion of Third Reich Cinema* (Houndmills, 2007).

VERHEY, J., 'Some Lessons of the War: The Discourse on Propaganda and Public Opinion in Germany in the 1920s', in B. Hüppauf (ed.), *War, Violence and the Modern Condition* (Berlin, 1997).

—— *The Spirit of 1914: Militarism, Myth and Mobilization in Germany* (Cambridge, 2000).

VOGT, S., *Nationaler Sozialismus und Soziale Demokratie. Die sozialdemokratische Junge Rechte 1918–1945* (Bonn, 2006).

VOIGT, G., 'Goebbels als Markentechniker', in W. Haug (ed.), *Warenästhetik. Beiträge zur Diskussion, Weiterentwicklung und Vermittlung ihrer Kritik* (Frankfurt a. M., 1977).

VONDUNG, K. (ed.), *Das wilhelminische Bildungsbürgertum: Zur Sozialgeschichte seiner Ideen* (Göttingen, 1975).

WARSTAT, D. H., *Frühes Kino der Kleinstadt* (Berlin, 1982).

WEICHLEIN, S., *Sozialmilieus und politische Kultur in der Weimarer Republik. Lebenswelt, Vereinskultur, Politik in Hessen* (Göttingen, 1996).

WEIN, F., *Deutschlands Strom—Frankreichs Grenze. Geschichte und Propaganda am Rhein 1919–1930* (Essen, 1992).

WEITZ, E., 'Communism and the Public Spheres of Weimar Germany', in Barclay and Weitz (eds.), *Between Reform.*

WELCH, D., *Propaganda and the German Cinema 1933–45* (Oxford, 1983).

—— *Germany, Propaganda and Total War, 1914–1918: The Sins of Omission* (London, 2000).

—— *The Third, Reich: Politics and Propaganda*, 2nd edn. (London, 2002).

WERNECKE, K., 'Kinobesuch als Freizeitvergnügen. Der Spielfilm als klassenübergreifendes Mittel in der Weimarer Republik', *MkF* 15 (1992), 92–100.

WETTE, W., BREMER, R., and VOGEL, D. (eds.), *Das letzte halbe Jahr. Stimmungsberichte der Wehrmachtpropaganda 1944/45* (Essen, 2001).

WICKE, P., *Von Mozart zu Madonna. Eine Kulturgeschichte der Popmusik* (Leipzig, 1998).

WILKE, J., 'Deutsche Auslandspropaganda im Ersten Weltkrieg: Die Zentralstelle für Auslandsdienst', in J. Wilke (ed.), *Pressepolitik und Propaganda. Historische Studien vom Vormärz bis zum Kalten Krieg* (Cologne, 1997).

—— *Grundzüge der Medien- und Kommunikationsgeschichte. Von den Anfängen bis ins 20. Jahrhundert* (Cologne, 2000).

WILKENDING, G., 'Die Kommerzialisierung der Jugendliteratur und die Jugendschruiftenbewegung um 1900', in Kaschuba and Maase (eds.), *Schund.*

WILLETT, J., *The New Sobriety, 1917–1933: Art and Politics in the Weimar Period* (London, 1978).

WIPPERMANN, K., *Politische Propaganda und staatsbürgerliche Bildung. Die Reichszentrale für Heimatdienst in der Weimarer Republik* (Bonn, 1976).

WITTE, K., *Lachende Erben, Toller Tag. Filmkomödie im Dritten Reich* (Berlin, 1995).

WITTENBRINK, T., 'Rundfunk und literarische Tradition', in Leonhard (ed.), *Programmgeschichte.*

—— 'Zeitgenössische Schriftsteller im Rundfunk', in Leonhard (ed.), *Programmgeschichte.*

WOLFFRAM, K., *Tanzdielen und Vergnügungspaläste. Berliner Nachtleben in den dreissiger und vierziger Jahren* (Berlin, 1992).

WOLTER, H.-W., *Generalanzeiger. Das pragmatische Prinzip. Zur Entwicklungsgeschichte und Typologie des Pressewesens im späten 19. Jahrhundert mit einer Studie über die Zeitungsunternehmungen Wilhelm Girardets (1838–1918)* (Bochum, 1981).

WULF, J., *Presse und Funk im Dritten Reich. Eine Dokumentation* (Gütersloh, 1964).

YOUNG, R. J., *Marketing Marianne: French Propaganda in America, 1900–1940* (Piscataway, NJ, 2004).

ZIMMERMANN, C., 'Landkino im Nationalsozialismus', *AfS* 41 (2001), 231–43.

—— 'From Propaganda to Modernization: Media Policy and Media Audiences Under National Socialism', *GH* 24 (2006), 431–54.

—— and Schmeling, M. (eds.), *Die Zeitschrift—Medium der Moderne* (Bielefeld, 2006).

Index